The Psalms
through
Three Thousand Years

PRAYERBOOK OF A CLOUD OF WITNESSES

WILLIAM L. HOLLADAY

FORTRESS PRESS   MINNEAPOLIS

THE PSALMS THROUGH THREE THOUSAND YEARS
Prayerbook of a Cloud of Witnesses

First paperback edition 1996

Interior design by Publisher's Workgroup
Cover design by Patricia Boman/David Meyer

The Library of Congress has cataloged the hardcover edition as follows:

Library of Congress Cataloging-in-Publication Data

Holladay, William Lee.
    The Psalms through three thousand years : prayerbook of a cloud of
witnesses / William L. Holladay.
      p.   cm.
    Includes bibliographical references and index.
    ISBN 0-8006-2752-0
    1. Bible. O.T. Psalms—Commentaries. 1. Title.
BS 1430.3.H65 1993
223'.2'009—dc20   93-6577
                                                CIP

ISBN 0-8006-3014-9 (paperback edition)

Manufactured in the U.S.A.   AF 1-3014

00   99   98   97   2   3   4   5   6   7   8   9   10

Contents

PART THREE
CURRENT THEOLOGICAL ISSUES

Abbreviations

AAR	American Academy of Religion
AAS	*Acta apostolicae sedis*
AB	Anchor Bible
ACW	Ancient Christian Writers
BARev	*Biblical Archaeology Review*
BASOR	*Bulletin of the American Schools of Oriental Research*
Bib	*Biblica*
BZ	*Biblische Zeitschrift*
BZAW	Beihefte zur *Zeitschrift für die alttestamentliche Wissenschaft*
CBQ	*Catholic Biblical Quarterly*
CBQMS	Catholic Biblical Quarterly—Monograph Series
CChr	Corpus Christianorum
chap(s).	chapter(s)
col.	column
ConBNT	Coniectanea biblica, New Testament
CRINT	Compendia rerum iudaicarum ad novum testamentum
CSEL	Corpus scriptorum ecclesiasticorum latinorum
Ebib	Etudes bibliques
ed(s).	editor(s)
EncJud	*Encyclopaedia judaica*
FC	Fathers of the Church
fig(s).	figure(s)
HAT	Handbuch zum Alten Testament
HDR	Harvard Dissertations in Religion
HSM	Harvard Semitic Monographs
HSS	Harvard Semitic Studies
HTS	Harvard Theological Studies

HUCA	*Hebrew Union College Annual*
IB	*Interpreter's Bible*
ICC	International Critical Commentary
IDB	G. A. Buttrick (ed.), *Interpreter's Dictionary of the Bible*
IDBSup	*Interpreter's Dictionary of the Bible*, Supplementary Volume
JAOS	*Journal of the American Oriental Society*
JB	Jerusalem Bible
JBL	*Journal of Biblical Literature*
JR	*Journal of Religion*
JSOT	*Journal for the Study of the Old Testament*
JSOTSup	*Journal for the Study of the Old Testament*—Supplement Series
JSS	*Journal of Semitic Studies*
KJV	King James Version
LCC	Library of Christian Classics
NAB	New American Bible
NCE	M.R.P. McGuire et al. (eds.), *New Catholic Encyclopedia*
NEB	New English Bible
NJB	H. Wansbrough (ed.), *New Jerusalem Bible*
no(s).	number(s)
NovTSup	Novum Testamentum, Supplements
NRSV	New Revised Standard Version
NRT	*La nouvelle revue théologique*
OTL	Old Testament Library
par(s).	parallel(s)
PG	Jacques-Paul Migne (ed.), *Patrologia graeca*
PL	Jacques-Paul Migne (ed.), *Patrologia latina*
RB	*Revue biblique*
REB	Revised English Bible
RHR	*Revue de l'histoire des religions*
RSV	Revised Standard Version
RTL	*Revue théologique de Louvain*
SBLDS	Society of Biblical Literature Dissertation Series
SBLMS	Society of Biblical Literature Monograph Series
SC	Sources chretiennes
TDNT	G. Kittel and G. Friedrich (eds.), *Theological Dictionary of the New Testament*
TEV	Today's English Version
TS	*Theological Studies*
v(v).	verse(s)
vol(s).	volume(s)
VT	*Vetus Testamentum*

Short Titles

Barrett, *Second Corinthians*
Charles K. Barrett, *A Commentary on the Second Epistle to the Corinthians* (New York: Harper & Row, 1973)

Beare, *Matthew*
Francis Wright Beare, *The Gospel according to Matthew* (San Francisco: Harper & Row, 1981)

Briggs
Charles Augustus Briggs and Emilie Grace Briggs, *A Critical and Exegetical Commentary on the Book of Psalms* (ICC; New York: Charles Scribner's Sons, 1906–7)

Brueggemann, *Finally Comes the Poet*
Walter Brueggemann, *Finally Comes the Poet: Daring Speech for Proclamation* (Minneapolis: Fortress, 1989)

Brueggemann, *Israel's Praise*
Walter Brueggemann, *Israel's Praise: Doxology against Idolatry and Ideology* (Philadelphia: Fortress, 1988)

Brueggemann, *Message of the Psalms*
Walter Brueggemann, *The Message of the Psalms: A Theological Commentary* (Augsburg Old Testament Studies; Minneapolis: Augsburg, 1984)

Calvin, *Psalms*
Calvin's Commentaries: Psalms (Edinburgh: Calvin Translation Society, 1843–55; reprint, Grand Rapids: Eerdmans, 1948–49)

Cambridge History of the Bible, I, II, III
Peter R. Ackroyd and C. F. Evans (eds.), *The Cambridge History of the Bible*, vol. 1: *From the Beginnings to Jerome* (Cambridge: Cambridge University Press, 1970); G.W.H. Lampe (ed.), *The Cambridge History of the Bible*, vol. 2: *The West from the Fathers to the Reformation* (Cambridge: Cambridge University Press, 1969); S. L. Greenslade (ed.), *The Cambridge History of the Bible*, vol. 3: *The West from the Reformation to the Present Day* (Cambridge: Cambridge University Press, 1963)

Conzelmann, *Acts*
Hans Conzelmann, *Acts of the Apostles* (Hermeneia; Philadelphia: Fortress, 1987)

Conzelmann, *1 Corinthians*
Hans Conzelmann, *1 Corinthians* (Hermeneia; Philadelphia: Fortress, 1975)

Dahood, *Psalms I, II, III*
Mitchell Dahood, *Psalms I: 1–50* (AB 16; Garden City, N.Y.: Doubleday, 1966); idem, *Psalms II: 51–100* (AB 17; Garden City, N.Y.: Doubleday, 1968); idem, *Psalms III: 101–150* (AB 17A; Garden City, N.Y.: Doubleday, 1970)

Fitzmyer, *Luke*
Joseph A. Fitzmyer, *The Gospel according to Luke I–IX, X–XXIV* (AB 28, 28A; Garden City, N.Y.: Doubleday, 1981, 1985)

Gerstenberger, *Psalms: Part I*
Erhard S. Gerstenberger, *Psalms: Part I, with an Introduction to Cultic Poetry* (The Forms of the Old Testament Literature 14; Grand Rapids: Eerdmans, 1988)

History of the Jewish People
Haim Hillel Ben-Sasson (ed.), *A History of the Jewish People* (Cambridge: Harvard University Press, 1976)

Holladay, *Jeremiah 1*
William L. Holladay, *Jeremiah 1* (Hermeneia; Philadelphia: Fortress, 1986)

Holladay, *Jeremiah 2*
William L. Holladay, *Jeremiah 2* (Minneapolis: Fortress, 1989)

Kraus, *Psalms 1–59*
Hans-Joachim Kraus, *Psalms 1–59: A Commentary* (Minneapolis: Augsburg, 1988)

Kraus, *Psalms 60–150*
Hans-Joachim Kraus, *Psalms 60–150: A Commentary* (Minneapolis: Augsburg, 1989)

Latourette, *History of Christianity*
Kenneth Scott Latourette, *A History of Christianity* (New York: Harper, 1953)

Latourette, *History of the Expansion of Christianity*
Kenneth Scott Latourette, *A History of the Expansion of Christianity* (7 vols.; New York: Harper, 1937–45)

Liturgy of the Hours
Christian Prayer: The Liturgy of the Hours (Boston: Daughters of St. Paul, 1976)

Lutheran Book of Worship (1978)
Inter-Lutheran Commission on Worship, *Lutheran Book of Worship* (Minneapolis: Augsburg, 1978)

Luther's Works
  Luther's Works (St. Louis: Concordia, 1955–86)

Mikra
  Martin Jan Mulder (ed.), *Mikra: Text, Translation, Reading and Interpretation of the Hebrew Bible in Ancient Judaism and Early Christianity* (CRINT II, 1; Assen and Maastricht: Van Gorcum; Philadelphia: Fortress, 1988)

New Jerome Biblical Commentary
  Raymond E. Brown, Joseph A. Fitzmyer, and Roland E. Murphy (eds.), *The New Jerome Biblical Commentary* (Englewood Cliffs, N.J.: Prentice Hall, 1990)

Pilgrim Hymnal (1958)
  Pilgrim Hymnal (Boston: Pilgrim, 1958)

Study of Liturgy
  Cheslyn Jones, Geoffrey Wainwright, and Edward Yarnold (eds.), *The Study of Liturgy* (New York: Oxford University Press, 1978)

The (Episcopal) *Hymnal 1982*
  The Hymnal 1982 (New York: The [Episcopal] Church Hymnal Corporation, 1982)

The Presbyterian Hymnal (1990)
  The Presbyterian Hymnal: Hymns, Psalms, and Spiritual Songs (Louisville: Westminster/John Knox, 1990)

The United Methodist Hymnal (1989)
  The United Methodist Hymnal: Book of United Methodist Worship (Nashville: United Methodist Publishing House, 1989)

Introduction

When I was a soldier in the American army in 1946, there was distributed at the chapels, I believe by the courtesy of the Gideons or the Y.M.C.A., a small edition of the Scriptures that would fit in our Ike-jacket pockets, and I took one. It was not, however, a full Bible—it was simply the New Testament and the Psalms. I knew, of course, that the rationale for this edition was a matter of economics and convenience. A full Bible that could have fitted in my pocket would need to have been printed on India paper, an impractical measure for the thousands of copies to be offered to members of the armed forces. But still, subliminally or not so subliminally, the edition suggested that the New Testament and Psalms were all that was really needed. And theologically untrained though I was at the time, the matter bothered me. Why is the Old Testament only represented by a single book?

From my vantage point today I know that 1946 was not the only year when an edition of the New Testament and Psalms appeared: only recently I received a volume containing the New Testament and Psalms in the New Revised Standard Version.[1] Indeed in the eighth century, in the Balkans, a sect emerged called the "Bogomils"; they accepted only the New Testament and the Psalms, holding the rest of the Old Testament to be the work of the devil. For this belief and others the group was declared heretical by the church.[2]

But, in a way, the answer to my question as a soldier is obvious: the book of Psalms has held a unique place in the lives of both Christians and Jews—the Psalms have been a primary vehicle for worship. For two millennia this collection of 150 individual psalms has helped to shape the public and private worship of Jews and Christians; I am not aware of any other body of religious poetry that has been so influential for so long a period of time, and for such a variety of religious communities.

The uniqueness of the Psalms has always been recognized. Athanasius, who was a bishop in Alexandria, Egypt, in the fourth century, wrote a letter to a man named Marcellinus, who was perhaps a deacon in the church in Alexandria; Marcellinus, during an illness, had set himself to study the Bible and wanted guidance from Athanasius on the Psalms. The bishop wrote, "All Scripture of ours, my

1

son—both ancient and new—is inspired by God and profitable for teaching, as it is written [2 Tim. 3:16]. But the Book of Psalms possesses a certain winning exactitude for those who are prayerful."[3]

Yet, curiously, we have not had a handbook that combines a treatment of the origin of the Psalms with attention to their use by Jews and Christians through history. One would have to piece together such a story from books that treat of the origin of the Psalms in Israel and from books that treat of Jewish and Christian liturgy and culture.

To those who center their religious loyalties in the Bible, whether Jews or Christians, it would seem important to tell the whole story of the Psalms. It would seem particularly important to Christians. For example, it is not enough to offer a Christian pastor guidance on the presumed original meaning of a psalm. If the pastor is to preach on a text from the psalm, then he or she must also be given some guidance on how legitimately to get from there to here. Theological issues abound. Thus when Protestants use Psalm 139 as a responsive reading, vv. 19-22 are commonly omitted, and these same four verses are omitted in this psalm when it occurs in Roman Catholic daily prayer; these are verses in which the psalmist expresses hatred for the enemies of God. Clearly the omission of these verses simplifies the process of worship, but is such an omission an appropriate treatment of the psalm? How, indeed, is one to read the "hard psalms," if at all?

Beyond matters of theological understanding, it is clear that the continued use of the psalms in music (to take only one example, Igor Stravinsky's *Symphony of Psalms*, composed in 1930, which draws from the Latin texts of Psalms 39, 40, and 150) and the influence of the psalms on religious and artistic expression are themselves matters of humanistic interest for our civilization. This book aims to set the whole story forth in a way accessible to the nonspecialist.

After an opening chapter that touches on some of the issues with which the book deals, this book has three sections. Part One, "The Psalms Take Shape—A Reconstruction" (chapters 2–6), attempts to discern the origin of the Psalms and psalm collections. Part 2, "The Psalter through History" (chapters 7–14), describes the use of the psalms at Qumran (the Dead Sea Scroll community), in the New Testament, and in the Jewish and Christian communities down through the ages. Part 3, "Current Theological Issues" (chapters 15–19), explores some of the questions of the use, translation, and interpretation of the Psalms that confront us today.

The emphasis of this book is on topics of interest to those who read the Psalms in English. But even beyond that focus, my treatment at every point in this study has had to be severely selective. When I spoke to a friend of my plans for this book, he remarked, "Oh, so you're going to tell the story of the entire Judeo-Christian tradition." In each chapter I have offered illustrative examples that have caught my eye, but clearly they are a few out of a vast number; there is no way I could have done otherwise.

If the book is for nonspecialists, then I most emphatically affirm that in most of the chapters I have moved far out beyond my own field of specialization, and I have been heavily dependent on the advice of many colleagues who have kindly helped me avoid gross errors. I express here my thanks to the following colleagues and friends at Andover Newton Theological School: Charles E. Carlston, Carole R. Fontaine, Mark and Melissa Heim, Robin Jensen, Elsie A. McKee, Eddie S. O'Neal, and Sze-kar Wan; to professors from other schools as well: Horace T. Allen, Jr., and Geoffrey Hill of Boston University; Mark C. Carnes of Barnard College; Janet Fishburn of Drew University; William R. Hutchison of Harvard University; Albert J. Raboteau of Princeton University; Jeremiah Unterman of Barry University; Roland E. Murphy, emeritus professor of the Divinity School of Duke University; Professor Peter B. Dirksen of the Faculty of Theology of the State University of Leiden, the Netherlands; Dr. Franz D. Hubmann of the Catholic Theological College, Linz, Austria; and to other friends and colleagues: Dr. Janice P. Leary, of Natick, Fr. Stavros Kortmas, of West Roxbury, and Faith A. Kaufmann, of Amherst, Massachusetts.

And here I acknowledge my deep debt to my wife Patricia Appelbaum, to whom this work is dedicated. In the course of her own research in various areas of church history she has for two years kept a sharp eye out for references to the Psalms, and we have steadily talked through the issues raised in this book. I owe her more than I can express.

I am an amateur (in the etymological sense of that word, a "lover") of all the topics in this book; and it may be helpful to indicate to the reader how this could be, by setting down a few of the stages of my own peculiar journey. After my undergraduate studies (with a major in Greek and a minor in Latin), my first theological degree, at the Pacific School of Religion in California (1948–51), allowed me to specialize in the Old Testament. During those years I became a member of the Berkeley Society of Friends, and in that community I steadily pondered questions that today are summed up under the term "spirituality." Then I was ordained into the ministry of the Congregational Christian churches (later the United Church of Christ) and served two rural churches in California; during the first five Sundays of Lent in 1954 I preached a series of sermons on "A Christian Uses the Psalms," and I find that some of the matters that I discuss in chapter 19 of this book were on my mind when I drafted those sermons more than thirty-five years ago.

After three years of doctoral study (again specializing in the Old Testament) and two years in campus ministry, I began teaching the Bible, first to undergraduates at Elmhurst College for three years and then for seven years (1963–70) to Protestant theological students at the Near East School of Theology in Beirut, Lebanon. During one summer of those years (1964) I was a member of the staff at the archeological excavation of the biblical city of Shechem on the West Bank; and throughout that time in and near the Holy Land I was constantly stimulated to see the Bible in its original context. Since 1970 I have taught the Old Testament to (mostly) Protestant theological students at Andover Newton Theological School. And in 1972 I began serving on the translation committee for the New Revised Standard Version (see chapter 14); my experience there helped to sharpen my perceptions of the issues of translation (see chapters 17 and 18).

In 1985, having struggled with questions of liturgy and spirituality, I entered the Roman Catholic Church, whereupon I reverted to lay status. Since that time I have, for morning and evening prayers, used the Roman Catholic Liturgy of the Hours (see chapter 14), usually alone or with friends but once, for a few days, in a Dominican community. My daily worship has been at daily Mass, though not on a regular basis, and since 1988 I have helped sing Sunday Mass in the Men's Schola, along with the Boston Archdiocesan Choir School, at St. Paul Roman Catholic Church in Cambridge, Massachusetts; in these ways I regularly participate in the use of the Psalms in Christian worship.

There is one troublesome matter that must be dealt with here and now, and that is the numeration of the chapters and verses of the Psalms. Though both the Hebrew tradition and the Greek tradition (the Septuagint translation; see chapter 6) reckon 150 psalms in the book of Psalms, there is a difference in their respective numerations. The two agree for Psalms 1 to 8. The Hebrew Psalms 9 and 10 are reckoned in the Septuagint as Psalm 9. Then the Hebrew Psalms 11 to 113 are the Septuagint Psalms 10 to 112, respectively, so that for this span the Septuagint numeration is one behind the Hebrew. The Hebrew Psalms 114 and 115 are again reckoned by the Septuagint as one psalm, Psalm 113. Then the Hebrew Psalm 116 is divided in two by the Septuagint, Hebrew Ps. 116:1-9 being the Septuagint Psalm 114 and Hebrew Ps. 116:10-19 being the Septuagint Psalm 115. Then the Hebrew Psalms 117 to 146 are the Septuagint Psalms 116 to 145, respectively, the Septuagint numeration again falling one behind the Hebrew. Then the Hebrew Psalm 147 is divided in two, Hebrew Ps. 147:1-11 being the Septuagint Psalm 146 and Hebrew Ps. 147:12-20 being the full Septuagint Psalm 147. The last three Psalms are then numbered identically, 148 to 150.

This problem of numeration would be of concern only to specialists except for the fact that the Septuagint numeration became that of the Latin Vulgate and therefore the numeration of Roman Catholic translations until recently, whereas Protestant Bibles have used the traditional Hebrew numeration. For example, in the score of Stravinsky's *Symphony of Psalms*, referred to above, the (Latin) Psalms that he employs are cited as Psalms 38, 39, and 150 instead of Psalms 39, 40, and 150. *In this book I shall use the Hebrew numeration even when referring to Psalms in their Greek or Latin translation*: when Augustine refers to "Psalm 21" (see chapter 10), it is the psalm known to us as Psalm 22 and is therefore so designated here.

But there is still more. Some of the psalms have superscriptions (notes on the psalms from ancient times); for example, the New Revised Standard Version for Psalm 51 reads, "To the leader. A Psalm of David, when the prophet Nathan came to him, after he had gone in to Bathsheba." The Hebrew text reckons many of these superscriptions as one or two verses, so that (in the case of Psalm 51, for example) the Hebrew text numbers the first verse of the psalm proper ("Have mercy on me, O God . . . ,") as v. 3. This practice is continued in Jewish translations, as one might expect (see *The Holy Scriptures*, 1917, and the new Jewish version called *Tanakh*, 1985).[4] But it is also the practice of earlier Roman Catholic translations: the Douay Version (1609) numbers "Have mercy on me, O God . . ."

as v. 3 (but, of course, of Psalm 50!—see above). By contrast, Protestant translations have reckoned the first verse of the psalm proper as v. 1 (so the KJV, the RSV, and the NRSV, as well as the NEB and the REB). Current Roman Catholic translations differ: the JB and the NJB follow the Protestant pattern, but the NAB follows the Jewish one. In this book, when the versification differs, *I shall give the Hebrew verse number first, followed by the Protestant verse number in parentheses or brackets*: thus "Have mercy on me, O God . . ." will be referred to as Ps. 51:3 (1). In this way the reader can look either before the parentheses or within them, according to the versification scheme employed in the Bible that he or she uses.

I trust that a work that offers an overview of the Psalms—chanted, sung, and recited by so great a cloud of witnesses (see Heb. 12:1) through the past three thousand years—will help to inform and edify the present generation of those witnesses.

NOTES

1. *The New Revised Standard Version: New Testament and Psalms* (Iowa Falls, Iowa: World Bible Publishers, 1989).

2. "Bogomils," in F. L. Cross (ed.), *The Oxford Dictionary of the Christian Church* (Oxford: Oxford University Press, 1983), 184.

3. Athanasius, *The Life of Antony and the Letter to Marcellinus* (The Classics of Western Spirituality; New York: Paulist, 1980), 101.

4. *The Holy Scriptures according to the Masoretic Text: A New Translation* (Philadelphia: Jewish Publication Society, 1917); *Tanakh: A New Translation of the Holy Scriptures according to the Traditional Hebrew Text* (Philadelphia: Jewish Publication Society, 1985).

1

The Lord Is My Shepherd, Then and Now

Thirty-five years ago, in a parish I served in California, there was a woman named Beth. She had been crippled by a stroke; she was unable to speak or even to move, except for some nods and moans and vague gestures with her left hand. She was not only confined to her home but bedridden, waited on by her husband. Word came to me that she wished to be baptized and then taken into membership in the church, and her wishes were granted in due course.

When I would visit her, I would find myself carrying on both sides of the conversation, as one does with someone who is mute; yet her mind was active, and she could still spell. So when she wanted to communicate anything, I would go through the laborious process of naming the letters, one at a time, from a child's slate that displayed the alphabet and the numbers. "Is it in this line?" I would ask. She would shake her head, "No." "Then is it in this line?" and she would grunt, "Yes." "Is it M? Is it N? Is it O? Is it P?"—I would go down the line. The letter was P; I would write down P. And so it went, until a word or abbreviation took shape. And usually her message was "PS 23," the Twenty-third Psalm. She would want me to recite for her the Twenty-third Psalm. Occasionally I would try to talk with her about some other psalm and read it to her, but she could not be bothered with complications: Beth's faith, so far as I could discern, began and ended with the Twenty-third Psalm. That was what she asked for, and that was what I could give her.

And it is striking, the hold that this particular psalm has in the popular religion of our culture. Parents whose hold on Christian belief is not too secure may still teach their children the Lord's Prayer and the Twenty-third Psalm as a kind of double summary of the faith.

Eldridge Cleaver, the former leader of the Black Panther organization, writes of his conversion in 1975 to the Christian faith. He had fled to France to avoid arrest after a shoot-out with police in Oakland, California. In deep depression one night, he writes:

I just crumbled and started crying. I fell to my knees, grabbing hold of the banister; and in the midst of this shaking and crying the Lord's Prayer and the 23rd Psalm came into my mind. I hadn't thought about these prayers for years. I started repeating them, and after a time I gained some control over the trembling and crying. Then I jumped up and ran to my bookshelf and got the Bible. . . . I discovered that my memory really had not served me that well. I got lost somewhere between the Valley of the Shadow of Death and the overflowing cup. But it was the Bible in which I searched and found that psalm. I read through it. At that time I didn't even know where to find the Lord's Prayer. I looked for it desperately. Pretty soon the type started swimming before my eyes, and I lay down on the bed and went to sleep.[1]

This double summary of the faith is embedded in the souls of firm Christians as well: I have heard a pastor who intended to lead his congregation in the Lord's Prayer begin mistakenly, "The Lord is my shepherd." The psalm has been recited eagerly by young soldiers in foxholes; and elderly folk on their deathbeds may welcome its recitation, eager for its reassurance, particularly in the "valley of the shadow of death."

Indeed the psalm is thoroughly at home in our secular culture. Garrison Keillor, in one of his childhood "reminiscences" of his (mythical) hometown of Lake Wobegon, Minnesota, recalls the Memorial Day celebrations, when schoolchildren were primed by their teacher, Miss Lewis, to recite on demand either Abraham Lincoln's *Gettysburg Address*, John McCrae's poem "In Flanders Fields," or the Twenty-third Psalm.[2] How the psalm came to be lodged so thoroughly in American culture I shall explore in the Epilogue.

One may ask, then: What is going on when I recite this psalm, or some similar psalm? What is happening is somewhat different from what happens when I recite other portions of Scripture. When I say, "In the beginning God created the heavens and the earth," I am repeating an affirmation about God's creative work at the beginning of time, and at the same time I am identifying myself with all the company of people through time and space who share that affirmation; and similarly, when I read a passage from Isaiah or from the Gospels in the New Testament, I am affirming, "This is what people heard God say" or "This is what people heard Jesus say." But when I repeat the Twenty-third Psalm, I am addressing God—the words in the middle of the psalm are in the second person, "I shall fear no evil, for you are with me." And when I address God, I am not only acknowledging God's presence, I am also interacting with God: I am shifting reality, if ever so slightly. The recitation is *performative*: I am helping to create a new situation between myself and God.[3] And if I am reciting or singing the psalm with a company of fellow believers, then all of us, together, are helping to create a new situation between our company and God. (I shall explore this matter in more detail in chapter 15.)

This is utterly crucial. This is what Beth knew, and this is what all those countless foxhole soldiers and dying patients and just plain people have known all along.

And more: people today who recite the psalm are putting themselves in solidarity with numberless others in earlier times and places who have recited the same psalm, in dozens of different languages. The same verses of the psalm have nourished them, too, as the psalm nourishes us.

But now we come upon a curious problem, as we think about the history of the Twenty-third Psalm through the centuries and about the history of the other psalms that make up the 150 in our book of Psalms. It is clear, if we think about it, that people's styles and outlook and way of life are constantly changing. Words shift in implication and meaning: we know that in eighteenth-century novels people do not speak as they do today. And particularly for the Psalms, coming to us as they do from hundreds of years ago, the symbols and assumptions at the time of their composition are likely to be altogether different from those today. To take the example right at hand, it is all fine to recite, "The Lord is my shepherd, I shall not want," but there are not so many shepherds around as there used to be. You and I may know that there used to be whole communities sustained by sheepherding, but nowadays many city people have never seen a shepherd with a flock of sheep. What was once a vivid metaphor now simply conjures up for many of us a quaint four-color picture from Sunday school.

And the matter is even more complicated than that. Most of us realize that the New Testament was originally written in Greek and the Old Testament in Hebrew, and we can recognize, too, if we have had experience with foreign languages, that every translation inevitably shifts (if ever so slightly) the style of thinking, since every language brings with it its own ways of thinking. We may say, "The Lord is my shepherd, I shall not want," but even though that is as accurate a translation as is possible, our English words may not call up in our minds quite what the Hebrew words *yahweh rō'î lō' 'ehsār* did in the mind of the poet who first sang the poem.

Let us allow ourselves, then, to ponder the distance between the words of the poet (*yahweh rō'î lō' 'ehsār*) and our words (The Lord is my shepherd, I shall not want), because that distance and the turns taken by these words and other words of the Psalms are what this book is all about.

There is no way to know for sure who the poet was who created the Twenty-third Psalm, or when he lived (and it probably was a "he," given the social and institutional structure of ancient Israel). Of course, we know the tradition that King David wrote the Psalms, and indeed the Twenty-third Psalm has a superscription translated in the RSV and the NRSV as "A Psalm of David"; but, as we shall see, the tradition that David wrote the Psalms developed much later than the original composition (see chapter 6).

But even though there is no way to be certain of the original setting of the psalm—it is, after all, only six verses long—scholars have made some informed suggestions. One recent authority has suggested that the psalm might have been a prayer offered by an individual in the context of a worship service held within a small circle composed of family or clan members, in which the petitioner, having survived danger ("even though I walk through the darkest valley," v. 4), offers defiant trust in God ("in the presence of my enemies," v. 5).[4]

Others, however, suggest that the setting of the psalm was originally royal: that is to say, that it was spoken by the king in the context of worship in Jerusalem—hence the mention of the "house of Yahweh" (usually translated "house of the Lord") in v. 6—and that the "enemies" mentioned in v. 5 are probably Israelites plotting against the king or, less likely, national enemies.[5]

So I shall make a suggestion: even though I do not accept the view that King David wrote all the Psalms, I think it is worth pursuing the possibility that King David wrote this one. Let us at least ponder the possibility for the moment. If the psalm *was* written by David, then we must date it to the early tenth century B.C.E., when David reigned. And if it was written by David, then there are two points to be considered in the use of "shepherd" for God. The first is that David himself had been a shepherd as a boy (1 Sam. 16:11). If David is the singer, then it is ironic that he, the erstwhile shepherd, now elevated to the highest position of the nation Israel, himself acknowledges a divine shepherd, God, so that he, David, has an identity as a sheep of God's (vv. 2-3).

The second point, of which many people are not aware, is that in the ancient Near East a ruler was called "shepherd" of his people: this is the regular usage in Assyrian and in Homeric Greek.[6] In Jer. 2:8, for example, the prophet uses "shepherds" to mean the rulers of Israel (in the RSV and NRSV the footnote states the literal meaning of the Hebrew text). So if David had been a literal shepherd as a boy, he became a metaphorical shepherd as king: but here, too, if David "shepherds" his people, then there is a divine shepherd, a divine ruler, above David. Indeed Psalm 78 is almost a commentary on the Twenty-third Psalm: in Ps. 78:52, God "led out his people like sheep, and guided them in the wilderness like a flock," and then, in vv. 70-71, God "chose his servant David, and took him from the sheepfolds; from tending the nursing ewes he brought him to be the shepherd of his people Jacob, of Israel, his inheritance."

Furthermore, if the phrase "you anoint my head with oil" implies that the psalmist is a guest to whom the divine host is being hospitable (compare Amos 6:6, and Luke 7:46 particularly)—is the setting a sacred meal in the sanctuary? one wonders—then, if David is the psalmist, "anointing" here also suggests the anointing he received in becoming king (2 Sam. 2:4).

Now the first phrase of the psalm also offers a feature to which we must pay heed: in Hebrew it reads, "Yahweh is my shepherd" ("Yahweh" being indicated in the RSV and the NRSV by the phrase "the LORD," with small capital letters—see below). "Yahweh," we must understand, was the name of the God of Israel; we may recall the elaborate narrative in Exodus 3, when God vouchsafed this divine name to Moses. For King David, as for Israelites until the time of the exile in Babylon in the sixth century B.C.E., Yahweh was understood as the God who had covenanted with the Israelite people at Sinai and led them into the land of Canaan; but Yahweh was nevertheless understood as one God among the many gods of the many nations of the world. Indeed, in Psalm 82, God confronts the gods of the nations (for this psalm, see chapter 2). There is a notable narrative in 1 Samuel 26 in which David, not yet king, is trying to keep away from the power of King Saul; Saul wants to kill the young David before he can take over the throne. David comes upon Saul's encampment during the night and begs for a reconciliation with the king. In v. 19 David speaks to Saul: "Now therefore let my lord the king hear the words of his servant. If it is Yahweh who has stirred you up against me, may he accept an offering; but if it is mortals, may they be cursed before Yahweh, for they have driven me out today from my share in Yahweh's heritage, saying, 'Go, serve other gods.'" That is to say, David wants to know the source of Saul's enmity: if it is God, David assumes that offering an animal sacrifice will take care of the matter, but if it is human beings, he can only curse them, because they want to drive him out of the territory of the Israelites, and if he is driven out of the territory of the Israelites, then he will be forced to worship some other god, which he most emphatically does not want to do. Indeed in the next chapter of 1 Samuel we are told how David slipped over into Philistine territory (1 Sam. 27:1-7)—but how could someone like David be content to worship Philistine gods? So, if David was the author of the psalm, then a plausible implication of "Yahweh is my shepherd" is "It is Yahweh who is my shepherd" (rather than some other god).

What I am stressing here is that whatever the original author or setting of the psalm, we must visualize its context in the culture of early Israel, a culture in some ways very distant from our own. The German commentator Hans-Joachim Kraus describes our own "lyric-romantic understanding of the song" but insists that "Psalm 23 is not tangled up in the bliss of trust which is here displayed in idyllic and lovely pictures of pious submission."[7]

We must go on to understand, however, that even in ancient times the psalm was undergoing shifts in its reference points as the centuries passed. Subsequent worship leaders would sing the song in the temple in Jerusalem, whether they were kings or commoners. Individuals could make the song their own—after all, there is nothing that is restrictively royal about the diction of the psalm. In this way the psalm became democratized.

But then, in 587 B.C.E., the temple in Jerusalem was destroyed and the leading citizens taken off in exile to Babylon (2 Kings 25; see especially vv. 9 and 11 there). In the years of exile, then, the phrase "I shall dwell in the house of Yahweh" either had to become a promise for the future or had to be spiritualized into something like "I shall stay within the household of Yahweh." But it is clear that the metaphor of Yahweh as shepherd continued its hold on the exilic community: in Ezekiel 34 we read the words of that prophet of the early exile about Yahweh the true shepherd, faithful to his sheep, the people of Israel, when human shepherds (the rulers) of Israel have been exploitive and negligent of their people. There can be bad shepherds as well as good shepherds!

Now by the time Babylon had collapsed and the Persian king allowed those who so wished to return to Jerusalem, in 538 B.C.E. (2 Chron. 36:22-23), two related developments had taken place. The first was that the Jewish people were convinced that the God of Israel was the God of all the world (compare the affirmations of the prophet of the exile, whose words are now found in Isaiah 40), so that the "Yahweh" who is "my shepherd" was no longer thought of as over against other gods—Yahweh was the sole God of the world. The second development was that by the time those who returned to Jerusalem rebuilt the temple there—it was dedicated in 515 B.C.E.—they became convinced that the name of God, "Yahweh," was too holy to be pronounced routinely: wherever the name appeared in a text, the reciter was obligated to use a substitute word instead, namely, "Adonay" (which means, simply, "the Lord"). Of course, if the God of Israel is the only God, then it was clear who is meant by "the Lord." (This usage of the post-exilic Jewish community is the explanation for the translation of "Yahweh" by "the LORD" in the RSV and NRSV Bibles; the small capital letters signal to the reader that the original Hebrew text has "Yahweh." It will be noted, by the way, that the JB and the NJB do continue to use the name "Yahweh.") So here is another shift of tone: we no longer hear the specificity of "Yahweh is my shepherd" but rather the generic "The Lord is my shepherd."

I should like to note two other issues that come up in the phrasing of this psalm. The first is the phrase translated in the KJV and the RSV as "the valley of the shadow of death" in v. 4. This phrase is a high point of the psalm for many who recite it today: I have already mentioned how dear the psalm is to those facing death. But, curiously, scholars are not sure precisely what the Hebrew phrase means. The Hebrew says "the valley of *ṣalmāwet.*" The question is the meaning of the word preserved as *ṣalmāwet.* The sequence can be taken as two words, *ṣal* (shadow of) and *māwet* (death). The word appears also in Pss. 44:20 (19) and 107:10 and 14; in these contexts (especially 44:20 [19]) "death" is not necessarily at issue. So some commentators have thought that the word is not a compound meaning "shadow of death" at all and that the vowels are wrongly transmitted: by this opinion the word should be taken as *ṣalmût*, with the meaning "dense darkness."[8] According to this understanding, the poet has in mind the deep, dark valleys as night comes on. Recently, however, opinion has swung back in the other direction, but with a twist: it has been suggested that the expression does literally mean "shadow of death" but that this is a kind of superlative, something like "a deathly shadow";[9] hence the NRSV rendering, "through the darkest valley." In any event, its connotation for the original poet was doubtless different from its connotation for Christians, with a Christian view of death.

In passing it may be noted that the Christian perspective on death has shaped the Christian hearing of not only the "valley of the shadow of death" but also the last phrase of the psalm, "dwell in the house of the Lord for ever" (KJV, RSV). The Hebrew here means "dwell in the house of Yahweh for length of days," and the phrase undoubtedly reflects its parallel, "all the days of my life," so that the rendition of the NRSV, "my whole life long," is appropriate.

If the "valley of the shadow of death" is a high point of the psalm for many today, then the phrase in v. 5, "in the presence of my enemies," is not necessarily a high point: that God would prepare a table before me in the presence of my enemies is not, I suspect, a concept that communicates anything very positive. But it meant much to the poet: v. 5 shifts the metaphor for God from a shepherd to a host, and the phrase "in the presence of my enemies" is the operative phrase of half the verse. The occurrence of these words reminds us of the distance between the poet's outlook and our own.

Clearly the picture is that the speaker gloats over the humiliation of his enemies. Years ago, the Psalms scholar Hermann Gunkel cited a noteworthy passage from one of the Amarna letters, letters written by princes in Palestine to the pharaoh of Egypt in the fourteenth century B.C.E. In this particular letter, from a city called Irqata, we read, "May the king our lord [the pharaoh] listen to the words of his faithful servants and give gifts to his servants [the writers] while our enemies look on and eat dust."[10] The psalmist's concern is that God's mighty protective power be obvious to his enemies, so that they may be shamed and humiliated. Israelite culture was a shame culture, like that of others since that time around the Mediterranean Sea: in Israel it was important to be able to hold one's head high in public and not be shamed.[11] The Bible offers many parallels. Thus in the first line of Jer. 2:26 we read, "As a thief is shamed when caught"—not "As a thief is accused when caught" but "is shamed." Paul makes the same point in Rom. 12:20 when he quotes Prov. 25:21-22: one shames one's enemies by meeting their evil with good. But for Christians, who know they are to love their enemies (Matt. 5:44), the line in the Twenty-third Psalm is a problem and tends to pass us by.

These considerations lead us to ponder the greatest distance of all between ourselves and the original poet, if we ourselves are Christians: that Jesus himself spoke again and again of his own shepherding role. In Mark 6:34 we heard that Jesus had compassion on the crowds because they were like sheep without a shepherd; in Luke 12:32 he is remembered as saying, "Do not be afraid, little flock," and according to Matt. 15:24 he said, "I was sent only to the lost sheep of the house of Israel." Then there is the parable of the shepherd who goes after the lost sheep (Luke 15:3-6). And we hear of Jesus the Good Shepherd preeminently in John 10:11—"I am the good shepherd; the good shepherd lays down his life for the sheep"—and indeed in the whole passage, John 10:1-16.

This metaphor of Jesus as the good shepherd became a central image for the Christian church: it was the favorite symbol of Christ among those who constructed and worshiped in the catacombs in Rome—when one visits the catacombs, there one can see paintings of the Good Shepherd and carvings of the Good Shepherd on tomb after tomb from the second century onward;[12] and from when the Christian faith became the faith of the Roman empire, one finds impressive statues of Christ as the Good Shepherd.[13]

And surely for Christians the image of Jesus as the Good Shepherd overlies the Twenty-third Psalm: if the convention of Jews since the post-exilic period is to use "the Lord" for the name of God, and if "the Lord" is used in the Gospels to refer to Jesus (Matt. 7:21-22; Luke 24:34; and *passim*), then Christians will inevitably hear the Twenty-third Psalm as a description of Jesus the Good Shepherd.

Furthermore, it is almost inevitable that Christians, on hearing "you prepare a table before me," will understand a reference to the last supper and the sacrament of communion. For example, it is said that this verse was a favorite text for communion in London churches during the German bombings during World War II.[14]

But the association is much older. Athanasius, the bishop of Alexandria in the fourth century, in his exposition of the psalm states that "he leads me beside still waters" is "perhaps to be understood as holy baptism," that "you anoint my head with oil" means "the mystic chrism" (the consecrated oil used in baptism, confirmation, and ordination), and "you prepare a table before me" means "the mystic table."[15] And Cyril of Alexandria (?370–444) expanded on the idea of the "table" as that of the Eucharist (service of communion), explaining "enemies" as well:

> Perhaps this too might be said by the faithful: You have prepared for us a spiritual table, so that by eating and being strengthened we will be able to face our persecutors at any time. For spiritual food, by encouraging the soul, enables it to resist impure spirits and the teachers of errors. But the mystic table, the flesh of the Lord, also makes us strong against passions and demons. For Satan fears those who become pious participants in the mysteries.[16]

This Christianization of the psalm brings with it a Christian understanding of Christ as bringing his people from death to life in the phrases "even though I walk through the valley of the shadow of death" and "I shall dwell in the house of the Lord for ever" (RSV). It will be interesting to see how English-speaking Christians react to the shifts of translation in the NRSV for this psalm (compare the discussion in chapter 17).

For us in the twentieth century, as I have already noted, even the vividness of the metaphor of "shepherd" has faded. And because sheep are not noted for being very bright animals ("All we like sheep have gone astray," Isa. 53:6), you and I may not take kindly to the notion that we are in need of shepherding. The danger, then, as I have already said, is a sentimentalizing of the psalm, shaped by Sunday-school pictures, and, to the extent that the psalm defines our faith, a sentimentalizing of our faith.

As we survey the journey of the Twenty-third Psalm from then to now, it is clear that some of its original implications are lost on us and that it has taken on the baggage of later implications. How much of this loss and gain is legitimate, to be encouraged? How much of it is illegitimate, to be fought against? To put it in the strongest terms: Is it possible that the Holy Spirit urged on the original poet, in pre-exilic Israel, words whose true import is only to be understood in later centuries, in the light of further revelation?

These are not questions that my parishioner Beth could know or care about, but they may well be questions to be pondered by those of us who do not perceive ourselves yet to be at death's door. They are the kind of questions with which this book will deal.

NOTES

1. Eldridge Cleaver, *Soul on Fire* (Waco, Tex.: Word, 1978), 211–12.
2. Garrison Keillor, *Lake Wobegon Days* (New York: Viking, 1985), 118–23.

3. See Walter Brueggemann, *Israel's Praise: Doxology against Idolatry and Ideology* (Philadelphia: Fortress, 1988), 1–28.

4. For this view, see Erhard S. Gerstenberger, *Psalms: Part I, with an Introduction to Cultic Poetry* (The Forms of the Old Testament Literature 14; Grand Rapids: Eerdmans, 1988), 115–16.

5. Arthur C. Merrill, "Psalm 23 and the Jerusalem Tradition," *VT* 15 (1965):354–60; cf. John Eaton, "Problems of Translation in Psalm 23, 3f," *Bible Translator* 16 (1965): 171–76; Hans-Joachim Kraus, *Psalms 1–59, A Commentary* (Minneapolis: Augsburg, 1988), 305–6.

6. Francis Brown, Samuel R. Driver, and Charles A. Briggs, *A Hebrew and English Lexicon of the Old Testament* (Oxford: Clarendon, 1907), 945a, I *rā'â*, 1d; Walter Baumgartner and others, *Hebräisches und Aramäisches Lexikon zum Alten Testament* (Leiden: Brill, 1967–90), 1176a, I *r'h*, B 3.

7. Kraus, *Psalms 1–59*, 309.

8. Charles Augustus Briggs and Emilie Grace Briggs, *A Critical and Exegetical Commentary on the Book of Psalms* (ICC; New York: Charles Scribner's Sons, 1906–7), 1:211–12.

9. D. Winton Thomas, "*ṣalmāwet* in the Old Testament," *JSS* 7 (1962): 191–200, and, in general, the bibliography in Baumgartner and others, *Lexikon*, 964b.

10. Jorgen A. Knudtzon, *Die El-Amarna-Tafeln* (Leipzig: Hinrichs, 1907–15), no. 100, 31–36.

11. For biblical Israel, see Johannes Pedersen, *Israel: Its Life and Culture* (I/II; London: Oxford University Press; Copenhagen: Branner, 1926), 213–44. For current anthropological investigations of these phenomena today and with copious bibliography, see David D. Gilmore (ed.), *Honor and Shame and the Unity of the Mediterranean* (Washington, D.C.: American Anthropological Association, 1987). More accessible are David W. Augsburger, *Pastoral Counseling across Cultures* (Philadelphia: Westminster, 1986), 111–32, where the author analyzes shame cultures from a psychological point of view; and John J. Pilch, *Introducing the Cultural Context of the Old Testament* (Hear the Word 1; New York: Paulist, 1991), 49–70. Pilch suggests we ponder the assumptions in a film such as *Prizzi's Honor*.

12. Jack Finegan, *Light from the Ancient Past* (Princeton: Princeton University Press, 1946), 383–84, figs. 163, 167.

13. See the marble statue in the Lateran Museum, Rome, depicted in G.W.H. Lampe (ed.), *The Cambridge History of the Bible*, vol. 2: *The West from the Fathers to the Reformation* (Cambridge: Cambridge University Press, 1969), plate 6.

14. J.R.P. Sclater, "Exposition, Psalm 23," in *IB* 4:128b.

15. *PG* 27:col. 140.

16. *PG* 69:841–42.

PART ONE

THE PSALMS
TAKE SHAPE—
A RECONSTRUCTION

2

In the Beginning:
Psalms
Sung in David's Day

There have always been songs. As long as men and women have used words, they must have used words with rhythm: words with power; words to be repeated; words with which to recall the heroism of battle, to bring success to the hunt, to celebrate the joy of birth and the sorrow of death. Indeed researchers have recently reported that the long songs of the humpback whale give evidence of rhymelike schemes![1] So one may assume that words have been sung as long as there have been men and women communicating at all.

When we look at the ancient Near East, we see wall paintings from earliest times in Egypt depicting dancers, musicians, and singers,[2] and bas-reliefs from Assyria of the same sort.[3] And we have texts of hymns from both Egypt on the one hand and Assyria and Babylonia on the other.[4]

Now, when we examine the biblical book of Psalms, what can we say about its origin? The tradition among both Christians and Jews is that King David wrote the Psalms. For example, Heb. 4:7 in the New Testament attributes the words of Ps. 95:7-8 to David, even though that psalm in the Old Testament has no specific notation associating it with David. There is a remark in Jewish tradition from the second century C.E. that implies that David at least edited the Psalms.[5]

But this tradition seems to have arisen late in the biblical period. Scholars today believe it is altogether plausible that David wrote *some* psalms, but the tradition that David wrote the *whole* book of Psalms appears to be a late one that arose when the Psalms were being collected; we shall examine the matter in chapter 6. If David wrote some psalms, then the tradition that he wrote the whole book of Psalms was an expansion of that memory, reinforced by the record of his skill on the lyre (1 Sam. 16:14-23; 18:10), of his laments over Saul and Jonathan (2 Sam. 1:19-27) and over Abner (2 Sam. 3:33-34), and of his organization of the musicians at the sanctuary in Jerusalem (1 Chron. 6:16-17 [Protestant numeration vv. 31-32]; 16:4-7; 25:1; 2 Chron. 23:18).

Scholars who have worked on the Psalms in the last hundred years or so have detected within them the kind of variations of style and emphasis that suggest that they are the product of many poets and singers over many centuries. In this chapter and in the next three chapters, I offer a plausible reconstruction of the origin of the Psalms; but it is only fair to say that there are not enough clues within the Psalms for certainty, and scholars therefore continue to differ on many details.

The Historical Framework of the Old Testament

In chapter 1 I offered a few details of the history of the Old Testament people as we looked at the way Psalm 23 might have fared through the course of that history. Now, however, I want to offer a historical framework into which we can fit the remarks on various psalms with which we deal in this and the following three chapters.

It is convenient to begin the story with Moses; a good guess for a date for Moses' career would be 1250 B.C.E. By 1220 B.C.E. there were evidently Israelites settled in the land of Canaan (Palestine), worshiping the God whom they called Yahweh. They worshiped at various sanctuaries; notable among these were two sanctuaries where at one time or another was kept the Ark of the Covenant, that symbol of the presence of Yahweh with the covenant people. One of these sanctuaries was at Bethel, eight kilometers (five miles) north of Jerusalem (Judg. 20:26-27); the other was at Shiloh, where the boy Samuel grew up, thirty-two kilometers (twenty miles) north of Jerusalem (1 Samuel 1–3, especially 3:3). Another important early sanctuary was at Dan, where the headwaters of the River Jordan are to be found at the base of Mount Hermon in the far north, 170 kilometers (106 miles) north of Jerusalem; there a grandson of Moses was installed as priest (Judg. 18:30).

A variety of political and military pressures resulted in the establishment of the kingship in Israel, first under Saul, then under his son-in-law David, about 1000 B.C.E. King David captured the city of Jerusalem for himself; in that city David installed the Ark of the Covenant (2 Sam. 6:1-15), and David's son Solomon built a permanent temple for it on the mountain in Jerusalem called "Zion" (1 Kings 5–8, especially 8:1).

After Solomon's death, about 922 B.C.E., the kingdom of Israel split in two, north and south. The northern kingdom continued to call itself the kingdom of Israel, and it comprised ten of the Israelite tribes. This kingdom had its capital in three successive cities: first at Shechem, an old city forty-nine kilometers (thirty miles) north of Jerusalem; then at two nearby cities—Tirzah, ten kilometers (six miles) northeast of Shechem, and a new city, Samaria, which was built by King Omri in about 875 B.C.E. (1 Kings 16:24) and was located twelve kilometers (seven and one-half miles) northwest of Shechem. The throne in the north was frequently overthrown by usurpers, notable among whom was the general Jehu, who took over from the house of Ahab in about 842 B.C.E. By contrast, the southern kingdom, called the kingdom of Judah, maintained its capital in Jerusalem and maintained its kingship in the line of King David.

The northern kingdom came to an end when Samaria was captured by the

Assyrians (invaders from what is present-day northern Iraq) in 721 B.C.E. Many of its leaders were taken east into exile, some seem to have taken refuge in the southern kingdom, and the so-called Samaritan community that emerged two hundred years later seems to have drawn on northern traditions. On the other hand, the southern kingdom was able to continue its existence for another 134 years. Then Jerusalem was captured by the Babylonians (invaders from what is present-day southern Iraq) in 587 B.C.E.

Much of the leadership from Jerusalem was taken into exile in Babylon; there they and their descendants remained until allowed to return to Jerusalem in 538 B.C.E. by Cyrus, king of Persia, who had defeated Babylonia.[6] I continue an outline of the history of the Jews in chapter 5.

The Discovery of the Ugaritic Texts

Surprisingly, there are indications that a handful of psalms have their origin long before David's time. To understand this we must touch on an archeological discovery made in 1928.

In the spring of that year an Arab peasant was plowing his land, about twelve kilometers (seven and one-half miles) north of the port of Latakia in Syria, when his plow struck a slab of stone, part of an ancient tomb. The Department of Antiquities was alerted, and the following year an archeological campaign was begun on a neighboring mound, locally known as Ras Shamra (Fennel Promontory). The mound turned out to be the remains of an ancient city named Ugarit, a city previously known from Babylonian, Hittite, and Egyptian records. The archeological excavations have continued in the decades since, and the site has been enormously productive.[7]

The crucial matter for our purposes is the extensive series of texts, written on clay tablets in a previously unknown language, that have been unearthed from the mound. This language (now called Ugaritic) is related to biblical Hebrew but dates earlier than Hebrew. The texts in question were, it seems, copied during the period 1375–1340 B.C.E., but in many cases the origin of these texts was centuries earlier. (Recall the dates given above: Moses evidently flourished about 1250 B.C.E., and the reign of King David began about 1000 B.C.E.) The texts of greatest interest to us are the myths of Canaanite gods and goddesses and the legends of ancient heroes. In many cases the names of the Canaanite gods mentioned in these new texts are already known from references in the Old Testament—the fertility god Baal, for example (see Judg. 6:25 and the narratives in 1 Kings 18 and 2 Kings 10:18-27). What we have here, then, is a collection of the pagan religious lore of the Canaanites, a reflection of the religious practices against which the leaders of Israel later struggled.

But what became apparent as scholars studied these texts in detail was that the texts in many instances offered words and phrases that occurred in the Old Testament as well, especially in the Psalms—and, more than words and phrases, grammatical peculiarities and poetic structures. Indeed this Ugaritic literature, as it is now called, has been able to elucidate many puzzling sequences in the Psalms that had been thought by earlier scholars simply to be copyists' errors or that had been misunderstood.

A few examples may make the matter clear. The second half of Ps. 29:2 is a line that in the KJV was translated, "Worship the Lord in the beauty of holiness" (it gave rise to a nineteenth-century hymn opening with those words).[8] Now a frequent pattern in Hebrew is two nouns in an "of" pattern (X of Y), but this structure is often better rendered in English by an adjectival structure; for example, in Ps. 2:6 the literal Hebrew "hill of my holiness" really means "my holy hill." So "in the beauty of holiness" was assumed by commentators to mean "in holy ornaments";[9] hence the RSV translation "in holy array." By this understanding the heavenly host was summoned to worship Yahweh in splendid vestments or the like. But the same word that has been translated "beauty" or "array" (Hebrew, *hadrat*) turns up in a Ugaritic text in parallelism with the word meaning "dream" or "vision." One of these texts is the legend of King Keret, who is supposed to be a son of the god El and thus half divine. Keret had a dream of the god; the two lines in question read, "Keret awoke, and it was a dream; the servant of El, and it was a visitation."[10] That is to say, the word in Ugaritic does not mean "beauty" or "ornament" but "(splendor of) divine visitation" or "revelation." It refers to a theophany, an appearance of the god. Because Psalm 29 turns out to be a very old psalm indeed (see below), the line in v. 2 means "Worship [prostrate yourselves before] Yahweh in (his) holy visitation."[11] The word does not then refer to the vestments of the worshipers but to the glory of God. (The NRSV is ambiguous: "Worship the Lord in holy splendor.")

Now, it is striking that the Ugaritic texts offer the same kind of parallelism as is found in Hebrew poetry, as we can see in the case of the two parallel words in the Ugaritic lines, "dream" and "visitation." And not only do the two bodies of literature both offer parallelisms, but in some cases the same pairs of parallel words occur in both bodies of literature. For example, "hand" (Hebrew, *yād*) is often paired with "right hand" (Hebrew, *yāmîn*). Thus in Psalm 89 there are two verses with this pairing, vv. 14 (13) and 26 (25); the latter reads, "I will set his [David's] hand on the sea and his right hand on the rivers." In the Ugaritic texts, too, this is a frequent pairing; for example, "Take the cup from my hand, the goblet from my right hand."[12]

Again, there are in the Psalms examples of a type of poetic parallelism that has been called "stair-step" parallelism, where the elements are repeated in a form such as A + B + C // A + B + D // A + D + E. In the Psalms one can note Ps. 96:1-2a,

Sing to Yahweh a new song,
Sing to Yahweh, all the earth,
Sing to Yahweh, bless his name.

Another example is Psalm 29, where vv. 1-2 are translated in the NRSV, "Ascribe to the Lord, O heavenly beings, ascribe to the Lord glory and strength. Ascribe to the Lord the glory of his name; worship the Lord in holy splendor" (for more on

Psalm 29, see below). In the Ugaritic texts this type of parallelism was a favorite: for example,

> Like the heart of a cow (yearning) for her calf,
> like the heart of a ewe (yearning) for her lamb,
> so the heart of Anat (yearned) after Baal.[13]

From a great array of such evidence, of which I have offered only a few examples, one can draw a remarkable conclusion: that there was in Syria–Palestine a shared cultural tradition of poetry-building that included both the Canaanites in the Late Bronze Age (1500–1200 B.C.E.) or earlier, from whom we have the Ugaritic texts, and the Israelites who had settled in the land of Canaan by a time just before 1200 B.C.E., from whom we have early Hebrew poetry, including early psalms. And the existence of this shared cultural tradition suggests that the Israelites are marked off from the Canaanites not so much by any ethnic distinctiveness as by their religious conviction that they are the covenant people called together by Yahweh.[14]

Psalms with Canaanite Antecedents

I have already mentioned the second verse of Psalm 29, where the word "visitation" appears, and I have mentioned the stair-step parallelism of the first two verses of that psalm. But there is more to be said about Psalm 29. In this psalm Yahweh is manifested in thunder, lightning, and storm:

> The voice of Yahweh is over the waters;
>   the God of glory thunders,
> Yahweh, over mighty waters.
> . . .
> The voice of Yahweh breaks the cedars;
>   Yahweh breaks the cedars of Lebanon.
> He makes Lebanon skip like a calf,
>   and Sirion like a young wild ox.
> The voice of Yahweh flashes forth flames of fire. (vv. 3, 5-7)

Now, thunder, lightning, and storm are precisely the manifestations of the Canaanite god Baal in the Ugaritic texts: "Now at last Baal may appoint a time for his rain, a time for (his) ship (to appear) in the snow and for the sounding of his voice in the clouds, for him to release (his) lightnings on the earth."[15] That is to say, Yahweh is described in Psalm 29 in just the way Baal had been described by the Canaanites. But there is more: if one actually substitutes the word "Baal" (Hebrew, *ba'al*) for the word "Yahweh" (Hebrew, *yahweh*) in the Hebrew text of the psalm, a number of alliterations appear. Thus the first line of v. 3 would be not *qôl yahweh 'al-hammáyim* but *qol ba'al 'al-hammáyim*, and v. 7 would be not *qôl yahweh ḥōṣēb laḥăbôt 'ēš* but *qôl ba'al ḥōṣēb laḥăbôt 'ēš*. And if one substitutes *ba'al* for *yahweh* in vv. 5 and 6, the name of the god would be echoed by the double occurrence of the word "Lebanon" (Hebrew, *lĕbānôn*). In sum, the present Hebrew text of the psalm has so great a number of occurrences of the consonants *b* and *l* and of the syllable 'al as to lead us to suspect that the original form of the psalm was a hymn to the god Baal and that it was later adapted for the worship of Yahweh by the simple expedient of substituting the name "Yahweh" for "Baal."[16] Whether the adaptation was so simple or was more complex is impossible to say, but it is clear that at the very least Psalm 29 is a Yahwistic adaptation of an older Canaanite hymn.[17] A Canaanite background for the psalm would explain the curious address in the first line of the psalm to the *běnê 'ēlîm*—literally, "sons of gods" (see the footnote in the RSV and the NRSV)—that is, various "gods" or "godlings." These divine personages are referred to again in Ps. 89:7 (6); they give no difficulty in a polytheistic context but are certainly in tension with monotheism after it emerged.[18] (Commentaries written before the discovery of the Ugaritic material usually explain the phrase as a reference to angels.)[19] Here, then, is a psalm that appears to come from a time much earlier than that of King David. (However, it may be noted in passing that it was not only that the Israelites borrowed from the pagans; borrowing could go in the other direction as well. For example, a pagan adaptation of part of Psalm 20 has turned up in Egypt—see chapter 4.)

Another psalm that is likely to be from the premonarchical period is Psalm 82. It appears to be a vision of the divine council in heaven, perhaps a vision originally delivered by a prophet. It portrays a trial in which God, as the head of the divine council, puts the pagan gods on trial; here, it is clear, we have a fine polemic against the Canaanite gods, who are found guilty of not looking after the afflicted and the poor (vv. 2-3). The verdict is astonishing (vv. 6-7); God speaks: "You are gods," but "you shall die like mortals!" The phraseology in this psalm is very old. Thus the gods are called *běnê 'elyôn*, "children of Elyon" (NRSV, "children of the Most High"). But, most remarkably, the psalm has phraseology that reminds one of the Ugaritic legend of King Keret. Keret is ill and threatened with death, and his son asks, "Shall you die, father, as men? . . . or shall gods die?"[20] And it appears that, because of his weakness, he had not been defending the poor, the orphan, and the widow.[21] Whether or not the Israelite psalm was deliberately playing on the motifs of the Canaanite Keret legend, at least the psalm comes out of a time when the struggle between the Canaanite gods and Yahweh was perceived to be hanging in the balance; one is safe therefore in looking for its origin in the earliest period of Israel.[22]

Another psalm (or, rather, half-psalm) that is likely to stem from this period is Ps. 19:2-7 (1-6). Verses 5b-7 (4b-6) are a unique sequence, describing the sun in its path across the sky; this description is a complement to the affirmation of the glory of the heavens and the firmament (the dome of the sky) that silently proclaim the revelation of God (vv. 2-5a [1-4a]). Mitchell Dahood suggests that what we have here is an Israelite adaptation of a Canaanite hymn to the sun.[23] I am not aware of any Canaanite model that would urge this conclusion, but it is altogether likely, given the preoccupation of pagans with "signs of the heavens." In any event, the half-psalm is probably pre-Davidic; the closest parallel is Judg. 5:31, the end of the song of Deborah: "So perish all your enemies, O Lord! But may your friends be like the sun as it rises in its might." The song of Deborah is by common opinion the oldest long poetic sequence in the Old Testament, dating probably to the late twelfth century B.C.E.[24] It is possible, then, to imagine Ps. 19:2-7 (1-6) originating in this period. It should be noted that the last half of the psalm, vv. 8-15 (7-14), is clearly a post-exilic addition, perhaps from the fifth century B.C.E.; I discuss it in chapter 5.

In these psalms, then, and perhaps a few others, one may be in touch, even though distantly, with the imagery of people who flourished *before* the time of David. These psalms span the full period of three thousand years referred to in the title of this book. The phrases of these psalms have undergone the greatest transformation of all: they underwent an adaption out of paganism into the Israelite faith in Yahweh.

Psalms from David's Reign

Now, are there any psalms that may plausibly be attributed to the reign of David? I set forth in chapter 1 a scenario that would emerge if Psalm 23 really originated with David, and I think that scenario is not simply a sentimental exercise but a plausible one; but there is no way to be sure with a psalm of only six verses. At this point I suggest three other psalms that appear to have originated in David's reign.

I begin with Psalm 2, which is a psalm for the day of the king's coronation—God says, "I have set my king on Zion, my holy hill" (v. 6). It was common in the ancient Near East for vassal states to take advantage of a change in rule to rebel against an oppressive ruler.[25] But Yahweh has put his king in place in Jerusalem, and Yahweh will keep rebellious peoples at bay (vv. 4-6, 10-12)! Who speaks in this psalm? Who is the "I" in v. 7? It sounds like the declaration of a priest or even of a prophet: the words of Yahweh to the king, "You are my son, today I have begotten you," are certainly reminiscent of the words of Yahweh in the oracle of the prophet Nathan about King David in 2 Sam. 7:13, "I will be a father to him, and he shall be a son to me." Earlier in Nathan's oracle there is reference to Yahweh's cutting off David's enemies for him (2 Sam. 7:8-11), as there is in this psalm. And one notes that both passages use the word "rod" for punishment (Ps. 2:9; 2 Sam. 7:14). The language of the psalm is certainly archaic—one authority suggests a date in the tenth century B.C.E.,[26] and I think it altogether likely that it was a psalm sung by Nathan at David's coronation.

A psalm of similar content and background is Psalm 110. Unfortunately, the meaning of the Hebrew text of this psalm is at several points very uncertain. The Hebrew phrasing of the first half of v. 1 is, literally, "The revelation of Yahweh to my lord: 'Sit down at my right hand,'" where "my lord" means something like "your majesty" (compare the use of "my lord" in 1 Sam. 24:8-10). The Hebrew word translated "revelation" suggests the oracle of a prophet, and because the oracle is addressed to the king, one thinks again of Nathan and David. The oracle is evidently spoken in the context of a coronation in Jerusalem (v. 2).[27] One of the most curious expressions in the Psalms is to be found in v. 4: "You are a priest forever according to the order of Melchizedek." The figure of Melchizedek was of importance for the sect at the Dead Sea (see chapter 7) and in the argumentation of the Letter to the Hebrews in the New Testament (see chapter 8). The name "Melchizedek" occurs in a short passage in Genesis (Gen. 14:18), where a king by that name is said to have dealt with the patriarch Abraham. But, in truth, in the present text of Psalm 110 the name may be a misunderstanding of what might have lain in the original text: because "Melchizedek" in Hebrew may mean "my king is legitimate," the original meaning of the phrase in the psalm may be, simply, "You are a priest forever, according to my decree my legitimate king."[28] In any event, the text seems to indicate that the king was to be a priest as well (v. 4); and because 2 Sam. 8:18 seems to imply that David could function as a priest (compare 1 Kings 3:4), we are again led to the possibility that the psalm was originally sung at David's coronation. But of course there can be no certainty in the matter.

The third psalm that might plausibly be linked to David is Psalm 18, a hymn of thanksgiving after a successful battle. Strikingly, this psalm is duplicated in 2 Samuel 22, and there it is specifically attributed to David (2 Sam 22:1). The context given for the psalm in 2 Samuel 22 might itself be unhistorical, but that this psalm, which appears to offer archaic language, is preserved in two different parts of the Old Testament suggests that the attribution to David should be taken seriously; most scholars at least date it to the tenth century B.C.E.[29]

Although we cannot with confidence locate more than a handful of psalms from David's day, there are certainly a few, and these few can stretch our minds back to the worship that took place in the days of his reign. Fortunately, there are a substantial number of psalms that we can date to the next few centuries, and it is to these that we turn in the next two chapters.

NOTES

1. Linda N. Guinee and Katharine B. Payne, "Rhyme-like Repetitions in Songs of Humpback Whales," *Ethology* 79 (1988):295–306.

2. Othmar Keel, *The Symbolism of the Biblical World* (New York: Seabury, 1978), 335–52; James B. Pritchard, *The Ancient Near East in Pictures* (Princeton: Princeton University Press, 1954), 65–66, figs. 206–11.

3. Keel, *Symbolism of the Biblical World*, plate 27.

4. James B. Pritchard, *Ancient Near East Texts relating to the Old Testament* (Princeton: Princeton University Press, 1955), 365–92.

5. Charles Augustus Briggs and Emilie Grace Briggs, *A Critical and Exegetical Commentary on the Book of Psalms* (ICC; New York: Charles Scribner's Sons, 1906–7), 1:liv.

6. See, conveniently, John Bright, *A History of Israel* (Philadelphia: Westminster, 1981).

7. J.C.L. Gibson, *Canaanite Myths and Legends* (Edinburgh: T. & T. Clark, 1978), 1; Mitchell Dahood, *Psalms I: 1–50* (AB 16; Garden City, N.Y.: Doubleday, 1966), xviii.

8. John S. B. Monsell (1811–1875), "Worship the Lord in the Beauty of Holiness"; see, e.g., *Pilgrim Hymnal* (Boston: Pilgrim, 1958), no. 31; *The Hymn Book of the Anglican Church of Canada and the United Church of Canada* (Toronto: Anglican Church of Canada and the United Church of Canada, 1971), no. 33.

9. So Briggs, *Commentary*, 1:251, 252.

10. Ugaritic Text 14 (Krt), line 155; see, conveniently, Gibson, *Canaanite Myths*, 86.

11. Frank M. Cross, Jr., "Notes on a Canaanite Psalm in the Old Testament," *BASOR* 117 (February 1950): 20–21; Hans-Joachim Kraus, *Psalms 1–59: A Commentary* (Minneapolis: Augsburg, 1988), 344.

12. Ugaritic Text 19 (Aqhat), lines 215–16.

13. Ugaritic Text 6.ii.28–30.

14. Cf. the remarks by James L. Kugel, "Topics in the History of the Spirituality of the Psalms," in Arthur Green (ed.), *Jewish Spirituality from the Bible through the Middle Ages* (World Spirituality, An Encyclopedic History of the Religious Quest 13; New York: Crossroad, 1988), 119–20.

15. Ugaritic Text 4.v.68–71; see Gibson, *Canaanite Myths*, 60–61.

16. For this suggestion, see Aloysius Fitzgerald, "A Note on Psalm 29," *BASOR* 215 (October 1974): 61–63.

17. See the literature cited in Dahood, *Psalms I*, 175; Kraus, *Psalms 1–59*, 346, and full discussion there.

18. For a recent discussion of the possibility of polytheism in the monarchical period of Israel, see Mark S. Smith, *The Early History of God, Yahweh and the Other Deities in Ancient Israel* (San Francisco: Harper & Row, 1990); for "sons of gods," see 9.

19. So Briggs, *Commentary*, 1:252.

20. Ugaritic Text 16 (Krt) vi.47–50; see Gibson, *Canaanite Myths*, 95.

21. Ugaritic Text 16 (Krt) i.17–18, 22; see Gibson, *Canaanite Myths*, 102. On the resemblances with Keret, see Roger T. O'Callaghan, "A Note on the Canaanite Background of Psalm 82," *CBQ* 15 (1953):311–14.

22. Mitchell Dahood, *Psalms II: 51–100* (AB 17; Garden City, N.Y.: Doubleday, 1968), 269; Leopold Sabourin, *The Psalms: Their Origin and Meaning* (New York: Alba House, 1974), 308–9, with further bibliography.

23. Dahood, *Psalms I*, 121.

24. Bright, *History of Israel*, 147.

25. Kraus, *Psalms 1–59*, 126.

26. Dahood, *Psalms I*, 7.

27. Hans-Joachim Kraus, *Psalms 60—150: A Commentary* (Minneapolis: Augsburg, 1989), 347.

28. Mitchell Dahood, *Psalms III: 101–150* (AB 17A; Garden City, N.Y.: Doubleday, 1970), 117–18; but this understanding of the verse began years ago with Theodor Gaster: see Sabourin, *Psalms*, 361–62.

29. See the basic study by Frank M. Cross, Jr., and David Noel Freedman, "A Royal Song of Thanksgiving: II Samuel 22 = Psalm 18," *JBL* 72 (1953):15–34. For recent discussion, see Dahood, *Psalms I*, 104; Kraus, *Psalms 1—59*, 256–58; Sabourin, *Psalms*, 342–44; P. Kyle McCarter, Jr., *II Samuel* (AB 9; Garden City, N.Y.: Doubleday, 1984), 474–75.

3

Psalms
from the North

In chapter 2 we examined a handful of psalms that may have been known during David's kingship. As for his son Solomon, there are no psalms that can be attributed to the time of his kingship. It is true, Psalm 72 carries the superscription "Of Solomon," but this note doubtless reflects a late tradition based on the expression "king's son" in v. 1, understood as "David's son." There is at least the possibility that Psalm 104 was adapted from an Egyptian source during Solomon's reign (see the discussion in chapter 4), but there is no way to prove it.

We remind ourselves that the kingdom broke in two after Solomon's death, and so we ask ourselves whether we can trace any of the Psalms to the northern kingdom of Israel. As a matter of fact, scholars have recently begun to work on evidence that there are indeed a good many such psalms within our biblical book. Before we consider this evidence, however, we need to think through how such psalms would have come to us.

We must remind ourselves that the present book of Psalms, as a collection, is a product of the post-exilic Jewish community in Jerusalem (see chapter 6), so that any psalms of northern origin would be psalms that later proved useful in the south and were preserved in the south. Such psalms would be of two sorts. The first sort is psalms written by northerners and used at one or another of the northern sanctuaries before the fall of Samaria in 721 B.C.E. These psalms would have been brought south by refugees and adapted or adopted by worshipers in Jerusalem. The second sort of psalm would be psalms written by northerners who were not loyal to northern sanctuaries but who continued to remain loyal to Solomon's temple in Jerusalem. Such psalms could have originated either before 721 B.C.E. or thereafter: in Jer. 41:4-5 we read of some pilgrims from the north who came south to worship at Jerusalem at a time just after the fall of that city in 587 B.C.E. Psalms of this sort could of course be adopted without any change by the south.

But it is safe to say that any psalm from the north would have its origin before the fall of Jerusalem in 587 B.C.E.: there are not likely to have been any self-identified northerners among the exiles from Jerusalem to Babylon, and the Jews

26

that rebuilt the temple two generations later, in 520 B.C.E., had no interest in the participation of any northerners (Ezra 4:1-3).

The Nature of the Evidence

With these considerations in mind, how might we recognize the psalms from the north? There are two interlocking kinds of evidence. The first is any *references to geographical features or tribes of the north*. For example, several scholars have noticed that the references to "the Jordan," "Mount Hermon," and "the thunder of your cataracts" in Ps. 42:6-7 (5-6) suggest a locale at the headwaters of the River Jordan in Upper Galilee; similarly, the references to "Joseph," "Ephraim," and Manasseh" in Ps. 80:2-3 (1-2) suggest a northern locale for the psalm, inasmuch as Ephraim and Manasseh are the two half-tribes of "Joseph" (Gen. 48:13-14) and both were northern territories. (But the contrary is not true; a psalm that speaks of "Zion" or "Jerusalem" could still have a northern origin—it could be a northern psalm later adapted for the south by the addition of "Zion" or the like, or it could be a psalm of a northerner loyal to the south.)

The second kind of evidence is *language usage* in the Hebrew text that exhibits northern dialect: if one finds a striking number of words or grammatical forms that are characteristic of the north, then one may conclude that the text is of northern origin. What resources are there for determining northern dialect? Scholars may examine the text of the book of Hosea, a northern prophet. They also reach out beyond the Old Testament to the inscriptions of this historical period from Phoenicia (present-day Lebanon) and from Ammonite territory (territory adjoining the northern kingdom east of the Jordan River): the dialects of Phoenician and Ammonite are very closely related to biblical Hebrew. And beyond these closely related dialects, scholars look to Aramaic, a language then centered in Damascus; and, more distantly, to the Ugaritic texts: even though the Ugaritic texts are earlier than those of the biblical period, they reflect the language of southwest Syria north of present-day Lebanon (see chapter 2). From the texts of these dialects and languages scholars can isolate many northern features.

Much of the evidence is technical, a matter of the details of the Hebrew language, but one example may illustrate evidence of language usage. Psalm 10 has a curious expression for the negative, the word *bal*; it occurs five times in the psalm, in vv. 4, 6, 11, 15, and 18. By contrast, the normal Hebrew negative is *lō'*. The negative *bal* appears also in the short Psalm 16, in vv. 2, 4 (twice), and 8. Now, *bal* is the only negative to occur in Phoenician, and it is common in Ugaritic as well. It occurs sporadically in other psalms that appear to have a northern origin; outside the Psalms it appears twice in the book of Hosea, who was a northern prophet, and once in the book of Job. One may conclude that the use of *bal* is an evidence of northern dialect.

Gary A. Rendsburg, a young scholar at Cornell University, has recently submitted all the Psalms to examination for evidence of northern dialect;[1] he has concluded that the following thirty-five psalms are of northern origin: Psalms 9–10 (originally a single psalm); 16; 29; 36; the Korahite psalms (Psalms 42–49; 84; 85; 87; 88); 53; 58; the psalms of Asaph (Psalms 50; 73–83); 116; 132; 133; 140; and 141.

With regard to Psalms 29 and 82, our discussion of these psalms in chapter 2 has made it plain that they reflect Canaanite phraseology such as occurs in the Ugaritic texts, so it is not surprising to learn that they offer northern linguistic features. In this chapter I discuss the other thirty-three psalms. I begin with Psalm 45, one of the Korahite psalms, a psalm unlike any other. Then I discuss the other Korahite psalms, then the psalms of Asaph, and then the remainder that Rendsburg has specified.

Psalm 45

Psalm 45 is unique in not being addressed to God at all, but rather to a king and queen on the occasion of their wedding. The king is not named, but the reference to the Phoenician city of Tyre in v. 13 (12) suggests that the queen in question was Jezebel, the princess from Sidon (1 Kings 16:31—the cities of Tyre and Sidon were at that time united under one king),[2] who was given in marriage to Ahab, a king of the northern kingdom of Israel, whose father Omri built the capital of Samaria. And the "ivory palaces" in v. 9 (8) remind one of the "ivory house" that Ahab built (1 Kings 22:39); that phrase was doubtless a reference to the ivory inlay work in the royal palace in Samaria, pieces of which were preserved in the ruins of that palace and excavated by archeologists in recent times.[3] The plausibility of this identification of the king is increased if the verb "you love" in v. 8 (7) (Hebrew 'āhabtā) is seen as a play on the name of Ahab (Hebrew, 'aḥ'āb).[4] The likelihood is that this psalm was composed for the wedding of Ahab and Jezebel;[5] the date then would be approximately 869 B.C.E.[6]

The Other Korahite Psalms

Rendsburg finds northern linguistic features in the whole series of psalms that have the superscription "Of the Korahites," that is, Psalms 42–43, which were originally a single psalm (see below); 44–49; 84; 85; 87; and 88. He is, however, by no means the first scholar to propose that the Korahite psalms have a northern origin;[7] in particular, a young British scholar named Michael D. Goulder has put forward a daring and plausible theory of the origin of these psalms. I set forth this theory here; though there is no way to be certain, it is a possible explanation for them and a useful way for us to envisage their earliest setting.

Goulder proposes that these psalms were used in the autumn liturgy at the Israelite sanctuary of Dan, in the far north of the kingdom.[8] This festival is the so-called Festival of Booths, the only festival recorded for the northern kingdom (1 Kings 12:32-33; compare Hos. 9:5); there it was established to be celebrated for one week beginning on the fifteenth day of the eighth month (October/November), in contrast to the custom in the south, where it was celebrated on the corresponding days of the seventh month (Lev. 23:33-43). Now, who were the Korahites, and what does the superscription mean? According to 2 Chron. 20:19, the Korahites were a guild of singers, but their antecedents are obscure; the original Korah was a Levite (Exod. 6:21), but whether the guild of singers was genealogically descended from Korah or whether they only believed themselves to be so cannot be known.[9] Goulder believes that they had become the Levitical priesthood at Dan.[10]

The first two psalms in the series are Psalms 42–43, which, as I have noted, were originally one psalm. The evidence for their unity lies both in the fact that there is no separate superscription on Psalm 43 and in the fact that there is language shared between the two psalms. Thus an almost identical "refrain" is repeated three times, in Ps. 42:6-7 (5-6), 12 (11), and Ps. 43:5; and the wording of Ps. 43:2 is a variation on Ps. 42:10 (9).

I have already called attention to the geographical references in Ps. 42:6-7 (5-6); the description of waterfalls and cataracts is appropriate to the area of Baniyas at the base of Mount Hermon, at which was to be found the sanctuary of Dan (1 Kings 12:29-30).[11] Though scholars have generally thought the psalm to be a lament of someone who is ill, Goulder makes a strong case that the psalm is the utterance of a king or leading citizen of the north who mourns the sad plight of his realm in the past year and who looks forward to making a pilgrimage to the sanctuary at Dan. This would be the logic of 42:7 (6), "Therefore I remember you from the land of Jordan and of Hermon," and the logic of "walk" in 42:10 (9) and 43:2 (as the new Jewish version has it, not "walk about" as the NRSV has it)—he is on pilgrimage.[12]

Psalm 44 is a community lament: Israel has suffered a humiliating defeat (vv. 10-17 [9-16]). Because the speaker shifts repeatedly from "we" (v. 2 [1]) to "I" (v. 5 [4]) to "we" again (v. 6 [5]), the speaker is likely to be the king; the speaker's mention of his "sword" and "bow" strengthens this supposition. One has the impression that the community has prostrated itself at a sanctuary (v. 26 [25]).[13] Is there any way to suggest a historical circumstance for this psalm? Goulder notes the circumstances of 732 B.C.E., when the Assyrian king Tiglath-pileser ravaged Galilee and other northern areas, though he left Dan intact (2 Kings 15:29); at that time Pekah, the king of Israel, was killed and Hoshea (Hebrew, *hôšēaʿ*) came on the throne. Now, four times in the first seven verses the psalmist uses the verb *yšʿ* (save): v. 4 (3), *hôšîʿâ*; "victories" (literally, "salvations"), v. 5 (4), *yěšûʿôt*; "save me," v. 7 (6), *hôšîʿēnî*; "you have saved us," v. 8 (7), *hôšaʿtānû*. One could imagine the psalmist looking on the name of the new king as a hopeful omen and salvation and working the word repeatedly into his song.[14]

Scholars have assumed that Psalm 46 is a song celebrating God's victorious work in the city of Jerusalem; but it is noteworthy that neither Zion nor Jerusalem is mentioned, and if the "city" (vv. 5-6 [4-5]) is Jerusalem, the "river" would have to be an apocalyptic development. It is simpler to take the geographical details of "waters" and "river" (vv. 4-5 [3-4]) as descriptions of the headwaters of the Jordan at Dan, much like the references in Psalm 42.[15] The psalm then celebrates God's victory both over the subterranean waters of chaos (vv. 3-4 [2-3]) and over Israel's enemies (vv. 7-10 [6-9]).[16]

Again, Psalm 47 celebrates God's kingship over all the nations: indeed, "God has gone up with a shout" (v. 6 [5]) suggests the worshipers going up to the altar, and perhaps God's mounting the divine throne as well.[17]

Psalm 48 celebrates the impregnability of the "city of our God," but in contrast to Psalm 46, in which the "city of God" is unnamed, here the focus is Zion (vv. 3, 12, 13 [2, 11, 12]) and Judah (v. 12 [11]). Can this psalm really be of northern origin? The description of Mount Zion as being "in the far north" (v. 3 [2]) is odd, as it stands. The Canaanites had a belief in a mountain of their "north," a mountain in southwest Syria that the Romans called Mons Casius and that the Syrians today call Jebel al-Aqra', where the gods gathered, and that belief in a mountain of the north which is holy to the deity seems to have been adopted here.[18] But the description of such a mountain as "beautiful in elevation" would fit Mount Hermon admirably—better certainly than Mount Zion in Jerusalem, which is dwarfed by a mountain range to its north. Goulder therefore proposes that the words "Mount Zion" in v. 3 (2) are a later insertion from when the psalm was adapted to southern use.[19] He further suggests that the original form of the last line of v. 11 (10) and vv. 12-13 (11-12) was shorter, perhaps reading "Your right hand is filled with victory, let Hermon be glad; Walk about Dan, and go all around it, count its towers," and that when "Hermon" and "Dan" were changed to "Mount Zion" and "Zion," a portion of Ps. 97:8 was inserted, namely, "The towns [literally, "daughters"] of Judah rejoice, because of your judgments." Such a proposal could explain both the reference to the "far north" and the northern linguistic features of the psalm.[20]

Psalm 49 is a curiosity: it appears to be a wisdom psalm, concerned with the transient nature of human life and wealth. At the same time, it is heavy with northern dialect features: Mitchell Dahood calls its language "probably the most dialectal in the Psalter."[21] But it appears to Goulder, to the contrary, to be a warning to the nations of the world that to invade Israel is to court death.[22] He proposes that "those who supplant me" (the literal meaning of "my persecutors" in v. 6 [5]; see the new Jewish version) are either Israelites who are attempting to usurp the throne or external enemies who wish to bring down the kingdom of Israel. The word translated "wealth" in v. 7 (6) should be understood here as "(military) power"; it is used of the "might" of a war-horse in Ps. 33:17. Such a background helps make sense of the mysterious v. 8 (7), which says, literally, "A brother no one shall in any way ransom" (see the footnote in the NRSV). The point is, no foreign king will be able to ransom a fellow king who has been captured by the Israelites: captives belong to Yahweh and are to be done to death (one thinks of Oreb and Zeeb, Zebah and Zalmunna, Midianite leaders who were killed in Gideon's campaign [Judg. 7:25; 8:21]). This is the train of thought in vv. 9-15 (8-14): enemy armies will go down to Sheol, the abode of the dead. The psalm then affirms Yahweh's protection of Israel against those who would challenge the throne.

Psalm 84 is a pilgrim-song that has much in common with Psalms 42–43: there is mention of God's dwelling place (Pss. 43:3; 84:2 [1]), and pilgrims are on the move (Pss. 42:10 [9]; 43:2; 84:7, 8 [6, 7]). Yet, in contrast to Psalms 42–43, which imply a locale in the north, Psalm 84 mentions Zion—not in v. 6 (5), where the words are supplied in the NRSV (see the footnote there), but in v. 8 (7); there Goulder proposes that "in Zion" was either a late insertion or a replacement for an expression such as "in Hermon." As for "Baca" in v. 7 (6), according to the Jewish historian Josephus there was a small town in Galilee carrying that name,[23] and it is possible that this is the place referred to in the psalm; the name means "balsam tree" in Hebrew, and in the early days the psalm may have simply spoken of the "Valley of the Balsam Tree" rather than to the valley of a village with the name "Baca."[24] Goulder makes the point that if these psalms were part of the autumn festival, then the reference to "early rain" (v. 7 [6]) is appropriate to the north, where the rains begin earlier than in the south.

If Psalm 84 resembles Psalms 42–43, Psalm 85 resembles Psalm 44: both are community laments, and both begin by a review of God's gracious acts to the nation in the past (Pss. 44:2-9 [1-8]; 85:2-4 [1-3]). But whereas the catastrophe to the nation in Psalm 44 was a military defeat, the catastrophe in Psalm 85 is a drought: rainfall is never completely to be depended on in Palestine, and drought is a recurrent possibility.

As Psalm 84 resembles Psalms 42–43 and as Psalm 85 resembles Psalm 44, so Psalm 87 resembles Psalm 48: both are psalms that focus on "the city of God" (Pss. 48:2, 9 [1, 8]; 87:3). But the text has appeared obscure at many points. Goulder again suggests, as he has with Psalms 48 and 84, that the phrases "the gates of Zion" (v. 2) and "of Zion" (v. 5) were added when the psalm was adapted for use in Jerusalem—as well as the phrase "with Ethiopia" in v. 4, which is awkward in Hebrew. He then groups the words of the first two verses differently: with the omission of "the gates of Zion" they read, "His foundation in the holy mountains Yahweh loves, more than all the dwellings of Jacob." The plural "mountains" certainly suggests the range of Mount Hermon more than Mount Zion in Jerusalem. Again, in vv. 4 and 6 Goulder takes the words "This one was born here" as the announcement of a royal birth, of the same form as we find in Isa. 9:5 (Protestant numeration v. 6), "To us a child is born." He takes "Philistia and Tyre" as vocative (words of address) and the expression "this one and that one" in v. 5 in the normal Hebrew meaning of "each man," linking it with "say" just before. His translation of vv. 4-6 is, then:

> I will declare Egypt and Babylon as among them that know me:
> Behold, O Philistia and Tyre,
> This one was born there!
> Each man shall say, He was born in her;
> And the Most High himself shall establish her.
> Yahweh shall declare when he writes down the peoples,
> This one was born there!

By this understanding, the psalm is the celebration of the city (Dan) in which a royal birth has taken place: neighboring peoples are summoned to witness Yahweh's grace in this event. But in the reuse of the psalm in Jerusalem, the old phrases became awkward and were to some degree misunderstood, according to Goulder.[25]

Psalm 88, the last Korahite psalm, is normally taken as an individual lament of someone stricken by a lifelong illness (v. 16 [15]). But there are difficulties with this view: though the description of the plight of the psalmist is grim—he is in the "Pit" (v. 5 [4]), all God's waves have gone over him (v. 8 [7]), he is a horror to his friends (v. 9 [8])—nevertheless he looks forward to God's deliverance in the morning (v. 14 [13]). Indeed, there seems to be a shift in what may be called the tense references in the Hebrew verbs of that verse that is ignored in the standard translations: the words seem to mean "I for my part, to you, O Yahweh, have cried out, and [or 'but'] in the morning my prayer will come before you." The wording of vv. 2-3 (1-2) is similar, and again the translations do not reflect what the Hebrew seems to say: it is, literally, "O Yahweh, God of my salvation, (on) the day of my having cried out in the night before you, let my prayer enter your presence, incline your ear to my cry." Curious also is the expression "I am shut in" (v. 9 [8]); the verb suggests being imprisoned or restrained. Goulder's proposal is that the psalm is spoken by a representative of the nation, perhaps a priest, who is ritually made a scapegoat and driven from the community for a day, shut up in a watery pit near the sanctuary at Dan. He suggests that the same mode of thinking may lie behind Lamentations 3 (see vv. 6-9 and 55-57 there) and Isaiah 53. There is, he acknowledges, no way to prove that such a ritual existed at the sanctuary of Dan, but such a theory does explain the specificity of the words of the psalm with regard to "pit" and "waters." If such a ritual existed at Dan, it may well have been thought semibarbarous by those in Jerusalem who inherited the psalm, even though the theological thought continued into the exilic period in Lamentations 3 and Isaiah 53.[26]

Goulder offers a suggestion to explain the parallels between Psalm 84 and Psalms 42–43, between Psalm 85 and Psalm 44, and between Psalm 87 and Psalm 48. He proposes that Psalms 84, 85, and 87 were early, joyful psalms in the sequence of the week of liturgy, composed in the ninth century B.C.E.; Psalms 42–43, 44, and 48 were later replacements in the sequence with a more anxious tone, at a time when the northern kingdom was facing military reverses, after 750 B.C.E. What we would have, therefore, in Psalms 42–49 is the final form of the liturgical sequence in the north, and the sequence in Psalms 84–87 includes those psalms that had been replaced in the liturgy but were preserved elsewhere nevertheless.[27] Though Goulder has many other suggestions to make in regard to these psalms, I do not pursue them here.

The Psalms of Asaph

As with the Korahite psalms, the psalms with the superscription "of Asaph" (Psalms 50 and 73–83) share features of northern dialect, and again, Rendsburg is not the first to reach this conclusion.[28] Who was Asaph? A notice in 1 Chron. 15:19 names him as a singer in David's court, but whether this collection of psalms originates with the singer Asaph himself or whether we simply have an "Asaphite" collection cannot be determined.

In three of these psalms, the people of God is referred to as "Joseph." We recall that the two "Joseph" tribes, Ephraim and Manasseh, were northern tribes. These references are Pss. 77:16 (15); 80:2 (1); and 81:6 (5). I deal first with Psalm 81 and then with Psalms 77 and 80.

Psalm 81 is an exhortation to celebrate a festival; since both new moon and full moon are mentioned (v. 4 [3]), the festival is doubtless the great autumnal festival that begins with the new moon of the new year (Rosh Hashanah) (Num. 29:1, 6) and ends two weeks later with the Feast of Booths (Num. 29:12). We have already examined Goulder's proposal that the Korahite psalms reflect the celebration of the Feast of Booths at Dan. Psalm 81 touches on the Ten Commandments and the rescue from Egypt (vv. 10-11 [9-10]).

Though Psalm 77 appears to be the lament of an individual (vv. 2-11 [1-10]) to which a hymn has been added (vv. 12-21 [11-20]), the psalmist's complaint hints at national concerns (vv. 8-10 [7-9]), so the psalmist could well be dealing with a national crisis.

Psalm 80 is certainly a lament of the community, beset by a military enemy (v. 14 [13]). The most plausible assumption is that this psalm comes from the last days of the northern kingdom, when Assyria threatened Samaria, and the fact that in the Greek translation of the psalm (the Septuagint; see chapter 6) the psalm carries the superscription "about Assyria" is also suggestive; but certainty is impossible.[29] The question then arises in our minds: If the Korahite psalms originated at Dan, and if the sanctuary at Dan was devastated by the invasion of the Assyrian king Tiglath-pileser in 732 (2 Kings 15:29), then did the psalms of Asaph originate in the other major northern sanctuary, at Bethel?[30] It is altogether possible.

I shall touch on the other psalms in this collection briefly. They are of various types. Psalms 74, 79, and 83, like Psalms 77 and 80 already considered, are laments of the community.

Psalms 74 and 79 resemble each other closely; both appear to describe the destruction of "the sanctuary in Jerusalem" (74:2-8; 79:1, 3). But the specific mentions of "Zion" or "Jerusalem" are few (74:2; 79:1, 3) and could well be later additions, adaptations to fit the destruction of the Jerusalem temple.

Psalm 83 lists various enemies that have conspired against the people (vv. 7-9 [6-8]). The mention of Assyria (v. 9 [8]) doubtless points to the threat of that empire against the northern kingdom.

There are five other Asaphite psalms: Psalms 50, 73, 75, 76, and 78. Psalm 50 is unique in the psalms in offering a judgment against the appropriateness of sacrifice (vv. 7-15), a message coming out of prophetic circles. This psalm has close ties to the northern prophet Hosea (among others), not only in the relativization of sacrifice (compare Hos. 6:6) but in other ways as well. Thus v. 22 appears to be a shortened version of Hos. 5:14.

Psalm 73 is a wisdom psalm that offers a striking number of northern dialect features.

Psalm 75 is a community thanksgiving that at the same time depicts the judgment of Yahweh on all the nations of the earth.

Psalm 76, though it exalts Judah and Zion (vv. 2-3 [1-2]), again contains northern dialect forms and therefore may be the work of a northerner celebrating his
loyalty to the temple in Jerusalem.

Psalm 78 is a long psalm that recites God's mighty acts in Israel.

Other Psalms from the North

There remain ten psalms in Rendsburg's group of northern psalms. I deal first
with the more unusual psalms, beginning with Psalm 132, a psalm that is doubtless
quite early. The wording of vv. 6-10 celebrates David's bringing the Ark of the
Covenant from the north to Jerusalem (2 Sam. 6:1-15), and vv. 11-12 remind
the hearer of Nathan's prophecy to David (2 Samuel 7). Though one scholar has
suggested that the psalmist might be the prophet Nathan and that the psalm might
have been sung during the moving of the Ark,[31] given the northern linguistic
features of the psalm, it is safer to understand it as a reflection of a northern
community loyal to the religious claims of Jerusalem, a community that celebrated
the moving of the Ark to its resting place in Jerusalem.[32]

I now turn to Psalm 16, a psalm that offers four occurrences of the northern
negative *bal*, as we saw at the beginning of this chapter. The psalm is a profession of
faith in Yahweh; Dahood has proposed that it is the profession of a former Canaanite
believer who became a convert to belief in Yahweh.[33] If this is the correct understanding of the original context of the psalm, then it is a nice counterbalance to
the accusations made by prophets such as Hosea and Jeremiah against those of the
people of Yahweh who backslid to worship Baal.

Psalm 133 is a short psalm of three verses that exalts family solidarity; beyond
the features of northern dialect in the poem, one notes the mention of Mount
Hermon in the north. The psalm may be the work of a northerner loyal to the cult
in Jerusalem.[34]

Psalm 53 is unusual in that it is a virtual duplication of Psalm 14, but Psalm 53
offers northern dialect features, whereas Psalm 14 offers the more expected Hebrew
of the south. In Psalm 53 the psalmist expresses regret over the godlessness of
his age.

Psalm 58 is a lament of the community that offers a series of curses on enemies. Is this invective against human enemies or against pagan gods? In favor of the
latter alternative is some of the phrasing in Hebrew, which reminds one of Psalm
82 (see chapter 2). But the state of the text of this psalm leaves one uncertain.[35]

Two of the remaining northern psalms are laments of the individual, Psalms
140 and 141. Both psalms have occurrences of the negative *bal* (Pss. 140:11, 12 [10,
11]; 141:4). These two psalms beg God for deliverance from personal enemies.

Psalms 9–10 were originally a single psalm, and they are still reckoned as a
single psalm in the Greek Septuagint tradition (see introduction and chapter 6).
The double psalm appears at first to be an acrostic: every second verse begins with
a successive letter of the Hebrew alphabet, though as a matter of fact five letters are
missing in the sequence, so the text appears to be damaged or altered in transmis-

sion. Whether we have to do here with a thanksgiving of the individual, as Psalm 9 appears to be, or a lament, as Psalm 10 appears to be, is debated;[36] the text shares features of both.

Psalm 116, finally, is a thanksgiving in which the psalmist expresses gratitude at his recovery from illness.

Several of the psalms that have been considered here describe the action of enemies: Ps. 10:2–11 describes them in lurid terms. This is a topic that needs extensive discussion, but because there are so many psalms of southern origin with this feature, I save until chapter 4 an exploration of this matter.

Here, then, is an array of psalms that give indication of their origin in the northern kingdom of Israel, incorporated into the repertory of psalms in the south at various points in history.

NOTES

1. Gary A. Rendsburg, *Linguistic Evidence for the Northern Origin of Selected Psalms* (SBLMS 43; Atlanta: Scholars Press, 1990).

2. Arvid S. Kapelrud, "Sidon," in *IDB* 4:344a.

3. James B. Pritchard, "Ivory," in *IDB* 2:775, with illustration.

4. The suggestion of Hans Schmidt, *Die Psalmen* (HAT 15; Tübingen: Mohr, 1934), 87.

5. So Ferdinand Hitzig, *Die Psalmen* (Leipzig and Heidelberg: Winter, 1863), 246; for recent discussion, see Hans-Joachim Kraus, *Psalms 1–59: A Commentary* (Minneapolis: Augsburg, 1988), 453–54.

6. John Bright, *A History of Israel* (Philadelphia: Westminster, 1981), 241.

7. Martin J. Buss, "The Psalms of Asaph and Korah," *JBL* 82 (1963):387.

8. Michael D. Goulder, *The Psalms of the Sons of Korah* (JSOTSup 20; Sheffield: JSOT, 1982).

9. Kraus, *Psalms 1–59*, 438–39.

10. Goulder, *Sons of Korah*, 59.

11. Rendsburg, *Linguistic Evidence*, 52.

12. Goulder, *Sons of Korah*, 23–35.

13. Ibid., 85–98.

14. Ibid., 90.

15. Ibid., 139.

16. Ibid., 137–49.

17. Ibid., 151–59.

18. Richard J. Clifford, *The Cosmic Mountain in Canaan and the Old Testament* (HSM 4; Cambridge: Harvard University Press, 1972), 142–44.

19. Goulder, *Sons of Korah*, 162–63.

20. Ibid., 167–68.

21. Mitchell Dahood, *Psalms I* (Garden City, N.Y.: Doubleday, 1966), 296.

22. Goulder, *Sons of Korah*, 181–95.

23. Josephus, *Wars of the Jews*, 3.3.1.

24. Goulder, *Sons of Korah*, 40.

25. Ibid., 170–80.

26. Ibid., 195–210.

27. Ibid., 17–19.

28. Cf. Buss, "Psalms of Asaph and Korah," 382–92, esp. 384; Harry P. Nasuti, *Tradition History and the Psalms of Asaph* (SBLDS 88; Atlanta: Scholars Press, 1988), esp. 115–16, 193.

29. Hans-Joachim Kraus, *Psalms 60–150: A Commentary* (Minneapolis: Augsburg, 1989), 139–41; Mitchell Dahood, *Psalms II* (Garden City, N.Y.: Doubleday, 1968), 255.

30. The suggestion of Goulder, *Sons of Korah*, 220.

31. Mitchell Dahood, *Psalms III* (Garden City, N.Y.: Doubleday, 1970), 241.

32. Rendsburg, *Linguistic Evidence*, 89–90.

33. Dahood, *Psalms I*, 87.

34. Rendsburg, *Linguistic Evidence*, 93.

35. Kraus, *Psalms 1–59*, 534–35; Leopold Sabourin, *The Psalms: Their Origin and Meaning* (New York: Alb House, 1974), 299–300.

36. Kraus, *Psalms 1–59*, 191–94; Dahood, *Psalms I*, 54; Sabourin, *Psalms*, 280; Erhard S. Gerstenberger, *Psalms: Part I, with an Introduction to Cultic Poetry* (Grand Rapids: Eerdmans, 1988), 72–75.

4

Psalms for the Temple of Solomon

I turn now to psalms that appear to have arisen in the southern kingdom of Judah between the death of Solomon in 922 B.C.E. and the fall of Jerusalem in 587 B.C.E. We remind ourselves that there were several sanctuaries in the southern kingdom other than Solomon's temple in Jerusalem. For example, the prophet Amos (approximately 755 B.C.E.) refers to a sanctuary at Beersheba (Amos 5:5; 8:14), forty-five miles (seventy-two kilometers) southeast of Jerusalem. It was only in 622 B.C.E. that King Josiah centralized worship at the temple in Jerusalem and forbade worship at outlying sanctuaries (2 Kings 22–23). One surmises then that there must have been psalms developed at these outlying sanctuaries, but we have no way to determine whether any of them survived into our biblical collection. We therefore turn to psalms that originated at the Jerusalem temple. One caution is necessary, however: as we attempt to visualize psalms in this context, we must be careful not to imagine that Jerusalem too grandly. Recent estimates suggest that the population of Jerusalem in David's day was approximately two thousand, and that it grew to roughly thirty thousand by the time of Hezekiah (700 B.C.E.), remaining at that level until the fall of the city in 587 B.C.E.[1] It was a modest city, at least by present-day standards.

The Nature of Our Evidence

How might we identify these pre-exilic Jerusalemite psalms? I can think of three kinds of evidence that can be brought to bear. The first is the identification of royal psalms: psalms that presuppose the king as speaker or addressee, if they are not of northern origin, must be southern psalms from the monarchical period, because royal psalms would not have been written after the monarchy had ceased to be. The second is the identification of psalms offering unique features of theology or phraseology appropriate to the pre-exilic period. The third is the identification of psalms from which the pre-exilic prophets drew: if a prophetic oracle is genuine to one of the pre-exilic prophets (who can be dated), and that oracle draws on a given psalm, then that psalm was clearly already in existence in the pre-exilic period. These categories overlap to some degree, and they surely do not exhaust the body of pre-exilic psalms, but together they specify twenty-one psalms, which we will consider in the present chapter.

Royal Psalms

Scholars isolate eleven royal psalms. I have already discussed five of these: Psalms 2, 18, and 110 in chapter 2, which I surmise were associated with David's reign; and Psalms 45 and 132 in chapter 3, of northern origin. There remain six more: Psalms 20, 21, 72, 89, 101, and 144. I first discuss Psalm 72 and then take up the rest in numerical order.

Psalm 72 is similar to Psalm 2, discussed in chapter 2; because both psalms call down Yahweh's blessing on the king, perhaps the former also was composed for a coronation.[2] Psalm 72 offers language as extravagant as that in Psalm 2: if Ps. 2:10 is a warning to the "rulers of the earth" that Yahweh's king is invincible, then Psalm 72 expresses the wish that the king live as long as the sun and the moon (v. 5) and that his realm reach from the Mediterranean to the "River" (that is, the Euphrates, v. 8). But such grandiloquence is typical of court language in the ancient Near East; we may note, in a later century, that when Nehemiah came into the presence of the Persian king Artaxerxes, his first words were, "May the king live forever!" (Neh. 2:3).

Psalm 20 is a prayer of the congregation in the Jerusalem temple (v. 3 [2]) as the king sets out for battle (vv. 5-6 [4-5]).[3] In passing it may be noted, as a curiosity, that vv. 2-6 (1-5) of this psalm have turned up in a collection of pagan prayers from Egypt, from the first century B.C.E.; the words of these verses had been translated into Aramaic but written in an Egyptian script, and where "Yahweh" appears in our psalm, "Horus" (an Egyptian god) appears in the pagan version! I suggested in chapter 2, in my discussion of Psalm 29, that in that psalm Israel perhaps took over a pre-Israelite psalm to Baal. Now we see how the Egyptians borrowed one of the biblical psalms from Aramaic-speaking Jews living there and adapted it for one of their gods.[4]

In Psalm 21, Yahweh has given the king victory. Was it the victory that was prayed for in Psalm 20?[5] Compare the wording of Ps. 20:5 (4) with Ps. 21:3 (2).[6]

Psalm 89 implies the experience of a king who has lost a battle (vv. 44-45 [43-44]). A recent study suggests that the psalm is the complaint of a prophet about God's nonfulfillment of an earlier prophetic oracle (vv. 4-5 [3-4]): kingship has fallen. If this analysis is correct, the historical situation is likely to have been the fall of Jerusalem in 587 B.C.E.[7]

Psalm 101 is also the declaration of a king (see particularly the diction of v. 8); it may originally have been the king's vow of moral purity (on his coronation day?).[8]

And Psalm 144, like Psalm 20, could well have been a prayer before battle, or at least vv. 1-11 could be; vv. 12-15 may be a later addition to the psalm.[9]

In addition, one must mention three other psalms, Psalms 28, 61, and 63. In these psalms there is mention of the king in the third person (Pss. 28:8; 61:7-8 [6-7];

and 63:12 [11]). These psalms too must come from the time of the monarchy; indeed they may in the first instance have been prayers offered by the king, and the third-person references may be his references to himself.[10]

Psalms Offering Unique Wording
Appropriate to the Period

I now turn to three psalms that are prime candidates for this period because of their striking or archaic theology or phraseology: Psalms 24, 104, and 131.

Psalm 24 surely belongs at the beginning of the period of Solomon's temple.[11] It is what may be called a "torah" liturgy, a liturgy before the gates of the temple, beginning with ritual questions as to who may enter; it ends with a repeated acclamation of the entrance of Yahweh the divine leader in battle (v. 8), a circumstance that leads scholars to believe that the psalm was originally sung as the Ark of the Covenant was being brought in procession into the temple (see the discussion of Psalm 132 in chapter 3).[12] The psalm reminds us of the old traditions of Yahweh's leadership in battle during the time the people were in the wilderness, when the Ark of the Covenant was the symbol of Yahweh's protection (Num. 11:33-36).

It may be helpful here to discuss briefly the phrase "Yahweh Sabaoth," which occurs in v. 10 (RSV and NRSV "the Lord of hosts"). This is an old liturgical phrase that seems to have had its origin in the sanctuary at Shiloh,[13] where Samuel grew up (1 Samuel 1); later the phrase was transferred to the temple of Solomon.[14] Its meaning, however, is not altogether certain: the most plausible explanation is that it means "Yahweh of armies," that is, the armies of Israel in holy war (compare the description in the old war song in Exod. 15:3). The context of the phrase in Psalm 24 reinforces that explanation.[15] In any event, this psalm must have originated at a time when the primary description of Yahweh was as a warrior, which is to say, early in the pre-exilic period.

I turn now to Psalm 104, a psalm expressing joy in God's creation. A concentrated interest in creation is unusual in the Psalms, but more remarkable is the striking resemblance between expressions in this psalm and expressions in an Egyptian hymn, the so-called Hymn to the Aton. The "Aton" in Egypt was the sun disk, the source of life, and that hymn stems from the reign of Akh-en-Aton (also spelled Ikhnaton or Akhenaten) in the decades around 1365 B.C.E.[16] About one-third of the biblical psalm is strongly reminiscent of passages in the Egyptian hymn. In Ps. 104:20-21 we read:

> You make darkness, and it is night,
>   when all the animals of the forest come creeping out.
> The young lions roar for their prey,
>   seeking their food from God.

The corresponding lines in the Egyptian hymn read:

When thou settest in the western horizon,
The land is in darkness, in the manner of death.
They sleep in a room, with heads wrapped up,
Nor sees one eye the other.
All their goods which are under their heads might be stolen,
(But) they would not perceive (it).
Every lion is come forth from his den;
All creeping things, they sting.
Darkness is a shroud, and the earth is in stillness,
For he who made them rests in his horizon.

Again, vv. 25–26 read:

Yonder is the sea, great and wide,
   creeping things innumerable are there,
   living things both small and great.
There go the ships,
   and Leviathan that you formed to sport in it.

In the Egyptian hymn we find:

The ships are sailing north and south as well,
For every way is open at thy appearance.
The fish in the river dart before thy face;
Thy rays are in the midst of the great green sea.

These resemblances are not coincidental; the biblical psalm has in some way drawn on the Egyptian hymn. But it is clear that it is an adaptation rather than a direct translation. It is altogether possible that the Egyptian material was mediated through Phoenicia (the reference to the cedars of Lebanon in v. 16 is striking, as is the reference to "wild goats" in v. 18). But however this material entered into the liturgical life of Israel, it is far more likely to have done so in the period of Solomon, for example, or at least before the Babylonian exile, than in the post-exilic period, when the Jewish community was less open to foreign influences.[17]

The other unusual psalm that I wish to discuss here is Psalm 131, a psalm only three verses long. As one reads it, one gains the suspicion that the last verse is a liturgical addition to what is otherwise a unique expression: the psalmist's heart is calmed as a weaned child is calmed. Recently the German scholar Gottfried Quell put forth a strong argument that vv. 1-2 were written by a woman.[18] In his analysis, vv. 1-2a are a statement of modesty, a statement of serenity; he points out, however, that at the end of v. 2a ("Truly I have calmed and quieted my soul") the Hebrew text marks a strong pause. Verse 2b then takes a fresh turn, perhaps a self-quotation: "Like a weaned child on his mother, like a weaned child on me is my soul," the implication of the last line being "like a weaned child on me is my soul on God." If this understanding is correct, then clearly the poem is written by a woman. Quell speculates that the poem might have been deposited in the temple on the occasion of a thank-offering (Lev. 7:12-13); found later by the compiler of pilgrim songs; and, with the addition of v. 3, accepted into the collection of pilgrim songs, Psalms 120–134 (for which, see chapter 6). There is no way to determine the date of such a short poem, but because we have the narrative of at least one woman who took religious leadership in the pre-exilic period (Huldah the prophetess; 2 Kings 22:14-20), a pre-exilic date seems plausible.

Psalms from Which Amos and Jeremiah Drew

As we seek to identify other psalms whose origin is in this period, there is one more resource at our disposal. The dates of the prophets of pre-exilic times are known within narrow limits, and there are several instances in which part of a given psalm seems to have been quoted by one of the prophets—one instance, to my knowledge, by Amos (whose date is roughly 755 B.C.E.), and other instances by Jeremiah (whose dates are roughly 627–586 B.C.E.). If the prophet really cites a given psalm, then of course the psalm must predate the prophet; but the problem obviously is to be sure that the borrowing is not the other way around—that the psalmist is not quoting the prophet—or that both texts are not simply conventional language. The matter is best dealt with by examples.

There are two such parallels in the book of Jeremiah to Psalm 1, namely, Jer. 12:1b-2 and 17:5-8; and in each of them Psalm 1 is deformed in a different way. If both the passages in Jeremiah are genuine to the prophet (and I have become convinced that they are), then the psalm must be prior.[19] Similarly, both Amos 9:2-3 and Jer. 23:23-24 draw on Ps. 139:7-12, and Amos in particular uses the material ironically; the psalm must be prior.[20] Even if to a psalm passage there is only a single prophetic parallel, if the prophet (Jeremiah) uses the phraseology ironically, then the psalm is surely prior; irony is not a characteristic of the psalms. Thus Jer. 10:25 cites Ps. 79:6-7.[21] The two verses just before the Jeremiah verse in question similarly offer an expansion of Prov. 16:9 and 20:24 and an expansion of Ps. 6:2 (1) or 38:2 (1). These citations, I am convinced, are genuine to Jeremiah: he is citing passages that are repeated by people who are unwilling to accept any covenant responsibility. (I return to Jeremiah's citation of Ps. 79:6-7 in chapter 16.) The psalms in question are therefore prior.

By contrast, if there is reason to think that Jeremiah originated a phrase, then if it occurs in a psalm, the Jeremiah usage is prior to the psalm in question. For example, the phrase "terror on every side" occurs five times in Jeremiah (Jer. 6:25; 20:3, 10; 46:5; 49:29); it seems to have been a favorite phrase of his and probably originated in the particular incident in which a temple priest, Pashhur, locked the prophet in the stocks overnight (Jer. 20:1-6). Because the phrase occurs in Ps. 31:14 (13), one must conclude that Psalm 31, or at least vv. 10-25 (9-24) of that psalm (which form an intact section of their own), must be dated after Jeremiah's time (see chapter 5).[22]

In this way I have concluded that sixteen psalms—namely, Psalms 1, 2, 6, 7, 9–10, 22, 35, 38, 63, 64, 78, 79, 83, 84, 122, and 139—are older than Jeremiah.[23] (I have also specified seven psalms that are to be dated *later* than Jeremiah; I will discuss these, as already indicated, in chapter 5.) Of these, Psalm 2, a royal psalm which I have surmised comes from David's time, was discussed in chapter 2; Psalms 9–10, 78, 79, 83, and 84 have been identified as northern psalms and were discussed in chapter 3; and Psalm 63 has already been referred to in this chapter as a psalm that mentions the king. And I have already illustrated the principle of my conclusions by reference to Ps. 79:6–7 and Jer. 10:25. Because I have already dealt with these psalms in earlier chapters, it would serve no purpose here to offer all the parallels in Jeremiah that have brought me to my conclusions; I shall simply offer two more for illustration.

Psalm 78:60 offers the only mention of the fall of the old sanctuary at Shiloh other than Jeremiah's temple sermon (Jer. 7:12, 14; 26:6). Furthermore, in the narrative of the sermon Jeremiah speaks of Israel's obligation "to walk in my law," a phrase occurring also in Ps. 78:10 (and elsewhere in early material). And in one of Jeremiah's "confessions," Jer. 20:11, Yahweh is spoken of as "like a warrior," and the prophet also speaks of the everlasting disgrace or shame of adversaries; for these phrases, see Ps. 78:65-66.[24]

Again, in Ps. 84:8 (7) we read that the pilgrims "go from strength to strength"; in Jer. 9:2 (Protestant numeration v. 3) the prophet speaks of people who "proceed from evil to evil," surely a parody on the psalmist's phrase.[25]

I now turn to the remaining nine psalms, namely, Psalms 1, 6, 7, 22, 35, 38, 64, 122, and 139. Seven of these psalms are laments of the individual, and I discuss them first, beginning with Psalm 22 and then dealing with the others in sequential order, namely, Psalms 6, 7, 35, 38, and 64. Then I discuss Psalm 122, a pilgrim song; then Psalm 139, a hymnic declaration of innocence; and, finally, Psalm 1, an instruction in covenant norms.

These laments sound as if they are intensely personal, but we must realize that all the pre-exilic psalms, even the laments, were closely tied with the cult. That is to say, the psalms must be understood as part of the liturgy in the temple, part of recurrent acts of worship. Psalms that, to us at least, may appear to be the spontaneous outpouring of poets were not necessarily so in the first instance at all; the language of the psalms was stylized and traditional, associated with cultic acts.

I begin, then, with Psalm 22. (Jeremiah made use of phrases from vv. 2, 8-11, and 15 [1, 7-10, and 14], especially in Jer. 20:7-18.)[26] The psalmist alternates complaints with affirmations of confidence in God. He first accuses God of having abandoned him (vv. 2-3 [1-2]), then affirms his trust in God (vv. 4-6 [3-5]). He complains that everyone who sees him mocks his plight (vv. 7-9 [6-8]), then affirms his confident dependence on God (vv. 10-11 [9-10]). Then, curiously, his complaint is renewed—at great length (vv. 12-19 [11-18]), beginning with a petition in v. 12 (11): "Do not be far from me." He then describes his plight, both symptoms of illness—fever and the like—and the hostility of enemies. The psalmist renews his petition ("But you, Yahweh, do not be far away") in vv. 20-22 (19-21). Then suddenly there is a hymn of thanksgiving (vv. 23-27 [22-26]): the psalmist makes a vow for his deliverance. And, finally, there is a general hymn of praise (vv. 28-32 [27-31]). As to the last five verses, scholars believe they could be a post-exilic addition to the psalm.[27] My own suspicion is that the hymn of thanksgiving (vv. 23-27 [22-26]) was added in the post-exilic period as well, perhaps earlier in that period; its diction closely resembles that of Ps. 40:10-11 (9-10), and Ps. 40:2-12 (1-11) is, by my understanding, post-exilic (for this, see chapter 5). In any event, the alternation of complaint and affirmation of confidence is the kind of repetition appropriate to liturgy (compare Lev. 4:6; 2 Kings 13:18), and the hymn of thanksgiving suggests that at some stage the suppliant, in the completion of the ritual of lament, was assured of God's answer to his plea.[28]

Who might the suppliant of vv. 2-22 (1-21) have been? The fulsomeness of the expressions[29] suggests that the words of the psalmist are those of a kind of archetypal figure, quite possibly a king; one thinks of notices in the historical books of illnesses suffered by kings of Judah, such as Uzziah's skin disease (conventionally called "leprosy"; 2 Kings 15:5) or Hezekiah's illness (2 Kings 20:1-7). But of course there is no way to know.

The remaining six laments of the individual have many of the characteristics of Psalm 22—stereotyped descriptions by the psalmist of the mockery he has suffered from his enemies and of the symptoms of illness.

Psalm 6 offers complaint to God and imprecation against enemies. Jeremiah 15:15—"Do not, because of the slowness of your anger, take me away"—is evidently an ironic variation on Ps. 6:2 (1)—"Do not rebuke me in your anger."[30]

Psalm 7 has many of the characteristics of laments; Jeremiah evidently drew on v. 10 (9) for the phrase "you who test the mind and heart," which occurs in Jer. 11:20 (= 20:12) and 17:10a.[31] The psalmist prays that Yahweh might save him from his pursuers (v. 2 [1]), and in this respect the Psalm is like Psalm 22. But there is in this psalm something new, a declaration of innocence (vv. 4-6 [3-5]): one must conclude that the speaker has fled to the temple to affirm with an oath of cleansing his innocence from the accusation of an enemy, and he appeals to Yahweh for a righteous verdict;[32] it is the same procedure set forth in 1 Kings 8:31-32. We see this setting again in our discussion of Psalm 139, below.

Personal enemies again loom large in Psalm 35. In vv. 5-6 the psalmist is speaking of his enemies: "Let them be like chaff before the wind, with the angel of Yahweh driving them on. Let their way be dark and slippery, with the angel of Yahweh pursuing them." In Jer. 23:12 the prophet is speaking for God of those prophets who are not proclaiming God's word: "Therefore their way shall be to them like slippery paths in the darkness, into which they shall be driven and fall."[33]

Psalm 38 may be the self-description of one suffering from a skin disease ("leprosy"; compare the remarks on Psalm 22, above).[34] It is noteworthy that in Jer. 15:17 the prophet states that Yahweh's hand is upon him, as Ps. 38:3 (2) says of the psalmist, and that later in Jer. 15:17 the prophet states that he has "sat alone," the situation prescribed in Lev. 13:46 for "leprosy."[35]

In Psalm 64 the psalmist broods about the secrecy of his enemies' plotting, and he says (v. 7 [6]), "The human heart and mind [literally, "inner organs and heart"] are deep [Hebrew, *'āmōq*]." Jeremiah is evidently offering a wordplay on the adjective when he says, "The heart is devious [Hebrew, *'āqōb*] above all else" (Jer. 17:9)— "devious" being more alarming than "deep."[36]

I now turn to Psalm 122, a pilgrim song. The psalmist rejoices with his fellow pilgrims that he has been able to enter Jerusalem; in vv. 6-8 he plays on the popular etymology that connects the name of "Jerusalem" with "peace" as he seeks the peace of Jerusalem. Jeremiah evidently drew on vv. 6-8 of the psalm: Jer. 15:5 says, literally, "Ask for the peace of Jerusalem."[37]

I turn now to two psalms that appear to be unrelated to temple liturgy but may be so related after all. The first is Psalm 139. As I have already noted, this psalm was drawn upon both by the prophet Amos in the eighth century B.C.E. and by Jeremiah in the seventh; both prophets drew on vv. 7-12 (see Amos 9:2-3 and Jer. 23:23-24). The present-day reader sees in this psalm an affirmation of God's omniscience and omnipresence (see chapter 15), a psalm marred however by the imprecations of vv. 19-22. But these four verses, often omitted in present-day reading of the psalm (see the Introduction and the discussion in chapter 16), are in its original setting the climax of the psalm; some of its innuendos are lost on us, at least in the usual translations. For one thing, the verses of cursing center on what in Hebrew are called *'anšê dāmîm*, literally, "men of blood" (v. 19; NRSV, "the bloodthirsty"). But there is evidence of a play on words here, that what is meant is not only "men of blood" but "men of idols" as well.[38] Furthermore, the phrase in the first line of v. 24, "wicked way" (NRSV), is, literally, "way of an idol" (the same word "idol" is found in Isa. 48:5). The word "way" here would then imply "cult practice," as it does in Jer. 2:23. There is a strong likelihood, then, that the psalm was originally the public declaration of innocence by someone who had been accused of idol worship: the psalm begins and ends with an appeal to Yahweh to investigate personally, on the basis of divine knowledge, the charges of idolatry brought against him.[39] The strong words of vv. 19-22 then become more plausible: the "wicked" (v. 19), or rather the "guilty" (see the last section of this chapter), are those who reject Yahweh in favor of pagan gods; Yahweh is against them, and the worshiper wants to be sure that Yahweh knows that he is against them too. We must then understand the same kind of setting of a declaration of innocence in the temple as I have already suggested for Psalm 7.

The last psalm to be considered, from which Jeremiah drew, is Psalm 1. This psalm is usually classified as a "wisdom" psalm, and it is assumed that it is a late (post-exilic) composition.[40] But the fact that the psalm was drawn on by Jeremiah in two different ways, as I have already noted, indicates that it must be pre-exilic. And there is another clue that it is pre-exilic: in v. 2 there appears to be a wordplay between *yahweh* (Yahweh), translated in the NRSV as "the LORD," and *yehgeh* (he meditates), a wordplay that would not be possible in the post-exilic temple when the name "Yahweh" was no longer pronounced (see chapter 5).

In current translations Psalm 1 contrasts the way of the "righteous" and the "wicked," though I would prefer the terms "innocent" and "guilty," respectively (see the last section of this chapter), and it sets forth the ideal of piety for *tôrâ* (in current translations, the "law"). But *tôrâ* (usually spelled "torah") was in the pre-exilic period not so much "law" in our sense as "teaching, instruction": one notes the translation "teaching" for *tôrâ* in the NRSV for Isa. 1:10, and the translation "instruction" for the same word in Jer. 18:18. It is the kind of instruction in covenant norms we saw listed in Ps. 24:4. And Jer. 18:18 likewise indicates that in the pre-exilic period this "instruction" on covenant norms of behavior was the responsibility of priests, so again one is led to the Jerusalem temple and perhaps, before the centralization of cultic observance at the Jerusalem temple under King Josiah, to outlying cult centers where priests and Levites would have given instruction. Indeed, does the word "way" in v. 6 have the overtone of "cult practice" that we found in Psalm 139? It would seem altogether likely.

How Do We Reconstruct a Vanished Culture?

Let us pause now for a moment to get our bearings. In this chapter we have discussed nineteen psalms whose origins can be attributed to the period of Solomon's temple in Jerusalem. Some of these psalms are "easy" to read; that is to say, we can sense their various contexts, even if the culture that gave rise to them is far away and long ago. For example, if present-day readers read Psalm 72, they will recognize the connection with kingship and can imagine the worship at the temple. In other instances, however, readers are forced to take the word of scholars that a psalm is royal and a part of temple worship—Psalm 101 strikes readers simply as a tiresome sequence of self-righteousness. I shall come back to this matter presently. But clearly we cannot always grasp the assumptions of these psalms, or of the seven psalms discussed in chapter 2 or the thirty-five psalms discussed in chapter 3, for that matter. So the question becomes: How can we find a way as fully as possible to recapture and grasp that culture, in order that these various psalms may speak most directly to us?

Of course we can take the trouble to visit the territory settled by the Israelites so long ago; there are still areas whose appearance is little changed from ancient times, where the houses are made of the local limestone blocks and mud bricks. But even these areas will be dotted with Coca-Cola signs and visited by buses.

We can visit ancient archeological sites such as Megiddo and Shechem, but it is difficult to envisage the houses and palaces and sanctuaries simply from the remaining foundation stones, let alone to envisage the inhabitants of these buildings.

We can visit museums such as the Israel Museum in West Jerusalem (or the British Museum in London or some other museum) and peer at Israelite artifacts from the pre-exilic period. But what survive to our day are pottery and implements of stone and bone and ivory and metal, leaving us only to imagine what has disappeared, the wooden implements and leather and cloth and foodstuffs and the rest of what people used in their daily round.

We can examine Assyrian bas-reliefs in the museums of the Near East or Europe or North America, or we can examine Egyptian wall paintings. When we do, we will see plenty of Assyrians or Egyptians, but in the rare cases when we see Israelites, it is usually as prisoners of war, and we cannot be sure that when we see Egyptian brewers and bakers and farmers they resemble their Israelite counterparts very much.[41]

But we wish we could gain a sense of the social organization of the Israelites—their class structure; the relations between city, village, and country; their clan structure; the relations between nuclear families and the clan; and the relations between men and women within families—and of their economic structures—their land tenure system; the extent to which their agriculture was for subsistence and the extent to which there was surplus for trade; how the trading patterns worked; and the extent to which crafts such as pottery and metal craft were specialized. We wish we could gain a better grip on the details of their daily life: their infant mortality rate and their life expectancy and how often they ate meat. And, above all, we wish we could discern their thoughts and their yearnings, what their assumptions were about the nature of human beings and about life and death. Some of these details we can glean from a careful reading of the Old Testament, but the Old Testament in its present state is largely a product of the post-exilic period and a product of urban men in Jerusalem, priests and Levites and scribes. Much, therefore, is left undescribed or unexplained.

And so we have these psalms, and questions crowd into our minds. What, we wonder, was the liturgy of the temple like in this period, and how did the psalms fit into it? How did the psalms sound when they were sung or recited? Scholars have tried to gain clarity about these questions, without much success. The psalms were doubtless sung or chanted, and they were probably given musical accompaniment: Ps. 68:26 (25) offers enticing hints. (The ranks of musicians said to be organized by David [1 Chronicles 25] are evidently the understanding of the post-exilic period projected back onto the early pre-exilic period.)[42] But though we do not know how they sounded, we can at least recognize the poetic skill of the psalmists, and to this we turn for a moment.

The Poetic Skill of the Psalmists

What is clear from the Hebrew text is the skill of the poets in this period—not only their ability to move hearts but their skill with the structure of sounds and words. I have already touched briefly on the matter of parallelism in chapter 2, and it need not be repeated here. But it may be useful to be reminded that, however accurate and helpful a translation may be, no translation can do justice to the sound effects of the original (compare the discussion in chapter 17).

For a brief sample, let us take the first three verses of Psalm 6, a lament already discussed:

(2) *yahweh 'al-bĕ'appĕkā tôkîḥēnî*
    wĕ'al-baḥămātĕkā tĕyassĕrēnî
(3) *ḥonnēnî yahweh kî-'umlal 'ānî*
    rĕpā'ēnî yahweh kî-nibḥălû 'aṣāmāy
(4) *wĕnapšî nibḥălâ mĕ'ōd*
    wĕ'attā yahweh 'ad-mātāy

Word by word:

(2 [1]) Yahweh do-not-in-your-anger rebuke-me
    and-do-not-in-your-wrath discipline-me
(3 [2]) be-gracious-to-me Yahweh for-languishing I-am
    heal-me Yahweh for-are-shaking my-bones
(4 [3]) and-my-self is-shaking greatly
    and-you Yahweh until-when?

Each verse consists of a pair of lines, and both lines of each pair are closely parallel with each other. In v. 2 (1) the first line begins with "O Yahweh," and then the rest of that line is balanced word by word with the second line: "do not in your anger" is matched by "do not in your wrath" not only in meaning but by the sound of the grammatical tags *'al-b-* and *-kā*, and "rebuke me" and "discipline me" are parallel not only in meaning but by the sound of the grammatical tags *t-* and *-ēnî*. In v. 3 (2) "Yahweh" comes second in both lines, followed immediately by the particle *kî* (for). The first position of each line is taken by positive verbs (in contrast to the negative expressions in the previous verse), "be gracious to me" and "heal me," and these match again not only in meaning but in sound, echoing the *-ēnî* of the previous verse. "My bones" at the end of the second line is matched by the emphatic pronoun "I" *('ānî)* at the end of the first line. Verse 4 (3) not only contains two balancing lines but lines that are closely bound to the lines of v. 3 (2) as well. In the first line of v. 4 (3) the verb is the singular form, "is shaking" *(nibḥălâ)*, of the plural verb in the second line of the previous verse, "are shaking" *(nibḥălû)*. And the subject of the verb in the first line, "my self" *(napšî)*, is a standard parallel to the emphatic first-person pronoun "I" *('ānî)* in the first line of the previous verse. The second line of v. 4 (3) not only addresses "Yahweh" but precedes the name by the emphatic second-person pronoun "you" *('attā)*, matching "I" *('ānî)* in the previous verse. And the abrupt and unexpected question at the end of the verse, *'ad-mātāy* (how long?), is a sound echo not only of the last word of the first line, *mĕ'ōd* (greatly), but even more of the last word of v. 3 (2), *'ăṣāmāy* (my bones).

Here at least we can gain a glimpse of some of the ways the poet builds up the poem; the aesthetic satisfaction to be gained in the psalms was surely an important contributing factor in the religious sensibilities of the worshipers, and a factor, too, in the ease with which they were committed to memory: we have seen how Amos in the eighth century and Jeremiah in the seventh could incorporate phrases and passages of these psalms into their own oracles.

The Faith and Outlook of the
Pre-exilic Psalms

There is one more matter to consider, in many ways the most important matter of all: What sort of belief system, what sort of theology is set forth in these pre-exilic psalms? In some ways the faith reflected in these psalms is recognizably the faith of people today, but again one must be careful not to modernize the old belief system in too facile a way. Let us see what we can glean from the psalms we have examined.

Utterly central, of course, is Yahweh, Israel's God. We hear little about Yahweh's activity beyond the circle of Israel. True, Yahweh is creator of the heavens and the earth (Pss. 19:2-7 [1-6]; 89:12-13 [11-12]) and all that is in them (Psalm 104), but creation is a minor note in these psalms. Preeminently, Yahweh is celebrated for the mighty deeds of the past: Yahweh brought Israel out of Egypt, gave the nation the law, fought the wars that would settle Israel in the land of Canaan (in detail, Psalm 78; in general, Pss. 9:2, 12 [1, 11]; 22:5-6 [4-5]; 46:9-10 [8-9]; 68:18 [17]; 83:10-13 [9-12]).

Though Yahweh's divine council is mentioned (Ps. 89:8 [7]), there is really no God but Yahweh (18:32 [31]—at least in the context of singing this psalm!). Yahweh is depicted as leader in battle (24:7-10), as king (10:16), and as judge (7:9 [8]), indeed, as the judge of other gods (82:1); actually, king and judge are a single metaphor (9:5, 8 [4, 7]).

The overwhelming bulk of these texts is concerned with Yahweh's dealings with the protagonist, whether king or commoner. Both king and pilgrim affirm that Yahweh has covenanted forever with David and his house (king: 89:4-5, 20-38, 50 [3-4, 19-37, 49]; 132:11-12; pilgrim: 122:5), and linked with the house of David is Yahweh's choice of Zion in Jerusalem to dwell in (9:12 [11]; 84:8 [7]; 122:4-5), where the congregation of Israel (22:23 [22]; 35:18; 68:27 [26]) may meet Yahweh and offer sacrifice (20:4 [3]).

In these psalms Israel perceives itself to be embattled, surrounded by hostile "nations" and "peoples" and "kings of the earth." This is true in Psalm 2, where Yahweh will terrify the enemy kings and defeat them through the Davidic king, but it is true in other psalms as well: Yahweh trains the king for war (18:35 [34]; 144:1); Yahweh judges the nations (7:7-9 [6-8]; 9:20 [19]); when the kings see Yahweh in Zion, they flee in panic (48:6-7 [5-6]), they cringe and lick the dust before the king (18:45-46 [44-45]; 72:9); Yahweh destroys the nation's enemies (9:6 [5]; 18:41 [40]) and brings victory to the king (20:7 [6]). Israel's dependence on Yahweh counts for more than the dependence of other nations on chariots and horses (20:8-9 [7-8]). Some of this rhetoric is surely stylized and a feature of the life situation of these psalms, but it reinforced both Israel's conviction of the distinctiveness of the covenant between the nation and Yahweh and the sense the nation had of vulnerability to outside forces. These psalms speak constantly of "us" beset by "them." A recent American novel picks up this note:

He [the pastor at a funeral] read a psalm, something about a lovely dwelling place, which came as a relief to Maggie because of her experience, most of the Book of Psalms tended to go on in a paranoid way about enemies and evil plots.[43]

But what is even more astonishing is that the same mentality of "us" or even "me" beset by "them" is transferred to the domestic front, as the psalmist pours out his soul to Yahweh concerning his personal enemies (6:8 [7]), who are often referred to as "neighbors" (89:42 [41]; 101:5) or "friends" (38:12 [11]). And what are these enemies accused of doing? They pursue the psalmist (7:2 [1]); occasionally his language implies that they wish to murder him (7:2-3 [1-2]; 22:21-22 [20-21]). They plot against him (64:3, 7 [2, 6]). Sometimes the rhetoric borrows from the mythic world of Yahweh's cosmic enemies: the psalmist is entrapped by the "mighty waters" (18:17 [16]; 144:7).

But most of the offenses of his personal enemies lie in the semantic field of talking (10:7; 64:3): the enemies mock him (22:8 [7]; 35:21) and scorn him (89:42 [41]) and slander him (101:5), they curse him and utter lies against him (7:15 [14]). They are false witnesses (35:11). We must remind ourselves of the perception the Israelites had of the power of the word, not only of blessings and curses but of words in general; compare the classic statement regarding the power of Yahweh's word to effect change (Isa. 55:10-11).

The psalmist is baffled: they render him evil for good (38:21 [20]; and, by implication, 7:4-5 [3-4]). And he is devastated. He weeps and moans in the night (6:7-8 [6-7]), he grows weak and ill (22:15-16 [14-15]) and is in danger of entering Sheol, the realm of the dead (6:5-6 [4-5]; 9:14 [13]; 18:5-6 [4-5]). Again, much of this phraseology is stylized, but one must reckon with a culture in which even leading citizens sense themselves to be vulnerable to the gibes and whisperings of other people. We recall the discussion of Ps. 23:5 in chapter 1, the matter of the shaming of one's enemies. Since, in the contexts we are now discussing, the psalmist wishes to shame his enemies (6:11 [10]; 35:4, 26; 83:17-18 [16-17]), it is clear that the fear of the psalmist is that he himself will be shamed (compare 89:46 [45]).

The psalmist, then, affirming himself to be helpless in the face of this activity of his enemies, turns to Yahweh for help. Yahweh is a refuge of the oppressed (9:10 [9]; 18:2-4 [1-3]), and again and again in these laments the psalmist turns to Yahweh for retribution, that the wicked deeds of his enemies might be turned back on them (10:2); indeed, once the psalmist calls for sevenfold retribution (79:12). If Yahweh sometimes seems absent or far away (10:1; 22:3 [2]), the psalmist can only cry out and trust that his cry will be heard.

Most surprising to our modern sensibility, the psalmist is utterly convinced of his own innocence and the guilt of his enemies. The notion that he might have sinned is a marginal one; once, when he brings the matter up, it is simply a rhetorical flourish (7:4-6 [3-5]). Sin might be inherited from his ancestors (79:8), but only occasionally does he really think his present predicament might be due to his sin (38:4-5, 19 [3-4, 18]). In current translations the terms the psalmist uses to speak of himself and his enemies are "righteous" and "wicked," respectively. The Hebrew terms, *ṣaddîq* and *rāšāʿ*, do have these ethical connotations, but it may be helpful for us to try another pair of translations that equally well render the Hebrew words, namely, "innocent" and "guilty" (compare my discussions of Psalms 139 and 1, above). If there is a quarrel or dispute between the psalmist and his enemies, then he affirms before Yahweh that he is innocent and his enemies are the guilty party.

Indeed we have seen more than one psalm in which a declaration of innocence plays an important role (7:4-6 [3-5]; 18:21-25 [20-24]; 101; 139:19-22). Yahweh is *ṣaddîq* (righteous or innocent) and exemplifies *ṣedeq* (righteousness or innocence; 7:18 [17]); so the folk who rejoice in Yahweh are likewise understood to be righteous or innocent (64:11 [10]; 68:4 [3]), among whom the psalmist reckons himself. He is, after all, worshiping Yahweh by the very act of singing the psalm. And, by contrast, the one who is *rāšāʿ*, "guilty" or "wicked," is an enemy of Yahweh, and Yahweh will drive all such away (68:2-3 [1-2]). The psalmist hates all who hate Yahweh (139:21-22). It is this contrast between the ways of the "innocent" or "righteous" and the "guilty" or "wicked" that is set forth in Psalm 1.

Now, we ask: Did the psalmist really have so many enemies? Who in actuality were these people about whom he is talking? To answer, we must first understand that plots and factions were a very real part of court life. Even the cliché-ridden narrative in 1 and 2 Kings from the historian of the seventh century B.C.E. offers many possible situations in which a protagonist could know himself to be surrounded by enemies: around 922 B.C.E. the old priest Abiathar was banished from Jerusalem to Anathoth (1 Kings 2:26-27); around 842 B.C.E. the priest Jehoiada, loyal to Yahweh, revolted against Athaliah, queen of Judah, who was a daughter of King Ahab of Israel and who was a devotee of the god Baal (2 Kings 8:26; 11:1-20, especially 2, 9, 18); around 800 B.C.E. there was war between King Amaziah of Judah and King Jehoash of Israel (2 Kings 14:1-22); during Manasseh's reign (roughly 687–642 B.C.E.) it is said that the king sponsored Baal worship at the temple (2 Kings 21:3), and the practice of Baal worship continued in Jerusalem during the early years of Josiah's reign (roughly 630 B.C.E.; Zeph. 1:4-6)—loyal Yahwists could well have been embattled.

And we know almost nothing of the enemies of people outside court circles, although there come to mind the opposition to the prophet Amos on the part of Amaziah, the priest of Bethel (Amos 7:10-17); the arrest and trial of the prophet Jeremiah after his temple sermon (Jer. 26:1-19); Jeremiah's later arrest by the temple priest Pashhur (Jer. 20:1-6); and the repeated plots of Jeremiah's unnamed enemies against him (Jer. 11:18—12:6; 15:10, 15-18; 17:18; 18:18-23; 20:7-12). And we only suspect power struggles between the country gentry and the court in Jerusalem (but compare 2 Kings 23:30 and 34), to say nothing of the factions within towns and villages, but everyone knows that disputes between families can fester for years. One does not lack, then, for circumstances in which the psalmist's perception of the work of enemies might be expressed. At countless points those who sang these psalms would be right: they had enemies. If one was a Yahwist, one would be aware of devotees of Baal in the land. If one was a sincere Yahwist, concerned about widows and orphans, then one would constantly be reminded that there were those who oppressed widows and orphans, to say nothing of those who persecuted people who were concerned about widows and orphans.

And we must remind ourselves of the obvious: the culture was almost completely an oral one. In times nearer our own, situations of social conflict call forth pamphlet wars, anonymous manifestos on public walls, and the like—one thinks of the period of the Reformation or the period just before the French Revolution. But in pre-exilic Israel the medium of social conflict was word of mouth.

And there is another factor in the matter. Sickness was understood to be punishment for sin; we have touched on the matter already (Ps. 38:4-5, 19 [3-4, 18]). Therefore when someone fell ill, though his own conscience might be clear (again those protestations of innocence), there would be others who would ask, "What did he do to deserve this?" Though the poem of the book of Job evidently comes from a slightly later period, it reflects this mentality: though Job is an innocent man (Job 1:1), his friend Eliphaz lists the sins that must correspond to his disease (Job 22:1-11). To someone who was ill it must have been maddening to be half aware of such speculation on the part of people who were part of one's own community.

Further, to be ill is by definition to feel particularly helpless and vulnerable; if a person was sleepless with fever, then feverish notions and nightmares would be bound to contribute to that sense of being surrounded by enemies ready to take advantage of one's weakness, particularly when one is concerned to maintain one's honor. And doubtless many who sang these psalms projected their own unacknowledged faults onto their friends and neighbors.[44]

So the psalmist is convinced that his help lies in Yahweh: it is Yahweh who will vindicate all the downtrodden, the weak, the oppressed, the prisoner, the widow, and the orphan, who do not have the strength and the means to gain justice for themselves (9:10, 13, 19 [9, 12, 18]; 10:14; 68:6-7 [5-6]). Indeed the word normally translated "vengeance" (Hebrew, *nĕqāmâ*) may be better translated "vindication" (compare 79:10; I shall return to this matter in chapter 17).[45] And the king—to revert to that figure once more—is charged to maintain justice for the poor on Yahweh's behalf (72:2, 4, 12-14).

The topic of justice for the poor invites us to ponder for a moment who these "poor" were (Hebrew, *'ānî* or *'ānāw*). Are we to understand that the reference is to those suffering economic poverty, or are there other connotations to these terms? It is clear from the contexts that these words often refer to those who are victimized, who are without legal resources. But the diction of 9:16-17 (17-18) attracts our attention: there the "wicked" or "guilty" and "the nations" are parallel, and "the needy" and the "poor" are parallel. Whether or not Psalms 9–10 were originally spoken by the king, in any event it is clear that the speaker identifies himself with the "poor." The "poor," then, are those who frequent the temple (9:15 [14]), whom Yahweh loves, and whose recourse is to Yahweh.[46]

It is useful to visualize the covenant community in this period as a community whose ultimate government was Yahweh: it was Yahweh who was ultimately responsible for the defense of the realm against enemies, for upholding justice in the realm, and for maintaining the prosperity of the realm. Then, when human monarchy was established under Saul and David, that monarch was the representative of the ultimate government, which was Yahweh. Phrases in the psalms that sometimes seem to the modern reader self-righteous turn out to be expressions of loyalty to Yahweh's divine governance. I have referred, as a parallel, to the French Revolution. It may be useful to recall how easy it was in France in the years just after the revolution to accuse someone of being a "traitor of the people" (or, in our own century in the Soviet Union, of being an "enemy of the people"). One may suspect the same dynamic to be at work.

Thus may we glimpse, somewhat through a glass darkly, the hymns sung in the temple of Solomon.

NOTES

1. Magen Broshi, "Estimating the Population of Jerusalem," *BARev* 4, no. 2 (June 1978):12.

2. This possibility is suggested in Hans-Joachim Kraus, *Psalms 60–150: A Commentary* (Minneapolis: Augsburg, 1989), 76–77.

3. So Hermann Gunkel, *Die Psalmen* (Göttingen: Vandenhoeck & Ruprecht, 1929), 81; and Mitchell Dahood, *Psalms I: 1–50* (Garden City, N.Y.: Doubleday, 1966), 127. Hans-Joachim Kraus (*Psalms 1–59: A Commentary* [Minneapolis: Augsburg, 1988], 278–79) accepts the possibility of this explanation for the psalm.

4. See Charles F. Nims and Richard C. Steiner, "A Paganized Version of Psalm 20:2-6 from the Aramaic Text in Demotic Script," *JAOS* 103 (1983):261–74; and, recently, Ziony Zevit, "The Common Origin of Aramaicized Prayer to Horus and of Psalm 20," *JAOS* 110 (1990):213–28.

5. The suggestion of Dahood, *Psalms I*, 131.

6. But Sigmund Mowinckel believed it likely that Psalm 21 was sung before battle and that the success described in the psalm was an anticipated prophetic oracle; see Sigmund Mowinckel, *The Psalms in Israel's Worship* (New York and Nashville: Abingdon, 1962), 2:62.

7. Michael H. Floyd, "Psalm lxxxix: A Prophetic Complaint about the Fulfillment of an Oracle," *VT* 42(1992), 442–57.

8. Kraus, *Psalms 60–150*, 277–78; Mitchell Dahood, *Psalms III: 101–150* (Garden City, N.Y.: Doubleday, 1970), 2.

9. Cf. Kraus, *Psalms 60–150*, 541–42.

10. Mowinckel, *Psalms in Israel's Worship* 1:220, 226; Dahood, *Psalms I*, 172; idem, *Psalms II: 51–100* (Garden City, N.Y.: Doubleday, 1968), 83–84, 96.

11. Kraus, *Psalms 1–59*, 312.

12. Ibid.; Dahood, *Psalms I*, 151.

13. See J. P. Ross, "Jahweh Seba'ot in Samuel and Psalms," *VT* 17 (1967):76–92, esp. 79.

14. Tryggve N. D. Mettinger, "YHWH SABAOTH—The Heavenly King on the Cherubim Throne," in Tomoo Ishida (ed.), *Studies in the Period of David and Solomon and Other Essays: Papers Read at the International Symposium for Biblical Studies, Tokyo, 5–7 December 1979* (Winona Lake, Ind.: Eisenbrauns, 1982), 109–38.

15. For this matter, see Kraus, *Psalms 1–59*, 85–86.

16. For a convenient translation, see John A. Wilson in James Pritchard (ed.), *Ancient Near Eastern Texts relating to the Old Testament* (Princeton: Princeton University Press, 1955), 369–71.

17. See Georges Nagel, "A propos des rapports du psaume 104 avec les textes égyptiens," in Walter Baumgartner and others (eds.), *Festschrift für Alfred Bertholet* (Tübingen: J.C.B. Mohr [Paul Siebeck], 1950), 395–403.

18. Gottfried Quell, "Struktur und Sinn des Psalms 131," in Fritz Maass (ed.), *Das Ferne und Nahe Wort: Festschrift Leonard Rost* (BZAW 105; Berlin: Töpelmann, 1967), 173–85.

19. See William L. Holladay, *Jeremiah 1* (Hermeneia; Philadelphia: Fortress, 1986), 376–77, 489–90; idem, *Jeremiah 2* (Hermeneia; Minneapolis: Fortress, 1989), 65.

20. Holladay, *Jeremiah 1*, 640; idem, *Jeremiah 2*, 68.

21. Holladay, *Jeremiah 1*, 339, 344.

22. Holladay, *Jeremiah 2*, 68–69.

23. Ibid., 65.

24. Ibid., 65–66.

25. Ibid., 68.

26. William L. Holladay, "The Background of Jeremiah's Self-Understanding: Moses, Samuel, and Psalm 22," *JBL* 83 (1964):156–59; idem, *Jeremiah 2*, 66.

27. Erhard S. Gerstenberger, *Psalms: Part I, with an Introduction to Cultic Poetry* (Grand Rapids: Eerdmans, 1988), 112–13, with bibliography.

28. Ibid., 112; Kraus, *Psalms 1–59*, 294.

29. Ibid.

30. Holladay, *Jeremiah 2*, 67.

31. Ibid., 67–68.

32. Kraus, *Psalms 1–59*, 169.

33. Holladay, *Jeremiah 2*, 67.

34. Kraus, *Psalms 1–59*, 411.

35. Holladay, *Jeremiah 2*, 67.

36. Ibid., 66–67.

37. Ibid., 66.

38. So Dahood, *Psalms III*, 297, building on Jan C. M. Holman, "Analysis of the Text of Ps 139," *BZ* 14 (1970):37–71, 198–227.

39. Dahood, *Psalms III*, 284; see further Leopold Sabourin, *The Psalms: Their Origin and Meaning* (New York: Alba House, 1974), 386–87.

40. Kraus, *Psalms 1–59*, 114–15.

41. Though for a splendid attempt to visualize Israelite life, see Othmar Keel, *The Symbolism of the Biblical World: Ancient Near Eastern Iconography and the Book of Psalms* (New York: Seabury, 1978).

42. Jacob M. Myers, *I Chronicles* (AB 12; Garden City, N.Y.: Doubleday, 1965), xix–xl.

43. Anne Tyler, *Breathing Lessons* (New York: Knopf, 1988), 68.

44. See Kraus, *Psalms 1–59*, 95–99.

45. George E. Mendenhall, *The Tenth Generation: The Origins of the Biblical Tradition* (Baltimore: Johns Hopkins University Press, 1973), 69–104.

46. Kraus, *Psalms 1–59*, 92–95.

5

Hymns
for the Second Temple

The Jews in the Hundred Years after the
Fall of Jerusalem in 587 B.C.E.

The Babylonian capture of Jerusalem in 587 B.C.E. was catastrophic. The city fell in July of that year; the last king of Judah, Zedekiah, was captured, blinded, and taken off in chains to Babylon. Then in August the local Babylonian military commander entered the city; burned the temple, the palace, and the larger residences; broke down the city walls; and began the deportation of leading citizens to Babylon. The chief priests and military officers were led off and executed (2 Kings 25:1-12, 18-21). The city could not be used for the capital of the newly constituted Babylonian province of Judea; the capital instead was set up at Mizpah, a military stronghold to the north of the city (Jer. 40:5-6). The Edomites, a perennial enemy of Judah from the southeast, took advantage of the prostration of the city both to jeer and to loot (Obad. 1, 11-14; Ps.137:7; Lam. 4:21-22). Within the city there was widespread starvation and even reports of cannibalism (Lam. 4:5, 9-10). It is worth noting, as we survey the events of those days, that the book of Lamentations offers five communal laments from the catastrophe of the fall of the city that continue that literary type in these specific circumstances.

The exiles, deported to Babylon five hundred miles to the east, had to endure not only the knowledge that their beloved city Jerusalem had been physically destroyed and its people scattered but, more particularly, that kingship in the line of David was at an end, at least temporarily, and above all that the temple in Zion, Yahweh's throne, was destroyed. And their fellow exile Ezekiel, the prophet, shared with them his vision that even before the temple was physically destroyed, it had been forsaken by the glorious presence of Yahweh (Ezek. 10:1-22; 11:22-25).

Then, about 540 B.C.E., a prophet arose among the exiles (he is conventionally called "Second Isaiah," his words being preserved in Isaiah 40–55); he proclaimed the good news that release was coming by the agency of King Cyrus of Persia (Isa. 44:28; 45:1). And, indeed, in 538 B.C.E. Cyrus did conquer Babylon, and he soon decreed that any Jewish exiles who wished could return to Jerusalem—he even set aside funds to aid their return (Ezra 1:1-11). Accordingly, an expedition of people did return (Ezra 2:1-70) under the leadership of Sheshbazzar, a man of royal descent (Ezra 1:8). When the group arrived in Jerusalem, they made a beginning at rebuilding the temple (Ezra 5:13-16), but thereafter the work lapsed; work on the temple would not be taken up again for another generation.

Then, in 520 B.C.E., Darius, king of Persia, a successor of Cyrus, issued a fresh decree that encouraged a second group of Jews to return from Babylon to Jerusalem; they were led by the priest Jeshua or Joshua and by a man named Zerubbabel, who was appointed governor of the Jewish community in Jerusalem (Hag. 2:1-4; Ezra 3:1-2). One of the prophets in Jerusalem, Haggai, was the immediate stimulus for a fresh start on the rebuilding of the temple (Hag. 1:1-15). The community set the altar and immediately began offering sacrifices and observing the appointed feasts (Ezra 3:1-5). Then they relaid the foundation for the new temple and held a liturgical celebration (Ezra 3:10-11). The narrative in the book of Ezra records that the people sang responsively a joyful verse (Ezra 3:11) that is a variation on one that appears in the Psalms several times (Pss. 106:1; 107:1; 118:1, 29; 136:1).

Nevertheless, it was a bittersweet occasion, for alongside the joy of the moment the narrative also records the disappointment of those who could remember the proportions of Solomon's temple (Ezra 3:12-13; compare Hag. 2:3-4). And it took another five years for this second temple to be completed (515 B.C.E., Ezra 6:13-18).

But as for the royal palace, there was no need to rebuild it. It is true, there seems to have been an effort to crown Zerubbabel king (Hag. 2:20-23; compare Zech. 3:1-10; 6:9-15), but the attempt came to nothing, and it was in the temple that the community found its center. (There were also some Jews, we must remind ourselves, who remained in Babylon for one reason or another, and there was a substantial community of Jews in Egypt [compare Jeremiah 44]; but we know nothing about the extent to which these communities made use of the Psalms. In chapter 6 we return to the matter of the Jewish community in Egypt.)

The Jews in Jerusalem made up a small community indeed: if the population in Jerusalem had been about 30,000 just before the exile, it is estimated at about 4,500 after the exile.[1] Archeologists excavating in our day have found few architectural remains in Palestine from the Persian period:[2] people must simply have moved back into ruined buildings and patched them up to live in. The wall of Jerusalem remained broken down, leaving people vulnerable to raiding parties (compare Neh. 2:17): the city wall would not be rebuilt for another seventy years, until Nehemiah in 445 B.C.E. (Neh. 2:1; 2:8—6:15).

And if the people felt themselves vulnerable to raiding parties, they were also haunted by the enmity of the Samaritans, whose early offer to help in rebuilding the temple the Jews spurned (so, evidently, the import of Ezra 4:1-5).

The little community was itself split into factions: if there were prophets who supported the priestly authorities in the temple (Hag. 2:15-19; Zech. 7:1-14), there were also those who opposed the same priestly leaders (Isa. 66:1-6). And later, when Nehemiah began his work on the wall, there would be opposition not only from

Samaritans but also from Ammonites and Arabs (Neh. 2:10, 19; 4:1-2 [Protestant numeration vv. 7-8]).

Bilingualism among the Returnees

There is one more development of which we must take account before we turn to the post-exilic psalms, and that is a linguistic one. The traditional language of the Israelites had been Hebrew, of course, but in the last 150 years of the pre-exilic period some officials in the court had gained knowledge of a sister language, Aramaic (see 2 Kings 18:26). Aramaic was about as close to Hebrew as Portuguese now is to Spanish, or as Dutch now is to German. It had arisen originally among the Aramaean (Syrian) people, centered in Damascus, and it slowly became the common language between the subject peoples within the Assyrian and Babylonian empires. That process continued in the western provinces of the Persian Empire after 538 B.C.E. The Jewish exiles in Babylon had therefore gained a knowledge of Aramaic, and they returned to Jerusalem speaking it alongside Hebrew; Hebrew then became more and more the elevated language of religious discourse, the language of the books that became Scripture. By the time Ezra brought the full book of the law to Jerusalem at the end of the fifth century B.C.E., those who listened to it needed to have it "interpreted" (Neh. 8:8), an expression that probably suggests a running interpretation into Aramaic. Because fresh psalms continued to be composed in Hebrew in this period, we must ask ourselves how these two languages functioned side by side in one community.

The answer is that we do not know in detail. Bilingualism is a complicated phenomenon and can take many forms. One thinks of the Swiss and Austrian dialects of German, spoken in homes and shops but not written except for humorous or intimate effect, while the standard "High German" is the language of newspapers, radio, and television, and of sermons and other public discourse.

I think too of the situation I encountered in Beirut. The only written form of Arabic is classical Arabic, the language of the Qur'ān and of the great Arabic literary heritage, but today the forms of spoken Arabic vary from nation to nation, and all of these colloquial dialects are as much in contrast to classical Arabic as Italian and Spanish today are to classical Latin. Now, the pastor of the Arab Presbyterian Church in Beirut, when I was there, delivered his sermons in classical Arabic, as he would be required to do; indeed, some members of the congregation were of the opinion that the higher and more elaborate the pastor's Arabic (which they could not always follow in detail), the more admirable was his preaching skill. But in his children's sermons he spoke in colloquial Lebanese Arabic, and the striking thing was that the congregation loved the children's sermons, because then they could hear the gospel preached directly and freshly. Their emotions, therefore, were divided: admiration and pride for the rich classical Arabic of the adult sermons; delight at the immediacy of the colloquial Arabic, which spoke to them intimately.

I offer these analogies as models by which to grasp the linguistic situation of those who returned to Jerusalem. So what was the feeling-tone associated with the use of Hebrew in this community? It was associated with the traditional discourse of the temple, certainly. It would sound stately, dignified; it would be associated with the beloved past. It would be more familiar to those who could read and write than to those who could not. It would probably be more familiar to men and boys than to women and girls, and it would probably be more familiar to those in the city of Jerusalem than to those in outlying areas.[3]

Psalm 137: A Psalm Composed during the Exile

Now let us go back to the situation of the exiles in Babylon, before they returned to Jerusalem, and to the Psalms. There is one psalm that was clearly composed during the exile, Psalm 137; this is a lament of the people that depicts unforgettably the desolation of the Jewish exiles suddenly far from home: "By the rivers of Babylon—there we sat down and there we wept when we remembered Zion. . . . How could we sing Yahweh's song in a foreign land?" (137:1, 4). And their bitter, helpless rage against the raiding Edomites and against the Babylonian oppressors becomes at least comprehensible (vv. 7-9).

The Pre-exilic Psalms in the Exilic Context

During the time of the exile, of course, the people would have continued to sing the old pre-exilic psalms. Psalms originating in the north that had described a northern disaster were now sung with the fall of Jerusalem in mind. This must have been the case for Psalm 74 (see chapter 3); once "Mount Zion" was added in v. 2, the description of the destruction of the sanctuary (vv. 4-8) would speak to the exiles of the destruction of Solomon's temple, and, after the death of Ezekiel, the words of v. 9 would come alive.

And, in general, all the psalms of the pre-exilic period would have shifted their connotations when sung by Jewish exiles in Babylon. Royal psalms would have been sung with both nostalgia for what was gone and with hope for what was coming; for after all, had Yahweh not promised that David's line would continue forever, as long as the sun and moon endure (Ps. 89:37-38 [36-37])? The psalms of lament would take on fresh meaning when the community was surrounded by foreign enemies on every side, and the pilgrim songs would encourage the people with the hope that the day would come when they could see Jerusalem once more.

Linguistic Clues for the Post-exilic Period and Post-exilic Psalms Dependent on Jeremiah

When we move to the post-exilic period, we find fewer clues for a definitive identification of fresh psalms. One might think that the Hebrew language would have shifted to a new stage in such a way that later vocabulary or phraseology might indicate that specific psalms are post-exilic. And, indeed, there have been convincing attempts in recent years to specify post-exilic psalms on this basis. One Israeli scholar has recently suggested criteria by which to specify the following psalms as post-exilic: Psalms 103, 117, 119, 124, 125, and 145.[4] Of these, Psalms 103 and 119 are discussed below; Psalm 117 is very short; and Psalms 124, 125, and 145 may all plausibly be assigned to the post-exilic period on other grounds.[5] But, in general, the diction of the Psalms is too stylized to allow us to detect much of a shift in language between the pre-exilic and the post-exilic periods.

There are a few psalms whose general diction has led some scholars to assume a post-exilic setting. One of these is the short Psalm 126: the phrases of this psalm, as conventionally translated (see the NRSV), would certainly fit this period,[6] but we lack complete certainty.[7]

The best clue of which I am aware for specifying an origin in the post-exilic period is offered by psalms that borrow from Jeremiah or from other datable material (see chapter 4). I discuss below seven psalms that appear to borrow from Jeremiah: four laments of the individual, Psalms 51, 69, 31, and 55:2-19 (1-18), in that order; a thanksgiving of the individual, Ps. 40:2-12 (1-11); and two hymns, Psalms 135 and 148. In addition, I discuss Psalm 103, which draws primarily from Isaiah 40–66 (material from the sixth century) but perhaps also from Jeremiah.

Laments of the Individual

Psalm 51 is universally acknowledged to come from this period. The most obvious clue is in v. 20 (18): "rebuild the walls of Jerusalem" suggests a time before Nehemiah's work. (It may be pointed out that the Hebrew verb means simply "build," but the point remains the same.) Some critics, however, suggest the possibility that vv. 20-21 (18-19) are a later addition to the psalm,[8] in which case the date of the rest of the psalm would be earlier. But the psalmist of vv. 3-19 (1-17) appears to be dependent on Jeremiah. The reason is somewhat intricate but may be summarized as follows.

Both vv. 4 and 9 (2 and 7), on the one hand, and Jer. 2:22 and 4:14, on the other hand, share the verb "wash" (Hebrew, *kābas*) for purification from sin. But for the imagery of Jer. 2:21 the prophet seems to have drawn on Isa. 5:1-7, and for the imagery of Jer. 2:22 he seems to have drawn on Isa. 1:15-20; however, in Isa. 1:16 another verb for "wash" is used. I suggest, then, that Jer. 2:21-22 drew on the *imagery* of two passages of Isaiah, and that the psalmist of Psalm 51 in his turn drew on the *specific phrases* of Jeremiah. Furthermore, Ps. 51:12 (10) seems to be dependent on Jer. 31:33, part of the "new covenant" passage (the verses share the root "[re]new"—Hebrew, *ḥdš*—and "heart"—Hebrew, *lēb*.)[9] So whether or not vv. 20-21 (18-19) belong to the original psalm, the original psalm appears to date from the exilic or the early post-exilic period. Though on the face of it the psalm is an individual's prayer of contrition, it is not out of the question that the psalm originally functioned as a collective lament from the exilic period—this is, as least, the view of one scholar.[10] The psalm is a profound expression of the awareness of sin that emerged in the exilic and post-exilic period (I return to this matter later).

Psalm 69 is clearly from the early post-exilic period, as vv. 36-37 (35-36) indicate—verses much like Ps. 51:20-21 (18-19), already examined. The psalm draws on Jeremiah: Jer. 15:15b reads, literally, "Know my bearing on your account disgrace"; this phrase is simplified in Ps. 69:8a (7a) to "for on your account I have borne disgrace."[11] Though the diction of the psalm resembles that of the laments of the pre-exilic period, it offers some striking features. The lament proper (vv. 2-30 [1-29]) is long and elaborate. The psalmist is zealous for God's house (v. 10 [9]), and that zeal has attracted personal enemies, deliverance from whom he asks from God. The speaker appears to have been accused of theft (v. 5 [4]); one wonders: Is he languishing in prison (v. 15 [14]), or is the diction simply imitative of Jeremiah's predicament (Jer. 38:6)? The wording of v. 34 (33) might suggest he is in prison. One wonders also: Does the notion that praise is better than sacrifice (v. 32 [31]) suggest that the psalm was originally composed in Babylon, away from temple sacrifice, in which case "God's house" (v. 10 [9]) would be metaphorical (God's household, company, or the like)? Or is it simply a reflection of prophetic teaching?

Psalm 31, another lament, was used in chapter 4 as an illustration of a psalm drawing from Jeremiah: the phrase borrowed is "terror on every side" (v. 14 [13]), which was not only a favorite of Jeremiah's but one that he evidently was the first to use (see Jer. 20:1-6). In this psalm the lament proper is vv. 2-19 (1-18); to this a thanksgiving has been added (vv. 20-25 [19-24]), exactly as with Psalm 22 (see chapter 4). The psalmist appears to cite not only "terror on every side" from Jeremiah but to offer reminiscences of other passages of Isaiah, Jeremiah, Ezekiel, and earlier psalms.[12] It is a good example of how a psalmist of this period was able to weave older material into a fresh context.

Psalm 55, like Psalm 69, resembles in its phraseology the individual laments we examined in chapter 4. Verses 7-12 (6-11) are a variation on Jer. 9:1-7 (Protestant numeration 2-8). One notes the theme of fleeing to lodge in the wilderness (Ps. 55:8 [7]; compare Jer. 9:1 [2]), the theme of the "tongue" (Ps. 55:10 [9]—NRSV, "speech"; compare Jer. 9:2, 7 [3, 8]), and the phrase "oppression and fraud" (Ps. 55:12 [11]; compare Jer. 9:5 [6]—NRSV, "oppression" and "deceit"). But the psalmist tones down Jeremiah's diction: whereas Jeremiah evidently understands Yahweh to wish to flee to the desert to get away from the people, the psalmist wishes to flee to the desert to be rid of his enemies.[13] The psalmist affirms that he could deal with enemies or adversaries, but what is shattering is that he is betrayed by his familiar friend (vv. 13-15, 21 [12-14, 20]).

Psalm 40:2-12 (1-11) is a thanksgiving for healing. (Verses 13-18 [12-17] of this psalm did not originally belong with the first portion: these verses are a lament, and vv. 14-18 [13-17] are virtually identical with Psalm 70.) Beyond the borrowing from Jeremiah—vv. 4-5 (3-4) imitate Jer. 17:5-8, which I am convinced is genuine to the prophet[14]—this sequence is a low-key summary of the prophetic rejection of sacrifice (v. 7 [6]) and in this respect resembles 69:32 (31), which we have just examined. Furthermore, the wording of vv. 8-11 (7-10) suggests the torah piety of the period.[15]

Hymns

I now turn to two hymns that drew on Jeremiah, Psalms 135 and 148. Psalm 135 is a hymn in which the psalmist praises the greatness of God. Verse 7 duplicates with minor variations the last three lines of Jer. 10:13.[16] Though Jer. 10:1-16 is widely thought not to be original to that prophet, I have cautiously concluded that it is genuine to him;[17] but beyond that, the psalm imitates verses from other psalms, from Exodus, and from Deuteronomy.[18] The psalm reviews the mighty acts of God in delivering Israel from Egypt, and it insists on Yahweh's power in contrast to heathen idols (v. 7, already cited, implies this because of the message of all of Jer. 10:1-16; vv. 15-18 say it directly, but doubtless vv. 15-20 are dependent on Ps. 115:4-11).

Psalm 148, a hymn calling upon everything in heaven and earth to praise God, is the last psalm I cite that is dependent on Jeremiah. Verse 6 bears a complicated relation to Jer. 5:22. In the Jeremiah verse there is a double meaning of the Hebrew verb *'ābar* (surpass, and pass away)—there it is affirmed that Yahweh "established the sand as a bound for the sea, a limit forever" (my trans.), and (1) that "it (the sea) shall not surpass it" (my trans.) and (2) that "it (the sand) shall not pass away for it (the sea)" (my trans.). In Ps. 148:6 the subject is the sun, moon, stars, and waters above the heavens that are established forever; there, it is affirmed, Yahweh (1) "fixed a limit that cannot be passed" and (2) "set a law that cannot pass away" (see both the RSV and NRSV and footnote at that verse). Furthermore, the listing in the psalm of the features of nature reflects the wisdom interests of the post-exilic period.

Psalm 103

There are, in addition, psalms that have borrowed from other prophetic material, for example, Psalm 103. This hymn, described by Mitchell Dahood as "an Old Testament *Te Deum*,"[19] seems to have borrowed the phrase "he will not be angry forever" (v. 9) from both Jer. 3:12 and Isa. 57:16 (the date for the latter being about 520 B.C.E.), vv. 15-16 (humans being like grass) from Isa. 40:6-8, and perhaps vv. 11-12 ("as the heavens are high above the earth") from Isa. 55:7-9 (a reminder: Isaiah 40–55, "Second Isaiah," is to be dated about 540 B.C.E.).

The Faith of
the Early Post-exilic Community

Let us pause now and see if we can bring into focus the religious concerns of the community in this period, using not only these psalms but other writings of the same period (Haggai, Zechariah 1–8, Isaiah 56–66, Ezra, and Nehemiah), and thereby hear the psalms of the Second Temple in their context.

To be sure, it was in a real sense the same faith as in pre-exilic times. God is the creator and sustainer of the sun and moon and waters (Pss. 69:35 [34]; 74:12-17; 135:6-7; 148:5-13). God has chosen Israel (Ps. 135:4) and covenanted with its people (Ps. 74:20) to be a people of obedience, and the people remember his acts of deliverance in the past (Pss. 103:7; 135:8-12). God is king (Ps. 74:12) and rules over all (Ps. 103:19). The old creed of Exod. 34:6-7 is recalled, that God is merciful and gracious, slow to anger and abounding in steadfast love (Ps. 103:8).

But there are shifts of emphasis. No longer do we suspect the real existence of other gods—the expression in Ps. 135:5 is simply traditional (compare vv. 15-18). However much Zion may be the mountain where God chooses to dwell (Pss. 51:20 [18]; 69:36 [35]; 87:2-3), there is no longer any assumption that God is confined to a particular land. The metaphor of God as a warrior has faded (Ps. 69:25-26 [24-25]), for there are no armies of Israel at God's disposal.

As I have already stated, God's ancient name, "Yahweh," was suppressed at the time the Second Temple was built; in texts employing the name, the term "Adonay" (the Lord) was substituted (see chapter 1). And the "hosts" in the phrase "the Lord of hosts" (compare chapter 4) would at this time have been understood as "angels" (so, evidently, the implication of Pss. 103:20-21; 148:2).

The sociological situation of the community profoundly shaped its stance before God. I have given some indication of this already, but it bears repeating as we think about the community's self-understanding. Their numbers were greatly reduced in comparison with the population level in pre-exilic times; such shrinking brings with it a kind of existential panic, particularly as the community could recall their tradition that God promised Jacob that his offspring would be like the dust of the earth, and that he would spread abroad to the west and to the east and to the north and to the south (Gen. 28:14). Those who returned to Jerusalem were economically poor, especially at first (Hag. 1:6). And they were vulnerable: in the pre-exilic period they may have been a nation surrounded by other nations that were hostile, but as a nation they had borders and an army and, above all, a king, one sponsored by God himself. Now kingship was gone, or at least its reestablishment was postponed to the indefinite future; there was no army and there were no borders—no borders for Judea, which was now simply a province of the Persian Empire, and no wall even for the city of Jerusalem until Nehemiah's time. Furthermore, many Jews remained in Babylon or were scattered in Egypt; the community was no longer located within a given territory. This lack of what might be called "external liminality" would have been profoundly disorienting to a people accustomed to old ways of thinking and behaving.

And, above all, the fall of Jerusalem itself was a watershed experience: a Jeremiah might have proclaimed that Yahweh could destroy his temple (Jer. 7:14), and an Ezekiel might have affirmed that Yahweh had already taken his glory from the temple (Ezek. 10:1—11:25), but until the actual fall of the city in 587 B.C.E., most people would have held onto Yahweh's word spoken through Isaiah: "I will defend this city to save it, for my own sake and for the sake of my servant David" (2 Kings 19:34). The fall of the city, then, was stunning; the people were forced to take account of the word of Jeremiah and Ezekiel, that God had brought the catastrophe upon them for their sins, and to become convinced that that word was valid. Lamentations 4:12-13 sums the matter up well:

> The kings of the earth did not believe, nor did any of the inhabitants of the world, that foe or enemy could enter the gates of Jerusalem. It was for the sins

of her prophets and the iniquities of her priests, who shed the blood of the righteous in the midst of her.

It is in this context that we must hear the profound acknowledgment of sin in Psalm 51 (and elsewhere as well—Ps. 69:6 [5]), and the affirmation, too, that God is more gracious toward the people than their sins would merit (Ps. 103:11).

Along with the acknowledgment of sin comes what one might call a new inwardness, a willingness to ponder the self in both chagrin and joy. One sees this in Psalm 51 (see vv. 8 [6] and 19 [17]), but also in Psalm 103, where in the first five verses the psalmist addresses his own "self" (the literal meaning of the Hebrew *nepeš*, usually translated "soul").

Did the worshiping community have a deepened sense of awe before God? One wonders whether this is the explanation for the conventional phrase "those who fear God" that appears in Pss. 31:20 (19), 40:4 (3), and 103:11 and 17 (and compare 22:24 [23], part of the thanksgiving section of Psalm 22, discussed in chapter 4).

The psalmists in the post-exilic period took to heart not only the prophets' preaching on the fall of Jerusalem but their word also that God loves a responsive heart more than sacrifice (40:7 [6]; 51:18-19 [16-17]; 69:31-32 [30-31]). Yet the ancient ritual led by the priests in the temple would have reassured the worshiping community of their continuity with the past: we note that the phrases "house of Israel" and "those who fear the Lord" in Ps. 135:19-20 enclose the phrases "house of Aaron" and "house of Levi," references to the priests and Levites, respectively. And, one wonders, what is the nuance of the phrase "the great congregation"? The phrase is found in Pss. 35:18 and 40:10-11 (9-10) (and also 22:26 [25], in the thanksgiving section of Psalm 22; see chapter 4). Does it refer to the worshiping community in Jerusalem, in contrast to smaller communities elsewhere?

As already noted, the diction of these psalms' laments follows closely the diction of the laments from pre-exilic times: there is the same insistence on the innocence or righteousness of the psalmist and his partisans (31:19 [18]; 69:29 [28]) and on the guilt or wickedness of the enemies (31:18 [17]; 55:4 [3]), the same concern for the speech of the enemies (55:10, 22 [9, 21]; 69:12-13 [11-12]), the same reaction of weeping (31:10 [9]; 69:4 [3]), the same effort to be free of shame and to heap shame on the enemies (31:2, 18 [1, 17]; 69:7-8 [6-7]). But Psalm 69 introduces some new motifs, not only the accusation, already noted, that the psalmist has stolen something (69:5 [4]), but also, "They gave me poison for food, and for my thirst they gave me vinegar to drink" (69:22 [21], NRSV). And the very length of Psalm 69 is striking; clearly the occasion for laments was still very much present.

Yet praise to God was innovative, too: the psalmist of Psalm 40 affirms that God has "put a new song in my mouth" (v. 4 [3]).

Torah-Psalms 19:8-15; 119; and
the Motif of Wisdom

There are two more fresh motifs that appear in the psalms of this period. The first is a renewed emphasis on torah. We discussed the Hebrew word *tôrâ* in chapter 4 with regard to Psalm 1; there I suggested that in the pre-exilic period the nuance of the word was "teaching"or "instruction" in covenant norms, norms such as those mentioned in Ps. 24:4. The word appears in post-exilic psalms as well: in 40:9 (8) we read, "I delight to do your will [literally, "what you favor"], O my God; your *tôrâ* is within my heart." Here the word could still mean "instruction."

But there are two psalms where the word clearly means "law," and both of them, I am convinced, are from the post-exilic period. The first is Ps. 19:8-15 (7-14): here *tôrâ* is parallel with the synonyms "precepts" (v. 9 [8]) and "ordinances" (v. 10 [9]). These verses offer us a piety of torah, the concentration on God's will in written form. They are evidently a post-exilic extension of vv. 2-7 (1-6) (see chapter 2).

The other psalm in which *tôrâ* means "law" is Psalm 119, which is a baroque example of torah piety. This psalm is the most elaborate acrostic in the Old Testament. In chapter 3 it was explained that Psalms 9–10 originally made up a single acrostic psalm. There are other acrostic psalms, but Psalm 119 is the champion: each of the first eight verses begins with the first letter of the Hebrew alphabet (aleph), each of the next eight verses with the second letter (beth), and so on through the twenty-two letters, 176 verses.[20] In this psalm, too, the word *tôrâ* is matched by the synonyms "precepts" and "statutes": *tôrâ* occurs twenty-four times in the psalm,[21] "precepts" occurs twenty-one times,[22] and "statutes" occurs twenty-two times.[23] More importantly, however, the words are interchangeable: one has the phrases "keep your precepts" (vv. 4, 63, 134, 168) and "keep your statutes" (vv. 5, 145) alongside "keep your *tôrâ*" (vv. 34, 44, 55, 136).

In Psalms 19 and 119, then, *tôrâ* implies "the body of legal formulations"; these psalms are products of a period when written legal collections were evidently being made and when the community was shifting to a concern for the precise meaning of those written collections. One thinks of the coming of Ezra the scribe from Babylon to Jerusalem in the second half of the fifth century B.C.E. with a copy of the "torah of Moses" (Ezra 7:1-26; Neh. 7:73—8:18), which he read and taught to the assembled people in Jerusalem.

The second fresh motif is a greater integration of "wisdom" resources into the psalms. In chapter 4 Jer. 18:18 was cited as a passage in which "torah" is translated in the NRSV as "instruction"; this verse links the function of the priest—to hand on "instruction" or "law"—and the function of the prophet—to hand on "the word" (of God)—with the function of "the wise" as well—to hand on "counsel." The summing up of advice and expertise, not only by the use of maxims within the family but by the use of counsel within the court and schools, was an important feature of the culture of Israel (it is summed up in the book of Proverbs). The organization in Psalm 148, category by category, of all creation in a universal appeal to praise the Lord is certainly evidence of the kind of systematic pondering of the universe that was part of wisdom.[24]

The Pre-exilic Psalms in the Post-exilic Context

It was in this sad, timid, and joyous community of the Second Temple that new psalms were sung. But, we remind ourselves, not only were the old pre-exilic psalms sung during the exile; they were sung in this post-exilic community as well.

So we must pause to ponder how the old psalms would have been heard by the community in the period of the Second Temple.

Some songs would have been heard and understood with few shifts of perception. For example, pilgrims could glory in the sight of the temple once more, so that pilgrim songs such as Psalms 84 and 122 would be sung as they had been sung in earlier centuries.

But for most of the pre-exilic psalms there would of necessity have been shifts in understanding[25]—the royal psalms, for example, after the collapse of the movement to crown Zerubbabel king. Some royal psalms were so explicit that they could be used only to anticipate a future restoration of the Davidic monarchy (Psalms 2 and 72). But other royal psalms, less overtly so, would have been "democratized"— Psalm 101, for example, the psalm of declaration of innocence. Indeed the process of democratization must have been a steady, though complicated, one: if the context of pre-exilic worship was strongly centered in the royal court, now there was no court, and the experience of the people in exile would have strengthened their perception that the psalms were a vehicle for the worship of a people bereft of royal leadership, where any head of family might find touch with God.[26]

The pre-exilic communal laments, like pilgrim songs, were always relevant; indeed, the description of the destruction of Jerusalem in Psalm 79 would have been more relevant than ever in the early post-exilic period. And individual laments were equally relevant: there are misery and distress in human lives in every generation. Nevertheless, there must have been a shift even here. If the laments in pre-exilic times were confident affirmations to Yahweh of innocence over against the wiles of personal and national enemies, the laments of the post-exilic community would have been sung out of the conservatism and defensiveness of a small ecclesial minority looking for signs of God in a remote corner of the Persian Empire. Phrases in Isaiah give some sense of the mood of the community: "O that you would tear open the heavens and come down . . . Zion has become a wilderness . . . Will you keep silent, and punish us so severely?" (Isa. 63:19; 64:9, 11 [Protestant numeration 64:1, 10, 12]). In this context, words such as "My God, my God, why have you forsaken me?" (Ps. 22:2 [1]) would speak out of the depths of community despair.

If *tôrâ* shifted to the meaning of "the body of legal formulations," as I have indicated, then the phraseology of Psalm 1—"their delight [that is, of the righteous] is in the law of the Lord, and on his law they meditate day and night"—takes on the meaning that is more familiar to us: the righteous glorying in the piety of torah.

By the same token, if wisdom motifs became more integrated into psalm language, then Psalm 139 would have helped the worshiper to glory in the infinite awareness of God and God's scrutiny of each worshiper.

And it remains only to note that if pre-exilic psalms continued to be used in worship, patterns existent in the Psalms could always be incorporated into other literature that would become Scripture: the poetry of the book of Job is probably to be dated in the exilic or early post-exilic period, and Psalm 139 has evidently been mined for phraseology in Job. Thus one may compare Job 10:8-11 with Ps.

139:13-16 and Job 17:12-13 with Ps. 139:8, 11-12. If wisdom motifs entered into the psalms, psalm motifs entered into wisdom.

By the same token, the book of 1 Chronicles was prepared in the late post-exilic period, probably about 400 B.C.E., and the poem in 1 Chron. 16:8-36 is a composite psalm put together from previous material in the Psalms: thus 1 Chron. 16:8-22 is from Ps. 105:1-15; 1 Chron. 16:23-33 is from Ps. 96:1-13; and 1 Chron. 16:34-36 is from Ps. 106:1, 47-48.

In these ways the Psalms influenced literature beyond the book itself.

NOTES

1. Magen Broshi, "Estimating the Population of Ancient Jerusalem," *BARev* 4, no. 2 (June 1978):10–15.

2. Shalom M. Paul and William G. Dever, *Biblical Archaeology* (New York: Quadrangle/New York Times, 1974), 25.

3. John Bright, *A History of Israel* (Philadelphia: Westminster, 1981), 411–12.

4. The work is published in Hebrew: Avi Hurvitz, *Ben Lashon Lelashon* (Jerusalem: Mossad Bialik, 1972). The full English descriptive title is *The Transition Period in Biblical Hebrew—A Study in Post-exilic Hebrew and Its Implications for the Dating of Psalms.* See the reference in Nahum M. Waldman, *The Recent Study of Hebrew: A Survey of the Literature with Selected Bibliography* (Cincinnati: Hebrew Union College Press, 1989), 80.

5. Hans-Joachim Kraus, *Psalms 60–150: A Commentary* (Minneapolis: Augsburg, 1989), 391, 441, 444, 547.

6. So Kraus, *Psalms 60–150*, 449.

7. Leopold Sabourin, *The Psalms: Their Origin and Meaning* (New York: Alba House, 1974), 317–18.

8. Hermann Gunkel, *Die Psalmen* (Göttingen: Vandenhoeck & Ruprecht, 1929), 226; Hans-Joachim Kraus, *Psalms 1–59: A Commentary* (Minneapolis: Augsburg, 1988), 501.

9. William L. Holladay, *Jeremiah 2* (Minneapolis: Fortress, 1989), 69.

10. So André Caquot, "Purification et expiation selon le psaume LI," *RHR* 169 (1966):133–54.

11. Holladay, *Jeremiah 2*, 70.

12. Charles Augustus Briggs and Emilie Grace Briggs, *A Critical and Exegetical Commentary on the Book of Psalms* (New York: Charles Scribner's Sons, 1906–7), 1:264, offers a long list, though not all the presumed citations are cogent.

13. Holladay, *Jeremiah 2*, 69–70.

14. Ibid., 69.

15. Kraus, *Psalms 1–59*, 424.

16. Holladay, *Jeremiah 2*, 69.

17. William L. Holladay, *Jeremiah 1* (Philadelphia: Fortress, 1986), 324–26.

18. Kraus, *Psalms 60–150*, 492.

19. Mitchell Dahood, *Psalms III: 101–150* (Garden City, N.Y.: Doubleday, 1970), 24.

20. The other acrostic psalms are 25, 34, 37, 111, 112, and 145; in addition, Prov. 31:10-31 and each of the first four chapters of Lamentations are arranged as acrostics, and Nah. 1:2-8 shows traces of part of an original acrostic.

21. Verses 18, 29, 34, 44, 51, 53, 55, 61, 70, 72, 77, 85, 92, 97, 109, 113, 126, 136, 142, 150, 153, 163, 165, 174.

22. Verses 4, 15, 27, 40, 45, 56, 63, 69, 78, 87, 93, 94, 100, 104, 110, 128, 134, 141, 159, 168, 173.

23. Verses 5, 8, 12, 16, 23, 26, 33, 48, 54, 64, 68, 71, 80, 83, 112, 117, 118, 124, 135, 145, 155, 171.

24. Kraus, *Psalms 60–150*, 561–62.

25. For the whole matter, see James L. Kugel, "Topics in the History of the Spirituality of the Psalms," in Arthur Green (ed.), *Jewish Spirituality: From the Bible through the Middle Ages* (New York: Crossroad, 1988), 130–31.

26. Sigmund Mowinckel, *The Psalms in Israel's Worship* (New York and Nashville: Abingdon, 1962), 1:78; Kugel, "Topics," 131.

6

Steps toward the Status of Scripture: The Psalms are Collected, Annotated, and Translated

In chapters 2 through 5 we established with fair probability the period of time for the origin of roughly 70 of the 150 psalms. For a few more there might be clues similar to those I have employed, but at this stage of scholarly research it does not seem possible to reach any certainty for the origin of the remainder of the psalms.

Nevertheless, we can be sure that at a certain stage there emerged a collection of 150 psalms, more or less, which has come to be called "the Psalter." In this chapter I shall treat of three activities clustering around the development of the collection of the Psalms: the collecting process itself, the annotations made on various psalms, and the venture of translating the psalms out of the Hebrew language. All these activities were taking place during a period of time when the collection of Psalms was on its way to being considered scriptural, and that process, too, needs our attention.

The Jews: The Fifth through the Third Centuries B.C.E.

First, however, let us touch briefly on the history of the period after Ezra and Nehemiah. Judea continued to be part of the Persian Empire, and the Jews continued their existence there without interruption. Influences from Greek culture, marginal at an earlier time, must have become more pronounced in this period, but they exploded upon Palestine with the coming of Alexander the Great. Alexander defeated the last king of the Persian Empire, Darius III, at Issus at the northeast corner of the Mediterranean Sea in 333 B.C.E.; the Greek king then marched south along the Mediterranean and took Egypt in 332. In these months, then, Jerusalem came under his control. After campaigns that took Alexander all the way to northwest India, he died in Babylon in 323. After his death the territory of Egypt passed to the control of Ptolemy, one of his generals, while the territories of Babylonia and westward to Syria and eastward to Iran came under the control of another general, Seleucus. Both of them coveted Palestine, but for the first century or so after

Alexander's death it was to the Ptolemaic Empire of Egypt, with its capital at the new city of Alexandria, that Palestine and thus Jerusalem and the Jewish community of the Second Temple belonged.[1] It was in the late Persian period and the early Greek period that the Psalter began to take on its final shape.

Fresh Psalms:
The Collection of 150 Psalms

Two contrary developments emerged at this period. The first is that psalms continued to be written; it is possible that Psalm 119 comes as late as from this period (see chapter 5). However, beyond a psalm such as this one, which was included in the final collection of biblical psalms, other psalms were written that were not included in that final collection. Copies of some of the excluded ones have turned up among the Dead Sea Scrolls, but we will postpone a discussion of them until chapter 7.

The contrary development is the urge to confine the number of psalms to 150. But, as we noted in the Introduction, the specific numeration of individual psalms differs between the Hebrew tradition that has come down to us and the Greek one (which I shall discuss presently): that is to say, there is an arbitrariness in the way the psalms are numbered. Thus in chapter 3 we noted that both Psalms 9–10 and Psalms 42–43 were originally single psalms. By contrast, Psalm 147 is made up of two psalms, 147:1-11 and 147:12-20, and the two psalms carry different numbers in the Greek tradition. We have the situation, then, that although everyone agreed that there were 150 psalms, there was not agreement on the numeration that would arrive at the number of 150.

The Types of Psalms

As I have referred to various psalms in chapters 2 through 5 I have mentioned their type or form (also called *genre* or *Gattung*); it is useful now to summarize these various types.[2]

There are *hymns*, psalms that praise God. We discussed Ps. 19:2-7 (1-6) and Psalm 29 in chapter 2; Psalm 104 in chapter 4; and Psalms 103, 135, and 148 in chapter 5.[3] Three subgroups may be mentioned. There are *psalms of Yahweh's kingship*, of which Psalm 47, discussed in chapter 3, is an example.[4] There are *canticles of Zion*, exemplified by Psalms 46, 48, 76, and 87, discussed in chapter 3. And there are *pilgrim songs* such as Psalm 84, discussed in chapter 3, and Psalm 122, discussed in chapter 4.

There are *laments of the community*: Psalms 74, 79, 80, 83, and 85, discussed in chapter 3; and Psalm 137, discussed in chapter 5.[5] There are also *laments of the individual*: Psalms 42–43, 86, 88, 140, and 141, discussed in chapter 3; Psalms 22, 35, 38, 63, and 64, discussed in chapter 4, and Psalms 6, 7, 31, 51, 55, and 69, discussed in chapter 5.[6]

There are *thanksgivings of the community*, though we have discussed none so far; an example would be Psalm 68.[7] There are also *thanksgivings of the individual*, exemplified by Psalm 40:2-12 (1-11); see chapter 5.[8]

There are *psalms of confidence of the community*, though we have discussed none so far; an example would be Psalm 125.[9] And there are *psalms of confidence of the individual*: Psalms 23 (see chapter 1), 16 (see chapter 3), and 131 (see chapter 4).[10]

There are *royal psalms*, psalms that originally, at least, were associated with the exercise of kingship: there is the hymn for a royal wedding, Psalm 45 (see chapter 3); Psalms 2, 18, and 110 (see chapter 2); Psalm 132 (see chapter 3); and Psalms 20, 21, 72, 89, 101, and 144 (see chapter 4).

Finally, there are some minor types: *liturgies*, such as Psalm 82, a prophetic liturgy (see chapter 2), and Psalm 24, a torah liturgy (see chapter 4); a *prophetic announcement of judgment*, Psalm 81 (see chapter 3); *historical psalms*, such as Psalm 78 (see chapter 3);[11] an *instruction in covenant norms*, Psalm 1 (see chapter 4); and *torah-psalms*, such as Ps. 19:8-15 (7-14) and Psalm 119 (see chapter 5).

Inevitably, there are psalms of mixed types: Psalms 9–10 appear to be so (see chapter 3). Also inevitably, scholars will argue about the classification of particular psalms: Psalm 139 has been classified as a hymn, an individual song of thanksgiving and confidence, a declaration of innocence, and a didactic (wisdom) psalm (see chapter 4). But in general the categories that are here set forth remind of us the range of psalms to be found within the Psalter.

Clues to Subcollections
within the Psalms

The Psalter offers clues that it came into existence not as an arbitrary series of 150 individual psalms but rather as a series of subcollections. Unfortunately, however, the precise identity of these subcollections and the steps by which they were compiled to produce our present Psalter are not at all clear. Indeed there are at least three overlapping ways by which to glimpse the subcollections.

The first and most obvious clue into possible subcollections is that of the "superscriptions," those notations at the head of most of the psalms that categorize them or characterize them in various ways. We have already determined that the psalms of the Korahites and the psalms of Asaph are of northern origin (see chapter 3).

The second clue to possible subcollections is the existence of four "doxological postscripts" scattered through the Psalter—that is, expressions of general benediction that appear at the ends of four separate psalms, expressions that are not connected in any direct way with the psalms to which they are attached. These postscripts are as follows: Ps. 41:14 (13) reads, "Blessed be the Lord, the God of Israel, from everlasting to everlasting. Amen and Amen." Psalm 72:18-20 reads, "Blessed be the Lord, the God of Israel, who alone does wondrous things. Blessed be his glorious name forever; may his glory fill the whole earth. Amen and Amen. The prayers of David son of Jesse are ended." Psalm 89:53 (52) reads, "Blessed be the Lord forever, Amen and Amen." Psalm 106:48 reads, "Blessed be the Lord, the God of Israel, from everlasting to everlasting. And let all the people say, 'Amen.' Praise the Lord!"

These four postscripts have been taken to mark the ends of the first four "books" of the Psalter, namely, Psalms 1–41, Psalms 42–72, Psalms 73–89, and Psalms 90–106; Psalms 107–150 would then be the fifth and final "book." Accordingly, the headings "Book I," "Book II," and so on are inserted at the heads of these "books" in the RSV and the NRSV. But it should be stressed that this numeration of "books" in the Psalter is not in the original Hebrew text (or in the text of the Greek translation, for that matter) but is inserted simply for the convenience of the modern reader. It should also be noted that the notation in Ps. 72:20 just cited—"The prayers of David son of Jesse are ended"—appears to contradict the repeated superscription "Of David," which, as one can see, continues through Psalm 145. Clearly, the matter is complicated.

The third clue into possible subcollections is afforded by occasional duplications within the Psalter. For example, Psalm 108 is a combination of sections of two other psalms: Ps. 108:2-6 (1-5) is virtually the same as Ps. 57:8-12 (7-11), and Ps. 108:7-14 (6-13) is virtually the same as Ps. 60:7-14 (5-12). The existence of such a duplication suggests that the same psalm material had been in two different subcollections that were later combined. But even more suggestive is the duplication between Psalms 14 and 53; these psalms are virtually the same, the major difference being that Psalm 14 uses the name "Yahweh" (translated "the LORD" in the RSV and the NRSV), whereas Psalm 53 uses the generic term "God" (Hebrew, 'ĕlōhîm).

And, it seems, this contrast points to a significant clue: Psalms 1–41 overwhelmingly use "Yahweh," Psalms 42–83 overwhelmingly use the generic term "God," and Psalms 84–150 return once more to the overwhelming use of "Yahweh." This striking shift has led scholars to designate Psalms 42–83 as the "Elohistic Psalter" ("Elohistic" from the Hebrew 'ĕlōhîm [God]); those psalms outside the Elohistic Psalter could be characterized as "Yahwistic." Thus one can see Psalm 14 (= 53) turning up in both the Elohistic Psalter and a Yahwistic collection; and because Psalm 53, by the analysis of chapter 3, has its origin in the north, one can assume that Psalm 14 was in an originally southern collection. And it is certainly striking that Psalms 1–41, the first sequence to use "Yahweh," correspond to "Book I" of the Psalms, and the Elohistic Psalter begins where "Book II" begins (though, as we can see, it does not end where "Book II" ends).

But these are clues only, and the matter of subcollections is clearly complex. I first deal with the superscriptions, and then I return to the more general question of the process by which the Psalter came to have its present shape.

The Superscriptions

The various notations that now stand at the heads of most psalms give much difficulty to interpreters, but a few matters have become clear to scholars. One of the most surprising things must be explained at the start: some types of superscriptions seem originally to have been *postscripts* of the *preceding* psalm.[12] Two passages will make the matter clear. The first is Habakkuk 3, which is an isolated psalm. It begins (v. 1) with a notation of the perceived type (genre) of psalm (NRSV, "A prayer"), continues with an attribution to the author ("of the prophet Habakkuk"), and concludes with what is evidently a reference to an analogous genre or type ("according to Shigionoth"). The psalm ends (v. 19) with instructions for performance (NRSV, "To the choirmaster: with stringed instruments"). In this psalm, then, the notes on genre and authorship are at the beginning, and the notes for performance are at the end.

The second passage is Psalm 88. The superscriptions at the head of this psalm are many and confusing. First we have "A Song. A Psalm of the Korahites," that is, notations on type (genre) and authorship. Then we have "To the leader [this is the same Hebrew expression as 'to the choirmaster' in Hab. 3:19]: according to Mahalath Leannoth," that is, instructions on performance. Then we have "A Maskil of Heman the Ezrahite," that is, another set of notations on type (genre) and authorship, notations that contradict the ones that began the superscription. But now we notice that "A Song. A Psalm of the Korahites" matches the superscription of Psalm 87, "Of the Korahites. A Psalm. A Song." So we see what has happened at the beginning of Psalm 88: "A Song. A Psalm of the Korahites" has simply duplicated the superscription of Psalm 87, and that duplication originally belonged *at the end of Psalm 87*, along with the notations of performance, "To the leader: according to Mahalath Leannoth"—just like the similar notes at the end of Habakkuk 3. The only notation that originally belonged at the head of Psalm 88 is "A Maskil of Heman the Ezrahite." Evidently, what happened in the post-exilic period, when scribes had already forgotten the meaning of many of these notations and when manuscripts were written out with one word following directly after another and without breaks between the psalms, was that the prose notations at the ends of psalms were conflated with the prose notations at the beginnings of the psalms that followed. It is striking to think how doggedly scribes would copy what they had before them, even when they had lost a full understanding of what they were copying.

With this survey, let us look briefly at the types of notations that occur in what are now superscriptions. We begin with notations of attribution, typified by "of the Korahites" and "of Asaph" (see chapter 3) and the repeated "of David." We must realize that, though some of these attributions are real clues to authorship, others, like many of the occurrences of the attribution "of David," may represent the unhistorical assumptions of later generations rather than actual authorship.

In the Hebrew text, seventy-four of the psalms carry the attribution to David;[13] interestingly, in the Greek translation (the Septuagint; see below) this attribution is given to fourteen more.[14]

Eleven psalms are attributed to the "Korahites" (literally, "sons of Korah"), and twelve psalms are attributed to Asaph; as we have seen, these names are associated with musicians in David's court (see chapter 3).

Then there are single psalms attributed to other musicians in David's court.

The attribution that originally belonged to Psalm 88, as we have seen, is to Heman the Ezrahite. The following psalm, Psalm 89, is attributed to Ethan the Ezrahite. Now, 1 Chron. 15:19 associates Asaph, Heman, and Ethan as singers in David's time. Likewise, Psalm 39 is attributed to Jeduthun; Jeduthun is mentioned along with Heman in 1 Chron. 16:41 as a singer in David's court. One may suspect, then, that, given the collections of the Korahites and of Asaph, single attributions to Heman, Ethan, and Jeduthun were made to honor other singers remembered from David's time.[15]

To summarize the coincidence of these attributions with the boundaries of the first three "books" of the Psalter: if "Book II" begins the Elohistic Psalter, it also begins the Korahite psalms; the "Davidic" collection ends temporarily at Psalm 70, near the end of "Book II" (Psalm 71 has no superscription, and Psalm 72 is attributed to Solomon); "Book III" begins the sequence of psalms of Asaph (except for the lone Psalm 50) and closes with the last sequence of Korahite psalms. That is to say, there is the possibility of seeing a pattern in the building up of each of the first three "books."

I return now to attributions themselves. Two more are doubtless products of fancy—to Solomon (Psalm 72—see chapter 4—and Psalm 127, probably from the phrase "builds the house") and to Moses (Psalm 90). In addition, there is one pseudonym (Psalm 102)—to 'ānî (one afflicted).

I now turn to the superscriptions that appear to be ancient classifications of types (genres) of psalms. A few of these terms are clear, but most of them, alas, are not. I take them up below, one by one. Two or three of them are attached to short sequences of psalms and so suggest subcollections.

(1) Hebrew, šîr: this term is found, unmodified, in the superscriptions of Psalms 30, 48, 65–68, 75, 76, 83, 87, 88, 92, and 108. The word means, literally, "song," and is so translated in the superscriptions of the NRSV. But the word doubtless had a technical sense, referring to a particular kind of song; perhaps it was one accompanied by instruments, since "musical instruments" in Hebrew are literally called "gear of song" (kĕlê šîr; see, e.g., 1 Chron. 15:16). The term occurs specifically in the Hebrew phrase šîr hamma'ălôt, translated in the NRSV as "a song of ascents"; this phrase occurs as a superscription in a straight sequence of psalms, Psalms 120–134. Again, no one is certain what "ascents" refers to, but the traditional explanation is still perhaps the most satisfactory—"a song sung when ascending (as a pilgrim) to Jerusalem"—because Jerusalem is elevated above the surrounding countryside. However, even though this explanation would indeed fit a psalm such as Psalm 122, it would not fit some of the others so well. But perhaps we must think of Psalms 120–134 as a "songbook for pilgrimage," psalms sung at various points along the way.

(2) Hebrew, mizmôr: this term occurs fifty-seven times in the superscriptions to the psalms; it is translated simply "psalm" in the NRSV, for example, in Psalm 98. In most cases it is associated with an attribution; for example, with Psalm 3 in the NRSV the superscription is translated "a psalm of David." The term mizmôr, like šîr,

suggests a "song," but the distinction between it and *šîr* is lost on us; indeed, Psalm 92 is called both a *mizmôr* and a *šîr*.

(3) Hebrew, *miktām*: this term occurs in the superscriptions of Psalms 16 and 56–60; it is left untranslated in the NRSV (Miktam). The Greek Septuagint translates the term as "(a poem) to be inscribed on a stele," but whether this is a clue to its original meaning is uncertain.

(4) Hebrew, *maśkîl*: this term occurs in the superscriptions of Psalms 32, 42, 44, 45, 52–55, 74, 78, 88, 89, 142, and in the text of 47:8 (7). The NRSV has left this word untranslated (Maskil). Scholars have suggested, in view of the meanings of the verb associated with this word, that it means a "didactic song"—an interpretation that would apply to Psalm 78—or else an "artistic song"—perhaps one that was newly composed (compare the phraseology of 2 Chron. 30:22, where the Levites "showed skill [the same word in the plural, *maśkîlîm*] in the service of the Lord").

(5) Hebrew, *šiggāyôn*: this term occurs in the superscription of Psalm 7, left untranslated by the NRSV (Shiggaion). It evidently means "lamentation," but why that term is applied only to a single psalm is not known.

(6) Hebrew, *tĕhillâ*: this term occurs in the superscription of Psalm 145. It is translated "praise" in the NRSV; it is a term that appears often in the body of psalm texts, both in expressions of individual thanksgiving (e.g., Ps. 22:26 [25]) and in a hymn of the congregation (Ps. 100:4).

(7) Hebrew, *tĕpillâ*: this term appears in the superscriptions to Psalms 17, 86, 90, 102, and 142. It is translated "prayer" in the NRSV; more precisely, it means a prayer of lament, or of bidding, or of intercession (for the last, see Ps. 109:4).

Now we must notice what we might call the notations of circumstance: there are thirteen psalms "of David" whose superscriptions contain reference to certain incidents at which a given psalm was presumed to be appropriate (Psalms 3, 7, 18, 34, 51, 52, 54, 56, 57, 59, 60, 63, and 142). For example, at Psalm 51 one finds, "[A Psalm of David,] when the prophet Nathan came to him, after he had gone in to Bathsheba."

I now turn to the notations that, by the analysis I have already offered, appear originally to have been postscripts, that is, instructions for performance, and I begin with the Hebrew expression *lamnaṣṣēaḥ*, which occurs fifty-five times. It is the expression that the NRSV translates "to the choirmaster" in Hab. 3:19 and "to the leader" in the Psalms but, in truth, neither translation is secure. Most of the occurrences of this superscription are encompassed by Psalms 4–88 (that is, within Books I through III); the only exceptions are Psalms 109, 139, and 140 (that is, within Book V). There are two verbs to which the word could be referred, one meaning "excel" and the other meaning something like "make music." If the word refers to "excelling," it might mean something like "from him who excels (as poet and singer)." But then "excel" may mean nothing more than "direct" or "lead"— hence the translation "to the leader." But if the word derives from "make music," it may not refer to a person at all but may mean something like "for the performance." The matter has not been solved.

Beyond the expression "to the leader," there are several other notations that appear originally to have been intended as postscripts on the preceding psalms, though the listing below identifies the psalms where these notations are now among the superscriptions. All of these notations begin with prepositions, and they appear to pertain to performance. They are as follows:

(1) Hebrew, *bingînôt*: this expression is found in the superscriptions of Psalms 4, 6, 54, 55, 67, and 76. The NRSV rightly translates "with stringed instruments," that is, various types of lyres or harps (compare 33:2-3).

(2) Hebrew, *'el-hannĕḥîlôt*: this expression is found in the superscription of Psalm 5. Though there is some hesitation about the nature of this notation, most scholars agree that it refers to some type of wind instrument; the NRSV translates "for the flutes."

There are two terms that appear to be correlative, in that they occur contrastively in 1 Chron. 15:20-21.

The first is (3) Hebrew, *'al-haššĕmînît*, in Psalms 6 and 12; the second is (4) Hebrew, *'al-'ălōmôt*, in Psalm 46. Both expressions are simply transliterated in the NRSV: "according to The Sheminith" and "according to Alamoth." The first appears to mean "according to the eighth" ("eighth" of what? one wonders), and the second, "according to the young women." Because of the reference in 1 Chronicles, some have thought the first means "with bass voices" (on the eighth string?) and the second, "with soprano voices," but the matter is uncertain; the first expression may mean "on the eight-stringed instrument." The second, for its part, may be connected with another notation, (5) Hebrew, *'almût labbēn*, found in the superscription of Psalm 9 (NRSV, "according to Muth-labben"). Or this entire group of notations may refer to tunes (compare the following).

One or two more notations may be either for the occasion of the psalm or for the tune.

(6) Hebrew, *'al-haggittît* (NRSV "according to The Gittith"): this expression is found in the superscriptions of Psalms 8, 81, and 84. It may be a musical instruction ("upon the harp of Gath," or "according to the Gath tune"), or it may be a reference to a particular tune ("The Woman of Gath"); again, no one knows.

(7) Hebrew, *'al-māḥălat*: this expression in Psalms 53 and 88 is completely opaque (NRSV "according to Mahalath"). One derivation suggests that it might mean "for illness," or perhaps it is a reference to a tune that begins "The Illness of" so-and-so. Another derivation suggests that it might refer to a round dance, a roundelay or the like. But no one knows.

There remains a whole series of notations, most if not all of which evidently refer to well-known tunes: "Do Not Destroy" (Psalms 57, 58, 59, 75); "The Deer of the Dawn" (Psalm 22); "The Dove on Far-off Terebinths" (Psalm 56); "Lilies" (Psalms 45, 69); "Lily of the Covenant" (Psalm 60); and "Lilies, a Covenant" (Psalm 80).

Then there are notations concerning the situation in which the psalm is to be used. Psalm 92 is assigned to the Sabbath (and it should be added that in the Greek Septuagint translation other psalms are assigned to other days of the week: Psalm 24 to the first day, Psalm 48 to the second day, Psalm 94 to the third day, and

Psalm 93 to the sixth day). Psalms 38 and 70 are given the rubric "for the memorial offering" (see Lev. 2:2: RSV, "memorial portion"; NRSV, "token portion"). Psalm 100 has the notation "of thanksgiving," probably referring to the offering of thanksgiving (Lev. 7:12). Psalm 30 has the notation (literally) "(at the) dedication of the house," but whether at the dedication of the Second Temple or the rededication in 164 B.C.E. after its desecration by Antiochus Epiphanes (see chapter 7) would be impossible to say.

Now, as we examine all these various kinds of superscriptions, what are we to conclude?

The superscriptions occur in both the Hebrew text that has come down to us and in the Greek Septuagint translation, which was probably made about 150 B.C.E. (see below), though, as we have noted, there are some variations in the details between the two traditions. The activity of adding the notations, then, took place at some time before 150 B.C.E. Such classifying and annotating must have been a part of the activity of collecting that took place in this period. And it must have taken place well after the close of the period of active composition of the Psalms. The activity of collecting and annotating, perhaps the work of the Levites, must have taken place during the fourth and third centuries B.C.E., that is, in the last part of the Persian period and in the Ptolemaic period, two centuries for which we have very little historical information. It was a time in Jerusalem not of innovation but of consolidation.

The notations that cite the circumstances of David's life when he is presumed to have uttered a given psalm are expressions of the same kind of view of David as that which gave rise to the present books of Chronicles: David as the organizer of worship in Jerusalem. And again and again in the books of Chronicles we have found references for this or that detail of the superscriptions.[16]

"Selah," "Higgaion," and "Hallelujah"

It is convenient here to discuss three other terms that occur not in the superscriptions but in the body of the Psalms. Two of them are mysterious and evidently have something to do with performance: "Selah" and "Higgaion." "Selah," (Hebrew, *selâ*) occurs seventy-one times in the Psalms (ninety-two times in the Greek Septuagint translation!), beginning with Ps. 3:3 (2). All current translations simply transliterate the word "Selah"; there is no agreed-upon etymology for the word, and it would not be helpful here to list all the various suggestions that have been made. Two current explanations are that it was the signal either for an instrumental interlude or for a congregational response of some sort. But Michael Goulder, whose analysis of the Korahite psalms I used in chapter 3, has a new suggestion that looks promising: that it means "recitative," marking a pause at which there should be the recitation of a prayer or story from Israelite tradition.[17] For example, he suggests that after Ps. 85:3 (2) there might have been a recitation of the core of Exodus 32–34. Perhaps scholars will yet solve the mystery.

The Hebrew term *higgāyôn* occurs only once, just before "Selah" in Ps. 9:17

(16) (NRSV, "Higgaion"), and appears to mean "meditation" or the like. It may be a call for an instrumental interlude. It also occurs in the text of 92:4 (3), where the NRSV translates it as "melody." But we are not really sure of its meaning.

The third term is well understood: the Hebrew expression *halĕlû-yāh*, normally written in English as "Hallelujah" and transliterated into Greek and Latin as "Alleluia." The Hebrew *halĕlû* is a plural imperative, "praise," and *yāh* is evidently an archaic shortened form of the name of God, *Yahweh*; hence the translation "praise ye the Lord" (KJV) and "praise the LORD" (RSV and NRSV). In the Hebrew text the phrase occurs twenty-three times, only in the Psalms, from Ps. 104:35 to Ps. 150:6; it should be noted that the verb in question occurs freely in other combinations, and the shortened form *yāh* occurs occasionally outside the Psalms, for example, in Exod. 15:2 (see JB and NJB at that verse). The phrase normally does not share in the poetry of its context (that is, it is not paired with a parallel phrase) and most often occurs at the beginning or end of a given psalm, or both: for example, Psalm 106 begins and ends with the phrase.

Indeed the phrase is distinctive enough that when it occurs at the beginning of a psalm, the Septuagint translation (see below) took it as a superscription, and in the Septuagint it appears more often than it does in the Hebrew text (for example, at the beginning of the acrostic Psalm 119). Yet the meaning of the phrase was always clear, and when it occurs in the middle of a psalm the Septuagint translates it (e.g., Ps. 135:3) instead of transliterating it. But it is evident that the phrase always had a special significance and served as the word of praise par excellence. It occurs twice in the Deuterocanonical literature with that implication (Tob. 13:18; 3 Macc. 7:13) and four times in a liturgical passage of Revelation in the New Testament (Rev. 19:1, 3, 4, 6; see chapter 8). In the Greek and Latin form "Alleluia" it entered deeply into Christian liturgy (see chapter 10), and in the form "Hallelujah" began to take on unexpected secular overtones in the nineteenth century (see chapter 13).

The Compilation of the Psalter

I now return to the earlier question: Can we discern any of the steps by which the present 150 psalms were compiled? Here I draw heavily on the recent study of a young scholar at George Fox College in Newberg, Oregon, Gerald Henry Wilson.[18]

There is a clear contrast between the compilation of Books I to III and that of Books IV to V of the Psalter: Books I to III were stabilized before Books IV to V. Of the sixty-one psalms that I have determined to be pre-exilic, all but twelve are in Books I to III.

And reinforcing evidence is provided by texts of the Psalms that have been found among the Dead Sea Scrolls: though I shall discuss this evidence in detail in chapter 7, I must mention it here. Among the Dead Sea Scrolls are many that contain texts of the Psalms, although there are no complete ones. One of the scrolls contains portions of psalms from Psalm 6 through Psalm 69, as well as Psalm 71. The order of these psalms is more or less that of our traditional order (the only exceptions are the joining of Psalms 31 and 33 and of 38 and 71);[19] and there are other fragments that support the traditional order of Psalms 76 through 85.[20] By contrast, another Psalms scroll contains a scattering of psalms from Psalm 93 to the end of the Psalter, but this scroll offers its psalms in an altogether different order and intermixes them with other psalmlike material that is not in the traditional Psalter; and there are other fragments that support this nontraditional order. This evidence suggests that the order of the psalms in Books I to III was a settled matter before the time of the Dead Sea Scrolls, whereas the order of psalms in Books IV to V, or even the matter of what psalms would be included in those books in the Dead Sea community, was not settled by that time.

The final arrangement of Books I to III, taken as a whole, appears to be a presentation of devotion to God seen through the experience of David.[21] I shall set this forth after we examine each of these three books separately.

As one looks at Book I, it is striking that almost all the psalms from Psalm 3 to Psalm 41 carry a superscription of attribution to David; the only exceptions are Psalm 10, which, as we have seen, was originally linked to Psalm 9 (see chapter 3), and Psalm 33, which seems to have had a peculiar relation to Psalm 32 (one notes the likeness of 32:11 and 33:1).[22] One can imagine how Psalm 2, a psalm that may well be from David's coronation (see chapter 2) but in any event was seen to affirm the covenant made with David at his coronation, might have been prefixed to the sequence of "Davidic" psalms (Psalms 3–41); Psalm 41, the closing psalm, would be heard to balance Psalm 2—as Yahweh's assurance of continued protection to David against his scheming enemies. (Later the full Psalter would have been introduced by Psalm 1, the instruction in covenant norms.)[23]

Book II, as we have already seen, begins the Elohistic collection, and again there is a strong interest in authorship. It contains the first Korahite sequences, Psalms 42–49 (43 being originally attached to 42), while Psalms 51–65 and 68–70 are attributed to David. This leaves out of account Psalms 50, 66, 67, and 72. Of these, Psalms 66 and 67 are without any attribution (again, excluding Psalm 43). As for Psalm 50, an isolated psalm attributed to Asaph, it appears within the sequence of Psalms 47–51, all given the title of *mizmôr* (NRSV, "a psalm"), a notation that appears to *bridge* the first sequence of Korahite psalms on the one hand and those attributed to David on the other.[24] Again, with Psalms 66 and 67, which have no attribution, the titles of *šîr* (NRSV, "a song") and *mizmôr* ("a psalm") evidently bridge the sequence of Psalms 65–68, and *mizmôr* alone in Psalms 62–64 continues that function. We have already noted the peculiarity of the attribution of Psalm 72 to Solomon;[25] one could imagine that this Elohistic collection of Book II, understood in a later century as made up of psalms composed both by David and by his musicians, was completed by a single psalm understood to be from David's son Solomon.

In Book III the Elohistic Psalter concludes with the sequence of Asaph psalms (Psalms 73–83), and as the book reverts to Yahwistic psalms, we have the last four Korahite psalms (Psalms 84, 85, 87, 88) interrupted by a psalm attributed to David (Psalm 86) and closed by a psalm attributed to Ethan. It is to be noted, however, that this closing Psalm 89 is explicitly concerned with the Davidic covenant (vv. 4-5 [3-4], 21-22 [20-21], 29 [28]); but it is a covenant in the dim past (vv. 20 [19], 50

[49]), a covenant concerned for David's descendants (vv. 5 [4], 30 [29], 37 [36]). The covenant introduced in Psalm 2 has come to nothing, and David's descendants wait for a restoration: "How long, Yahweh?" (89:47 [46]). In the final collection, then, Books I to III view the psalms through the interpretive glass of David as Yahweh's chosen one.

Now, within each book, and each subcollection within a book, there were doubtless other modes of arrangement of sequences of psalms. One recent study suggests that the psalms within Book I may be linked by a chain of repeated words and phrases. Thus Psalms 1 and 2 may be linked by the word "happy" (Hebrew, 'ašrê: 1:1 and 2:11), by the verb "meditate" or "plot" (Hebrew singular, yehgeh: 1:2; and plural, yehgû: 2:1), and by the combination of "way" and "perish" (1:6 and 2:12); Psalms 2 and 3 may be linked by the phrase "holy hill" (2:6 and 3:5 [4]); and so on.[26] But obviously there are limits to our ability to discern such a process; sometimes a psalm may have been copied simply because there was space on a scroll of papyrus for one more psalm.

When we turn to Books IV and V, the territory is more uncertain than is the case for Books I to III, because, as we have seen, the order of the psalms was more fluid for a longer period of time. Book IV (Psalms 90–106) has a high proportion of untitled psalms (thirteen out of seventeen). This book appears to function as the editorial "center" of the Psalter, and these seventeen psalms, interwoven in theme and structure, set forth answers to the plaintive question raised by Psalm 89. The answers are, essentially: Yahweh is king; Yahweh has been our refuge in the past, long before the monarchy existed, and will be our refuge now that the monarchy is gone; blessed are those who trust in Yahweh![27] This book begins and ends with Moses, who led Israel before there was a monarchy: Psalm 90 is attributed to Moses, and Psalms 105 and Psalm 106 deal with the events of Moses' career (105:23-45; 106:7-33). Psalm 90 asks the "How long?" question that was raised in Ps. 89:47 [46], but the question is raised in a fresh way, not in the context of the lost monarchy but in the context of Israel's sin. Psalm 91 continues the motif of God as refuge (90:1; 91:1-2).[28] (Indeed there are Hebrew manuscripts that combine Psalms 90 and 91 as a single psalm.)[29] Psalm 92 is a bridge from the "refuge" psalms (90 and 91) to the "Yahweh is king" psalms that begin with Psalm 93: Yahweh is Israel's rock (92:16 [15]) and refuge, and at the same time Yahweh is "on high" forever (92:9 [8]; compare 93:4).

Psalms 93 and 95 to 99 are a series of psalms that exalt Yahweh as king (93:1; 95:3; 96:10; 97:1; 98:6; 99:1); this series is interrupted by Psalm 94, which reverts to the problem that prevents Israel from recognizing the kingship of Yahweh: "How long" will the wicked prevail (v. 3)? Yet Yahweh is the "rock of my refuge" (v. 22). With Psalm 95 we return to divine kingship: Yahweh is king as well as rock (vv. 1, 3); yet there the memory of Israel's rebellion in the wilderness (vv. 7-11) is a backdrop for the present situation. Psalms 96–99 are a litany of praise, ringing the changes on Yahweh's kingship and reverting to Moses in 99:6. Psalm 100 picks up the theme of Israel as the sheep of Yahweh's pasture (v. 3) that was heard in 95:6-7.

Psalms 101–106 are miscellaneous, rounding out the book in various ways.

Thus in Psalm 101, attributed to David, the psalmist contrasts those who do and those who do not seek Yahweh. Then in Psalm 102 there is reversion to the themes of Psalm 90—the transience of human beings and the everlastingness of God. Psalm 103, even more than Psalm 102, picks up multiple themes from Psalm 90 and in a way answers the questions raised in that psalm: Yahweh forgives human iniquity (vv. 3, 10, 12; compare 90:7-8), responding to human beings with steadfast love and mercy (vv. 4, 8, 11, 17-18; compare 90:14); Yahweh satisfies human beings with good as long as they live (v. 5; compare 90:14); Moses is mediator of the divine will (v. 7); human beings are as transient as grass (v. 15; compare 90:5-6). "Yahweh has established his throne in the heavens, and his kingdom rules over all" (v. 19).

Psalms 104–106 close the book; they are the first of the Hallelujah psalms, each ending with that acclamation (Psalm 106 begins with it as well). As such they are a bridge to Book V. At the same time, Psalm 104 matches Psalm 103 in that both of them begin and end with "Bless Yahweh, O my soul," and the former reintroduces some of the themes of the "Yahweh is king" psalms (for example, "You are clothed with honor and majesty" matches "Honor and majesty are before him" in Ps. 96:6). And, as we have seen, Psalms 105 and 106 revert to the theme of Moses.[30]

Book V is a long book (Psalms 107–150), and it has several clear subcollections within it: Davidic psalms (Psalms 108–110; 138–145), Hallelujah psalms (Psalms 111–117, 135, 146–150), and "Songs of Ascents" (Psalms 120–134). One may tentatively discern its overall shape;[31] it is easiest to begin at the center and to work outward. There are two parts to the center. The first part is the gigantic Psalm 119, which, in its emphasis on torah (law), balances Psalm 1, the introduction to the whole Psalter. The second part is the unbroken sequence of Songs of Ascents (Psalms 120–134), psalms that repeatedly affirm the necessity to rely on Yahweh alone. This central section is bracketed by two sets of psalms (Psalms 108–117 and 138–150): each of these sets is composed of Davidic psalms (Psalms 108–110, 138–145) followed by Hallelujah psalms (Psalms 111–117, 146–150). This simple scheme leaves several "bridge" psalms.

Psalms 107 and 118 are bridge psalms. Psalm 107 is a bridge from Book IV, in that it picks up the theme of the "gathering" of the exiles (107:2-3) with which Book IV ended (106:47). At the same time, it opens with the verse, "O give thanks to Yahweh, for he is good, for his steadfast love endures forever!" with which Psalm 118 also opens, the latter psalm being a bridge from the first Hallelujah set to the great Psalm 119.

Psalm 135 reinforces the last "ascent" psalm, Psalm 134: the opening verses of Psalm 135 expand Ps. 134:1, while the closing verse (135:21) expands 134:3. In other ways Psalm 135 matches Psalm 118: Psalm 118 opens with an exhortation of three groups to prayer to Yahweh—"Israel," "the house of Aaron," and "those who fear Yahweh" (118:2-4); Psalm 135 concludes with these same groups (vv. 19-20, with the addition of "house of Levi").[32]

Psalm 136 opens with the same verse with which Psalms 107 and 118 open, namely, "O give thanks to Yahweh, for he is good, for his steadfast love endures forever!" Indeed the last line of that verse is repeated as a refrain through the whole psalm. At the same time, Psalm 136 looks forward to Psalm 145: the latter psalm, too, celebrates Yahweh's steadfast love (145:8); both speak of Yahweh's "wonders" (136:4; 145:5) and of his sustenance to his creatures (136:25; 145:15-16); and both speak of "all flesh" (136:25; 145:21).[33]

The last set of Davidic and Hallelujah psalms is introduced by Psalm 137: the plaintive cry of the exiles is answered by the sequence of Davidic psalms that offers David's praise of Yahweh.

In a way, the last of the Davidic psalms, Psalm 145, is the climax of Book V. It has connections with Psalm 1 and with the opening psalm of the book (the contrasting ways of the righteous and the wicked, v. 20; compare Pss. 1:6; 107:42); it also connects with the "Yahweh is king" psalms of Book IV, both as to the kingship of Yahweh and the celebration of his wonders (for vv. 1, 11-13, compare Psalms 93, 95–99; for vv. 4-7, compare Ps. 96:3). The book then closes with the final set of Hallelujah psalms, Psalms 146–150.

Book V, then, appears to be a final answer to the plea of the exiles, and, as with Books I to III, David is seen to model the attitude of reliance and dependence on Yahweh.

The Process of Canonization

I now turn to a basic question: How did the Psalter become Scripture? That is: How did it happen that the collection of 150 psalms became not simply useful, not simply a vehicle for worship, like a hymnal in our day, but an authoritative text, revelatory for the faith of the community? To put it still another way: How did it happen that the collection of 150 psalms was definitively completed, so that no more psalms might be added? To pose the question technically: How did the book of Psalms become canonical?

Some brief background will be useful. The first body of Jewish Scriptures to become canonical was the Torah (Law), also called the Pentateuch—that is, the first five books of the Old Testament, Genesis through Deuteronomy. Both Jews and Samaritans view the Torah as canonical, so that body of material must have been canonical or on its way to being considered canonical before the final split between Samaritans and Jews. One suspects that something like the present text of the Torah was what Ezra brought to Jerusalem from Babylon in the fifth century B.C.E. (Ezra 7:21; Neh. 8:1). One notes that in Neh. 8:1 it is called "the law of Moses": by that time it was assumed that Moses wrote the Pentateuch.

The second body of Jewish Scriptures to become canonical was the so-called Prophets, that is, the books of Joshua, Judges, 1 and 2 Samuel, 1 and 2 Kings, Isaiah, Jeremiah, Ezekiel, and the twelve minor prophets. The Samaritans do not reckon these books to be scriptural and do not use them. The origins of these books are various, but in the course of time this body of material came to be laid alongside the Pentateuch as scriptural. We see it in the words attributed to Jesus in the Gospels, for example, "Do not think that I have come to abolish the law or the prophets" (Matt. 5:17) and "beginning with Moses and all the prophets" (Luke

24:27). We can see it earlier: in chapters 44 to 49 of the Deuterocanonical book of Sirach (Ecclesiasticus), written about 180 B.C.E. ("Let us now praise famous men"), the author reviews the great ancestors in Israel, beginning with the great men in Genesis and continuing with (among others) Moses, Joshua, Nathan and David and Solomon, Hezekiah, Isaiah, Josiah, Jeremiah, Ezekiel, and the twelve prophets, and closing with Zerubbabel, Jeshua, and Nehemiah; and there is no sense of division between the story in the Pentateuch and that in the later books of the Prophets.

In the Jewish classification of the Scriptures, the book of Psalms is reckoned in the third body of material, the so-called Writings, which consists also of Job, Proverbs, the so-called five scrolls (Ruth, Song of Songs, Ecclesiastes, Lamentations, and Esther), Daniel, Ezra, Nehemiah, and 1 and 2 Chronicles. During the period of history that we are discussing in this chapter and for some centuries thereafter, this category of Writings was an imprecise one. If there are passages in the Gospels in which Jesus is remembered as speaking of the "law" and the "prophets," there is also one that includes the psalms—"that everything written about me in the law of Moses, the prophets, and the psalms must be fulfilled" (Luke 24:44)— and tradition recalls that Jesus cited some psalm passages as Scripture (Psalm 110, in Mark 12:35-37 and pars.; see chapter 8). And, earlier, the grandson of Sirach, writing just after 132 B.C.E., begins the prologue that he appended to Sirach as follows: "Many great teachings have been given to us through the Law and the Prophets and the others [or other books] that followed them." We may presume, then, that the Psalter was in the process of becoming canonical during the latter part of the Persian period and in the Ptolemaic period.

It should be pointed out that for Jews of the time, who accepted the Law and the Prophets as canonical, there would have been an obvious difficulty in accepting the Psalms as canonical. Moses was a lawgiver and a prophet through whom, it was understood, God has spoken. The books of Joshua, Judges, Samuel, and Kings describe (among other things) the lives of prophets, and the books of Isaiah, Jeremiah, Ezekiel, and the twelve minor prophets offer the words of the prophets, through whom, it was understood, God has spoken. But the Psalms are, by and large, poems addressed *to* God: it would be more difficult to understand these poems as revelatory, as spoken by God, in the same way. (This issue will emerge quite specifically in the Jewish debate in the Middle Ages about the very nature of the book of Psalms; see chapter 9.) Nevertheless, the status of David as the king with whom God had covenanted forever—the king who (as the Chronicler narrated) had organized the guilds of musicians for the temple—and above all the centrality of the Psalter in worship would have been powerful incentives for the heightened status of the collection of Psalms.

And, as we have already had occasion to note, among the Dead Sea Scrolls the text of the Psalms scroll from Cave 11 offers us psalms from Books IV and V of our Psalter intermixed with noncanonical psalms, and in an altogether different order from that of the Psalter. That scroll represents a transitional situation, in which the choice of psalms that became Scripture and the sequence of those psalms had not yet become stabilized (see chapter 7).

The Scattering of Jews beyond Palestine
and the Use of the Psalms
beyond Palestine

I now turn to a related matter: the extent to which Jews were scattered through-out the Near East. There were Jews who had stayed in Babylon: Ezra the scribe had returned from there to Jerusalem in the second half of the fifth century (Ezra 7:6). Indeed Babylon would remain a center of Jewish life for centuries to come.[34] There had been settlements of Jews in Egypt since before Jeremiah's time (Jer. 44:1-30), and we have Aramaic documents from Jewish mercenaries at the First Cataract of the Nile from throughout the period of the fifth century B.C.E. (the colony of Elephantine, near the present Aswan Dam).[35] The population of Jews in Egypt received a strong boost after the founding of the new port city of Alexandria, named for the great general after his death; the city would grow immensely, and became a world center of Jewish culture.[36] And, finally, we must not forget the population of Jews in cities and towns in Palestine, outside of Jerusalem.

Because the traditional ritual of animal sacrifices could take place only in Jerusalem, one wonders about the religious life of those who lived at a distance from that city. As for the Jewish mercenary colony at Elephantine in Egypt, there is evidence that these folk were half pagan,[37] but Elephantine was an enormous dis-tance from Jerusalem; those who were closer to that center of religious life must have been orthodox in their faith, led by Levites and others. But how was the religious sensibility of Jews far from Jerusalem nourished?

There must have been synagogues, centers where Jews could meet for study and prayer; but, curiously, we are entirely in the dark about the origin of that important institution. Perhaps it is natural that there are no clear-cut references to synagogues in the Old Testament, since that body of literature is a product of Jewish scribes in Jerusalem. By contrast, synagogues are mentioned everywhere in the New Testament.

Synagogues would have served as centers where Scripture, especially the Torah, was read and studied and where prayers were offered. There may have been attempts at some synagogues to match the readings and prayers that would have been employed in the Jerusalem temple on the same occasion, but we simply do not know.

What is clear is that the books of the Hebrew Scriptures would have been a kind of portable shrine, a religious home, for Jews wherever they settled. For these communities the Psalter would have been available as a prayer book. For Jews residing away from Jerusalem, then, the psalms would inevitably have become detached from their cultic associations and would have become an autonomous medium for the worship of God.

Translations

The First Translation: The Septuagint

In about 250 B.C.E., the Jewish community in Alexandria, Egypt, began a project with enormous consequences for the future, namely, the translation of the Hebrew Scriptures into Greek.

It is not self-evident that the text of a scripture is translatable. It is a cliché, of course, that no translation is ever completely successful—when a text moves from one language to another, something is lost. I shall return to this matter in chapter 17. But if a literary work has become Scripture, then can one make a translation at all? It is useful at this point to compare the attitude of Muslims toward the idea of translating the Qur'ān from the original Arabic. For the Muslims, the very words of the Qur'ān *in the Arabic language* are holy, and therefore a true translation of the Qur'ān into another language is by definition impossible: if one is to learn the Qur'ān, one will do it in Arabic. Of course, translations of the Qur'ān have been made, even by Muslims, but such translations are considered simply to be commentaries that do not have the status of the original.[38] Such a theological stance is dependent on the Muslim understanding of the inspiration of the specific Arabic words. But the attitude of the Jews in Egypt toward their Scriptures was clearly different: they came to the conclusion that their Scriptures, translated into another language, would still be their Scriptures.

Since Alexander's time, the coast of Egypt and the port of Alexandria above all were a part of the Hellenistic world, and the time came when the Jews were Greek-speaking and could no longer easily understand their Scriptures in the original Hebrew. In the conviction that they needed to hear their Scriptures in a language they could understand, therefore, the work of translation was begun, evidently in piecemeal fashion: the Torah was probably done in about 250 B.C.E. and the Prophets in about 200 B.C.E. Then the Psalms (and the various other books of the Writings) were likewise translated, probably between 200 and 150 B.C.E.[39] So emerged the translation that in total has come to be known as the Septuagint (because of the legend that seventy [or seventy-two] translators produced the work: *septuaginta* is "seventy" in Latin).

It is worth taking a moment to ponder what such a process of translation must have been like. First of all, it is important to understand that the Hebrew texts of the time were written with consonants only: the vowel markings of the texts were developed later, in the Middle Ages. It is true, the structure of the Hebrew language is such that somewhat more linguistic information is given by a consonantal text than would be given by an English text with consonants only; but still, the Hebrew consonantal text offers itself more as a memory guide for a reader who has already half-memorized the text than as a clear guide to a reader who is unfamiliar with the text.

Second, no dictionaries or word lists or grammars were available, so far as our knowledge goes. A translation would simply depend upon the skill of those who were familiar with the Hebrew text and at the same time were able to write Greek fluently.

Third, Hebrew and Greek are completely unrelated languages. In chapter 5 the shift from Hebrew to Aramaic in Palestine was discussed. But Hebrew and Aramaic are sisters: they are both northwest Semitic languages, having a similar structure and much common vocabulary. Greek, by contrast, is an Indo-European language. Hebrew and Greek were as far apart in those days as English and Arabic are today. The verb system in Greek is structured differently than it is in Hebrew; sentences go together differently. Indeed it has often been maintained that Hebrew and Greek ways of thinking are altogether different.[40]

Fourth, there was no "theory of translation" in those days (see chapter 17); the translators had to learn by doing. (By contrast, we have evidence of Jerome's reflection on his task when he came to translate the Old Testament into Latin in the fourth century C.E.;[41] see below.) The Septuagint translators were without card files, without verse references, without even the convenience of books made of leaves bound at the spine—this development would emerge particularly among Christians beginning in the first and second centuries C.E. And they doubtless never thought of "first drafts": papyrus was expensive. They just began.

The result, for the Torah, is a wooden translation that is largely word by word, a translation that sounds very "un-Greek." The translation of the Prophets was freer but still had the sound of "translation Greek." But, we must remind ourselves, when the Jews first began to learn and speak Greek in Alexandria it was street Greek, everybody's second language; they were a long way from the elegance of Demosthenes and Plato. But even if the Greek of the Septuagint was to some degree translation Greek, nevertheless it was Scripture for Greek-speaking Jews, and it eventually came to have a kind of holy appropriateness about it. So it was that by the middle of the second century B.C.E. the Psalms were being recited in the synagogues of Alexandria in Greek.

We must further understand that the wording of that translation is not altogether what we know from the traditional Hebrew text. There are many textual variations between the traditional Hebrew text that has come down to us and the Septuagint translation that has come down to us; this is inevitable, given the way copies were made of copies in ancient times. The Hebrew text would not be stabilized until the end of the first century C.E. (see chapter 9), and variations of all sorts were common in the period we are now discussing.

As an example, let us compare the Hebrew and the Greek texts of Psalm 1. There are two variations between the Hebrew text (which itself is well rendered into English in our current translations) and the Greek text. The first line of v. 4 in the Hebrew reads, literally, "Not so the wicked," but the Greek reads, "Not so the wicked, not so." Here many scholars believe that the Greek text is right and that in the Hebrew text the second "not so" has dropped out.[42] Then to the second line of the verse, "but are like chaff that the wind blows away," the Greek text adds, "from the face of the earth." Here the extra words in the Greek may be a secondary addition for clarity,[43] though I personally believe the addition is correct: the Hebrew pĕnê (face of) would make a nice alliterative addition to the Hebrew tidpennû (drives away).

Another example is Ps. 95:6: the Hebrew text reads, as current English translations have it, "O come, let us worship and bow down, let us kneel before the Lord our maker"; the consonantal text for "let us kneel" is nbrkh. The Greek text, however, reads, "let us weep" (nbkh), from a text that omitted one consonant by mistake.

Furthermore, beyond the kind of variations that would naturally grow up between two forms of text, there are occasions when it is clear that the translator did not understand a particular word or expression. For example, in Pss. 60:10 (8) and 108:10 (9) the Hebrew phrase *sîr raḥṣî*, "my wash basin"—literally, "basin of my washing"—is translated into Greek as *lebēs tēs elpidos mou*, "basin of my hope," because in Aramaic the verb *rĕḥēṣ* means "hope."[44]

At points where, in the judgment of the translators of the RSV and the NRSV, the Hebrew text of the Psalms is defective and the Greek Septuagint offers a superior reading, one can see some of the evidence for their decision, because those translations offer notes on the text. For example, in Ps. 20:10 (9), as the footnote in those translations indicates, the Hebrew (abbreviation "Heb") says, "Give victory, O Lord; let the King answer us when we call," but the RSV and NRSV have followed the Greek Septuagint (abbreviation "Gk"), which reads, "Give victory to the king, O Lord; answer us when we call." (It is only fair, however, to add that on this verse—and many others!—there are scholars who offer still other solutions.)[45]

But I raise another sort of question, not about the small details of wording but about the general reaction the translation would inspire in the Greek-speaking Jewish community. It is a good translation; the parallelisms of the poetry of the Psalms are well reproduced. It would have been a good vehicle for synagogue prayer. True, it softens some of the sharpness of the Hebrew: for example, when in Ps. 3:4 (3) the Hebrew says, "But you, O Lord, are a shield around me," the Septuagint translates, "But you, O Lord, are my support"; and when in Ps. 18:3 (2) the Hebrew says, "My God my rock," the Septuagint translates, "My God my help."[46] But the Septuagint does not soften the stark anthropomorphisms of the Hebrew (that is, the use of language for God that is derived from the characteristics of human beings). When the Hebrew speaks of the "face" of God, the Septuagint uses the Greek word for "face," not a word meaning "presence" or the like.[47]

Where the Septuagint does seem to be interpretive, it is because it is a theological product of its time—but that should not surprise us. Thus when Ps. 97:7 mentions "gods," the Septuagint interprets this to be "angels" (see the discussion in chapter 8 on Heb. 1:6). But, strikingly, the Septuagint leaves the term "gods" in Ps. 82:6 (see chapter 2).

And one more curiosity may be mentioned here: the Septuagint text contains more material than the Hebrew tradition does. The extra material is of two sorts. First, a few books known in the Hebrew tradition have insertions in the Septuagint text: for example, the book of Daniel is expanded by several additions, including a prayer offered by Azariah (Abednego) and a psalmlike hymn sung by Hananiah, Mishael, and Azariah (Shadrach, Meshach, and Abednego) in the fiery furnace, with some intervening prose material; this sequence is inserted in the Septuagint text between Dan. 3:23 and 3:24. Clearly, such later liturgical material continued to draw on the model of the Psalms.[48]

Second, there are extra books in the Septuagint that do not appear in the Hebrew tradition. These extra books, such as Sirach and 1 and 2 Maccabees, were considered Scripture by the early Christians but rejected by the Jewish authorities (for 1 and 2 Maccabees, see chapter 7; for the exclusion of these books from the Jewish canon, see chapter 9). They remain part of canonical Scripture for the Eastern Orthodox (who use the Greek Bible) and for Roman Catholics (who until recently depended on the Latin Vulgate). Protestants have not placed them on the same level as Scripture and have called them the books of the "Apocrypha." In this study I shall use the neutral term for these books now favored by the NRSV, namely, "Deuterocanonical."

The Use of the Septuagint in the New Testament

Although it is getting ahead of the story, it is convenient here to indicate some of the subsequent history of the Septuagint and to mention as well the other major translations of ancient times.

Soon the Septuagint was used by Greek-speaking Jews in the whole eastern Mediterranean area. Then, when the Christian church emerged as a Greek-speaking movement in the same area (we remind ourselves that the New Testament was written in Greek), it was natural for Christians to use the Septuagint as its Old Testament. This, by the way, explains why some of the citations of the Old Testament that appear in the New Testament do not exactly correspond with what we today read in the Old Testament: our present-day translations of the Old Testament are made from the Hebrew text, whereas the Christians writing the New Testament quoted from their Old Testament in Greek. For example, Paul, who grew up as a Greek-speaking Jew in Tarsus (in what is now southern Turkey), cited the Old Testament in the Septuagint version (see the discussion in chapter 8 of Paul's citation of Ps. 51:6 [4] in Rom. 3:4).

Then the Jewish authorities at the end of the first century C.E. rejected any Jewish use of the Septuagint; the Jewish Scriptures would have to be cited by an authoritative Hebrew text (or by translations made from such a text). There were, however, three later Jewish Greek translations of the Old Testament, efforts to replace the Septuagint for Greek-speaking Jews; these translations are known by the names of Aquila, Symmachus, and Theodotion. But they have survived to our day only in fragments, as part of a great work called the *Hexapla*, which contains versions of the Old Testament in six parallel columns and was organized about 230–245 C.E. by Origen, a church father and biblical scholar.[49] (We shall examine Origen's commentary on the Psalms in chapter 10.)

And it may be added, as a postscript here, that there were Jews who later came to regret the translations of their Scriptures into Greek: in a later rabbinic work it was said, "It once happened that five elders wrote the Torah for King Ptolemy in Greek, and that day was as ominous for Israel as the day on which the golden calf was made, since the Torah could not be accurately translated."[50] That Christians would quote the Scriptures to Jews in forms that furthered Christian doctrine was a source of great pain to Jews (see chapter 10).

The Aramaic Targums

Meanwhile, the traditional Aramaic interpretations of the Scriptures (discussed earlier in this chapter) were collected and standardized by the Jewish authorities:

the so-called Targums.[51] In Ps. 11:1 the footnote in the RSV and the NRSV prefers the reading of the Targum (abbreviation "Tg"), among others, to the Hebrew text.

The Syriac Peshitta

There are two important Christian translations that were made in ancient times. The first is a translation into Syriac, a dialect of Aramaic that was current in the Mesopotamian area in the early centuries of the Christian era; the translation is known as the Peshitta (the Syriac word for "common"). It is possible, at least for the Psalms and perhaps for other books, that the Syriac translation was based upon the Jewish Targum, but the matter is uncertain.[52] In Ps. 11:1, just cited, the Syriac (abbreviation "Syr") is among the texts followed in the RSV and NRSV.

The Latin Translations

The story of the Latin translations, the second important ancient Christian body of translations, is particularly interesting, given the importance of the Latin Psalter. As the Christian church moved from the Greek-speaking eastern Mediterranean area to the Latin-speaking area of the western Mediterranean, the Bible was translated into Latin, and the source language for both Testaments was Greek: the New Testament of course was originally written in Greek, but the Old Testament, including the book of Psalms, was translated into Latin from the Greek Septuagint—a translation that was two steps removed from the original language. This translation, the so-called Old Latin, emerged in North Africa, but there is evidence that there may have been several competing local translations that differed from each other: both Tertullian (about 220 C.E.) and Cyprian (about 250 C.E.) quoted from such a Latin Psalter, but these readings sometimes differed.[53] Only fragments of the Old Latin have survived to our day.

But after the Christian faith became a legal religion of the Roman Empire, the leaders of the church became less and less content with the quality of the Old Latin translation: it was not satisfying Latin.[54] Accordingly, about the year 382 C.E. the reigning pope, Damasus I, asked Jerome, one of the best biblical scholars of ancient times, to undertake a revision of the Latin Bible. (We shall examine Jerome's commentaries on the Psalms in chapter 10.) He worked first on the New Testament and then turned to the Old Testament, which he translated directly from the Hebrew; he worked on the Old Testament for fifteen years (390–405 C.E.). The resulting Bible, the so-called Vulgate, became the Latin Bible for the Roman Catholic Church.[55]

The story of Jerome's work of translating the Psalms, specifically, is a more complicated one. People had grown accustomed, in the recitation of the Psalms, to using the Old Latin, unsatisfactory though it may have been. Jerome made two separate revisions of that Old Latin Psalter. The first, evidently a fairly light revision, was made about 383 C.E., and this so-called Roman Psalter was used until modern times in the churches of St. Peter's in Rome and St. Mark's in Venice, as well as in Milan. The second revision, probably based on a consultation of Origen's *Hexapla*, was made about 392 C.E.; this is the so-called Gallican Psalter, since it was immediately adopted by the churches in Gaul. This revision of the Psalter was the one that entered into the Vulgate and has therefore been used in almost all portions of the Roman Catholic Church until modern times. (This rendering is also known by its Latin title, *Psalterium juxta Graecos*.) It is ironic that the Gallican Psalter was the version that perhaps pleased Jerome the least of all his renderings of the Psalter, and he agreed to it simply because it was the one that the church demanded and would accept.[56] Then, in the course of his general translation of the Old Testament, Jerome retranslated the Psalms directly from the Hebrew; this translation, known by its Latin title *Psalterium juxta Hebraeos*, is valuable in indicating the reading of the Hebrew text of the Psalms that was available to Jerome in the fourth century, but this translation was never used in the liturgy.[57] This would not be the last time that Christians favored for the Psalms an older and more familiar translation (see chapter 11).

In the textual footnotes in the Psalms of the RSV and NRSV, the designation "Jerome" means the text of the *Psalterium juxta Hebraeos* (see Ps. 11:1), whereas the abbreviation "Vg" refers to the Vulgate and, in the case of the Psalms, therefore to the *Psalterium juxta Graecos* (see Ps. 22:30 [29]).

Later Translations from the Septuagint

In later centuries there were further translations made into other languages from the Greek Septuagint. In the fourth century C.E. a translation was made into the Gothic language for the tribes of Goths living in what are now Bulgaria and Slovakia. In the fifth and sixth centuries, translations were made into two dialects of Coptic (known as Sahidic and Bohairic), that is, the forms of language descended from ancient Egyptian that were spoken by those in Egypt who were not Greek-speaking. A translation was made into classical Armenian, evidently in the fifth century, and is still used by the traditional Armenian Gregorian church; a translation was made into classical Georgian, probably in the fifth or sixth century, that is used by the church in the Republic of Georgia (in the south Caucasus area). And a translation was made into Old Church Slavonic (essentially Old Bulgarian) in the ninth century; this translation, modified to some degree in the various Slavic-speaking regions, has held its ground through the centuries in Slavic Orthodox churches.[58] And one must not forget that the Septuagint itself continued to be the Old Testament of the Greek-speaking Eastern church, the Greek Orthodox Church today.

Psalm 151

There is a postscript to this part of the story. In one of the great manuscripts of the Greek Septuagint (Sinaiticus), there are 151 psalms: at the end of the book of Psalms, the subscription reads, "The 151 Psalms of David." In other great Septuagint manuscripts (for example, Alexandrinus), Psalm 151 is in an appendix, and its superscription reads, "This psalm is ascribed to David as his own composition (though it is outside the number [some manuscripts add "of the one hundred fifty"]), after he had fought in single combat with Goliath."[59] Psalm 151 is likewise found at the end of the Psalter in the Old Latin version[60] and in the Sahidic Coptic version. And a slightly different version of this psalm, in Hebrew, has been discovered among the Dead Sea Scrolls (see chapter 7). Furthermore, there is a manuscript in the Syriac language from the twelfth century C.E., found in Mosul in northern Iraq, that offers *five* apocryphal psalms, Psalms 151—155; Psalm 151 is the same as that found in the Septuagint and among the Dead Sea Scrolls, but Psalms 154 and 155 also turn up, in the original Hebrew, among the Dead Sea Scrolls (see again chapter 7). In spite of the strong conviction, then, that the Psalms numbered 150, there was a contrary tendency to add "just one more" or "just a few more"!

And since Psalm 151 is part of scriptural canon for the Greek Orthodox Church, which today is part of the National Council of Churches of Christ in the U.S.A., the RSV (in 1977) and the NRSV, which have been sponsored by the council, offer Psalm 151 among the Deuterocanonical books. It is a bonus that only dramatizes the complicated story of how the separate psalms were collected, annotated, and translated by successive generations of Jews and Christians.

NOTES

1. John Bright, *A History of Israel* (Philadelphia: Westminster, 1981), 408–14.
2. See Hans-Joachim Kraus, *Psalms 1–59: A Commentary* (Minneapolis: Augsburg, 1988), 38–62; Leopold Sabourin, *The Psalms: Their Origin and Meaning* (New York: Alba House, 1974).
3. Others are Psalms 8, 33, 100, 111, 113, 114, 117, 136, 145, 146, 147, 149, and 150.
4. Others are Psalms 93, 96, 97, 98, and 99.
5. Others are Psalms 60 and 90.
6. Others are Psalms 3, 5, 13, 17, 25, 26, 27, 28, 39, 41, 54, 56, 57, 59, 61, 71, 102, 109, 130, and 143.
7. Others are Psalms 65, 66, and 124.
8. Others are Psalms 30, 34, 92, and 138.
9. Another is Psalm 129.
10. Others are Psalms 4, 11, and 62.
11. Another is Psalm 105.
12. Bruce K. Waltke, "Superscripts, Postscripts, or Both," *JBL* 110 (1991):583–96.
13. Psalms 3–9, 11–32, 34–41, 51–65, 68–70, 86, 101, 103, 108–110, 122, 124, 131, 133, 138–145.
14. Psalms 33, 43, 67, 71, 91, 93–99, 104, and 137.
15. Cf. Sigmund Mowinckel, *The Psalms in Israel's Worship* (New York and Nashville: Abingdon, 1962), 2:95–96.
16. Kraus, *Psalms 1–59*, 21–32; Sabourin, *Psalms*, 11–17.
17. Michael D. Goulder, *The Psalms of the Sons of Korah* (Sheffield: JSOT, 1982), 103–5.
18. Gerald Henry Wilson, *The Editing of the Hebrew Psalter* (SBLDS 76; Chico, Calif.: Scholars Press, 1985).
19. Ibid., 117.
20. Ibid., 116, 120.
21. Ibid., 209–14.

22. Ibid., 174–76.

23. Ibid., 173, 204–6.

24. Ibid., 163.

25. Cf. ibid., 210–11.

26. Cristoph Barth, "Concatenatio im ersten Buch des Psalters," *Wort und Wirklich-keit: Studien zur Afrikanistik und Orientalistik: Eugen Ludwig Rapp zum 70 Geburtstag,* Brigitta Benzing and others (eds.) (Meisenheim am Glan: Anton Hain, 1976), 1:30–40.

27. Wilson, *Editing of the Hebrew Psalter,* 214–15.

28. Ibid., 215–16.

29. Ibid., 177.

30. Ibid., 214–19.

31. Ibid., 220–28.

32. Ibid., 188–89.

33. Ibid., 189–90.

34. Bright, *History of Israel,* 375.

35. Ibid., 376.

36. Ibid., 414–15; and, in more detail, William O. E. Oesterley and Theodore H. Robinson, *A History of Israel* (Oxford: Oxford University Press, 1932), 2:410–11.

37. Bright, *History of Israel,* 376.

38. See, e.g., the translation into English by Marmaduke Pickthall, *The Meaning of the Glorious Koran* (1930; reprint, New York: New American Library, 1953; bilingual ed., Albany: State University of New York Press, 1976); and see there esp. the translator's foreword.

39. Charles Augustus Briggs and Emilie Grace Briggs, *A Critical and Exegetical Commentary on the Book of Psalms* (New York: Charles Scribner's Sons, 1906–7), 1:xxv.

40. For an effort to isolate these matters, see Thorleif Boman, *Hebrew Thought Compared with Greek* (London: SCM, 1960); for a thorough criticism of Boman's work, see James Barr, *The Semantics of Biblical Language* (Oxford: Oxford University Press, 1961), notably 46–79.

41. Benjamin Kedar, "The Latin Translations," in Martin Jan Mulder (ed.), *Mikra: Text, Translation, Reading and Interpretation of the Hebrew Bible in Ancient Judaism and Early Christianity* (CRINT II, 1; Assen and Maastricht: Van Gorcum; Philadelphia: Fortress, 1988), 323–29.

42. So Kraus, *Psalms 1–59,* 113.

43. Ibid.

44. For this illustration I am indebted to Emanuel Tov, "The Septuagint," in Mulder (ed.), *Mikra,* 170–71.

45. See, e.g., Mitchell Dahood, *Psalms I: 1–50* (Garden City, N.Y.: Doubleday, 1966), 126, 129.

46. For these examples, see Henry B. Swete, *An Introduction to the Old Testament in Greek* (Cambridge: Cambridge University Press, 1902; reprint, New York: Ktav, 1968), 326.

47. Arthur Soffer, "The Treatment of Anthropomorphisms and Anthropopathisms in the Septuagint of Psalms," *HUCA* 28 (1957):85–107.

48. See, conveniently, Carey A. Moore, *Daniel, Esther and Jeremiah: The Additions* (AB 44; Garden City, N.Y.: Doubleday, 1977).

49. Bleddyn J. Roberts, *The Old Testament Text and Versions* (Cardiff: University of Wales Press, 1951), 120–38.

50. *Sopherim* 1.7. This late tractate is one of the appendices to the Babylonian Talmud; see A. Cohen (ed.), *The Minor Tractates of the Talmud* (London: Soncino, 1965), 1:212–13.

51. For the details, see Roberts, *Old Testament Text*, 197–213; Philip S. Alexander, "Jewish Aramaic Translations of Hebrew Scriptures," in Mulder (ed.), *Mikra*, 224–25.

52. See Roberts, *Old Testament Text*, 214–28; Peter B. Dirksen, "The Old Testament Peshitta," in Mulder (ed.), *Mikra*, 285.

53. Roberts, *Old Testament Text*, 237–46, esp. 239.

54. For a careful assessment of the Old Latin in general, see Kedar, "Latin Translations," 302–13.

55. For an assessment of Jerome and the Vulgate Old Testament, see ibid., 313–35.

56. Roberts, *Old Testament Text*, 250.

57. Ibid., 247–59.

58. For all these, see ibid., 229–33, 236.

59. For the Greek text, see, conveniently, Alfred Rahlfs, *Septuaginta id est Vetus Testamentum Graece* (Stuttgart: Privilegierte Württembergische Bibelanstalt, 1935), 2:163–64.

60. James A. Sanders, *The Dead Sea Psalms Scroll* (Ithaca, N.Y.: Cornell University Press, 1967), 6.

PART TWO

THE PSALTER
THROUGH HISTORY

7

Psalms
at the Dead Sea

It is now time to turn from a reconstruction of the formation of the book of Psalms to a consideration of the use of the Psalms through history. This consideration turns us into many paths, including the use of Psalms by Jews through the centuries and the use of Psalms in the New Testament and by Christians through the centuries, in liturgy and in study, in hymns and in recitation.

After I finished writing my own treatment of these topics in this section, there came to my attention a little book from eighty years ago, *The Psalms in Human Life* by Rowland E. Prothero.[1] In spite of its title this work does not touch at all on Jewish use of the Psalms or on the Psalms in the New Testament; it does not deal with the Eastern Orthodox Church or with the Roman Catholic Church after the sixteenth century. It does not analyze liturgy or commentaries. It essentially offers stories from church history, beginning with the church fathers and continuing through the Middle Ages and the Reformation, with the emphasis on Great Britain and France and on Protestants; we learn, for example, the favorite psalm of Charlemagne (Psalm 68, "Let God rise up").[2] Though there are no footnotes, the author does include a full bibliography of sources, and his book is a gold mine of examples from church history: there are two chapters, for example, on the French Huguenots. It is therefore a useful supplement to my treatment here.

The Jews, 323–63 B.C.E.:
The Challenge of Hellenism

After the death of Alexander the Great, as we noted in chapter 6, Palestine found itself part of the Ptolemaic Empire, that portion of Alexander's realm that lay in Egypt. What happened in the following two centuries is complex, but at least an outline of events is necessary here.

The basic issue for the Jews of the time was how they would respond to the challenge of Hellenism. The Greek language and the Greek way of life were everywhere. It was not simply a matter of the Jews in Alexandria translating the Jewish

Scriptures into Greek. Greek adventurers and colonists were to be found all over the Mediterranean area. Greek ideas of free thinking, of a cosmopolitan unity among various ethnic groups, caught fire; thus the Jewish writer Philo of Alexandria presented Moses as the ideal philosopher-king.[3]

But to the Jews of Palestine the challenge of Hellenism took a different turn. The territory of Palestine had been coveted by the Seleucid Empire, that portion of Alexander's realm that included Syria and Babylon, and in the year 198 B.C.E., after a decisive battle with the Ptolemaic army, the Seleucid Empire annexed Palestine.

Though the Seleucid realm was led by a small group of Greek-speaking people, the empire was so far-flung and its population so heterogeneous and lacking in unity that its leaders felt threatened on every hand; there was therefore a strong impulse to urge Greek ways upon the peoples of the empire as a means to loyalty. Matters came to a head when Antiochus IV became the Seleucid ruler in 175 B.C.E. He sponsored pro-Hellenizing high priests over the Jews in Jerusalem, who in turn established a gymnasium in Jerusalem where races could be run in Greek fashion (those competing ran naked, to the horror of conservative Jews). Eventually, the king, his head swollen with notions of his own divinity, enforced Hellenization upon the Jewish people: pagan altars were erected throughout the land, Jews were forced on pain of death to eat pork, and in December 167 B.C.E. the cult of Olympian Zeus was introduced in the Jerusalem temple and swine's flesh offered on the altar to Zeus; the whole story is narrated in the Deuterocanonical books of 1 and 2 Maccabees, and it is clear that the book of Daniel was drafted in this period (the figure of Nebuchadnezzar there was a code for Antiochus IV) to encourage resistance to paganism.

Armed rebellion broke out in a village northwest of Jerusalem, as a family of brothers took to the hills against the Seleucid forces; the greatest of these was Judas, who came to be called Maccabeus ("the Hammerer"). In December 164 B.C.E. the Jewish patriots liberated the Jerusalem temple and purified it (the Jewish festival of Hanukkah celebrates this purification) and thereupon were able to create a small state with political autonomy.[4]

We pause here to note that there is in 1 Macc. 7:16-17 a reminiscence of Ps. 79:2-3. The passage describes a delegation of Jewish scribes who in 161 B.C.E. came to the Seleucid governor Bacchides to sue for peace. Though the governor assured them of their safety, "he seized sixty of them and killed them in one day"; and the narrative continues, "in accordance with the word which was written, 'The flesh of thy saints and their blood they poured out round about Jerusalem, and there was none to bury them,'" a paraphrase of the Psalms passage. And, it may be added, there are several other bursts of poetry in 1 Maccabees that draw from community laments among the psalms—Psalms 44, 74, and 79 (1 Macc. 1:36-40; 2:7-13; 3:45). The Maccabean period, alas, continued to offer incidents in which such community laments were appropriate.

The office of high priest had the ultimate loyalty of Jews, and the Maccabean leader Jonathan, the successor of his brother Judas, assumed the title of high priest (152 B.C.E.), and in this office he was succeeded by his brother Simon.[5] This family therefore replaced the Zadokite priests, the family that had held the office of high priest since David's time (2 Sam. 15:24; 1 Kings 1:34; compare Ezek. 44:15), and began the so-called Hasmonean dynasty of priest-kings. Unfortunately, this dynasty proved to be both oppressive and corrupt as the Hasmoneans threaded their way through the alliances and plots sponsored by various factions in Rome and by the clients of the various factions of Rome in the Near East. The Roman general Pompey conquered Jerusalem in 63 B.C.E., though the Hasmoneans continued to rule as clients of Rome.[6]

The Psalms of Solomon

Before I turn to the community at the Dead Sea, however, I must take note of a collection called the *Psalms of Solomon*. These are eighteen psalms that bear a close resemblance to the biblical Psalms; the name suggests a contrast with the canonical Psalms, presumed to be the work of David. The *Psalms of Solomon* are to be found in some editions of the Greek Septuagint (and also in Syriac),[7] but it is clear that the Greek text of these psalms is a translation from a lost Hebrew original.

These psalms are to be dated to about 70–45 B.C.E.; their phrases imitate the biblical Psalms and reflect the religious crisis in the hearts of devout Jews in Jerusalem that had been brought about by the invasion of the Roman army of Pompey in 63 B.C.E. Most scholars assume that these devout Jews were Pharisees or belonged to the circle that became the Pharisees;[8] in any event, they voice dismay at foreign invasion and corrupt government. *Psalm of Solomon* 1 reads:

> I cried out to the Lord when I was severely troubled,
>   to God when sinners set upon me.
> Suddenly, the clamor of war was heard before me;
>   "He will hear me, for I am full of righteousness."
> I considered in my heart that I was full of righteousness,
>   for I had prospered and had many children.
> Their wealth was extended to the whole earth,
>   and their glory to the end of the earth.
> They exalted themselves to the stars,
>   they said they would never fall.
> They were arrogant in the possessions,
>   and they did not acknowledge God.
> Their sins were in secret,
>   and even I did not know.
> Their lawless actions surpassed the gentiles before them;
>   they completely profaned the sanctuary of the Lord.

Psalm of Solomon 17 is a long poem of forty-six verses that sets forth a picture of the coming Messiah, a son of David (v. 21, not a supernatural figure) who will rule justly.

> He will be a righteous king over them, taught by God. There will be no unrighteousness among them in his days, for all shall be holy, and their king shall be the Lord Messiah. (v. 32)

Psalms, then, continued to be composed, though those beyond the 150 in the Psalter gained only limited acceptance.

The Discovery of the Dead Sea Scrolls

It was earlier, in the turmoil of events at the beginning of the Hasmonean dynasty, that the community of sectarians at the Dead Sea was formed. The life of this sect and its use of the Psalms are an important part of our story for several reasons, not the least of which is that the texts of the portions of the Psalms that have been found among the Dead Sea Scrolls are the earliest manuscripts of the Psalms to have survived to our day.

The story of the discovery of the sect and its scrolls is one of the archeological romances of modern times.[9] In the spring of 1947, a Bedouin shepherd boy was watching his flock about eight miles south of Jericho, near the Dead Sea, and he idly tossed a pebble into the opening of one of the dozens of caves in the area. To his alarm he heard not the expected sound of the pebble striking the cave floor but the shattering of pottery, and he fled. But he came back the next day with an older boy of his clan and they explored the cave together, finding several scrolls of leather, which they removed from the cave. The Bedouin know the value of antiquities, and these scrolls might have had value. Some months later these scrolls came into the hands of a shoemaker in Bethlehem, a Syrian Christian named Kando, who dealt with antiquities on the side. Kando thought the script in the scrolls might be Syriac and took them to be examined by priests at the Syrian Convent of St. Mark's in Jerusalem. The priest who looked at them knew they were not Syriac and asked for help from the American School of Oriental Research in Jerusalem.

It was then the spring of 1948, just before the state of Israel was declared, and because there was sporadic fighting in the city between the Jewish forces and the Arab forces, most of the staff of the American School had been evacuated; the only staff member to stay on was John Trever, a graduate student who had come to Palestine to prepare a set of color photographs of Palestinian wildflowers.

Trever looked at the scroll he was shown and asked to keep it overnight. He recognized the script as Hebrew; compared it with a specimen set of Hebrew scripts of various periods that was in the school library; took a few photographs of sample columns of the scroll, which he saw to be part of the book of Isaiah; and airmailed the photographs to William F. Albright, of Johns Hopkins University, recognized as the dean of American archeologists of the Near East. Albright examined the photographs and cabled Trever his congratulations on bringing to light the greatest archeological discovery of modern times. The scrolls from that first cave ("Cave 1") turned out to be a complete scroll of Isaiah;[10] a sectarian *Commentary on Habakkuk*,[11] and several other sectarian documents, notably the so-called *Community Rule* (formerly called the *Manual of Discipline*, a kind of constitution and bylaws for the sect),[12] the so-called *War Rule* (an apocalyptic description of the final war between the "children of light" and the "children of darkness"),[13] and the so-called *Thanksgiving Hymns*.[14]

Then, in the spring of 1949, the original cave was explored; and between 1951 and 1956 other caves in the area were explored, ten of which likewise yielded manuscript finds, and the ruins of the settlement nearby were excavated. It is clear that here, for roughly two centuries, an important Jewish community had lived out its life.

History and Beliefs of the Community

Unfortunately, the members of the sect did not leave behind any historical account of their origin and life, so scholars must try to piece together, often from very oblique and symbolic language, what can be known about them.

It is likely that the sect was founded by one of the Zadokite priests of Jerusalem, the family of priests who had been displaced by the Hasmoneans, for the Dead Sea sect refers to itself as "sons of Zadok."[15] The founder of the sect and his followers differed with the priestly authorities in Jerusalem over many details of the interpretation of Jewish law; the sectarian documents speak of a "Wicked Priest," who may be the Maccabean Jonathan—Jonathan, as we have seen, assumed the high priesthood in 152 B.C.E. Accordingly, the founder, called by the sect the "Teacher of Righteousness"—his actual name we do not know—took his followers to the wilderness of Judea, probably about 150 B.C.E.; there they might hope to live a life uncorrupted by the compromises of the power politics of Jerusalem. The location is now known by its local Arabic name Qumran. It is a region that is not only exceedingly dry but exceedingly hot. In this seemingly inhospitable region they evidently reoccupied a building dating from roughly the eighth century B.C.E., constructed an aqueduct from a spring in the hills to the west, and then in the period 150–140 B.C.E. built new buildings nearby. Except for a gap in occupation after a catastrophic earthquake in 31 B.C.E., the settlement was occupied until 68 C.E., when it was destroyed by an invading Roman army.

The community consisted, so far as we know, of men only. It was grouped into priests (sons of Aaron), Levites, and "men of Israel" and was organized hierarchically.[16]

The sectarians were keenly concerned for the details of Jewish law; they were also convinced they were living in the end time, and they wished to be ready for it. They took the word seriously of a "voice crying in the wilderness" (Isa. 40:3), and scholars have suggested that John the Baptist was reared by the sect (compare Luke 1:80: "The child [John] grew and became strong in spirit, and he was in the wilderness until the day he appeared publicly to Israel"); certainly, what the Gospels tell us of John's teaching fits very closely with what we have learned of the beliefs of the sect at the Dead Sea.[17]

The Scrolls

What are important for our purposes are the manuscript finds from the sect that were preserved in the dry climate in caves near the Dead Sea for two thousand years—though, it must be said, not always preserved very well. The scrolls that had been stored in large jars, such as those in Cave 1, were relatively well preserved, but those that had simply lain on the floor of their cave, such as those from Cave 4, had become fragmented into small bits with frayed edges, leaving scholars with a gigantic series of jigsaw puzzles.

The Dead Sea Scrolls, almost all of them in Hebrew, fall into two categories of texts. The first is copies of Scripture, or, to be more exact, copies of books that we have known heretofore, including both books that have been accepted as Scripture and books that at that time were being circulated as having scriptural status. The second is sectarian texts: texts produced by the sect for the use of its own members. I have already mentioned the sectarian works that were found in Cave 1—the *Community Rule*, the *Commentary on Habakkuk*, the *War Rule*, and the *Thanksgiving Hymns*. But many more sectarian documents have turned up in the other caves. What is of interest to us in the present study is the use of the book of Psalms within the community, so it is to that topic that I now turn.

The Psalms Scroll from Cave 11

Among the texts from the Dead Sea Scrolls are at least thirty copies of the Psalms, more than for any other biblical book.[18] The remains of these thirty copies contain in total at least fragments of 115 of the biblical Psalms.[19] Among these by far the most substantial is a scroll from Cave 11, discovered in 1956 but not unrolled until 1961.[20] The scroll is of leather; the beginning portion is missing, but what remains measures in all about thirteen and a half feet in length. There are on this scroll twenty-eight columns of text, plus a handful of detached fragments. These columns consisted originally of twenty-one to twenty-three lines of text each; unfortunately, the bottom edge of the scroll is worn away, so that about one-quarter to one-third of the lines of each column is missing. What remain for us, then, are between fourteen and seventeen lines of text. By handwriting style it is estimated that the scroll was copied in the period 30–50 C.E.[21] The psalms in this scroll (and other scrolls from Qumran) are, of course, not marked with numbers: the overt numeration is a feature of later centuries. But each fresh psalm is marked by a space, a third of a line or so in length, before the opening words.

The text of this Psalms scroll has three startling features. The first is that although the scroll as presently constituted contains all or parts of thirty-nine canonical psalms (psalms that are a part of our book of Psalms), the sequence of these psalms is altogether different from that in the traditional Hebrew text. The second feature is that intermixed with the thirty-nine canonical psalms are other poetic sequences: 2 Sam. 23:1-7 (which in 2 Sam. 23:1 is called "the last words of David"); part of 51:13-30 of the Deuterocanonical book of Sirach (Ecclesiasticus), which is an acrostic poem but not attributed to David in Sirach; Psalms 151, 154, and 155 (psalms beyond the traditional 150, discussed at the end of chapter 6); three more poetic sequences heretofore unknown; and a prose statement about David's compositions.[22] The third feature is that, in the case of the canonical psalms, the text is not always what we have known from the traditional Hebrew text. I discuss each of these features in detail.

The first feature is the order of the psalms. The contents of the scroll are arranged in the following order: Psalms 101–103; 109; 118; 104; 147; 105; 146; 148; 121–132; 119; 135–136; 145; 154 (noncanonical); "A Plea for Deliverance" (noncanonical); 139; 137–138; Sir. 51:13-30 (Deuterocanonical); "Apostrophe to Zion" (noncanonical); 93; 141; 133; 144; 155 (noncanonical); 142–143; 149–150; "Hymn to the Creator" (noncanonical); 2 Sam. 23:7; prose statement on David's compositions (noncanonical); 140; 134; 151A and B (noncanonical).[23] Thus, except for the sequences of Psalms 121–132 and for one sequence of three psalms (101–103) and for four pairs of psalms (135–136, 137–138, 142–143, and 149–150), the order of these psalms in no way matches the canonical order familiar to us.

Several rather unsystematic observations may be made on this matter. One is that every psalm from Psalm 118 to Psalm 150 is present except for Psalm 120, which may originally have been present in one of the extant columns but entirely within the lower portion (now missing) of such a column. Psalm 120 has seven verses, and at the bottom of column xiv, seven verses of Psalm 135 are missing.

Another observation on the order of the psalms is that in a separate Psalms scroll, one found in Cave 4[24] containing portions from Psalm 6 to Psalm 69, the order is more or less that of the traditional order, a circumstance suggesting that the order of the psalms in Books I and II may have been settled sooner than the order of the psalms in Books IV and V, to which most of the psalms in the scroll from Cave 11 belong.[25] I discussed this matter in chapter 6.

Again, some of the psalms do appear in our traditional order: Psalms 121–132 are all "songs of ascents" (see chapter 6), though it is true that these twelve psalms are not the complete sequence of songs of ascents in our Bible.

Now, it is striking that the remains of another Psalms scroll were found in Cave 11, a scroll written by a different scribe but from the same period of time, that is, the first half of the first century C.E. The remains of this scroll,[26] which consist of six small fragments, offer Psalms 141, 133, and 144 without intervening material and in that order, exactly the sequence in the long scroll we have just discussed; and the fragmentary scroll also includes "A Plea for Deliverance," one of the noncanonical poems in the long scroll. This circumstance suggests that the contents of the long scroll are not idiosyncratic but form a standard collection, copied and recopied.[27]

It is noteworthy that the superscriptions to the psalms in the long scroll are almost exactly as they are in the traditional Hebrew text that has come down to us. One must conclude that the superscriptions were added to the psalms even while the order of the various psalms was still fluid. There is one interesting variation in a superscription: in Psalm 145, where the traditional text has *těhillâ* (praise), the scroll has *těpillâ* (prayer; see chapter 6), a difference of only one letter; since "praise" appears as a superscription only for this psalm and "prayer" appears in five psalms, one wonders whether the Qumran scroll does not have a preferred reading. One may add that "Selah" occurs here just as it does in the traditional text (143:6).

The second startling feature of the Psalms scroll is the intermixture of canonical psalms with noncanonical material. Now, in Cave 11 there was found still another scroll, a mere zigzag scrap, that offers something even more surprising: a series of apocryphal (noncanonical) psalms ending with a single canonical psalm, Psalm 91.[28] Scholars tend to believe that these noncanonical psalms were not freshly composed by the sect but rather were earlier compositions copied and preserved by the sect.[29]

Now, there appear to be two possibilities to explain the existence of scrolls like these that intermixed canonical and noncanonical psalm material. One is that such a scroll might simply offer a given collection of psalms that were used in the community and that the notion of "only 150 psalms" and "only these psalms" had not taken over. If this is the situation, then the Cave 11 scroll is evidence of a stage on the way to canonicity, when there was not yet an agreed list of the 150 Psalms. The other possibility is that what we have here is the equivalent, in the Dead Sea sect, of a medieval breviary of the Roman Catholic Church (compare chapter 10). In a breviary a series of psalms are interwoven with New Testament material and with noncanonical prayers. If this is the situation, then what we have in the Cave 11 scroll could simply be an arrangement of psalms for liturgical recitation.[30] Given the paucity of our data, it is impossible to decide for sure what we have before us.

The third startling feature of the Psalms scroll is the nature of the text of some of the canonical psalms: the scroll offers significant differences from the traditional text of the Psalms that has come down to us. For example, because Psalm 136 closely resembles Psalm 118 (in the refrain, "O give thanks to the Lord, for he is good, for his steadfast love endures forever"), we find that the text of Psalm 136 in the scroll adds verses from Psalm 118 at the end: after 136:26, the last verse in the form of the psalm as we know it, we find added 118:1 (the refrain), then 118:15-16, then 118:8-9, then a new pair of lines ("It is better to trust in the Lord than to put confidence in a thousand people"), and then once more the refrain, completed by the new words "Praise the Lord." Because the scroll has the text of Psalm 118 elsewhere,[31] these lines at the end of Psalm 136 are not a mangled version of Psalm 118 but rather an extension of Psalm 136 derived from the similar Psalm 118.[32]

Some of the noncanonical material also contains verses known from elsewhere. For example, the close of the "Hymn to the Creator," which occurs in the scroll after Psalm 150 and before 2 Sam. 23:1-7, is made up of material from Jer. 10:12-13 and from Ps. 135:7. What we have, then, are floating bits of liturgical poetry that find a home in a fresh sequence.[33]

This scroll, then, represents a fascinating phenomenon: a specimen of a collection of psalms as it existed before the canonical process was completed. It is, in short, an example of the process we tried to envisage in chapter 6.

Chains of Proof Texts

There are several other types of literature among the Dead Sea Scrolls that involve the Psalms. One of them is the so-called *Florilegium* (anthology) found in Cave 4.[34] This little work, probably from the first century B.C.E., quotes a chain of "proof texts" from Scripture and intersperses these texts with comments that present the interpretation of them by the sect. These comments identify the community with the (ideal) temple in Jerusalem, and they proclaim the coming of two Messiahs, called the "Branch of David" and the "Interpreter of the Law," that is, a Davidic or kingly Messiah and an Aaronic or priestly Messiah.

The text begins with 2 Sam. 7:10; continues with Exod. 15:17-18; then takes up again 2 Sam. 7:11-14; moves to Amos 9:11; then Ps. 1:1; Isa. 8:11; Ezek. 44:10; Ps. 2:1; and, finally, Dan. 12:10. About the two psalm verses we read, "Explanation of 'How blessed is the man who does not walk in the counsel of the wicked': interpreted, this saying concerns those who turn aside from the way of (the people)";[35] and again (though unfortunately there are a couple of gaps in the manuscript):

> "Why do the nations rage and the peoples meditate vanity, the kings of the earth rise up, and the princes take counsel together against the Lord and against His Messiah?" Interpreted, this saying concerns the kings of the nations who shall rage against the elect of Israel in the last days. This shall be the time of the time to come over the house of Judah to perfect . . . Belial,[36] and a remnant of the people shall be left according to the lot assigned to them, and they shall practise the whole Law . . . Moses.[37]

The striking thing about this anthology of proof texts is that the first two chapters of the Letter to the Hebrews in the New Testament have much the same format of a chain of proof texts, indeed using some of the same texts as the Dead Sea anthology does—Heb. 1:5 quotes both Ps. 2:7 and 2 Sam. 7:14. That is to say, two religious communities—one a sect of Jews at the Dead Sea, another a sect moving out of Judaism (the Christians)—used texts from the Old Testament to justify their teaching and even drew on some of the same texts, among which are the Psalms (see chapter 8).

A similar document survives in fragments from Cave 11, a description of the events of the last days in which the heavenly deliverer is Melchizedek.[38] Melchizedek is a mysterious figure whom we have already encountered in Ps. 110:4 (see chapter 2). It is curious that in this sectarian document he is not a human king who encountered Abraham (Gen. 14:18) but rather a heavenly figure identical with the archangel Michael, the head of the "children of heaven" (angelic figures). It is also curious that in this document no reference is made to Ps. 110:4, the passage that is so central to the elaboration of the Melchizedek figure in the Letter to the Hebrews (see chapter 8). The psalm that is most central in the material we have of this text is Ps. 82:1-2, in which God challenges the pagan gods in a heavenly court (see chapter 2). A quotation will give the flavor of the document.

> For this [the final liberation] is the moment of the Year of Grace for Melchizedek. And he will, by his strength, judge the holy ones of God, executing judgment as it is written concerning him in the Songs of David, who said, "Elohim has taken his place in the divine council; in the midst of the gods he holds judgment" [Ps. 82:1]. And it was concerning him that he said, "Let the assembly of the peoples return to the height above them; God will judge the peoples" [Ps. 7:8-9 (7-8)]. As for that which he said, "How long will you judge unjustly and show partiality to the wicked? Selah" [Ps. 82:2], its interpre-

tation concerns Satan and the spirit of his lot who rebelled by turning away from the precepts of God to . . . And Melchizedek will avenge the vengeance of the judgments of God.[39]

This notion of Melchizedek as a heavenly figure helps put into perspective the description of Melchizedek in the Letter to the Hebrews as one who prefigures Jesus Christ (see again chapter 8).

Sectarian Commentaries

Another related type of literature among the scrolls is the commentary proper. From Cave 1 there are fragments remaining from a commentary on Psalm 68,[40] but more substantially there remains a manuscript found in Cave 4 of a commentary on Psalm 37.[41] Psalm 37 is a wisdom psalm, an acrostic; it is an affirmation that the wicked will receive their retribution and is therefore the kind of psalm that the sect could read in the light of its own history—as indeed it did.

Some of the interpretive comments are of a general nature, whereas others are more specific; a few quotations will give the flavor of the document. Thus to Ps. 37:7—"Be still before the Lord, and wait patiently for him; do not fret over those who prosper in their way, over those who carry out evil devices"—the comment reads, "Its interpretation concerns the Liar who has led astray many by his lying words so that they chose frivolous things and heeded not the interpreter of knowledge, so that they perish by sword and famine and pestilence." To v. 10—"Yet a little while, and the wicked will be no more; though you look diligently for their place, they will not be there"—the comment reads, "Interpreted, this concerns all wickedness at the end of the forty years, for they shall be blotted out and not an evil man shall be found on the earth." To v. 11—"But the meek shall inherit the land, and delight themselves in abundant prosperity"—the comment reads, "Interpreted, this concerns the congregation of the Poor who shall accept the season of penance and shall be delivered from all the snares of Belial. Afterwards, all who possess the earth shall delight and prosper on exquisite food."

But sometimes the interpretation becomes more specific. To vv. 18-19a—"The Lord knows the days of the blameless, and their heritage will abide forever; they are not put to shame in evil times"—the comment reads, "(Its interpretation concerns) the penitents of the desert who, saved, shall live for a thousand generations and to whom all the inheritance of Adam shall belong, as also to their seed for ever." To vv. 21-22—"The wicked borrow, and do not pay back, but the righteous are generous and keep giving; for those blessed by the Lord shall inherit the land, but those cursed by him shall be cut off"—the comment is, "Interpreted, this concerns the congregation of the Poor, who shall possess the whole world as an inheritance. They shall possess the High Mountain of Israel for ever, and in his sanctuary shall delight. But 'those cursed by him shall be cut off,' they are the violent of the covenant (?) and the wicked of Israel; they shall be cut off and blotted out for ever." To vv. 32-33—"The wicked watch for the righteous, and seek to kill them; the Lord will not abandon them to their power, or let them be condemned when they are brought to trial"—the comment is, "Its interpretation concerns the Wicked (Pri)est who watch(ed) the Right(eous one and sought) to kill him, . . . and the Law which he sent to him. But God will not aban(don him) and will not (condemn him when) he is brought to trial. And God (will) pay h(im) his (re)ward by delivering him into the hand of the violent of the nations that they may execute (judgment) on him."

Echoes of Phrases from the Psalms

We also have, within the sectarian documents, various citations and echoes of the Psalms. For example, in the *Community Rule*[42] there is an echo of Ps. 1:2; the passage reads, "And where ten [men of the Community] are, there shall never lack a man among them who shall study the Law continually, day and night, concerning the right conduct of a man with his companion."[43] Again, in the same document the phrase "broken spirit" from Ps. 51:19 (17) appears in a description of the character of those making up the council of the community; this passage is an excellent example of how the rhetoric of the sect was saturated with biblical phrases:

> In the Council of the Community there shall be twelve men and three priests, perfect in everything that is revealed of all the Law, to do truth, righteousness, justice, to love kindness, humbly to walk [compare Mic. 6:8] each with his fellow, to keep fidelity in the land with steadfast mind [Isa. 26:3] and broken spirit [Ps. 51:19 (17)], to pardon iniquity [Isa. 40:2] for those who do justice, and (to bear) the affliction of the crucible, and to walk with everyone according to the measure of truth and the ordering of time.[44]

Again, there are reminiscences of the Psalms in the so-called *War Rule*,[45] several copies of which survive among the scrolls; it is a document that depicts the coming eschatological war between the "children of light" (that is, the members of the sect) and the "children of darkness" (the enemies of the sect). The latter are called "the army of Belial," made up (among others) of "the band of Edom, Moab, and the sons of Ammon, the Philistines, and the bands of the Kittim of Assyria." (The "Kittim" are a vague designation in the Old Testament, beginning in Gen. 10:4. The term probably referred originally to the inhabitants of Cyprus, but it became generalized to refer to any pagan power, and in the documents of the sect it evidently referred primarily to the Romans.)[46] The document offers a detailed description of the military preparations for the war; its spirit derives from the wars in the wilderness described in the book of Numbers, but the specific military details are based on Roman army practice. It must be stressed, however, that the war that is described is not a historical war but a war at the end of the age, like the "Armageddon" referred to in Rev. 16:16.

Reminiscences of the Psalms (and of other Scriptures) are scattered through this document, but I refer particularly to two sorts of reminiscences.

The first is in a list of phrases that are to appear on the various war trumpets that are designated, phrases intended to attract the attention of God. We read, "On the trumpets for breaking camp they shall write, 'The mighty Deeds of God shall crush the Enemy, putting to Flight all those who hate Righteousness and bringing Shame on those who hate Him.'" This inscription is derived from Num. 10:35 or Ps. 68:2 (1).[47]

The second sort of reminiscence is in a hymn of enthusiasm to be sung at the final battle. I cite the first of three strophes of the hymn.

And you, God, are terrible [Deut. 7:21] in the glory of your kingdom [Ps. 145:11],
  and the congregation of your saints is in our midst for everlasting help.
We (offer) contempt for kings,
  mockery and scorn for heroes,
for holy is the Lord [Ps. 99:9],
  and the king of glory [Ps. 24:7-10] is with us;
the people of the heroic saints [Dan. 7:27; 8:24] and the host of angels are in our levy,
  the one Mighty in bat(tle) [Ps. 24:8] is in our congregation,
  and the host of his spirits are with our infantrymen and our cavalrymen.
(They are like) clouds and mists of dew covering the earth [Ezek. 38:9, 16; Isa. 18:4],
  like a shower of rain drenching with righteousness all its growth [Isa. 28:2; 34:1].[48]

Here we see how Psalm 24, the old torah liturgy that celebrates Yahweh's leadership in battle (see chapter 4), has been used once more to celebrate God's final victory over the forces of darkness at the end of time.

Further Noncanonical Psalms
Copied by the Sect

We have already seen how the Psalms scroll from Cave 11 interspersed canonical and noncanonical psalms. Beyond these we have scraps from Cave 4 of still other psalms heretofore unknown,[49] which appear to come from the same period, before the founding of the sect.[50] Unfortunately, the scraps of text are so fragmentary that no full lines remain.

The Thanksgiving Hymns

Finally, the biblical Psalms had deep influence on some fresh hymns composed within the community: the so-called *Thanksgiving Hymns*, roughly twenty-five of them, that are preserved on a single manuscript found in Cave 1.[51] Unfortunately, the scroll has suffered some deterioration, so that at points there are gaps in the wording.

Each hymn begins with the words "I thank you, O Lord," or the like. Many of the hymns give expression to sentiments common to all members of the sect, but others appear to refer to the experiences of a teacher abandoned by his friends and persecuted by his enemies. It is easy, then, to imagine that the author of these hymns was the founder of the sect, the Teacher of Righteousness himself, though obviously there is no way to determine this.[52] Nevertheless, these hymns give us a precious window into the spiritual sensibility of the community.

The matter of interest to us here, obviously, is the way in which the poet draws on the models of the laments in the biblical Psalms and produces something fresh. I quote the hymn that Geza Vermes calls "hymn 9":[53]

I thank you, O Lord [Ps. 57:10 (9)],
  that you have not abandoned me while I sojourn among a (foreign?) people,

(and not) according to my guilt have you judged me,
nor have you abandoned me among the designs of my inclination,
but you have helped my life from the Pit [Jon. 2:7 (Protestant numeration
v. 6)],
and you have given (your servant deliverance)
in the midst of lions destined for the children of guilt [Ps. 57:5 (4)],
of lionesses that break the bones of the mighty [Isa. 38:13 and Dan. 6:25
(Protestant numeration v. 24)]
and drink the blood of the brave [compare Num. 23:24].
You have put me in sojourning (or, with a pun, "in terror") with many
fishermen,
who spread a net on the face of the waters,
and with the hunters of the children of iniquity [Jer. 16:16 and Isa. 19:8],
and there in justice you have established me.
And the counsel of truth you have confirmed in my heart,
and the waters of the covenant for those who seek it.
You have shut the mouths of the young lions [Dan. 6:23 (Protestant
numeration v. 22), cited also in Heb. 11:33],
whose teeth are like a sword,
and whose fangs are like a sharp spear [Pss. 57:5 (4) and 58:7 (6)];
like the poison of serpents [Deut. 32:33].
All their design is for robbery and they have lain in wait [Prov. 23:28],
but they have not opened wide their mouths at me [Ps. 22:14 (13), or Lam.
2:16; 3:46].
For you, my God, have sheltered me
in the presence of the children of men [Ps. 31:20-21 (19-20)],
and your Law you have hidden (in me
un)til the time when you reveal your salvation to me.
For in the distress of my soul you have not abandoned me,
and my cry you have heard [Ps. 40:2 (1)] in the bitterness of my soul [Job
3:20; 7:11; 10:1],
and you have considered my sorrow
and recognized my sighing.
You have saved the soul of the poor one [compare Jer. 20:13]
in the den of lionesses
who whet like a sword their tongues [Ps. 64:4 (3)].
You, my God, have closed up their teeth,
so that they do not tear the soul [Ps. 7:3 (2)] of the poor and needy one
[Ps. 82:3];
you again bring back their tongue like a sword into its sheath [Jer. 47:6],
so as not (to strike down) the soul of your servant [Ps. 86:4];
so that you show yourself strong in me
before the children of men [again Ps. 31:20 (19)],
you have shown yourself marvelous in the poor one.
You have brought him into the cru(cible
like gol)d in the works of fire,
and like silver refined in the smelters' furnace,
to be purified seven times [Prov. 27:21; Ps. 12:7 (6)].
And the wicked of the peoples have rushed against me with their torments,

and all the day they crushed my soul [compare Ps. 143:3].
But you, my God, turn the storm to quiet [Ps. 107:29; note that "their
       torments" (above) occurs in Ps. 107:28],
   and the soul of the poor you have freed,
like . . .
       prey from the power of the lionesses [compare Amos 3:12 and Ps. 22:22
       (21)].[54]

This hymn of thanksgiving, like the others in this collection, is not a lament:
the poet does not cry out to God for help but offers God thanks for divine help
already given. In this respect the poet is in a state of confidence before God.

I have noted in this hymn twenty-nine reminiscences of phrases of Scripture,
fifteen from the Psalms and fourteen from other material (two from the Pentateuch; six from Isaiah, Jeremiah, and Jonah, and six from books of the Writings—
Job, Proverbs, Lamentations, and Daniel). Perhaps not all of these references are
equally cogent, but doubtless a few other reminiscences might be added to the list.
Of the reminiscences noted from the Psalms, all but two are from laments; the
remaining two (Psalms 40 and 107) are from songs of thanksgiving. Particularly
striking are the two reminiscences of Ps. 57:5 (4), which reads, "I lie down among
lions that greedily devour human prey; their teeth are spears and arrows, their
tongues sharp swords"; one might almost say that this hymn of thanksgiving is a
meditation on this verse of Psalm 57.

Here, then, is a body of hymns whose writer had drunk deep from all the
poetry of Scripture, but most particularly from the Psalms. So even if the contents
and text of the book of Psalms were not altogether stabilized during the period of
time when the sect lived out its life, nevertheless the book of Psalms functioned as a
scriptural resource.

Summary

Now, let us summarize what we can learn from the scrolls of the Qumran
community, both those we have examined and others like them. The documents
of the Dead Sea community offer us our first opportunity to see the use a worshiping community made of the Psalter. The community made copies of the
Psalms, commented on the Psalms, and drew on phrases of the Psalms in fresh
works.

The copies of the Psalms give evidence that the community knew the 150
Psalms that are our Psalter, or almost all of them, and that in addition the community looked upon a handful of other psalms as having equal status, psalms that were
not finally accepted as part of the Hebrew canon (though three are found elsewhere, in the Greek or Syriac tradition). That there were more copies of the
Psalms in the Qumran library than of any other biblical book itself underlines
the importance of the Psalms for the community.

The commentary material at Qumran takes biblical material and applies it
directly to the experience of the community. This is true for their commentaries on
various prophetic books and the like, and it is true for the *Florilegium* and the

commentary on Psalm 37, which are of more immediate interest to us. The commentator takes a verse and says, for example, "This concerns the Wicked Priest, who tried to kill the Teacher of Righteousness." We in our day would be more content if the commentator had said, "We may apply this verse to the Wicked Priest and to the Teacher of Righteousness," but undoubtedly, given the mind-set of the community, the commentator believed that these words were given at the foundation of the world to apply specifically to the community's own experience. The community, after all, believed it was living in the climax of history and that its members were God's righteous remnant; the final separation of the wicked and the righteous would soon take place. That is, the Qumran community exhibited sharply the mentality of "us versus them" that was a part of the covenant community from the beginning (see chapter 4).

That mentality is strongest in the psalms of lament; and we have seen how deeply the *Thanksgiving Hymns* drew from those laments, in spite of the fact that, strikingly, the *Thanksgiving Hymns* do not lament the persecution the community endures from the wicked of the world but rather rejoice in God's ultimate victory over the wicked.

We have seen how the metaphor of "God the warrior" in Psalm 24 was applied to God's activity in the final battle. Curiously, however, although there was a doctrine of the return of both a kingly Messiah and a priestly Messiah at the end of the age, little use seems to have been made of what Christians have designated the "messianic" psalms, such as Psalms 2, 72, or 110. Psalm 2:1-2, we note, is explained as the persecution of the community by the wicked kings, but as far as I am aware there are no citations to Ps. 2:6 or to the body of Psalm 72 (only the closing benediction, vv. 18-19) or to any of Psalm 110. The explanation may be that the community had a strong priestly concern, with correspondingly little interest in the royal ideology as such.

The sect was deeply preoccupied with the Law of Moses; not only are there several references to Psalm 1 (such as in the *Community Rule* and the *Florilegium*) but many to Psalm 119—for example, the phrase "those whose way is blameless" (Ps. 119:1 and Prov. 11:20) occurs seven times in the *Community Rule* and three times elsewhere in the scrolls.[55] The first passage in the *Community Rule* states that the leader of the community is "to instruct the upright in the knowledge of the Most High and to teach the wisdom of the children of heaven [i.e., the angels] to those whose way is blameless."

Yet, if the general mentality of the sect was of the righteousness of its members and the wickedness of its enemies, the poet of the *Thanksgiving Hymns* was profoundly aware of the depth of sin and of the wonder of his creation by God. It is therefore appropriate to close this study of the use of the Psalms at the Dead Sea by quoting from a portion of another *Thanksgiving Hymn* that reflects the spirit of Psalm 51 and images of Psalm 139.[56] Noteworthy here is the play on the two meanings of *qāw*, namely, "measuring-cord" and "sound" (compare the diction of Ps. 19:5 [4] and the note there in the RSV and NRSV). According to the poet, God not only knows our words before they are on our tongues but has even created the rules of poetry.

And yet I, a shape of clay
  kneaded in water,
a counsel of shame
  and a source of pollution,
a melting-pot of wickedness
  and an edifice of sin,
a straying and perverted spirit
  of no understanding,
    fearful of righteous judgments,
what shall I speak that is not foreknown,
  what shall I announce that is not foretold?
All things are graven before you
  with a stylus of remembrance
    for all perpetual ages,
and for the numbered cycles of eternal years
  in all their seasons;
they are not hidden or absent
  from your presence.
How shall a man tell his sin,
  and how plead concerning his iniquities?
How shall an ungodly man reply
  to righteous judgment?
Yours, O God of knowledge,
  are all righteous deeds
  and counsel of truth;
but to the children of men is the work of iniquity
  and the deeds of deceit.
It is you who have created breath on the tongue
  and known its words;
you established the fruit of the lips
  before they ever were.
You have determined words with a measuring-cord,
  the spouting of breath from the lips with a gauge,
you bring forth sounds according to their mysteries,
  the spouting of breath according to its reckoning,
to make known your glory
  and recount your wonders,
in all your works of truth
  and your right(eous judgments),
and to praise your name
  by the mouths of all who know you,
according to their understanding
  they shall bless you for ever and ever.[57]

NOTES

1. Rowland E. Prothero, *The Psalms in Human Life* (London: Murray, 1913).
2. Ibid., 75.

3. Erwin R. Goodenough, *By Light, Light: The Mystic Gospel of Hellenistic Judaism* (New Haven: Yale University Press, 1935).

4. See, conveniently, John Bright, *A History of Israel* (Philadelphia: Westminster, 1981), 415–27.

5. Menahem Stern, "The Period of the Second Temple," in Haim Hillel Ben-Sasson (ed.), *A History of the Jewish People* (Cambridge: Harvard University Press, 1976), 213.

6. Ibid., 185–223.

7. For the Greek text, see, conveniently, Alfred Rahlfs, *Septuaginta id est Vetus Testamentum Graece* (Stuttgart: Privilegierte Württembergische Bibelanstalt, 1935), 2:471–89; for a translation and introduction, see Robert B. Wright, "Psalms of Solomon," in James H. Charlesworth (ed.), *The Old Testament Pseudepigrapha* (Garden City, N.Y.: Doubleday, 1983, 1985), 2:639–70.

8. Paul Winter, "Psalms of Solomon," in *IDB* 3:959; cf. Wright, "Psalms of Solomon," 642.

9. See, conveniently, John C. Trever, *The Dead Sea Scrolls: A Personal Account* (Grand Rapids: Eerdmans, 1977).

10. Now technically designated 1QIsa[a].

11. Designation: 1QpHab.

12. Designation: 1QS.

13. Designation: 1QM.

14. Desgination: 1QH.

15. Geza Vermes, *The Dead Sea Scrolls in English* (London: Penguin, 1987), xvii.

16. Ibid., 19–35.

17. For a full discussion, see Joseph A. Fitzmyer, *The Gospel according to Luke I–IX* (AB 28; Garden City, N.Y.: Doubleday, 1981), 388–89.

18. James A. Sanders, *The Dead Sea Psalms Scroll* (Ithaca, N.Y.: Cornell University Press, 1967), 9.

19. Ibid., 146–48.

20. Designation: 11QPs[a]. The most convenient study of the scroll is Sanders, *Dead Sea Psalms Scroll.*

21. Sanders, *Dead Sea Psalms Scroll,* 6.

22. For the text of the noncanonical material, see, conveniently, Vermes, *Dead Sea Scrolls in English,* 208–14.

23. Sanders, *Dead Sea Psalms Scroll,* 34–89, 160–65; see also 144–45; Joseph A. Fitzmyer, *The Dead Sea Scrolls: Major Publications and Tools for Study* (Sources for Biblical Study 8; Missoula, Mont.: Scholars Press, 1975), 37–38.

24. Designation: 4QPs[a].

25. Sanders, *Dead Sea Psalms Scroll,* 13–14.

26. Designation: 11QPs[b]; see J.P.M. van der Ploeg, "Fragments d'un manuscrit de psaumes de Qumran (11QPs[b])," *RB* 74 (1967): 408–13.

27. Ibid., 412.

28. Designation: 11QPsAp[a]; see J.P.M. van der Ploeg, "Le Psaume XCI dans une recension de Qumran," *RB* 72 (1965):210–17.

29. For a recent discussion of the question, see Eileen M. Schuller, *Non-canonical Psalms from Qumran: A Pseudepigraphic Collection* (HSS 28; Atlanta: Scholars Press, 1986), 9–13.

30. For this suggestion, see van der Ploeg, "Le Psaume XCI," 216; see also James L. Kugel, "Topics in the History of the Spirituality of the Psalms," in Arthur Green

(ed.), *Jewish Spirituality: From the Bible through the Middle Ages* (New York: Crossroad, 1988), 133. For a recent exploration of the whole problem, see Gerald H. Wilson, "The Qumran Psalms Scroll Reconsidered: Analysis of the Debate," *CBQ* 47 (1985):624–42.

31. Fragment E1; see Sanders, *Dead Sea Psalms Scroll*, 160–61.

32. Ibid., 156.

33. Ibid., 130–31.

34. Designation: 4QFlor, also called 4Q174; see, conveniently, Vermes, *Dead Sea Scrolls in English*, 293–94; George J. Brooke, *Exegesis at Qumran: 4QFlorilegium in Its Jewish Context* (JSOTSup 29; Sheffield: JSOT, 1985).

35. Parentheses enclose words restored by scholars at gaps in the manuscript.

36. "Belial" or "Beliar" is a designation of Satan; see 2 Cor. 6:15.

37. See, conveniently, Vermes, *Dead Sea Scrolls in English*, 293–94.

38. Designation: 11QMelch; see, conveniently, Vermes, *Dead Sea Scrolls in English*, 300–301; cf. Harold W. Attridge, *Hebrews* (Hermeneia; Philadelphia: Fortress, 1989), 192–93.

39. Vermes, *Dead Sea Scrolls in English*, 301.

40. Designation: 1QpPs 68, also called 1Q16. For a translation of the text (in French), see Jean Carmignac and Pierre Guilbert, *Les Textes de Qumran, traduits et annotés* (Paris: Letouzey et Ané, 1961–63), 2:128; see further Maurya P. Horgan, *Pesharim: Qumran Interpretations of Biblical Texts* (CBQMS 8; Washington, D.C.: Catholic Biblical Association of America, 1979), 65–70, and texts, 13–15.

41. Designation: 4QpPsᵃ, also called 4Q171; for a translation, see, conveniently, Vermes, *Dead Sea Scrolls in English*, 290–92; see further Horgan, *Pesharim*, and texts, 51–57.

42. 1QS.

43. 1QS VI.6–7.

44. 1QS VIII.1–4.

45. 1QM; 4QM.

46. See Vermes, *Dead Sea Scrolls in English*, 28–29.

47. 1QM III. 5–6; see Vermes, *Dead Sea Scrolls in English*, 107.

48. 1QM XII. 7–10; see Vermes, *Dead Sea Scrolls in English*, 117.

49. Designation: 4Q380 and 4Q381; see Schuller, *Non-canonical Psalms*.

50. Schuller, *Non-canonical Psalms*, 5–14, 21–25.

51. 1QH.

52. Vermes, *Dead Sea Scrolls in English*, 166.

53. 1QH V.5–19.

54. My trans., adapted from Vermes, *Dead Sea Scrolls in English*, 162–64, compared with the French translation of Carmignac and Guilbert, *Les Textes de Qumran*.

55. 1QS IV.22; VIII.10, 18, 21; IX.2, 5, 9; 1QSa (= 1Q28a) I.28; 1QM XIV.7.

56. 1QH I.21–31.

57. My trans., adapted from Vermes, *Dead Sea Scrolls in English*, 146–47, compared with the French translation of Carmignac and Guilbert, *Les Textes de Qumran*.

8

Texts for
the First Christians:
The Psalms in the New Testament

The New Testament and the Documents
from the Dead Sea

We turn now from what is, for most present-day readers, unfamiliar material—the literature of the Jewish sect at the Dead Sea—to what is, for most readers, eminently familiar territory—the new Christian Scriptures. Already in chapter 7 we noted the seeming parallel between the two bodies of literature, the chain of proof texts in the Qumran *Florilegium* and the chain of proof texts in the first two chapters of the Letter to the Hebrews, and one possible link between the Dead Sea community and the New Testament as well, the figure of John the Baptist. And we find further links between the two communities, for the Qumran community, founded by the Teacher of Righteousness, saw itself as the true remnant of Judaism, whereas the Christian community, founded by Jesus of Nazareth, saw itself in the beginning as the true Israel of God (Gal. 6:16).[1]

The Jews, 63 B.C.E. to 70 C.E.

The Hasmonean priest-kings continued to rule in Jerusalem, but the squabbles of their factions continued to involve Rome. As we have seen, in 63 B.C.E., during the reign of Hyrcanus II, the Roman general Pompey occupied Jerusalem and thereby integrated Palestine into the Roman Empire; but Rome continued to sponsor various rulers of the Hasmonean line. The last of this line, and the most powerful, was Herod the Great (37–4 B.C.E.), an Idumean (that is, an inhabitant of the territory of the old Edomites southeast of the Dead Sea) who came to power through his marriage to Hyrcanus's granddaughter Mariamne. Though Herod was a powerful king, who enlarged and beautified the temple in Jerusalem, he remained a vassal to the Roman emperor Augustus throughout his reign. It is this Herod to whom Matt. 2:1 refers.

When Herod died in 4 B.C.E., Palestine was divided among his three sons; one of them, Archelaus, was given control of Judea, Samaria, and Idumea. But in 6 C.E.

complaints were lodged against Archelaus, and he was banished. Thereafter, those three territories were incorporated directly into the Roman system and ruled by a Roman governor (procurator). Pontius Pilate was the procurator (26–36 C.E.) before whom Jesus was tried. In the meantime, Herod's son Antipas was tetrarch (ruler) over Galilee (in the far north) and Perea (a narrow strip in Transjordan, east of Jericho); this is the Herod mentioned in Luke 3:1, who beheaded John the Baptist (Mark 6:17-28). Herod Antipas died in 39 C.E. Another Herod, Herod Agrippa I, was tetrarch of Judea, Galilee, and Perea during the period 41–44 C.E.; this is the Herod mentioned in Acts 12:1-24. He was succeeded by Herod Agrippa II, the Agrippa mentioned in Acts 25:13—26:32.

Palestine was thus divided and ruled directly or indirectly by Rome, and Jewish patriots became more and more restless; the last straw was the violation of the temple treasury by the Roman procurator Gessius Florus in 66 C.E. The Jews revolted, first in Jerusalem and later throughout the country. The revolt lasted seven years. In the year 68 the Romans destroyed the Qumran community, and in 70 the Roman Titus, son of the emperor Vespasian, captured Jerusalem; for this victory the Arch of Titus was erected in Rome. Finally, the last outpost of Jews, Masada, fell to the Romans in 73. This is the historical situation in which the events of the life of Jesus of Nazareth and of the lives of his early followers were played out—events reflected in the New Testament.[2]

The Nature of
the New Testament Sources

The difficulties in reconstructing the historical realities behind the New Testament are well known; only an outline will be offered here.

Jesus' public ministry took place largely in Galilee; it ended in Jerusalem about 30 C.E. But the earliest Gospel (that of Mark) must be dated roughly forty years later, to 70 C.E. The writers of the Gospels of Matthew and Luke drew on Mark and also on a special Sayings Source (conventionally called "Q"); both Matthew and Luke are to be dated to about 85 C.E. In contrast to Matthew, Mark, and Luke (the so-called Synoptic Gospels), the Gospel of John offers a rather different tradition about Jesus; this Gospel may be dated to about 90 C.E. That is to say, all of the detailed written accounts of Jesus' words and actions date to from one or two generations after the events themselves.[3]

The earliest written material in the New Testament is actually Paul's letters; those cited here, the Letters to the Corinthians and to the Romans, were written in the last half of the 50s. These literary circumstances render it exceedingly difficult to determine how the historical Jesus may have used the Psalms—indeed, it makes it difficult even to set forth the data from the New Testament in any coherent way.

I begin with the narratives in the Synoptic Gospels that portray Jesus as citing Psalms; I then deal with passages in the Synoptics in which the evangelists themselves cite Psalms; thereafter, I shall examine citations of the Psalms in the Gospel of John; and then I shall try to summarize Jesus' use of the Psalms. Thereupon, I shall deal with the material in the Acts of the Apostles, the material in Paul's authentic letters, the material in the Letter to the Ephesians, and then the material in the Letter to the Hebrews.

Narratives That Portray Jesus and
His Disciples Using Psalms in Worship

I begin with a reference to the singing of psalms by Jesus and his disciples. At the end of the narrative of the last supper, Mark 14:26 states, "When they had sung the hymn, they went out to the Mount of Olives" (par. in Matt. 26:30). One assumes that the hymn referred to here is the Hallel, Psalms 113–118, sung in praise to God at the Passover meal (see chapter 9);[4] at least in the tradition recorded in Mark, Jesus and his disciples followed on that occasion the customary celebration of Passover.

And there is a similar note in Acts 4:24:

> After they [Peter and John] were released [from their arrest], they went to their friends and reported what the chief priests and the elders had said to them. And when they heard it, they lifted their voices together to God and said, "Sovereign Lord, who made the heaven and the earth, the sea, and everything in them [Ps. 146:6], it is you who said by the Holy Spirit through our ancestor David, your servant."

This is followed by a citation of Ps. 2:1-2 (see below, on the Acts of the Apostles).

Again, whether or not this scene is exact history, these details are precious reminders that the disciples had constant recourse to the Psalms in worship, just as did traditional, faithful Jews.[5] One also has references to Christians singing "psalms" in 1 Cor. 14:26 (NRSV, "a hymn"); Eph. 5:19; and Col. 3:16; but it is uncertain whether these passages refer to the psalms of the Old Testament or to freshly minted Christian "psalms" similar to the *Thanksgiving Hymns* of the Dead Sea sect, or to both.[6]

Citations of the Psalms in
the New Testament

By one count there are fifty-five citations of the Psalms in the New Testament,[7] counting parallels in the Gospels as individual items; and these are found in all sections of the New Testament.[8] There are thus roughly as many citations and reminiscences of the Psalms as of Isaiah (there are fewer of Isaiah—forty-seven— but Isaiah is a shorter book than the Psalms). These citations are of thirty-five psalms. Functionally, then, the Psalms are treated as Scripture, whatever their precise canonical status was in the various circles of the first-century church.

Jesus' Citations of the Psalms
in the Synoptic Narratives before Holy Week

I begin with narratives in which Jesus is said to have used the Psalms. The first, in the sequence of the Gospels, is from the so-called Q source (the Sayings Source behind Matthew and Luke but not Mark), in the narrative of the temptation in the wilderness; here, according to the testimony, it is not Jesus himself who uses the psalm but the devil! The devil is said to have quoted Ps. 91:11-12 as a temptation (Matt. 4:6; Luke 4:10-11), and Jesus replies by citing Deut. 6:16. This is an astonishing window into Jesus' understanding of Scripture, or at least into the tradition of the first-century church about Jesus' understanding of Scripture: there is a devilish use of Scripture as well as a godly one.[9] One is reminded of Jeremiah's use in Jer. 10:25 of Ps. 79:6-7 as a psalm that is *not* appropriate, in his time, to cite (see chapter 4).[10]

There are a handful of citations or reminiscences of the Psalms in Jesus' Sermon on the Mount. Thus Matt. 5:5—"Blessed are the meek, for they will inherit the earth"—is a reminiscence of Ps. 37:11—"the meek shall inherit the land" ("land" and "earth" represent the same word in Hebrew).[11]

Again, Matt. 5:34-35—"Do not swear at all, either by heaven, for it is the throne of God, or by the earth, for it is his footstool, or by Jerusalem, for it is the city of the great King"—combines Isa. 66:1—"Heaven is my throne and the earth is my footstool"—with Ps. 48:3 (2)—"Mount Zion, in the far north, the city of the great King."[12]

The parallel of Matt. 6:26—"Look at the birds of the air; they neither sow nor reap nor gather into barns, and yet your heavenly Father feeds them. Are you not of more value than they?"—in Luke 12:24—"Consider the ravens"—reminds one of Ps. 147:9—"He gives to the animals their food, and to the young ravens when they cry." It appears that Jesus used "ravens" and that Matthew has generalized the saying.[13]

And Jesus' word to those at the end time who say, "Lord, Lord," but do not do God's will—"Depart from me, you evildoers" (Matt. 7:23, compare Luke 13:27)—is taken from Ps. 6:9 (8)—"Depart from me, all you workers of evil."[14]

In each of the Synoptic Gospels, after the narrative of Peter's confession to Jesus at Caesarea Philippi, there is a discourse by Jesus on discipleship and cross-bearing. In Matthew's wording, Jesus says, "For the Son of Man is to come with his angels in the glory of his Father, and then he will repay everyone for what has been done" (Matt. 16:27). The last phrase, though seemingly commonplace, appears to be taken from Ps. 62:13 (12), "For you repay to all according to their work."

Citations of the Psalms
in the Synoptic Narratives of Holy Week

There is a particular cluster of citations of the Psalms in the narratives of the last week of Jesus' earthly ministry. One may conclude that those who gathered the traditions that came to form the Gospels were particularly concerned for the details of that last week, and that they were most particularly aware of anticipations in the Psalms that to them pointed to Jesus' suffering and death.

Various verses from Psalm 118 are cited at several points in these narratives. We first hear the psalm in the narrative of the triumphal entry into Jerusalem. The three Synoptic Gospels differ in the details of the words shouted by the crowd, but all of them derive material from Psalm 118: according to Mark, the onlookers shouted, "Hosanna! Blessed is he who comes in the name of the Lord! Blessed is the kingdom of our father David that is coming! Hosanna in the highest!" (Mark 11:9-10); Matthew shortens this to "Hosanna to the Son of David! Blessed is he who comes in the name of the Lord! Hosanna in the highest!" (Matt. 21:9); and according to Luke, they shouted, "Blessed is the king who comes in the name of the Lord! Peace in heaven, and glory in the highest!" (Luke 19:38). It is to be noted that Ps. 118:26a reads, "Blessed is he who comes in the name of the Lord." As to the word "hosanna," it is a rendering in Greek of the Hebrew expression *hôšî'â nnā'*, literally, "Save, please!"; it occurs in the first line of Ps. 118:25, but in the psalm verse the imperative "save, please" is addressed to Yahweh, whereas in Matthew the reference is "to the Son of David." As to the phrase of Ps. 118:26a, it will be noticed that Luke has inserted "the king" in the phrase, an insertion derived from the wording of Zech. 9:9. And the last part of the Lucan phrase appears to be a reiteration of Luke 2:14.

The evangelists all imply that Jesus accepted the identification of the figure in Ps. 118:26: one recalls that when Jesus is remembered as lamenting over Jerusalem, he apostrophizes to the city, "For I tell you, you will not see me again, until you say, 'Blessed is he who comes in the name of the Lord.'" (Matthew places that lament later in the week in Jerusalem [Matt. 23:39]; Luke places it earlier in Jesus' ministry [Luke 13:35].)[15]

According to the Gospel of Mark, Jesus cited two verses earlier in Psalm 118, namely, vv. 22-23, to close the parable of the vineyard, the telling of which is likewise during the last week in Jerusalem: "The stone that the builders rejected has become the cornerstone; this was the Lord's doing, and it is amazing in our eyes" (Mark 12:10-11; parallels in Matt. 21:42 and Luke 20:17).[16] This psalm passage, it is to be noted, is cited again in the New Testament—in Acts 4:11 in the course of a sermon of Peter's,[17] and again in 1 Peter 2:7.[18] Though it is clear that the details of Jesus' passion and later Christian thinking have reshaped some of the details of the parable of the vineyard, one may assume that Jesus intended the parable to refer to himself.[19]

Matthew adds a detail when Jesus was in the Jerusalem temple: as he was healing the sick, the children among the bystanders repeated the acclamation "Hosanna to the Son of David," whereupon the chief priests and scribes became indignant. Jesus then cited Ps. 8:3 (2), "Out of the mouths of infants and nursing babies you have prepared praise for yourself" (Matt. 21:16). This scene is doubtless an elaboration by Matthew.[20]

The Use of Psalm 110 in the New Testament:
Its Presumed Use by Jesus

The narrative of Jesus' use of Ps. 110:1, again during the last week of his ministry, is far from transparent in meaning. This verse, as it happens, is cited several times in the New Testament; it was an important text for Christians.[21] Thus Peter is reported to have used the verse in his Pentecost sermon (Acts 2:34-35), and the verse is cited in the chain of quotations at the beginning of the Letter to the Hebrews (Heb. 1:13). (Psalm 110:1 is also alluded to in 1 Cor. 15:25: see below.) But Jesus' use of the verse is remarkable: he uses it to make a teaching point, according to Mark 12:35-37 (with pars. in Matt. 22:41-46 and Luke 20:41-44).[22]

I established in chapter 2 that the first verse of this psalm originally implied that a prophet addressed the king with an oracle from God. But by the time of the New Testament, as we have seen, everyone believed that David was the author of all the Psalms. Now, the use of Ps. 110:1 in Acts 2:34-35 and Heb. 1:13 is identical.[23] The passage in Acts narrates Peter's sermon at Pentecost, and in that sermon he cites Pss. 16:8-11 and 132:11 and then the verse in question, to demonstrate that David predicted that Jesus was raised from the dead and that God made him both Lord and Christ. And in Hebrews 1 the writer is affirming that Christ is superior to the angels. Both passages, then, assume that the psalmist (David) refers to Jesus when he says "my lord."

But in the Synoptic Gospels, Jesus is reported to be doing something different with the psalm verse: he is rejecting the doctrine of the scribes and Pharisees about the identity of the Messiah. He takes it for granted in the psalm that David is speaking and addressing the Messiah, who will rule at the end of the age. But, Jesus reasons, David would not call any "son" of his "my lord." Therefore, by this reasoning, one cannot equate "Messiah" and "Son of David."

Now, it is far from clear what is going on here. It is altogether likely that, at least on one level, this unit in the Synoptic Gospels reflects a dispute between factions of the New Testament church over the "correct" title for Jesus—whether "Son of David" or "Messiah." Indeed some scholars believe that the narrative was simply formulated by the community.[24] However, since the Dead Sea community, so far as we know, did not use Psalm 110 in its speculation about the Messiah (nor indeed does any other Jewish source of the time known to us),[25] and because it was a central proof text in the New Testament and thereafter, it is altogether likely that Jesus, after all, began the process, offering some kind of teaching about the psalm. Sorting all this out, however, is difficult.

If the Synoptic Gospels preserve the historical memory of a saying of Jesus, is there any way for us to grasp the point that Jesus was trying to make? Jesus appears to deny the identity of Messiah and Son of David. But all Jews assumed, from Old Testament texts, that the Messiah would be a son of David (to stay only with prophetic texts: Isa. 9:1-6 [Protestant numeration 2-7]; 11:1-9; Jer. 23:5-6; Ezek. 34:23-24; 37:24),[26] and there is no evidence within the Gospels that Jesus was ever challenged by his opponents for denying such a basic belief. Therefore, if he is said to have denied the identity of the Messiah and the Son of David, he must have been saying something about himself. Conceivably he could be saying, "I am the Messiah but I am not the Son of David." But both Matthew and Luke include the narrative, and at the same time both these evangelists affirm Jesus' descent from David (Matt. 1:1-17; Luke 3:23-31), so at least in the minds of these evangelists this cannot be the point of Jesus' word. Further, in Mark 10:46-52 blind Bartimaeus calls Jesus "Son of David" and Jesus does not deny it.

So if Jesus acknowledged himself to be descended from David, he might in this incident be denying himself messianic status or, while accepting messianic status, raising the issue of the kind of Messiah he was. Mark, for his part, presents Jesus as accepting messiahship but telling the disciples to keep it a secret (Mark 8:27-30); indeed, Mark uses the notion of the "messianic secret" as an organizing principle.[27] The incident of Jesus' use of Psalm 110, then, at least in Mark, could be an effort of the evangelist to portray Jesus as half concealing and half revealing the messianic secret;[28] Matthew and Luke then would have taken the incident over from Mark.

But if Jesus himself used the psalm in some way, and if his use was to some degree ironic or allusive, what might he have intended? Was it to suggest that he, the Messiah, was not a royal figure at all, as the scribes and Pharisees might have thought, but a Messiah of a very different sort, a poor outcast with a supernatural origin?[29] Was it to suggest that David could indeed call the Messiah "Lord," even if he is David's son, because he is also God's Son?[30] It is impossible to be certain.[31]

A Reminiscence of the Psalms
in the Narrative of the Last Supper

In Mark 14:18, in the narrative of the last supper, Jesus said, "Truly I tell you, one of you will betray me, one who is eating with me"; this wording suggests Ps. 41:10 (9), "Even my bosom friend in whom I trusted, who ate of my bread, has lifted the heel against me." The wording in Mark three verses later (v. 21)—"For the Son of Man goes as it is written of him"—suggests that Mark had Scripture in his mind, and this citation is made explicit in John 13:18 (see below).[32]

Psalm 22 from the Cross

The Gospels record two utterances by Jesus from the cross that are citations of psalms. One is the cry of dereliction, "My God, my God, why have you forsaken me?" (Ps. 22:2 [1]), cited in Mark 15:34 and Matt. 27:46.[33] Scholars have assumed that the tradition of this recitation is historical, for it appears to cut across the Christian conviction that Jesus Christ is the very incarnation of God.[34]

More recent investigation, however, suggests that the lament psalms were a primary tool in the early church for theological interpretation of the passion narrative.[35] It is noteworthy that this particular psalm became a resource for the evangelists in supplying details for the crucifixion story. Thus Mark 15:24 and parallels recall Ps. 22:19 (18), a reminiscence made explicit in John 19:24.[36] And Matt. 27:43 recalls Ps. 22:9 (8).[37] Beyond the Gospels, the Letter to the Hebrews also understands the psalm to be spoken by Jesus: Heb. 2:12 cites Ps. 22:23 (22).[38]

A Second Psalm Citation from the Cross

The Gospel of Luke testifies to another utterance from the cross: "Father, into your hands I commend my spirit" (Luke 23:46). This wording is taken from Ps. 31:6 (5).[39] One assumes that it is a touch that originated with the evangelist.[40]

The Synoptic Evangelists' Use
of the Psalms

Beyond the evangelists' testimony of Jesus' use of the Psalms are instances in which the evangelists themselves use verses from the Psalms in their narration.

Thus, in the narrative of the baptism of Jesus in Mark 1:11 (and parallels in Matt. 3:17 and Luke 3:22), a voice from heaven was heard to say, "You are my Son, the Beloved; with you I am well pleased," a citation of Ps. 2:7.[41]

Again, in Matt. 13:35 the evangelist explains Jesus' teaching in parables this way: "This was to fulfill what had been spoken through the prophet: 'I will open my mouth to speak in parables; I will proclaim what has been hidden from the foundation of the world.'" This is a citation of Ps. 78:2, "I will open my mouth in a parable; I will utter dark sayings from of old."[42] Now, in contrast to the voice from heaven, repeated in all three Synoptic Gospels, this explanation of parables by Matthew has no parallels in the other Synoptic Gospels and is doubtless a secondary touch by Matthew.[43]

Citations from the Psalms in the Gospel of John

I now turn to the Gospel of John. This Gospel offers further instances in which Jesus is said to have cited psalms. Thus John 6:31 has Jesus say, "As it is written, 'He gave them bread from heaven to eat'"; this is a conflation of the lines of Ps. 78:24, "He rained down on them manna to eat, and gave them the grain of heaven."[44] John 10:34 has Jesus cite Ps. 82:6: "I said, 'You are gods.'" In the original intention of the psalm, the high God confronts the pagan gods (see chapter 2), whereas in John the reasoning is, if God addressed his audience (to whom the Word of God came) as "gods," then how much more may Jesus himself, whom God sent, be addressed as "Son of God."[45] In John 13:18, in the narrative of the last supper, Jesus says, "It is to fulfill the scripture, 'The one who ate my bread has lifted his heel against me'"; this is a citation of Ps. 41:10 (9), "Even my bosom friend in whom I trusted, who ate of my bread, has lifted the heel against me" (for this citation compare Mark 14:18, already discussed[46]—it is possible that John is here dependent on Mark).[47]

And in Jesus' farewell discourse, John 15:25, he says, "It was to fulfill the word that is written in their law, 'They hated me without a cause.'" This is a reference to two Psalms passages: Ps. 35:19, where God will not give joy to "those who have hated me without cause"; and Ps. 69:5 (4), "More in number than the hairs of my head are those who hate me without cause."[48] In these two passages in the Gospel of John, then, the evangelist testifies that Jesus, in the course of the last supper discourse, used verses from the laments to apply to himself.

As a postscript, one could add John 2:17: when Jesus drove the money changers out of the temple, "his disciples remembered that it was written, 'Zeal for your house will consume me'"—a citation of Ps. 69:10 (9), "It is zeal for your house that has consumed me." Here the citation is doubtless an editorial comment of the evangelist.[49]

Jesus' Use of the Psalms: Summary

Can we reach any conclusions about Jesus' use of the Psalms? It is clear that he drew on verses of the Psalms (as he drew from the Prophets and from other material in the Jewish Scriptures) to clarify his identity and mission, but it is difficult to be more specific. Let me make one simple observation, however: although he made use of at least one of the psalms of lament (Ps. 22:2 [1])—perhaps more (Ps. 62:13 [12])—astonishingly, he does not take on any of the spirit of "us against them" with which those psalms are filled (see chapter 4). In his teaching Jesus affirms the existence of good people and bad people, but the separation of the two categories will be made by God at the end of the age; this is the point of the parable of the weeds in the wheat (Matt. 13:24-30), and it is the point of the saying, "I tell you, on that night there will be two in one bed; one will be taken and the other left; there will be two women grinding meal together; one will be taken and the other left" (Luke 17:34-35). Indeed it is the point of the teaching about not judging (Matt. 7:1-2; Luke 6:37), for in the present age God makes his sun rise on the evil and on the good and sends rain on the righteous and on the unrighteous (Matt. 5:45; Luke 6:35). Jesus accepts that stance in his own conduct, and he urges his disciples to do the same (Matt. 5:46-48; Luke 6:36); compare the use of the psalms of lament in the *Thanksgiving Hymns* at the Dead Sea (see chapter 7).

The Canticles in Luke

It is also to be observed that, in the nativity narratives of Luke 1–2, the evangelist preserves several canticles, notably the "Magnificat" of Mary in 1:46-55, the "Benedictus" of Zechariah in 1:68-79, and the "Nunc Dimittis" of Simeon in 2:29-32. These canticles strongly resemble the *Thanksgiving Hymns* of the Dead Sea sect and thus were shaped by the models of the Psalms, as the *Thanksgiving Hymns* were.[50] For example, with Luke 1:50—"His mercy is for those who fear him from generation to generation"—compare Ps. 103:17a—"The steadfast love of the Lord is from everlasting to everlasting on those who fear him."

Citations to the Psalms in the
Narratives in Acts

I turn now to the Acts of the Apostles. In the first chapter, in the narrative of the replacement of Judas, we have two citations from the Psalms (Acts 1:20). The first is intended as the expression of a curse on Judas: "Let his homestead become desolate, and let there be no one to live in it." This is an adaptation of Ps. 69:26 (25), part of a sequence of curses in a psalm of lament at the attacks of personal enemies; the plural reference to enemies has been shifted to singular to fit Judas alone. This is followed by the second citation, "Let another take his position of overseer," an adaptation of Ps. 109:8; Psalm 109, again, has a sequence of curses, and the verse in question takes advantage of the Septuagint translation of the Hebrew expression for his "position" (*episkopē*), since for New Testament Christians it suggests a church office.[51]

I have already mentioned Peter's Pentecost sermon (Acts 2:25-35) in my discussion of Jesus' use of Ps. 110:1. In that sermon he is remembered as having cited Pss. 16:8-11; 132:11; and 110:1.

And I have already mentioned the citations in Acts 4:11, 24-26. In that chapter Peter and John are arrested by the Jewish authorities and then released. In his address to the authorities, Peter adapted Ps. 118:22: "This Jesus is 'the stone that was rejected by you, the builders; it has become the cornerstone.' " And after they were released from their arrest, Peter and John are said to have adapted the beginning of Ps. 146:6 as an invocation and then cited Ps. 2:1-2: "Why did the Gentiles rage, and the peoples imagine vain things? The kings of the earth took their stand, and the rulers have gathered together against the Lord and his Messiah." In this narrative the psalm verses serve both as worship and as testimony. The term "Anointed" (or "Messiah") in Ps. 2:2 is, of course, understood as a reference to Jesus Christ, and the verses are used to explain how "both Herod and Pontius Pilate, with the Gentiles and the peoples of Israel, gathered together against" Jesus (Acts 4:27).

Later in Acts, Paul, in a sermon in Antioch of Pisidia, cites Ps. 2:7; Isa. 55:3; and Ps. 16:10 to demonstrate that Jesus Christ is raised from the dead and suffers corruption no more (Acts 13:33-35).[52]

These citations in Acts show how passages from the Psalms came to the minds and lips of the earliest Christian preachers: they drew from old psalms of cursing in connection with the loss of Judas; and they drew from the royal psalms—Psalms 2 and 110—and from a psalm of trust in which the poet affirms that he will not suffer death, Psalm 16 (as well as, of course, from other Scripture, particularly the prophets), to tell the story of Jesus Christ.

Citations in the Letters to the Corinthians

I now turn to Paul's letters.[53] In Paul's Corinthian correspondence there are four passages offering citations from the Psalms. Three of them are grace notes to his discourse rather than being central to his argument. In 1 Cor. 3:20 he cites Ps. 94:11—"The Lord knows the thoughts of the wise, that they are futile";[54] in 2 Cor. 4:13 he cites Ps. 116:10—"I believed, and so I spoke";[55] and in 2 Cor. 9:9 he cites Ps. 112:9—"He scatters abroad, he gives to the poor; his righteousness endures forever."[56]

But more substantially, in 1 Cor. 15:25, "For he must reign until he has put all his enemies under his feet," he alludes to Ps. 110:1, and in v. 27 he specifically cites Ps. 8:7 (6), "For he [God] has put all things in subjection under his feet." Paul asserts that "his feet" are Christ's feet, an interpretation reinforced by the occurrence of "son of man" two verses earlier in Psalm 8; for this term was, of course, understood by Christians to be a title of Jesus Christ (this is also the argumentation of Heb. 2:6-9, for which see below).[57]

Citations in the Letter to the Romans

It is in his Letter to the Romans, however, that Paul offers a whole series of citations of the Psalms, more than a dozen of them, which are central to his theological discourse.

In Romans 3:4, Paul alludes to Ps. 116:11 and then cites Ps. 51:6 (4); interestingly, the latter is a verse where the Septuagint translation diverges from the traditional Hebrew text, and, as we noted in chapter 6, Paul, having grown up in the world of Greek-speaking Jews, cites the Septuagint. The Hebrew of the second half of 51:6 (4) says, literally, "so that you are justified in your word (of sentencing) and blameless when you judge"; the Septuagint, however, has "that you may be justified in your words and might overcome when you are judged." But the contrast makes no real difference to Paul's argument, which is that God is just even when human beings are unjust.[58]

Then, in Rom. 3:10-18, we have a whole cascade of citations, all but one from the Psalms: vv. 10-12 are an adaptation of Pss. 14:1-3 and 53:2-4 (1-3), which are virtually identical (see chapter 6); v. 13a is Ps. 5:10b (9b) and v. 13b is Ps. 140:4b (3b); v. 14 is Ps. 10:7a; vv. 15-17 are Isa. 59:7-8; and v. 18 is Ps. 36:2b (1b). All these citations from the Psalms are descriptions of the wicked in laments; Paul uses these phrases to describe all men, all under the power of sin, both Jews and Greeks.[59]

In Rom. 4:7-8, Paul cites Ps. 32:1-2. This is a psalm of thanksgiving for healing, but given the connection in the Psalms between sickness and sin, the psalmist in the first two verses says, "Happy are those whose transgression is forgiven, whose sin is covered. Happy are those to whom the Lord imputes no iniquity, and in whose spirit there is no deceit"; and it is these verses that Paul cites to describe the person whose faith accepts God's gift of forgiveness.[60]

Paul cites Ps. 44:23 (22) in Rom. 8:36. The psalm is a prayer for deliverance from national enemies, and the verse in question describes the perilous state of the covenant people: "Because of you we are being killed all day long, and accounted as sheep for the slaughter." Paul uses these words to describe the difficulties and dangers faced by Christians.[61]

In Rom. 10:18, Paul quotes Ps. 19:5 (4): "Their voice goes out through all the earth, and their words to the end of the world." In its original context the verse described the handiwork of God in the heavens ("The heavens are telling the glory of God"); Paul uses the verse to describe the spread of the gospel to all the world.[62]

In Rom. 11:9-10, Paul reverts once more to the issue of those within Israel who have rejected the gospel; they were hardened, he maintains, and he uses a sequence of curses from Ps. 69:23-24 (22-23) to apply to them: for example, "Let their eyes be darkened so that they cannot see."[63]

In Rom. 15:3, Paul cites a verse earlier in Psalm 69, namely, v. 10 (9). In that verse the psalmist is addressing God—"The insults of those who insult you have fallen on me"—and Paul assumes the verse to be on the lips of Jesus, an expression of the self-abasement of Christ.[64] Finally, in Rom. 15:9 and 11, Paul quotes two hymnic verses, Pss. 18:50 (49)—"For this I will extol you, O Lord, among the nations, and sing praises to your name"—and 117:1—"Praise the Lord, all you nations! Extol him, all you peoples!"[65]

Paul thus takes the diction of the psalms of lament but uses that diction within his own theological framework: the descriptions of the wicked are used for those who have not accepted the gospel (Rom. 3:10-18; 11:9-10), and the descriptions of the suffering of the innocent are used for the suffering of Christians in the present age (Rom. 8:36) and of Jesus Christ himself (Rom. 15:3)—not, note well, specifically for Paul's own sufferings. He also sees the spreading of the gospel among the Gentiles as an activity appropriately described in terms of God's heavenly handiwork (Rom. 10:18), an activity worthy of hymnic thanksgiving (Rom. 15:9, 11).

A Citation in the Letter to
the Ephesians

There is a single quotation from the Psalms in the Letter to the Ephesians, a letter judged by most scholars to have been drafted by a disciple of Paul:[66] in Eph. 4:8 there is a quotation from Ps. 68:19a (18a). The Hebrew wording of this psalm is far from clear. The half-verse addresses God and refers to a divine victory; it seems to mean, "You ascended the high mount [Sinai?], you made captives, you took gifts among human beings" (or, conceivably, "you took gifts from their hands"). The Septuagint has taken this somewhat opaque text and translated, similarly, "You have gone up on high, you led captivity captive, you have taken gifts in human beings." The author of Ephesians has shifted "you" to "he" and "take" to "give": "When he ascended on high he made captivity itself a captive; he gave gifts to his people." Some of the manuscripts of the Septuagint have accommodated their translation to this reading in Ephesians. The author takes the subject of the verbs to be not God but Jesus Christ, and he derives a whole scenario of Christ's work from this rendering (Eph. 4:9-10).[67]

Citations in the Letter to
the Hebrews

Finally, the Letter to the Hebrews is particularly heavy with Old Testament citations, all of which are cited in the form in which the Septuagint gives them. The contrast in some instances between the Septuagint and the traditional Hebrew text causes difficulties (see below).

The author of the Letter to the Hebrews draws particularly from the Psalms[68]—there are citations from eleven psalms all told. Indeed, as we noticed in chapter 7, the first two chapters of Hebrews offer a chain of nine quotations, passages cited to demonstrate the superiority of Christ over the angels.[69] Thus Heb. 1:5 cites Ps. 2:7 and 2 Sam. 7:14; Heb. 1:6 cites a phrase from Ps. 97:7; Heb. 1:7 cites Ps. 104:4 (see below); Heb. 1:8-9 cites Ps. 45:7-8 (6-7); Heb. 1:10-12 cites Ps. 102:26-28 (25-27); Heb. 1:13 cites Ps. 110:1; Heb. 2:6-8 cites Ps. 8:5-7 (4-6); and Heb. 2:12 cites Ps. 22:23 (22).[70]

Let us pause to get our bearings. In three of the citations in the first two chapters the author uses the verses in ways that strike present-day readers as appropriate, given the theological stance of the New Testament. Thus two of the psalms cited are royal psalms, probably composed for coronations (Psalms 2 and 110); both of the verses cited are ones in which God addresses the king (Pss. 2:7; 110:1), so the author of Hebrews understands God to be addressing Jesus Christ. Again, Psalm 22 is a psalm remembered as having been uttered by Jesus on the cross, and the psalm was heavily used in the narrative of the passion; so here the author cites v. 23 (22), "I will proclaim your name to my brothers," as being spoken by Jesus.

But the use the author makes of the other five citations is likely to strike us as arbitrary. Three of them depend on the occurrence of the word "angels" in the Septuagint (Pss. 8:6 [5]; 97:7; 104:4). In the first two of these, the word in Hebrew is *'ĕlōhîm*, which means either "God" or "gods." In Ps. 8:6 (5) the line is ambiguous in Hebrew, either "You have made the human being a little less than God" or "You have made the human being a little less than the gods" (see NRSV and footnote at the verse). In Ps. 97:7, however, *'ĕlōhîm* takes a plural verb and so must mean "gods"; the context is of idols and their worshipers. But in the period of the Septuagint translation, it is understandable that an expression such as "gods" would be softened, and in both passages the translation is "angels." In Ps. 104:4 the situation is still different: the Hebrew says *mal'ākîm* (messengers, whether human or divine), so that the Greek translation *angeloi* (messengers, whether human or divine) is precise, and the assumption of "angels" is justified.

Psalm 45:7 (6) is a citation that offers a more complex problem than the first three but is a splendid example of shifts in perception as one moves from one language to another. Psalm 45 is, as we saw in chapter 3, a song for a royal wedding; as such, the singer addresses vv. 3-10 (2-9) to the king himself. The seeming exception, and a glaring one, is v. 7a (6a): the Hebrew line consists of three expressions that seem to mean, in sequence, "your throne," "God," and "forever and ever." By the normal understanding of Hebrew grammar, these can be construed to mean either "your throne, O God, is forever and ever" or "your throne is God forever and ever." The first interpretation is highly unlikely in this context: the king is hardly to be addressed as "God," given the traditional theology of Israel. And the second is equally unlikely: if the king is being addressed, the metaphor of his being enthroned on God is dubious.

The solution is easily at hand, first suggested, I believe, by Mitchell Dahood: the Hebrew word *kis'ăkā* should be understood not as "your throne" but as a verb, "has enthroned you."[71] This verb is otherwise unattested in the Old Testament but would be built according to well-known Hebrew patterns. We would then translate "God has enthroned you forever and ever," and the line would be parallel to v. 3b (2b)—"Therefore God has blessed you forever"—and to v. 8b (7b)—"Therefore God, your God, has anointed you." If that is the solution to the original meaning of the verse, the knowledge of the existence of a verb "to enthrone" was lost on later generations, and the Septuagint did the best it could—"Your throne, O God, is forever and ever"—allowing the author of the Letter to the Hebrews to use the line to refer to Jesus Christ as God incarnate. (I discuss this verse again in chapter 17.)

Finally, Ps. 102:26-28 (25-27) is a sequence of hymnic verses (in the context of the whole psalm they conclude the lament of a sick person). In the Septuagint the first line reads, "In the beginning, you, O Lord, laid the foundations of the earth"; though the traditional Hebrew text lacks "O Lord," the expression is not alien to the context. The author of the Letter to the Hebrews has taken the vocative "O Lord" as an address to Jesus Christ.

Beyond the first two chapters of the letter, we have Heb. 3:7—4:11, which is exhortation. In Heb. 3:7-11 the author cites Ps. 95:7b-11; then Heb. 3:15 and 4:7 repeat Ps. 95:7b-8a, and Heb. 4:3 and 5 repeat Ps. 95:11.[72] Psalm 95:7b-11 is itself an admonition not to repeat the mistakes of Israel in the wilderness but to be obedient to God, and this admonitory passage is taken over by the author in his address to fellow Christians without any theological shift.[73]

Then in Heb. 5:5 the author once more cites Ps. 2:7—"You are my Son, today I have begotten you"—as he did in 1:5; and in 5:6 and in 7:17 and 21 he cites Ps. 110:4: "You are a priest forever, according to the order of Melchizedek."[74]

Now, Psalm 110 is very old (see chapter 2). Whatever the original meaning of v. 4, at least by the time of the Septuagint the verse was understood to be a reference to the Melchizedek of Gen. 14:18-20; and we have seen the speculation in the Dead Sea sect on the figure of Melchizedek. In Heb. 7:17 and 21 the author gives his own interpretation, that Jesus Christ is the priest in the pattern of Melchizedek.[75]

In Heb. 10:5-7 the author cites Ps. 40:7-9 (6-8);[76] the wording of the Septuagint, which the author uses, differs at several points from the original Hebrew, and the author rearranges and shortens the Septuagint at the end of the citation, but the details are not important for our consideration here. Psalm 40:2-12 (1-11) is a prayer of thanksgiving for healing; we examined this half-psalm in chapter 5, in particular the statement in vv. 7-9 (6-8) that God does not require sacrifice and offering. That statement and the statement that follows ("Lo, I am coming to do your will") are taken by the author as statements of Jesus, that he abolishes animal sacrifice in order to do God's will (10:9).[77]

Finally, in Heb. 13:6 the author cites Ps. 118:6, a thanksgiving for deliverance. He offers the verse as something that both he and his audience can affirm: "The Lord is my helper, I will not be afraid; what can anyone do to me?"[78]

"Hallelujah" in Revelation 19

In Rev. 19:1, 3, 4, and 6 there appears the expression "Hallelujah" in the midst of words of joy of the heavenly host. Here this expression, found in certain psalms (see chapter 6), has been taken over into the language of Christian worship. As we see in chapter 10, its use would be greatly expanded in the elaboration of Christian worship in later centuries.

Shifts Made in the Meaning
of Psalm Verses by the New Testament

We have seen how the use of some of the citations in the Letter to the Hebrews appears somewhat arbitrary, the writer having taken the intention of the wording some distance from that of the original psalmists. But this kind of shifting needs to be seen in the larger context of the use of the Psalms (and of other Old Testament Scripture) by the New Testament as a whole, and, indeed, by the Jewish authorities in this period. I discuss the theological issues raised by this shifting at several points later in this study, especially in chapter 19, but we must ponder some historical issues here.

The first observation to be made is that there are many resemblances between the way the Dead Sea sect used the Psalms and the way the New Testament writers used the Psalms. I have noted this already. Both communities took the Psalms (and other Old Testament material) and applied them directly and immediately to their own stories. The Dead Sea sect could say, "This passage applies to the Teacher of Righteousness," and Christians could say, "That passage applies to Jesus Christ." Indeed this is clearly what generations of Jews had done before this time: wherever the texts were considered authoritative, they were used to shape and to highlight the experience of the worshipers who used the texts. Our notion of historical investigation, our wish to answer the question "What did the text mean to its original author?" was never possible for them.

In particular, both the Dead Sea community and the New Testament Christian writers were convinced that they were living at the end of the present age, and that the age to come would soon dawn. Scripture, then, for both communities, offered clues to the reality of God's breaking in on their lives at their present point of history.

However, there are contrasts between the way the Dead Sea sect used the Psalms and the way the New Testament used them. It is clear that the speaker or writer in the New Testament usually did not have written texts at hand from which to cite a passage; the narrative in Luke 4:16-30 of Jesus' appearance in the synagogue at Nazareth, when he *read* from the scroll of Isaiah and applied the passage to himself, is a great exception. Normally we must assume that the writer was quoting from memory.[79] This activity differs from that of the Dead Sea sect. The material from the Dead Sea is scribal, the work of commentators dealing with written texts before them, whereas to a greater or lesser degree the New Testament writers were preachers and catechists whose use of Old Testament texts was much less systematic.

This leads us to a crucial question, and one unfortunately not susceptible to simple answers: How do these texts from the Psalms function for the New Testament writers? Are they really proof texts, texts used to prove a theological point? Or are they ornaments, citations that lend depth to the discourse; or something in between? Does the discourse depend crucially on the citations, or could the discourse dispense with them altogether? Clearly, each instance of a citation stands somewhere on a spectrum of possible answers. Jesus' citations appear to be crucial to his discourse: one cannot have the narrative of the temptations in the wilderness or his discourse on Ps. 110:1 without the citations. Indeed one might almost say that the Psalms text shapes Jesus' understanding of the truth as much as the text fortifies or undergirds his understanding of the truth. By contrast, the writer of the Letter to the Ephesians does not need Ps. 68:19 (18). God gives gifts, and Paul can detail the gifts in 1 Corinthians 12; a verse from a psalm, whether quoted accurately or inaccurately, is not necessary for the affirmation. And the various writers in the New Testament differ in the extent to which they depend on citations. For example, Matthew cites the Old Testament far more than Luke does, but Luke's Gospel does not suffer by the relative lack of citations.

Another contrast between the New Testament use of the Psalms and that of the Dead Sea sect is a function of the place of the communities' respective belief systems within Judaism. The Dead Sea sect remained within Judaism and doubtless would have continued to remain within Judaism, if it had been allowed to survive; by contrast, the New Testament community seems to have been clearly destined to move out of its Jewish context, even if the apostle Paul had not come on the scene. As far as the Dead Sea sect is concerned, it is noteworthy that there was a discovery in the eighth century of the Christian era of what were evidently some of the Dead Sea Scrolls, a discovery that stimulated a Jewish sect called the Karaites—if indeed the discovery of these scrolls did not actually precipitate the formation of that sect.[80] But the Karaites continued to remain within the context of Judaism (I shall discuss the Karaites in chapter 9). By contrast, two factors predisposed the New Testament community to move out of its Jewish context. The first was its proclamation of the resurrection of Jesus and his messiahship, and in general its conviction that the new age in some sense had begun. The other was the movement of the faith into Samaritan and Greek-speaking areas under the leadership of Peter, Philip, Barnabas, and others, even before Paul's mission to the Gentiles was underway (Acts 8, 10–11). It is instructive in this regard to compare another messianic movement that emerged in Judaism in the seventeenth century, that of Sabbatai Ṣevi, which originated in the Near East and spread to Europe. Though this movement did not seek gentile converts, its messianism and its unorthodox attitude toward Jewish festivals and laws aroused the consistent opposition of the Jewish authorities.[81]

Thus, inasmuch as the Christian faith offered a more drastic transmutation of the Old Testament faith than did the beliefs of the Dead Sea sect, the Christian interpretations of passages from the Psalms were inevitably more of a transmutation than was the case with the sectarians at the Dead Sea.

It is important, however, to observe that the writers of the New Testament were not altogether arbitrary in their interpretation of texts from the Old Testament. By tradition, the great Jewish teacher Hillel (first century B.C.E.) had formulated seven logical rules for drawing meaning out of Scripture, and one can trace some of the same patterns of logic in the New Testament interpretations. For example, rule 1 was called "light and heavy," that is, deriving a "heavy" conclusion from a "light" premise, typified by the expression "how much more." Thus the ravens neither sow nor reap, and God feeds them (Ps. 147:9)—of how much more value are you (Luke 12:24); if the Scripture calls "gods" those whom God addressed (Ps. 82:6), how much more may he whom God sent into the world be called "son of God" (John 10:34-36). Rule 4 was called "building a father from two passages," that is, a general principle established on the basis of a teaching contained in two texts. Thus the uncircumcised Abraham (Gen. 15:6) and the circumcised David (Ps. 32:1-2) establish the general principle that the righteousness of God is graciously given to the circumcised Jew and to the uncircumcised Gentile apart from works (Romans 4).[82]

Beyond these rules of exegesis, the New Testament writers took for granted that verses from the Psalms (and, indeed, all of Scripture) may be open to midrashic interpretation: that is, that verses may be adapted to the present to instruct or edify current readers. The New Testament writers could apply the Psalm verse to some aspect of Jesus' life and ministry: they began with Jesus and the messianic events associated with him and then used the Psalm verse to explain or illuminate those events. Thus, in Acts 4:11, Peter shifts Ps. 118:22—"The stone that the builders rejected has become the chief cornerstone"—so as to accuse the Jewish authorities—"This Jesus is 'the stone that was rejected by you, the builders; it has become the cornerstone.'"

The New Testament interpretation takes for granted that Old Testament notions may prefigure Christian realities—thus Psalm 8, which contains the terms "Adam" (man) and "son of man," was directly applied to Jesus Christ (1 Cor. 15:27; Heb. 2:6-9); that Old Testament notions of corporate Israel or the king may be applied to Jesus Christ ("the stone that the builders rejected" [Ps. 118:22] in Matt. 21:42; Acts 4:11; 1 Pet. 2:7); that Old Testament expressions applied to God can be applied to Jesus Christ (John 6:31, from Ps. 78:24; Heb. 1:10-12, from Ps. 102:26-28 [25-27]); and that Old Testament expressions are in some instances a "mystery," which charismatic Christian interpretation can explain—a charismatic interpretation the style of which, at least, goes back to Jesus himself (Matt. 13:35, from Ps. 78:2).[83]

The existence of these modes of interpretation in the New Testament leads to the question of the theological issues that that they raise for Christians. The Dead Sea sect did not consider its own sectarian works—the *Florilegium*, the various commentaries, the *Thanksgiving Hymns* and the *War Rule*—to be canonical, and therefore the sect did not produce any commentaries on the existing sectarian texts. But because the New Testament became canonical for Christians, its mode of using the Psalms (and other Old Testament material) became canonical. This circumstance immediately raises for Christians the question of how one deals theologically with any disparity between a given text in the Old Testament and a use of the same text in the New Testament. This is a question that the church fathers had to deal with as soon as commentaries began to be written.

For example, Jerome, in his fourth-century commentary on the Gospel of Matthew, remarks on the problem presented by Matt. 27:9-10, a reflection of Judas's betrayal of Jesus. The verses in Matthew read, "Then was fulfilled what had been spoken by the prophet Jeremiah, saying, 'And they took the thirty pieces of silver, the price of him on whom a price had been set by some of the sons of Israel, and they gave them for the potter's field, as the Lord directed me." As is well known, the passage is not from Jeremiah at all but is a paraphrase of Zech. 11:13, with a slight reminiscence of Jer. 18:2-3 and 32:6-15. Remember, Jerome had no concordances or other such reference aids. He writes:

> This testimony is not to be found in Jeremiah; but in Zechariah, which is almost the last of the twelve [minor] prophets, there is a certain likeness, and even though the meaning does not greatly disagree, nevertheless both the arrangement and the words are different. I have recently read in a certain Hebrew volume that a Hebrew of a Nazarene sect showed me, an apocryphal [book] of Jeremiah, in which I have found these things written word for word. Nevertheless the aforementioned testimony seems to me more likely from Zechariah, in the normal manner of the evangelists and apostles, who offer so

much of the meaning from the Old Testament in a given instance but neglect the arrangement of the words.[84]

(For more on Jerome's commentary on the Psalms, see chapter 10.)

The question of discrepancies between the Old Testament wording and that of the New Testament, then, is an old one; but it is particularly insistent for Christians today, who can gain an awareness of the shifts that have taken place in the meaning of texts as the centuries pass. One important source of this discrepancy, as we have seen, is the contrast between the Hebrew text and the Septuagint, but this contrast is by no means the only cause of the discrepancy.

A flat and unnuanced conception of the mode by which the Holy Spirit works in canonical texts must inevitably lead to difficult conclusions. Thus, if the interpretation of a psalm verse in the New Testament is the "real" meaning of that verse, then was the psalmist who composed the psalm ignorant of its "real" meaning, and were the Jewish worshipers who sang the psalm through the centuries likewise ignorant?

And related questions are bound to be raised. What psalms are useful for Christian worship? If all the psalms are useful, how may the "difficult" ones be interpreted to render them useful? These questions will be dealt with particularly in chapters 16 and 19. But we are getting ahead of our story; we first need to see how the psalms have actually been used by Jews and Christians during the past twenty centuries.

NOTES

1. See the essays in Krister Stendahl (ed.), *The Scrolls and the New Testament* (New York: Harper, 1957); and more recent bibliography in Geza Vermes, "Dead Sea Scrolls," in *IDBSup* 219b.

2. See, in detail, Menahem Stern, in Haim Hillel Ben-Sasson (ed.), *A History of the Jewish People* (Cambridge: Harvard University Press, 1976), 223–303.

3. The number of attempts to discern the historical Jesus is enormous. For a current assessment of the difficulties in the quest, see John P. Meier, *A Marginal Jew: Rethinking the Historical Jesus*, vol. 1 (AB Reference Library; Garden City, N.Y.: Doubleday, 1991); for a current attempt that draws heavily on social anthropology and Greco-Roman history, see John Dominic Crossan, *The Historical Jesus: The Life of a Mediterranean Jewish Peasant* (San Francisco: Harper, 1991).

4. Vincent Taylor, *The Gospel according to St. Mark* (London: Macmillan; New York: St. Martin's, 1952), 548.

5. Hans Conzelmann, *Acts of the Apostles* (Hermeneia; Philadelphia: Fortress, 1987), 34.

6. Hans Conzelmann, *1 Corinthians* (Hermeneia; Philadelphia: Fortress, 1975), 244; Eduard Lohse, *Colossians and Philemon* (Hermeneia; Philadelphia: Fortress, 1971), 151; Markus Barth, *Ephesians* (AB 34, 34A; Garden City, N.Y.: Doubleday, 1974), 582–83.

7. D. Eberhard Nestle, *Novum Testamentum Graece* (Stuttgart: Privilegierte Württembergische Bibelanstalt, 1952), 662–65.

8. On the topic in general, see Donald Juel, *Messianic Exegesis: Christological Interpretation of the Old Testament in Early Christianity* (Philadelphia: Fortress, 1988), 89–117.

9. There is an enormous literature on the temptation narratives. The following are useful on this temptation: Thomas W. Manson, *The Sayings of Jesus* (= *The Mission and Message of Jesus*, part 2) (London: SCM, 1949), 44–46; Francis Wright Beare, *The Gospel according to Matthew* (San Francisco: Harper & Row, 1981), 110–11; Joseph A. Fitzmyer, *The Gospel according to Luke I–IX, X–XXIV* (AB 28, 28A; Garden City, N.Y.: Doubleday, 1981, 1985), 509, 517; and see, in detail, Birger Gerhardsson, *The Testing of God's Son (Matt 4:1-11 & par): An Analysis of an Early Christian Midrash* (ConBNT; Lund: Gleerup, 1966), esp 60–61.

10. William L. Holladay, *Jeremiah 1* (Philadelphia: Fortress, 1986), 340–41, 344.

11. Manson, *Sayings of Jesus*, 47; Beare, *Matthew*, 130.

12. Eduard Schweizer, *The Good News according to Matthew* (Atlanta: John Knox, 1975), 127.

13. Manson, *Sayings of Jesus*, 112; Beare, *Matthew*, 187; Fitzmyer, *Luke*, 978.

14. Beare, *Matthew*, 198; Fitzmyer, *Luke*, 1025–26.

15. On these various matters, see Taylor, *Mark*, 456–57; Manson, *Sayings of Jesus*, 318; Beare, *Matthew.*, 461; Fitzmyer, *Luke*, 666–67, 1035–37, 1251.

16. Taylor, *Mark*, 476–77; Dennis E. Nineham, *Saint Mark* (Philadelphia: Westminster, 1963), 313; Beare, *Matthew*, 430; Fitzmyer, *Luke*, 1285.

17. Conzelmann, *Acts*, 33.

18. Francis W. Beare, *The First Epistle of Peter* (Oxford: Blackwell, 1947), 94, 99.

19. See the thorough treatment of this parable by Fitzmyer, *Luke*, 1277–82.

20. Manson, *Sayings of Jesus*, 221; Beare, *Matthew*, 417–18.

21. For a thorough treatment of this text, see David M. Hay, *Glory at the Right Hand: Psalm 110 in Early Christianity* (SBLMS 18; Nashville and New York: Abingdon, 1973); Juel, *Messianic Exegesis*, 135–50.

22. For discussion on this passage, see Taylor, *Mark*, 490–93; Beare, *Matthew*, 444–45; Fitzmyer, *Luke*, 1309–16, with further bibliography; and see, recently, Ragnar Leivestad, *Jesus in His Own Perspective* (Minneapolis: Augsburg, 1987), 113–15.

23. Conzelmann, *Acts*, 21; Harold W. Attridge, *Hebrews* (Philadelphia: Fortress, 1989), 62–63.

24. See the discussion in Taylor, *Mark*, 493; and Fitzmyer, *Luke*, 1310.

25. Fitzmyer, *Luke*, 1311.

26. Taylor, *Mark*, 491.

27. On this matter, see, conveniently, Sherman E. Johnson, "Secret, Messianic," in *IDB* 4:261a.

28. Taylor, *Mark*, 493.

29. Ibid., 492–93.

30. Leivestad, *Jesus*, 114–15.

31. See the thorough survey of the whole matter in Fitzmyer, *Luke*, 1309–14.

32. Taylor, *Mark*, 540.

33. For the use of this psalm in the New Testament, see Juel, *Messianic Exegesis*, 110–16.

34. Taylor, *Mark*, 593–94.

35. Meier, *Marginal Jew*, 170; Crossan, *Historical Jesus*, 367–87, esp. 387.

36. Taylor, *Mark*, 589.

37. Beare, *Matthew*, 534; Raymond E. Brown, *The Gospel according to John* (AB 29, 29A; Garden City, N.Y.: Doubleday, 1966, 1970), 920–22.

38. Attridge, *Hebrews*, 90.

39. Fitzmyer, *Luke*, 1514, 1519.

40. See ibid., 193.

41. Taylor, *Mark*, 162; Beare, *Matthew*, 100–104; Fitzmyer, *Luke*, 485.

42. Beare, *Matthew*, 310.

43. See Robert H. Gundry, *The Use of the Old Testament in St. Matthew's Gospel* (NovTSup 18; Leiden: Brill, 1967), 210, 211; O. Lamar Cope, *Matthew: A Scribe Trained for the Kingdom of Heaven* (CBQMS 5; Washington, D.C.: Catholic Biblical Association, 1976), 14.

44. Cf. Brown, *John*, 262.

45. Ibid., 409–11; E. Earle Ellis, "Biblical Interpretation in the New Testament Church," in Martin Jan Mulder (ed.), *Mikra: Text, Translation, Reading and Interpretation of the Hebrew Bible in Ancient Judaism and Early Christianity* (Assen and Maastricht: Van Gorcum; Philadelphia: Fortress, 1988), 700.

46. Brown, *John*, 554, 571.

47. So Charles K. Barrett, *The Gospel according to St. John* (London: SPCK, 1962), 372.

48. Brown, *John*, 689.

49. Ibid., 115, 119.

50. Raymond E. Brown, *The Birth of the Messiah* (Garden City, N.Y.: Doubleday, 1977), 346–65, 377–92, 456–60; Fitzmyer, *Luke*, 359–62, 376–79, 422.

51. For a discussion of these interpretations, see, in detail, Ernst Haenchen, *The Acts of the Apostles: A Commentary* (Oxford: Blackwell, 1971), 161; Gerhard A. Krodel, *Acts* (Augsburg Commentary on the New Testament; Minneapolis: Augsburg, 1986), 65–66.

52. Conzelmann, *Acts*, 105.

53. For a general analysis of Paul's use of the Old Testament, see, recently, Richard B. Hays, *Echoes of Scripture in the Letters of Paul* (New Haven: Yale University Press, 1989).

54. Conzelmann, *1 Corinthians*, 78.

55. Charles K. Barrett, *A Commentary on the Second Epistle to the Corinthians* (New York: Harper & Row, 1973), 142–43; Victor P. Furnish, *II Corinthians* (AB 32A; Garden City, N.Y.: Doubleday, 1984), 258.

56. Barrett, *Second Epistle to the Corinthians*, 238; Furnish, *II Corinthians*, 442; Hans Dieter Betz, *2 Corinthians 8 and 9* (Hermeneia; Philadelphia: Fortress, 1985), 111.

57. Conzelmann, *1 Corinthians*, 272–74.

58. Ernst Käsemann, *Commentary on Romans* (Grand Rapids: Eerdmans, 1980), 80–81.

59. Ibid., 86–87.

60. Ibid., 113.

61. Ibid., 249–50.

62. Ibid., 295–96.

63. Ibid., 301–2.

64. Ibid., 381–82.

65. Ibid., 386.

66. See, recently, Nils A. Dahl, "Ephesians, Letter to the," *IDBSup* 268; idem, "Ephesians," in James L. Mays (ed.), *Harper's Bible Commentary* (San Francisco: Harper & Row, 1988), 1212–13.

67. Barth, *Ephesians*, 472–77.

68. See, in detail, Simon E. Kistemaker, *The Psalm Citations in the Epistle to the Hebrews* (Amsterdam: Soest, 1961).

69. For the chain of quotations in general, see Attridge, *Hebrews*, 50–51.

70. See, in detail, ibid., 53–54, 57–62, 70–72.

71. Mitchell Dahood, *Psalms I:1–50* (Garden City, N.Y.: Doubleday, 1966), 273.

72. Kistemaker, *Psalm Citations*, 108–16.

73. Attridge, *Hebrews*, 114–16, 119–20, 123–24, 126–30.

74. Ibid., 145–46, 199, 203, 207, 208; Kistemaker, *Psalm Citations*, 116–24.

75. For Melchizedek, see Attridge, *Hebrews*, 192–95.

76. Kistemaker, *Psalm Citations*, 124–30.

77. Attridge, *Hebrews*, 274.

78. Ibid., 389.

79. Paul J. Achtemeier, "*Omne verbum sonat*: The New Testament and the Oral Environment of Late Western Antiquity," *JBL* 109 (1990): 3–27.

80. See James A. Sanders, *The Dead Sea Psalms Scroll* (Ithaca, N.Y.: Cornell University Press, 1967), 7; John M. Allegro, *The Dead Sea Scrolls* (Harmondsworth: Penguin, 1958), 166–67.

81. Gershom Scholem, *Sabbetai Ṣevi: The Mystical Messiah* (Bollingen Series 93; Princeton: Princeton University Press, 1973).

82. Ellis, "Biblical Interpretation", 699–702.

83. See, in detail, ibid., 702–24.

84. Jerome, *(S.) Hieronymi Presbyteri Opera, Part I, Opera Exegetica, 7: Commentarium in Mattheum Libri IV* (CChr Series Latina 77; Turnhout: Brepols, 1969), 265–66.

9

The Psalms for Jews, from the First Century of the Common Era

As we turn from the New Testament to study the use of the Psalms by Jews from the first century of the common era until modern times, we move into a world with which too few people today are acquainted in detail. Present-day readers who are observant Jews may know parts of the story; by contrast, present-day readers reared in a Christian environment typically know almost nothing of the story. The ebb and flow of Jewish life in the last twenty centuries is far too often unknown territory; but it is a rich territory and deserves to be better known.

There is no way to offer more than a sketch of Jewish life during the extent of time in question, but we must at least touch the high spots in order to learn the place of the Psalms in that life.

Five major topics make up this chapter: (1) the fixing of the canon and text of the Jewish Scriptures at the end of the first century; (2) the dispersion of Jewish communities through the Middle Ages and into the modern period; (3) the use of the Psalms in Jewish liturgy; (4) the way that the Psalms were used in the Mishnah, Talmud, and midrashim, monuments of Jewish literature that arose in the Middle Ages from the second to the thirteenth centuries, particularly in Babylon; and (5) the debate over the nature of the Psalms and the commentaries that were written on the Psalms in Europe from the tenth to the thirteenth centuries. I close the chapter by touching more briefly on four further items: (1) Jewish translations of the Psalms into various vernaculars; (2) hymns taking their model from the Psalms; (3) the influence of the Psalms in art and music; and (4) the way the Psalms have entered into present-day Jewish secular life.

The fall of Jerusalem to the Romans in 70 C.E. was a shattering experience for Jews, fully as shattering to them as the fall of that city to the Babylonians had been in 587 B.C.E. And again, as with the catastrophe of 587 B.C.E., it was the destruction of the temple that was the focus of their tragedy. This time, however, the temple would not be rebuilt; from this time forward Jewish worship would center in the synagogue.

The Fixing of the Canon and Text of
the Jewish Scriptures

The challenge to the Jews to find a center for their lives and hope for the future was compounded by challenges from the Christian community, which by then was beginning to be a real threat. Christian documents from that period, especially the Gospel of John, with its reiterated reference to "the Jews" over against Jesus, reflect the enmity between church and synagogue; John 2:18 is the first of several dozen such passages. In particular, Christians argued with Jews about the meaning of Old Testament passages, and often the two communities used different wordings for the same texts.

The result was that the rabbinic academy at Jamnia, a city west of Jerusalem toward the coast (the Old Testament Jabneel [Josh. 15:11] or Jabneh [2 Chron. 26:6]), where central authority for the Jewish community resided during the period 70–100, settled two related questions. The first question was to confirm the list of books that were canonical Scripture (see chapter 6); though the issue of canonicity was settled for the most part long since, there was evidently uncertainty at least about the status of Ecclesiastes and the Song of Solomon,[1] and during this period the authorities appear to have confirmed the list of books which from then on made up the Hebrew Scriptures (and which thus led Martin Luther to the list of the Old Testament without the Deuterocanonical books like Maccabees).[2]

The second question was to begin to establish an authoritative text of the Hebrew Scriptures: this was the process of overcoming the variations in the Hebrew wording in Scripture, of which we have taken note in chapters 6 and 7. The aim was to produce a uniform text of the Scriptures, and this activity was accompanied by a conviction of the sanctity and divine inspiration of the precise wording of the Bible. It was an activity associated with the name of Rabbi Akiba (ca. 50–132).[3]

The Dispersion of Jewish Communities
through the Middle Ages and into
the Modern Period

In the matter of the history of the Jewish communities, I can only offer a handful of details and encourage readers to learn more.

In the first century of our era there were Jewish communities all across the Roman Empire, particularly around the Mediterranean Sea. The Jews were particularly strong in Egypt (especially Alexandria); Palestine; and Syria, to the north of Palestine. There were Jews on the mainland of Greece and the islands of Greece, and in the city of Rome (readers of the New Testament will recall the visits made by Paul, recorded in the book of Acts, to synagogues in those regions). There was also a strong community of Jews in Babylon, which was then part of the Parthian Empire (the Parthians were Persians); these were the descendants of Jews who had stayed in Babylon after the exile from Jerusalem in the sixth century B.C.E.[4]

As we have seen, when Jerusalem fell in 70 C.E. as a consequence of the Jewish revolt against Rome, the temple was destroyed and the Jewish population scattered. There was a supreme religious council of Jewish authorities that doubtless had its origin in the Persian period, called the Sanhedrin (for this term see, e.g., John 11:47 in the NAB; the word is translated "council" in the RSV and the NRSV); this council survived the fall of the city and settled in Jamnia, and its authority reached—at least theoretically—even to the Jewish communities in Babylon.[5]

Then, in Palestine in 132–35, there was a second, unavailing Jewish revolt against Rome (the revolt of Bar Kokhba [Simon bar-Koseba]). The result was that Jews were forbidden to enter Jerusalem except on one day a year, to mourn. Jewish communities in Palestine did survive and even thrive, particularly in Galilee; it was in these circumstances that the Mishnah was produced, as I describe below. But the fortune of the Palestinian Jewish communities faded in the century thereafter as the energies of the Roman Empire deteriorated and the economy turned downward. Thus in the third century there was steady war between the Roman and Parthian empires, and Jews, as so often, were caught in the middle. Then, in the beginning of the fourth century, came the edict of the emperor Constantine, making the Christian faith a legal religion of the empire; a consequence was that Jews everywhere in the empire suffered from anti-Jewish laws, and the population of Jews dwindled in Palestine.

Now, ever since the Middle Ages, Jews in the dispersion outside Palestine have recognized two divisions of their communities, the so-called Sephardim and the Ashkenazim. The Sephardic Jews were those in Babylon, Egypt and North Africa, Spain, and southern France (Marseilles). The Ashkenazic Jews were those in Italy who spread north into northern France and England and settled in Cologne and elsewhere in the Rhine Valley of Germany; later these German Jews moved east into Poland, Lithuania, and western Russia. I describe first the Sephardim and then turn to the Ashkenazim.

Though, as I have said, Jewish life in Palestine declined in the third century and thereafter, in Babylon, Jewish communities throve. At the beginning of the third century the Babylonian Jewish community founded two great academies, in Sura and Nehardea (later moved to Pumbadita); these cities were located along the Euphrates from the city of Babylon northward, roughly forty-five miles (seventy-five kilometers) from the neighborhood of present-day Baghdad. These academies accomplished two tasks of importance to us here: they finally fixed the tradition of vowels in the text of Scripture—we recall that early manuscripts were written in consonants only (see chapter 6)—and they produced the (Babylonian) Talmud, which I describe below.

There were Jewish communities in the Arabian peninsula. There are passages reflecting Jewish lore in the Muslim Qur'ān, suggesting contact between Muḥammad and the Jews in the early seventh century; thus twice in the Qur'ān it is mentioned that God gave the revelation of the Psalms to David.[6]

By the beginning of the seventh century, the Persians were expanding their empire (by then, the so-called Sassanian dynasty), particularly against Constantinople (the Byzantine [= eastern Roman] Empire), and as part of that drive they captured Jerusalem in 614. The Persians handed Jerusalem over to Jewish settlers, who then expelled the Christians and removed their churches. Three years later, however, the Persians shifted, making peace with the Christians and war on the Jews, and in 629 the Byzantine emperor took back Jerusalem and restored all the Christian relics to the Church of the Holy Sepulchre; the Jews were consequently forced to flee.

In 632 another military force appeared: Arab armies fired by the new religion of Islam. And in 638 the patriarch of Jerusalem surrendered the city to the Muslim caliph Omar. That same year (Muslim) Arab armies also overran Mesopotamia, thus bringing an end to the rule of the Sassanian dynasty over the Jews in Babylonia.

The fate of Jews in the western Roman Empire in general sank as that empire collapsed, but there were some bright spots. Thus there was a distinguished Jewish community in Visigothic Spain;[7] when the Visigoths conquered Spain, they were Arian Christians (that is, they adhered to the form of belief that was rejected by the Council of Nicaea in 325). When the kings in Spain became Catholic, however, they tried to force the Jews in their realm to convert to the Christian faith. From the sixth to the eighth century, then, the Jews in Spain suffered much mistreatment.

In the meantime, the (Arab) Muslim conquests continued into Egypt and west across North Africa and north into Spain. Spain fell to the Muslims in 711, and the Arab armies were stopped in France only by Charles Martel at Tours in 732.

In general, Jews and Christians fared well in Muslim lands in the Middle Ages; the Qur'ān honors both Jews and Christians as "people of the book," that is, those having Scriptures revealed by God.[8] Thus there were Jews who through their own talents rose to political leadership in Muslim Spain, such as Rabbi Samuel Hanagid and his son Joseph in the eleventh century.[9]

By contrast, more often than not Christian lands emerging from the Middle Ages were inhospitable to Jews. Thus all Jews were expelled from England by Edward I in 1290 (Jews were not allowed into England again until the time of Cromwell in the second half of the seventeenth century), from France in 1394, and from Spain by Ferdinand and Isabella in 1492. Specifically, the status of Jews in Europe was worsened in the context of the Crusades; the religious emotions of Christians were turned against Jews as well as against Muslims.

In the early modern period the Jewish population increased in Palestine, particularly as refugees from Spain found sanctuary there; the holy city of Safed, about seven miles (eleven kilometers) northwest of the Sea of Galilee, became an important Jewish center alongside of Jerusalem.[10] And refugees from Spain found sanctuary in Holland, where Sephardic Jews developed a vigorous community, particularly in Amsterdam, bringing with them their mode of speech, called Judeo-Spanish or Ladino.[11]

In the meantime, the Ashkenazic Jews centered in the Rhine Valley of Germany suffered particularly during the Crusades (the twelfth century), and Jews streamed eastward to settle in Poland, Lithuania, and western Russia. They took with them their speech, a German dialect in which a proportion of the vocabulary was Hebrew, the language that came to be called Judeo-German or Yiddish. Through the centuries these Jews were often subject to dreadful persecutions (pogroms), perhaps the most horrible of which (until the Holocaust under Adolf Hitler) were the massacres of Jews by the Cossack chief Chmielnicki in the Ukraine (1648–55).[12]

Jews not only migrated throughout North Africa and Europe but to the Western Hemisphere as well. There was a Jewish colony in Recife, Brazil, in the middle of the seventeenth century, and this colony later moved to New Amsterdam (New York).[13] Jews continued to migrate to the New World, culminating in the immigration of two and a half million Jews into the United States during the thirty-year period 1890–1920.[14]

Finally, one must note the immigration into Palestine beginning at the end of the nineteenth century under the inspiration of Jewish nationalism (Zionism). This movement has continued to the present day, both in the context of flight during the murder of six million Jews by the Nazis in the Holocaust of 1941–45[15] and in the context of the establishment of the state of Israel in 1948.[16]

It was in all these disparate circumstances that traditional Judaism (that is, the so-called Orthodox Judaism) evolved. This traditional Judaism has adhered faithfully to the norms of observance, which are set forth in their fullness in the Babylonian Talmud (for which, see below). Yet central though Torah (the Jewish Law) has been, it would be unfortunate to conclude that Jewish faith is a matter of legal observance. It is true, adherence to the Law has elicited from Jews a piety and love that is deeply appealing, but the history of Judaism has been marked by a variety of movements that have reshaped piety in significant ways. I later make mention of the Karaite sect that arose in the ninth and tenth centuries; and one may note the emergence of esoteric mystical speculation (the so-called Kabbala) in the fifteenth century, especially in Safed,[17] and the rise in eastern Europe, especially in the course of the eighteenth century, of the ideal of joyous communion with God in the movement called Ḥasidism.[18] Judaism has always offered rich variety. Nevertheless, until the last two centuries it could be understood as the faith of a single religious community, that of Orthodox Judaism. (Today, it may be noted, Orthodox Jews in the United States are associated in the Union of Orthodox Jewish Congregations of America).

In the meantime, in the last two centuries some Jews have reconceived their religious life in several different ways, and we must turn our attention now to these. The first is the movement that came to be called Reform Judaism; it began in Germany in 1818 and gathered force thereafter, particularly in the 1840s. This movement has been an effort to accommodate Judaism to the culture around it. Jews in this tradition pray in the language of the locality rather than in Hebrew and in general have modified Jewish liturgy and practice in significant ways, and they place their primary emphasis on the ethical values of Judaism rather than on the traditional details of Torah.[19] In the United States, Reform Jews are associated in the Union of American Hebrew Congregations; their center for higher learning is the Hebrew Union College–Jewish Institute of Religion in Cincinnati.

The second movement has come to be called Conservative Judaism. This is a mediating position that has won favor particularly in the United States. Jews in this tradition retain as many of the requirements of Torah as are possible within a non-Jewish majority culture, and their liturgical practices largely conform to traditional (Orthodox) practice.

> Orthodoxy would say: we obey because God wants us to perform this particular law; we know that for all eternity Jews will be bound by all the rules set down in the divinely dictated Torah. Conservatism would say: we obey this law because it has always been dear to the Jewish people; it conveys a meaningful message to them. We will abide by it as long as the people—by unanimous and unspoken consent—wish to retain it.[20]

In the United States, Conservative Jews are associated in the United Synagogue of America, and their rabbis in the Rabbinical Assembly of America; their spiritual center and institution of higher learning is the Jewish Theological Seminary of America in New York City.

One more movement is of significance, the so-called neo-Orthodoxy in Germany, associated with Samson Raphael Hirsch (1808–88). Hirsch's ideal was absolute faithfulness to Torah combined with the highest scholastic and educational standards of European culture. It was a movement that did not survive the Nazi destruction of German Judaism.[21]

It is impossible to obtain exact statistics, but the most recent *World Almanac* offers the following for the United States: Orthodox Jews—1,000 congregations, 1,000,000 members; Conservative Jews—850 congregations, 2,000,000 members; Reform Jews—839 congregations, 1,300,000 members.[22] Thus, in the United States, the proportion is roughly: Orthodox, 23 percent; Conservative, 47 percent; Reform, 30 percent.

Here, then, in the merest sketch, is some background for visualizing the Jewish communities through the ages, communities that were nourished on the Psalms.

The Use of the Psalms in Jewish Liturgy

The tragedy of the destruction of the temple in 70 C.E. was so overwhelming that we possess little coherent understanding of the nature of Jewish liturgy before the destruction.[23] However, there are scattered references in both the New Testament and in the Jewish Mishnah (a compilation from the end of the second century; see below) that allow us some understanding of the patterns of worship in this period.

Worship in the Jerusalem Temple centered on animal sacrifice, provision for which is given in the Pentateuch: morning sacrifice and evening sacrifice, with additions for the Sabbath, the New Moon, and the great annual feasts.[24] The Mishnah recalls that Levites recited Psalm 24 on Sunday, Psalm 48 on Monday, Psalm 82 on Tuesday, Psalm 94 on Wednesday, Psalm 81 on Thursday, Psalm 93 on Friday, and Psalm 92 on Saturday,[25] and these traditions are likely to be correct: it was noted in chapter 6 that superscriptions in the Septuagint text of the Psalms designate Psalm 24 for Sunday, Psalm 48 for Monday, Psalm 82 for Tuesday, Psalm 93 for Friday, and Psalm 92 for Saturday; of these five notations, only the designation for Tuesday is different. But it is impossible to reconstruct the order of liturgy of the temple services. And as to the forms of worship outside the temple, in the synagogues of the period, we are almost completely uninformed.[26]

Jewish liturgy, as one might expect, developed gradually in the centuries after the fall of Jerusalem. The full system, like all liturgical practice, is intricate, and practices have varied not only in the course of history but among the different branches of Judaism—between Sephardic and Ashkenazic Jews, for example.[27] In this work I offer only enough detail to indicate how the Psalms are used.

The liturgies of the Orthodox Jews and the Conservative Jews are virtually the same, and no distinctions are dealt with here. Both communities recite their prayers and psalms in Hebrew, the language of liturgy. As for Reform Jews, they use the local language for most, if not all, of their liturgy. I do not describe here the varied practices of Reform congregations, though Reform prayer books likewise draw deeply from the Psalms.

I begin with a few preliminary observations. The first is that Jews, when reciting the Psalms, always recite any superscription along with the psalm proper; the superscription is considered part of the text. (This is never true in Christian practice.)

One must also note that every Jewish blessing begins with the words *bārûk 'attâ 'ădōnāy*—"Blessed art Thou, O Lord"—the words of Ps. 119:12a; and these words are always extended by the words *'ĕlōhênû melek hā'ōlām*, so that the whole phrase is "Blessed art Thou, O Lord our God, King of the universe." For example, the blessing before eating bread at a meal is "Blessed art Thou, O Lord our God, King of the universe, who brings forth bread from the earth"; when putting on a fringed tallith (prayer shawl) in the synagogue, the blessing recited is "Blessed art Thou, Lord our God, King of the universe, who sanctified us with His commandments, and commanded us to wrap ourselves in the *tzitzit* [fringes]."

As one surveys the use of the Psalms in Jewish liturgy, one must begin by making an obvious distinction between the statutory use of various psalms in the Jewish liturgy and nonstatutory uses. During the period of the formation of the Talmud (third to fifth centuries), few psalms were required to be recited, but the custom of using various psalms slowly penetrated into the liturgy over the course of the centuries, so that at the present time the liturgy draws richly from the Psalter.[28]

There is a threefold rhythm to the succession of synagogue services: there are (1) daily services, (2) Sabbath services, and (3) services for occasions beyond the week—for the New Moon and for the annual festivals. (This threefold rhythm is comparable to the Christian liturgy, which is likewise organized around daily liturgy, Sunday liturgy, and special annual observances; see chapter 10.)

Jewish daily services are built around the injunction to pray three times a day—in the morning, the afternoon, and the evening;[29] in practice, the afternoon service on weekdays is often held late enough so that the evening service follows without a break.[30] The prayer used on each of these three occasions is the same, a prayer called either the Amidah (Standing; from the posture of prayer) or the *Shemoneh Esrei* (Eighteen [Blessings]; now actually nineteen but still so called). The Amidah is central to Jewish piety. Though I shall not describe it in detail,[31] because it does not bear directly on the use of the Psalms, nevertheless it must be said that the blessings in the prayer contain frequent phrases from the Psalms. Thus the second of these blessings, called *Gevurot* (that is, the "Powers" of God), in describing God uses the phrases "who supports the falling," taken from Ps. 145:10, and "who frees the captives," taken from Ps. 146:7. And after this blessing there is one called the *Kedushah* (Holiness), the heart of which is made up of the recitations of Isa. 6:3; Ezek. 3:12; and Ps. 146:10.

In the morning service (in Hebrew, *Shaharit*), the Amidah is preceded by four elements. One is the *Birkhot ha-Shahar* (Morning Blessings [or Benedictions]), various prayers that were originally intended to be said privately but were gradually transferred to the synagogue. But even before the Morning Blessings, the first prayer prescribed on entering the synagogue is the *Mah Tovu* (How Goodly), made up of Num. 24:5 followed by Pss. 5:8 (7); 26:8; 95:6 (modified to first person singular); and 69:14 (13).[32]

After the Morning Blessings, Psalm 30 is recited as a bridge to the third element of the morning service, the so-called *Pesukei d'Zimra* (Verses of Song), the core of which is the sequence of Psalms 145–150.[33] Psalm 145, it must be explained, is called the *Ashrei* (Blessed), inasmuch as its recitation is always preceded by Pss. 84:5 (4) and 144:15, both of which begin with "Blessed." In the *Pesukei d'Zimra* the sequence of Psalms 145–150 is preceded by various passages; in one tradition, after certain prayers one hears 1 Chron. 16:8-36, followed by a chain of the following verses of the Psalms: Pss. 99:5, 9; 78:38; 40:12 (11); 25:6; 68:35-36 (34-35); 94:1-2; 3:9 (8); 46:8 (7) (= 12 [11]); 84:13 (12); 20:10 (9); 28:9; 33:20-22; 85:8 (7); 44:27 (26); 81:11 (10); 144:15; and 13:6 (5-6).[34] And the sequence *Pesukei d'Zimra* has been followed, since the Middle Ages, by the Song of the Sea (Exod. 15:1-18), then by a thanksgiving prayer, and then by Psalm 100 (called, from the Hebrew superscription, *Mizmor l'Todah*).

The fourth element, directly preceding the Amidah, is the Shema ("Hear, O Israel"; Deut. 6:4).

Following the Amidah, there ordinarily follows the *Tahanun* (Supplication), which, since the fourteenth century, has consisted of a psalm; in the Ashkenazic tradition it is Psalm 6, whereas in the Sephardic tradition it is Psalm 25.[35] This psalm is preceded and followed by set prayers that are interspersed with phrases from the Psalms. But the *Tahanun* is omitted on many occasions, including the Sabbath, the New Moon, and various festivals.

The morning service then concludes with the *Ashrei* once more (Psalm 145 with two prefixed verses), followed by Psalm 20, two traditional prayers, and then the Psalm of the Day. Since the Middle Ages it has been customary to recite the psalm that had been designated for the day of the week by the Levites in the temple: Psalm 24 on Sunday, Psalm 48 on Monday, Psalm 82 on Tuesday, Psalm 94 on Wednesday, Psalm 81 on Thursday, Psalm 93 on Friday, and Psalm 92 on Saturday.

In the afternoon service (in Hebrew, *Minḥa* [Gift]), the Amidah is preceded by the third recitation of the day of the *Ashrei* (Psalm 145 with two prefixed verses) and is followed by a closing prayer.

The evening service (in Hebrew, *Maariv*) is opened with Pss. 78:38 and 20:10 (9), followed in turn by the short Psalm 134. Then follows the Shema, preceded by two blessings and followed by two blessings; then follow the Amidah and a closing prayer.

The weekly rhythm of Jewish worship is built around the Sabbath.[36] The Sabbath morning service has two focuses: the first is the Amidah (which is shortened for the Sabbath service, as it is for the morning service of the great festivals; see below), and the second is the reading of the Torah. The Torah (Pentateuch) is divided into consecutive readings so that the reading of the whole Torah is completed in the course of one year. The Torah is also read, it may be noted, during the Sabbath afternoon service and in the Monday and Thursday morning services; the assigned reading for each of these three occasions is standard, namely, the reading following the one the previous Sabbath morning.[37]

In the Sabbath morning service, the Torah reading is followed by a selected reading from the Prophets (this reading is called *Haftarah* [Concluding Portion]). It is to be recalled (see chapter 6) that the Prophets in the Hebrew Bible consists of the books of Joshua, Judges, 1 and 2 Samuel, 1 and 2 Kings, Isaiah, Jeremiah, Ezekiel, and the twelve minor prophets. The *Haftarah* is a given selection from one of these books.

For the Sabbath morning service, and for the morning services of the great festivals (see below), there is a great expansion of the *Pesukei d'Zimra*. Thus, after the opening prayers and the recitation of 1 Chron. 16:8-36 and the chain of psalm verses already described, and before the recitation of Psalms 145–150, in the Ashkenazic tradition the following nine psalms are recited: Psalms 19; 34; 90; 91; 135; 136 (the so-called *Hallel HaGadol*—Great Hallel [Praise]); 33; 92; and 93; in the Sephardic tradition fourteen psalms are recited, in the following order: Psalms 103, 19, 33, 90, 91, 98, 121–124, 135, 136, 92, and 93.[38] Then, following the reading of the Torah and the selection from the Prophets, there is in the morning service for the Sabbath (and for the new moon and great festivals as well) a portion of the service called *Musaf* (Additional) or *Musaf Amidah*, originally a separate service but now joined to the morning service. As its name implies, it is a repetition of the Amidah, shortened for this portion of the service. The morning service then closes with various prayers.

On Friday evening there is a special service preceding *Maariv* (the normal evening service), and that is the so-called *Kabbalat Shabbat* (Welcoming the Sabbath); this service has not been obligatory but has become customary. The service begins with the recitation of at least Psalm 29; among Ashkenazic Jews, beginning in the sixteenth century, the tradition arose of reciting Psalms 95–99 before Psalm

29.[39] The service then follows with a short prayer of the mystics (*Ana bekhoaḥ*). This is followed by *Lekhah Dodi* ("Come, dear friend, to meet the bride," the bride being the Sabbath), a hymn composed by Rabbi Shlomo Halevy Alkabetz, a Palestinian poet of the sixteenth century. The service concludes with the recitation of Psalms 92 and 93.[40]

In the afternoon service for the Sabbath during the winter months (between Sukkot and Passover), the Ashkenazic Jews began the custom, in the twelfth century, of reciting Psalm 104 and Psalms 120–134 after the Amidah and various prayers.[41]

There are three great annual festivals, the so-called pilgrim festivals, that are enjoined in the Old Testament: (1) Passover (Hebrew, *Pesaḥ*) or the Feast of the Unleavened Bread, celebrated on the fourteenth through the twenty-first days of Nisan (the first month, March/April); (2) Shavuot (Pentecost, also called the Feast of First Fruits or Weeks), celebrated forty-nine days after the first night of Passover; and (3) Sukkot (the Feast of Booths or Tabernacles), celebrated from the fifteenth to the twenty-second of Tishri (the seventh month, September/October).[42] For the liturgy of these festivals and Ḥanukkah (which falls in December) and Rosh Ḥodesh (the day of the New Moon) as well, the so-called Hallel (Praise) is recited, that is, the sequence of Psalms 113–118.[43] This is the recitation, it should be noted, to which one assumes Mark 14:26 is referring in the narrative of Jesus' last supper with his disciples (see chapter 8). (Though not directly relevant to this study, one must make mention of two other great festivals of the Jewish year: Rosh Hashanah [the New Year], celebrated fourteen days before Sukkot, and Yom Kippur [the Day of Atonement], celebrated five days before Sukkot. These are the two longest liturgies of the Jewish year.)

In the evening that begins Passover, the Jewish custom is to hold the Passover meal at home, the so-called Passover Seder (Order of Service). At that service the Hallel is recited, Psalms 113–114 just before the seder meal and Psalms 115–118 afterward.[44] It may be helpful to note that, in contrast to the so-called Great Hallel (Psalm 136), Psalms 113–118 are often called the Egyptian Hallel, given both the reference in Ps. 114:1 and the association of the sequence with Passover.

The whole Passover festival lasts eight days; the Hallel is recited each day of the festival in the morning service, though on the last six days of Passover the Hallel is shortened (as it is for the festival of the New Moon as well), the so-called Half Hallel: Ps. 115:1-11 and Ps. 116:1-11 are omitted.[45] However, it is recited in full during the morning service for Shavuot and during the service on each of the successive mornings of the seven days of Sukkot.[46] For each of the morning services of these festivals, after the recitation of the Amidah in the shortened form (prescribed also for the Sabbath morning service), the Hallel is recited, followed directly by the reading of the Torah passage prescribed for the given day of the festival.[47] It may be added that there are festivals on which the Hallel is not recited: for instance, Rosh Hashanah, Yom Kippur, and Purim (which occurs in February or March).[48]

Beyond the three pilgrim festivals, there are other occasions during the year when special psalms are added to the daily psalm. Psalm 27 is added to the morning and evening services from the first of the month Elul (the sixth month, August/

September; thus the month before Sukkot) until the last day of Sukkot. During the week of Ḥanukkah, Psalm 30 is said. On Rosh Ḥodesh (New Moon), Psalm 104 is added.

We have seen how the Hallel is said at the Passover Seder in the home. There are other traditional prayers said in the home in which the Psalms have a place. One is *Shiva* (Seven; i.e., the number of days of mourning), when mourners stay home and the morning and evening services take place there. At these services certain adjustments are made: for example, *Taḥanun*, which includes Psalm 6, is omitted, as is Psalm 20 at the conclusion of the morning service; the Hallel is omitted for a service for mourners on the New Moon or Ḥanukkah; Psalm 16 is added in place of *Taḥanun* for mourners on the New Moon or Ḥanukkah; and Psalm 49 is added to the end of the mourners' morning and evening services.

Another prayer that takes place in the home is the *Birkat Hamazon* (Blessing of the Meal), the grace said after the meal. This grace customarily begins with the recitation of Psalm 137 during the week or Psalm 126 on a Sabbath or feast day. Then follow four blessings—for food, for the land (of Israel) and for Torah, for Jerusalem, and for the good that God affords his people.

Similarly, other psalms are to be found in miscellaneous services: prayer before going on a journey, night prayer before retiring to rest, the memorial service for the dead, and the like.[49]

Beyond the full psalms specified on various occasions, single verses of psalms occur often in Jewish liturgies: mention has already been made of the psalm verses of the *Mah Tovu*, recited before the Morning Blessings; of the long chain of Psalm verses that precedes the recitation of the *Ashrei* (Psalm 145) and the two verses (Pss. 84:5 [4] and 144:15) that are used immediately before that Psalm 145; and of Pss. 78:38 and 20:10 (9), used to open the evening service. But one may mention in addition that on the Sabbath afternoon service, after the Amidah, there follows a short passage made up of Pss. 119:142; 71:19; and 36:7 (6), each of which begins with "your righteousness."[50]

Now, how might one summarize the use of the Psalms in Jewish liturgy? I have cited fifty-seven psalms that play a role in the liturgy. If one classifies these psalms by genre,[51] some striking patterns emerge. The fifty-seven psalms represent 38 percent of the Psalter. Of the major genres, the following are overrepresented: hymns proper, fifteen out of nineteen;[52] psalms of Yahweh's kingship, five out of six;[53] psalms of confidence, seven out of twelve;[54] seven out of seventeen of the psalms of thanksgiving;[55] five out of eleven wisdom psalms;[56] two out of two prophetic exhortations;[57] and the torah liturgy (Psalm 24) and the small liturgy (Psalm 134).

Underrepresented are royal psalms, three out of eleven.[58] And, it is worth noting, the psalms deemed "messianic" by Christians (Psalms 2, 72, 110) are not represented.

Spectacularly underrepresented are laments, especially laments of the individual: there are three out of thirty-eight laments of the individual,[59] and six out of eighteen of the laments of the community.[60]

And it is instructive to see where in the liturgy the nine laments that do occur are to be found. Four of them are said in the course of reciting Psalms 120–134 (laments: Psalms 120, 123, 126, 130) in the Sabbath afternoon service during the winter months. Two of them (Psalms 82 and 94) are Psalms of the Day, recited at the close of the morning service. Psalm 90 is one of the many psalms recited before Psalms 145–150 in the *Pesukei d'Zimra* in the morning service for Sabbath and festivals. There are only two laments that take a central place in the liturgy. One is Psalm 6, a lament of the individual recited daily by those in the Ashkenazic tradition (the *Taḥanun*); during the recitation of the psalm, the person reciting it assumes a seated posture, bent over, with the face lowered on the left forearm.[61] In this psalm, the worshiper gives voice to his weakness, and enemies are mentioned, but the enemies do not loom as large in this psalm as they do in many of the laments of the Psalter. Similar remarks might be made regarding the Sephardic equivalent in the *Taḥanun*, Psalm 25. (It is striking that, in Christian tradition, Psalm 6 is the first of seven so-called Penitential Psalms; five of the others—Psalms 32, 38, 51, 102, 143—are absent from this survey of Jewish liturgy, and Psalm 130 occurs only in the recitation of Psalms 120–134.)

The other lament that takes a central place in Jewish attention is a lament of the community, Psalm 137 ("By the waters of Babylon"), which is recited on weekdays at the beginning of the blessing after meals. The sensibility here is that the meal is a reminder of the altar of sacrifice in the temple, and thus it is the loss of the temple in Jerusalem of which the worshiper is reminded.[62] Lamentation, then, plays an important but not a dominant role in Jewish liturgy.

Almost two-thirds (thirty-six) of the psalms represented are hymns, psalms of confidence, or psalms of thanksgiving. Overwhelmingly, then, the psalms in Jewish liturgy are those of praise and thanksgiving. Again and again the rabbis and sages have spoken of the joy that the worshiper gains by being in the presence of God.[63]

This sense of joy can also be glimpsed in the chain of eighteen portions of psalms that is recited at the beginning of the *Pesukei d'Zimra*. This sequence reinforces in as many ways as possible the awesomeness of God, the compassion of God, the trust that the community places in God. Strikingly, of these eighteen short passages (most of them single verses), eleven close the psalm from which they are taken; that is, they round off or summarize the psalm in question. For example, the first two quotations are from a psalm of Yahweh's kingship, Ps. 95:5 and 9, parallel verses: v. 5 reads, "Extol the Lord our God; worship at his footstool. Holy is he!" and v. 9 reads, "Extol the Lord our God, and worship at this holy mountain; for the Lord our God is holy." In these ways the psalms selected for the liturgy have built up the piety of Jewish communities through the ages.

One may note also that the custom has grown up in recent years among Conservative and Reform Jews of celebrating a Brith Habbat (covenant of the daughter), to mark the birth of a baby girl, as a feminine analogue to the Brith Milah (covenant of circumcision); and in this freely evolving rite one or more psalms may be used—for example, Psalm 127 (using "children" instead of "sons") or Psalm 128—or specific verses from the Psalms, or the various eight-verse sections of the acrostic Psalm 119 will be recited in the order of the letters spelling the girl's name in Hebrew.[64]

Beyond whole psalms and psalm verses that have a place in Jewish liturgy, there is a strong tradition that it is a pious act to recite the complete Psalter, and various sects have drawn up schemes by which the whole Psalter may be completed in a month or, alternatively, in a week,[65] exactly like the Christian breviary (see chapter 10). Indeed "societies of reciters of Psalms" (*ḥevrot tehillim*) have been formed: in Jerusalem today a special society has been set up whereby two separate groups recite the whole Psalter daily at the Western Wall,[66] and for this purpose the text of the book of Psalms is published separately in pocket editions. And there are a variety of folk practices employing the Psalms. For example, exactly as with the ceremony on the birth of a girl baby, one may recite on behalf of a sick person successive sections of Psalm 119, letter by letter, corresponding with the Hebrew spelling of the name of the sick person; following this, the verses are recited that correspond to the six letters of the Hebrew words for "Tear away Satan" (*koph, resh, ayin; shin, teth, nun*).[67]

The Use of the Psalms in the Mishnah, the Talmud, and Midrashic Literature

I now turn to the great monuments of Jewish literature that were compiled in the course of the Middle Ages.[68] The first was the Mishnah: this is a compendium of traditional judgments on Torah (Jewish Law) that was compiled at the end of the second century of our era. A standard translation in English takes up 789 pages.[69] It consists of sixty-three short books (Tractates), each dealing with a particular topic— thus *Shabbath* deals with questions of the Sabbath; *Ketuboth* (Marriage Deeds) deals with marriage laws. These legal judgments have shaped conduct for Orthodox Jews; they are based on interpretations of the laws of the Pentateuch, and specific judgments often have the names of individual rabbis attached.

By the very nature of this work, references to the Psalms in the Mishnah are few—only forty-one references in Herbert Danby's edition.[70] These references are of two sorts. The first is prescriptions for the recitation of given psalms. I have already made reference to one of these prescriptions, the tradition for the singing of the Psalm of the Day on successive days of the week by the Levites in the temple. This prescription is incorporated into synagogue liturgy. And there is another such prescription, the procedure to be carried out in the case of a drought in Palestine. In the Tractate *Taanith* (Fasting) the procedure is given for a fast during the ninth month (November/December) if no rain had fallen: a three-day fast is declared; then, if after these three days there was still no rain, an additional seven days of fasting was prescribed, and in the prayer during those additional seven days the leader of the congregation was to add to the Eighteen Blessings (thus the early form of Amidah; see above) six further benedictions, among which are four psalms, namely, Psalms 120, 121, 130, and 102.[71] It is striking that all of these psalms are psalms of the individual, three of them being laments (Psalms 120, 130, and 102):

Psalm 130 begins, "Out of the depths I cry to you, O Lord." In this instance, psalms of the individual are used in the most corporate of prayers, that God relieve the drought in the land.

But most of the references to the Psalms in the Mishnah are simply a kind of scriptural reinforcement for the matter at hand. I offer two examples. In *Aboth* (Fathers), a collection of maxims and saying on the law, we read:

> Rabbi Hananiah ben Teradion [who was killed in the Bar-Kokhba revolt in 135 C.E.] said: If two sit together and no words of the Law [are spoken] between them, there is the seat of the scoffers, as it is written, *Nor sit in the seat of scoffers* [Ps. 1:1]. But if two sit together and words of the Law [are spoken] between them, the Shekinah [Divine Presence] rests between them, as it is written, *Then those who revered the Lord spoke with one another. The Lord took note and listened, and a book of remembrance was written before him of those who revered the Lord and thought on his name* [Mal. 3:16].[72]

Again, there is a compact notice toward the beginning of the Tractate *Rosh ha-Shanah* (Feast of the New Year) that incorporates a psalm verse:

> At four times in the year is the world judged [by God, through his manifestations in nature]: at Passover, through grain; at Pentecost, through the fruits of the tree; on New Year's Day all that come into the world pass before him like legions of soldiers, for it is written, *He who fashions the hearts of them all, and observes all their deeds* [Ps. 33:15]; and at the Feast [of Tabernacles] they are judged through water [that is, rain, because rain at the Feast of Tabernacles is a sign of God's anger; *Taanith* 1.1].[73]

I now turn to the Talmud. The Talmud is a commentary on the Mishnah. Actually, there are two Talmuds. One is the Jerusalem (or Palestinian) Talmud, prepared in the rabbinic schools in Palestine in the third and fourth centuries, a work that has survived only in parts. The other is the (longer) Babylonian Talmud, prepared in the rabbinic schools of Babylon in the course of the sixth century; this compilation became the standard collection of rabbinic teaching. An English edition of the Babylonian Talmud is published in thirty-four volumes, comprising roughly 16,500 pages.[74]

The Talmud consists of the sequence of passages of the Mishnah, followed by further material called *Gemara* (Aramaic for "Study"). This further material is of two sorts: one is legal material (the general term in Hebrew being "halakah" ["practice"], and the other is various kinds of homiletic material—ethical reflections, tales of Israel's past, all sorts of edifying matters (the general term in Hebrew being "haggadah" [telling or homiletics]).[75] In this vast collection, citations from Psalms of course have a place.

One illustration must here suffice for dozens. In the Tractate *Yoma* we read the determination of the rabbis that the manna given to the Israelites in the wilderness was piled at least sixty cubits high (this is roughly ninety feet or thirty meters). The reasoning is as follows. In Gen. 7:11 it is said that the *windows* of the heavens were opened, allowing the waters of the deluge to fall, and in v. 20 of that passage it is stated that the waters of the flood covered the mountains fifteen cubits deep. The measure of the deluge is the measure of punishment. By contrast, for the falling of the manna one reads in Ps. 78:19, "Can God spread a table in the wilderness?" and in vv. 23-24 of that psalm we read that God commanded the skies above and opened the *doors* of heaven so that manna rained down on them to eat. Here, then, is the measure of goodness, the measure of the manna. A rabbi in the Tannaitic period (the second century) asked, How many windows has a door? The answer is four; therefore the manna that fell on Israel was at least sixty cubits high. Indeed, as Rabbi Issi ben Judah (of the second century) taught, "The manna which fell down for Israel rose so high that all the kings of the east and west could see it, as it is said, [*You prepare a table before me in the presence of my enemies;*] *my cup overflows* [Ps. 23:5]." The enemies of Israel could thus see the manna manifest.[76]

I turn now to midrash. "Midrash" (expounding) is a general term for this mode of free exposition of the Bible that was employed by the rabbinic schools in ancient Palestine.[77] We have seen midrashic technique at Qumran and within the New Testament, as writers expounded Scripture within their own perspectives.

But there also arose specific collections of midrash for specific books of the Old Testament, beginning with the books of the Pentateuch and continuing with some of the other books. In these collections midrashic material is organized sequentially for a given biblical book. There does exist a Midrash on the Psalms, but it played only a minor part in Jewish literature, having been completed at a late date, perhaps in the thirteenth century.[78]

The Midrash on Psalm 23 covers more than six pages in the English printed edition. The comments on the first verse alone ("The Lord is my shepherd, I shall not want") take up almost four pages. Much of it is a series of comparable passages; it begins as follows.

> *The Lord is my shepherd; I shall not want.* These words are to be considered in the light of the verse *My beloved is mine and I am his; he pastures his flock among the lilies* [Song of Sol. 2:16], by which is meant that the congregation of Israel said to the Holy One, blessed be He: As He is God to me, so am I a people to Him. As He is God to me, having said: *I am the Lord your God* [Exod. 20:2], so am I His people to Him, He having said: *Listen to me, my people* [Isa. 51:4]. As He is father to me, having said: *I have become a father to Israel* [Jer. 31:9], so am I son to Him, He having said: *Israel is My . . . son* [Exod. 4:22]. As he is shepherd to me, Asaph having said: *Give ear, O Shepherd of Israel* [Ps. 80:2 (1)], so am I sheep to Him, He having said: *You are my sheep, the sheep of my pasture* [Ezek. 34:31]. As He is brother to me, Solomon having said: *O that you were like a brother to me* [Song of Sol. 8:1], so am I sister to Him, He having said: *Open to me, my sister, my love* [Song of Sol. 5:2].

In its comment on Ps. 23:5, the Midrash states that the "table" is a table of manna and quail. It notes the opinion, already cited, that the heaps of manna were sixty cubits high and comments, "He who does not believe this—he shall not look upon the sweetness [to come], as is said: *They will not look on the rivers, the streams flowing with honey and curds* [Job 20:17]."

The Karaites and the Debate on the
Nature of the Psalms

There were several developments within Judaism, especially in southern Europe, that stimulated a movement away from what was called *derash* (applied meaning), that is, the activity of (free) exposition of Scripture (midrash), to what was called *peshaṭ* (literally, "specific statement"), that is, the plain meaning of the text or, perhaps better, the meaning of the text in its context.[79] The movement began with debates between traditional rabbinic Judaism and the sect called the Karaites (see below), and in the case of the Psalms it developed into a debate, now almost forgotten, on the very nature of that book. The concern for the plain meaning of the text in turn began to stimulate real commentary literature, beginning in the tenth century and flowering in Europe in the eleventh, twelfth, and thirteenth centuries, which would make a lasting contribution to scriptural studies.

The factors leading to this development are complicated, but the following at least may be mentioned. First, Europe in general was growing more prosperous, emerging from the instabilities of the early Middle Ages. Second, Greek philosophical works, having been preserved by Muslims, were helping to shape Muslim thinking, and where there was interaction between Muslims and Jews, as there was in areas having a substantial population of Sephardic Jews (particularly in Spain), this awareness had an effect on Jewish thinkers as well. Third, the study of Arabic grammar and lexicography, branches of learning stimulated by the earlier work of Greek grammarians, in turn stimulated Jewish scholars to be more self-conscious about the nature of the Hebrew language and to undertake the preparation of Hebrew grammars and word lists.

Then there was an additional, quite specific development within Judaism, the emergence at the end of the eighth century of a sect known as Karaites (i.e., "Biblicists"). In our day scholars have come to realize that there is a striking resemblance between the teachings of the Karaites and the teachings of the Qumran community centuries before, so much so that it is altogether possible that the sect owed its origin to an early discovery of some of the Dead Sea Scrolls, or at least that the sect was stimulated by such a discovery (see chapter 7).[80] In any event, the Karaites rejected the rabbinic authority embodied in the Talmud and relied instead on their own intelligence to read the Scriptures independently.[81] Therefore even commentators who were anti-Karaite were forced to take scriptural studies with fresh seriousness.[82]

I begin the story in Mesopotamia, with Saadiah Gaon (882–942 C.E.), who was born in the Fayyum in Upper Egypt and eventually became head of the Jewish academy at Sura, north of Babylon. He was a scholar of wide-ranging interests, concerned above all to counter the teachings of the Karaites. He translated several books of the Bible into Arabic, among which were the Psalms, and he wrote two different introductions to the Psalms.[83]

His theory about the nature of the Psalms was a curious one. He insisted that the Psalms were a second Torah: as God had revealed the first Torah to Moses, so

God revealed the Psalms to David. In this insistence Saadiah not only ignored any variation in style among the Psalms but also the form-critical contrast between the Psalms and the Pentateuch—whereas the Pentateuch can be understood as words of God to the covenant people, the Psalms, at least on the surface, are words from the people to God, prayers and the like. Doubtless Saadiah was motivated by the centrality of the Psalms for Jewish life and by the fivefold division of the Psalter (see chapter 6). But his more particular motive was clearly to counter the approach of the Karaites, who taught that the Psalms are prophetic prayers.

Two Karaite teachers came forth to try to refute Saadiah, namely, Salmon ben Yeruḥam, born in Palestine or Egypt about 910; and Yefet ben 'Ali, born in Fez, Morocco, about the middle of the tenth century. We have commentaries on the Psalms from both teachers. They taught that the Psalms are prayers written under prophetic inspiration not only by David but by other prophets as well, such as Moses (see the superscription of Psalm 90), and that, being prophetic, the Psalms predicted the fall of the temple in 70 C.E. and the coming redemption of the Jews. Because in the Karaite view these prayers came by prophetic inspiration, the Psalter was to be the mandatory prayer book for Israel; and because the Karaites employed for their prayers only this prophetic material, their prayers were to be considered superior to those of Jews of the rabbinic tradition, who employed nonprophetic prayers (such as the Amidah).

A third view of the Psalms was espoused by Moses Ibn Giqatilah, who was born in Cordoba, Spain, at the beginning of the eleventh century. Only fragments of his commentary on the Psalms are available, but this commentary was drawn upon by Abraham Ibn Ezra (see below). Ibn Giqatilah was active in Saragossa, Spain, in the middle of the century, and spent some time in southern France. In his approach to Scripture he minimized the place of miracle, made free use of Christian commentaries and translations of the Bible, and viewed the Psalms not as prophecies but as prayers and poems produced by different authors and referring to historical events that occurred in proximity to their utterance.

Still a fourth view of the Psalms was set forth by Abraham Ibn Ezra, born in Toledo, Spain (ca. 1090–1167). Ibn Ezra had a wide-ranging intellect and traveled widely as well; he has been remembered as a poet, scientist, and philosopher, as well as a grammarian and biblical commentator. He wrote two commentaries on the Psalms, an earlier one (that survives only in part) alongside the "standard" one, which was written in France. He refers more than once to Ibn Giqatilah; in contrast to the earlier figure, Ibn Ezra returned to the belief held by the writers of the Talmud, that the Psalms are inspired poetry—poetry (rather than primarily prayers) written under prophetic inspiration.[84] I return to Ibn Ezra in a moment.

Commentaries on the Psalms

Three commentaries on the Psalms in Hebrew have survived from this period to become central for Jewish interpretation of the book. In chronological order, they are those of Rabbi Solomon ben Isaac (popularly known as Rashi, from the acronym of his name); Ibn Ezra; and Rabbi David ben Qimḥi. It is to these commentaries that I now turn.[85] Given the vastness of this commentary literature, I offer only a handful of samples here, choosing them from the commentary treatments of Psalms 23, 2, and 137, respectively.

Rashi

The commentaries of Rashi (1040–1105) have been the most popular. Rashi lived his whole life in Troyes in central France. He wrote commentaries on almost every book of the Old Testament[86] and on the Talmud as well; they are direct, simple, and often homely.

Given the superscription of Psalm 23, Rashi takes it for granted that David is the psalmist. For the first verse—"The Lord is my shepherd, I shall not want"—Rashi simply understands David to say, "In this wilderness in which I walk I trust that nothing will be lacking for me"; and on v. 5—"You anoint my head with oil"—Rashi has David say, "I have already been anointed by your word to be king."

In Psalm 2 there are several difficult or rare words, and Rashi is at pains to offer Hebrew synonyms or, in several cases, words in his vernacular, Old French (which he spelled in the Hebrew alphabet!). (These Old French "glosses" in Rashi's commentaries turn out to be of great value to historians of the French language; there are several hundred of them, and they are some of the earliest specimens of Old French.) He begins his comments on Psalm 2 by stating, "Our rabbis explain this text to refer to the Messiah-king, but according to the literal sense it will be more appropriate to explain it in reference to David himself; compare the verse, *and the Philistines heard that the Israelites had anointed David king* [2 Sam. 5:17]." For verse 2 he explains the Hebrew noun *rōzĕnîm* (NRSV, "rulers") by the vernacular word *šyntrš*, possibly *sendres*, modern French *sires* (lords), or *senatours*, modern French *sénateurs* (senators); and he connects the Hebrew verb *nōsĕdû* (NRSV, "take counsel") with the common Hebrew noun *sôd* (counsel) and explains the verb by the vernacular word *pyrqynšylrwnṭ*, that is, *perkensileront*, a verb related to the modern French *conseilleront*.

In Ps. 137:3 there is a Hebrew word that appears only here in the Old Testament, *tôlālênû* (NRSV, "our tormentors"). Rashi explains the word as "kinds of musical instruments," given the reference to "our harps" in v. 2; he connects the word to the word *tālînû* in v. 2 (NRSV, "we hung up"), assuming that "they raise them," that is, the instruments. (A modern commentator would see the wordplay between the two verses but deny such an etymological connection.)

Ibn Ezra

I now return to Ibn Ezra, whose place in the debate on the nature of the Psalms I have already described.[87] For "still waters" in Ps. 23:2, Ibn Ezra points out that they are the opposite of a rushing brook. In Ps. 2:2 Ibn Ezra, like Rashi, connects *nôsĕdû* to *sôd*. On the word *tôlālênû* in Ps. 137:3, Ibn Ezra remarks that it is a difficult word. He cites several rabbinic opinions: one is that the word is related to *tālûl*, a word that appears in Ezek. 17:22 (NRSV, "lofty"); another, that the word is to be compared with *yĕlālâ* (howling), in which case the word would have a *t-* prefix, like *tôšābênû* (our sojourners) from the verb *yāšab* (dwell)—our tormentors want joy, but they cause us to howl. All of this demonstrates how a scholar of that epoch struggled with the details of etymology.

Qimḥi

The third commentator I mention is Qimḥi (often spelled Kimḥi or Kimchi; ca. 1160–1235), known by his acronym as Radak. He lived in Narbonne, a city in Provence (southwestern France) near the Mediterranean Sea.[88]

Qimḥi becomes specific in identifying the context of Psalm 23: "before me a table" is the kingship (given to David); "in the presence of my enemies" refers to Doeg and Ahitophel (Doeg betrayed David [1 Sam. 22:9], and Ahitophel conspired with Absalom against David [2 Sam. 15:31]).

On the word *nôsĕdû* in Ps. 2:2, Qimḥi connects the word to *sôd*, as the other commentators do, but he is uneasy because the word appears to be related to the verb root *yāsad* (establish, found); so he also cites the latter possibility, suggesting that "counsel is to actual performance as the foundation to a building." (As a matter of fact, modern lexicographers still debate which derivation is correct.)[89]

In Ps. 137:3, Qimḥi simply says that the meaning of the phrase is that "they required of us 'words of song' and asked us to make merry with our harps." But he also cites the derivation from "wailing," just as Ibn Ezra did.

And one may mention one more curiosity: In discussing the Edomites (Ps. 137:7), Qimḥi relates the reference not only to the destruction of Solomon's temple in 587 B.C.E. but (by prediction) to the destruction of the Second Temple by the Roman Titus. The Edomites were identified with the Romans evidently because Herod, the Idumean (and thus ultimately an Edomite), was a client of Rome.

These three commentators, and others like them, have helped generations of Jewish readers to refocus their attention on the "plain meaning" of the text.

Translations, Hymns, Poems, Musical Works:
The Psalms as a Jewish Treasure

Four more items must be mentioned as we round off our study. The first is translations. I have already mentioned medieval translations of the Psalms into Arabic, and Jews continued steadily to make translations of the Scriptures into their vernaculars—translations that, of course, included the Psalms. For example, there is evidence of many Jewish translations into various Judeo-Romance languages; there is a Ladino (Judeo-Spanish) translation of the Psalms that was published in Constantinople in 1540.[90] There was a Yiddish translation of several books that included the Psalms prepared before 1490; a Yiddish translation of the Psalms was published in Venice in 1545.[91] But there was little call for a Yiddish translation of the Scriptures in eastern Europe; boys and men learned their Hebrew, Yiddish books were for women, and women were marginal in the use of the Scriptures.[92] There was more call for such translations in central and western Europe and, particularly, in the United States; the most serious was the Bible of "Yehoash," the pen name of Solomon Bloomgarden (1870–1927), whose entire translation was finally published in 1937.[93]

There have been many Jewish translations of the Scriptures into English. One notable one in the nineteenth century was that of Isaac Leeser (1806–1868); his translation was an adaptation of the KJV.[94] Then the Jewish Publication Society produced in 1917 a Jewish version that prevailed for almost half a century, though only the Conservative and Reform movements supported this translation; the Orthodox issued a ban on it.[95] Again, it was a light revision of the KJV.[96] But after the Second World War a new Jewish version into current English was prepared, this time with the support of the Orthodox movement as well;[97] this translation is now referred to as *Tanakh*.[98]

The second item one must acknowledge is the range of hymns (Hebrew, *Piyyutim*) that have the Psalms as a model, some of which have entered Jewish liturgy. I have already mentioned the hymn *Lekhah Dodi* (Come my beloved), sung at the service to welcome the Sabbath. Three more hymns may be mentioned here. Two of them are recited at the end of the liturgy for Friday evening and for festivals. The first is the *Yigdal*, a poem composed by Daniel ben Judah of Rome in the fourteenth century; it is a poem based on the thirteen articles of faith of Maimonides the philosopher.[99] This hymn was translated into English in 1770 by Thomas Olivers, a Wesleyan minister, as "The God of Abraham Praise," and in this form has entered into the repertory of Christian hymnody; the (Episcopal) *Hymnal 1982* uses both this translation and a more literal one, "Praise to the Living God."[100] The second hymn is the *Adon Olam* (Lord of the world), supposed to have been composed by Solomon Ibn Gabirol (1021–1058); the last words of the hymn are from Ps. 118:6. Finally, I mention the hymn *Maoz Tsur* (Rock of ages), sung after the kindling of the Ḥanukkah lights both in the synagogue and in homes; it is of German origin, perhaps from the thirteenth century,[101] and it has become known beyond Jewish circles.[102] Jewish prayer books contain the texts of many such hymns; again, the topic is too vast to explore here.[103]

Many of these hymns are not sung in the synagogue at all but are Sabbath *Zemirot* (songs) sung at Sabbath meals;[104] but it must be added that among the *Zemirot* the biblical Psalms themselves also play an important part.[105]

The third item one must acknowledge is the way in which the Psalms have entered Jewish art and music.[106] One thinks, for example, of the work of the Swiss Jewish composer Ernest Bloch (1880–1959), *Avodath Hakodesh* (*Sacred Service*), completed in 1933, a musical rendering of the Sabbath morning service of the *Union Prayer Book* (of Reform Judaism), which thereby incorporates passages from the Psalms. Thus the work begins with the *Mah Tovu*, which, as we have noted, includes four psalm verses, and ends, just before the benediction, with a moving setting of the hymn *Adom Olam*. And mention may also be made of the *Service sacré* (1947) of Darius Milhaud (1892–1974), based on the Provençal Jewish traditions he had known as a child.

The fourth item to be mentioned is that, strikingly, as the Hebrew language has been revived as a living language, particularly for those living in the present-day state of Israel, the Hebrew Scriptures and most especially the Psalms have become central to the "national heritage." We must understand that only 10 or 15 percent of those living in Israel are religiously observant, but in secular Israeli schools the Hebrew Bible is treated as the basic text of Jewish civilization. Indeed Israeli popular music and rock music often contains biblical themes, some borrowed from the Psalms among them. As an instance of how the Psalms have entered into popular discourse, one may note that Ps. 126:5-6—"They who sow in tears shall reap with songs of joy; though he goes along weeping, carrying the seed-bag, he shall come back with songs of joy, carrying his sheaves" (*Tanakh* translation)—has become a proverb in Israeli agricultural settlements. Again, on June 7, 1967, the news announcer for The Voice of Israel in Jerusalem could find no more appropriate way to announce the taking of the eastern portion of Jerusalem, formerly held by the Arabs, than the recitation of Psalm 122 ("Our feet are standing within your gates, O Jerusalem. Jerusalem—built as a city that is bound firmly together"). The Psalms then live in Jewish consciousness in ways that defy delimitation.[107]

Occasionally a non-Jew can be allowed to experience what the Hebrew Scriptures can mean to Jews, and that experience is afforded by a recent collection of essays by North American Jewish writers on various books of the Bible. The title of the collection is *Congregation: Contemporary Writers Read the Jewish Bible.*[108] Two contributors to this collection write on the Psalms: Allen Mandelbaum (1926–   ), who is professor emeritus of English and comparative literature at the Graduate Center of the City University of New York; and John Hollander (1929–   ), who is a professor of English literature at Yale University. In their essays these writers ponder the layer of misunderstandings they had of lines of the Psalms as boys, the collision of the Hebrew they learned and the King James Version they also learned, the layers of interpretation of the Jewish sages and the paraphrases of (Christian) English poets, and above all the steady marvel of the action of the Psalms upon the writers. Mandelbaum affirms, "*Tehillim* (Psalms) is one text that, I now can see, has had a strange constancy for me,"[109] and Hollander closes his essay with the suggestion that

> the layers of misreadings and rereadings are part of the poetry of the text itself in the poetic portions of the Bible. And the problems and puzzles of the psalms will remain eternal occasions for the reader's negative capability as well as for the interpretive wit that turns every reader into a poet, if only momentarily.[110]

In the course of their essays these writers touch on many of the concerns of the present study.

I close this chapter with a personal reminiscence. Some years ago a friend of mine, a fine amateur musician, began training to follow in his grandfather's footsteps as a Jewish cantor; he is one of the founding members of a communal farm in the Catholic Worker tradition. The first time he sang as a cantor, it was before a

Jewish congregation not far from the farm, at the evening service before Rosh Hashanah (New Year's). It was an occasion of joy: his parents had come from another state, and the congregation was enlarged with many of his friends. As I sat with a couple of Roman Catholic priests, waiting for the service to begin, one of the priests opened the prayer book, which was printed with Hebrew and English on facing pages. The first thing he saw, at the beginning of the book, was Psalm 95. "Oh look," he said, "they have the invitatory psalm!"—that is, the psalm that Catholics who use the prayers of the hours recite before daily morning prayer. Here was a link between two traditions that have been separated by almost two millennia: the same psalm, fulfilling the same function, to open the act of worshiping Almighty God; and that brief moment of surprised recognition was an acknowledgment of a shared heritage.

NOTES

1. See Mishnah *Yadaim* 3.5.

2. For a recent assessment of the place of Jamnia in the process of establishing the canon, see Roger T. Beckwith, "Formation of the Hebrew Bible," in Martin Jan Mulder (ed.), *Mikra: Text, Translation, Reading and Interpretation of the Hebrew Bible in Ancient Judaism and Early Christianity* (Assen and Maastricht: Van Gorcum; Philadelphia: Fortress, 1988), 58–61; and David E. Aune, "On the Origins of the 'Council of Javneh' Myth," *JBL* 110 (1991):491–93.

3. Bleddyn J. Roberts, *The Old Testament Text and Versions* (Cardiff: University of Wales Press, 1951), 20–23; idem, "Text, OT," in *IDB* 4:585; Dominique Barthélemy, "Text, Hebrew, History of," in *IDBSup* 880–82.

4. Menahem Stern, "The Period of the Second Temple," in Haim Hillel Ben-Sasson (ed.), *A History of the Jewish People* (Cambridge: Harvard University Press, 1976), 277–78.

5. See T. Alec Burkill, "Sanhedrin," in *IDB* 4:214–18; Shmuel Safrai, "The Era of the Mishnah and Talmud (70–640)," in Ben-Sasson (ed.), *History of the Jewish People*, 307–11.

6. Qur'ān 4.163; 17.55.

7. See Solomon Katz, *The Jews in the Visigothic and Frankish Kingdoms of Spain and Gaul* (Cambridge, Mass.: Mediaeval Academy of America, 1937).

8. Cf. Qur'ān 3.64–65; see Haim Hillel Ben-Sasson, "The Middle Ages," in idem (ed.), *History of the Jewish People*, 404–6.

9. Ibid., 454–58.

10. Ibid., 661–63.

11. Ibid., 633–39.

12. Ibid., 654–57; and, in detail, Nathan Ben Moses Hanover, *Abyss of Despair (Yeven Metzulah)* (New York: Bloch, 1950).

13. Shmuel Ettinger, "The Modern Period," in Ben-Sasson (ed.), *History of the Jewish People*, 735.

14. Ibid., 860–64.

15. Ibid., 1017–39.

16. Ibid., 1048–62, 1075–96.

17. Ben-Sasson, "Middle Ages," 695–701; and see Frank Talmage, "Apples of Gold: The Inner Meaning of Sacred Texts in Medieval Judaism"; Ivan G. Marcus, "The Devotional Ideals of Ashkenazic Pietism"; Daniel C. Matt, "The Mystic and the *Miẓwot*"; and Moshe Idel, "*Hitbodedut* as Concentration in Ecstatic Kabbalah," all in Arthur Green (ed.), *Jewish Spirituality from the Bible through the Middle Ages* (New York: Crossroad, 1988), 313–55, 356–66, 367–404, and 405–38, respectively; and R. J. Zwi Werblowsky, "The Safed Revival and Its Aftermath"; Jacob Katz, "Halakhah and Kabbalah as Competing Disciplines of Study"; Lawrence Fine, "The Contemplative Practice of Yiḥudim in Lurianic Kabbalah"; and Louis Jacobs, "The Uplifting of Sparks in Later Jewish Mysticism," all in Arthur Green (ed.), *Jewish Spirituality from the Sixteenth-Century Revival to the Present* (World Spirituality, An Encyclopedic History of the Religious Quest 14; New York: Crossroad, 1989), 7–33, 34–63, 64–98, and 99–126, respectively.

18. Ettinger, "Modern Period" 768–76; and Louis Jacobs, "Typologies of Leadership and the Hasidic Ẓaddiq"; and Rachel Elior, "ḤaBaD: The Contemplative Ascent to God," both in Green (ed.), *Sixteenth-Century Revival*, 127–56 and 157–205, respectively; Martin Buber, *Tales of the Hasidim: Early Masters* (New York: Schocken, 1947); idem, *Tales of the Hasidim: Later Masters* (New York: Schocken, 1948); idem, *Hasidism and Modern Man* (Harper Torchbooks 839; New York: Harper & Row, 1966); and see, in general, for both kabbalism and Ḥasidism, Gershom G. Scholem, *Major Trends in Jewish Mysticism* (New York: Schocken, 1961).

19. Ettinger, "Modern Period," 834–37; and see, conveniently, Leo Trepp, *Eternal Faith, Eternal People: A Journey into Judaism* (Englewood Cliffs, N.J.: Prentice-Hall, 1962), 299–304. For a thorough history of the movement, see Michael A. Meyer, *Response to Modernity: A History of the Reform Movement in Judaism* (Oxford: Oxford University Press, 1988).

20. Trepp, *Eternal Faith*, 307.

21. For Reform and neo-Orthodoxy, see Ettinger, "Modern Period," 834–40.

22. *The World Almanac and Book of Facts, 1991*, 609.

23. For a useful sketch, see Abraham Cronbach, "Worship in NT Times, Jewish," in *IDB* 4:894–903; see also Raphael Posner, Uri Kaploun, and Shalom Cohen (eds.), *Jewish Liturgy, Prayer and Synagogue Service through the Ages* (Jerusalem: Keter, 1975), 118, 246.

24. See, conveniently, G. Henton Davies, "Worship in the OT," in *IDB* 4:882.

25. See Mishnah *Tamid* 7.4; cf. Cronbach, "Worship in NT Times," in *IDB* 4:896.

26. Cf. Cronbach, "Worship in NT Times," *IDB* 4:895.

27. For non-Jews and for nonpracticing Jews, helpful explanations of synagogue liturgy and of Jewish prayer books may be found in Hayim Halevy Donin, *To Pray as a Jew: A Guide to the Prayer Book and the Synagogue Service* (New York: Basic Books, 1980), and in Posner, Kaploun, and Cohen (eds.), *Jewish Liturgy*. For a fuller treatment of the evolution of the details of Jewish liturgy, see Lawrence A. Hoffman, *The Canonization of the Synagogue Service* (University of Notre Dame Center for the Study of Judaism and Christianity in Antiquity 4; Notre Dame, Ind.: University of Notre Dame Press, 1979). More technical and dealing with the earlier period is Joseph Heinemann, *Prayer in the Talmud: Forms and Patterns* (Berlin and New York: de Gruyter, 1977).

28. Louis Isaac Rabinowitz, "Psalms, Book of," in *EncJud* 13:1323.

29. Mishnah *Berakoth* 4.1.

30. Posner, Kaploun, and Cohen (eds.), *Jewish Liturgy*, 119.

31. For a description, see Cronbach, "Worship in NT Times," in *IDB* 4:898; Donin, *To Pray as a Jew*, 69–108; Posner, Kaploun, and Cohen (eds.), *Jewish Liturgy*, 81–84.

32. Posner, Kaploun, and Cohen (eds.), *Jewish Liturgy*, 120; cf. Donin, *To Pray as a Jew*, 200.

33. For a description of the development of the *Pesukei d'Zimra*, see Leon J. Liebreich, "The Compilation of the Pesuke de-Zimra," *Proceedings of the American Academy of Jewish Research* 18 (1948–49):255–67.

34. Cf. Rabinowitz, "Psalms," *EncJud* 13:1334.

35. Donin, *To Pray as a Jew*, 202–5; Posner, Kaploun, and Cohen (eds.), *Jewish Liturgy*, 107.

36. See Posner, Kaploun, and Cohen (eds.), *Jewish Liturgy*, 130–41.

37. Donin, *To Pray as a Jew*, 234.

38. Rabinowitz, "Psalms," *EncJud* 13:1324.

39. Ibid.; and see Posner, Kaploun, and Cohen (eds.), *Jewish Liturgy*, 131.

40. Donin, *To Pray as a Jew*, 257–61.

41. Rabinowitz, "Psalms," in *EncJud*, 13:1324; Posner, Kaploun, and Cohen (eds.), *Jewish Liturgy*, 19, 137.

42. Posner, Kaploun and Cohen (eds.), *Jewish Liturgy*, 141–59.

43. See Johannes Hempel, "Hallel," in *IDB* 2:514; Posner, Kaploun, and Cohen (eds.), *Jewish Liturgy*, 108–9.

44. Donin, *To Pray as a Jew*, 267; see Mishnah *Pesaḥim* 10.6.

45. Donin, *To Pray as a Jew*, 265–66.

46. Ibid., 266.

47. Ibid., 68.

48. Ibid., 265.

49. Rabinowitz, "Psalms," in *EncJud* 13:1324.

50. Posner, Kaploun, and Cohen (eds.), *Jewish Liturgy*, 137.

51. For convenience I use the classifications in Leopold Sabourin, *The Psalms: Their Origin and Meaning* (New York: Alba House, 1974), 175–410.

52. Psalms 19, 29, 33, 100, 113, 114, 117, 135, 136, 145—150.

53. Psalms 93, 96—99.

54. Four psalms of confidence of the individual out of nine: Psalms 16, 27, 121, 131—and all three psalms of confidence of the community—Psalms 115, 125, 129.

55. Four psalms of thanksgiving of the individual out of eleven—Psalms 30, 34, 92, 116—three psalms of thanksgiving of the community out of six—Psalms 68, 118, 124.

56. Psalms 49, 91, 127, 128, 133.

57. Psalms 81 and 95.

58. Psalms 20, 132, 144.

59. Psalms 6, 120, 130.

60. Psalms 82, 90, 94, 123, 126, 137.

61. Donin, *To Pray as a Jew*, 204; Posner, Kaploun, and Cohen (eds.), *Jewish Liturgy*, 107–8.

62. Donin, *To Pray as a Jew*, 301.

63. The literature on Jewish piety is immense. Useful are Scholem, *Jewish Mysticism*; Marcus, "Ashkenazic Pietism."

64. Jeremiah Unterman, personal correspondence.

65. Rabbi Avrohom Chaim Feuer and others, *Tehillim* (ArtScroll Tanach Series; New York: Mesorah, 1985), 1746.

66. Rabinowitz, "Psalms," *EncJud* 13:1325.

67. For this procedure, see Feuer et al., *Tehillim*, 1745.

68. A useful introduction is Isidore Epstein, "Talmud," in *IDB* 4:511–15.

69. Herbert Danby, *The Mishnah* (Oxford: Oxford University Press, 1958); and see, recently, Jacob Neusner, *The Mishnah: A New Translation* (New Haven: Yale University Press, 1988).

70. Danby, *The Mishnah*, 810.

71. Mishnah *Taanith* 3.2.

72. Mishnah *Aboth* 3.2.

73. Mishnah *Rosh ha-Shanah* 1.2.

74. Isidore Epstein (ed.), *The Babylonian Talmud* (London: Soncino, 1935–48).

75. A useful introduction to this literature is Jacob Neusner, *Invitation to the Talmud* (New York: Harper & Row, 1973). Selections may be found in Ben Zion Bokser and others, *The Talmud: Selected Writings* (New York: Paulist, 1989).

76. Babylonian Talmud *Yoma* 76a; in Epstein (ed.), *Babylonian Talmud*, the page citation in *Yoma* is 369–70.

77. Isidore Epstein, "Midrash," in *IDB* 3:376–77; Jacob Neusner, *What is Midrash?* (Philadelphia: Fortress, 1987); idem, *A Midrash Reader* (Philadelphia: Fortress, 1990).

78. See William G. Braude, *The Midrash on Psalms*, 2 vols. (Yale Judaica Series 13; New Haven: Yale University Press, 1959).

79. The matter is not simple; see David Weiss Halivni, *Peshat and Derash: Plain and Applied Meaning in Rabbinic Exegesis* (Oxford: Oxford University Press, 1991).

80. For the link, see John A. Allegro, *The Dead Sea Scrolls* (Harmondsworth: Penguin, 1958), 166–67; for the parallels in doctrine between the two groups, see Naphtali Wieder, *The Judean Scrolls and Karaism* (London: East and West Library, 1962).

81. Ben-Sasson, "Middle Ages," 448–49.

82. See Erwin I. J. Rosenthal, "The Study of the Bible in Medieval Judaism," in Geoffrey W. H. Lampe (ed.), *The Cambridge History of the Bible*, Vol. 2; *The West from the Fathers to the Reformation* (Cambridge: Cambridge University Press, 1969), 255–58; Joshua Baker and Ernest W. Nicholson, *The Commentary of Rabbi David Kimḥi on Psalms CXX–CL* (University of Cambridge Oriental Publications 22; Cambridge: Cambridge University Press, 1973), xv–xvi.

83. For a translation into English of his longer introduction, see Moshe Sokolow, "Saadiah Gaon's Prolegomenon to Psalms," *Proceedings of the American Academy of Jewish Research* 51 (1984):131–74.

84. For this survey of the debate among Saadiah Gaon, the Karaites, Ibn Giqatilah, and Ibn Ezra, I am indebted to Uriel Simon, *Four Approaches to the Book of Psalms: From Saadiah Gaon to Abraham Ibn Ezra* (Albany: SUNY Press, 1991).

85. For a convenient assessment of the three, see Rosenthal, "Study of the Bible," 261–71.

86. Unfortunately, translations of Rashi's commentary material into modern European languages are limited to those on the Pentateuch. There are scattered details of Rashi's comments on the Psalms in Feuer et al., *Tehillim*. I have used the text of Rashi printed in a standard rabbinic Bible, *Miqre'ot Gedolot* (Warsaw, 1874–77; reprint, New York: Pardes, 1951), supplemented by reference to a Latin translation (Johann Friedrich Breithaupt [ed.]), Jarchi, *Commentarius Hebraicus in Biblia: Latine Versus* (Gotha; 1710–14).

87. I use here the text in the *Miqre'ot Gedolot.*

88. Qimḥi's commentary on the Psalms is not included in the edition of *Miqre'ot Gedolot* available to me. A critical (Hebrew) edition of Psalms 1–41 appeared in S. M. Schiller-Szinessy, *The First Book of the Psalms . . . with the Longer Commentary of R. David Qimchi* (Cambridge: Deighton Bell; Leipzig: Brockhaus, 1883); an English translation of the commentary on some of these psalms—namely, Psalms 1–10, 15–17, 19, 22, 24—is found in Rowland G. Finch and George H. Box, *The Longer Commentary of R. David Ḳimḥi on the First Book of Psalms* (Translations of Early Documents Series III, Rabbinic Texts; London: SPCK; New York: Macmillan, 1919). A critical (Hebrew) edition of Psalms 42–72 appears in Sidney I. Esterson, "The Commentary of Rabbi David Ḳimḥi on Psalms 42–72, Edited on the Basis of Manuscripts and Early Editions," *HUCA* 10 (1935): 309–450. A critical (Hebrew) edition, with English translation, of Psalms 120–150 is found in Baker and Nicholson, *Commentary of Rabbi David Kimḥi.* An excellent assessment of Qimḥi is Frank E. Talmage, *David Kimḥi: The Man and the Commentaries* (Harvard Judaic Monographs 1; Cambridge: Harvard University Press, 1975).

89. Francis Brown, Samuel R. Driver, and Charles A. Briggs, *A Hebrew and English Lexicon of the Old Testament* (Oxford: Clarendon, 1907), 414a, chooses *yāsad*, translating "seat themselves close together, sit in conclave"; whereas Walter Baumgartner and others, *Hebräisches und Aramäisches Lexikon zum Alten Testament* (Leiden: Brill, 1967–90), 399a, assumes that alongside the verb "found" there is a homonym that is a by-form of *swd* ("take counsel").

90. "Bible," in *EncJud* 4:865–66; see further Margherita Morreale, "Vernacular Scriptures in Spain," in Lampe (ed.), *Cambridge History of the Bible*, 2:474–75.

91. "Bible," in *EncJud* 4:866; Chone Shmeruk, "Yiddish Literature," in *EncJud* 16:800.

92. Harry M. Orlinsky and Robert G. Bratcher, *A History of Bible Translation and the North American Contribution* (SBL Centennial Publications; Atlanta: Scholars Press, 1991), 125.

93. Harry M. Orlinsky, "Yehoash's Yiddish Translation of the Bible," *JBL* 60 (1941): 173–77; and Orlinsky and Bratcher, *History of Bible Translation*, 126–27.

94. Orlinsky and Bratcher, *History of Bible Translation*, 131–38.

95. Ibid., 183–84, n. 5.

96. *The Holy Scriptures according to the Masoretic Text: A New Translation* (Philadelphia: Jewish Publication Society of America, 1917).

97. *The Torah, The Prophets and The Writings* (Philadelphia: Jewish Publication Society of America, 1962, 1978, 1982). See Orlinsky and Bratcher, *History of Bible Translation*, 179–91.

98. *Tanakh: A New Translation of the Holy Scriptures according to the Traditional Hebrew Text* (Philadelphia: Jewish Publication Society of America, 1985).

99. Aaron Rothkoff, "Yigdal," in *EncJud* 16:833–35.

100. *The Hymnal 1982* (New York: The [Episcopal] Church Hymnal Corporation, 1982), nos. 401 and 372. "The God of Abraham Praise" is a standard item in recent hymnals: Inter-Lutheran Commission on Worship, *Lutheran Book of Worship* (Minneapolis: Augsburg, 1978), no. 544; *The United Methodist Hymnal: Book of the United Methodist Church* (Nashville: United Methodist Publishing House, 1989), no. 116; *The Presbyterian Hymnal: Hymns, Psalms, and Spiritual Songs* (Louisville: Westminster/John Knox, 1990), no. 488. See further Bathja Bayer, "Yigdal," in *EncJud* 16:835.

101. "Ma'oz Ẓur," in *EncJud* 11:910.

102. See, e.g., "Rock of Strength," in Florence Hudson Botsford (ed.), *The Universal Folk Songster* (New York: Schirmer, 1937), 97.

103. See Donin, *To Pray as a Jew*, 280–83; and extensively in Ezra Fleischer, "Piyyut," in *EncJud* 13:573–602.

104. Donin, *To Pray as a Jew*, 283.

105. Unterman, personal correspondence.

106. "Psalms, Book of," in *EncJud* 13:1325–34.

107. Unterman, personal correspondence.

108. David Rosenberg (ed.), *Congregation: Contemporary Writers Read the Jewish Bible* (New York: Harcourt Brace Jovanovich, 1987).

109. Ibid., 285.

110. Ibid., 312.

10

The Psalms for Christians: In the West until the Reformation, and in the East

We turn back now to the Christian communities, to trace their use of the Psalms. I deal in this chapter with the use of the Psalms in the early church, in the Western church until the time of the Reformation (the beginning of the sixteenth century), and in the Eastern church. Thus we are dealing with a span of time almost as long as that covered in our survey of Judaism in chapter 9, and it will be clear that the life of Christian communities manifested almost as much variety as we have glimpsed in Jewish communities.

Because the story of the spread of the Christian faith is well known to present-day readers, I shall not devote much space to the matter.

The Christian churches that produced the books of the New Testament in the second half of the first century were small, Greek-speaking communities scattered across the cities of the eastern Mediterranean Sea, reaching as far as Rome. In the course of the second and third centuries the faith spread, but at best the Christian faith lived outside legal recognition and during several periods was actively persecuted. When the Roman emperor Constantine suddenly allowed the Christian faith to be a legal religion of the Roman Empire (312 C.E.), Christian communities were Greek-speaking in the eastern Mediterranean and (to some extent) in Gaul, and Latin-speaking in Italy, North Africa, southern Spain, and Roman Britain. The faith had also spread into Syriac-speaking areas of Mesopotamia and among the Armenian people (north of Mesopotamia, toward the Caucasus Mountains), but for purposes of this chapter we must confine ourselves to the Greek- and Latin-speaking churches.

Constantine rebuilt the ancient city of Byzantium and named it after himself, Constantinople (present-day Istanbul); in 330 he transferred the imperial capital from Rome to Constantinople. Constantinople would understand itself to be the capital of the Roman Empire until it fell to the Turks (in 1453), but, in a real sense, from 330 until the fall of Rome to the Germanic general Odoacer (476) the western Roman Empire (speaking Latin) and the eastern Roman Empire (speaking Greek) were two separate entities, and the two cities continued as twin centers of Christian authority, in the West and in the East, through the Middle Ages.

In spite of the barbarian migrations of the Middle Ages, the Christian faith continued to spread: Western Christianity into Ireland in the fifth century and into Scandinavia in the tenth and eleventh centuries, and Eastern Christianity into Russia and other Slavic territories in the tenth century. By the sixteenth century, then, the conversion of the population of Europe had been completed.

Given the use of the Psalms in Jewish worship, one assumes that recitation of the Psalms was a part of earliest Christian worship as well (see chapter 9), but we lack any details.

I take up six topics in this chapter: (1) citations of the Psalms in the early church fathers; (2) the place of the Psalms in the eucharistic liturgy (the liturgy of word and sacrament), especially as it developed in the West; (3) the commentaries on the Psalms in the church fathers; (4) the use of the Psalms in the Divine Office, especially as it, too, developed in the West; (5) the use of the Psalms in the Eastern church; and, finally, (6) vernacular translations, and some popular uses of verses and phrases of the Psalms.

Citations of Psalm Material in the Earliest Church Fathers

The writings of the church fathers are extensive; one can only cite a small number of examples of their use of the Psalms. I am more thorough with regard to the earliest period, as we see how this literature moved out from the New Testament. Citations of the Psalms in the church fathers generally follow the pattern already set forth in the New Testament, although there are occasional surprises.

I begin with two works that were included in some early canons of the New Testament, namely, *1 Clement* and *Barnabas*.[1] The first named, *1 Clement*, was written from Rome to Corinth about 96 C.E., presumably by Clement, the bishop of Rome at that time.[2] It is a long letter, almost as long as 1 and 2 Corinthians combined, and is particularly full of citations from the Old Testament; it contains some 172 Old Testament citations, among which are 49 citations from thirty-two of the psalms. Both Psalms 2 and 110 are cited, psalms that in the New Testament are given a messianic interpretation; in *1 Clement* they are understood as they are in the Letter to the Hebrews—indeed, the citations of those psalms are offered along with citations from Hebrews itself.[3] Some passages cited from the Psalms are extensive.

The work cites Ps. 22:7-9 (6-8), and the words of the passage are attributed to Jesus, whom we are to emulate;[4] and it cites Ps. 51:3-19 (1-17) as words of David, whom we are likewise to emulate.[5] Psalm 50:16-23, the word of God to the sinner, is cited directly as cautionary words to the Christian.[6] And in another passage of moral exhortation, there is a chain of citations from the Psalms (and other biblical material): Pss. 37:9, 38, 35-37; 78:36-37; 62:5 (4); 31:19 (18); and 12:4-6 (3-5) are cited.[7] To sum up: though the author is lavish in his use of passages of the Psalms, there are no surprising turns of interpretation; the passages are used largely for moral appeal.

Barnabas was written about 130 C.E.[8] It offers about a dozen citations from ten psalms; the interpretation of this material is often fanciful. Thus the three clauses of Ps. 1:1 are associated with three sorts of meat forbidden by Moses: forbidden seafood with "the man who does not follow the counsel of the ungodly," pork with "the man who does not stand in the way of sinners," and forbidden birds with "the man who does not sit in the seat of scorners."[9] "He is like a tree planted by rivers of water" (Ps. 1:3) refers both to the waters of baptism and to the (tree of the) cross.[10] Psalm 51:19 (17), "A sacrifice pleasing to God is a broken spirit," proves that Jewish sacrifices are now abolished.[11] But at other points the author reflects New Testament interpretation: verses in Psalm 22 predict the suffering of Christ,[12] and Ps. 110:1 demonstrates that Christ was not the son of David.[13]

The *Didache*, a short church manual from the second century,[14] cites Ps. 4:2— "they love vanity"[15]—and Ps. 37:11—"the humble will inherit the earth,"[16] a phrase reinforced by Matt. 5:5. But the most surprising citation is Ps. 118:26, "who comes in the name of the Lord,"[17] a phrase applied not to Jesus but to visiting teachers and prophets. Here, then, "the Lord" is understood to refer to Jesus himself, in whose name the visitor comes: one should "welcome him as the Lord."[18]

By contrast, there are early works of the church fathers that are almost devoid of citations of the Psalms: among these are the letters of Ignatius of Antioch (ca. 98–117)[19] and Polycarp's *Letter to the Philippians* (ca. 155).[20] Both of these bodies of material offer many citations and reminiscences of New Testament passages but are virtually devoid of citations of the Psalms.[21]

The writings of Justin Martyr (from about 150 C.E.) are full of references to the Psalms; one could say that Justin uses the Old Testament in the way Matthew does.[22] In his *Apology*, a defense of the Christian faith addressed to pagans, the central section cites extensive material from the Psalms as predictions of Christ;[23] and in his *Dialogue with Trypho* (Trypho was a Jew), where he attempts to show the false position of the Jews with regard to the Christian faith, there are some forty-seven references to twenty-four psalms.

One of the key psalms for Justin is Psalm 22; very simply for him, in this psalm David predicts the story of Christ. In the *Apology* he cites scattered verses of the psalm with this understanding;[24] in the *Dialogue* he devotes a long section to this psalm, explaining it christologically, verse by verse. Indeed, for him the conclusion of the psalm, beginning with v. 23 (22)—"I will tell of your name to my brothers"— is a prediction of the resurrection.[25]

Two successive chapters of the *Apology* offer extensive portions of four psalms.[26] Justin first cites Ps. 19:3-6 (2-5) as a prediction of those who were to proclaim Christian teaching (in this he follows Rom. 10:18); then, strikingly, he cites the totality of Psalms 1 and 2 without a break between them—Psalm 1 as a statement about how the prophetic spirit teaches human beings to live, and Psalm 2 as a testimony of the conspiracy against Christ between Herod and the Jews on the one hand and Pilate on the other (compare the beginning of Origen's commentary on Psalm 2, discussed below). Finally, he cites Ps. 96:1, 2, 4-10 as a prediction of how Christ will rule after being crucified. (His version of vv. 9-10, it may be noted, is eccentric: "Let all the earth fear before him, and be set upright and not shaken. Let them exult among the nations; the Lord has reigned from the tree"—for "from the tree," see below.) He uses the same psalms extensively in the *Dialogue*: Ps. 19:2-7 (1-6) describes how Christ comes forth from the heavens and returns there;[27] Ps. 2:7 ("You are my son, today I have begotten you") is cited three times;[28] and he spends a whole chapter insisting that the Jews have omitted "from the tree," a presumed reference to the crucifixion, from their copies of Psalm 96.[29] (Actually, these words seem to have been added by a Christian glossator in the Greek and Latin versions; there is no evidence that it was ever to be found in a Hebrew text.)[30]

Justin cites Psalm 110 extensively. In the *Apology* he cites vv. 1-3 as David's prediction that God the Father would take Christ into heaven after raising him from the dead.[31] In the *Dialogue* he cites the psalm six times. Twice he is at pains to insist that the psalm refers to Christ rather than to Hezekiah, the latter opinion (according to Justin) being that of Trypho[32]—though there is at hand today no evidence that any Jewish authority ever so interpreted the psalm.[33] Justin insists that the first verse of the psalm demonstrates that not only God but Jesus must be called "Lord,"[34] and that vv. 3-4 demonstrate that he has been from the beginning of time.[35] In the *Dialogue* he cites Psalm 45 four times, understanding it as a description of Christ: he cites it once in its entirety[36] and three more times in part.[37] Another psalm he cites frequently is Psalm 19 (both sections of the psalm):[38] remarkably, he interprets "strong as a giant to run his race" (v. 6 [5]) to refer not to the sun but to Christ![39]

Irenaeus, bishop of Lyons in the second half of the second century, in his long work *Against Heresies* uses verses from the Psalms with equal imagination.[40] He cites Ps. 80:2 (1)—"You who are enthroned upon the cherubim, show yourself"—as indicating the necessity for four Gospels, inasmuch as the cherubim have four faces (a datum implied by Ezekiel 1 and 10) and their faces are images of the activity of the Son of God;[41] and he cites Ps. 85:12 (11)—"Truth has come forth from the earth"—as a prediction by David about the resurrection of Jesus.[42]

It is useful to remind ourselves that Christians in the early centuries were by no means united in their understanding of the Old Testament, the Psalms included; so a word here might be said about Marcion, a nonconformist in the church at Rome about 140 C.E.[43] Marcion believed that the God revealed in the Old Testament, a God of justice, was altogether separate from the God of love who is the Father of Jesus Christ: the Old Testament was Jewish history and must be laid aside now that the definitive event of history had come, the event of Jesus Christ. Marcion not only laid aside the Old Testament but confined his scriptural canon to the Gospel of Luke and to ten Pauline letters, and both Luke and Paul's letters he edited.[44] He was literal-minded and almost alone of his age rejected allegory;[45] he denied that the Old Testament prophesies a suffering Messiah.[46] For him, Psalm 2 did not refer to Jesus Christ but described the future national hope of the Jews; Ps. 132:11 was fulfilled in Solomon (against Acts 2:30).[47] Marcion was excommunicated from the church at Rome about 144 C.E., but the churches founded by him continued for another two or three centuries; the Marcionites in Mesopotamia at the beginning of the fifth century were said to have composed psalms of their own for use instead of the Davidic psalms in their meetings for worship.[48]

The Use of the Psalms in Christian Worship in the Earliest Centuries

By the fourth century the memorization of the Psalms by many Christians and their habitual use as songs in worship by all Christians about whom we know were matters of long-standing tradition.[49] In passing, in the Introduction to this work I briefly cited the *Letter to Marcellinus* of Athanasius (ca. 295–373), bishop of Alexandria; this letter concerns the nature of the Psalms. It is a rich and elaborate description of how various psalms can fit the spiritual need of a Christian.[50] Athanasius traces the events in the life of Jesus Christ that are, he declares, foretold in the Psalms; but there is more.

> He who takes up this book—the Psalter—goes through the prophecies about the Savior, as is customary in the other Scriptures, with admiration and adoration, but the other psalms he recognizes as being his own words. And the one who hears is deeply moved, as though he himself were speaking, and is affected by the words of the songs, as if they were his own songs.[51]

> And it seems to me that these words become like a mirror to the person singing them, so that he might perceive himself and the emotions of his soul, and thus affected, he might recite them.[52]

He then lists the psalms that manifest the various literary types—narrative, entreaty, thanksgiving, confession, and the like. And he offers specific prescriptions for the various situations in which Christians find themselves:

> When you see that you are despised and persecuted for the truth's sake by all your friends and relatives, do not give up concern either for them or for yourself. And if you see your acquaintances turning against you, do not be alarmed, but separate yourself from them and turn your mind to the future and sing Psalm 30 [that is, Psalm 31].[53]

We saw already in chapter 1 that Athanasius saw in Psalm 23 a reference to baptism, to anointing, and to the sacrament of communion. We have an impression of baptismal liturgy from a letter written by Paulinus of Nola (353–431); Nola is located about fifteen miles (twenty-five kilometers) east of Naples. Paulinus was bishop there and corresponded with Jerome and Augustine. He described the baptistery built by his friend Sulpicius Severus in south Gaul in the late fourth century; in a letter to Severus, he submitted the text of an inscription that would be set over the murals that decorated the baptistery. The text describes the sacred water in the celestial font into which the new Christians plunge:

> The guilt perishes but life returns; the old Adam dies,
>   and the new Adam is reborn to eternal sovereignty.

The text ends,

> From that place the presiding priest leads from the sacred font,
>> babes, snowy-white in body, heart, and garb.
> And walking the novice lambs around the festive altars,
>> he imbues their tender mouths with the health-giving food.
> From here the older generation of the community rejoice together in a noisy
>> throng,
>> and the fold bleats along with their new chorus, Alleluia![54]

The phraseology here suggests that the metaphor of sheep and the literary movement of the psalm from waters to table has been incarnated in the liturgy of baptism.

There emerged two recurrent acts of Christian worship. One was the communal reenactment of Jesus' last supper with his disciples, that is, the eucharistic liturgy, which became known in the West as the Mass. The other was what became known as the Divine Office, that is, the set prayers at various times through the period of twenty-four hours (Vigils, Lauds, Prime, and so on), a form of worship that developed both from the organized communal prayers of monastic communities and from the noneucharistic public devotions of the great cathedral churches.[55]

The Eucharistic Liturgy

The evolution of various practices in the eucharistic liturgy during the early centuries is a complex story, just as we have seen the evolution of Jewish liturgy to be. I offer only enough detail to clarify the place of the Psalms.

In a certain respect the whole liturgy is heavy with the influence of the Psalms. Thus early in the service the phrase *Kyrie eleison* (Lord have mercy) and its variant *Christe eleison* (Christ have mercy) are recited, always in Greek; the former is an adaptation of a recurrent phrase in the Septuagint Psalms (e.g., Ps. 57:2 (1); the NRSV there has "Be merciful to me, O God"). The acclamation "Alleluia" is discussed below.

In our effort to understand the place of the Psalms in the eucharistic liturgy, we must be careful not to forget their emotional effect. In his *Confessions*, Augustine (354–430), describing his baptism by Ambrose, notes, "How did I weep, in Thy Hymns and Canticles, touched to the quick by the voices of Thy sweet-attuned Church!" Then he remarks that the church in Milan had begun to take over the manner of the Eastern churches, that "Hymns and Psalms should be sung, lest the people should wax faint through the tediousness of sorrow: and from that day to this the custom is retained, divers, yea, almost all Thy congregations, throughout other parts of the world, following herein."[56]

Already early in the history of the church there were two parts to the eucharistic liturgy: the first was the liturgy of the catechumens (the liturgy of the word),[57] centering on the Scripture readings; the second was the liturgy of the faithful (the liturgy of the sacrament), centering on the Eucharist (Communion). Catechumens (those preparing for baptism) were urged to be present at the liturgy of the word, but only baptized members were allowed at the liturgy of the faithful.

The Liturgy of the Word

As early as Tertullian (end of the second century) there is evidence of the use of the Psalter in the liturgy of the word.[58] By the fourth century there is evidence that, when psalms were used in the liturgy, they were sung responsorily: that is, a cantor would sing successive sections of the psalm, to which the congregation would respond with a refrain.[59] For Sunday liturgy the earliest custom was to have three readings—one from the Old Testament, one from the Epistles, and one from the Gospels, though in the Roman rite the Old Testament lesson soon began to be dropped (it must be understood that the psalm was considered not a substantive reading as much as a response to the previous reading). The position of the psalm varied in relation to the three readings: at Rome, when there were three readings, the psalm was sung between the first and the second readings, whereas in Augustine's day at Hippo (in present-day Tunisia), where he was bishop, the psalm was sung between the Epistle and the Gospel.[60]

In the earliest centuries there was no fixed lectionary, that is, no readings prescribed for particular days: the selection of lessons was at the bishop's discretion.[61] Gradually there began to be more fixity in the choice of readings, especially in the case of the important occasions of the church year—Christmas, Holy Week and Easter, and Pentecost.

It is useful to linger with Augustine; hundreds of his sermons have been preserved, and in the course of these sermons he often specifies the readings on which he is preaching.

Thus in five sermons for Christmas Day he notes that the psalm is Psalm 85;[62] he cites specifically vv. 11-12 (10-11): "Steadfast love and faithfulness will meet; righteousness and peace will kiss each other; faithfulness will spring up from the ground, and righteousness will look down from the sky." Similarly, in a sermon for the "Octave" of Christmas (the eighth day after Christmas, counting inclusively; that is, one week later, January 1), Psalm 106 is chosen; he cites v. 47: "Save us, O Lord our God, and gather us from among the nations, that we may give thanks to your holy name."[63]

We have several psalm choices for the period of Lent, during which Augustine preached sequentially on passages from the Gospel of John. These are: for the Wednesday after the Fourth Sunday of Lent, Psalm 50 (he cites v. 3);[64] for the Friday of that week, Psalm 2 (he cites v. 8);[65] for the Fifth Sunday of Lent, Psalm 74 (he refers to vv. 21-23);[66] for the Wednesday of that week, Psalm 82 (he cites v. 8);[67] for the Thursday of that week, Psalm 35 (he cites vv. 13-16 and 20).[68] On Good Friday, Psalm 22 was used, the obvious choice.[69]

For the vigil of Easter (the liturgy of the night before Easter) he uses Psalm 118 (he cites v. 24: "This is the day that the Lord has made; let us rejoice and be glad in it").[70] For the Thursday of Easter Week he uses Psalm 147.[71] For the First Sunday after Easter he uses either Psalm 116:10-19 (a full psalm in the Greek and Latin tradition)—he cites v. 11, "Everyone is a liar"[72]—or Psalm 118 (as for the vigil of Easter).[73]

And for a few more specific days we have knowledge of the psalms he chooses. Thus for the eve of Pentecost he uses Psalm 141; in one sermon he cites vv. 3-4 and in another, v. 5.[74] For the Monday after Pentecost he uses Psalm 2;[75] for the Friday after Pentecost, Psalm 105 (he refers to v. 3, "Let the hearts of those who seek the Lord rejoice");[76] and there are a few more such occasions for which we know the psalm.[77]

The Alleluia Acclamation

I must pause here to discuss the use of the "Alleluia" acclamation. It was explained in chapter 6 that the Hebrew phrase *hallēlû-yāh* (Hallelujah) was used as a special expression of praise to God in certain psalms and that the phrase was then taken over into Christian liturgy (in both Greek and Latin) as "Alleluia." This word in the early centuries of Christian worship was associated with the Gospel reading, though in the earliest period the specific practice varied. Thus at Milan it was evidently sung during the Gospel procession, whereas in Spain it was sung after the Gospel; in Rome, in the middle of the fifth century, it was used only on Easter Day, whereas in North Africa, Augustine knew of it on all Sundays.[78] The evolution of the Alleluia is complicated, and the details are at some points obscure.[79] But in the Middle Ages it became the settled custom to put away the Alleluia during Lent, indeed, starting some days before the beginning of Lent: the Alleluia was said for the final time on the Saturday before Septuagesima Sunday (the ninth Sunday before Easter) and would not be used again until the vigil the night before Easter. There was, until modern times, a quaint custom observed in the cathedral at Langres (about 150 miles [240 kilometers] southeast of Paris), called the "Scourging of the Alleluia": on the day in which, according to the ritual, the Alleluia began to be omitted from the liturgy, a top on which the word "Alleluia" was written was whipped out of the church to the singing of psalms by the choirboys, who wished it bon voyage until Easter.[80]

The Liturgy of the Faithful

As for the liturgy of the faithful,[81] Augustine notes that the custom had recently arisen at Carthage of having psalms sung by a cantor while Communion was being distributed.[82] His remarks are engaging:

> Meanwhile, a certain Hilary, a Catholic layman of tribunitial rank, incited to anger, for some reason or other, against the ministers of God, as often happens, in abusive, censorious language, wherever it was possible, was violently attacking the custom which, at the time, had been introduced in Carthage, of singing hymns from the Book of Psalms either before the oblation or when what had been offered was being distributed to the people; he insisted that this should not be done.[83]

According to Cyril of Jerusalem (ca. 315–386), the prescribed psalm portion is Ps. 34:9 (8)—"O taste and see that the Lord is good"—whereas Chrysostom (?–407) speaks of Psalm 145—"I will extol you, my God and King."[84]

Commentaries on the Psalms in
the Church Fathers

I pause now in our survey of the use of the Psalms in worship to consider the commentaries that were written by the church fathers on the Psalms in this period.[85] The teachers in the church were always dealing with the Psalms, and there was never any distinction, such as we might make, between theology on the one hand and the critical interpretation of a commentary on the other. Scripture was always interpreted on the basis of the stated faith of the church, so that the commentaries that were produced were not overly distinct from sermons.

At an early stage there emerged in the church a conflict between two styles of interpretation, that of Alexandria (Egypt) and that of Antioch (Syria). These two cities were the second and third in population in the Roman Empire, and in both of them learning had flourished long before the advent of the church. We have already become acquainted with Alexandria as the site of the Septuagint translation (chapter 6). This city had been an intellectual center, specifically of Neoplatonism,[86] and the Jewish writer Philo of Alexandria (20 B.C.E.–45 C.E.) had worked out in that intellectual tradition an allegorical understanding of Judaism that indeed owed more to Plato than to the original thought-world of the Old Testament.[87] Christian commentators trained in Alexandria were prone, then, to allegorize passages of Scripture, particularly in order to avoid the anthropomorphisms of the Old Testament. In contrast, the school of Antioch was noted for its sober, literal interpretation of the Bible.[88]

Origen

The greatest biblical scholar of Alexandria was Origen (ca. 185–254).[89] At the age of seventeen he took charge of the catechetical school of Alexandria. We have already mentioned Origen for his preparation of the *Hexapla*, an enormous six-column work covering the text of the entire Old Testament (see chapter 6). He also prepared full commentaries on many books of the Bible, including the Psalms.[90] I refer here to Origen's comments on Psalms 2, 23, and 137, which were the psalms discussed in chapter 9 in the analysis of medieval Jewish commentators. I cannot reproduce in full his extensive comments (those on Psalm 2, for example, cover 460 lines of Greek). I content myself with brief samples.

He begins his commentary on Psalm 2[91] by citing two Hebrew manuscripts he has consulted, in one of which Psalms 1 and 2 are separated and in the other of which Psalms 1 and 2 are written as a single psalm (we may compare Justin Martyr's citation of Psalms 1–2 without a break). He then cites a reading of Acts 13:33 familiar to him, which cites Ps. 2:7b as taken from "the first psalm," likewise indicating the tradition that Psalms 1–2 made up a single psalm.[92]

We must remind ourselves that in the Septuagint the word "anointed" in v. 2 is *Christos*, so that (given the precedent of Acts 4:25-28) Origen takes it for granted that the psalm deals with Jesus Christ.

In commenting on the meaning of vv. 1-2, Origen affirms the rhetoric of Peter and John in Acts 4:25-29, who understood the words to refer to "Herod and Pontius Pilate, with the Gentiles and the peoples of Israel" (see chapter 8). He pauses to note that for the first verb of v. 1 the Septuagint has *ephryaxan* ("were unruly, growled"), whereas Aquila (see chapter 6) more accurately has *ethorybēthēsan* ("were in an uproar").

To understand what Origen says about v. 3, we must understand that the word "saying" at the end of v. 2 in the KJV, RSV, and NRSV is an interpretive addition: neither the Hebrew text nor the Septuagint has such a transitional word to soften the roughness of the rhetorical shift. The fact that all present-day scholars agree that v. 3 is spoken by the kings does not gainsay the lack of an explicit clue within the text itself to alert the reader to the shift. Now, at the beginning of his comment on the psalm, Origen has noted a shift of speaker at the beginning of v. 3. He proposes that it is Christ who speaks the verse, but the first person plural there is a problem, so he proposes that Christ addresses the angels, who, he suggests, speak the words of the first two verses.

> It seems to me that the first four lines are spoken by the angels who had come down with the Savior; they are full of rage at the ambush laid against Christ by the invisible kings and princes and at the same time are unsure what in the world it is all about. So since the kings and princes were the ones who bound human beings and imposed their yoke on them, the Son of God responds to his angels and urges them to imitate him in breaking the bonds of sinners and throwing off their yoke. Let us for our part break the bonds by which we are bound when we sin, since everyone is constricted by the cords of his sins. And perhaps it is better to break bonds like Samson than to loose them, as the sin of Jerusalem has been loosed, since she has received from the Lord's hand double for her sins [Isa. 40:2]. Now whoever throws off from himself the predicted yoke can take up Jesus' easy yoke and carry his light burden [Matt. 11:30], and become his draught animal: and the disciples will loose his bond [Matt. 18:18]. (my trans.)

Origen's comments on Psalm 23[93] show his philosophical bent. On v. 1 he remarks, "Just as sheep are nourished on grass and water, so the human being is made to live by action [Greek, *praxis*] and knowledge [*gnōsis*]." On v. 3—"He restores my soul; he leads me in the paths of righteousness for his name's sake"—Origen says, "If the path is of righteousness, it is also of prudence [*sōphrosynē*], love [*agapē*] and self-control [*egkrateia*], by which anyone enters into the kingdom of heaven." He notes the shift from speaking about God in the third person (vv. 1-3) to speaking to God in the second person (vv. 4-5). He also makes the point that the psalmist speaks of "walking" in the midst of the shadow of death, not "sitting," and that God accompanies the one walking; and he cites the passage from Isaiah (in the Septuagint), "those who dwell [or "sit"; the verb means both in Hebrew] in the region and the shadow of death, on them has light shined" (Isa 9:1 [Protestant numeration v. 2]). The phrase "in the presence of my enemies" in v. 5 is, in the Septuagint, "in the presence of those who afflict me," so Origen asks about the nature of those afflictions. He compares the afflictions to the struggles of athletes, who, when they win, gain prizes; so, similarly, a table that is spiritual (*pneumatikos*) and intellectual (*noētos*) is prepared because of affliction. "Thus every time you are afflicted, a spiritual table will be placed before you." He quotes Paul: "Not only that, but we also boast in our sufferings" (Rom. 5:3; the Greek word is the same word meaning "afflictions"). And he quotes Jesus' words: "And I confer on you, just as my Father has conferred on me, a kingdom, so that you may eat and drink at my table in my kingdom" (Luke 22:29).

In regard to Psalm 137,[94] Origen first comments on v. 1—"By the rivers of Babylon, there we sat and wept when we remembered Zion" (Septuagint wording)—that it expressed the great yearning of the men of the city (of Jerusalem). Then he asks why they should have sat down by the rivers, and answers that because they were captives, taken from a hostile land, they had to live outside walls and cities. Astonishingly, for v. 2— "On the willows in the midst of it we hung up our instruments" (Septuagint wording)—he says, "It is to be understood that every soul that sits in shadow and ignorance has barren reason [*logos akarpos*], hanging up the instruments that take care of practical matters." And for v. 3—"For there those who had taken us captive asked us words of songs, and those who had carried us away, a hymn: 'Sing us from the songs of Zion!'" (Septuagint wording)—he remarks, "I have known demons to force us to recite psalms and spiritual songs in which there is some command which we have transgressed, so that those listening may laugh at us who speak but do not act."

We may sum up what we have seen of Origen's commentaries as follows. His training in rhetoric makes him alert to form-critical and rhetorical shifts in the text (Ps. 2:2-3; 23:4). He is keenly aware of variant Greek translations of the Hebrew text (Ps. 2:1). From time to time he can recognize the historical context of a given psalmist (Ps. 137:1). Following the lead of the New Testament, he finds Christian meaning in the text (Ps. 2:1-3) and apt New Testament as well as Old Testament parallels (Ps. 23:4). But he also quickly finds opportunity for the kind of philosophical reflection that is more an expression of his Neoplatonic culture than of the mind-set of the Old Testament.

Jerome

I now turn to Jerome (ca. 342–420), the greatest biblical scholar of the ancient Western church. We have already met him as a translator of the Bible into Latin (see chapter 6); now we must take account of his commentary work on the Psalms.[95] In his approach Jerome stands midway between the allegorical interpretations of Alexandria and the literal interpretations of Antioch; in his commentaries he frequently refers to Origen's work.

The last half of Jerome's life was spent in Bethlehem. There he wrote a small commentary on the Psalms, consisting really of brief annotations, perhaps in the year 391; we also have "tractates" on the Psalms, not quite homilies (although they carry that alternative title), given by Jerome to his fellow monks in Bethlehem.[96] Again, I restrict myself to some of Jerome's comments on Psalms 2, 23, and 137; for Psalms 2 and 23 we have only his remarks in his little commentary, whereas for Psalm 137 we have material both in the little commentary and the tractates.

For Psalm 2 Jerome draws from Origen's interpretation and takes it for granted that the psalm refers to Jesus Christ, but he moves off in an independent direction. "It is something daring to want to interpret this psalm after Peter [has done so], or rather to expect something else from it than he has said in Acts," he remarks. Then, commenting on "the kings of the earth stood up" in v. 2 (the Old Latin reading), he says, "Not only King Herod [Peter's interpretation in Acts 4:27] but also those kings stood firm against the Lord whose kingdoms the devil showed him in a point of time [Matt. 4:8]." That is, Christ's opponents are not simply the heads of state at the time of his crucifixion, as Peter understood, but all the kings of the world mentioned at Christ's temptation in the wilderness. With regard to v. 3—"let us break their chains"—Jerome follows Origen's identification of the speaker as Christ and his general train of thought, but he offers his own interpretation of what the "chains" represent:

> The four preceding lines are spoken either by the prophet or by angels, who marvel at how human heedlessness has arisen against the Son of God. But from the fifth line the Lord himself responds, urging the people of the Gentiles and all of the Jews who would trust them, to break the legal chains and throw off the heavy burden of the law which their fathers could not bear, and rather to follow him whose yoke is sweet and burden light.

Jerome has only two comments on Psalm 23. On "The Lord is my shepherd, I shall not want" he says, "Ezekiel speaks about this shepherd: 'I shall set over them a shepherd, and he shall feed them, my servant David' [Ezek. 34:23]." And for "Your rod and your staff—they comfort me" he cites Prov. 3:12a—"For the Lord reproves the one he loves"—presumably because a rod is often an instrument of punishment (Ps. 89:33 [32]).

As I have already indicated, we have more from Jerome on Psalm 137; even the remarks in his little commentary are extensive. He begins:

> This psalm can be understood in three ways, not only about the exile which befell the Jewish people when they were taken to Babylon and were mocked there in various ways, but also about sinners who are expelled from the church and are delivered to the power of the devil, and about the superior exile, whenever we wish it, by which a sometimes noble company is led forth into the vale of tears.

On the verse "On the willows in its midst we hung up our instruments" he comments:

> Whoever sits on the rivers of Babylon and remembers Zion can neither hold back tears, nor wholly give up hope for salvation. But the willow is an unfruitful tree that always takes delight in moisture, always takes delight in water and rain [Jerome seems to imply that the willows welcome the exiles' tears]. It is the same with us if and when we are holy: if we for our part give ourselves to vices, to lust, to wantonness, then the instruments with which we used to sing to God we hang up on unfruitful trees.

Jerome becomes even more homiletic in his tractate on this psalm. He begins:

Unless one is ill, he does not know how precious good health is; again, those who are lame do not know the strength of those whose feet are whole; and similarly with the blind and those who see. I say all this because the psalm says, "On the rivers of Babylon, there we sat down and wept, when we remembered Zion." Babylon means "confusion" [Gen. 11:9]: therefore Babylon is this world. Therefore the sinner who has fallen out of paradise and comes into the vale of tears, that is, into Babylon, into this world, says—or rather the prophet, speaking out of his identity as the one who has fallen says—"On the rivers of Babylon."

He then paints a picture of someone who is in the prime of life and then falls ill and sees his beauty fade, passing away like water: "Thus we sit there and weep, when we remember Zion." He then quickly reminds us of our fall from paradise and our memory of that earlier happiness. Then he mentions the man who went down from Jerusalem to Jericho (Hebrew, *yĕrîḫô*, which means, by his understanding, "the moon" [Hebrew, *yārēaḫ*], which is always changing, a characteristic of this world) and fell among thieves, and a Samaritan picked him up and healed him with oil and wine (Luke 10:29-37).

In summary, Jerome brought a lively mind to the craft of commentary work; his commentaries are full of all kinds of learning. And where Origen would draw a philosophical conclusion from a text, Jerome from the same text prefers to draw theological and ethical conclusions. Indeed sometimes his mind is so lively that he offers us a kind of stream of consciousness: this is certainly the case in his treatment of the first verse or two of Psalm 137.

Theodore of Mopsuestia

I now turn to the best representative of the school of Antioch whose work has come down to us, Theodore of Mopsuestia (ca. 350–428).[97] Theodore was born in Antioch; in the year 390 he became bishop of Mopsuestia, a city north of Antioch, site of the present town of Misis, about fifteen miles (twenty-five kilometers) east of Adana in southern Turkey. Theodore made a clear distinction between the task of an exegete—namely, preparing a commentary—and that of a preacher. "I judge the exegete's task," he writes, "to be to explain words that most people find difficult; it is the preacher's task to reflect also on words that are perfectly clear and to speak about them."[98]

The first commentary he wrote, as it happens, was on the Psalms. Later in his life he confessed that he was aware of imperfections in the work.[99] Even so, it demonstrates a sober, independent mind at work. The commentary has not survived complete, but what we do have is a fairly complete representation, partly in the original Greek and partly in Latin translation, of his work on the first eighty-one psalms.[100]

We have his commentary on Psalm 2 in full (in Latin translation). He begins it this way: "In the second psalm the blessed David prophesies and narrates everything that has been fulfilled at the time of the Lord's passion by the Jews." He cites Peter's testimony in Acts 4 and adds the words of Heb. 1:5, attributing them to Paul. He then argues against Jewish teachers who attempt to twist the reference of the psalm from the Lord, to whom it belongs, to Zerubbabel or David. He then returns to reinforce Peter's interpretation: the kings who "stood up" (v. 2, Septuagint) are Herod and Pilate; many "gathered together" (v. 2, Septuagint) when God in his might veiled the sun and left the whole earth in darkness (Mark 15:33 and pars.). He identifies the "princes" (NRSV, "rulers") as the scribes and Pharisees; "the Lord and his anointed" are for him, of course, the Father and the Son. In contrast to Origen and Jerome, he denies that there can be any shifts in speaker within a psalm; thus on the diction of v. 3 he affirms that it is the words of the rulers and of their people as well, who say in effect, "Let us remove from ourselves the sovereignty of the Father and the Son and not be subjected any further to their rule."[101]

On Psalm 23, only two remarks from his commentary have survived. On v. 3— "He leads me in the path of righteousness"—he says, "He has instructed us by the tribulations of captivity, so that he might call us into the track of discipline and teach us to follow the ways of justice and truth." And on "your rod and your staff" (v. 4) he explains the rod and the staff as the help of God.

Theodore's commentary on Psalm 137 has not survived. To fill out our impression of his approach, I note a few of his comments on Psalm 72. We must understand that both Origen and Jerome affirm that the psalm refers to Christ: v. 5— "And he shall continue as long as the sun"—is the clue for Jerome.[102] But Theodore begins, "Some have said the details of the psalm refer to Solomon, others that they refer to Christ; it is all laughable—how could anyone confuse human affairs and prophecies about Christ?" He earnestly defends the reference of the psalm to Solomon: the verb in v. 5 does not refer to Christ but rather to the "peace" (NRSV, "prosperity") mentioned in v. 3—peace shall continue as long as the sun. This interpretation of the psalm is reinforced for him by the Septuagint's reading of v. 9—"Before him the Ethiopians shall fall down, and his enemies shall lick the dust"; Theodore remarks, "This happened at the coming of the queen of Ethiopia, who was stirred by the glory around him [that is, Solomon: 1 Kings 10:1-10]."

Further commentaries were written during the Middle Ages, but, at the risk of oversimplifying a rich array of material, it still may be said that these commentaries were homiletical rather than exegetical, imitative rather than original—handbooks compiled from the works of Jerome and Augustine.[103] Yet a perusal of specialists' studies on the Bible in the Middle Ages will convince us of the theological riches of the period.[104]

The Psalms in the Liturgy in the Seventh Century

I return now to the place of the Psalms in the evolving worship practices of the church. By the seventh century the variety of local practices in the eucharistic liturgy had given way to unity, both in the East and in the West; we have several documents that set forth the procedure during this period.

In Spain there were a whole series of prayers said by the priest as he was vesting, including Psalm 26, which contains the words "I wash my hands in innocence, and go around your altar, O Lord" (v. 6).[105] (Compare the vesting prayers in the Eastern church, analyzed below.)

The liturgy of the word proper began with the Introit, that is, the singing of a psalm or portion of a psalm to cover the entrance of the priest;[106] like the Alleluia, the procedure of the Introit varied and its evolution is somewhat obscure.[107] The Introit was then followed by other items—the Kyrie, the Gloria, and the Collect.

There followed three Scripture readings: an Old Testament lesson, followed by the psalm (sung responsively), then the Epistle lesson. In the East there then followed the Alleluia, interspersed between the verses of a psalm or portions of a psalm, followed by the Gospel;[108] in Spain the reading of the Gospel followed the Epistle, and the Gospel was followed by the "Lauda," that is, the Alleluia and a verse generally taken from a psalm.[109] But by the ninth century the Old Testament lesson had disappeared in both East and West, leaving the psalm or psalm portion alone before the Epistle;[110] in the West this became known as the "Gradual," evidently because it was recited on a step (Latin, *gradus*) above the congregation (compare chapter 12).

In the liturgy of the faithful the custom continued, in both East and West, of chanting a psalm during the distribution of communion.[111]

The Psalms in the Divine Office in the West[112]

The necessity of common prayer in the newly emerging monastic communities led to a novel use of the Psalter—the practice of reciting the whole Psalter, in its biblical order, over a given period of time—normally a week—without any reference to the hour, the day or the season[113] (compare the parallel recitation of the complete Psalter by Jews; chapter 9). And there were similar public noneucharistic services of prayer in the great cathedral churches, in which the Psalms had a large place; at some of these services the leadership was taken by monks and nuns, while at others the bishop or other clergy presided.

There eventually emerged eight offices (times of prayer): a night office (because of Ps. 119:62, "At midnight I arise to praise thee"), called "Vigils" or "Nocturns"; and seven day offices (because of Ps. 119:164, "Seven times a day I praise thee"), namely, "Lauds" (at daybreak), "Prime" (at the "first hour," roughly seven o'clock), "Terce" (at the "third hour," roughly nine o'clock), "Sext" (at the "sixth hour," roughly noon), "None" (at the "ninth hour," roughly three o'clock), "Vespers" (in the evening), and "Compline" (on retiring to bed).[114] (It should also be said that the frequently used term "Matins" is ambiguous. Strictly speaking, it refers to the first morning service [Lauds]; but because that term has also been used for the night office, which was later celebrated in the early morning without a break before Lauds, it is best to avoid the term altogether.)[115]

Each of these occasions of prayer, it should be understood, centered on the recitation of psalms; but other readings from the Old and New Testaments and various prayers were also involved.

The selection of psalms at each occasion of prayer varied widely: indeed, at Constantinople in 1204, secular and monastic churches had two entirely different arrangements.[116] But there were some constants: universally, Lauds always concluded with the praising Psalms 148 through 150 (hence the name "Lauds").[117]

It is impossible here to review all of the schemes, but we must pause to take account of a landmark in the development of the daily office in the early Middle Ages, namely, the office prescribed in the Rule of Saint Benedict for Benedictine communities (ca. 530).[118] The Psalter was to be completed once each week. His assignments were as follows.

Vigils consisted of Psalms 3 and 95, followed by a selection of twelve psalms according to the day of the week. Lauds always began with Psalms 67 and 51, and continued with the following selection, day by day: on Sunday, Psalms 118 and 63; on Monday, Psalms 5 and 36; on Tuesday, Psalms 43 and 57; on Wednesday, Psalms 64 and 65; on Thursday, Psalms 88 and 90; on Friday, Psalms 76 and 92; and on Saturday, Psalm 143 and, instead of another psalm, Deut. 32:1-43. Lauds was then completed each day by Psalms 148, 149, and 150. Prime on Sunday used the first four sections of Psalm 119 and on Monday through Saturday used three psalms each day: on Monday, Psalms 1, 2, and 6; on Tuesday, Psalms 7–9; on Wednesday, Psalms 10–12; on Thursday, Psalms 13–15; on Friday, Psalms 16, 17, and the first half of 18; on Saturday, the second half of Psalm 18 and Psalms 19 and 20. Terce, Sext, and None on Sunday used three successive sections of Psalm 119—vv. 33-56 for Terce, vv. 57-80 for Sext, and vv. 81-104 for None. Monday completed the recitation of Psalm 119: vv. 105-128 for Terce, vv. 129-152 for Sext, and vv. 153-176 for None. Tuesday through Saturday, Terce used Psalms 120–122, Sext used Psalms 123–125, and None used Psalms 126–128. Vespers used four psalms each day in a sequence from Psalm 110 to Psalm 147, deleting Psalms 118–128, 134, and 143, dividing each of the long psalms 139, 144, and 145 into two readings, and combining Ps. 116:10-19 (a single psalm by the reckoning of the Vulgate) and Psalm 117 into a single reading. That is, for Vespers on Sunday one read Psalms 110–113; on Monday, Psalms 114–115 (a single psalm by the reckoning of the Vulgate), 116:1-9 (a full psalm by the reckoning of the Vulgate), 116:10-19 plus 117, and 129; on Tuesday, Psalms 130–133; on Wednesday, Psalms 135–138; on Thursday, the two halves of Psalm 139 and Psalms 140 and 141; on Friday, Psalm 142, the two halves of Psalm 144, and the first half of Psalm 145; and on Saturday, the second half of Psalm 145, Psalm 146, and the two halves of Psalm 147 (two psalms by the reckoning of the Vulgate). Compline consisted every day of Psalms 4, 91, and 134. This scheme leaves roughly seventy-three psalms unspecified: these are to be distributed for the night office, twelve psalm readings each night, in accordance with the best judgment of the community.

In this way Benedict made an effort to assign particular psalms to the hours when they were most appropriate—for example, Psalms 5 and 36 to Lauds.

And one must not lose sight of the fact that this bare scheme outlined the prayer life of the community. It is appropriate to quote part of chapter 13 of the rule, which comes in the midst of the instructions of the psalms to be used.

> Of course, the Offices of Lauds and Vespers shall never be allowed to end without the superior finally reciting, in the hearing of all, the whole of the Lord's Prayer. The purpose of this is the removal of those thorns of scandal, or mutual offence, which are wont to arise in communities. For, being warned by the covenant which they make in that prayer, when they say, *Forgive us as we forgive*, the brethren will cleanse their souls of such faults. At the other Offices, however, only the last part of that prayer shall be said aloud, so that all may answer, *But deliver us from evil*.

The Benedictine scheme, for Christian communities, of prayer through the Psalms was so sensible that it stimulated similar but more rigorous rules. The Roman office that was standardized in the late Middle Ages is an adaptation of the Benedictine rule, but in it all 150 psalms are specifically assigned a place in the week of prayers (see Appendix 1).

In the centuries that followed, the recitation of the Divine Office became the regimen of prayer not only for monks and nuns but for communities of secular priests as well. Of course, its use depended on many factors: the ability of church authorities to impose these standards at a distance; the availability of books, copied by hand at great toil; and the literacy of those who would be expected to use these books. But there continued to be diversity in the Divine Office in the Western church. And there were other developments. Thus there was steadily increasing elaboration of the office as the centuries passed.

Where there were monastic communities that could be trained, the office was chanted to traditional melodies (plainsong) that have come to be called "Gregorian chant"—that is, under the assumption that this mode of chant was innovated by Gregory the Great (ca. 540–604), though historians of music cannot prove his connection with this chant.[119]

And there were efforts as well to impose the saying of the office on individual secular priests, particularly after the reforms of Charlemagne (802 C.E.), so that the custom spread of private recitation of the office.

Breviaries

If there was to be a recitation of the Divine Office (which also came to be called the "hours"), then there had to be books containing the office; so "breviaries" came into existence, books for monastic libraries that would offer a "conspectus" (for that is the meaning of breviary) of the offices for the entire year. And the Divine Office was recited not only by priests, monks, and nuns but by some lay people as well, particularly pious monarchs and nobility who had the leisure and the impulse to do so (and who had the learning as well; for the office, we must remember, was only in Latin). One thinks of Alfred the Great, who became king of the West Saxons in England in 871; he "was frequent in psalm-singing and prayer, at the hours both of the day and night,"[120] and he carried in his bosom a book "wherein the daily courses and psalms, and prayers which he had read in his youth, were written."[121]

On the continent of Europe the use of such books by lay people as well as clerics was encouraged by the new literacy that came during the Carolingian period (that is, after Charlemagne). One of the glories of the Carolingian age is the ninth-century manuscript of the Psalms in the Utrecht university library, with marvelous illustrations.[122]

In later centuries, copies of the Psalter and the breviaries that were often sumptuous in their illuminated illustration were prepared for pious members of the nobility; one thinks of the books of the hours prepared for the Duke of Berry (1340–1416), especially the one in the Cloisters in New York City.[123]

The illustrations in the Psalters and breviaries, it should be stressed, are frequently of New Testament scenes to which the psalm is understood to refer. For example, in the Stuttgart Psalter from 820–830 C.E. the illustration of Ps. 2:1-2— "Why do the nations conspire, and the peoples plot in vain? The kings of the earth set themselves, and the rulers take counsel together, against the Lord and his anointed"—is of Christ before Pilate[124] (an association that, as we have seen, goes back to Acts 4:25-29).

The Psalms, then, were perceived to be the property of lay Christians in a way that the rest of the Scriptures were not. Thus in a Frankish penitential (book of church discipline) of the early eighth century it is stated, "A layman may not read a lection in the church nor sing the alleluia but only the psalms and responses without the alleluia."[125] The "Earlier Rule" of St. Francis (1221) offers the following on the Divine Office:

> All the brothers, whether clerical or lay, should celebrate the Divine Office, the praises and prayers, as is required of them. The clerical [brothers] should celebrate the office and say it for the living and the dead according to the custom of the clergy. And for the failings and negligence of the brothers they should say daily the *Miserere mei, Deus* [Psalm 51], with the Our Father; and for the deceased brothers let them say the *De Profundis* [Psalm 130] with the Our Father. And they may have only the books necessary to fulfill their office. And the lay [brothers] who know how to read the Psalter may have it. But those who do not know how to read should not have any book.[126]

And the Council of Toulouse in 1229 reinforced this general approach: there it was decreed that the only portions of Scripture that lay people could possess were the Psalter and such passages as were in the breviary (which were, of course, chiefly Psalms).[127]

So it came about that the Psalter became the textbook through which the young clerk-to-be learned his letters; the Psalms were central for primary education.[128] Often the Psalms were learned by heart.[129]

Saying the Psalms as Penance

There developed a fresh use of the psalms, and that was the imposition of saying psalms as penance. The disciplines of penance originated in monastic communities, and various handbooks were compiled for the guidance of priests imposing penance for various sins. The penance was often fasting or other austerities for a given period of time, but sometimes penance could be the saying of a certain number of psalms. For example, the penitential of an Irish abbot named Cummean (ca. 650) states, "He who is willingly polluted during sleep [that is, has a nocturnal emission], shall arise and sing nine psalms in order, kneeling. On the following day he shall live on bread and water; or he shall sing thirty psalms, kneeling at the end of each."[130] Such a penance, of course, assumes that the Psalms were committed to memory.

Then there grew up equivalences: according to the penitential of Burchard, bishop of the city of Worms in the early eleventh century, if one had been assigned one month on bread and water, the penitent could redeem this penalty by singing "1200 psalms, kneeling; but if he cannot do this, he shall sing 1680 psalms, sitting or standing, without kneeling; if possible, in a church; but if not, in one place."[131] However, if one did not know the psalms (a layman, presumably), then he could redeem the penalty of a day on bread and water by a money payment—if he was rich, by three denarii, and if he was poor, by one denarius—and on that day he would then be free to eat anything except wine, meat, and fat.[132] And from the notion of such equivalences it was an easy step to vicarious penance, condemned at the Council of Cloveshoe (England) in 747: a wealthy man (again, presumably, a layman) would pay others to sing psalms, fast, and give alms on his behalf.[133]

Popular culture made other uses of the Psalms and psalm verses, but before I discuss these we must turn to the use of the Psalms in the Eastern church.

The Eastern Orthodox Church:
The Liturgy

Christians whose center of gravity is western Europe or the Western Hemisphere are guilty of a selective view of Christian history: as the early church moves into the Middle Ages they tend to concentrate on the Western church, ignoring other arms of Christendom.[134] But there is, of course, the Eastern church, whose patriarch has been in Constantinople (now Istanbul), whose branches are found in Greece and in various Slavic lands. (It is worth noting that today there are roughly 3,365,000 members of Orthodox churches in the United States.)[135] Indeed there exist still other Oriental Christian churches—those of Syriac, Armenian, Coptic, and Ethiopic liturgies—but we cannot linger for them here.[136]

Both the eucharistic liturgy and the Divine Office developed in a different way in the Eastern church.[137] The eucharistic liturgy (in the Eastern church called simply "the liturgy") may be divided, as we have seen in the early church, into the liturgy of the catechumens and the liturgy of the faithful. In the Eastern church the liturgy of the catechumens begins with what is called the *typika*, the portion of the liturgy before the reading of Scripture. In the *typika*, interwoven with litanies are three "antiphons" (psalms or hymns or portions of these) sung by the choir or, if there is no choir, by the deacon. In the liturgy apart from the great festivals, the first antiphon is the whole of Psalm 103, and the second antiphon is the whole of Psalm 146; these are the so-called "typical psalms."[138] (In the liturgy apart from the great festivals, the third antiphon uses material other than the Psalms.)

Before I turn to the remainder of the liturgy, I must pause to explain that it is organized into a cycle called the *Octoechos* (literally, "[the cycle of] eight notes"). There are eight "tones" (musical settings), one for each successive week through the year.

In the liturgy apart from the great feasts, the Psalms are used at two points in the portion of the liturgy of the catechumens devoted to the reading of Scripture, that is, the so-called *Prokimenon* and the Alleluia verses. The *Prokimenon* (literally, "what is set forth"; the plural is *prokimena*) is the remnant of the psalm passage in the liturgy of the word in the early church. We recall that by the ninth century, the Old Testament lesson having disappeared, the psalm, psalm portion, or psalm verse was simply sung before the reading of the Epistle; now this *prokimenon*, read by the designated reader, was simply one or two verses from a given psalm. The eight *prokimena* (in the cycle of eight weeks) are, successively: Pss. 33:22, 1; 118:14, 18; 47:7 (6), 2 (1); 104:24a, 1a; 12:8 (7), 2a (1a); 28:9a, 1a; 29:11; 1a; 76:12a (11a), 2 (1).

Then there are two verses of a psalm, read again by the reader, along with the Alleluia acclamation before the reading of the Gospel; these eight selections (in the cycle of eight weeks) are, successively: Pss. 18:48 (47), 51 (50); 20:2 (1), 10 (9); 31:2a (1a), 3b (2b); 45:5a (4a), 8a (7a); 89:2-3 (1-2); 91:1-2; 92:2-3 (1-2); 95:1-2.

During the liturgy of the faithful, at the distribution of the communion bread, Ps. 34:9 (8) is sung. It is noteworthy that in that verse, because of a shift of pronunciation in Greek, a wonderful wordplay has emerged: the Greek says, *Geusasthe kai idete hoti chrēstos ho kyrios*—"Taste and see that good is the Lord"—but *chrēstos* (good) is now heard as *Christos*—"Taste and see that *Christ* is the Lord."[139] Then, at the very end of the liturgy, there is a distribution to the congregation of bread taken from the loaves from which the eucharistic bread has been cut (the so-called *antidoron*). As this is distributed, the whole of Psalm 34 is sung;[140] today, often, a tape is played.

For the liturgy during the great feasts, such as the period from Lent through Easter to Pentecost, there are special antiphons in the *typika*, special *prokimena*, and special Alleluia verses; and there are verses taken from the Psalms that are sung by the choir during the distribution of Communion as well. It would serve no purpose to give the full system here; I simply set forth a few services by way of example.

On Palm Sunday, in the *typika* (the beginning of the liturgy), the three antiphons are Pss. 116:1-4; 116:10, 12-14; and 118:1-4, respectively. The *prokimenon*, appropriately, is Ps. 118:26a, 27a, 1 (v. 26a was the acclamation for Jesus at the entrance into Jerusalem), and the Alleluia verses are Ps. 98:1a, 3b. Then, after the reading of Scripture in the liturgy of the faithful, there is a Communion hymn that repeats Ps. 118:26a, 27a.

Similarly, for Easter the three antiphons in the *typika* are Pss. 66:1-4; 67:2-4 (1-3); and 68:2-4a (1-3a), respectively. The *prokimenon* is Ps. 118:24, 1, and the Alleluia verses are Pss. 102:14a (13a) and 33:13.

Other feast days also carry special psalm verses. Thus for Christmas the antiphons are Pss. 111:1-3; 112:1-4; and 110:1-3a, respectively; and then there is an Introit that uses Ps. 110:3b-4. The *prokimenon* is Ps. 66:4, 1-2, and the Alleluia verses are Ps. 19:2-3 (1-2).

And one more example: on the feast of the Nativity of the Virgin (September 8) the *prokimenon* is taken (understandably) from the Magnificat (Luke 2:46-48), but the Alleluia verses are Ps. 45:11 (10), 13b (12b).

One should also note that in the occasional services of the church appropriate psalms are used. Thus in the service of baptism, after the child has been baptized, the choir sings the whole of Psalm 32. Similarly, when a betrothal and wedding take place on the same day, then in the wedding service the priest says the whole of Psalm 146.

By contrast, verses from the Psalms play a major role in the prayers of the priest or bishop as he vests himself before the liturgy. (The Western church has had similar prayers on vesting, but they are not taken from the Psalms.) In the Eastern church there are fourteen such prayers. Of these, two are nonbiblical and two are taken from the New Testament; the remaining ten are either citations or adaptations from the Old Testament, and eight of these are from the Psalms.

1. On donning the *stoicharion* (alb; the basic linen garment reaching from the neck to the ankles) he repeats Isa. 61:10—"My soul will rejoice in the Lord, for he has clothed me with the cloak of salvation and with the robe of delight; he has crowned me with a mitre as a bridegroom and adorned me as a bride" (my trans.).

2. On donning the right *epimanikion* (sleeve cuff) he repeats Exod. 15:6— "Your right hand, Lord, is glorified in might; your right hand has shattered the enemy and by the immensity of your glory you have crushed your adversaries."

3. For the left *epimanikion* he repeats Ps. 119:73—"Your hands have made me and fashioned me; teach me and I will learn your commandments."

4. For the *epitrachelion* (stole; the narrow sash worn around the neck) he recites a nonbiblical prayer—"Blessed be God who pours forth his grace upon his priests"—to which the priests in the Russian church add Ps. 133:2—"like the precious ointment upon the head, running down upon the beard, upon the beard of Aaron, running down the skirts of his clothing."

5. For the *perizonion* (broad belt or girdle) he recites an adaptation of Ps. 18:33 (32)—"Blessed be God, who girds me with strength and makes my way blameless"—and the priests in the Russian church add the next verse— "making my feet like harts' feet, and has set me up on high."

6. For the *epigonation* (a large, diamond-shaped pendant with a cross embroidered on it, which hangs over the right thigh), if the priest has been given

one by the bishop, he recites Ps. 45:4-5a (3-4a)—"Gird your sword upon your thigh, O Mighty One; Go forth, prosper and reign in your beauty and vigor for the sake of truth, meekness and righteousness"—and priests in the Russian church add the next half verse.

7. For the *phelonion* (chasuble; the outer garment) he recites Ps. 132:9—"Your priests, Lord, will be clothed with righteousness and your saints will rejoice."

8. For the episcopal *omophorion* (long scarf worn on the shoulders, corresponding to the Roman pallium) the bishop recites a nonbiblical prayer—"Upon your shoulders, O Christ, you have brought our fallen nature to the Father."

9. For the pectoral cross the priest or bishop recites Matt. 16:24—"If anyone would come after me, let him deny himself and take up his cross and follow me."

10. For the episcopal *encolpion* (an oval medallion worn on a chain from the neck, usually with a depiction of Christ or the Virgin Mary on it) the bishop recites Ps. 51:12 (10)—"Create in me a clean heart, O God, and renew a right spirit within me."

11. For the episcopal miter (headdress) the bishop recites Ps. 21:4b (3b)—"You have put on his head a crown of precious stones" (though the Septuagint reads "stone," singular!).

12. For the episcopal crosier (crook-shaped staff) the bishop recites Ps. 110:2, which in the Septuagint reads, "The Lord will send to you a staff of strength from Zion, and rule among your enemies."

13. For the episcopal *dikerotrekera* (candles held in candlesticks with two and three branches, respectively) the bishop recites Matt 5:16—"Let your light so shine before men that they may see your good works and give glory to your Father who is in heaven."

Then, as the priest washes his hands, he recites Ps. 26:6-8—"I will wash my hands with the innocent, Lord."[141]

The Eastern Orthodox Church:
The Divine Office

The Psalms are likewise the backbone of the Divine Office in the Eastern church.[142] We must remind ourselves that the shift of the Divine Office to private recitation did not take place in the Eastern church; there the Divine Office remained the service of noneucharistic prayer through the hours of the day that has been maintained in the great churches and monasteries.

As in so many systems of liturgy, the system of the Divine Office in the Eastern church is complicated.

For purposes of recitation the whole Psalter is divided sequentially into twenty *kathismata* (literally, "sessions"; the singular is *kathisma*); each "cathism" thus contains approximately eight psalms. Each cathism is divided into three *staseis* (literally, "stations" or "stanzas"; the singular is *stasis*): these are sequences for reading, closed by prayer phrases such as the "Glory to the Father" and the like. Thus the first *stasis* of the first cathism consists of Psalms 1–3; the second *stasis*, of Psalms 4–6; and the third *stasis*, of Psalms 7 and 8 (for the full system, see Appendix 2). In ordinary weeks the full Psalter is completely recited once a week: one cathism is recited for Vespers and two cathisms for Matins. The cycle begins with Vespers on Saturday evening with the first cathism. The second and third cathisms are recited for Sunday Matins. Only for Sunday Vespers is a cathism not recited. Thus the fourth and fifth cathisms are recited for Monday Matins; the sixth, for Monday Vespers; and so on. The nineteenth and twentieth are recited for Saturday Matins. In this cycle no cathisms are read during the hours of Prime, Terce, Sext, and None.

There are five variations in this pattern (again, see Appendix 2). One of them is that during the first, second, third, fourth, and sixth weeks of "Great Lent" (that is, the six weeks before Easter) the Psalter is recited twice each week. During Vespers on Monday through Friday the eighteenth cathism is recited, three cathisms are recited during Matins, and one cathism is recited during most of the days for Prime, Terce, Sext, and None.

And, in addition to this sequential cycle of reading the Psalter, specific psalms are recited in the course of the hours. Thus Saturday evening for Vespers the introductory psalm, Psalm 104, is recited; then the first cathism, and then four evening psalms, namely, Psalms 141, 142, 130, and 117. During the service of Compline, when no cathism is recited, there is nevertheless a recitation of Psalms 51, 70, and 143; and for the service of "Great Compline" (used Monday through Thursday of Lent and for certain other evenings as well) there is a recitation of Psalms 4, 6, 13, 25, 31, 91; then, after certain prayers, Psalms 51 and 102; and then, to close the service, Psalms 70 and 143.

As one might expect, the Middle Ages saw illuminated Psalters prepared in the Eastern church that are as sumptuous as those in the West.[143]

This full regimen of the Divine Office in the Eastern church has been practical only in monasteries and the great churches; in the traditional Orthodox lands the monasteries and churches have continued to sing the Psalms in the Greek or Slavonic languages (Slavonic is essentially Old Bulgarian),[144] and these churches have been slow to modernize the language of liturgy so that it is easily accessible to the listener.

But the Orthodox tradition has always believed that the liturgy should be in the language of the people, and so in English-speaking lands the liturgy has been developed in English. Thus one finds the Psalms translated by the monks of the Orthodox monastery of New Skete (New York State), a translation first used in 1966 and revised in the following years.[145] This translation was largely made from the Hebrew text rather than from the Septuagint Greek; it is in fluent American English. Here is Psalm 1:

> Happy indeed is the man who follows not the counsel of the wicked, nor lingers along the path of sinners, nor sits in the company of cynics, but who

delights in the law of the Lord, and ponders his law day and night. He is like a tree planted near flowing waters, yielding fruit in due season, whose foliage never withers or fades. All that he does succeeds. But the wicked are not like this—not at all!—for they are like winnowed chaff blown about on the ground by the wind. No, evildoers will not survive judgment, nor will sinners stand among the just, but the Lord guards the way of the just, but the way of the wicked leads to doom.

Vernacular Translations
and Some Folk Uses of the Psalms

Translations of portions of the Bible did not begin with the Reformation; there were many vernacular translations in European languages in circulation—though that copies had to be made by hand limited that circulation.[146] The translation into English of John Wyclif and his associates, begun around 1382, is a landmark in English. But it must be remembered that these vernacular translations were made from the Latin Vulgate, so that in the case of Old Testament books such as the Psalms, these translations were two steps from the original. Only with the Protestant Reformation were Christian translations made directly from the Hebrew.

I close this chapter by returning to the place of the Psalms in the lives of common folk. The Psalms were so central that they penetrated into folk belief. Thus the opening verse of Psalm 91—"He who dwells in the shelter of the Most High, in the care of the God of Heaven will abide"—was a favorite inscription for a protective amulet.[147] Again, the psalm verse heard so often during the distribution of Communion in the liturgy in the Eastern church, "O taste and see that the Lord is good," could be used to prevent wine from turning; one was instructed to write the verse on an apple and then throw the apple into the wine.[148]

Finally, there is always the temptation to misuse ritual. There is a purely legendary account of Quendreda, the sister of Kenelm who became king of Mercia (England) in 819 C.E. According to the legend, after the king was killed in a plot she wanted to curse him; she took up a Psalter and sang, as an incantation, Psalm 119 backward, beginning with the last verse and continuing to the first, at which point her eyes fell out of their sockets onto the page from which she had been reading.[149] One's reponse to this story today could well be that Psalm 119 is a psalm that makes as much sense read verse by verse backward as forward; but this is not the point. The legend partakes of the folk motif of reverse magic, by which magical results are sought by doing the reverse of the normal ritual act.[150] For the purposes of our study of the Psalms, one can sense in this strange story an awe for the power of the word, for the power of reading, for the power of the Psalms.

NOTES

1. Edgar J. Goodspeed, "The Canon of the New Testament," in *IB* 1:65.

2. Massey H. Shepherd, Jr., "Clement, Epistles of," in *IDB* 1:648–49; "Apostolic Fathers," in *IDBSup* 36, 38. For a commentary and translation, see Cyril C. Richardson

(trans.), in *Early Christian Fathers* (LCC 1; Philadelphia: Westminster, 1953), 33–73; Robert M. Grant and Holt H. Graham, *The Apostolic Fathers: A New Translation*, vol. 2: *First and Second Clement* (New York: Nelson, 1965), 1–106.

   3. *1 Clement* 36.
   4. *1 Clement* 16.15–16.
   5. *1 Clement* 18.2–7.
   6. *1 Clement* 35.7–12.
   7. *1 Clement* 14—15.
   8. Walther Eltester, "Barnabas, Epistle of," in *IDB* 1:357–58. For a commentary and translation, see Robert A. Kraft, *The Apostolic Fathers: A New Translation and Commentary*, vol. 3: *Barnabas and the Didache* (New York: Nelson, 1965), 17-56, 80–162.
   9. *Barnabas* 10.10.
   10. *Barnabas* 11.6.
   11. *Barnabas* 2.10.
   12. *Barnabas* 5.13; 6.6.
   13. *Barnabas* 12.10; cf. Matt. 22:43-45.
   14. Massey H. Shepherd, Jr., "Didache," in *IDB* 1:841–43. For commentary and translation, see Richardson (trans.), in *Early Christian Fathers*, 161–79; Kraft, *Apostolic Fathers*, 3:57–77, 134–77.
   15. *Didache* 5.2.
   16. *Didache* 3.7.
   17. *Didache* 12.1.
   18. *Didache* 11.2.
   19. Massey H. Shepherd, Jr., "Ignatius, Epistles of," in *IDB* 2:678–80. For commentary and translation, see Richardson (trans.), in *Early Christian Fathers*, 74–120; Robert M. Grant, *The Apostolic Fathers: A New Translation and Commentary*, vol. 4: *Ignatius of Antioch* (New York: Nelson, 1966).
   20. Massey H. Shepherd, Jr., "Polycarp, Epistle of," in *IDB* 3:839–40. For commentary and translation, see Richardson (trans.), in *Early Christian Fathers*, 121–37; William R. Schoedel, *The Apostolic Fathers: A New Translation and Commentary*, vol. 5: *Polycarp, Martyrdom of Polycarp, Fragments of Papias* (New York: Nelson, 1967), 3–46.
   21. The only ones to be noted are Ps. 1:3 in Ignatius, *Magnesians*, 13.1; Ps. 33:9 in Ignatius, *Ephesians*, 15.1; Ps. 4:5 in Polycarp, *Philippians*, 12.1; and Ps. 150:6 in Polycarp, *Philippians*, 2.1.
   22. For Justin's use of the Bible, see Willis A. Shotwell, *The Biblical Exegesis of Justin Martyr* (London: SPCK, 1965), esp. 30–31. For a commentary and translation of Justin's works, see Justin Martyr, *The First Apology; The Second Apology; Dialogue with Trypho; Exhortation to the Greeks; Discourse to the Greeks; The Monarchy, or the Rule of God* (FC 6; Washington, D.C.: Catholic University of America, 1948). For a commentary and translation of selections from the *Apology*, see Richardson (trans.), in *Early Christian Fathers*, 242–89.
   23. Justin, *Apology*, 30—53.
   24. Ps. 22:17 (16) and 19 (18) in Justin, *Apology*, 35; Ps. 22:8-9 (7-8) in Justin, *Apology*, 38.
   25. Justin, *Dialogue*, 98—106.
   26. Justin, *Apology*, 40—41.
   27. Justin, *Dialogue*, 64.8.
   28. Justin, *Dialogue*, 88.8; 103.6; 122.6.

29. Justin, *Dialogue*, 73.

30. Charles Augustus Briggs and Emilie Grace Briggs, *A Critical and Exegetical Commentary on the Book of Psalms* (New York: Charles Scribner's Sons, 1906–7), 2:304–5.

31. Justin, *Apology*, 45.

32. Justin, *Dialogue*, 32—33; 83.

33. Shotwell, *Justin Martyr*, 78.

34. Justin, *Dialogue*, 56.14.

35. Justin, *Dialogue*, 63.3; cf. 118.1.

36. Justin, *Dialogue*, 38.3–5.

37. Justin, *Dialogue*, 56.14; 63.4–5; 86.3.

38. Justin, *Dialogue*, 30.2; 42.1; 64.7–8; 69.3.

39. Justin, *Dialogue*, 69.3.

40. There is no English translation available of the full work, though selections are available, e.g., in Richardson (trans.), in *Early Christian Fathers*, 343–97. For a complete French (and Latin) translation, see Irénée de Lyon, *Contre les hérésies*, ed. Adelin Rousseau and others (SC 100; 152–53, 210–11, 263–64, 293–94; Paris: Cerf, 1965–82).

41. Irenaeus, *Against Heresies*, 3.11.8.

42. Irenaeus, *Against Heresies*, 3.5.1.

43. With regard esp. to Marcion's use of Scripture, see Edwin C. Blackman, *Marcion and His Influence* (London: SPCK, 1948). There is also a recent study of Marcion's theology: R. Joseph Hoffman, *Marcion: On the Restitution of Christianity* (AAR Academy Series 46; Chico, Calif.: Scholars Press, 1984)—see the bibliography there.

44. Blackman, *Marcion and His Influence*, 23–41.

45. Ibid., 114–15, 116.

46. Ibid., 115.

47. Ibid., 117.

48. Ibid., 64.

49. William A. Clebsch, "Preface," in Athanasius, *The Life of Antony and the Letter to Marcellinus* (The Classics of Western Spirituality; New York: Paulist, 1980), xviii.

50. For the letter itself, see Athanasius, *Letter to Marcellinus*, ed. and trans. Clebsch, 101-29. For the Greek text and Latin translation, see *PG* 27:11–46.

51. Athanasius, *Letter to Marcellinus*, ed. and trans. Clebsch, 109.

52. Ibid., 111.

53. Ibid., 116.

54. Paulinus, *Epistula* 32 (ad Severum), 3.5; Latin text in *Sancti Pontii Meropii Paulini Nolani Epistulae* (CSEL 29; Vienna: Tempsky, 1894), 279–80; translation adapted from Robin M. Jensen, *Living Water: Images, Settings and Symbols of Early Christian Baptism in the West* (Ph.D. diss., Union Theological Seminary, 1990), 424–25.

55. W. Jardine Grisbrooke, "The Formative Period: Cathedral and Monastic Offices," in Cheslyn Jones, Geoffrey Wainwright, and Edward Yarnold (eds.), *The Study of Liturgy* (New York: Oxford University Press, 1978), 358–59.

56. Augustine, *Confessions*, 9.6.14; 9.7.15.

57. J. A. Lamb, "The Place of the Bible in the Liturgy," in Peter R. Ackroyd and C. F. Evans (eds.), *The Cambridge History of the Bible*, vol. 1: *From the Beginnings to Jerome* (Cambridge: Cambridge University Press, 1970), 568–70.

58. Tertullian, *De Anima*, 9.

59. Peter G. Cobb, "The Liturgy of the Word in the Early Church," in Jones, Wainwright, and Yarnold (eds.), *Study of Liturgy*, 186.

60. Geoffrey G. Willis, *St Augustine's Lectionary* (Alcuin Club 44; London: SPCK, 1962), 5, 21.

61. Ibid., 615–19.

62. Ibid., 58; the references are: Sermons 185.3; 189.2; 191.1, 2; 192.1; 193.2. For the Latin text, see *PL* 38. For English translations of these sermons, see Thomas C. Lawler (ed.), *St. Augustine: Sermons for Christmas and Epiphany* (ACW 15; London: Longmans, Green, & Co.; Westminster, Md.: Newman, 1952), Sermons 3, 7, 9, 10, and 11.

63. Sermon 198.1 (= Lawler [ed.], *St. Augustine*, Sermon 17).

64. Augustine, *In Iohannis Evangelium Tractatus CXXIV* (CChr Series Latina 36; Turnhout: Brepols, 1954), 4.2.

65. Ibid., 6.9.

66. Ibid., 7.1.

67. Ibid., 9.13.

68. Ibid., 10.1, 4, 7.

69. The sermon is *Enarrationes in Psalmos* 21.II; for an English translation, see Scholastica Hebgin and Felicitas Corrigan (eds.), *St. Augustine on the Psalms* (ACW 29; London: Longmans, Green, & Co.; Westminster, Md.: Newman, 1960), 1:207–28.

70. Sermons 225.4.4; 226; 230; 258.1; see *PL* 38. Sermon 258 is available in a French translation in Augustin d'Hippone, *Sermons pour la Pâque*, ed. Suzanne Poque (SC 116; Paris: Cerf, 1966), 345–51.

71. *In Iohannis Epistulam Tractatus* 4.3; see *PL* 35.

72. Sermon 257.

73. Sermon 258.1.

74. Sermons 29.3; 266.1.

75. Sermon 13.

76. Sermon 28.1.

77. Willis, *Augustine's Lectionary*, 22–57.

78. Cobb, "Liturgy of the Word," 186–87.

79. Rembert G. Weakland, "Alleluia," in *NCE* 1:321–23.

80. Georges Goyau, "Langres," in *Catholic Encyclopedia* 8:790.

81. See, briefly, Lamb, "Place of the Bible," 579.

82. Edward Yarnold, "The Liturgy of the Faithful in the Fourth and Early Fifth Centuries," in Jones, Wainwright, and Yarnold (eds.), *Study of the Liturgy*, 194.

83. Augustine, *Retractationes* 37; see Augustine, *The Retractations*, trans. Mary Inez Bogan (FC 60; Washington, D.C.: Catholic University of America Press, 1968), 140.

84. Yarnold, "Liturgy of the Faithful," 197.

85. For a brief survey of commentators, see Briggs, *Commentary*, 1:cii–cv.

86. See William R. Inge, "Neo-Platonism," in James Hastings (ed.), *Encyclopaedia of Religion and Ethics* (New York: Charles Scribner's Sons, 1908–27), 9:308.

87. See Erwin R. Goodenough, *By Light, Light: The Mystic Gospel of Hellenistic Judaism* (New Haven: Yale University Press, 1935), esp. 11–12.

88. See, conveniently, Robert M. Grant, "History of the Interpretation of the Bible. I: Ancient Period," in *IB* 1:109–11; and, in more detail, R.P.C. Hanson, "Biblical Exegesis in the Early Church," in Ackroyd and Evans (eds.), *Cambridge History of the Bible*, 1:412–53.

89. See M. F. Wiles, "Origen as Biblical Scholar," in Ackroyd and Evans (eds.), *Cambridge History of the Bible*, 1:454–88.

90. The Greek text, with a Latin translation, may be found in *PG* 12:1053–1686. Further fragments may be found in René Cadiou, *Commentaires inédits des Psaumes: Etude sur les textes d'Origène contenus dans le manuscrit Vindobonensis 8* (Paris: Société d'Edition "Les Belles Lettres," 1936).

91. *PG* 12:1099–1118.

92. On this matter, see, conveniently, G.H.R. Macgregor, "Acts of the Apostles, Exegesis," in *IB* 9:180.

93. *PG* 12:1259–66.

94. *PG* 12:1658–59.

95. For a recent biographical study of Jerome, see John N. D. Kelly, *Jerome: His Life, Writings and Controversies* (New York: Harper & Row, 1975). For Jerome as a Bible commentator, see H.F.D. Sparks, "Jerome as Biblical Scholar," in Ackroyd and Evans (eds.), *Cambridge History of the Bible*, 1:535–41.

96. For the small commentary see Germain Morin (ed.), *S. Hieronymi Presbyteri Commentarioli in Psalmos* (CChr Series Latina 72; Turnhout: Brepols, 1959), 165–242; for the text of the addresses, see idem (ed.), *Tractatus sive Homiliae in Psalmos* and *Tractatus in Psalmos Quattuordecim Novissime Reperti* (CChr Series Latina 78; Turnhout: Brepols, 1958), 1–447. For an analysis of the content and style of these works, see Arthur S. Pease, "Notes on St. Jerome's Tractates on the Psalms," *JBL* 26 (1907):107–31.

97. For a convenient summary of Theodore's biblical work, see M. F. Wiles, "Theodore of Mopsuestia as Representative of the Antiochene School," in Ackroyd and Evans (eds.), *Cambridge History of the Bible*, 1:489–510; for his commentary on the Psalms, see, esp., 497–501. For a fuller analysis of his understanding of the Old Testament, see Dimitri Z. Zaharopoulos, *Theodore of Mopsuestia on the Bible: A Study of His Old Testament Exegesis* (New York: Paulist, 1989); for the nature of the surviving text of his commentary on the Psalms, see 30–32; and for Theodore's general understanding of the Psalms, see 83–86.

98. This is from the introduction to his *Commentary on John*, cited in Wiles, "Theodore of Mopsuestia," 491.

99. Ibid., 497.

100. Robert Devreesse, *Le Commentaire de Théodore de Mopsueste sur les Psaumes (I—LXXX)* (Studi e Testi 93; Vatican City: Vatican City Press, 1939).

101. Cf. Wiles, "Theodore of Mopsuestia," 498.

102. See the little commentary of Jerome on this psalm.

103. A list of these may be found in Briggs, *Commentary*, 1:cv.

104. See Beryl Smalley, *The Study of the Bible in the Middle Ages* (Oxford: Blackwell, 1952); and the sections of part 6, in idem, "The Exposition and Exegesis of Scripture," in G.W.H. Lampe (ed.), *Cambridge History of the Bible*, vol. 2: *The West from the Fathers to the Reformation* (Cambridge: Cambridge University Press, 1969), 155–279.

105. D. N. Hope, "The Medieval Western Rites," in Jones, Wainwright, and Yarnold (eds.), *Study of Liturgy*, 230.

106. Cobb, "Liturgy of the Word," 182.

107. Francis A. Brunner, "Introit," in *NCE* 7:596.

108. Hugh Wybrew, "The Byzantine Liturgy from the *Apostolic Constitutions* to the Present Day," in Jones, Wainwright, and Yarnold (eds.), *Study of Liturgy*, 210–11.

109. Hope, "Medieval Western Rites," 231–32.

110. Wybrew, "Byzantine Liturgy," 216.

111. Ibid., 213.

112. See, briefly, Lamb, "Place of the Bible," 580–83. For a more extended treatment, see the articles on "The Divine Office" in Jones, Wainwright, and Yarnold (eds.), *Study of Liturgy*, 350–82; and Robert Taft, *The Liturgy of the Hours in East and West: The Origins of the Divine Office and Its Meaning for Today* (Collegeville, Minn.: Liturgical Press, 1986).

113. W. Jardine Grisbrooke, "The Divine Office: The Formative Period," in Jones, Wainwright, and Yarnold (eds.), *Study of Liturgy*, 360.

114. Ibid., 360–63.

115. Ibid., 361 n. 3.

116. Ibid., 364 n. 1.

117. Ibid., 364; J. D. Crichton, "The Divine Office—The Office in the West: The Early Middle Ages," in Jones, Wainwright, and Yarnold (eds.), *Study of Liturgy*, 371.

118. See, conveniently, Justin McCann (ed. and trans.), *The Rule of Saint Benedict* (London: Burns Oates, 1952), chaps. 8–18.

119. See Ruth Steiner, "Gregorian Chant," in *The New Grove Dictionary of Music and Musicians* (London: Macmillan, 1980), 7:697–98.

120. Asser of St. David's, *Annals of the Reign of Alfred the Great*, in John A. Giles, *Six Old English Chronicles* (London: Bell & Dadly, 1872), 68.

121. Ibid., 76.

122. Francis Wormald, "Bible Illustration in Medieval Manuscripts," in Lampe (ed.), *Cambridge History of the Bible*, 2:321–22, plate 36; André Grabar, *Christian Iconography: A Study of Its Origins* (Bollinger Series XXXV, 10; Princeton: Princeton University Press, 1968), plate 145.

123. *The Belles Heures of Jean, Duke of Berry* (New York: The Cloisters, Metropolitan Museum of Art, 1958). See further Millard Meiss, *French Painting in the Time of Jean de Berry: The Boucicaut Master* (New York: Phaidon, 1967).

124. Gertrud Schiller, *Iconography of Christian Art*, vol. 2: *The Passion of Jesus Christ* (Greenwich, Conn.: New York Graphic Society, 1972), plate 211.

125. John T. McNeill and Helena M. Gamer, *Medieval Handbooks of Penance* (Records of Civilization, Sources and Studies 29; New York: Columbia University Press, 1938), 273.

126. *Regula non bullata* 3.3–9, cited in Regis J. Armstrong and Ignatius C. Brady (trans.), *Francis and Clare: The Complete Works* (The Classics of Western Spirituality; New York: Paulist, 1982), 111.

127. Kenneth S. Latourette, *A History of Christianity* (New York: Harper, 1953), 456.

128. Smalley, *Study of the Bible in the Middle Ages*, xiv.

129. Dom Jean Leclercq, "The Exposition and Exegesis of Scripture, from Gregory the Great to St Bernard," in Lampe (eds.), *Cambridge History of the Bible*, 2:196.

130. McNeill and Gamer, *Medieval Handbooks*, 104.

131. Ibid., 344.

132. Ibid.

133. Ibid., 394.

134. E.g., *The Cambridge History of the Bible* does not deal with the Eastern church; nor in *Study of Liturgy* is there any material on the Eastern church in the section on the Divine Office.

135. *The World Almanac and Book of Facts, 1991*, 609.

136. For the Divine Office in these liturgical traditions, see Taft, *Liturgy of the Hours*, 219–71.

137. For those outside this tradition, it is difficult to locate the sources from which to understand the place of the Psalms in Orthodox liturgy; most of the available handbooks either are written for the Orthodox worshiper, who already knows the system; are too brief; or both. I have found the following to be useful: John Glen King, *The Rites and Ceremonies of the Great Church, in Russia, Containing an Account of Its Doctrine, Worship, and Discipline* (London, 1772; reprint, New York: AMS, 1970); Mother Mary and Archimandrite Kallistos Ware (trans.), *The Festal Menaion* (London: Faber & Faber, 1969); *The Divine Liturgy according to St. John Chrysostom, with Appendices* (New York: Russian Orthodox Greek Catholic Church of America, 1967). The French work, by Feuillen Mercenier and François Paris, *La Prière des églises de rite byzantin*, vol. 1, *L'Office divin, la liturgie, les sacrements* (Prieuré d'Amay-sur-Meuse, Belgium: 1937), describes the Divine Office and liturgy of the church that uses the Byzantine Rite but is in communion with Rome (the Melkite Church); it nevertheless brings understanding of the details of the liturgy used in the Eastern church.

138. Mary and Ware (trans.), *The Festal Menaion*, 79.

139. Dimitri E. Conomos, *The Late Byzantine and Slavonic Communion Cycle: Liturgy and Music* (Dumbarton Oaks Studies 21; Washington, D.C.: Dumbarton Oaks Research Library and Collection, 1985), 12.

140. Mary and Ware (trans.), *The Festal Menaion*, 80.

141. *The Liturgy of the Orthodox Church*, 60–65; King, *Rites and Ceremonies*, 140–42.

142. See Taft, *Liturgy of the Hours*, 273–91.

143. See Kurt Weitzmann, *Byzantine Liturgical Psalters and Gospels* (London: Variorum Reprints, 1980).

144. See, conveniently, Kenneth S. Latourette, *A History of the Expansion of Christianity*, vol. 2: *The Thousand Years of Uncertainty* (New York: Harper, 1938), 161.

145. *The Psalter* (New Skete, Cambridge, N.Y.: 1984).

146. For these translations, see the articles in part 9, "The Vernacular Scriptures," in Lampe (ed.), *Cambridge History of the Bible*, 2:338–491.

147. Eunice Dauterman Maguire and others, *Art and Holy Powers in the Early Christian House* (Illinois Byzantine Studies 2; Urbana and Chicago: University of Illinois Press, 1989), plates 134 and 136.

148. Ibid., 89.

149. Carl Horstman, *Nova Legenda Angliae* (Oxford: Clarendon, 1901), 2:112.

150. Stith Thompson, *The Motif-Index of Folk-Literature* (Bloomington, Ind.: Indiana University Press, 1955), motif D1782.

11

The Psalms for Reformation Protestants

In the year 1054 the split between the Eastern and Western churches became definitive, with mutual excommunications; it was a split that was the result of centuries of divergence between Greek-speaking and Latin-speaking Christians, between the erstwhile political centers of Constantinople and Rome. But the Reformation, the split within the Western church beginning in 1517 that resulted in the birth of various Protestant churches, was the result of theological, cultural, political, and economic causes that were by comparison sudden in their emergence and awesome in their consequences.

As with the historical background for chapters 9 and 10 (the history of the Jews in the last two millennia and the story of the spread of the Christian faith until the sixteenth century), I can only sketch a suggestion of the historical background for the Reformation. But I must note a few details, particularly as they bear on the use of the Psalms in the Reformation churches.

The perfection of the art of printing from movable type in about 1450 reshaped the lives of Europeans as much as the advent of television in the middle of our own century has reshaped our own lives. As the sixteenth century began, printed material was everywhere, not only books but pamphlets and leaflets, the latter two often illustrated with woodcuts to reinforce the word. And though the ecclesiastical and political authorities tried, they could not really control the production of printed material any more than the recent Communist government of Romania could insist on the governmental registration of typewriters, or the former Soviet Union on the control of photocopying machines. The spread of the printed word encouraged literacy, and literacy encouraged the spread of the printed word.

And that printed word was in vernacular languages as well as in Latin. It is a wonderful thing to see and comprehend, in neat ranks of letters, one's own tongue.

By this time, too, the knowledge of Greek was spreading in the West, reinforced by the Greek manuscripts that were brought west by refugees fleeing Constantinople as it fell to the Turks in 1453. Humanist scholarship encouraged the study of the New Testament in Greek and the comparison of the text traditions of various manuscripts; and the hunger grew for knowledge of Hebrew as well, so that the Old Testament began to be studied by Christians in the traditional Hebrew text. Thereby scholars became aware of the differences between the texts of the Hebrew Old Testament and of the Greek New Testament on the one hand and the text of the Latin Vulgate available to them on the other.

And discoveries were being made in the wider world as well. Seagoing exploration, beginning with the Portuguese on the west coast of Africa and the journeys of Christopher Columbus and others to the Western Hemisphere, made it clear that Aristotle and other ancient writers did not have all the answers. Suddenly many people began to sense that they could move beyond the settled conclusions of the past.

Northern Europe expanded its trade. No longer were Rome and Constantinople and the Mediterranean Sea the center of the world, and the cities in the Rhineland and the Low Countries were becoming more prosperous.

And the papacy had declined as a political, moral, and spiritual force during the fourteenth and fifteenth centuries. The details cannot concern us here, but many thoughtful Christians sought ways to reform and renew the church.[1]

One result of these new developments was the growing awareness of lay people of their place in the economy of God, and the growing awareness of Christians of the source book of the faith, namely, the Bible.

Martin Luther: His Career and
His Commentaries on the Psalms

The initiator of the Reformation, Martin Luther (1483–1546), was one of those who shaped modern Western history.[2] He was born in Eisleben, a town about 115 miles (185 kilometers) southwest of Berlin. In 1505 he became an Augustinian monk and in 1507, a priest. As a monk Luther was, of course, obligated to share the devotional life of his community, saying the canonical hours;[3] indeed, he did not give them up until 1520, three years after the beginning of the Reformation, when he was hiding, deeply involved in his dispute with Rome (he was depressed and had fallen three months in arrears in saying the office!).[4] But long after Luther had translated the Bible, he continued in his prayers to recite the Psalms in the Latin Vulgate in which he had been reared.[5]

He became a professor in the University of Wittenberg in 1511, and to relieve his spiritual distress, his confessor suggested that he gain his doctorate and assume the chair of professor of Bible.[6] He accordingly began the study of the Scriptures and in 1513–1515 delivered lectures on the Psalms. Luther's humanist studies had afforded him knowledge of Greek and Hebrew, and he prepared for these lectures by reading extensively in medieval commentaries. In these years, and in the years he lectured on Romans (1515–1516) and Galatians (1516–1517), he became convinced that salvation from God is not the result of one's confession of sins and the forgiveness of these sins but is rather a new relation with God, based not on any human merit but on God's grace and the faith of the believer; and in 1517 he posted his famous Ninety-five Theses, the basis of the Lutheran Reformation. We have his early lectures on the Psalms, which covered most of Psalms 1 through 126. We also have a second set of lectures on the Psalms that were offered in the next few years and, in some cases, subsequently revised.[7]

He begins his comments on Psalm 1:1 this way:

> *Blessed is the man.* He is the only blessed One and the only Man from whose fullness they have all received (John 1:16) that they might be blessed and men and everything that follows in this psalm. He is "the firstborn among many brethren" (Rom. 8:29).[8]

His assumption here that the psalm refers to Christ he takes from certain medieval commentators, but it is clear that "for him, as for his time, the Old Testament was a Christian book foreshadowing the life and death of the Redeemer."[9] Thus "the counsel of the ungodly" is the "designs of the Jews, who afterwards crucified Him."[10] And to his remarks on Psalm 1 he appends some explanations of vocabulary: the Latin Vulgate for the beginning of v. 2 says, "But his will is in the law of the Lord," and Luther notes, "*Will* is not taken as in the schools [that is, as the medieval scholastics understood it], but it denotes a cheerful and spontaneous readiness (see the word *ḥēpeṣ* in the dictionary) and willing good pleasure." Luther is right, and the English versions use "delight" in this verse.

But in his second lectures on the Psalms (probably begun in the latter half of 1518), he does not interpret Psalm 1 to refer to Christ; he writes, "The search for personal blessedness is common to all men. . . . Blessed is he who loves the Law of God."[11] In that lecture "the ungodly" are "those who through their rules, privileges, merits, doings, and regulations divide themselves in implacable discord";[12] here he is speaking against the Catholic system.

In his first lectures on the Psalms, he does not touch on general questions about Psalm 2 or about the first eight verses; on v. 9, he says that the "rod of iron" is "the holy Gospel, which is Christ's royal scepter in his Church."[13] In his second lecture on the psalm, however, he does deal with generalities. He says, "That David was the author of this psalm, and that it speaks of Christ, is established through the authority of the primitive church," and he then cites Peter's words in Acts 4:24-28. Luther then continues:

> Therefore the mind must be strengthened in this interpretation and not be blown about by other winds of doctrine (Eph. 4:14), for this understanding was confirmed by heaven when the place shook at the end of their prayers, as Luke also writes (Acts 4:31).

As to the "kings of the earth," he says, "It should be made clear that Herod and Pilate are understood as being 'the kings of the earth,' even though Pilate was not exactly a king."[14] One has the impression that Luther is at least aware of contrary opinion on this matter. In v. 3, according to Luther, it is the kings who speak; the "bonds" are the commandments of Christ, and he compares the words of the kings to the words of the nobleman's citizens, in a parable of Jesus, who declared, "We do not want this man to reign over us" (Luke 19:14).[15]

Luther lectured on Psalm 2 once more, in the spring of 1532. The whole of the lecture on this psalm covers ninety pages, and in it we find vivid polemic against Thomas Münzer, a leader of the radical (Anabaptist) Reformation; Huldrych Zwingli, the Swiss reformer; and, of course, the "papists" (Catholics).[16]

We have a commentary on Psalm 23 that originated in Luther's "table talk" and was later edited for publication (in 1535 or 1536). For Luther, the psalmist is David. The "fine, pleasant, green pasture; fresh water; the path of righteousness; a rod; a staff; a table," all are names applied to the word of God;[17] we should, then, learn from this psalm not to despise God's word: we should "hear and learn it, love and respect it, and join the little flock in which we find it."[18] In his remarks on "Thou preparest a table before me against my enemies," one finds this:

> In this way I also have been preserved by the grace of God the past eighteen years. I have let my enemies rage, threaten, slander, and damn me, take counsel against me without ceasing, invent many evil devices, and practice many a piece of knavery. I have let them worry anxiously how they might kill me and destroy my teaching, or rather God's. More, I have been happy and of good cheer—at one time better than at another—have not worried greatly about their raving and raging, but have clung to the staff of comfort and found my way to the Lord's table.[19]

These commentaries, written by Luther at various times during a busy life, sometimes deal thoughtfully with Hebrew words or nuances of interpretation but more often serve as homiletical vehicles for his insistence on God's justification of sinful human beings through faith and the utter adequacy of Scripture as the only basis of that faith. Jaroslav Pelikan has written:

> Throughout his career Luther paid very much attention to the Psalter. . . . His attention to it was personal, devotional, political, exegetical, polemical—all at the same time. . . . What unifies the commentaries is the way each of them succeeds in blending Luther's personality with the message of the sacred text.[20]

And Emil Kraeling remarks:

> He [Luther] reports that the Psalter does not tell of the works of the saints but reports their *words*—how they spoke with God and prayed to God. "Yea, it enables us to look into their hearts and see what thoughts they had and how their hearts reacted to all the happenings, exigencies and necessities of existence."[21]

Luther thus has the same sensibility as did Athanasius twelve centuries earlier (see chapter 10).

As is well known, Luther translated the Bible into German from the original Greek and Hebrew. As I have indicated in chapters 9 and 10, there had been vernacular translations before Luther's time of both the Psalms and other biblical books, but it was Luther who with his translation of the Bible really created the modern German language. He translated the New Testament first, and then early in 1522 he set to work on the Old Testament. "I endeavored," he said, "to make Moses so German that no one would suspect he was a Jew."[22] But he wrote, "Translating is not an art that everyone can practice. It requires a right pious, faithful, diligent, God-fearing, experienced, practical heart."[23]

The Psalter was issued separately in 1524 and then revised in 1525, 1528, and 1531.[24] Roland Bainton writes:

> Luther's liberties were greatest with the Psalms because here he was so completely at home. They were the record of the spiritual struggles through which he was constantly passing. . . . Where the English version of Ps. 90 speaks of "secret sins" Luther has "unrecognized sins." He was thinking of his fruitless efforts in the cloister to recall every wrongdoing, that it might be confessed and pardoned. Where the English translates, "So teach us to number our days, that we may apply our hearts unto wisdom," Luther is blunt: "Teach us so to reflect on death that we may be wise."
>
> Luther so lived his way into the Psalms that he improved them. In the original the transitions are sometimes abrupt and the meaning not always plain. Luther simplified and clarified. . . . Take his conclusion to the Seventy-third Psalm. "My heart is stricken and my bones fail, that I must be a fool and know nothing, that I must be as a beast before thee. Nevertheless I will ever cleave to thee. Thou holdest me by thy right hand and leadest me by thy counsel. Thou wilt crown me at last with honor [vv. 21-24]."[25]

In 1523 Luther set forth reforms for his services of worship.[26] Here he moves toward the notion of the congregation's hearing entire psalms and not just short sequences from them: "First, we approve and retain the introits for the Lord's days and the festivals of Christ, such as Easter, Pentecost, and the Nativity, although we prefer the Psalms from which they were taken as of old."[27] Again, "The whole Psalter, Psalm by Psalm, should remain in use, and the entire Scripture, lesson by lesson, should continue to be read to the people."[28]

In 1524 he brought out a hymnbook for congregational singing, with twenty-three hymns of which he was the author; six of these were metrical paraphrases of psalms. Thus Psalm 130, "Out of the depths I cry to you," became *Aus tiefer Not schrei' ich zu Dir*. His famous hymn *Ein feste Burg ist unser Gott* (A mighty fortress is our God), an adaptation of Psalm 46, was published in 1529. Bainton writes:

> Luther's people learned to sing. Practices were set during the week for the entire congregation, and in the home after the catechetical hour singing was commended to the family. A Jesuit testified that "the hymns of Luther killed more souls than his sermons."[29]

The Reformation was above all a shift in theological perspective, a movement of humanists, clergy, princes, and commoners in northern Europe to reclaim the Bible with great joy; and the religious scene in Europe was transformed.

John Calvin: His Career and His
Commentaries on the Psalms

I now turn to the second giant of the Reformation, John Calvin (1509–1564).[30] Calvin was born in Noyon, about 50 miles (80 kilometers) north of Paris; he was educated in Paris, first in arts and philosophy and then in law. He became leader of the Reformation in Geneva (1536–1538 and 1541–1564), and his *Institutes of the Christian Religion* (first edition, 1536; final revision, 1559) became the most important theological textbook of the Reformation. What is of interest to us first is his commentaries. He wrote on Genesis, a harmony of the rest of the Pentateuch, Joshua, the Psalms, the major and minor prophets, and all of the New Testament except 2 and 3 John and Revelation.[31]

The current English translation of his commentary on the Psalms covers 2,400 pages. The commentary was published in Latin in 1557 and in French in 1558.[32]

In the preface that Calvin wrote to his commentary on the Psalms, he lays out not only his understanding of the Psalms but his own religious development. In it he begins (as do Athanasius and Luther) by calling the Psalter "An Anatomy of all the Parts of the Soul,"

> for there is not an emotion of which any one can be conscious that is not here represented as in a mirror. . . . Here the prophets themselves, seeing they are exhibited to us as speaking to God, and laying open all their inmost thoughts and affections, call, or rather draw, each of us to the examination of himself in particular, in order that none of the many infirmities to which we are subject, and of the many vices with which we abound, may remain concealed.[33]

He finds the Psalms a reflection of his own personal experience: "For although I follow David at a great distance, and come far short of equalling him, . . . I have no hesitation in comparing myself with him." Then, after a short autobiography, he returns to David's career:

> It seemed to me that by his own footsteps he showed me the way, and from this I have experienced no small consolation. As that holy king was harassed by the Philistines and other foreign enemies with continual wars, while he was much more grievously afflicted by the malice and wickedness of some perfidious men amongst his own people, so I can say as to myself, that I have been assailed on all sides, and have scarcely been able to enjoy repose for a single moment, but have always had to sustain some conflict either from enemies without or within the Church.[34]

He complains with David, "For it was not an enemy that reproached me; but it was thou, a man mine equal, my guide, and mine acquaintance. We took sweet counsel together, and walked unto the house of God in company" (see Ps. 55:13-15 [12-14]).[35] "This knowledge and experience," he concludes, "have been of much service in enabling me to understand The Psalms, so that in my meditations upon them, I did not wander, as it were, in an unknown region."[36]

If, for Luther, Psalm 2 was spoken by David to apply to Christ, then for

Calvin, in Psalm 2 David is describing his own kingship. "We know how many conspired against David," he writes.[37]

> It is not certain from the words whether he speaks only of enemies in his own kingdom, or extends his complaints to foreign invaders. But since the fact was, that enemies rose up against him in all quarters, and that as soon as he had settled the disturbances among his own people, the neighbouring states, in their turn, became hostile to him, I am disposed to think that both classes of enemies are meant, Gentiles as well as Jews.[38]

But David was a "type" for Christ: "That David prophesied concerning Christ, is clearly manifest from this, that he knew his own kingdom to be merely a shadow."[39] And, Calvin concluded, if what happened to David was what happened to Christ, then when such things happen to us, we may be reassured by what God has done in Christ.

> As often as the world rages, in order to disturb and put an end to the prosperity of Christ's kingdom, we have only to remember that, in all this, there is just a fulfilment of what was long ago predicted, and no changes that can happen will greatly disquiet us.[40]

On v. 4—"He who sits in the heavens laughs"—Calvin remarks:

> David ascribes laughter to God . . . to teach us that he does not stand in need of great armies to repress the rebellion of wicked men, as if this were an arduous and difficult matter, but, on the contrary, could do this as often as he pleases with the most perfect ease.[41]

With regard to Psalm 23, Calvin, as we might imagine, waxes eloquent on the character of God as shepherd, on his tender love and care for his faithful ones. With regard to v. 4, Calvin stresses how God reassures us in our fears; he knows both interpretations, "valley of deep darkness" and "valley of the shadow of death," and speaks of both but does not stress the matter of transition into death.

If, for Luther, v. 5—"You prepare a table before me"—suggests the communion table, it does not for Calvin:

> He means that God furnished him [David] with sustenance without trouble or difficulty on his part, just as if a father should stretch forth his hand to give food to his child. He enhances this benefit from the additional consideration, that although many malicious persons envy his happiness, and desire his ruin, yea, endeavour to defraud him of the blessing of God; yet God does not desist from showing himself liberal towards him, and from doing him good.[42]

With regard to Psalm 137, Calvin does not insist that David wrote it: "The prophets in speaking of future events employ very different language,"[43] he says, and adds, "The writer of this Psalm, whose name is unknown, drew up a form of lamentation, that by giving expression to their sufferings in sighs and prayers, they might keep alive the hope of that deliverance which they despaired of."[44] Verse 2— "We hanged our harps on the willows"—moves him to say that "he [the psalmist] deplores the suspension of the songs of praise, which God had enjoined in his Temple";[45] "willows" suggests the coolness of the shade on the river banks, "but the Psalmist says that these shades, however delightful, could not dispel a grief which was too deeply seated to admit of common consolations or refreshment."[46]

Calvin had a wonderful ability to listen to the plain meaning, and his theological and psychological acuity allowed him to discern the depths of the plain meaning of the text; no wonder that Brevard Childs, a few years ago, urged pastors "to read deeply and widely in" Luther and Calvin. "Perhaps it is wise to start with Calvin, whose commentaries have appeared in paper back editions."[47]

The Commentaries of Katharina Schütz Zell and Justitia Sanger

There is no space here to pursue commentaries on the Psalms beyond those of Luther and Calvin. But because the Reformation brought a fresh view of the status of women,[48] I must acknowledge here a laywoman in Strasbourg, Katharina Schütz Zell, who published a commentary on Psalms 51 and 130 in 1558;[49] and Justitia Sanger, a blind woman from Braunschweig, who published a commentary on ninety-six psalms in 1593, dedicating it to King Frederick II of Denmark.[50]

Metrical Psalms: The First Stage

The Reformation was the occasion for a completely new development in the use of the Psalms, that is, metrical psalters. The Reformation marked the beginning of hymn-singing as we now understand it: singing became an activity for the whole congregation. Luther, as we have seen, adapted psalms for congregational singing; he also adapted earlier Latin hymns, such as *Nun komm, der Heiden Heiland* (published in 1523), a German translation of the Advent hymn of Ambrose, bishop of Milan in the fourth century, *Veni redemptor gentium*.[51]

But it was the Calvinist movement that was the primary source for the adaptation of psalms for congregational singing. "The singing of psalms was one of the incontestably distinguishing marks of Calvinist culture in Europe and America in the sixteenth and seventeenth centuries."[52] Indeed, "Calvinists were convinced that they could legitimately appropriate the psalms to themselves. . . . The psalms were *their* songs which they sang as the elect people of God in a covenant relationship with Him."[53]

In 1535, Calvin came to reside in Basel, Switzerland (a German-speaking area); it was there that he wrote the first, modest edition of the *Institutes*. While there, he must have heard the congregational singing of psalms prepared by Zwingli and other Swiss reformers.[54] In the third chapter of the *Institutes* he discusses prayer, and, incidentally in the course of that discussion, he deals with the singing of psalms as a way to arouse one's ardor for God.[55]

So when Calvin was invited to superintend the Reformation in Geneva (part of the French-speaking area of Switzerland) in 1537, and drew up the articles for the conduct of worship in that city, he stated:

> Furthermore it is a thing most expedient for the edification of the church to sing some psalms in the form of public prayers by which one prays to God or sings His praises so that the hearts of all may be aroused and stimulated to make similar prayers and to render similar praises and thanks to God with a common love.[56]

Later in the articles he complains, "Certainly at present the prayers of the faithful are so cold that we should be greatly ashamed and confused. The psalms can stimulate us to raise our hearts to God and arouse us to an ardor in invoking as well as in exalting with praises the glory of His name."[57] He then goes on to suggest a solution—children to lead the singing:

> The manner of beginning in this seemed to us well advised if some children who have previously practiced a modest church song sing in a loud and distinct voice, the people listening with complete attention and following with the heart what is sung with the mouth until little by little each one accustoms himself to singing communally.[58]

By this time, then, Calvin has become convinced that song is a necessary component of public worship, and it is the Psalms that are to be sung.

He was in Geneva only a few months in 1537 before he was expelled, and by the end of that year he had settled in Strasbourg (a German-speaking city on the Rhine River that had, nevertheless, a French-speaking minority). In a few months he had published a Psalter (1539) containing nineteen psalms in French translation, all but one of which were in rhyme. Of these, thirteen were the work of the French humanist Clément Marot, while the rest were written by Calvin;[59] the tunes were taken over from an antecedent German songbook used in Reformed worship in Strasbourg.[60] Then Calvin returned to Geneva in 1541 and prepared the *Ecclesiastical Ordinances* for church order, essentially an enlargement of his earlier articles. In it he reinforced his concern for singing the Psalms and the leadership therewith of children.[61] The next year he prepared an enlarged Psalter, the so-called first Geneva Psalter: he took over seventeen more metrical psalms of Marot and revised some of the earlier ones.[62] His musical editor was Louis Bourgeois, a composer whose name still graces present-day hymnals: in the Genevan Psalter of 1551 there appears the tune he wrote that is now called "Old Hundredth," because in English it is used for a metrical form of Psalm 100—"All people that on earth do dwell"; the same tune is used in many churches for the doxology ("Praise God from whom all blessings flow").

Steadily expanding Psalters continued to be produced in Geneva: in 1562 there appeared a metrical Psalter with all 150 Psalms.[63] This Psalter was reprinted sixty-two times in its first two years and was translated into twenty-four languages.[64]

As I have already indicated, Calvin's conviction that only the Psalms and other biblical material may be sung by the congregation had a firm theological basis. This basis is most cogently set out in the "Epistle to the Reader" prefixed to the 1542 Geneva Psalter.

> Now what Saint Augustine says is true, that no one is able to sing things worthy of God unless he has received them from him. Wherefore, when we have looked thoroughly everywhere and searched high and low, we shall find no better songs nor more appropriate for the purpose than the Psalms of David, which the Holy Spirit made and spoke through him. And furthermore, when we sing them, we are certain that God puts the words in our mouths, as if he himself were singing in us to exalt his glory.[65]

(We saw in chapter 10 the enthusiasm Augustine manifested for the singing of psalms, a custom that had come to Milan from the East.) Indeed Calvin reached the point where he suggested that Christians should never sing any secular songs at all in whatever circumstance, thereby understanding the injunction of Eph. 5:20— "giving thanks to God the Father at all times and for everything in the name of our Lord Jesus Christ"—as excluding any songs but the Psalms.[66]

In the meantime, collections of metrical psalms were likewise being published in English; the earliest collection was that of the biblical translator Miles Coverdale (probably in 1535), containing metrical versions of thirteen psalms, two of which have two versions: the title of the book was (in modern spelling) *Ghostly psalms and spiritual songs drawn out of the holy Scripture, for the comfort and consolation of such as love to rejoice in God and his word.*[67] One of the most notable of such editions was that of Thomas Sternhold and John Hopkins (1549), which contained forty-four metrical psalms.[68]

The Sternhold and Hopkins Psalter was expanded, probably by William Whittingham, into all 150 Psalms and published in London in 1562; each psalm was either supplied with music or printed with directions for using a tune printed with another psalm.[69] This so-called Old Version became the standard for metrical psalms, sung by Established (Anglican) and nonconformist churches alike; it went through seventy-eight editions before 1600.[70] I have already mentioned the English metrical version of Psalm 100, "All people that on earth do dwell": the words are those of William Kethe and first appeared in that edition of 1562.[71]

The version of Psalm 23 was written by William Whittingham:

> The Lord is only my support
>   and he that doth me feed:
> How can I then lack any thing
>   whereof I stand in need?
> In pastures green he feedeth me,
>   where I do safely lie:
> And after leads me to the streams,
>   which run most pleasantly.
> And when I find myself near lost,
>   then doth he me home take,
> Conducting me in his right paths,
>   e'en for his own name's sake.

And tho' I were e'en at death's door
   yet would I fear no ill:
For both thy rod and shepherd's crook,
   afford me comfort still.
Thou hast my table richly spread
   in presence of my foe;
Thou hast my head with balm refresh'd,
   my cup doth overflow.
And finally, while breath doth last,
   thy grace shall me defend:
And in the house of God will I
   my life for ever spend.[72]

English Translations of the Bible

We must pause now in our survey of metrical psalms to touch on the activity of translations of the whole Bible into English. The sixteenth century saw several efforts.[73] I begin with William Tyndale, who (like most) began his work of translation with the New Testament: he had it printed in Germany and it was selling in England by 1526. He then turned to the Old Testament; but it was not completed when he was burned at the stake in 1536, leaving the memory of his final prayer, "Lord, open the King of England's eyes." One of Tyndale's helpers was Coverdale, whom we have already met as the compiler of metrical psalms. Coverdale's Bible was continued in the so-called Great Bible of 1539, which was sponsored by Henry VIII.

In the meantime, the followers of John Knox, the Scottish Calvinist leader, produced the so-called Geneva Bible of 1560. A compromise was the "Bishops' Bible" of 1568, which was an improvement on the Great Bible but not as radical as the Geneva Bible. It was the rendering of the Psalms in the Bishops' Bible (Psalm 23 begins, "The Lord is my shepherd: therefore can I lack nothing") that was used in the *Book of Common Prayer* until the twentieth century; the *Book of Common Prayer* never adopted the Psalms of the King James Version (any more than the Latin Vulgate accepted Jerome's translation of the Psalms in Hebrew; see chapter 6).

That King James Version, in 1611, was the culmination of the activity of translation; it was a translation that appeared when the English language was being spread throughout the earth, and it shaped English literature and church sensibility for three hundred years. (It is the KJV's Twenty-third Psalm that so many people have memorized: "The Lord is my shepherd, I shall not want.")

Metrical Psalms: The Second Stage

We return now to the matter of metrical Psalters. The Psalter of Sternhold and Hopkins may have been popular, but it did not satisfy those whose persuasions were Calvinist (the followers of John Knox in Scotland) or Puritan (those who wished to "purify" the Church of England). They were convinced it was too much of a paraphrase: How could four words in Hebrew—"The-Lord(-is) my-shepherd, not

I-shall-lack"—be turned into a full stanza of four lines in Sternhold and Hopkins? Even granting a certain amount of shift of translation necessary for rhyme and regularity of line, still those who clung to fidelity to the Hebrew text were not satisfied.

They made fresh efforts, then, to render the Psalms in metrical form. One effort that is notable for Americans is *The Whole booke of psalmes, faithfully translated into English metre*, commonly known as the *Bay Psalm Book*, the first book published in New England (Cambridge, Mass.: 1640).[74] Of this work 1,700 copies were printed. The ministers who did the rendering were concerned to keep as close to the Hebrew original as metrical form would allow. The result was far more concise than Sternhold and Hopkins, but sometimes ungainly. It is clear that John Cotton was responsible for Psalm 23;[75] it is four lines shorter than the version of Sternhold and Hopkins. It is as follows (with modern spelling):

> The Lord to me a shepherd is,
>   want therefore shall not I.
> He in the folds of tender grass
>   doth cause me down to lie.
> To waters calm me gently leads
>   Restore my soul doth he;
> He doth in paths of righteousness
>   for his name's sake lead me.
> Yea though in valley of death's shade
>   I walk, none ill I'll fear,
> because thou art with me, thy rod
>   and staff my comfort are.
> For me a table thou hast spread,
>   in presence of my foes;
> thou dost anoint my head with oil,
>   my cup it overflows.
> Goodness and mercy surely shall
>   all my days follow me,
> and in the Lord's house I shall dwell
>   so long as days shall be.

In 1647 a second edition of the *Bay Psalm Book* appeared in England, but in the meantime a revision was published by the same Cambridge press in 1651. It became known as the *New England Psalm Book*, and it was reprinted more than fifty times during the next hundred years.[76] A comparison of Psalm 23 shows how several phrases were made smoother:

> The Lord himself my shepherd is,
>   want therefore shall not I:
> He in the folds of tender grass
>   soft makes me down to lie.
> He leads me to the waters still,
>   restore my soul does he;

> In paths of righteousness He will
>   for his name's sake lead me.
> Tho' in death's gloomy vale I walk,
>   yet I will fear no ill;
> For thou art with me, and thy rod
>   and staff me comfort will.
> Thou hast for me a table spread
>   in presence of my foes;
> Thou dost my head with oil anoint,
>   and my cup overflows.
> Goodness and mercy all my days
>   shall surely follow me;
> And in the Lord's house I shall dwell
>   as long as days shall be.[77]

It may be said in passing that the settlers in New England may not have had too good an ear for poetry: William Bradford, longtime governor of the Plymouth Colony, in 1654 wrote a poem entitled "Some Observations of God's Merciful Dealing with us in this Wilderness, and His Gracious Protection over us These Many Years, Blessed Be His Name," which begins, "In this wilderness we lived have here, In happy peace this four and thirty year";[78] so the continued presence in the *New England Psalm Book* of lines such as "want therefore not shall I" should not come as a surprise.

Out of many other metrical Psalters, two more claim our attention. One is the Scottish Psalter of 1650. There had been Scottish Psalters since 1564, directly stimulated, as one might expect, by the Genevan Psalters.[79] From the 1650 Psalter come several paraphrases that still appear in current hymnals, including a rendering of Psalm 23:[80] this hymn is still so popular in Scotland as to lead some Scots jokingly to call it the "Scots' National Anthem."[81]

> The Lord's my shepherd, I'll not want,
>   he makes me down to lie
> in pastures green; he leadeth me
>   the quiet waters by.
> My soul he doth restore again,
>   and me to walk doth make
> within the paths of righteousness,
>   e'en for his own name's sake.
> Yea, though I walk in death's dark vale,
>   yet will I fear no ill;
> for thou art with me, and thy rod
>   and staff me comfort still.
> My table thou hast furnishèd
>   in presence of my foes;
> my head thou dost with oil anoint,
>   and my cup overflows.

Goodness and mercy all my life
    shall surely follow me;
and in God's house forevermore
    my dwelling-place shall be.[82]

And one sees other psalms from that Psalter in current hymnals: for example, its version of Psalm 95—"O come, let us sing to the Lord"[83]—and of Psalm 121—"I to the hills will lift mine eyes."[84]

The other Psalter to be mentioned is that of Nahum Tate and Nicholas Brady, *New Version of the Psalms of David* (London: first edition, 1696; second edition, 1698), which slowly replaced the Old Version of Sternhold and Hopkins.[85] Psalm 23 in their version covers twenty-four lines, as it does in Sternhold and Hopkins, but the wording is completely fresh.

The Lord himself, the mighty Lord
    vouchsafes to be my guide;
The shepherd by whose constant care
    my wants are all supplied.
In tender grass he makes me feed,
    and gently there repose;
Then leads me to cool shades, and where
    refreshing water flows.
He does my wand'ring soul reclaim,
    and to his endless praise,
Instruct with humble zeal to walk
    in his most righteous ways.
I pass the gloomy vale of death,
    from fear and danger free;
For there his aiding rod and staff,
    defend and comfort me.
In presence of my spiteful foes,
    he does my table spread;
He crowns my cup with cheerful wine,
    with oil anoints my head.
Since God doth thus his wond'rous love
    through all my life extend,
That life to him I will devote,
    and in his temple spend.[86]

Metrical psalms from this version that are still sung include Psalm 34—"Through all the changing scenes of life"[87]—and Psalm 42—"As pants the hart for cooling streams,"[88] which in *The* (Episcopal) *Hymnal 1982* has been altered to "As longs the deer for cooling streams."[89] I note in passing that Tate and Brady issued a supplement in 1700, offering metrical versions of some New Testament passages, including the hymn "While shepherds watched their flocks by night," which is still used in current hymnals.

Hymns Based on the Psalms

Beyond these metrical Psalters, one must take notice of the great flowering of Protestant hymnody. Many hymn-writers were stimulated by the Psalms or wrote their own paraphrases of psalms. I must confine myself to two hymn-writers of the eighteenth century. The first is Isaac Watts (1674–1748). Watts wrote paraphrases of Psalm 23, at least two of which are still sung. The first is "The Lord my shepherd is."

> The Lord my shepherd is,
>   I shall be well supplied;
> Since He is mine and I am His,
>   What can I want beside?
> He leads me to the place
>   Where heavenly pasture grows,
> Where living waters gentle pass,
>   And full salvation flows.
> If e'er I go astray,
>   He doth my soul reclaim,
> And guides me in His own right way,
>   For His most holy name.
> While He affords His aid,
>   I cannot yield to fear;
> Though I should walk through death's dark shade,
>   My Shepherd's with me there.
> Amid surrounding foes
>   Thou dost my table spread;
> My cup with blessing overflows,
>   And joy exalts my head.
> The bounties of Thy love
>   shall crown my following days;
> Nor from Thy house will I remove,
>   Nor cease to speak Thy praise.[90]

The second is "My shepherd will supply my need"; the twentieth-century composer Virgil Thomson (b. 1896) has arranged the hymn as an anthem.

> My shepherd will supply my need;
>   Jehovah is His name;
> In pastures fresh He makes me feed,
>   Beside the living stream.
> He brings my wand'ring spirit back
>   When I forsake His ways,
> And leads me, for His mercy's sake
>   In paths of truth and grace.
> When I walk through the shades of death,
>   Thy presence is my stay;

> A word of thy supporting breath
>   Drives all my fears away.
> Thy hand, in sight of all my foes,
>   Doth still my table spread.
> My cup with blessings overflows,
>   Thine oil anoints my head.
> The sure provisions of my God
>   Attend me all my days;
> O, may thine house be mine abode,
>   And all my work be praise.
> There would I find a settled rest,
>   While others go and come—
> No more a stranger or a guest,
>   But like a child at home.[91]

Still sung are Watts's paraphrases of Psalm 19, "The heavens declare thy glory, Lord";[92] Psalm 36, "High in the heavens, eternal God";[93] Psalm 90, "Our God, our help in ages past,"[94] usually altered to "O God, our help";[95] Psalm 100, "Before the Lord Jehovah's throne," revised by John Wesley (1737) to "Before Jehovah's aweful throne,"[96] in the *Lutheran Book of Worship* to "Before Jehovah's awesome throne,"[97] and in *The* (Episcopal) *Hymnal 1982* to "Before the Lord's eternal throne";[98] and Psalm 117, "From all that dwell below the skies."[99]

In his paraphrases Watts deliberately Christianized the Psalms. Thus from Psalm 72 he created "Jesus shall reign where'er the sun."[100] He took Ps. 98:4-9 and made of it a hymn sung at the Christmas season, "Joy to the world." Indeed in the preface to his *Psalms of David imitated in the language of the New Testament* (1719), he wrote:

> It is necessary to divest *David* and *Asaph* etc. of every other character but that of a *psalmist* and a *saint*, and to make them *always speak the common sense of a Christian*. When the Psalmist describes Religion by the *Fear* of God, I have often joined *Faith* and *Love* to it. Where he talks of sacrificing *Goats and Bullocks*, I rather chuse to mention the sacrifice of *Christ, the Lamb of God*.[101]

The other hymn-writer of the eighteenth century to be mentioned here is Charles Wesley (1707–1788). In comparison with Watts, Wesley drew less from the Psalms than from New Testament passages and from his own personal experience; but one may mention "Praise the Lord who reigns above," based on Psalm 150,[102] and "O for a heart to praise my God,"[103] based on Ps. 51:12 (10).

We can see, then, how the innovation of metrical psalms in the sixteenth century, such as those of Sternhold and Hopkins, stimulated in the seventeenth century both stricter renderings (the *Bay Psalm Book*) and smoother renderings (Tate and Brady), and how the advent of metrical psalms in turn stimulated fresh hymns that loosely paraphrased and Christianized the antecedent psalms.[104]

Paraphrases Composed by the
Humanist Poets

I now turn back to the sixteenth century to mention two extraecclesial uses of the Psalms. The first of these is the paraphrases made of psalms by humanist poets. The humanists, who were trained in both the ancient languages and in the languages current in Europe, appreciated the Psalms as poetic expressions and used them as models in poetic composition.

Sir Thomas Wyatt the elder (1503–1542) was a courtier and diplomat in the service of Henry VIII. He was also a poet who drew deeply on Italian models; he translated some of Petrarch's poems into English as well as writing poetry of his own, some of it love poetry; but he also refashioned the "Penitential Psalms." His rendering of Psalm 130 uses terza rima, the interlocking rhyme scheme used by Dante in the *Divine Comedy*. Here are the first eleven of the thirty-one lines of the poem (in modern spelling):

> From depth of sin and from a deep despair,
>> From depth of death, from depth of heartès sorrow,
>> From this deep cave of darkness' deep repair,
> Thee have I call'd, O Lord, to be my burrow [shelter].
>> Thou in my voice, O Lord, perceive and hear
>> My heart, my hope, my plaint, my overthrow,
> My will to rise; and let by grant appear
>> That to my voice thine ears do well entend.
>> No place so far that to thee 'tis not near;
> No depth so deep that thou ne may'st extend
>> Thine ear thereto. Hear then my woeful plaint.[105]

Sir Philip Sidney (1554–1586) was a soldier and statesman in the court of Elizabeth I. He rendered the first forty-three psalms into verse; then his sister Mary, Countess of Pembroke (ca. 1561–1621), began by revising her brother's psalms and then continued with her own, Psalms 44 through 150.[106] These renderings of the Psalms were noteworthy enough to call forth from John Donne, after the Countess's death, a poetic tribute, "Upon the translation of the Psalmes by Sir Philip Sydney, and the Countesse of Pembroke his Sister," in which he celebrates "the Sydnean Psalmes."[107]

And they are worthy of his tribute. The rendering of Psalm 23 is in stunning form—four stanzas of six lines each; each stanza containing successive lines of eight, six, four, eight, six, and four syllables; in a rhyme scheme of A, B, B, A, C, and C. It is as follows:

> The Lord, the Lord my shepherd is,
>> And so can never I
>>> Taste misery.
> He rests me in green pasture his:
>> By waters still, and sweet

He guides my feet.
He me revives: leads me the way,
   Which righteousness doth take,
      For his name's sake.
Yea, though I should through valleys stray,
   Of death's dark shade, I will
      No whit fear ill.
For thou, dear Lord, thou me besett'st:
   Thy rod, and thy staff be
      To comfort me;
Before me thou a table sett'st,
   E'en when foe's envious eye
      Doth it espy.
Thou oil'st my head, thou fill'st my cup:
   Nay more thou endless good,
      Shalt give me food.
To thee, I say, ascended up,
   Where thou, the Lord of all,
      Dost hold thy hall.

For the short Psalm 117, Mary Sidney offers, surprisingly, a twelve-line acrostic that spells the meaning of the last line of the psalm:

*P*raise him that aye
*R*emains the same:
*A*ll tongues display
*I*ehovah's fame.
*S*ing, all that share
*T*his earthly ball:
*H*is mercies are
*E*xpose'd to all:
*L*ike as the word
*O*nce he doth give,
*R*oll'd in record,
*D*oth time outlive.

These paraphrases offer us the Psalms as personal expressions, as material for meditation; here the emphasis is not on the people of God but on religious emotion. Wyatt would not be expressing penitence for

some *specific* fault or sin as out of a sense of world-weariness. Self-disgust for vanities fruitlessly pursued and moral contempt for the vanities of others would have been closely intermeshed. The line between the penitential mode and the mode of secular "complaint" may not have been precisely drawn.[108]

It is Mary Sidney's "insistence on the validity of applying to the psalms knowledge and understanding gained from study and personal experience that makes them exemplary models for private meditation."[109]

The Psalms as Battle Hymns

The second extraecclesial use of the Psalms is a direct outgrowth of the Calvinist development of metrical psalms, and that is their use as battle hymns. This phenomenon is remarkable, though it is certainly understandable. Of all the Protestant groups, the Calvinists had the longest struggle with opposing forces: after the Peace of Augsburg (1555) the Lutherans no longer struggled with Roman Catholic authorities, and the Anabaptists, being pacifist, did not fight. But the Calvinists sustained years of persecution, and they fought with martial psalms.[110] Again and again one reads of imprisoned Huguenots (French Protestants) singing psalms, much to the annoyance of the authorities, or of the rage of Roman Catholic bishops as Protestants would gather before their doors to sing psalms. It is clear that this singing of psalms by the laity played an important part in the expansion of the Reformation.[111]

One of the most popular psalms in the Huguenot armies was Psalm 68—"Let God arise, let his enemies be scattered." Another was Psalm 118—"For the Lord is good, his mercy endures forever"; this psalm was sung by the forces of Henry of Navarre before the Battle of Coutras (about twenty-eight miles [forty-five kilometers] east-northeast of Bordeaux in southwestern France) on October 20, 1587: before the battle, when the Huguenots began to sing, the royal forces thought they were begging for mercy, but one of the officers said, "When the Huguenots do this they are ready to fight well."[112] (The Calvinists won the battle, but they ultimately lost their struggle.)

The situation was similar in the Low Countries. When, in 1568, William of Orange (William the Silent) published his "Justification" of his resistance to Philip of Spain—the beginning of the Eighty Years' War of liberation for the Netherlands—he commenced by quoting Ps. 37:32, "The wicked watch for the righteous, and seek to kill them." So those loyal to the House of Orange repeatedly sang psalms in their resistance.[113]

The same was the case in Scotland. One scene may do for many. John Durie was a minister in Edinburgh who had been exiled; when he returned to the city in 1582, he was met by a steadily increasing crowd. David Calderwood (1575–1650) describes the scene in striking fashion.

> John Durie cometh to Leith at night the 3rd of September. Upon Tuesday the 4th of September, as he is coming to Edinburgh, there met him at the Gallowgreen 200, but ere he came to the Nethbow their number increased to 400; but they were no sooner entered but they increased to 600 or 700, and within short space the whole street was replenished even to Saint Geiles Kirk: the number was esteemed 2000. At the Netherbow they took up the 124 Psalm, "Now Israel may say," etc., and sung in such a pleasant tune in four parts, known to the most part of the people, that coming up the street all bareheaded till they entered the Kirk with such a great sound and majestie, that it moved both themselves and all the huge multitude of the beholders, looking out at the shots and over stairs, with admiration and estonishment: the Duke [of

Lennox] himself beheld, and reave his beard for anger: he was more affrayed of this sight than anie thing that ever he had seen before in Scotland.[114]

This use by Protestants of the Psalms in the conviction that God is utterly on the side of those who struggle in battle is reflected in the rhetoric of so many in those days; one thinks of the Puritan Oliver Cromwell in the seventeenth century. Three days after the Battle of Marston Moor (near York, fought on July 2, 1644), Cromwell, the decisive leader in the parliamentary army, wrote a letter to Colonel Valentine Walton, offering his condolence on the death of his eldest son. Here are the first two paragraphs of the letter:

Dear Sir,
    It's our duty to sympathise in all mercies; that we may praise the Lord together in chastisements of trials, that so we may sorrow together.
    Truly England and the Church of God hath had a great favour from the Lord, in this great victory given unto us, such as the like never was since this war began. It had all the evidences of an absolute victory obtained by the Lord's blessing upon the godly party principally. We never charged but we routed the enemy. The left wing, which I commanded, being our own horse, saving a few Scots in our rear, beat all the Prince's horse. God made them as stubble to our swords [compare Ps. 83:14 (13)], we charged their regiments of foot with our horse, routed all we charged. The particulars I cannot relate now, but I believe, of twenty-thousand the Prince hath not four-thousand left. Give glory, all the glory, to God.[115]

Metrical Psalms in Anglican Worship

I now return to the use of psalms in the worship of the Church of England. The Anglican church, which broke with the Roman Catholic Church under Henry VIII in 1534, slowly and carefully reformed its liturgy under the direction of Thomas Cranmer (1489–1556), Archbishop of Canterbury. The liturgy shifted to English and was embodied in the *Book of Common Prayer*, much of it the work of Cranmer (first edition, 1549). In Anglican worship, metrical psalms were commonly used before and after the sermon. So the metrical psalms were commonly bound in with the *Book of Common Prayer* as a kind of quasi-official appendix.[116] (The edition of Sternhold and Hopkins that I have consulted, from 1783, is bound as an appendix to the *Book of Common Prayer*.) So it was that this development of the Reformation, metrical psalms, found its way into the liturgy of a church that in its singing was not confined to the Psalms.

Printed Psalms in the Lives
of Two Laymen

I began the chapter by mentioning the printing press; I return to the matter now. In 1566, in Cambrai, France, a Protestant linen-weaver explained to his judges about the book in his life:

I was led to knowledge of the Gospel by . . . my neighbor, who had a Bible printed at Lyon and who taught me the Psalms by heart. . . . The two of us used to go walking in the fields Sundays and feast days, conversing about the Scriptures and the abuses of priests.[117]

This one quotation could really serve as the emblem of this chapter: an artisan, who was touched by a neighbor, by a printed Bible in French, and above all by the Psalms.

Musical Works

I have said almost nothing in this chapter about the tunes to which metrical psalms were sung. Obviously, the effect of a sung psalm depends fully as much on the tune as on the words. But the history of the development of these tunes and of their borrowing across national lines is too complex a tale to relate here. Suffice it to say that the earliest tunes in Geneva resembled those of Gregorian chant (see chapter 10) or else were borrowed from Lutheran sources, but the work of Bourgeois (born ca. 1510) and Claude Goudimel (died 1572) in Geneva and Thomas Tallis (died 1585) and Thomas Ravenscroft (ca. 1592–1635) in England helped develop the singing experience of Protestant worshipers toward modern hymnody.[118]

And, let us remind ourselves, metrical psalms gave pleasure, not only in worship but sometimes in convivial singing as well. Samuel Pepys, in his diary entry for July 1, 1664, notes:

busy till the evening, and then by agreement came Mr. Hill and Andrews and one Cheswicke, a maister who plays very well upon the Spinette, and we sat singing Psalms till 9 at night, and so broke up with great pleasure, and very good company it is, and I hope I shall now and then have their company.[119]

In another direction, I must at least mention the enormous array of musical works that were either based directly on psalms or based on German hymns that (as we have seen) were often derived from the Psalms. A review of these works would take us too far afield, but for examples I mention a setting by Dietrich Buxtehude (ca. 1637–1707), of *Lauda anima mea Dominum*, the Latin text of Psalm 146, for soprano solo and instrumental accompaniment;[120] and the sacred concerto *Loben den Herrn in seinem Heiligtum*, the German text taken from Psalm 150, by Johann Pachelbel (1653–1706).[121] And, above all, one must mention the works of Johann Sebastian Bach (1685–1750). Bach wrote chorale preludes for organ based upon Lutheran hymns, many of which are themselves based on the Psalms; for two examples, there are chorale preludes on *In dich hab' ich gehoffet, Herr* (In thee have I hoped, O Lord), a hymn of Adam Reissner (1496–1575) based on Ps. 31:2-6 (1-5),[122] and on *An Wasserflüssen Babylon* (By the waters of Babylon), a hymn based on Psalm 137.[123] And his church cantatas are likewise based on Lutheran hymns: for example, Cantata no. 38, *Aus tiefer Not schrei' ich zu Dir* (first performance, 1724), is an expansion of a hymn written by Luther paraphrasing Psalm 130.

When we move into the baroque period, we find George Frederick Handel

(1685–1759) using psalm material in his oratorios. Thus for *Israel in Egypt* (first performance, 1739) he used verses from Psalms 78, 105, and 106.

But it is in that crown of Handel's music, *Messiah* (first performance, 1742), that psalm sequences are used most tellingly. In that work Handel took various passages from the Old and New Testaments to set forth the gospel. Most of the Old Testament passages are from Isaiah (chapters 9, 40, and 53), but the next most frequent source of texts from the Old Testament is the book of Psalms. Selections 27 and 28 use Ps. 22:8-9 (7-8)—"All they that see Him, laugh him to scorn" and "He trusted in God that He would deliver him"; selection 29 uses Ps. 69:21 (20)—"Thy rebuke hath broken His heart"; selection 32 uses Ps. 16:10—"But thou didst not leave His soul in hell" (note that the psalm actually says "my soul"); selection 33 is a memorable chorus using four verses from Psalm 24, vv. 7-10—"Lift up your heads, O ye gates"; selection 36 uses Ps. 68:19 (18)—"Thou art gone up on high"; selection 37 uses Ps. 68:12 (11)—"The Lord gave the word"; and selections 40–43 draw on five verses from Psalm 2, vv. 1-4 and 9—"Why do the nations so furiously rage together?" "Let us break their bonds asunder," "He that dwelleth in heaven," and "Thou shalt break them." Though some of these selections are transitional recitatives, others are substantial contributions to the whole work. Handel in *Messiah* has woven together in a seamless robe the classic Christian affirmations about Jesus Christ, using in that work these verses from the Psalms.

And those who recognize little from *Messiah* will usually know the "Hallelujah Chorus." The words from that chorus are taken from Rev. 19:6; 11:15; and 19:16. The words from Rev. 19:6 are preceded by the word "Hallelujah!"—indeed, that word also appears in vv. 1, 3, and 4 of that chapter. I discussed in chapter 10 the way in which the expression "Alleluia" or "Hallelujah" came from the book of Psalms into Christian worship. In *Messiah*, Handel has taken that word as it appears in Revelation and has opened it out in an awesome expression of Christian joy, so much so that this chorus is often sung in churches on Easter Sunday.

NOTES

1. A helpful recent study on the background of the Reformation is Steven Ozment, *The Age of Reform, 1250–1550: An Intellectual and Religious History of Late Medieval and Reformation Europe* (New Haven: Yale University Press, 1980); see esp. 182–222.

2. The most readable account of Luther's life and work is Roland Bainton, *Here I Stand: A Life of Martin Luther* (New York and Nashville: Abingdon, 1950).

3. Ibid., 37–38.

4. Ibid., 195–96.

5. Ibid., 345.

6. Ibid., 52–60.

7. For an English translation, see *Luther's Works* (St. Louis: Concordia); vols. 10 (1974) and 11 (1976) contain the *First Lectures on the Psalms*, and vols. 12 (1955), 13 (1956), and 14 (1958) contain the second set of lectures, *Selected Psalms*.

8. *Luther's Works*, 10:11.

9. Bainton, *Here I Stand*, 62.

10. Ibid.

11. *Luther's Works*, 14:287.

12. *Luther's Works*, 14:292.

13. *Luther's Works*, 10:35.

14. *Luther's Works*, 14:313.

15. *Luther's Works*, 14:318.

16. *Luther's Works*, 12:7.

17. *Luther's Works*, 12:148.

18. *Luther's Works*, 12:149.

19. *Luther's Works*, 12:175.

20. Jaroslav Pelikan, "Introduction" to *Luther's Works*, 14:ix.

21. Emil G. Kraeling, *The Old Testament since the Reformation* (New York: Harper, 1955), 18; for a summary of Luther's view of the Psalms, see 17–19.

22. Bainton, *Here I Stand*, 327.

23. Ibid., 331.

24. Hans Volz, "Continental Versions to c. 1600," in S. L. Greenslade (ed.), *The Cambridge History of the Bible*, vol. 3; *The West from the Reformation to the Present Day* (Cambridge: Cambridge University Press, 1963), 95, 97.

25. Bainton, *Here I Stand*, 335; see further the assessment in Volz, "Continental Versions," 103.

26. See Martin Luther, "Concerning an Order for Public Worship," in Timothy F. Lull (ed.), *Martin Luther's Basic Theological Writings* (Minneapolis: Fortress, 1989), 445–48; and idem, "An Order of Mass and Communion for the Church at Wittenberg," in ibid., 449–70.

27. Luther, "An Order of Mass," 452.

28. Ibid., 468.

29. Bainton, *Here I Stand*, 346.

30. The most recent biographies are: Thomas H. L. Parker, *John Calvin: A Biography* (Philadelphia: Westminster, 1975); and Alister E. McGrath, *A Life of John Calvin: A Study of the Shaping of Western Culture* (Oxford and Cambridge, Mass.: Blackwell, 1990). For a convenient summary of Calvin's life and work, see Ozment, *Age of Reform*, 352–80.

31. On Calvin as commentator, see, briefly, Basil Hall, "Biblical Scholarship: Editions and Commentaries," in Greenslade (ed.), *Cambridge History of the Bible*, 3:87–90; and, more extensively, Joseph Haroutunian, "Introduction," in John Calvin, *Commentaries* (LCC 23; Philadelphia: Westminster, 1958), 15–50; P. T. Fuhrmann, "Calvin the Expositor of Scripture," *Interpretation* 6 (1952):188–209, with bibliography; and Hans-Joachim Kraus, "Calvin's Exegetical Principles," *Interpretation* 31 (1977):8–18.

32. The current English translation is that of James Anderson, *Calvin's Commentaries: Psalms* (Edinburgh: Calvin Translation Society, 1843–55; reprint, Grand Rapids: Eerdmans, 1948–49).

33. Calvin, *Psalms*, 1.xxxvii.

34. Ibid., 1.xliv.

35. Ibid., 1.xlvi.

36. Ibid., 1.xlviii.

37. Ibid., 1.9.

38. Ibid., 1.10.

39. Ibid., 1.11.

40. Ibid., 1.12.

41. Ibid., 1.14.

42. Ibid., 1.396–97.

43. Ibid., 5.189.

44. Ibid.

45. Ibid., 5.191.

46. Ibid., 5.191–92.

47. Brevard S. Childs, *Old Testament Books for Pastor and Teacher* (Philadelphia: Westminster, 1977), 29.

48. Sherrin Marshall, "Introduction," in idem (ed.), *Women in Reformation and Counter-Reformation Europe* (Bloomington and Indianapolis: Indiana University Press, 1989), 1–7.

49. The title page in German reads, in part, *Den Psalmen Miserere mit dem Khünig David bedacht, gebettet und paraphrasiert von Katharina Zellin M. Mattei Zellen seligen nachgelassne Ehefraw*; for a reproduction of the full title page, see André Séguenny (ed.), *Bibliotheca Dissidentium* (Bibliotheca Bibliographica Aureliana 79; Baden-Baden: Koerner, 1980), 1:118.

50. Merry E. Wiesner, "Nuns, Wives, and Mothers: Women and the Reformation in Germany," in Marshall (ed.), *Women in the Reformation*, 17, citing C. F. Paullini, *Hoch- und Wohlgelehrtes Teutsches Frauenzimmer* (Frankfurt and Leipzig: Johann Michael Funcke, 1712), 146.

51. For a current English rendition, see "Savior of the Nations, Come," in Inter-Lutheran Commission on Worship, *Lutheran Book of Worship* (Minneapolis: Augsburg, 1978), no. 28; *The* (Episcopal) *Hymnal 1982* (New York: The [Episcopal] Church Hymnal Corporation, 1982) no. 54; *The United Methodist Hymnal: Book of United Methodist Worship* (Nashville: United Methodist Publishing House, 1989), no. 214; *The Presbyterian Hymnal: Hymns, Psalms, and Spiritual Songs* (Louisville: Westminster/John Knox, 1990), no. 14.

52. Charles Garside, Jr., *The Origins of Calvin's Theology of Music: 1536–1543* (Transactions of the American Philosophical Society 69, 4; Philadelphia: The American Philosophical Society, 1979), 5.

53. W. Stanford Reid, "The Battle Hymns of the Lord: Calvinist Psalmody of the Sixteenth Century," in Carl S. Meyer (ed.), *Sixteenth Century Essays and Studies* (St. Louis: The Foundation of Reformation Research, 1971), 2:43–44.

54. Markus Jenny, *Luther, Zwingli, Calvin, in ihren Liedern* (Zürich: Theologischer Verlag, 1983), 217.

55. Garside, *Calvin's Theology of Music*, 8–9.

56. John Calvin, in *Ioannis Calvini Opera Selecta*, Peter Barth and others (eds.), (Munich, 1926–36), 1.369; translation in Garside, *Calvin's Theology of Music*, 7–8.

57. *Opera Selecta*, 1.375; translation in Garside, *Calvin's Theology of Music*, 10.

58. Ibid.

59. Garside, *Calvin's Theology of Music*, 14–15.

60. Jenny, *Luther, Zwingli, Calvin*, 220, 224.

61. Garside, *Calvin's Theology of Music*, 16.

62. Jenny, *Luther, Zwingli, Calvin*, 225.

63. Ibid., 228.

64. Reid, "Battle Hymns," 42 n. 20.

65. *Opera Selecta*, 2.17; translation in Garside, *Calvin's Theology of Music*, 33. The

citation from Augustine is from his first sermon on Psalm 34 (Vulgate numbering), sec. 1: see CChr Series Latina 38 (Turnhout: Brepols, 1956), 300.

66. Garside, *Calvin's Theology of Music*, 26.

67. Rivkah Zim, *English Metrical Psalms: Poetry and Praise and Prayer, 1535–1601* (Cambridge: Cambridge University Press, 1987), 215–16; see further Robin Leaven, *Goostly Psalmes and Spirituall Songes: English and Dutch Metrical Psalms from Coverdale to Utenhove, 1535–1566* (Oxford: Oxford University Press, 1991).

68. Zim, *English Metrical Psalms*, 224.

69. Ibid., 232.

70. *The Hymnal 1940 Companion* (New York: [Episcopal] Church Pension Fund, 1949), 183.

71. Ibid. See *Lutheran Book of Worship*, no. 245; (Episcopal) *Hymnal 1982*, nos. 377, 378; *United Methodist Hymnal*, no. 75; *Presbyterian Hymnal*, no. 220.

72. See Thomas Sternhold and John Hopkins (1549; reprint, London: J. & J. March, 1783).

73. See S. L. Greenslade, "English Versions of the Bible, 1525–1611," in idem (ed.), *Cambridge History of the Bible*, 3:141–74.

74. See the facsimile edition (Chicago: University of Chicago Press, 1956).

75. Zoltán Haraszti, *The Enigma of the Bay Psalm Book* (Chicago: University of Chicago Press, 1956), vii.

76. Ibid., 28, 29.

77. *New England Psalm Book* (1651; reprint, Boston: Henchman and Kneeland, 1758).

78. George F. Willison, *Saints and Strangers* (New York: Reynal & Hitchcock, 1945), 339.

79. Millar Patrick, *Four Centuries of Scottish Psalmody* (London: Oxford University Press, 1949).

80. *Lutheran Book of Worship*, no. 451; *The United Methodist Hymnal*, no. 136; *Presbyterian Hymnal*, no. 170.

81. So my colleague, Meredith Handspicker, reflecting on his experience worshiping in the Church of Scotland congregation in Geneva.

82. For a tracing of the anterior derivation of each line of this rendering, see Patrick, *Scottish Psalmody*, 103.

83. See the Roman Catholic hymnal *Hymns, Psalms and Spiritual Canticles*, ed. Theodore Marier (Belmont, Mass.: BACS, 1972), no. 137. *The United Methodist Hymnal* offers the words as a chant (no. 91); *The Presbyterian Hymnal* has altered the words to "O Come and Sing to the Lord."

84. *Pilgrim Hymnal* (Boston: Pilgrim, 1958), no. 85; (Episcopal) *Hymnal 1982*, no. 668; *Presbyterian Hymnal*, no. 234.

85. See *Hymnal 1940 Companion*, 182–83.

86. Nahum Tate and Nicholas Brady, *New Version of the Psalms of David* (1696; reprint, London: Mein and Fleeming, 1768).

87. *Pilgrim Hymnal*, no. 81.

88. *Pilgrim Hymnal*, no. 390; *Lutheran Book of Worship*, no. 452.

89. (Episcopal) *Hymnal 1982*, no. 658.

90. See *The Hymnal* (of the Evangelical and Reformed Church) (St. Louis: Eden, 1941), no. 307.

91. (Episcopal) *Hymnal 1982*, no. 664; *Presbyterian Hymnal*, no. 172.

92. *Pilgrim Hymnal*, no. 257.

93. *Pilgrim Hymnal*, no. 82.

94. *Pilgrim Hymnal*, no. 1; *Presbyterian Hymnal*, no. 210.

95. *Lutheran Book of Worship*, no. 320; (Episcopal) *Hymnal 1982*, no. 680; *United Methodist Hymnal*, no. 117.

96. *Pilgrim Hymnal*, no. 9.

97. *Lutheran Book of Worship*, no. 531.

98. (Episcopal) *Hymnal 1982*, no. 391.

99. *Pilgrim Hymnal*, no. 11; *Lutheran Book of Worship*, no. 550; (Episcopal) *Hymnal 1982*, no. 380; *United Methodist Hymnal*, no. 101; *Presbyterian Hymnal*, no. 229.

100. *Pilgrim Hymnal*, no. 202; *Lutheran Book of Worship*, no. 530; (Episcopal) *Hymnal 1982*, no. 544; *United Methodist Hymnal*, no. 157; *Presbyterian Hymnal*, no. 423.

101. Issac Watts, *Psalms of David imitated in the language of the New Testament* (1719; reprint, Derby: Henry Mozley, 1816), iii–iv.

102. *United Methodist Hymnal*, no. 96.

103. *United Methodist Hymnal*, no. 417.

104. For a comparison of Psalm 58 in ten prose and metrical versions, see J.C.A. Rathmell (ed.), *The Psalms of Sir Philip Sidney and the Countess of Pembroke* (New York: New York University Press, 1963), 343–55.

105. Donald Davis (ed.), *The New Oxford Book of Christian Verse* (Oxford: Oxford University Press, 1981), 25.

106. For the text of all 150 Psalms, those of Philip Sidney revised by Mary Sidney, and Mary Sidney's own, see Rathmell, *Psalms of Sir Philip Sidney*; for a critical appraisal of Mary Sidney's work, see Beth Wynne Fisken, "Mary Sidney's *Psalmes*: Education and Wisdom," in Margaret Patterson Hannay (ed.), *Silent but for the Word: Tudor Women as Patrons, Translators, and Writers of Religious Works* (Kent, Ohio: Kent State University Press, 1985), 166–83.

107. John Donne, *The Divine Poems*, ed. Helen Gardner (Oxford: Clarendon, 1978), 33–35.

108. Geoffrey Hill, personal correspondence with author.

109. Fisken, "Mary Sidney's *Psalmes*," 183.

110. Reid, "Battle Hymns," 36–37.

111. Ibid., 44, 46.

112. Ibid., 47 and n. 39.

113. Ibid., 48–50.

114. David Calderwood, *The History of the Kirk of Scotland*, ed. D. Laing (Edinburgh: Wodrow Society, 1849), 8:226; cited in Reid, "Battle Hymns," 53, and in Patrick, *Scottish Psalmody*, 61.

115. Wilbur C. Abbott (ed.), *The Writings and Speeches of Oliver Cromwell* (Cambridge: Harvard University Press, 1937–47), 1:287.

116. Alan Dunstan, "Hymnody in Christian Worship," in Cheslyn Jones, Geoffrey Wainwright, and Edward Yarnold (eds.), *The Study of Liturgy* (New York: Oxford University Press, 1978), 457.

117. Natalie Z. Davis, *Society and Culture in Early Modern France* (Stanford, Calif.: Stanford University Press, 1975), 189.

118. For a full presentation of this matter, see Nicholas Temperley and others,

"Psalms, Metrical," in *The New Grove Dictionary of Music and Musicians* (London: Macmillan, 1980), 15:347–82.

119. Samuel Pepys, *The Diary of Samuel Pepys*, ed. Henry B. Wheatley (New York: Random House, n.d.), 1:925.

120. *New Grove Dictionary*, 3:534, s.v. "Buxtehude."

121. *New Grove Dictionary*, 14:53, s.v. "Pachelbel."

122. Johann Sebastian Bach, *Das Orgelbüchlein* (The Liturgical Year), no. 41 (= BWV 640).

123. BWV 653.

12

The Psalms in the Roman Catholic Church from the Council of Trent until the Second Vatican Council

The Roman Catholic Church reacted to the movement of the Protestant Reformation in complicated ways, but its essential stance for four hundred years was established by the Council of Trent in the middle of the sixteenth century.

The printing press was a major factor in the spread of Protestant teachings (see chapter 11), but, obviously, it was available to Roman Catholics as well. Thus Rome could enforce a uniformity in liturgical practice, if it so desired, by the circulation of identical books across the world.

Now, even before Martin Luther's time there had been various efforts at reform underway in the Roman Catholic Church, particularly in Spain and Italy; and as the Protestant Reformation gained ground there emerged fresh movements for reform from within the Roman church: one may take note, for example, of Ignatius of Loyola (ca. 1491–1556), who founded the Society of Jesus (Jesuits) in 1534; the Jesuits' rigor in missionary work won back many Protestant areas to the Roman Catholic Church (especially in what is now Czechoslovakia and Poland).[1] Nevertheless, it would be fair to say that the papacy was slow to respond to the Reformation and that even popes who were convinced of the need for reform found enormous obstacles to achieving it.[2]

The Psalms, as we have seen, had a place in the Roman Catholic Mass and formed the backbone of the daily office (see chapter 10). In the 1530s there was an attempt to reform the Divine Office: Pope Clement VII commissioned the Spanish Cardinal Quiñones to prepare a revision, and this revision was promulgated by the succeeding Pope Paul III (first edition, 1535; second edition, 1536). The office, which had been the mode of communal prayer in the early church, was now intended for private recitation by the individual cleric. Quiñones kept to the established principle that the whole of the Psalter should be recited once a week; he made no provision for liturgical seasons or saints' days.[3] Though this breviary was ultimately a failure and would be replaced, it nevertheless had a remarkable currency for thirty years and incidentally had an influence on the compilation of the *Book of Common Prayer* in England (see chapter 11).[4]

The Roman Catholic Church in the middle of the sixteenth century remained a church under attack, and the institutional reponse to that attack was the council held at Trent (a city in the extreme north of Italy), which met during three periods of time over a span of eighteen years (1545–1547; 1551–1552; 1562–1563). To this council came not only church leaders but secular princes as well. For the third session, in 1562, the pope of that time (Pius IV) instructed that all Christian princes be invited, whether "schismatic" or not, but the Protestant powers refused to attend. Though Catholic, the Holy Roman Emperor of the time, Ferdinand I, was sympathetic toward many of the aims of the Protestants, and he with the French bishops drew up a list of reforms they desired, among them that Mass be celebrated in the vernacular languages, that the service books be revised, that Communion be offered in both bread and wine, that priests be allowed to marry, and that the Roman Curia be reformed. Philip II of Spain and the Spanish bishops were equally concerned to reduce the power of the papacy, but they rejected any alteration in the ritual and practice of the church. These divisions among the Catholic powers gave the papacy the means to enforce its primacy, so that the end result of the council was the reassertion of church practices of the immediate past.[5]

Along with much else, the council fixed the shape of the Mass and the daily office. The language would continue to be Latin: the council reaffirmed the authority of the Vulgate Bible and Latin as the only language of ritual.[6] Pope Pius V appointed a commission to revise the liturgical books, but in this revision there would be no innovation; members of the commission were determined to restore what they understood to be the permanent practice of the church. In 1568 they produced the *Breviarium Romanum* (Roman Breviary) and in 1570, the *Missale Romanum* (Roman Missal).[7]

The Psalms in the Mass

I first discuss the use of the Psalms in the Mass.[8] The entire liturgy was said in Latin, but the custom gradually arose of repeating the Gospel reading in the vernacular, so that the priest's homily (which was also in the vernacular) could be better understood. The material from the Psalms, however, was recited only in Latin.

As the priest prepared for Mass he was to recite Psalms 84; 85; 86; 116:10-19 (a full psalm in the Vulgate); and 130. Then, for the chief Mass on Sundays, the priest sprinkled the altar three times with holy water and then himself, and he intoned an antiphon consisting of Ps. 51:9 (7): "Thou shalt sprinkle me with hyssop, O Lord, and I shall be cleansed; thou shalt wash me, and I shall be made whiter than snow."

Now, for the Mass proper it would be fair to say that the Psalter was used chiefly as a source for short transitional sequences. These are so various as to be difficult to summarize; I simply give a few illustrations.

The first occasion in the Mass for material from the Psalms was the "Introit," words used as the officiant enters the sanctuary. It consisted of two or three verses of Scripture that were almost always taken from a psalm, and they were often shaped in a curious fashion: a verse or two would be taken from the middle of a given psalm, and to this a response would be offered that consisted of the opening verse of the same psalm. For example, in the Mass for the Saturday of the second week of Lent, the Introit consisted of Ps. 19:8 (7)—"The law of the Lord is unspotted, converting souls; the testimony of the Lord is faithful, giving wisdom to little ones"; the response to this was v. 2 (1)—"The heavens show forth the glory of God, and the firmament declares the work of his hands." Similarly, for the Third Sunday in Lent the Introit consisted of Ps. 25:15-16 and the response of Ps. 25:1-2.

Then, after the reading from the Epistle (or from the Old Testament), came the so-called Gradual—that is, the remnant of the full psalm that was read at that point in the liturgy in the early centuries of the church (see chapter 10). The Gradual, again, usually consisted of two or three verses, again, not always consecutive. Thus the Gradual for the Mass for the Saturday of the second week of Lent (after the reading of Gen. 27:6-39) consisted of Ps. 92:2-3 (1-2), the second verse being a response to the first—"It is good to give praise to the Lord, and to sing to thy name, O Most High," followed by "To show forth thy mercy in the morning, and thy truth in the night." The Gradual for the Third Sunday in Lent (after the reading of Eph. 5:1-9) was Ps. 9:20 (19) plus 4 (3).

On Sundays and special days, such as Ash Wednesday, the Gradual was followed immediately by another selection from the Psalms, the so-called tract: for the Third Sunday of Lent, the tract was Ps. 123:1-2. After this there followed the reading of the Gospel (for the Third Sunday of Lent, Luke 11:14-28).

After the homily and the recitation of the creed came the "Offertory," and this was again a selection of a few verses from a psalm: for the Saturday of the Second Week of Lent the Offertory was Ps. 13:4b-5a (3b-4a)—"Enlighten my eyes, that I never sleep in death, lest at any time my enemy say, I have prevailed against him." And the Offertory for the Third Sunday in Lent was taken from Psalm 19, the same psalm from which the Introit was taken for the previous day. This Offertory is a curious mixture: "The justices of the Lord are right, rejoicing hearts, and his judgments are sweeter than honey and the honeycomb, for thy servant keepeth them"; that is, it consists of Ps. 19:9a (8a) plus a mixture of "his judgments" from v. 10b (9a), "sweeter than honey and the honeycomb" from v. 11b (10b), and "for thy servant keepeth them" from v. 12a (11a).

During the reception of the consecrated bread, the priest spoke what is called "communion," again frequently taken from the Psalms: for the Third Sunday of Lent it was Ps. 84:4-5 (3-4).

These passages are "bits and pieces," even in the case of a short psalm: thus Psalm 23 is represented only four times, once for v. 1 (the communion for Saturday of the Fourth Week of Lent) and three times for v. 4 (in the Gradual for Saturday of the third week of Lent and in the Graduals in the special Masses "for pilgrims and travelers" and "for a good death"). And one would be hard pressed to find a pattern or coherence to the use of these passages of the Psalms: for the Fourth Sunday of Lent both the Gradual and the communion are taken from Psalm 122, v. 1 plus vv. 7 and 3-4, respectively, but such reinforcement from a single psalm is not too common.

It should also be noted that when a given psalm is represented more than once, it is often the case that different selections of verses of that psalm are represented. For example, Ps. 2:7b plus 1 appears as the Introit in the Mass for the midnight preceding Christmas Day, and Ps. 2:11-12 appears as the communion for the Mass for Friday after Ash Wednesday.

In contrast to the usage for most of the year, in the liturgies of Maundy Thursday and Good Friday full psalms rather than short sections were recited. Thus in the Vespers of Maundy Thursday a sequence of psalms was recited, each psalm (except the last) having two closing antiphons (repetitions of specific verses) chosen in a curious chain fashion. The sequence was Psalm 116, with the repetition afterward of Pss. 116:13 and 120:7; Psalm 120, with the repetition afterward of v. 7 and a phrase of Ps. 140:5 (4); Psalm 140, with a repetition of the same phrase in v. 5 (4) and Ps. 141:9; Psalm 141, with a repetition of v. 9 and Ps. 142:5; Psalm 142, with the repetition of v. 5. Then, following the recitation of the Magnificat (Luke 1:46-55), Psalm 51 was recited, and then, after the stripping of the altar, Psalm 22, preceded and followed by the repetition of v. 19 (18) of that psalm. And during the ceremony of the washing of the feet in that liturgy, the narrative from the Gospel of John was interspersed with four psalm verses, namely, Pss. 48:2 (1); 85:2 (1); 49:2 (1); 84:2-3a (1-2a).

In the liturgy for Good Friday the full Psalm 140 served as a tract before the recitation of the passion (John 18–19).

And it must be affirmed that at many points the verses of a psalm were chosen for their aptness to the season. Thus the Gradual for the Masses for Easter Sunday and the weekdays of Easter week consisted (at least partly) of Ps. 118:24, "This is the day the Lord has made; let us rejoice and be glad in it."

Occasionally one of these units was made up of selections from two different psalms; for example, the Introit for the Sixteenth Sunday after Pentecost consisted of Ps. 102:16 (15), with a response consisting of Ps. 98:1a.

All told, in the Masses appointed for the liturgical year (the so-called Proper of the Time) verses from 111 psalms were recited (reckoning in the numeration of the Vulgate). Nineteen more psalms are represented in the "Proper for Saints" (Masses appointed for the commemoration of saints on specific dates in the year), and in other special Masses.

Particularly in various special Masses, the choice of some psalm sequences is obvious. Thus in the Nuptial Mass verses from Psalm 128 were used for the Introit, the Gradual, the tract, and the communion (e.g., v. 3: "Your wife will be like a fruitful vine within your house; your children will be like olive shoots around your table"); Psalm 67 is drawn upon for the Introit and Gradual of the Mass for the Propagation of the Faith (v. 2: "that your way may be known upon earth, your saving power among all nations"), and Ps. 96:3-5 and 7-9a supply the tract and Offertory for that Mass.

Material from psalms that deal with enemies figured in the "Mass against the Heathen," a Mass already instituted in the fifteenth century when the Muslim Turks were threatening Europe (Pss. 83:19 [18]; 80:20 [19]; 79:9-10a); in the "Mass for the Removal of Schism" (Pss. 106:47; 122:6-7; 76:2-4 [1-3]; 147:12-14); and in the "Mass in Time of War" (Pss. 77:15-16 [14-15]; 59:2, 17 [1, 16]; 31:3a [2a]).

Some psalms are used again and again: the second half of Psalm 45 is understandably used for the various Masses pertaining to the Virgin Mary and for those commemorating female saints.

However, one cannot help wondering about the distribution of some of the material of the Psalms. For instance, one might expect Psalm 42 to turn up often during the liturgical year. Verses 2-4 (103) are used as the Tract at the blessing of the baptismal font during the Easter Vigil, but otherwise one finds only the opening verse in the Gradual of the Mass for a saint (Francis Caracciolo, ca. 1564–1608, on June 4) whose Mass has now, after the Second Vatican Council, been removed from the liturgical calendar.

Twenty psalms (in the Vulgate reckoning) thus remained unrepresented in the liturgy of the Mass. In some instances one can see why these psalms were left untouched. Psalm 53 was not used, but that psalm is a virtual duplicate of Psalm 14, which was. Psalm 131 was not used; it is a short psalm of submission, a psalm (as I indicated in chapter 4) written from a woman's point of view. But the reason for the omission of other psalms is not so clear.

To summarize: for attentive listeners at Mass who knew their Latin, some of the piety of the psalmists would be apparent, if not the full integrity of the psalmists' poetry; but if the listeners' Latin was dim or lacking, it would be difficult from the liturgy of the Mass to perceive the Psalms in any depth. Lay Catholics were then not privy to the excitement experienced by lay Protestants as they heard full psalms in their vernaculars (chapter 11).

The Psalms in the Daily Office

I now turn to use of the Psalms in the daily office. As I have already indicated, the daily office was now an obligation laid on each cleric, and the breviary of 1568, like its predecessor of 1535, covered the whole Psalter in a week, roughly twenty-one psalms in the prayers of a single day.[9]

We remind ourselves that in theory there were eight times of prayer in the twenty-four hours (see chapter 10): night prayer (Vigils, Nocturns), Lauds (at daybreak), Prime (roughly seven o'clock), Terce (roughly nine o'clock), Sext (roughly noon), None (roughly three o'clock), Vespers (in the evening), and Compline (on retiring to bed). But only monastic communities could hold to eight times of prayer each day. In practice, a busy secular priest, burdened with pastoral duties, would say Vigils, Lauds, and Prime as a single sequence in the morning; Terce, Sext, and None as a single sequence about noon; Vespers before the evening meal; and Compline before retiring. (Compare the remarks by Thomas Merton at the end of this chapter.)

All 150 Psalms were used, and all verses of each psalm. Several psalms were used more than once: thus Vigils began every day with Psalm 95; and when the office was said in community, Lauds was begun on every day but Sunday with

Psalm 51. On Sunday (to give an example for a single day), Vigils continued with Psalms 1, 2, 3, 8, 9, and 10. Lauds consisted of Psalms 93; 100; 63; the Song of the Three Young Men (which is an addition to the book of Daniel in the Septuagint and therefore in the Vulgate, and is part of the Apocrypha in Protestant Bibles); 148; a hymn; and the Benedictus (Luke 1:68-79). Prime began with a hymn and continued with Psalms 118; 54; 119:1-16; and prayers. Terce, after a hymn, consisted of Ps. 119:33-80 and closed with prayers. Sext, after a hymn, continued with Ps. 119:81-128 and prayers. None, after a hymn, consisted of Ps. 119:129-176 and prayers. Vespers consisted of Psalms 110; 111; 112; 113; 114 and 115; 117; 116:10-19; 132; 147:12-20; a blessing; a hymn; and the Magnificat (Luke 1:46-55). Compline, after prayers, consisted of Psalms 4, 91, and 134, and closed with a hymn, prayers, the Nunc Dimittis (Luke 2:29-32), and final prayers.

Psalms that contain indications of time were assigned accordingly: thus Ps. 5:4 (3)—"O Lord, in the morning you hear my voice; in the morning I plead my case to you, and watch"—was assigned to Lauds for Monday. Again, Ps. 121:3b-4a— "He who keeps you will not slumber; he who keeps Israel will neither slumber nor sleep"—was assigned to Vespers for Monday.

But in general the psalms were recited sequentially: thus, for Friday, Matins consisted of Psalms 78 (a long psalm with seventy-two verses), 79, 81, and 83, and Psalms 80 and 82 were recited for Terce on that day; and Psalm 77 was recited during Compline on that day, given v. 5 (4) of that psalm—"You keep my eyelids from closing." In addition to the general weekly scheme, there were special sets of readings assigned for particular special days: for example, Vigils for Trinity Sunday consisted of Psalms 8, 19, 24, 47, 48, 72, 96, 97, and 98.

We remind ourselves that when the daily office was prayed in community, it was chanted. Gregorian chant continued to be the medium for the recitation of Scripture wherever men could be mustered to be trained in it. Monastic communities and cathedrals continued in this way to sing the Psalms and other liturgical sequences to the glory of God.

Musical Settings of the Psalms

If there were no fresh uses made of the Psalms in the Roman Catholic Church in this period, there were most emphatically fresh musical renderings of psalms. I cannot offer an adequate survey of Roman Catholic church music for this period, any more than I could of Protestant musical renderings of the Psalms mentioned in chapter 11;[10] let me simply offer five examples out of dozens.

There is a lovely motet of Giovanni Pierluigi da Palestrina (1525?–1594) for four voices on the text *Sicut cervus* ("As the deer"), Ps. 42:2 (1), first performed in 1581.[11] There are three motets from Claudio Monteverdi (1567–1643) on the text *Beatus vir*, that is, Psalm 1.[12] There is a setting for two choirs of *Lauda Jerusalem* ("Praise the Lord, O Jerusalem," the Latin text of Ps. 147:12-20, a full psalm in the Vulgate), by Antonio Vivaldi (1678–1741).[13] There is a setting by Wolfgang Amadeus Mozart (1756–1791) of *Laudate pueri Dominum*, the Latin text of Ps.

113:1, 5, 7-9.[14] And there is a setting by Anton Bruckner (1824–1896) of the German text of Psalm 150, first performed in 1892.[15]

The Effect of the Latin Language

I must now say a general word about the effect of the continued use of Latin as the liturgical language for Roman Catholics: Latin remained for them what Hebrew has been for Jews (see chapter 9). For centuries Latin was the sole language for liturgy, Scripture, and theology. Priests were educated through the medium of Latin; all textbooks and lectures were in Latin. Latin was the expression of the unchangeableness of matters divine. And Latin had about it the characteristic not only of permanence but of mystery: the very fact that it was not so much used for ordinary secular purposes allowed it to be reserved for what is holy.

Furthermore, Latin bound the Roman Catholic Church together; Catholics could follow the same Latin Mass in whatever nation of the world they happened to be. For example, there came to the United States Army base in Italy where I served after World War II an American Catholic chaplain named Walsh, who knew no Italian. He found himself working with an Italian priest named Renato, a chaplain in the Italian army who, among other duties, had spiritual responsibility for Italian prisoners of war. The easy and obvious means of communication between these two chaplains was Latin, in which both of them had been educated. But, of course, this language of liturgy, Scripture, and theology, which was universal for priests, was at the same time closed to lay Catholics unless they had been schooled in it.

The Place of the Psalms in the
Lives of Catholics

I now turn to the larger question of the place of Scripture, and the Psalms in particular, in the teaching and life of Roman Catholics in this period after the Council of Trent. Though I have stressed the reactive mode of the council, it did take some steps for reform to counter the practices of Protestants. Thus provision was made for the public interpretation of Scripture in the larger towns; bishops were bound to preach—and the parish clergy, to teach plainly—what was required for salvation.[16]

At the same time, provision was made for an index of forbidden books,[17] that is, books that had not been approved for Catholic use. In 1564, Pope Pius IV published rules for the newly established index; in these, he warned against those vernacular translations that were "indiscriminately circulated" and declared that "in this matter the judgment of the bishop or inquisitor must be sought, who on the advice of the pastor or the confessor may permit the reading of a Bible translated into the vernacular by Catholic authors."[18] The requirement of written permission from the bishop (1564) to read Scriptures in the vernacular was later hardened (1596) so that written permission of the pope became necessary. This regulation was relaxed only in 1757.[19]

Roman Catholics in the years after the Council of Trent produced a Bible in English. English Catholics exiled in Rheims, France, produced a translation of the New Testament in 1582 and of the Old Testament in 1609, the so-called Douay-Rheims Version. It was essentially a translation from the Latin Vulgate, of course, rather than directly from the Hebrew and Greek; it was based upon the best knowledge of the Vulgate available at the time.[20] Psalm 51:3 (1) was rendered (with spelling modernized) "Have mercy on me, O God, according to thy great mercy. And according to the multitude of thy commiserations take away mine iniquity." Then, in 1750 the Douay-Rheims Version was revised by Bishop Richard Challoner. Challoner gives no evidence of mastery of Hebrew;[21] he simply tried to smooth the wording of the Douay-Rheims Version, sometimes by making use of the Protestant King James Version (1611). Thus in the above verse he changed "commiserations" to "tender mercies" and "take away" to "blot out," following the King James Version, and shifted "mine" to "my."[22] It should be noted that when, in the last two centuries, a Roman Catholic Bible is called the "Douay Version," it is normally Challoner's revision that is meant. But the superior style of the King James Version led English-speaking Catholics to become increasingly defensive of the Douay.[23] Here I cite the first three verses of Psalm 23 in that version:

> The Lord ruleth me: and I shall want nothing. He hath set me in a place of pasture. He hath brought me up, on the water of refreshment: he hath converted my soul. He hath led me on the paths of justice, for his own name's sake.

During the ensuing centuries there were fresh movements within the Roman Catholic Church—new efforts at mission, new modes of piety, the founding of new orders—but it is fair to say that there was little that brought fresh understanding of the Psalms.

But it must not be forgotten that the Psalms continued to nourish Christians in many ways. The autobiography of Thérèse of Lisieux (1875–1897) contains many citations or reminiscences of the Bible, the *Imitation of Christ*, and other works; most of the reminiscences from the Old Testament are from the Psalms and from the Song of Solomon. Typical is her remark about earthly friendships:

> I shall always be grateful to our Lord for turning earthly friendships into bitterness for me, because, with a nature like mine, I could so easily have fallen into a snare and had my wings clipped; and then how should I have been able to "fly away and find rest" [Ps. 55:7 (6)]?[24]

And when, on a journey to Naples, she saw Mount Vesuvius, she said, "There's something terrifying about the traces of its activity left on Pompeii; what a proof of God's power! 'A glance from him makes earth tremble; at his touch, the mountains are wreathed in smoke' [Ps. 104:32]."[25]

Again, Dorothy Day (1897–1980), who became the pioneer of the Catholic Worker movement in the United States, speaks of how deeply the Psalms nourished her. In contrast to Thérèse of Lisieux, however, Day was nourished on the

Psalms as a child in a non-Roman Catholic tradition: she attended an Episcopal church as a child, and she writes, "I loved the Psalms and the Collect prayers and learned many of them by heart, and the anthems filled me with joy." And later, "When we moved to the North Side [of Chicago] I went to the Episcopal Church of Our Saviour, on Fullerton Avenue, and studied the catechism so that I could be baptized and confirmed. There too I learned the formal prayer of the Church in her Psalms."[26]

At university Day abandoned the church and became a socialist. Later, when she was jailed for picketing the White House on behalf of women's suffrage, she asked for a Bible, and when it was brought

> I read it with the sense of coming back to something of my childhood that I had lost. My heart swelled with joy and thankfulness for the Psalms. The man who sang these songs knew sorrow and expected joy. "When the Lord brought back the captivity of Sion we became like men comforted. Then was our mouth filled with gladness: and our tongue with joy. Then shall they say among the Gentiles: The Lord hath done great things for them. The Lord hath done great things for us: we are become joyful. Turn again our captivity, O Lord, as a stream in the south. They that sow in tears shall reap in joy. Going, they went and wept, casting their seeds. But coming, they shall come with joyfulness, carrying their sheaves" [Psalm 126]. If we had faith in what we were doing, making our protest against brutality and injustice, then we were indeed casting our seeds, and there was the promise of the harvest to come.[27]

The Struggle over Biblical Scholarship: New Translations

In the course of the nineteenth century, new biblical scholarship was gaining ground in Protestant and secular circles (a matter I describe in chapter 13). The response of the Roman Catholic Church to this scholarship was repression, a repression that is still vivid in the memory of older Catholic scholars today. This repression lasted until 1943, when the papal encyclical *Divino Afflante Spiritu* was issued; and to some degree it lasted even until the issuing of *Dei Verbum* at the close of the Second Vatican Council (1965). The story is a tragic one in retrospect, one that reflects a stance of the Roman Catholic Church in contrast with the one prevailing today, but it is one that must be told if developments since the Second Vatican Council (see chapter 14) are to be understood.

The century from 1860 to 1960 was a stirring period in the history of the Roman Catholic Church in many respects. It was a time of internal debate and struggle, and I can only indicate a few of the details here, particularly as they bear on the use and understanding of the Psalms.[28]

In the United States in the middle of the nineteenth century, there was an attempt by Francis P. Kenrick, bishop of Philadelphia (1842–1851) and archbishop of Baltimore (1851–1863), to improve both the Douay-Rheims Version and the revision of Challoner—really, to produce a fresh translation.[29] In this enterprise he tried to stay with the Vulgate, but he was aware of the many points at which the Hebrew and Greek diverge from the Vulgate, and he also had one eye on the King James Version. In all this he was aware of Protestant work, even while attempting to stay within the Catholic tradition.

His translation of the Psalms was published in 1857; he gave the numeration according to both the Vulgate and the Hebrew original. For the beginning of Psalm 23 he retained the Douay "the Lord ruleth me," but in a note he added that the Lord ruled "as a shepherd."[30] But, cautious as Kenrick's translation of the Bible was, it failed to gain the approval of the American bishops, and the pressure of Rome for conformity in doctrine meant that the translation was ultimately forgotten.[31]

The pressure of new research about the Bible resulted in the encyclical *Providentissimus Deus* of Pope Leo XIII in 1893. The document declared that the professor of Scripture

> will make use of the Vulgate as his text; for the Council of Trent decreed that "in public lectures, disputations, preaching, and exposition," the Vulgate is the "authentic" version. . . . Nevertheless, wherever there may be ambiguity or want of clearness, the "examination of older tongues [that is, the Hebrew and Greek texts]," to quote St. Augustine, will be useful and advantageous.[32]

It goes on to state that "professors of sacred Scripture and theologians should master those tongues in which the sacred books were originally written: and it would be well that ecclesiastical students also should cultivate them, more especially those who aspire to academic degrees."[33] Professors "should make themselves well and thoroughly acquainted with the art of true criticism"[34]—by which the document means *textual* criticism, because it goes on to say, "There has arisen, to the great detriment of religion, an inept method, dignified by the name of 'higher criticism,' which pretends to judge of the origin, integrity, and authority of each book from internal indications alone."[35]

The suspicion of historical biblical criticism was tied up with a larger issue faced by the Roman Catholic Church: the movement to which the name "modernism" was given. Modernism referred to the attempts to apply current methods of historical criticism to the history of the church, as well as to the study of the Scriptures, and it was declared a heresy in 1907 by Pope Pius X in his encyclical *Pascendi Dominici Gregis*.

There were several Catholic scholars who, during this period, published studies on the relation between history and inspiration. One may mention in particular Henry A. Poels (1868–1948), a Dutchman who was appointed professor of Old Testament at the Catholic University of America in 1904 but was dismissed five years later for his views;[36] and Marie-Joseph Lagrange (1855–1938), a French Dominican who, almost without any support, founded the École Biblique in Jerusalem in 1892 and the journal *Revue Biblique* in 1892. When some of Lagrange's works occasioned a warning from the Sacred Congregation of the Consistory (1912), he gave up Old Testament research and transferred his interests to New Testament investigation.[37]

Meanwhile, in 1901 Pope Leo XIII established the Pontifical Biblical Commission to rule on biblical questions. Poels, Lagrange, and others who were concerned for historical criticism contributed to the work of this commission, but the body was heavily weighted against the new scholarship. One must also take note here of the influence of an American Protestant, Charles Augustus Briggs. I tell the story of Briggs in detail in chapter 13; suffice it at this point to say that he was a Presbyterian, a professor of Old Testament, until he underwent a heresy trial in that church (1891–1893) for his views on the Bible. He then became an Episcopalian, and beginning in 1906 he contributed greatly to the discussion around the decisions of the Pontifical Biblical Commission, particularly in regard to the questions of the presumed authorship of the Pentateuch by Moses and of the Psalms by David.[38]

From 1905 to 1915 the commission issued a series of fourteen "responses" on questions of biblical criticism; one of them, issued in 1910, concerned eight questions regarding the Psalms. I cite three of these questions to give some impression of the nature of the teaching of the church on the Psalms at that time. The official English translation reflects the stiff Latin original; the questions are drawn up as indirect questions (beginning with "whether").

> Whether the aforesaid titles [i.e., the superscriptions of the Psalms], witnesses to the Jewish tradition, can be prudently called in question except when there is no solid reason against their genuine character. Answer: In the negative.[39]

> Whether, considering the not infrequent testimonies in the Bible to David's natural skill, a skill further illumined by the special gift of the Holy Spirit, for the composition of religious odes; whether, considering too, the arrangement drawn up by him for the liturgical chanting of the Psalms; the attributions also, both in the Old Testament and the New, of psalms to him, as also in the actual inscriptions anciently affixed to the Psalms [i.e., the superscriptions]; whether, considering, moreover, the common opinion of the Jews, and of the Fathers and Doctors of the Church, it can prudently be denied that David was the principal author of the odes contained in the Psalter. Whether, on the other hand, it can be maintained that only a few of these odes are to be attributed to the Royal Psalmist. Answer: In the negative to both questions.[40]

> Whether we can in particular deny the Davidic origin of the psalms which, in both the Old and New Testaments, are expressly cited under David's name, especially such as Ps. 2, *Why have the Gentiles raged*; Ps. 15, *Preserve me, O Lord*; Ps. 17, *I will love Thee, O Lord, my strength*; Ps. 31, *Blessed are they whose iniquities are forgiven*; Ps. 68, *Save me, O God*; Ps. 109, *The Lord said to my Lord.* Answer: In the negative.[41]

This negative style is hard to untangle. To put it positively, the commission stated that it is not necessary to maintain that David was the sole author of the Psalms, but one must maintain that David was the principal author, and in particular that he was the author of Psalms 2, 16, 18, 32, 69, and 110. But it must be understood that these decisions have been implicitly revoked by later decrees, by

Divino Afflante Spiritu in 1943 (see below), and by the Second Vatican Council (see chapter 14).[42]

In the meantime, Pope Pius X founded the Pontifical Biblical Institute in Rome (a key date in its initial development was 1909, when it was placed under the exclusive direction of the Jesuits), and moderate Catholic biblical scholarship slowly began to made headway within the Roman Catholic Church. In 1920 the institute began the publication of three journals—*Biblica, Orientalia*, and *Verbum Domini* (The word of the Lord)—and Catholic scholars produced some excellent works; I think, for example, of the series "Études bibliques," begun by Lagrange in 1902; the commentary in that series by Albert Condamin on the book of Jeremiah (1936) is still useful.[43] And I must mention in particular the life and work of a remarkable figure, Augustin Bea (1881–1968), who was eventually made cardinal (1959).[44] Bea became a member of the Pontifical Biblical Commission and was then rector of the Pontifical Biblical Institute from 1930 to 1949; and in 1960, in the context of the Second Vatican Council, Pope John XXIII appointed him president of the new Secretariat for Promoting Christian Unity. Though at the beginning of his career his position on some critical matters was conservative, he was a notable Old Testament scholar, and his strong leadership and ecumenical interests helped open the Roman Catholic Church to fresh ways of approaching the Bible.

In the United States there were several events that may serve as landmarks. There had been efforts to prepare a revision of the Douay Version; the Confraternity of Christian Doctrine (a standing committee of the American bishops) undertook to revise the New Testament, given current understanding of the Greek text. The revision was finally issued in 1941, amid much controversy,[45] but the work on the Old Testament was abandoned after Pope Pius XII permitted and encouraged official translations from the original languages (see below). When a complete English version sponsored by the American bishops would appear, it would be in a different context (the New American Bible, published in 1970; see chapter 14). In the meantime, in 1936 various Roman Catholic biblical scholars in the United States organized the Catholic Biblical Association, and in 1939 the new organization inaugurated a journal, the *Catholic Biblical Quarterly*. The association and the journal would become the rallying point for Catholic scholars who were attempting to enlarge biblical understanding in the Roman Catholic Church.[46]

In August 1943 the Pontifical Biblical Commission issued a "clarification," explicitly stating that translations of the Bible for the use of the faithful could be made from the original languages, but that the passages used in the liturgy were to be translated from the Vulgate.[47] And a month later Pope Pius XII issued his encyclical on biblical studies, *Divino afflante Spiritu*; this encyclical, largely the work of Bea, was a great turning point.[48] This document stresses the great importance of textual criticism[49] and makes specific that the "authenticity" of the Vulgate is primarily juridical (free from error in faith and morals) rather than critical (always an accurate translation).[50] It called for scholars to apply the historical method to biblical books, stating:

We ought to explain the original text which was written by the inspired author himself and has more authority and greater weight than any, even the very best, translation whether ancient or modern. This can be done all the more easily and fruitfully if to the knowledge of languages be joined a real skill in literary criticism of the same text.[51]

The interpretation is that to understand the Scriptures, one should (1) go to the original Hebrew and Greek, bypassing Jerome's Vulgate if necessary; (2) understand the literary forms of the original; and (3) grapple with difficult problems.

But this encouragement to deal with the original languages inevitably brought grave difficulties: How should one treat the form of the Divine Office, the obligation laid on priests to pray the Psalms in Latin daily, using not even Jerome's translation from the Hebrew (the *Liber Psalmorum iuxta Hebraicum*; see the discussion in chapter 6) but the Gallican Psalter (the Old Latin, based upon the Septuagint Greek)? In 1941, Pope Pius XII asked the professors at the Pontifical Biblical Institute to prepare a new version of the Psalter, translated into Latin from Hebrew. It was published in 1945,[52] and priests were given the right to use it in the daily office;[53] breviaries published thereafter used it.

This new Psalter is a curious work: the vocabulary has little of the relaxed Latin of Jerome's fourth century but is rather in a more elevated Latin, using words and phrases that are found in Pliny and Ovid.[54] I offer a couple of examples. In Ps. 1:3 the NRSV reads, "and their leaves do not wither"; the Septuagint reads, "and its foliage shall not fall off"; and the (Old Latin) Vulgate likewise reads *et folium eius non defluet*, and Jerome did not bother to change this reading in his translation from the Hebrew. The Hebrew verb used in the psalm (*yibbōl*; root, *nbl*) covers a wide range of meaning: in Isa. 40:7 the NRSV offers "the flower *fades*"; in Exod. 18:18, Moses' father-in-law tells him that, with all the legal cases to adjudicate, Moses and the people *will wear themselves out* (NRSV). The use of the verb in Isa. 34:4b (referring to leaves on the vine and fruit on a fig tree) certainly suggests "withering" as much as "falling off." The new Latin Psalter might have used a form such as *exsiccata* (dried up; so Jerome in Isa. 40:7), but instead it used *marcescunt*, which means "wither" or "pine away"—a good rendering, but one that, as far as I know, had not appeared in Jerome's translation. Again, in Ps. 23:5 current translations render the phrase "my cup overflows"; the Hebrew is, literally, "my cup is saturation." The Septuagint had read, "thy [*sic*] cup inebriates like the best [wine, presumably]," because the related verb in Hebrew (and Aramaic) is used of being drunk; and the Old Latin Vulgate, though correcting the possessor of the cup, reflects the same verb: *et calix meus inebrians quam praeclarus est*. Jerome, in his translation from the Hebrew, retained "my cup inebriates," only omitting the suggestion of the best wine. But the new translation deprives the reciters of the psalm of any suggestion of inebriation, offering instead *calix meus uberrimus est*—"my cup is most copious."

This Psalter was an important event in the Catholic rediscovery of the Bible.[55] But even from the point of view of current understanding of Hebrew, the translation could be criticized,[56] and this Latin translation did not enjoy the use that had been hoped for it; the Latin was felt to be difficult to recite and sing. But it is to be noted that an English translation appeared simultaneously with it,[57] in which the aforementioned phrases appear as "and whose leaves wither not" (Ps. 1:3) and "my cup brims over" (Ps. 23:5). This was the English translation referred to by Merton (see below).

In the meantime, others were busy with translations. There was an English translation of the Psalms by a conservative American scholar, Charles J. Callan (1877–1960),[58] that does not move too much beyond Challoner's revision of the Douay-Rheims Bible; it is now scarcely remembered. (Psalm 23:1-3: "The Lord rules me, and I want for nothing; In the place of pasture, there He puts me. He leads me to refreshing streams. He revives my soul. He guides me in the paths of righteousness for His name's sake.")

But the work of Ronald A. Knox (1888–1957) was another matter altogether. Knox was a British convert to the Roman Catholic Church who offered his own translation of the Bible into English (New Testament, 1944; Old Testament, 1948–1950);[59] his translation of the Psalms appeared separately in 1947.[60] He had been trained in the classics at Oxford and was known as an accomplished English stylist. He wrote an account of his work as a translator;[61] he clearly believed in the translation principle known today as "dynamic equivalence" (see chapter 17), turning statements into rhetorical questions and reshaping phrases into what he considered English idiom. To read Knox's translation is suddenly to breathe fresh air: for example, Ps. 23:1—"The Lord is my shepherd; how can I lack anything?"—and verse 5 of that psalm—"Envious my foes watch, while thou dost spread a banquet for me; richly thou dost anoint my head with oil, well filled my cup"; Ps. 42:2-4 (1-3)—"O God, my whole soul longs for thee, as a deer for running water; my whole soul thirsts for God, the living God; shall I never again make my pilgrimage into God's presence? Morning and evening, my diet still of tears! Daily I must listen to the taunt, Where is thy God now?"; and Ps. 46:2-3 (1-2)—"God is our refuge and stronghold; sovereign aid he has brought us in the hour of peril. Not for us to be afraid, though earth should tumble about us, and the hills be carried away into the depths of the sea."

One notable thing that Knox did in the acrostic psalms was to create English acrostics, with the initial acrostic letters in bold type. Thus in Ps. 119:161-163 he has "*V*exed by the causeless malice of princes, my heart still dreads thy warnings. *V*ictors rejoice not more over rich spoils, than I in thy promises. *V*illainy I abhor and renounce; thy law is all my love."[62]

With the encyclical of 1943, Roman Catholic biblical scholarship came of age. A signal achievement was the production by the Dominicans at the École Biblique in Jerusalem of *La Bible de Jérusalem* (1948–1954), a striking French version.[63] The Psalms therein were the work of Raymond Jacques Tournay (b. 1912), a translation that was later modified by Joseph Gelineau, who attended to matters of rhythm and appropriateness for chanting (for a further discussion of Gelineau's Psalter, see below). One decision the translators made for this Bible that had particular consequence for the Psalms was to transliterate the Old Testament name of God, "Yahweh," rather than to use the expression "the Lord": thus instead of "The Lord is my shepherd," one finds *Yahvé est mon pasteur*—"Yahweh is my shepherd" (on this matter, compare chapter 1). I may add that a parallel English version, the Jerusalem Bible, employing very British English, would be published in 1966; a greatly improved French edition would appear in 1973; and, in English, the New Jerusalem Bible would appear in 1985 (I shall discuss these in chapter 14). This was a Bible that would have great circulation not only among Catholics but among Protestants as well.

Nevertheless, there were those within the Catholic hierarchy who continued to exercise vigorous opposition to the new directions in Catholic biblical scholarship.[64] It was only with the approval by the bishops at the Second Vatican Council of the Constitution on Divine Revelation, *Dei Verbum* (1965), that this opposition was overcome (see chapter 14).

Praying the Psalms on the Eve of Vatican II: Gelineau and Merton

I close this chapter by turning once more to the matter of worship through the Psalms, in a discussion of two notable figures: the Frenchman Joseph Gelineau (b. 1921) and the American Thomas Merton (1915–1968).

Gelineau, as we have just noted, adapted the translation of the Psalms in the original (French) Jerusalem Bible for chanting. He began to compose musical settings for four voice parts, based on Gregorian chant, for his rendering of some of the Psalms, and from 1953 onward this way of singing the Psalms spread among French Catholics; his first musical settings were published in 1954 and a setting of the whole Psalter in 1969.[65] Then a group called "The Grail" in England made a rendering into English of Gelineau's Psalms for singing—a translation, it should be noted, that was independent of the Psalms in the English version of the Jerusalem Bible (see above and chapter 14).[66] The Psalms have been sung in this arrangement not only in Catholic churches but in Protestant churches as well: the new American *Presbyterian Hymnal* of 1990, for example, contains two psalms in Gelineau's settings.[67]

Here, then, in a striking way, the old Catholic tradition of chanting the Psalms was brought into the twentieth century.[68] Gelineau's work has been largely eclipsed since the liturgical changes brought on by the Second Vatican Council, and it may be fair to say that there have been better ways to adapt the Psalms in vernacular languages for singing.[69]

Merton was an intellectual in New York City who spent his early adult years in and out of various radical groups; then, in 1941, he became a Roman Catholic and entered the austere discipline of the Trappists at the monastery in Gethsemani, Kentucky, later becoming a priest. His book *The Seven Storey Mountain* (1948), an account of his early years in the monastery, became a surprising best-seller in the United States;[70] suddenly the English-speaking world became conscious of the possibilities of the contemplative life.[71]

In 1956, Merton published a little book of thirty-nine pages, *Praying the Psalms.*[72] In 1947, Pope Pius XII had issued an encyclical on the sacred liturgy, *Mediator Dei;*[73] among other points, the document stated that because the Divine Office is the prayer of the mystical body of Jesus Christ (that is, the whole church, laity as well as clerics), greater participation in the office by the laity is urged.[74] Merton suggests that all church members learn how to pray by using the Psalms; the Psalms, he says, are not for priests only but for the whole church.

> No one can doubt that the Church considers the Psalms the ideal prayer for her clerics and religious. They form the largest part of the divine office. But the main purpose of this short essay is to remind the reader that the Psalter is also a perfect form of prayer for the layman.[75]

Indeed "Christ prays in us when we *meditate* on the Psalms, and does so perhaps even more perfectly than when we recite them vocally."[76]

There are three groups of people, says Merton, who pray the Psalms. The first group of people admit "that the Psalms are a perfect form of prayer (otherwise the Church would not use them), but they are unable to use them in their own prayer and never in fact do so. If they are bound to say the Office, they say it without much appreciation or understanding." The second group are convinced of the value of the Psalms, and as they say or sing the Psalms they do it with reverence; but still, the observance is external, and they do not really care to know the meaning of the Psalms—their business "is simply to recite them with meticulous care." Only the third group knows by experience that the Psalms are a perfect prayer.[77]

Now, "How does one arrive at such an appreciation of the Psalms?" Here Merton sets out plainly what we could have surmised: that the lay Christian can have an advantage over the busy priest, who must almost inevitably hurry his saying of the Daily Office.

> It is possible that a layman who does not recite the Office out of obligation may have an advantage over the cleric *in sacris* who is bound to the breviary. The fact that the Psalms become a habit is certainly of little value if they become a bad habit. And it is not a good habit to rush through the Psalms without any attention to their meaning, simply in order to fulfill an obligation as speedily as possible. Of course everyone is aware that it is practically unavoidable that a priest should sometimes say his Office in a hurry: he can hardly do otherwise, with the amount of work that he has to do. But that still does not make the rapid recitation of the Psalms a good habit. On the contrary, a conscientious cleric may come to the point when he has so few opportunities to pray his Office that he is fraught with tension and feelings of guilt and frustration which do not help his union with God.[78]

(One recalls Luther's guilt when he fell behind in his saying the breviary; see chapter 10.)

> One of the best ways to learn to appreciate the Psalms is to acquire the habit of reciting them slowly and well. And for this it is decidedly helpful to be able to limit one's recitation to just a few Psalms or to one only. . . . There is

nothing to prevent a layman from taking just one Psalm a day, for instance in his night prayers, and reciting it thoughtfully, pausing to meditate on the lines which have the deepest meaning for him. A priest can achieve the same effect by making his morning meditation on a favorite Psalm.[79]

Merton then goes on to describe the variety of psalms, and the way in which the Psalms bring us to *"the peace that comes from submission to God's will and from perfect confidence in Him."*[80] He recommends the English version issued at the time of the Latin Psalter of Pope Pius XII.[81]

Here Merton, concerned to teach Christians how to pray, has found through his own Catholic spirituality—especially as it was shaped by that of John of the Cross[82]—that which the Protestant Reformers had discovered and proclaimed in the sixteenth century: that the Psalms in one's own language, whether read to oneself, recited in company, chanted, or sung, are a treasure for the whole people of God.

NOTES

1. Kenneth Scott Latourette, *A History of Christianity* (New York: Harper, 1953), 840–49.

2. Ibid., 860–61.

3. J. D. Crichton, "The Office in the West: The Roman Rite from the Sixteenth Century," in Cheslyn Jones, Geoffrey Wainwright, and Edward Yarnold (eds.), *The Study of Liturgy* (New York: Oxford University Press, 1978), 383.

4. Ibid., 384.

5. Latourette, *History of Christianity*, 866–67.

6. R. V. Laurence, "The Church and Reform," in *Cambridge Modern History* (New York: Macmillan, 1904), 2:675.

7. Crichton, "Office in the West," 384; and Clifford Howell, "The Eucharist: From Trent to Vatican II," in Jones, Wainwright, and Yarnold (eds.), *Study of Liturgy*, 241.

8. The missal I have consulted is Fernand Cabrol, *The Roman Missal* (New York: Kenedy, 1934).

9. I have used *Breviarium Romanum ex decreto sacrosancti concilii tridentini restitutum* (New York and Boston: Benziger, 1943).

10. The articles in *NCE* 10:118–27 are useful.

11. F. X. Haberl and others (eds.), *G. P. da Palestrina: Werke* (Leipzig, 1862–1903), 5:148; R. Casimiri and others (eds.), *G. P. da Palestrina: Le Opere complete* (Rome: 1939–), 11:42; see *The New Grove Dictionary of Music and Musicians* (London: Macmillan, 1980), 14:133.

12. G. F. Malipiero (ed.), *C. Monteverdi: Tutte le opere* (Asolo: 1926–42), 15:368, 418; 16:167; see *New Grove Dictionary*, 12:532.

13. Ryom-Verzeichnis 609; see *New Grove Dictionary*, 20:43.

14. Part of the *Vesperae solennes de confessore* (Köchel-Verzeichnis 339); see *New Grove Dictionary*, 12:726.

15. See *New Grove Dictionary*, 3:368.

16. *The Canons and Decrees of the Sacred and Oecumenical Council of Trent* (London: Dolman, 1848), 24–26.

17. Ibid., 279.

18. Carl Mirbt, *Quellen zur Geschichte des Pabsttums und des römischen Kotholizismus* (Freiburg: J.C.B. Mohr, 1895); cited in English in Robert E. McNally, "The Council of Trent and Vernacular Bibles," *TS* 27 (June 1966):226.

19. Guy Bedouelle and Bernard Roussel (eds.), *Le Temps des réformes et la Bible* (Bible de tous les temps 5; Paris: Beauchesne, 1989), chap. 14 ("Eloge et réticences"), esp. 468–69.

20. F. J. Crehan, "The Bible in the Roman Catholic Church from Trent to the Present Day," in S. L. Greenslade (ed.), *The Cambridge History of the Bible*, vol. 3: *The West from the Reformation to the Present Day* (Cambridge: Cambridge University Press, 1963), 211–13.

21. Edwin H. Burton, *The Life and Times of Bishop Challoner (1691–1781)* (London: Longmans, Green, & Co., 1909), 1:273.

22. Ibid., 1:281–82.

23. Gerald P. Fogarty, *American Catholic Biblical Scholarship: A History from the Early Republic to Vatican II* (San Francisco: Harper & Row, 1989), 5.

24. Thérèse of Lisieux, *Autobiography of a Saint* (London: Harvill, 1958), 113.

25. Ibid., 172.

26. Dorothy Day, *The Long Loneliness* (New York: Harper & Row, 1952), 28, 29.

27. Ibid., 80–81.

28. The relevant papal enactments and decrees of the Pontifical Biblical Commission, translated into English, are conveniently collected in *Rome and the Study of Scripture* (7th ed.; St. Meinrad, Ind.: Grail, 1962); for the text in Latin, see *Enchiridion Biblicum* (Naples: D'Auria; Rome: Arnodo, 1954). For a convenient summary of the import of the documents, see Raymond E. Brown and Thomas Aquinas Collins, "Church Pronouncements," in Raymond E. Brown, Joseph A. Fitzmyer, and Roland E. Murphy (eds.), *The New Jerome Biblical Commentary* (Englewood Cliffs, N.J.: Prentice Hall, 1990), 1166–74. The story of the repression from an American perspective is set forth in Fogarty, *American Catholic Biblical Scholarship*.

29. Fogarty, *American Catholic Biblical Scholarship*, 14–34.

30. Ibid., 19–20.

31. Ibid., 34.

32. Paragraph 106; see *Rome and the Study of Scripture*, 13.

33. Paragraph 118; see *Rome and the Study of Scripture*, 20.

34. Paragraph 119; see *Rome and the Study of Scripture*, 20.

35. Ibid.

36. Fogarty, *American Catholic Biblical Scholarship*, 83–116.

37. Alexa Suelzer and John Kselman, "Modern Old Testament Criticism," in Brown et al. (eds.), *New Jerome Biblical Commentary*, 1126, sec. 55.

38. Fogarty, *American Catholic Biblical Scholarship*, 140–70; Mark S. Massa, *Charles Augustus Briggs and the Crisis of Historical Criticism* (HDR 25; Minneapolis: Fortress, 1990), 126–35.

39. Responsum VII, 3; see *Rome and the Study of Scripture*, 125.

40. Responsum VII, 4; see *Rome and the Study of Scripture*, 125.

41. Responsum VII, 5; see *Rome and the Study of Scripture*, 125. Note that the psalms named after Psalm 2 are given in the Vulgate numeration; they are, in the accepted numeration today, Psalms 16, 18, 32, 69, and 110.

42. Brown and Collins, "Church Pronouncements," 1171, sec. 25.

43. Albert Condamin, *Le Livre de Jérémie* (Ebib; Paris: Gabalda, 1936).

44. See, briefly, Suelzer and Kselman, "Modern Old Testament Criticism," 1126, sec. 58; and, in more detail, R.A.F. MacKenzie, "Augustin Bea (1881–1968)," *Bib* 49 (1968):453–56.

45. Fogarty, *American Catholic Biblical Scholarship*, 199–221.

46. Ibid., 222–49.

47. Ibid., 216–17.

48. MacKenzie, "Augustin Bea," 454.

49. Paragraphs 17–19; see *Rome and the Study of Scripture*, 90–91.

50. Paragraph 21; see *Rome and the Study of Scripture*, 91–92.

51. Paragraph 16; see *Rome and the Study of Scripture*, 89–90.

52. "Liber Psalmorum Nova e Textibus Primigeniis Interpretatio Latina Cura Professorum Pontificii Instituti Biblici Edita"; see, conveniently, the edition with an English translation in *The Psalms: A Prayer Book* (New York: Benziger, 1946).

53. See the Apostolic Letter of Pope Pius XII, *In Cotidianis Precibus*, recommending the new Psalter; for an English translation, see *Rome and the Study of Scripture*, 108–11.

54. For an explanation and defense of the work, see Augustine Bea, "The New Psalter: Its Origin and Spirit," *CBQ* 8 (1946): 4–35.

55. *CBQ* published a series of exegetical articles on Psalms 1–34, but then the series was discontinued: Ernest Lussier, "The New Latin Psalter: An Exegetical Commentary," beginning in *CBQ* 9 (1947): 226–34; and ending in *CBQ* 12 (1950):450–57.

56. A series of articles that did this was Thomas E. Bird, "Some Queries on the New Psalter," beginning in *CBQ* 11 (1949): 76–81; and continuing through *CBQ* 12 (1950): 301–10.

57. *The Psalms: A Prayer Book.*

58. Charles J. Callan (trans.), *The Psalms, Translated from the Latin Psalter, in the Light of the Hebrew, of the Septuagint and Peshitta Versions, and of the Psalterium Juxta Hebraeos of St. Jerome* (New York: Wagner, 1944).

59. Ronald A. Knox (trans.), *The Holy Bible: A Translation from the Latin Vulgate in the Light of the Hebrew and Greek Originals* (New York: Sheed & Ward, 1954).

60. Ronald A. Knox (trans.), *The Psalms* (New York: Sheed & Ward, 1947).

61. Ronald A. Knox, *On Englishing the Bible* (London: Burns, Oates, 1949) = idem, *The Trials of a Translator* (New York: Sheed & Ward, 1949).

62. For a critical but appreciative review of Knox's translation of the Psalms, see Michael J. Grunhanes, "Monsignor Knox's Version of the Psalms," *CBQ* 10 (1948): 42–54.

63. *La Sainte Bible, traduite en français sous la direction de l'Ecole Biblique de Jérusalem* (Paris: Desclée de Brouwer, 1955).

64. See Fogarty, *American Catholic Biblical Scholarship*, 281–333.

65. Joseph Gelineau, *Psalmodier en français* (Document Eglise qui Chante 2; Paris: Eglise qui Chante, 1969).

66. For the full Psalter in this translation, see *The Psalms: A New Translation, Translated from the Hebrew and Arranged for Singing to the Psalmody of Joseph Gelineau* (Philadelphia: Westminster, 1964). For the musical edition of all the Psalms in English, see Joseph Gelineau, *The Psalms: A Singing Version* (New York: Paulist, 1968).

67. *The Presbyterian Hymnal: Hymns, Psalms, and Spiritual Songs* (Louisville: Westminster/John Knox, 1990), nos. 173, 190.

68. For Gelineau's own theory of chanting the Psalms, see Joseph Gelineau, "Le Chant des psaumes," in idem, *Dans von assemblées: Sens et pratique de la célébration liturgique* (Paris: Desclée, 1971), 1:219–24.

69. For a negative assessment of Gelineau's work that nevertheless gives some of the flavor of liturgical controversy, see Thomas Day, *Why Catholics Can't Sing* (New York: Crossroad, 1990), 94–95.

70. Thomas Merton, *The Seven Storey Mountain* (New York: Harcourt Brace, 1948).

71. For biographical treatments of Merton, see Monica Furlong, *Merton: A Biography* (San Francisco: Harper & Row, 1980); Michael Mott, *The Seven Mountains of Thomas Merton* (Boston: Houghton Mifflin, 1986).

72. Thomas Merton, *Praying the Psalms* (Collegeville, Minn.: Liturgical Press, 1956).

73. For the Latin text, see *AAS* 39 (1947):521–95; I have been unable to consult an English text.

74. Paragraph 138; *AAS* 39 (1947):573 (paragraph 148).

75. Merton, *Praying the Psalms*, 15.

76. Ibid., 18.

77. Ibid., 20–21.

78. Ibid., 21–22.

79. Ibid., 22.

80. Ibid., 26.

81. Ibid., 23.

82. Thomas Merton, "St. John of the Cross," in Clare Booth Luce (ed.), *Saints for Now* (New York: Sheed & Ward, 1952), 250–60.

13

The Psalms
across Space and Time:
The Nineteenth Century

A Psalm Verse That Was a Beacon
for American Slaves

The nineteenth century was a period of optimism. The world was largely at peace, and during the course of the century trade and learning expanded enormously. But before we turn to take note of this optimism, we must ponder the enormity of the institution of slavery in the Western Hemisphere. By the beginning of the nineteenth century the slave trade was waning, but in the United States, in the census of 1860, 4,441,830 African Americans were counted, of whom 487,970 were free; the remainder were slaves.[1]

Under great disabilities this population gradually embraced the Christian faith.[2] African Americans embraced the biblical story of the Exodus out of Egypt as their own; one has only to think of a spiritual such as "Go Down, Moses" to recognize this fact. Again and again, America was understood as Egypt, and the African Americans understood themselves to be Israel in need of liberation.

But there is another Old Testament text that ignited their hope. That was Ps. 68:32 (31), which in the KJV reads, "Princes shall come out of Egypt; Ethiopia shall soon stretch out her hands unto God."[3]

The verse had already been used by Phillis Wheatley, a woman born in Senegal who had been kidnapped onto a slave ship and became the servant of a Boston woman. Wheatley became a poet and an important voice for her people. In a letter written to the Reverend Samuel Hopkins, dated February 9, 1774, she wrote, in part:

> Methinks, Rev. Sir, this is the beginning of that happy period foretold by the Prophets, when all shall know the Lord from the least to the greatest, and that without the assistance of human Art of Eloquence. My heart expands with sympathetic joy to see at distant time the thick cloud of ignorance dispersing from the face of my benighted country. Europe and America have long been fed with the heavenly provision, and I fear they loath it, while Africa is perishing with a spiritual Famine. O that they could partake of the crumbs, the

238

precious crumbs, which fall from the table of these distinguished children of the kingdom.

Their minds are unprejudiced against the truth, therefore 'tis to be hoped they would receive it with their whole heart, I hope that which the divine royal Psalmist says by inspiration is now on the point of being accomplished, namely, Ethiopia shall soon stretch forth her hands unto God.[4]

James Theodore Holly, an Episcopalian priest who was an African American, wrote in 1884 a striking reversal of the curse of Canaan (Gen. 9:25), which had been used to justify slavery. Holly stated that there have been three historic periods of human redemption, named after the three sons of Noah (compare Genesis 10): the first belongs to the Semitic people, whose task it was to formulate and preserve the word of God; the second was the Japhetic phase, the age of the Europeans who were commissioned to preach the gospel; and the third, the Hamitic phase, will soon complete the divine plan of human redemption, when the Hamites will finally put the word of God into practice.[5]

And preaching on this verse has continued: a sermon based on the text was cited in 1933, teaching African Americans to be satisfied with their race and stop imitating others.[6]

The Psalms into All the World

Two new developments related to the Bible emerged in the course of the nineteenth century, and these developments were interwoven: the dramatic movement of Christian mission emissaries out across the world, a movement that involved the translation of the Bible, including the Psalms, into dozens of languages that in many instances had not until that time been reduced to writing; and, at the same time, the steady attempt to recover the original historical context of the Bible. The Psalms went across space into all the world, and the Psalms began to be heard, once more, across time from their earliest singers. Both developments took place for the most part in the context of Protestant churches, though Roman Catholics were touched by them as well, as we saw in chapter 12.

The Christian churches had always sent out missionaries into new areas of the world,[7] and there were Protestants at work in the mission field well before the nineteenth century.[8] One thinks, for example, of the Moravians: in Bethlehem, Pennsylvania, a center was instituted for the preparation of missionaries to the native Americans. One of the most famous of the eighteenth-century Moravian missionaries was David Zeisberger, who became adept at the Mohawk language, gained the confidence of the Iroquois, and was initiated into some of their tribes.[9] He prepared a harmony of the Gospels in the Delaware language that was published in 1821.[10]

But the great Protestant foreign mission movement[11] was inaugurated in England with the Baptist Missionary Society (1792),[12] the London Missionary Society (1795),[13] and the Church Missionary Society (1799).[14] In the United States, mission work began in 1810 with the founding of the American Board of Commissioners for Foreign Missions at the initiative of Congregational ministers in New England, themselves impelled by the piety of a group of students at Andover Seminary in Massachusetts.[15]

Adoniram Judson and the Burmese

Among those students at Andover was one whose work I shall describe here, Adoniram Judson (1788–1850).[16] Judson set sail on Feburary 19, 1812, from Salem, Massachusetts, bound for India, though he had earlier also considered Burma as an ultimate destination.[17] While at sea, he and his wife, Ann, reluctantly came to the conclusion that baptism should be reserved for adult believers and be by immersion rather than by sprinkling; accordingly, when he arrived in Calcutta, they were immersed by a Baptist missionary there. He was convinced then that he must sever his relation to the American Board, and later, in 1814, he came under the support of a newly organized board, the General Missionary Convention of the Baptist Denomination in the United States of America for Foreign Missions.[18] After a sequence of circumstances that cannot be detailed here, Judson and his wife were expelled from India by the East India Company and landed in the port of Rangoon, Burma, on July 13, 1813, almost seventeen months after leaving Salem.

There had already been some British Baptist activity in Burma. A British missionary, Felix Carey, had a toehold and had made a start at compiling a grammar and dictionary of Burmese and a translation of some of the New Testament,[19] but the mission had not prospered.[20]

The Burmese language had had a written literature for centuries; their alphabet was derived from India, whence it had come along with the Buddhist faith. But there were no printed books: traditionally, Burmese literary material was written on dried palm leaves and without any divisions between the words. So Judson really had to begin at the beginning, without any adequate language resources and, essentially, without a settled Christian vocabulary from which he could draw; and it was to language study that he and Ann applied themselves. After a year had passed, he and Ann could read, write, and converse easily in Burmese. But then he began to saturate himself with Buddhist legend and poetry, so that he might enter into the religious spirit of the language. Not for six years did he attempt to preach in public.[21]

Then, along a busy thoroughfare, he erected a *zayat*, a type of building appropriate to Burma where a teacher would sit and teach those who came by; but it was six years before he baptized his first convert. On July 12, 1823, one day short of exactly ten years since he had first set foot in Burma, he could enter in his "Autobiographical Record," "Completed the translation of the New Testament in Burmese."[22] In 1824 he moved to the then capital, Ava, in the central part of the country south of Mandalay. But when the first Anglo–Burmese war broke out, he was thrown into jail as a suspected English-speaking foreigner, and he underwent eleven months of privation. One of the great stories of this remarkable life is the way in which his wife, Ann, sewed the manuscript of his translation of the New Testament into the pillow on which he lay while in jail; after many vicissitudes that manuscript was preserved,[23] and in 1832, after a press and a font of Burmese type had been installed in Rangoon, the New Testament was printed.

In the meantime, in 1826 his first wife died, and Judson essentially avoided all other activity in order to complete his translation of the Bible. We could wish to have more than terse entries in his journals and correspondence on the details of his translation work. In his journal for July 5, 1827, is the laconic notice, "Commenced a translation of the Book of Psalms."[24] Then we have a letter to the corresponding secretary of the mission society that he wrote from Rangoon on November 21, 1830:

> Dear Sir, Since my return to this place, I have chiefly confined myself to the garret of the house we occupy, in order to get a little time to go on with the translation of the Psalms, which was begun three years ago, but has been hitherto postponed for more important missionary work, which was ever pressing upon us.[25]

Then in a letter to the Rev. Dr. Boles on February 5, 1831, he wrote:

> Since my return from Promoe, I have been chiefly employed in finishing the Psalms, the book of Daniel, &c. which were begun some time ago. . . . Our house is frequently crowded with company; but I am obliged to leave them to Moung En, (one of the best of assistants,) in order to get time for the translation. Is this right? Happy is the missionary, who goes to a country, where the Bible is translated to his hand.[26]

In 1834 he completed his translation of the entire Bible into Burmese,[27] a work that saw print in 1835.[28] He then married the widow of a fellow missionary, Sarah Hall Boardman.

This circumstance bears on an incident connected with Judson's rendering of a verse in the Psalms. Just after his second marriage a faithful old Burmese Christian came to him, much troubled, and told him of his fear that his teacher was to be among the lost. "You know," he said, "the Bible says that God will deliver his children from the snare of the widow: but he has not delivered you; you have been snared by the widow." They turned to Ps. 91:3 and found that it read just as the old man had said. The feminine form of the word "fowler" had been used, which in Burmese is the word for "widow." Judson lost no time in revising that passage.[29]

Indeed he was constantly revising: he completed a revision of the New Testament in 1829, and a second revision in 1837; and he completed a revision of the Old Testament in 1835, and a second revision in 1840.[30] He continued for years working on a dictionary; by 1848 the English–Burmese section was complete, and it was printed the following year, but he was still working on the Burmese–English section at the time of his death (1850), and it had to be completed by others.

What resources did Judson bring to bear to the task? It was a great temptation for Bible translators to translate from the King James Version; among Protestants this version carried enormous authority. But Judson insisted on translating from the original Greek and Hebrew. He used the materials of biblical study taught him at Andover Seminary by Moses Stuart, one of the first to make German biblical scholarship known in the United States.[31] He had the use of Wilhelm Gesenius's Hebrew lexicon. For the Psalms he made use of Samuel Horsley's annotated translation.[32] In 1839 he wrote to the corresponding secretary of his mission board:

> Allow me to suggest whether the exegetical works of [Moses] Stuart, [Edward] Robinson, [Calvin] Stowe, [Henry J.] Ripley, [George] Bush, [George] Noyes, and such like, with some of the best German works, ought not to be sent out to the library, as soon as they come from the press, without waiting for an application to be made for them. I frequently see a sterling work on the cover of the Herald or Magazine, and am ready to scream, with some variations, "The book, the book! my kingdom for the book!" Yes, a kingdom, if the same ship which brought the notice had brought the work too; whereas I have to wait for letters to cross the ocean twice or three times, at least, and thus two or three years' use of the book is lost, during which time I am, perhaps, working upon that very portion of Scripture which that book is intended to illustrate.[33]

In 1840 Judson sent a copy of the revised Burmese Bible to the United States and wrote:

> I have bestowed more time and labor on the revision than on the first translation of the work, and more, perhaps, than is proportionate to the actual improvement made. Long and toilsome research among the biblical critics and commentators, especially the German, was frequently requisite to satisfy my mind that my first position was the right one. Considerable improvement, however, has been made, I trust, both in point of style and approximation to the real meaning of the original. But the *beau ideal* of translation, so far as it concerns the poetical and prophetical books of the Old Testament, I profess not to have attained. If I live many years, of which I have no expectation, I shall have to bestow much more labor upon those books. With the New Testament I am rather better satisfied, and the testimony of those acquainted with the language is rather encouraging. At least, I hope that I have laid a good foundation for my successors to build upon.[34]

In a similar letter in 1840 to the corresponding secretary of the mission board he wrote, "In the first edition of the Old Testament, I paid too much regard to the critical emendations of [Robert] Lowth, [Samuel] Horsley, and others. In the present edition, I have adhered more strictly to the Hebrew text."[35]

Emily Judson, his third wife, whom he married in 1846, wrote, "He felt, when making his translation, an almost overpowering sense of the awfulness [that is, the awesomeness] of his work, and an ever-present conviction that every word was as from the lips of God."[36] One of Judson's missionary colleagues wrote, after his death:

> The translation of the Holy Scriptures into the Burman language is admitted to be the best translation in India; that is, the translation has given more satisfaction to his contemporaries and successors than any translation of the Bible into any other eastern language has done to associate missionaries in any other parts of India. It is free from obscurity to the Burmese mind. It is read and understood perfectly. Its style and diction are as choice and elegant as the

language itself, peculiarly honorific, would afford, and conveys, doubtless, the mind of the Spirit as perfectly as can be.[37]

Nevertheless, even a very good work may be revised or replaced. The British and Foreign Bible Society issued a Burmese version of the New Testament in 1909 and of the full Bible in 1926.[38] In the meantime, Judson's Bible was revised by a committee of Baptists—the New Testament was completed in 1924 and the full Bible in 1933. There was an attempt in 1915 to combine the two translation committees, but their ideals of translation and publication were so different that the effort was abandoned.[39] It was clear, at least in the 1950s, that the Baptist church in Burma, numerically the largest, revered the Judson version and wished to keep it unchanged.[40]

One issue will perhaps illustrate the kind of questions that come up in translation. A Western professor working in Rangoon in 1950 wrote:

> Judson did his translation in the decaying period of Burmese monarchy, when the Court made up for their lack of power by extravagant language, honorifics, etc., applicable primarily to the Court, secondarily (a fortiori) to the hierarchy of the Buddhist Order in Burma, and thirdly by courtesy to the hierarchy of other religions. A Burmese king never merely "goes"; he "royally does a going." Judson (wrongly, in my opinion) adopted this court-jargon. When Jesus goes into Capernaum, he "royally did a going." Even when "Jesus wept," his "tears royally did a falling." Honorifics, none of which are in the Greek, are commonly tacked on to pronouns.[41]

The question of the use of these honorifics leads to more general questions of the theory of translation, to which I shall return in chapter 17.

In the meantime, work was going on in Burma among other peoples, of whom I shall mention one: the Karens. The Karens are a hill people centered in Tavoy, in the extreme southeast of the country (14°N, 98°E). A Karen who spoke Burmese, Ko Tha Byu, was converted to the Christian faith and helped the Baptist missionaries in their work among his people. In 1832 one of the missionaries, Jonathan Wade (1798–1872), reduced the Karen language to writing, adapting the Burmese alphabet for that purpose. In a letter written from Moulmein that year he stated:

> I commenced the study of this language more than a year ago, at first without any intention of reducing it to writing; but I found it necessary in order to assist my memory, to write down words, and my teacher understanding both Taling and Burman, I found that many of the Karen sounds could be expressed by the Taling character, which could not by the Burman; this suggested the idea of trying how far an arrangement of the Taling and Burman combined would go towards giving the Karens a written language. On going to Rangoon, as I expected to remain there, I gave up the work; but when I was again stationed here, and the Karens of this province came upon my hands, I resumed it, at the same time, however, writing to brother Mason to know whether he had pursued the study so far as to have formed a plan of reducing the language to writing, intending if he had got a plan arranged to adopt it here. His answer did not touch the main point of inquiry, but sister Boardman said in a letter to

Mrs. Wade, that brother Mason's poor health, and his being unable to have intercourse with the Karens during the rains, had prevented him from attending much to the study of their language, and that she was therefore glad that I had resumed the work, so that there was a prospect of the Karens having the scriptures in their own language.[42]

Then, in 1834, the "brother Mason" to whom Wade referred, Francis Mason (1799–1874), began translating the New Testament into the Sgau dialect of Karen; this was published in 1843.[43] In the meantime, in 1838 he had translated several psalms,[44] and the full Bible was published in 1853.[45] In the English introduction to that Bible, Mason offers examples of the difficulties he encountered, and he also indicates the resources he used. In Ps. 16:10, where various Hebrew texts differ between "your pious one" and "your pious ones," he cites the Greek, Latin, Syriac, and Aramaic versions (see chapter 6) from the Walton London Polyglot of 1657, as well as various commentaries available in his day.

Justin Perkins and the Syriac-speaking Nestorian Christians

I now describe another mission, one that illustrates a different set of translation issues: the mission of the American Board of Commissioners for Foreign Missions (essentially Congregationalists and Presbyterians) to the Nestorian Christians in the area of Lake Urmia in northwestern Persia (Iran). Here the issue was the contrast between the traditional ancient language of Christian liturgy and the current spoken language of the community: the Nestorians are one of the ancient Christian communities whose language for the Bible and for liturgy is Syriac[46] (I described in chapter 6 the translation of the Bible in the early Christian centuries into Syriac [the so-called Peshitta]). During the early Middle Ages, the Nestorian church was active in sending out missions from its center in Baghdad to adjoining territories, reaching as far as western China in the seventh century. But under pressure from Islam and the depredations of Mongol nomads, the population of Nestorians shrank to the area west and north of Lake Urmia; this lake has a high elevation, 4,183 feet (1,275 meters), and the mountains north and west of the lake sheltered the Nestorians.

To this community there went out from the American Board in 1833 a young seminary graduate, Justin Perkins (1805–1869), and his wife;[47] as with Judson and his wife, it is worth noting the length of time taken up in their travel. They sailed from Boston on September 21, 1833; arrived on Malta on November 8 and in Constantinople (Istanbul) on December 21, remaining there until May 17, 1834; then set sail for Trabzon, on the Black Sea, where they arrived May 30. From there they set out, on June 10, on horseback thirteen days to Erzurum (Turkey); they report carefully that they did not ride on the two intervening Sabbaths! Then they set out on July 15 for Yerevan (today the capital of the Republic of Armenia), arriving there August 8; on August 9 they set out for the south, only to be delayed several days by passport difficulties on the Persian frontier, which they passed on August 20. They arrived in Tabriz on August 23; three days later, one learns,

Perkins's wife delivered a daughter! Over eleven months had passed since they set out from Boston.

They and the missionaries who later joined them based themselves in the city of Urmia (now Reza'iyeh, Iran), west of the lake. They became associated with local Nestorian priests and bishops, a few of whom spoke some English; the missionaries opened schools and began medical work. The Nestorian priests knew their liturgy and to some degree their Scriptures, but, as can be imagined, the Syriac of the Nestorian liturgy and Scriptures was a form of the language fifteen hundred years older than the current spoken Syriac. Furthermore, their books of liturgy and Scripture were in manuscript form; no printed books were available to them.

Perkins had brought with him copies of Syriac books printed in the West; they were, however, printed in the Syriac alphabet called "Serto" (or "Jacobite"), different from the "Nestorian" alphabet (or "Chaldean") and detested by the Nestorians because of sectarian rivalries.[48] It should be stressed that the local vernacular Syriac had not to that time been reduced to written form; literacy meant that priests could read manuscripts written in ancient Syriac. (Compare the present-day situation of classical Arabic, which I described in chapter 5.)

The priests were eager for learning; we read in Perkins's journal:

> *Dec.* 11 [1836]. This evening priest Dunka, our translator from the mountains, commenced studying Hebrew. . . . This priest is naturally a fine scholar, and as the Hebrew much resembles the Syriac, it will cost him but little effort to acquire it; and a knowledge of it may prove invaluable in his qualifications as a translator. *Dec.* 12. Priest Yohannan, the teacher of our seminary, requested permission to spend his evenings in studying Hebrew with priest Dunka. I could not refuse him the privilege, as he labors hard in the school, during the day, and I hope he also may be aided by the exercise to a better understanding of the Scriptures. Our fine Nestorian boy, John, also preferred his request to join the Hebrew class, but I advised him to defer Hebrew until he shall have advanced farther in English. *Dec.* 15. We have recently introduced the practice of reciting verses of Scripture in our family, at our meals. This recital is now generally made in four different languages; in the ancient Syriac by myself; in the modern Syriac, i.e. the Nestorian dialect, by Mrs. Perkins; in Hebrew, by priests Dunka and Yohannan; and in English by priest Abraham and John. In addition to the agreeable intellectual exercise thus afforded, as we are all learners in these respective languages, the Scripture recited always presents matter for practical conversation and reflection.[49]

All this linguistic activity suggests that, in regard to the Bible, the missionaries had twin goals: a fresh translation of the Bible into modern Syriac and the development of facilities for printing. These twin goals are deftly summarized in Perkins's journal entries for December 29, 1835, and for February 14, 1836: "*Dec. 29.* We also need a press at our mission"[50]; "*Feb.* 14. We commenced the great work of translating the Bible into the Nestorian language. May the Lord prosper this, his own work, in our feeble hands."[51]

A printing press was dispatched on January 7, 1837, along with a font of "Syro-

Chaldaic" type obtained in London, as a second missionary couple went out to the
Urmia mission,[52] Albert L. Holladay (1805–1856) and his wife.[53] Unfortunately,
however, there was no printer to accompany the press. It arrived along with the
missionaries on June 7; the report of the mission for 1838 states:

> The printing establishment has arrived, and the manifold copying-powers of
> the press would have superseded these labors of the pen, on which the mission
> hitherto has been chiefly dependent for school-books and tracts, were there a
> printer to put it in operation. The Committee hope to be enabled to send one
> soon.

And, just following that statement, "Mr. Perkins is making progress in his translation of the Scriptures into modern Syriac."[54]

It may be recalled that in chapter 10 there was a description of the Psalms
commentaries of Theodore of Mopsuestia in the early fifth century; it is therefore
worth mentioning here two conversations that Albert Holladay had about eighteen
months after his arrival at the Urmia mission. The first was with Mar Elias, a
Nestorian bishop in the village of Geog Tapa, just east of Urmia. In his journal
Holladay records:

> *December* 11, 1838. . . . In the course of my conversation with the bishop today,
> I inquired if he knew any thing of such an author as Theodore of Mopsuestia.
> To my surprise he answered in the affirmative, and said that some extracts
> from his writings still exist in this province, and that many of his works are to
> be found among the Nestorians of the mountains . . . . *December* 12. Desiring
> to know something more about the works of Theodore of Mopsuestia, I made
> the same inquiry of priest Dunka, which I had before made of Mar Elias. He
> also declared that many of Theodore's works are still preserved in the moun-
> tains; but added, that this Theodore was once a Mussulman [Muslim]![55]

(To round off this part of the narrative, it may be said that Holladay and his wife
had to return to the United States in 1846 because of his wife's ill health.)

Nothing more is reported at this time about the press that arrived at the Urmia
mission in 1837; it evidently remained inoperative for lack of a printer. Then we
learn that among those sent out to Urmia in 1840 was Edward Breath, printer, who
embarked from Boston on July 21, taking with him "a press constructed expressly
for the mission, composed of so many separate pieces as to be conveniently trans-
ported across the country on horseback to Ooroomiah [Urmia]."[56] Perkins reports
in his journal: "*Nov.* 9. We took the press from the boxes in which it was brought
and set it up. . . . It appears like an exotic, in this dark, remote land; and still, like a
familiar old acquaintance, whose arrival is inexpressibly welcome." And again:

> *Nov.* 21. We put our press in operation, by printing, on small scraps, a few
> copies of the Lord's prayer, in the ancient Syriac, merely to gratify the curios-
> ity of the natives who had never before witnessed printing. The "Press" is now
> the *lion* here. Numbers call daily to see it. The Nestorians are inexpressibly
> delighted with it, alike as a curiosity and as holding out a pledge of opening a
> new era upon their people.[57]

And nine days later he reported:

> *Nov.* 30. We commenced printing the Psalms in the ancient Syriac language, a
> work we had long promised to the clergy, as the *first* labor of the press. They
> are very anxious that we should print the *rubrics* with red ink, according to
> their own style of illuminating books with the pen. This would considerably
> augment the labor; but the increased acceptance with which this portion of the
> Scriptures would meet, particularly in their church service, renders it quite
> desirable to comply with their wishes, if we can find materials for red ink. We
> also print this edition of the Psalms with *references*, with which the Nestorians
> are exceedingly pleased, possessing as they do no *concordance*, and never before
> having had anything in the form of references, which they pertinently denom-
> inate "witnesses." Those who are able to read English, use our reference Bibles
> with great satisfaction.[58]

Soon the press was printing material in modern Syriac. Once more, Perkins's
journal documents the progress:

> *March* 13 [1841]. The proof-sheets of our *first* tract in the Nestorian language
> was brought into my study for correction. This is indeed the *first sheet*, ever
> printed in that language and character. As it was laid upon my table, before our
> translators, priest Abraham and Dunka, they were struck with mute astonish-
> ment and rapture, to see *their* language in *print;* though they had themselves
> assisted me, a few days before, in preparing the same matter for the press. As
> soon as recovery from their surprise allowed them utterance, "it is time to give
> glory to God," they mutually exclaimed, "that our eyes are permitted to behold
> the commencement of *printing books* for our people!"[59]

One incident recorded by Perkins bears directly on the Psalms. In his journal
for March 21, 1841, he records:

> We recently translated the 51st Psalm, to insert in the chapter in our first tract,
> on the necessity of a new heart. As I was admiring the spirit of the Psalm,
> priest Dunka reminded me, that the Nestorians repeat it daily in the ancient
> Syriac, in their regular devotions. They always go to a brook or spring and
> wash the face and hands, immediately before worship, and while washing,
> repeat in a whisper a part of this Psalm, beginning with the second verse,
> "Wash me thoroughly from mine iniquity and cleanse me from my sin," etc. At
> the commencement of their worship, in their churches, an invocation is offered,
> consisting mainly of several verses from the last part of the Psalm, viz., "O
> Lord, open thou my lips, and my mouth shall show forth thy praise. For thou
> desirest not sacrifice, else would I give it; thou delightest not in burnt-offering;
> the sacrifices of God are a broken spirit; a broken and a contrite heart, O God,
> thou wilt not despise." The very prominent place which this wonderful Psalm
> and other portions of Scripture of like import, hold in the Nestorian Liturgy,
> have often strongly impressed me with the former comparative purity of this
> ancient church, and the general excellence of the matter embodied in their
> church service. At the same time, there is more or less that is exceptionable in
> it, which ought never to be translated.[60]

The last sheets of the New Testament, with parallel columns in ancient and modern Syriac, came from the press in November 1846.[61] Perkins completed the translation of the Old Testament in January 1849; he remarked that the close relation of Hebrew to Syriac made his work easier. The Old Testament, in the same double-column format, was published in 1852. As an example of the effort, in ancient Syriac the first verse of Psalm 23 is *māryā' ner'ēn wĕmedem lā' nĕḥassar lī*— literally, "The-Lord pastures-me and-anything not shall-be-lacking to-me"; the verse was translated into modern Syriac as *māryā' ra'yī yĕle' le' ḥāsren*—"the-Lord (is) my-shepherd, nothing is-lacking-to-me."

After all this great effort, it is tragic to report that the Nestorian Christians suffered grievously during and after the First World War at the hands of the Turks, Kurds, and Muslim Persians; many of them fled into what is now northern Iraq, then under the control of the British. In 1933, when Iraq declared its independence, many of them fled into Syria. In comparison with their situation in the early nineteenth century, they are now a decimated and scattered community.

Johann Gottlieb Christaller and the Twi People

The impact of the work of biblical translation on groups of people who had been illiterate may be illustrated by a comment on the translation of the Psalms into Twi, done by Johann Gottlieb Christaller (1827–1895), a German linguist, who served with the Basel Mission in what is now Ghana. He became the foremost promoter of the Akan language and culture, especially Twi, into which he completed a translation of the Bible in 1871. An African contemporary, David Asante of Akropong, wrote to Christaller in 1866:

> The Psalms are translated perfectly and brilliantly. Nobody can read this translation without deep feelings of awe. They resemble in many ways the songs of mourning (*Kwadwom*) in our Twi language; the Twi people will be glad to read them. May the Lord give His blessing to your labours.[62]

The Work of Translation

The immense task of getting the Bible into the various languages of the world continued through the nineteenth century and continues at an increasing rate in the twentieth. As of the end of 1989, full Bibles have been translated into 7 languages of North America; 7 languages of Central America, South America, and the Caribbean; 58 languages of Europe; 119 languages of Africa; 96 languages of Asia; and 26 languages of Australia, New Zealand, and the Pacific islands, for a total of 313 translations of the full Bible; and there are more languages in which the Psalms but not the full Old Testament have been rendered.[63]

Here I make two general observations, and they are interrelated. The first is that this whole, vast enterprise of translation is based on a theological assumption: that there is no language on earth that is not a suitable vehicle for Scripture translation. By this assumption, it does not matter whether the language has never been reduced to writing or, on the contrary, has a tradition of centuries of written literature; nor does it matter whether its speakers are nomadic hunter-gatherers or, on the contrary, are the carriers of an urban civilization. Every human language, we assume, may become the vehicle of biblical translation.[64] This assumption cuts across the views that were common for centuries: that there are "primitive" languages with vocabularies of only a few hundred words, or that only a few languages are capable of expressing the nuances of Scripture.

In Chapter 6, in the discussion of the translation of the Old Testament into Greek (the Septuagint), I made the point that the Jews took a theological risk in embarking upon a translation of the Hebrew Scriptures. But Greek was the prestige language of the Mediterranean area in the centuries around the turn of the era. It might be thought to be another matter when it comes to the Bawn language of Bangladesh, in which the full Bible was published in 1989 by the Bangladesh Evangelical Christian Church; or the Lahu language, spoken by a population of that name in northeast Burma and the western part of Yunnan province in China, in which the full Bible likewise appeared in 1989 from the Bible Society in Thailand; or to the Uruund language of Zaire in Africa, into which the Psalms were recently translated (I shall return to the last-mentioned translation in a moment).

The second observation is that Bible translators today take advantage of current studies in linguistics, studies beyond the ken of the missionary translators of the early nineteenth century.[65] These studies involve the analysis of the sounds of a given language in such a way that an alphabet can be devised for it; the analysis of the morphology of words (their variations by prefixes, suffixes, and other modifications); the analysis of the syntax of sentences; and the analysis of discourse patterns. It turns out that languages across the world manifest far more variety in these matters than can be imagined by those who have stayed with European languages. The exploration of the patterning of languages, which began with the work of anthropologists such as Eduard Sapir, who recorded native American languages, has in itself been reinforced by the concerns of missionary Bible translators.

Bible translators today will usually have had some training in Greek for the New Testament but will not necessarily have studied Hebrew. Instead they depend on the variety of translations available today in languages such as English and the range of helps for translators issued by institutions such as the American Bible Society in the United States and the United Bible Societies in London.[66]

I offer here portions of a report by Anna E. Lerbak, who helped work on a translation of the Psalms into Uruund (also called Lunda), a language spoken by perhaps four hundred thousand people centered in Kapanga, southwestern Zaire (5°S, 17°E).[67] The language was first written down by Methodist missionaries; in 1952 there was a meeting of Protestant and Catholic missionaries and local native speakers to agree on spelling conventions.

> We have been aware of the fact that we were creating or stabilizing the religious vocabulary and terminology, or phraseology, a sober thought. We tried

all the time to write in such a way that it would be readily understood by new readers, and at the same time be a good and dignified language that the best and most advanced people would be glad for the young generation to learn, and that everybody would be glad to hear read in church and care to read at home.[68]

The translators had an earlier translation in Chokwe and two in Luba, both of which are related languages, and these helped. Their sources were not the Hebrew text but the American Standard Version of 1901 (for a description of this translation, see below); recent Danish and French translations; Elmer A. Leslie's commentary (1949);[69] and then, before the work was completed, the Revised Standard Version (1952; see chapter 14). The portion translated by Lerbak was gone over by local native speakers and then sent out to Kapanga and Sandoa (two cities), and the responses that came back were incorporated into revisions.

> A brief account about deciding on the names of God may be interesting. The word for God is *Nzamb* which has been used from the beginning, there is no question about that. The name "Jehovah" [Yahweh] had been used in some contexts, but I had the feeling that it did not mean much to the people, and when I asked the pastors they all said it didn't, and worse, it very often confused people, especially in the villages. During the conversation it was suggested that the name *Chinawej* be used in the place of "Jehovah," and this met with immediate approval. A few days later I was working on a Psalm in which "Jehovah" was used frequently, so I wrote *Chinawej* in its place and then read the Psalm to them. The response was about like this: "That is it, now people will understand, that is how *Chinawej* is. The Jews call God 'Jehovah,' we call Him *Chinawej*, it is the same God, but we know Him as *Chinawej* as the Jews know Him as 'Jehovah.' " They often call God *Chinawej* in prayer, it seems to indicate warmth and intimacy.
>
> The same word is used in two other ways. It is the name of a snake which never attacks human beings. And it is used as a response of approval. When told of something they are pleased to hear, something they find good, just, helpful, generous, they often respond by saying, *Chinawej*. When they call God *Chinawej*, it indicates that they think of Him as One Who is good and just and generous towards them. When it was suggested at the committee that we use *Chinawej* in place of "Jehovah" it was accepted immediately and unanimously.[70]

As with Judson's use of honorifics in Burmese, these choices in translation policy raise general questions about the nature of a translation, to which I shall return in chapter 17.

The Recovery of the World of the Psalms: Pioneers

I now turn to the other major development in the nineteenth century bearing on the Psalms: the expanding attempt to recover the original historical context of biblical material, so that the Psalms reach out to us across time.

There were a variety of developments in the nineteenth century that led to a profound shift in thinking about faith and history, a shift as profound in its way as the adjustment of the Jewish faith to Hellenism that began in the fourth century B.C.E. (see chapter 6). I can only allude here to a few of these developments. A literal reading of the biblical account of creation was challenged by the growing science of geology, exemplified by Charles Lyell's *Principles of Geology* (1830–1833),[71] and by the theory of evolution set forth by Charles R. Darwin in *The Origin of Species by Means of Natural Selection* (1859) and *The Descent of Man and Selection in Relation to Sex* (1872).[72] The exclusive claims of the Christian faith were implicitly challenged by a growing awareness of the scriptures of the faiths of east Asia, climaxed by the publication, under the editorship of F. Max Müller, of the fifty volumes of the series *Sacred Books of the East* (1879–1910).[73] These publications and many more like them implanted the idea among thoughtful people that everything has been in constant change and development—the inanimate world, all the species of plants and animals in the world, and all the varieties of human cultures with their various ideas and ideals—and that, in the domain of human culture, it is the task of historians to trace the details of these developments and to understand them without prejudging them.

These ideas suggested that both the Bible and the Christian faith were subject to historical development. In specific regard to the Bible, these ideas of development were reinforced by a great array of new information bearing on the Bible that emerged from fresh discoveries coming to light regarding the geography, antiquities, and languages of the ancient Near East. There was Napoleon's expedition into Egypt (1798);[74] and in Mesopotamia the excavations of Austin Henry Layard and Paul Émile Botta at Nineveh (1842) may be mentioned, out of many.[75] Edward Robinson began the serious identification of ancient sites in Palestine (1838, 1852).[76] Theretofore undeciphered languages of the ancient Near East spoke once more as Jacques Joseph Champollion began to read the hieroglyphics of Egypt (1822); and Assyrian and Babylonian cuneiform began to be understood, especially through the efforts of Henry C. Rawlinson on the Behistun inscription (1850 and thereafter).[77] The publication by George Smith (1873) of the recently translated Babylonian flood narrative, a narrative offering striking parallels to the flood narrative of Genesis, created a sensation.[78]

The beginning of the nineteenth century saw the inauguration of modern scholarship in the Hebrew language with the work of Wilhelm Gesenius (1786–1842), who published a grammar of Hebrew in 1813, which he continued to enlarge until his death, and a Hebrew–German lexicon in 1815, which he continued to improve for years. His Hebrew–Latin lexicon (1833) was translated into English by Robinson in 1836—the same man who explored Palestine. (We have seen how Judson depended upon Gesenius's works for the preparation of the Burmese Bible.)[79]

In those decades scholars, especially in Germany, began to analyze biblical texts with the techniques of literary and historical criticism, rather than to be content to view them simply as divine works beyond the reach of such inquiry. Both the New Testament Gospels and the books of the Pentateuch (Genesis through

Deuteronomy) appeared to yield to such historical-critical inquiry; one thinks of David F. Strauss's *Das Leben Jesu kritisch bearbeitet* (The life of Jesus treated critically [1835–36], translated into English in 1846), which caused such a storm that Strauss was removed from his teaching post,[80] and of the literary analysis of the Pentateuch associated with the names of Karl Heinrich Graf (1866) and Julius Wellhausen (*Geschichte Israels* [1878], translated into English as *Prolegomena to the History of Ancient Israel* [1885]), which proposed separating the first five books of the Old Testament into four literary sources, all of them from a time centuries after Moses.[81]

As for the book of Psalms, in chapter 2 it was briefly noted that, in the nineteenth century, critical scholars began to date many of the Psalms to long after David. And in chapter 12 we saw how the Roman Catholic Church violently resisted such proposals of biblical scholars. Now we must affirm that these ideas were equally dismaying to Protestants.

The Life and Work of Charles Augustus Briggs

Among the critical commentaries of this period that date most of the Psalms late, few were so carefully compiled as that of Charles Augustus Briggs (1841–1913) and his daughter Emilie Grace Briggs. The commentary appeared in 1906–1907 in the series called International Critical Commentary, a series that Charles Briggs planned and edited.[82] Though their late dating of the Psalms is rejected today, there is much in this commentary that remains of permanent value. Because Charles Briggs himself became a symbolic center of the debate in the Protestant churches of the United States over the use of the historical-critical method on the Bible, I choose to narrate his story.[83]

Charles Briggs was born in New York City in 1841 and accepted the Christian faith at a revival meeting in 1858, joining the denomination to which his mother belonged, the Presbyterian church. In 1861 he entered Union Theological Seminary in New York, a school that at that time was related to the Presbyterian church. There Briggs fell under the spell of Robinson, already mentioned as an explorer of ancient Palestinian sites and a translator of Gesenius's Hebrew lexicon. Robinson, having been trained in Germany in the new linguistic and archeological methods, in turn trained his students in these same methods, but at the same time he endowed them with the firm conviction that their critical studies would serve the beliefs of Presbyterian orthodoxy.[84] Briggs quickly became an outstanding student, and he, too, was convinced that his academic pursuits could be an expression of his piety. In a notebook he wrote:

> God's love, if truly presented, would call forth all the affections of our heart, mind and soul. Thus, our great duty is to examine into the nature of God and his loving relation to us. Let us cultivate our faculties of mind, as these are the best means for attaining our perfection.[85]

In 1866, Briggs and his bride set off for Berlin, where he imbibed the methods of historical criticism from the professor under whom he studied, Isaac August Dorner. Briggs wrote his uncle in 1867:

When new light dawns from above, most men cling to the old and can't believe any new light possible. But the world needs new views of the truth. The old doctrines are good but insufficient. . . . Let us seek more light under the guidance of the Holy Spirit. I cannot doubt but that I have been blessed with a new divine light. I feel a different man from what I was a few months ago. The Bible is lit up with a new light.[86]

In 1869 he returned to New York and became pastor of the First Presbyterian Church of Roselle, New Jersey. In the meantime, his interest in the Psalms was stimulated when he was asked to help translate and edit the *Commentary on the Psalms* of Karl Bernhard Moll; the English translation appeared in 1872.[87] On the basis of this and other work, he was named professor of Hebrew and cognate languages at Union Theological Seminary in 1874.

I pause here to note that in 1880–1881 there was a heresy trial in Scotland that anticipated in many respects the trials that Charles Augustus Briggs (see below) would undergo in 1891–1893. The defendant in that trial was W. Robertson Smith (1846–1894), who at the age of twenty-four was appointed to the chair of Old Testament studies at Aberdeen's Free Church College. Smith was a biblical critic and an editor of the ninth edition of the *Encyclopaedia Britannica*, and it was his article on "Bible" in that work, especially his espousal there of the views of Graf and Wellhausen on the Pentateuch, that caused controversy. The result was his trial for heresy in the General Assembly of the Scottish Free Church. This trial was as much of a sensation in American Protestantism as the so-called Scopes "Monkey" Trial would be in 1925; the *New York Times* offered its readers the text of speeches delivered in Aberdeen.[88] Smith was removed from his position in Aberdeen, and in 1883 he was appointed professor of Arabic at the University of Cambridge. And it may be noted that one of his works, *The Religion of the Semites* (1889),[89] became a classic—it was important enough to be reprinted by the Meridian Library in 1956.

In 1890 a professorship in biblical theology was founded at Union Theological Seminary in memory of Robinson, and Charles Briggs became the first incumbent in that chair. At the time of his induction into this chair he was already widely suspect among conservatives for his views on biblical criticism, and the inaugural address he gave on January 21, 1891, with the title "The Authority of Holy Scripture," was a defining moment in the religious history of the United States. He stated, "It is the testimony of human experience in all ages that God manifests Himself to men, and gives certainty of His presence and authority. There are historically three great fountains of divine authority—the Bible, the Church and the Reason."[90] He continued:

Men are influenced by their temperaments and environments which of the three ways of access to God they may pursue. There are obstructions thrown up by the folly of men in each one of these avenues, and it is our duty as servants of the living God, to remove the stumbling-block out of the way of all earnest seekers after God, in the avenues most familiar to us.[91]

Briggs insisted that the doctrines of verbal inspiration, literal inerrancy, and prophecy as minute prediction actually represented barriers to the divine word.

Against all such timid defenses he called for a new critical vision of Christianity itself.

> Criticism is at work with knife and fire. Let us cut down everything that is dead and harmful, every kind of dead orthodoxy, every species of effete ecclesiasticism, all those dry and brittle fences that constitute denominationalism and are the barriers of Church Unity. Let us remove every encumbrance out of the way for a new life; the life of God is moving throughout Christendom, and the springtime of a new age is about to come upon us.[92]

The address was discussed in the secular press as well as in the religious press. Later that spring, the Presbytery of New York appointed an investigating committee "to consider the Inaugural Address and its relation to the Confession of Faith."[93]

The ensuing legal process took more than two years and was an intricate affair. Essentially, the (local) Presbytery of New York undertook a case against Charles Briggs; then the (national) General Assembly, in the spring of 1891, recommended that the appointment of Briggs to the Robinson chair at Union Seminary be vetoed. The New York presbytery heard the case in the fall of 1891 and dismissed the charges. Then the conservatives in the presbytery voted to appeal the decision of the presbytery not to the (state) Synod of New York but to the General Assembly. The 1892 General Assembly reversed the dismissal of the case in presbytery and remanded it to the presbytery for a new trial; so, in the fall of 1892, the presbytery heard the matter again, with new charges, including the charge that Briggs rejected the "verbal inspiration" and "inerrancy" of the Bible.

In this trial, as in earlier ones, Briggs held his ground, affirming his loyalty to Holy Scripture. He pointed out that Jerome, Augustine, Luther, and Calvin had freely admitted to errors in Scripture; this admission in no way constituted a compromise of biblical authority. He also held his ground in his use of legal arguments on Presbyterian procedure. But his opponents were deeply convinced that beneath Briggs's affirmations of doctrinal correctness he was undermining the faith they had known. No compromise was possible, because a sea change had come into Protestant religious discourse with the advent of literary-historical criticism of the Bible.[94]

The presbytery acquitted Charles Briggs of all charges, but then the prosecuting committee again filed an appeal to the General Assembly; and that assembly, in the spring of 1893, after lengthy consideration declared that they found

> that Charles A. Briggs has uttered, taught and propagated views, doctrines and teachings as set forth in the said charges contrary to the essential doctrine of Holy Scripture and the [Westminster] Standards, and in violation of his ordination vow. . . . Wherefore this General Assembly does hereby suspend Charles A. Briggs, the said appellee, from the office of minister in the Presbyterian Church in the United States of America.[95]

In the midst of all this, in 1892 the Board of Directors of Union Seminary issued a public statement announcing that, in the light of the recent enactments of the General Assembly, "the agreement (of 1870) between the Union Theological Seminary and the General Assembly of the Presbyterian Church should be, and hereby is, terminated."[96] Thereafter, Union Seminary was independent of any denominational affiliation.

This whole story may seem only distantly related to a study of the Psalms; but Charles Briggs was the outstanding American biblical scholar of his day, and his trials crystallized the issues of biblical scholarship for that day and for the decades ahead.

And we must understand that, during this whole period, remarkably, Briggs continued his contributions to scholarship. In 1883 he undertook to collaborate with Francis Brown of Union Seminary and Samuel R. Driver of Oxford University in a new edition of Gesenius's Hebrew lexicon, which had been put into English by Robinson. Briggs contributed especially the articles on Hebrew words of psychological and theological import, and the first section of what came to be called Brown–Driver–Briggs appeared in 1891; the complete lexicon was published in 1907,[97] and for his share in this work Briggs received the degree of Doctor of Letters by Oxford University. And, as we have already seen, the commentary on the Psalms (written with his daughter) appeared in 1906–1907.[98]

As I have already indicated, from the vantage point of present-day scholarship, the Briggs's commentary is wide of the mark in the dates assigned to various psalms: for example, of Psalm 29, which present-day scholars take to be one of the oldest psalms, probably adapted from a pre-Israelite (Canaanite) poem (see chapter 2), Briggs says, "The Ps. seems to belong to the Persian period subsequent to Nehemiah"[99] (that is, to the end of the fifth century or beginning of the fourth). He further dismembers psalms whose sections need to be heard together; for example, he separates Psalm 139 into three separate psalms.[100] Nevertheless, his commentary is still a mine of carefully gathered data of permanent usefulness.

The rest of Briggs's story may be quickly told. In 1898 he severed his ties with the New York presbytery, and in the spring of 1899 he was ordained in the Episcopal church. During these years he gave himself more and more to the ecumenical movement; he became convinced that a historical understanding of the Bible and of the Christian faith would lead forward-looking Christians into church union. Thus in 1901 (as we saw in chapter 12) he went to Rome to lend his support to Catholic "modernists," and in 1904 he left the Robinson chair to accept a new chair at Union Seminary, that of "Theological Encyclopedia and Symbolics."

It is not too much to say that it was the struggles of scholars such as Briggs that laid the groundwork for the kind of understanding of the Psalms that is set forth in this study.

Revision of the King James Version

I now turn more briefly to other developments among Protestants in the nineteenth century that bear on the Psalms. The first is the work on a revision of the King James Version. By the middle of the nineteenth century it was clear that with better knowledge of Hebrew and Greek, and particularly with the discovery, from Egyptian papyri that had come to light, that the Greek of the New Testament was not some kind of special holy dialect but simply the ordinary Greek of the first century C.E., a revision of the King James Version would be appropriate. In 1870 the Convocation of the (Anglican) Province of Canterbury decided to undertake "a revision of the Authorized Version of the Holy Scriptures."

At first there was an American committee working with the British committee, but communication between them proved cumbersome, and the result was a British revision, the so-called Revised Version, published in 1885. The committee was instructed to retain the vocabulary and diction of the King James Bible, working simply for greater accuracy. It was agreed that the parallel American committee could make light revisions in the direction of American usage, and that revision, published in 1901, was the so-called American Standard Version.

But it soon became clear that both revisions were backward steps, losing the cadences of the King James Bible and often introducing fresh archaisms. The revision did shift "Holy Ghost" to "Holy Spirit" in the New Testament, and typographically it displayed the poetry of the Old Testament, including that of the Psalms, in a poetic format. But the phrase "his mercy endureth for ever" in Psalm 118 became "his lovingkindness endureth for ever," and, astonishingly, the Hebrew name "Yahweh," rendered "the Lord" in the King James Version, became "Jehovah"—"Jehovah is my shepherd; I shall not want"—thereby perpetuating an erroneous rendering of that divine name. Though this version gained somewhat in accuracy, it never replaced the King James Version in the use and affection of English-speaking Christians.[101]

Paraphrases of the Psalms

In chapter 11 there was a description of metrical psalms that were developed in the sixteenth, seventeenth, and eighteenth centuries. Psalms continued to be paraphrased for singing in the nineteenth century, though not so profusely. I mention here a nineteenth-century paraphrase of Psalm 23 that is still to be found in current hymnals, "The King of love my shepherd is;"[102] the hymn was written by Henry Williams Baker (1821–1877) in 1868. Baker was an Anglican priest and hymnwriter who was the chief promoter of the collection *Hymns Ancient and Modern* (1861), a publication that ranks as one of the great events in the history of hymnody of English-speaking churches; by 1912 it had sold sixty million copies.[103] In the hymn in question, Baker followed the lead of Isaac Watts and deeply Christianized the psalm.

> The King of love my shepherd is,
>   Whose goodness faileth never;
> I nothing lack if I am his,
>   And he is mine for ever.
> Where streams of living water flow,
>   My ransomed soul he leadeth,
> And where the verdant pastures grow,
>   With food celestial feedeth.

Perverse and foolish oft I strayed,
  But yet in love he sought me,
And on his shoulder gently laid,
  And home, rejoicing, brought me.
In death's dark vale I fear no ill,
  With thee, dear Lord, beside me;
Thy rod and staff my comfort still,
  Thy cross before to guide me.
Thou spread'st a table in my sight;
  Thy unction grace bestoweth;
And O what transport of delight
  From thy pure chalice floweth!
And so through all the length of days
  Thy goodness faileth never:
Good Shepherd, may I sing thy praise
  Within thy house for ever.

Musical Works

Composers continued to draw on the Psalms for resources in musical works. For many composers two must do here, Felix Mendelssohn (1809–1847) and Johannes Brahms (1833–1897). Mendelssohn's ancestry was Jewish; his father, however, had him and his sister baptized into the Lutheran church as children (we saw in chapter 9 how many Jews in Germany in this period wished to adapt to the culture around them). Mendelssohn set many psalms to music: one thinks particularly of his setting of Psalm 42 for chorus, first performed in 1837.[104] And the lyrics of his oratorios "St. Paul" and "Elijah" likewise draw on verses from the Psalms.

Brahms was not a conventional Christian believer, but he drew on passages of the Bible for his "German Requiem," most wonderfully in the fourth section of that work, "Wie lieblich sind deine Wohnungen" (How lovely is your dwelling-place), using Ps. 84:2-3, 5 (1-2, 4).

Responsive Readings

Even given the enlargement in the knowledge of the nature of the Bible that became available to Christians, which has been chronicled in this chapter, one must not lose sight of the fact that the Psalms continued, as they had done from the beginning, to nourish the faith of Christians both in public and private worship.

Notable in this regard is a fresh way of reciting the Psalms in various churches in the United States that arose in the nineteenth century—"responsive readings" of the Psalms, by which verses or half-verses of a given psalm are read alternately by the worship leader and the congregation. This mode of recitation evidently began in Presbyterian churches. We recall that the tradition in Calvinist (Reformed and Presbyterian) congregations in the sixteenth, seventeenth, and eighteenth centuries was to sing metrical versions of the Psalms (see chapter 11). But at the end of the eighteenth century and in the nineteenth century, these metrical psalms were being displaced by hymns in the worship of many Presbyterian congregations, hymns such as those of Isaac Watts and Charles Wesley. By the end of the nineteenth century, the urge to retain a place for the Psalms in worship led to the innovation of reading them responsively.

A key figure in this development appears to have been Leonard W. Bacon (1830–1907), a Congregational minister who eventually became a historian of American Christianity. Bacon was a supply pastor in St. Peter's Presbyterian Church of Rochester, New York, in 1855; in that year there appeared a printed *Church Book of St. Peter's, Rochester*, containing responsive readings, and in later life Bacon claimed to have compiled them.[105]

Now, Anglican (and thus American Episcopalian) churches with choirs had been accustomed to double chants in chanting the Psalms: that is, each half of the choir recited half a verse, alternately. In that way the usual parallelism of the poetry of a given psalm was apparent (on parallelism, see chapter 4). But Presbyterians and others were accustomed to seeing the Psalms in printed Bibles with numbered verses, so the tendency was to separate the two parts verse by verse rather than by half-verses. That is the situation in the Presbyterian hymnal of 1895, the earliest hymnal I have located that offers printed responsive readings of psalms.[106]

Other denominational hymnals took up the practice,[107] as did nondenominational hymnals as well.[108] In all these hymnals the selection of responsive readings was just that, a *selection* of psalms deemed suitable for congregational use; often verses were omitted that were deemed unnecessary or unsuitable (such as Ps. 139: 19-22; see the Introduction), and often, too, two or more psalms would be combined into a single reading. (I discuss the appropriateness of this procedure in chapter 16.) It may also be noted in passing that responsive readings of other biblical passages began to be offered, even from such books as the Letter to the Romans, where alternate recitation seems hardly appropriate.

"Alleluia" and "Hallelujah"

I have had occasion to touch on the use through Christian history of the acclamation "Hallelujah" or "Alleluia" (see chapters 10 and 11). Now, a curious split took place in English usage in the nineteenth century: whereas "Alleluia" stayed completely within liturgy and worship, not only for Roman Catholics but for Anglicans and others as well, the form "Hallelujah" began to be used in secular contexts as an expression of joy, at first, no doubt, ironically. A transition point might have been in the refrain of that half secular expression of culture Protestantism, Julia Ward Howe's "Battle Hymn of the Republic" (1861)—"Glory, glory, hallelujah!" The word was used in mild mocking of the Salvation Army, which was founded in 1865; it was perhaps because the term figured prominently in Salvation Army hymns and preaching on street corners. Thus a sympathetic, popular account of the Salvation Army appeared in 1961 with the title *The Hallelujah Army*.[109] Slang phrases were current, such as "hallelujah-lass" for a young female member of the

Salvation Army and "hallelujah-stew" for the soup served at a Salvation Army hostel.[110]

A curious instance of secular use of the word is the hobo song "Hallelujah, I'm a Bum," which began to be sung at the turn of the twentieth century. The first stanza of this song goes:

> Oh, why don't you work
>> like other men do?
> How the hell can I work
>> when there's no work to do?
> Hallelujah, I'm a bum!
>> Hallelujah, bum again.
> Hallelujah, give us a hand-out
>> To revive us again.[111]

This song is a parody of a gospel hymn that appears in the Salvation Army hymnal, "My God, I am Thine." The first stanza goes:

> My God, I am Thine,
>> What a comfort divine,
> What a blessing to know
>> That my Jesus is mine!
> Hallelujah! send the glory!
>> Hallelujah, Amen!
> Hallelujah! send the glory!
>> Revive us again![112]

The parody "Hallelujah, I'm a Bum," it is said, was sung outside Salvation Army missions for many years,[113] and was picked up by members of the Industrial Workers of the World (IWW's), who made verses of their own for it and gave it a wide fame.[114] Curiously enough, the chorus of the gospel hymn may be found with different verses in the current hymnal of the National Baptists; the first stanza reads:

> We praise Thee, O God,
>> for the Son of Thy love,
> For Jesus who died
>> And is now gone above.[115]

The parody reminds us in any event that the expression "Hallelujah" has drifted a long way from the Psalms.

In this discussion of the use of the Psalms in the nineteenth century, I offer one last vignette. Rufus M. Jones (1863–1948) was a member of the Religious Society of Friends (Quakers) who became professor of philosophy at Haverford College in Pennsylvania and was instrumental in founding the American Friends Service Committee. He recalls his boyhood on a farm near China, Maine: when he was eight years old, he was offered a new pair of mittens if he read all the way through the Psalms.[116] The passion to read the whole book of Psalms, which bestirs some Jews in Jerusalem today (see chapter 9) and shaped for centuries the daily prayer of Roman Catholic priests and religious orders (see chapter 12), touched a nineteenth-century Quaker family in rural Maine as well.

NOTES

1. W. O. Carver, "Negroes (United States)," in *Encyclopaedia of Religion and Ethics* 9:292–93.

2. Kenneth Scott Latourette, *A History of the Expansion of Christianity*, vol. 4 (7 vols.; New York: Harper, 1937–45), chapter 9.

3. For the importance of this text, see Albert J. Raboteau, "Exodus, Ethiopia, and Racial Messianism: Texts and Contexts of African American Chosenness," in William R. Hutchison (ed.), *Chosen People Themes in Western Nationalist Movements, 1880–1920* (HTS; Minneapolis: Fortress, forthcoming); and see further Randall C. Bailey, "Africans in Old Testament Poetry and Narratives," in Cain Hope Felder (ed.), *Stony the Road We Trod: African American Biblical Interpretation* (Minneapolis: Fortress, 1991), 177–78.

4. John Shields (ed.), *The Collected Works of Phillis Wheatley* (New York: Oxford University Press, 1988), 175–76.

5. James Theodore Holly, "The Divine Plan of Human Redemption, in Its Ethnological Development," *AME Church Review* 1 (October 1884): 79–85; cited in Raboteau, "Exodus, Ethiopia, and Racial Messianism."

6. Benjamin E. Mays and Joseph W. Nicholson, *The Negro's Church* (New York: Russell & Russell, 1933), 69–70.

7. See, conveniently, Latourette, *History of the Expansion of Christianity*.

8. Ibid., vol. 3.

9. Ibid., 3:223; and see, in detail, Edmund A. De Schweinitz, *The Life and Times of David Zeisberger* (Philadelphia: Lippincott, 1871).

10. Ibid., 689, 691.

11. Latourette calls the nineteenth century "the great century"; see the title of his *History of the Expansion of Christianity*, vols. 4–6.

12. Ibid., 4:68–69.

13. Ibid., 4:68–69.

14. Ibid., 4:70.

15. Ibid., 4:79–82.

16. The fullest account of Judson's work from the vantage point of this study is Francis Wayland, *A Memoir of the Life and Labors of the Rev. Adoniram Judson, D.D.* (Boston: Phillips, Sampson, 1853). I have also drawn on Stacy R. Warburton, *Eastward! The Story of Adoniram Judson* (New York: Round Table, 1937); and Courtney Anderson, *To the Golden Shore: The Life of Adoniram Judson* (Boston: Little, Brown & Co., 1956; reprint, Valley Forge, Pa.: Judson, 1987).

17. Anderson, *To the Golden Shore*, 54–56; cf. Warburton, *Eastward!*, 55.

18. Anderson, *To the Golden Shore*, 184; Latourette, *History of the Expansion of Christianity*, 4:82–83.

19. Warburton, *Eastward!*, 65.

20. Latourette, *History of the Expansion of Christianity*, 6:229.

21. Warburton, *Eastward!*, 65.

22. Ibid., 143.

23. Ibid., 102, 110.

24. *American Baptist Magazine* 8 (1828):129. (This journal, for vols. 1–4, is called *American Baptist Missionary Magazine and Intelligencer*; for vols. 16–29, *Baptist Missionary Magazine*.)

25. *American Baptist Magazine* 11 (1831):207–8.

26. Ibid., 343–44.

27. Latourette, *History of the Expansion of Christianity*, 6:229.

28. Warburton, *Eastward!*, 146.

29. Ibid., 145.

30. Ibid., 144–45.

31. For an appreciative sketch of Moses Stuart, see G. Ernest Wright, "The Phenomenon of American Archaeology in the Near East," in James A. Sanders (ed.), *Near Eastern Archaeology in the Twentieth Century* (Garden City, N.Y.: Doubleday, 1970), 5.

32. Samuel Horsley, *Book of Psalms: Translated from the Hebrew, with Notes* (2 vols.; London, 1815); see Warburton, *Eastward!*, 151–52.

33. Wayland, *Life and Labors*, 2:129.

34. Ibid., 2:160.

35. Ibid., 2:161.

36. Warburton, *Eastward!*, 154.

37. Cited in Wayland, *Life and Labors*, 2:168.

38. H. C. Willans, "Translators' Conference in Burma," *Bible Translator* 4 (1953):22.

39. Warburton, *Eastward!*, 155 n.

40. Willans, "Translators' Conference," 24.

41. Gordon H. Luce, "Three Major Problems in Taungthu Translation," *Bible Translator* 1 (1950):153.

42. *Baptist Missionary Magazine* 13 (1833):201.

43. *Baptist Missionary Magazine* 24 (1844):200.

44. *Baptist Missionary Magazine* 19 (1839): 141.

45. Francis Mason (trans.), *The Holy Bible, Containing the Old and New Testaments, in Sgau Karen* (Tavoy: Karen Mission Press, 1853).

46. I cannot offer a description of all the church communities using Syriac; see, in detail, Latourette, *History of the Expansion of Christianity*, 2:263–85.

47. For the mission, see, briefly, Latourette, *History of the Expansion of Christianity*, 6:57–58. For details of the early years, see esp. Justin Perkins, *A Residence of Eight Years in Persia, among the Nestorian Christians* (Andover, Mass.: Allen, Morrill and Ardwell, 1843); for later developments in the mission, see the issues of *Missionary Herald*.

48. Perkins, *Eight Years in Persia*, 258.

49. Ibid., 297–98.

50. Ibid., 246; see, in more detail, *Missionary Herald* 32 (1836):296–97.

51. Perkins, *Eight Years in Persia*, 258.

52. *Missionary Herald* 34 (1838):7.

53. One notes in passing that he and I share the same curiously spelled surname. He and I are both descended from John Holladay, who died in 1742 in Spotsylvania County, Virginia.

54. *Missionary Herald* 35 (1839):7.

55. Ibid., 449.

56. *Missionary Herald* 37 (1841):6.

57. Perkins, *Eight Years in Persia*, 444.

58. Ibid., 446.

59. Ibid., 456.

60. Ibid., 457.

61. *Missionary Herald* 43 (1847):128–29.

62. Hans W. Debrunner, *A History of Christianity in Ghana* (Accra: Waterville, 1967), 144; cited in Lamin Sanneh, *Translating the Message: The Missionary Impact on Culture* (American Society of Missiology Series 13; Maryknoll, N.Y.: Orbis Books, 1989), 181.

63. These statistics are taken from the United Bible Society report for 1989. For an accessible presentation of the enterprise of Bible translation across the world, see Eugene A. Nida, *God's Word in Man's Language* (New York: Harper, 1952).

64. Sanneh, *Translating the Message*, 29–31.

65. For a classic presentation of linguistics, see Leonard Bloomfield, *Language* (New York: Holt, 1933).

66. There is an enormous literature on these matters. I mention, almost at random, Eugene A. Nida, *Bible Translating: An Analysis of Principles and Procedures, with Special Reference to Aboriginal Languages* (New York: American Bible Society, 1947); Ernst R. Wendland, *Language, Society, and Bible Translation* (The Bible Society of South Africa, 1985); and the United Bible Societies Monograph Series, such as Philip C. Stine (ed.), *Issues in Bible Translation* (United Bible Societies Monograph Series 3; London: United Bible Societies, 1988).

67. Anna E. Lerbak, "Translating the Psalms to Uruund," *Bible Translator* 5 (1954):84–87.

68. Ibid., 85.

69. Elmer A. Leslie, *The Psalms: Translated and Interpreted in the Light of Hebrew Life and Worship* (New York and Nashville: Abingdon-Cokesbury, 1949).

70. Lerbak, "Translating the Psalms," 87.

71. See Charles C. Gillispie, *Genesis and Geology: The Impact of Scientific Discoveries upon Religious Beliefs in the Decades before Darwin* (Harvard Historical Studies 58; Cambridge: Harvard University Press, 1951; reprint, Harper Torchbooks 51; New York: Harper, 1959).

72. For a readable account of the impact of Darwin's work on religion at the time, esp. through the writing and speaking of Thomas H. Huxley, see William Irvine, *Apes, Angels, and Victorians: The Story of Darwin, Huxley, and Evolution* (New York: McGraw-Hill, 1955).

73. F. Max Müller (ed.), *Sacred Books of the East* (50 volumes; Oxford: Oxford University Press, 1879–1910).

74. See, e.g., John A. Wilson, *Signs and Wonders upon Pharaoh* (Chicago: University of Chicago Press, 1964), 14–17.

75. See, e.g., Seton Lloyd, *Foundations in the Dust: A Story of Mesopotamian Exploration* (Harmondsworth: Penguin, 1955), esp. chap. 7. For more detail, see Arnold C. Brackman, *The Luck of Nineveh: In Search of the Lost Assyrian Empire* (New York: Van Nostrand Reinhold, 1978).

76. See, e.g., Wright, "American Archaeology," 3–8.

77. For a readable account of these decipherments, see Philip E. Cleator, *Lost Languages* (New York: John Day, 1959). For Champollion, see Wilson, *Signs and Wonders*, 17–19; for Rawlinson, see Lloyd, *Foundations in the Dust*, 91–96.

78. Lloyd, *Foundations in the Dust*, 179–80.

79. For Gesenius's work, see John W. Rogerson, *Old Testament Criticism in the Nineteenth Century* (Philadelphia: Fortress, 1985), 50–57.

80. For Strauss's life and work, see Richard S. Cromwell, *David Friedrich Strauss and His Place in Modern Thought* (Fairlawn, N.J.: Burdick, 1974); Horton Harris, *David Friedrich Strauss and His Theology* (Cambridge: Cambridge University Press, 1973).

81. For the work and influence of Wellhausen, see Rogerson, *Old Testament Criticism*, 257–89.

82. Charles Augustus Briggs and Emilie Grace Briggs, *A Critical and Exegetical Commentary on the Book of Psalms* (New York: Charles Scribner's Sons, 1906–7), 1:211–12.

83. For a brief biography of Briggs, see *Dictionary of American Biography*, 3:40–41; for background and interpretation I have drawn on Mark S. Massa, *Charles Augustus Briggs and the Crisis of Historical Criticism* (Minneapolis: Fortress, 1990). Massa offers a generous bibliography of primary and secondary sources.

84. Massa, *Charles Augustus Briggs*, 30–31.

85. Cited in ibid., 29.

86. Ibid., 37.

87. Karl Bernhard Moll, *Der Psalter* (Bielefeld and Leipzig: Velhagen und Klasing, 1869–71); Carl Bernhard Moll, *The Psalms* (Commentary on the Holy Scriptures, Old Testament, 9; New York: Scribner and Armstrong, 1872).

88. Massa, *Charles Augustus Briggs*, 17–21; see further Rogerson, *Old Testament Criticism*, 275–84.

89. William Robertson Smith, *Lectures on the Religion of the Semites* (New York: Appleton, 1889).

90. Cited in Massa, *Charles Augustus Briggs*, 87.

91. Cited in ibid., 88.

92. Cited in ibid., 89.

93. Ibid., 93.

94. Ibid., 93–108.

95. Cited in ibid., 108–9.

96. Ibid., 103–4.

97. Francis Brown, Samuel R. Driver, and Charles A. Briggs, *A Hebrew and English Lexicon of the Old Testament* (Oxford: Clarendon, 1907).

98. Briggs, *Commentary*.

99. Briggs, *Commentary*, 1:252.

100. Ibid., 2:491–93.

101. See Luther A. Weigle, "English Versions since 1611," in S. L. Greenslade (ed.), *The Cambridge History of the Bible*, vol. 3: *The West from the Reformation to the Present Day* (Cambridge: Cambridge University Press, 1963), 371–74.

102. *Pilgrim Hymnal* (Boston: Pilgrim 1958), no. 80; Inter-Lutheran Commission on Worship, *Lutheran Book of Worship* (Minneapolis: Augsburg, 1978), no. 456; *The (Episcopal) Hymnal 1982* (New York: The [Episcopal] Church Hymnal Corporation, 1982), nos. 645, 646; *The United Methodist Hymnal: Book of United Methodist Worship* (Nashville: United Methodist Publishing House, 1989), no. 138; *The Presbyterian Hymnal: Hymns, Psalms, and Spiritual Songs* (Louisville: Westminster/John Knox, 1990), no. 171.

103. *Hymns Ancient and Modern* (London: Novello, 1861). The work has been expanded and reprinted many times; see the discussion in "Hymn, Section IV, Protestant," in *The New Grove Dictionary of Music and Musicians* (London: Macmillan, 1980), 8:850.

104. Opus 42.

105. Julius Melton, *Presbyterian Worship in America: Changing Patterns since 1787* (Richmond: John Knox, 1967), 94–96.

106. *The Hymnal* (Philadelphia: Presbyterian Board of Publication and Sabbath School Work, 1895).

107. *The Methodist Hymnal* (New York: Methodist Book Concern, 1905).

108. *Hymns of Worship and Service* (New York: Century, 1905); Ivan L. Bennett (ed.), *The Hymnal: Army and Navy* (New York: Barnes, 1942).

109. Harry E. Neal, *The Hallelujah Army* (Philadelphia: Chilton, 1961).

110. See Eric Partridge, *A Dictionary of Slang and Unconventional English* (New York: Macmillan, 1984), 523.

111. For six stanzas, see Carl Sandburg, *The American Songbag* (1927; reprint, New York: Harcourt Brace Jovanovich, 1955); or Olin Downes and Elie Siegmeister, *A Treasury of American Song* (New York: Howell Soskin, 1940), 330–31.

112. For three stanzas, see William Booth (comp.), *Salvation Army Songs* (New York: Reliance Trading, 1901), no. 248.

113. Downes and Siegmeister, *American Song*, 331.

114. Sandburg, *American Songbag*.

115. *The New National Baptist Hymnal* (Nashville: National Baptist Publishing Board, 1977), no. 18.

116. Rufus M. Jones, *A Boy's Religion from Memory* (Philadelphia: Ferris & Leach, 1902), 42–43.

14

The Psalms
in the Churches Today:
Protestants and Roman Catholics

In this chapter I try to summarize the understanding and the use of psalms by Protestants roughly since the First World War and by Roman Catholics from the time of the Second Vatican Council. Even though the time span covered for Protestants is more extended than for Catholics, both branches of Christendom experienced a maturing of biblical scholarship and produced a range of new translations during these periods, and it is appropriate to treat the two branches of the church together because of the ways in which they have shared in both biblical scholarship and in lectionaries. Here I concentrate on "official" or "churchly" uses of the Psalms, and then in chapters 15 through 19, which will deal with current theological issues, I touch on several efforts to employ the Psalms in fresh and imaginative ways.

It is not easy to sum up current developments within the churches, both because of their variety and because of our own closeness to them. I begin by describing two major developments in scholarship on the Psalms in this century,[1] one by a Protestant and the other by a Roman Catholic. Next I discuss the array of recent biblical translations, taking them as much as possible in chronological order. Then I turn to describe the work of the Second Vatican Council with respect to two matters: the new freedom for biblical scholarship and the changes in the liturgy, both the eucharistic liturgy (the Mass) and the daily office (now called the "Liturgy of the Hours"). Next I discuss the movement toward a common lectionary, one shared by both Catholics and Protestants.[2] Then I discuss recent paraphrases of psalms that are part of current worship, both in hymnals and in such ventures as the Taizé community, closing with a few remarks on musical compositions that employ the Psalms.

Scholarship on the Psalms

In chapter 13 we surveyed the rediscovery of the ancient Near East by biblical scholars and the attempt to see the Psalms in their original context, exemplified by the commentary of Charles Augustus Briggs and Emilie Grace Briggs. In that survey I suggested points at which that commentary was inadequate by present-day standards.

Progress in the study of the Psalms moved out in a fresh direction in the work of Hermann Gunkel (1862–1932), a professor in various universities in Germany. Gunkel's interest was not so much in historical or literary criticism as in what came to be called "form criticism": he investigated the different "categories" or "types" (German, *Gattungen*) of psalms—or, if we use the French word, the *genres* of the Psalms. Gunkel classified the various psalms into the genres of "hymns," "songs of Yahweh's enthronement" (see below), "laments of the community," "royal psalms," "laments of the individual," "thanksgivings of the individual," and various minor genres. By and large this classification has become standard for scholars. And Gunkel linked the study of these genres with an attempt to reconstruct the life situation that brought a given genre into existence and kept it in being. This is the orientation that I have assumed in my presentation of the Psalms in chapters 3 through 5, and I return to the matter in chapter 15.

Gunkel began his work on the Psalms with a little book called *Ausgewählte Psalmen* (Selected Psalms), published in 1904; the fourth revised edition of this work appeared in 1917.[3] He then produced two monumental works on the Psalms, *Die Psalmen* (The Psalms), a commentary on all of the Psalms, published in 1926;[4] and *Einleitung in die Psalmen* (Introduction to the Psalms), completed after his death by Joachim Begrich (1933), in which he analyzed the various genres of the Psalms.[5]

Gunkel's work was extended by such scholars as Sigmund Mowinckel (1884–1965), a Norwegian; his great work was published in Norwegian in 1951.[6] Mowinckel stressed the place of the Psalms in the cultus (community worship) and extended Gunkel's theory of a festival of the reenthronement of Yahweh at the turn of the new year, a theory stimulated by Babylonian practice; this theory is now rejected by most scholars.[7] I also mention here the commentary of Artur Weiser (b. 1893),[8] who theorized that many psalms were related to a covenant renewal ceremony in the autumn, a theory that likewise has not held ground.[9] Current work in the form criticism of the Psalms is perhaps best represented by the work of Erhard S. Gerstenberger, a German who taught for many years in the United States and Brazil.[10]

The other fresh shift in Psalms research was stimulated by the discovery, beginning in 1928, of the pre-Israelite Ugaritic texts (see chapter 2); the scholar who has written most insistently on the importance of these ancient texts for an understanding of the Psalms was Mitchell Dahood (1922–1982), who was a Jesuit scholar at the Biblical Institute in Rome. Though his commentary on the Psalms (1966–1970)[11] is an extreme and experimental piece of work,[12] it has forced scholars to rethink their understanding of the language of the Psalms (see, again, chapter 2).

Fresh Translations of the Bible

This century has seen an unprecedented array of biblical translations, not only in English but in other languages as well. These translations have come about because of the confluence of two perceptions: first, that the diction of the translations of earlier centuries has become antiquated and misleading; and second, that the steadily increasing fund of new information in biblical scholarship needs to be reflected in the wording of the translations now in use. I deal with English translations first.

I described in chapter 13 the effort in the second half of the nineteenth century to revise the King James Bible that produced the (British) Revised Version of 1885 and the American Revised Version of 1901. Then, in the period between the First and Second World Wars, several "unofficial" translations appeared, of which two are notable. The first was that of James Moffatt (1870–1944), a Scottish scholar who came to the United States and taught at Union Theological Seminary. His New Testament first appeared in 1918 and his Old Testament in 1922; his final revision was published in 1934.[13] The second is the so-called American or Chicago Translation; Edgar J. Goodspeed (1871–1962) translated the New Testament (1923) and the Apocrypha (1938), while the Old Testament, which appeared in 1939, was the work of four scholars: J. M. Powis Smith (1866–1932), Theophile J. Meek (1881–1966), Leroy Waterman (1875–1972), and Alexander R. Gordon (1872–1930).[14] Both translations attempted to use current English: the pronoun "thou" and analogous forms continued to be used to address God, but in addressing a single human being "you" was used. Psalm 42:2 (1) was translated by Moffatt as "The deer is panting for the stream, and, O God, I pant for thee"; in the American Translation the verse is "As a deer longs for the water-courses, So my whole being longs for thee, O God." Here the King James Version "hart" has become "deer," and the somewhat misleading word "soul" in the King James Version is rendered as the simple pronoun "I" by Moffatt and by "my whole being" in the American Translation. (For a further discussion on the English translation "soul," see chapter 17.)

These translations were never generally adopted by congregations in public worship, but they were taken up widely for private use, and their circulation accustomed readers to a Bible in modern diction. It should also be noted that these translators and others like them published a great number of guides for Bible reading, such works as Goodspeed's *How to Read the Bible*.[15]

I now turn to the story of the Revised Standard Version. In 1928 the copyright of the American Standard Version was acquired by the International Council of Religious Education and thus passed into the ownership of the churches of the United States and Canada; the council included forty major denominations. The council appointed a committee of fifteen scholars to inquire whether further revision was necessary. Among that group, as it happened, were Moffatt, Goodspeed, Smith, Waterman, and Gordon. That committee recommended and in 1937 the council voted for a thorough revision of the American Standard Version; the resultant revision would therefore be an "official" translation, at least to the extent that it would be sponsored by a division of what became the National Council of Churches of Christ in the United States of America. The revision was called the Revised Standard Version; the New Testament appeared in 1946 and the Old Testament in 1952, and the Apocrypha followed in 1957.[16] This translation used "thou" and "you" as Moffatt and the American Translation had done, "thou" in addressing God and "you" in addressing one or more human beings.

This version was immediately popular; congregations chose it for their pulpit Bibles, so that in the 1950s and 1960s the KJV and the RSV were the major contenders for the loyalty of Protestant Christians—a divided loyalty symbolized by the layout of the commentary set called *The Interpreter's Bible*,[17] in which the texts of the KJV and the RSV appear in parallel columns at the top of the page. An edition of the Synoptic Gospels in the Revised Standard Version, exhibited in parallel, appeared;[18] a concordance to the RSV was prepared.[19] Denominational hymnals that printed responsive readings from the Psalms used the RSV,[20] so that the wording of the Psalms in this version, in particular, became familiar to worshipers.

Given the lack of an adequate English translation of the Bible for Roman Catholics in this period, Cardinal Cushing of Boston in 1966 gave his *imprimatur* to an unaltered edition of the RSV,[21] and it was a major event when in 1973 the so-called Common Bible, a Protestant–Catholic edition of the Revised Standard Version, was published.[22]

I described in chapter 12 the French *Bible de Jérusalem* (1948–1954), produced by the Dominicans at the École Biblique in Jerusalem. A parallel English version, the Jerusalem Bible, appeared in 1966;[23] in the years since its appearance it has become a favorite with English-speaking Roman Catholics who are serious about Bible reading, and with many non-Catholics as well. It was the earliest English translation with a large circulation to shift from "thou" to "you" in addressing God, and, like its French antecedent, it used "Yahweh" instead of "the Lord" (Ps. 23:1: "Yahweh is my shepherd"; v. 5: "You prepare a table before me in the presence of my enemies"). The French antecedent was revised and appeared in 1973, a Spanish edition appeared in 1976,[24] and the English version was revised in the light of the French revision and appeared as the New Jerusalem Bible in 1985.[25]

In Great Britain there was a parallel urge for a revision of the King James Version and the Revised Version, and in 1947 a committee representing several church bodies was appointed to prepare such a Bible. The resultant version, called the New English Bible, was published in sections, the New Testament in 1961 and the Old Testament and Apocrypha in 1970.[26] Whereas the RSV tended to stay within the tradition of the KJV and translate as much word for word as the idiom of English allows, the NEB was much freer in seeking a "dynamic equivalent": roughly, the answer to the question, "How would Isaiah or Paul say it if either of them were writing in English instead of Hebrew or Greek?" (I shall discuss this matter further in chapter 17.) The result is sometimes startling: in Ps. 23:5, "Thou hast richly bathed my head with oil"; in Ps. 139:3a, "Thou hast traced my journey and my resting places." And one further matter should be mentioned in connection with the Psalms: the NEB omitted the superscriptions (see chapter 6), given the assumption that these were not part of the original text of the Psalms. This decision was widely criticized (see on the Revised English Bible, below).

In the meantime, English-speaking Roman Catholics found themselves needing an English Bible to meet the needs of Catholic liturgy and the recitation of the daily office in English, in response to the shift from Latin to vernacular languages after the Second Vatican Council. The Confraternity of Christian Doctrine, a committee of American bishops, had issued, we recall (chapter 12), a translation of the New Testament in 1941, but work had lapsed on the Old Testament. Now that Roman Catholic scholars were completely free to translate from the original languages, work was renewed in the Old Testament and completed in 1969; the full Bible in this version, given the designation the New American Bible, appeared in 1970.[27] This translation, like the Jerusalem Bible, abandoned "thou" in addressing God (Ps. 23:5: "You spread the table before me in the sight of my foes"). It may be added that a revision of the New Testament appeared in 1987, and the Psalms of this version have recently been revised.[28]

During the same period, Pope Paul VI commissioned a revision of the Latin Vulgate. This "New Vulgate" was published in 1979, after the Second Vatican Council; I discuss it below.

And at this point we must remind ourselves of the appearance of a fresh English translation of the Old Testament by American Jewish scholars (1962–1982), a version now referred to as *Tanakh* (see chapter 9).[29] It, too, abandoned "thou" for God (Ps. 23:5: "You spread a table for me in full view of my enemies").

Two other English versions that appeared in the 1970s should be mentioned here. The first is the so-called Good News Bible, or Today's English Version, sponsored by the American Bible Society and intended particularly for those for whom English is a second language or for those who have difficulty in reading; the New Testament, called *Good News for Modern Man*, appeared in 1966; the Old Testament, in 1976; and the Apocrypha in 1979.[30] The second is the New International Version, sponsored by the New York Bible Society, which appeared in 1978.[31]

And it must be noted that, in Great Britain, the New English Bible has been substantially revised as the so-called Revised English Bible in 1989.[32] It, too, has abandoned "thou" for God; and it has restored the superscriptions of the Psalms, omitted by the NEB.

I now return to the translation committee that produced the RSV. This committee never disbanded, and in the years after 1952 it dealt with minor revisions. But it became clear that more than minor revisions were becoming necessary—for example, given the example of the JB and the NAB, the pronoun "thou" for God had begun to seem more and more out of date. So in 1974 the committee of the National Council of Churches that was charged with policy for the RSV authorized the preparation of a full revision of the RSV; the result is the so-called New Revised Standard Version (1990). Two notable features of this revision are the shift from the pronoun "thou" to "you" and the attempt to employ phraseology for human beings that is not gender-specific, when that is appropriate (Ps. 1:1: "blessed are those" rather than "blessed is the man"); for this issue, see the discussion in chapter 18. But this revision is an improvement in hundreds of other details.

The NRSV has now been adopted for the responsive readings in the new United

Methodist hymnal,[33] and doubtless other hymnals will follow suit; and there is now a concordance of the version.[34]

Let us pause here to ponder this outpouring of fresh translations; three matters call for consideration. The first is a double phenomenon not generally recognized by the public: both that in several instances biblical scholars have served in more than one translation effort, and that the translation panels of both the NAB and the NRSV were interconfessional. Thus Harry M. Orlinsky (1908–1992), a professor at Hebrew Union College–Jewish Institute of Religion, came on the translation committee of the RSV in 1945 and continued in the revision work of the NRSV; in the meantime, he was one of the major translators of the *Tanakh*. Similarly, George W. MacRae (1928–1985), Bruce Vawter (1921–1986), and Roland E. Murphy (b. 1917) worked on the NAB and then came on the committee for the NRSV—MacRae and Vawter in 1972 and Murphy in 1976. It is important to stress that, though one might casually assume that the NRSV has been solely a Protestant effort, this has not been the case. As a matter of fact, the National Council of Churches includes Orthodox churches in its membership, and one Orthodox scholar, Demetrios Constantelos, served as a translator; furthermore, even though Roman Catholics are not part of the National Council of Churches, Roman Catholics such as MacRae, Vawter, and Murphy participated in the work of the translation. By contrast, three Protestants were part of the translation team of the (Catholic) NAB—Frank M. Cross (b. 1921), David Noel Freedman (b. 1922), and James A. Sanders (b. 1927).

Second, as one could imagine, translators are glad to borrow phrasing from earlier Bibles. I can affirm that translators for the NRSV constantly had an eye on the JB, the NEB, the NAB, and available sections of the new Jewish version as they worked. Their effort was simply to find the best rendering in English, so similarities of phrasing are no accident.

Third, for every Protestant congregation that welcomes a variety of translations there are ten that manifest frustration and bewilderment at this multiplicity, a mood nicely caught by the title of a book published in 1974 by Broadman Press (the publishing arm of the Southern Baptist Convention), *What Bible Can You Trust?*[35] Even Protestants who understand the necessity of revisions and fresh translations wish that they could have a standard text for the memorization of passages, so that repetition can do its work in their awareness. Again, there is often a controversy as to which translation a congregation will adopt for normal use. It can happen, for example, that an RSV pulpit Bible was donated years ago to a congregation in someone's memory; shall that Bible be replaced by a pulpit Bible of the NRSV, and if so, what is to be done with the old one? Such questions can vex a board of deacons.

Now, as I have already indicated, similar new translations in the last half-century have appeared in other major European languages; I can mention here only a few. The Netherlands Bible Society commissioned a new translation in the early decades of this century; the New Testament appeared in 1939 and the full Bible in 1951, the so-called *Nieuwe Vertaling* (New Translation).[36] It began to replace the old *Statenvertaling* (States-General translation) of 1637 in the various Protestant churches in Holland in a way analogous to the adoption of the RSV in the United States. But by now this "New Translation" is perceived as out of date, and there are plans underway for its revision.[37]

A striking development for both French-speaking and German-speaking Christians has been the production in the last thirty years of joint Protestant–Catholic translations: in French, the so-called *Traduction oecuménique de la Bible* (Ecumenical Translation of the Bible) was published in 1976;[38] in German, the *Einheitsübersetzung* (Unity Translation) appeared in 1980.[39] And, as we noted in chapter 13, the translation of the Bible into more of the whole range of languages across the world has continued at an ever-increasing rate.

The Second Vatican Council: The Mass, the Divine Office, and the "New Vulgate"

The Second Vatican Council was a watershed event for the Roman Catholic Church. The Council, an assemblage of Roman Catholic bishops, was called by Pope John XXIII; he described the intent of the council by the Italian word *aggiornamento*, which means "renovation" or "modernization" but with the implication of the dawning of a new day.

Through the decisions of the council the Psalms have emerged with new power in Catholic liturgy, and by the achievement of shared lectionaries, congregations of many Protestant churches have been encouraged to incorporate the Psalms into their worship as well.

The council met in four sessions, from 1962 to 1965, during which time John XXIII died (1963) and was succeeded by Pope Paul VI. Among a whole array of decisions, there were three interrelated ones that bear on the use of the Psalms: new freedom for Catholic scholars in biblical studies; the use of vernacular languages and the reform of the Mass; and the new prayers of the hours (formerly known as the daily office). I discuss these matters in that order.

As to the matter of freedom to pursue biblical studies, we recall the discussion in chapter 12 regarding the establishment of the Pontifical Biblical Institute in Rome; the struggle of Catholic biblical scholars who had adopted the historical-critical method to pursue their scholarship freely, a struggle centered in the United States in the Catholic Biblical Association; and the issuing in 1943 of the papal encyclical *Divino afflante Spiritu*, which freed biblical scholars to work from the original Hebrew and Greek texts. But there continued to be powerful voices in the Roman hierarchy against the new learning. To take one example: in 1961 the then-apostolic delegate to the United States, Archbishop Egidio Vagnozzi, delivered a baccalaureate speech at Marquette University in Milwaukee in which he described a dangerous movement among some Catholic intellectuals "to build a bridge between modern secular thought and Catholic thought, even to the point of digressing from positions traditionally accepted in the past." He referred to the "dispute amongst Catholic scholars concerning the idea of history as applied to both the Old and New Testaments"; he thought exegetes should not "insist on presenting as definitive truth—to be accepted by all right-thinking people— theories and opinions which can receive the definitive stamp of truthfulness only from the 'magisterium' of the Church"; and he concluded by stating that the "the Sacred Books of the Bible are too basically fundamental, too basically essential to be left to the individual and private interpretation of even a large number of scholars."[40]

In the same way, the Biblical Institute in Rome had come under increasing attack during the late 1950s.[41] In all this, the nature of the Psalms was rarely at issue; inevitably, the center of these storms was the question of the literal historicity of the Gospels.

During the first session of the Second Vatican Council, a "schema" on the sources of revelation was offered; it aroused so much opposition that it was withdrawn after a little more than a month.[42] During the second session the schema was still being revised and was not submitted to the bishops for a vote, but meanwhile, at that same session, an important discussion was underway on religious liberty.[43] Then, during the time when the third session was meeting (April 1964), the Biblical Commission issued an important instruction on the truth of the Gospels; in it the commission gave due regard to the genre of the Gospels, that is, their origin in apostolic preaching, and the wording of this instruction fed into the debate on the schema on revelation.[44] The schema would not be voted on until the fourth session of the council, by which time new members were named to the Biblical Commission who were sympathetic to biblical scholarship. It was on November 18, 1964, that the bishops approved the Constitution of Divine Revelation, *Dei Verbum* (The word of God).[45]

Then, on December 7 of that year, the bishops accepted the revised text on religious liberty, *Dignitatis Humanae Personae* (Of the dignity of the human person). These two schemas, taken together, allowed the maturing of Roman Catholic biblical scholarship. One fruit of that scholarship in the United States was *The Jerome Biblical Commentary* (1968), prepared entirely by scholars of the Catholic Biblical Association;[46] another was the NAB (1970), already described.

In regard to liturgical renewal, this notion had taken hold in the Roman Catholic Church at the turn of the twentieth century—indeed, a long time before that. We noted in chapter 12 the effort of the emperor Ferdinand at the Council of Trent for a vernacular Mass, and the first bishop of Baltimore, John Carroll (1735–1815), was interested in the same matter.[47]

But by the turn of the twentieth century a variety of trends that became known as the "liturgical movement" were underway. Just as biblical scholars had begun to investigate biblical material historically, so liturgical scholars began to rediscover the existence of liturgical patterns that were earlier than the patterns of the late medieval period that had been confirmed at the Council of Trent; it began to be clear that the Mass is not a sacrifice to be performed by the priest and watched by the congregation but rather a celebration of the whole church, the mystical body of Christ, consisting of priests and people, who should all have part in it.[48] The way was prepared (for example, by the liturgical commission of American bishops, which was organized in 1958)[49] for the first document of Vatican II, the *Constitution on the Liturgy (Sacrosanctum Concilium)*, issued December 4, 1963; it was an extraordinary document, being published immediately, for example, by the *New York Times*.[50] The council ordered a reform of the liturgy, ruling that "full active participation by the people, demanded by the very nature of liturgy," should be "the aim to be considered before all else" as their "right and duty by reason of their baptism."[51] Pope Paul VI thereupon appointed a special commission to revise the liturgy; the system of lections (readings) in the liturgy of the word (*Ordo lectionum Missae:* "The order of readings of the Mass") was completed in 1969, and the details of the new missal and the new daily office (now called "Liturgy of the Hours") were completed in 1970.[52] The shift to the new pattern of the Mass was initiated gradually, beginning in 1964, but the completed *Sacramentary* was introduced for the First Sunday of Advent in 1974, and the Liturgy of the Hours on the First Sunday of Advent in 1977.[53]

I first discuss the Mass, and deal only with the changes that bear on the Psalms. The liturgical texts, as we know, are now in the vernacular language. At the beginning of the Mass, just after the entrance of the priest, there is an "entrance antiphon"—a verse, usually taken from the Psalms, that may be recited in unison by the the priest and the whole congregation. The liturgy of the word (see chapter 10) now includes a more extensive reading of Scripture than in the Mass from the Council of Trent (compare chapter 12).[54] The readings for Sunday Mass form a three-year cycle, and there are for this Mass three readings: the first is chosen from the Old Testament, the Book of Acts, or the Book of Revelation; the second is from the Epistles; and the third is from the Gospels. The readings for the daily Mass are in a two-year cycle, the first reading being from the Old Testament or from the New Testament other than the Gospels, and the second from the Gospels. And after the first reading, whether in Sunday Mass or daily Mass, there is a "responsorial psalm"—that is, a psalm or sizable section of a psalm, read by the reader or sung by the cantor or choir, usually in three or four sections, with an "antiphon" (congregational response) that is taken from the same psalm. The text of this psalm is usually chosen to "fit" in some way with one or more of the other readings; it is not selected arbitrarily. The reader (or cantor or choir) begins the responsorial psalm by reciting (or chanting or singing) the antiphon, which is then repeated by the congregation; the reader (or cantor or choir) then reads (or chants or sings) roughly two verses of the psalm, whereupon the congregation repeats the antiphon; and so on, to the end. Typical is the treatment of Psalm 18. The antiphon is "I love you, O Lord, my strength" (v. 2 [1]). The text that is then read or sung consists of vv. 2-3 (1-2), followed by the congregation saying or singing the antiphon; vv. 4 (3) and 47 (46), followed again by the antiphon; and, finally, vv. 50-51 (49-50), followed once more by the antiphon. For the liturgy of the word for Sunday Masses and for Masses for special saints' days, 79 psalms out of the 150 in the Psalter have been selected as responsorial psalms (treating Psalms 42–43 as a single psalm), and for weekday Masses, 124 psalms have been selected. And, because four psalms are used in Sunday Masses but not in weekday Masses, there are only twenty-two psalms that do not appear somewhere, in whole or in part, among the responsorial psalms.

Some psalms are divided: for example, Psalm 22 is represented both by the lament section—vv. 8-9, 17-18a, 19-20, 23-24 (7-8, 16-17a, 18-19, 22-23)—assigned to Palm Sunday, when the passion of Christ is also read; and by the hymnic section—vv. 26-28, 30-32 (25-27, 29-31)—which is assigned to the Fifth Sunday of Easter in the second year.

In this, as in so much else, there is a great restoration of the pattern of the early church; far more of the Psalms are heard than in the Graduals and tracts of the Mass of the Council of Trent. And my impression is that congregations really hear the words of the Psalms: that they are expected to respond with the antiphon helps in hearing, and they often follow the entire text in a "missalette" (a pamphlet available in the pew racks that allows the worshiper to follow the order of a specific Mass) or in a hymnal. But it must be added that the system of responsorial psalms has not been followed in every country. In Austria, for example, the custom, retained from the time before Vatican II, of substituting the singing of a hymn at this point of the Mass is still generally followed.

Finally, it must be noted that at each Mass there is a "Communion antiphon"— a verse, often (but not always) taken from the Psalms, that is recited by the priest and congregation just before the Eucharist is distributed.

The daily office (now the "Liturgy of the Hours") has been equally transformed.[55] Gone is the assumption that parish priests, like those in the monastic orders, should be expected to pray eight times a day and to complete the recitation of the whole Psalter in a week.[56] Instead, prayers are set forth for four times a day: morning prayer (a conflation of the former Vigils and Lauds; the former Prime is suppressed); daytime prayer is in three parts (a conflation of the former Terce, Sext, and None); evening prayer (the former Vespers); night prayer (the former Compline); and in addition, there is an office of readings. The morning, daytime, and evening prayers are on a four-week cycle, and night prayer is on a weekly cycle. In this way, over a period of four weeks, most if not all of the Psalms are recited (see below). Those in contemplative orders are obligated to recite the entire sequence, including the three sections of daytime prayer. Priests recite the entire sequence but may choose only one of the three sections of daytime prayer. What one may call "less urgent" psalms are assigned to daytime prayer; for example, with two exceptions, all the sequences of Psalm 119, the long wisdom psalm, are found in daytime prayer.[57] And as in the daily office promulgated at the Council of Trent, each psalm is completed by the "Gloria Patri" and is preceded and followed by an antiphon, in almost every instance drawn from the psalm itself.

Morning prayer every day begins with the "invitatory" psalm, usually Psalm 95, and is followed by three other readings: usually a psalm, followed by an Old Testament "canticle" (a poetic sequence from outside the Psalter) and by another psalm; then the "Benedictus" (Luke 1:68-79); intercessions; the Lord's Prayer; and a closing prayer. Daytime prayer consists of three psalms, along with other readings and prayers. Evening prayer consists of two psalms followed by a New Testament canticle; then the "Magnificat" is always recited, followed by intercessions, the Lord's Prayer, and a closing prayer. Night prayer consists of one or two psalms and various readings and prayers. Because the biblical psalms are of varying length, longer ones are divided into two or even three sections, each section then corresponding to a "normal" psalm: for example, Psalm 45 is divided into two sections for evening prayer for Monday in the second week, and the immense Psalm 119 is divided into its twenty-two alphabetical sections, each of eight verses. Beyond the basic four-week cycle there is (as there was in the daily office in earlier times) the so-called proper of seasons, special sequences of psalms and prayers to be used in Advent, Lent, Easter, and the like, as well as sequences for special holy days.

Within the four-week cycle there are psalms that are appropriate to given days and times: thus Ps. 110:1-5, 7, understood as a messianic psalm, is the first psalm recited for evening prayer each Sunday; and Psalm 51, the great penitential psalm, is the first psalm recited for morning prayer each Friday (to mark the crucifixion). Psalms that mention "morning" are naturally assigned to morning prayer: for example, because of the verse "It is you whom I invoke, O Lord. In the morning you hear me; in the morning I offer you my prayer, watching and waiting" (Ps. 5:4 [3]), Psalm 5 is the first psalm in morning prayer for Monday in the first week. Similarly, because of the verse "I will sing, I will sing your praise. Awake, my soul, awake, lyre and harp, I will awake the dawn" (Ps. 57:9 [8]), Psalm 57 is the first psalm in morning prayer for Thursday in the first week. And because of the verses "May he never allow you to stumble! Let him sleep not, your guard. No, he sleeps not nor slumbers, Israel's guard" (Ps. 121:3-4), Psalm 121 is the second psalm for evening prayer for Friday in the second week.

Though there are far fewer traces of any numerical sequence for the Psalms than in the Divine Office of the Council of Trent, there are still a few adjoining pairs: for example, Psalms 128 and 129 are the second and third psalms for daytime prayer for Thursday of the fourth week, and Psalms 137 and 138 are the first and second psalms for evening prayer for Tuesday of the fourth week.

There are occasional repetitions of psalms in contrasting parts of the day: thus the two sections of Psalm 45 are the first and second psalms for evening prayer for Monday in the second week and the second and third psalms for daytime prayer for Saturday of the fourth week.

In this way morning prayer uses forty psalms, plus Psalm 95 (the invitatory psalm), for a total of forty-one; evening prayer uses thirty-nine psalms, four of which are shared with morning prayer,[58] so that morning and evening prayer together use seventy-six psalms. Daytime prayer uses thirty-eight psalms, four of which are shared with either morning or evening prayer,[59] so that morning, daytime, and evening prayers together use 110 psalms. Night prayer uses nine psalms, five of which are shared with morning, daytime, or evening prayer,[60] so that the four fresh psalms bring the total to 114 psalms for all four times of prayer.

There are special psalms assigned for some special days in the year, but these psalms duplicate ones already occurring in the four-week Psalter.

If one recites only one section of daytime prayer, then one's recitation falls considerably short of the full Psalter, of course; there is therefore a "complementary" four-week Psalter that distributes virtually the remainder of the Psalms, day by day, through the cycle of four weeks, in such a way that those who recite all three sections of daytime prayer can complete the recitation of virtually all the Psalms in four weeks. These supplemental psalms are essentially given in numerical order: thus the supplemental psalms for Sunday of the first week are Psalms 1, 2, and 3; those for Monday of that week are Psalms 6 and 9, and so on.

I have said "virtually" because three psalms are left altogether untouched: Psalms 58, 83, and 109, each of them psalms of cursing (though it should be noted that a portion of Psalm 109 appears as a responsorial psalm in one weekday Mass). It should also be pointed out that within the psalms that are recited there are occasional verses or sequences that are omitted: for example, in Psalm 110, recited for Sunday evening prayer, v. 6, a verse of cursing, is omitted. (I return to the issue of omitting material from the Psalms in chapter 16.)

This Liturgy of the Hours offers a practical way not only for priests and those in monastic orders but for lay persons as well to allow their daily prayer to be shaped by the Psalms. And indeed the general instructions issued with the liturgy encourage such use by lay persons.[61]

Finally, in 1965, Pope Paul VI appointed a commission to produce a revision of the Latin Vulgate appropriate to the revisions in the Roman liturgy after Vatican II.[62] This *Nova Vulgata* ("New Vulgate") was issued in 1979.[63] It is not a revision of Jerome's translation (see chapter 6) but a new work, translating the original Hebrew of the Old Testament and the Greek of the New Testament into a Latin that is not as stiff and classical as was the revision of the Psalter that had been published in 1945 (see chapter 12). However, the revisers could not ignore Jerome's work. But by 1979 Roman Catholics were hearing Scripture in vernacular translations, so this Latin rendering has remained largely unused.[64]

Protestant Adaptations of the Roman Lectionary and the Common Lectionary

The movement in the English-speaking world toward a lectionary shared both by Roman Catholics and by the major Protestant churches is a surprising development of the last two decades.[65] When, in response to the *Constitution on the Liturgy* of Vatican II, the bishops first began their planning to reshape the lectionary, two Protestant leaders in the United States initiated unofficial correspondence with key figures in the Roman Catholic Church in North America, to see whether there could be agreement on common liturgical texts: a Presbyterian, Scott F. Brenner, wrote in 1964, and a Lutheran, Hans Boeringer, wrote in 1966. The result was a meeting sponsored by the Institute for Liturgical Studies at Valparaiso University in Indiana in 1966, which was attended by persons from the Inter-Lutheran Commission on Worship, the Protestant Episcopal Church, the United Presbyterian Church, the Worship Commission of the Consultation on Church Union (COCU, an effort of nine denominations to work toward church union), and the International Commission on English in the Liturgy of the Roman Catholic Church. A larger meeting followed in the next year; and a smaller working group on "Agreed Texts," meeting twice a year, began in 1968 to work on a common Psalter for liturgical use. In the ensuing years the group became more diverse with additional Presbyterian and Methodist representatives, and Canadian churches began to take part. The common Psalter was published in 1976;[66] the translation was that of Massey Shepherd, Jr., an Episcopalian.

After the publication in 1969 of the three-year Roman lectionary, the Consultation on Common Texts encouraged closer conformity in its use by Protestant denominations. The Episcopalian and Lutheran churches, churches that employ a lectionary as Roman Catholics do, adopted lectionaries close to the new Roman one rather quickly. Thus the Episcopalians included the lectionary in the *Draft Proposed Book of Common Prayer* in 1970[67] and then in the new edition of the *Book of Common Prayer* in 1979.[68] The Inter-Lutheran Commission on Worship, a joint body of various Lutheran churches planning for a merger, issued *The Church Year: Contemporary Worship 6* in 1973[69] and the *Lutheran Book of Worship* in 1978.[70]

And adaptations of the same lectionary were taken over or encouraged by churches or congregations of other Protestant traditions: Presbyterian, Methodist, and various churches in the "free church" tradition (such as the United Church of Christ and the Disciples of Christ). Thus in 1970 a version of the Roman lectionary appeared in *The Worshipbook*, a service book jointly produced by three Presbyterian churches in the United States.[71]

But here I must pause to discuss the attitude toward lectionaries on the part of Protestant churches other than the Episcopalian and Lutheran ones. The worship books of the Presbyterian, Methodist, and "free church" traditions had, it is true, offered lectionaries through the years, but it is fair to say that the use of these lectionaries had at best been sporadic. The focus of Sunday worship in these churches is the sermon, which is understood to be an exposition of a text chosen by the preacher from the whole range of the Bible. Pastors in these traditions had not been attracted to a lectionary because there are more texts in the Bible from which to preach than any lectionary can include. But clearly a lectionary helps prevent pastors from preaching only from their favorite few texts or from planning a sermon before locating a text that might fit. What has happened, therefore, is that in recent years more and more pastors from these churches have undertaken to preach from a lectionary; but even so, such pastors tend to center on a single text for a given Sunday, so that it may happen that the worship service for that Sunday will not include the full set of three readings and a Psalm.

The move toward preaching from the lectionary has been stimulated by ecumenical ventures wherein Roman Catholic priests and Protestant pastors have met together to discuss common readings and plan sermons together, particularly before Advent and Lent but sometimes on a steady schedule.

A thoughtful presentation of the lectionary for Presbyterians is Horace T. Allen, Jr.'s, *A Handbook for the Lectionary* (1980).[72] Allen is a professor in the Boston University School of Theology and has taken the lead for two decades in shaping an ecumenical lectionary. The *Handbook for the Lectionary* has two parts: the first is a presentation of what the lectionary is, facing not only the opportunities but the problems that a lectionary presents; the second is a guide, Sunday by Sunday, to the readings and how they are related.

But the variations from the Roman three-year lectionary among the different denominations led the Consultation on Common Texts to sponsor a conference on the lectionary, to try to bring harmony among these variations; accordingly, in March 1978 a meeting was held in Washington, D.C., of representatives from thirteen churches in Canada and the United States, chaired by Allen. The conference agreed to recommend improvements in the Roman lectionary and greater uniformity in its use; they thereupon set up a working group, the North American Committee on Calendar and Lectionary (N.A.C.C.L.), which has met twice yearly since then. The working group published a "Common Lectionary" in 1983. This lectionary, very close to the Roman Catholic, Episcopalian, and Lutheran lectionaries, has had wide distribution and is at the present time undergoing further revision. It should also be noted that pastors' helps are published that offer theological background on the readings of these related lectionaries,[73] and there is a journal, *Lectionary Homiletics*,[74] that offers resources for preaching from the lectionaries.

The Common Lectionary as now constituted uses 110 of the Psalms for the Sundays of the three-year cycle, along with special readings for Christmas Day, Ash Wednesday, the weekdays of Holy Week, and a few other special days. Not only do more psalms appear in this lectionary than in the Roman lectionary for Sunday Masses, but individual psalms are more complete. For example, both the Roman lectionary and the Common Lectionary use Psalm 47 for Ascension Day (or, for Protestants who do not celebrate that day, the Seventh Sunday of Easter), but the Roman lectionary uses only six verses of the psalm (vv. 2-3, 6-9 [1-2, 5-8]), whereas the Common Lectionary uses all nine verses. But the Common Lectionary does shorten some of the longer psalms: for example, Psalm 40, assigned to the Second Sunday of Epiphany in the first year and to the Feast of the Annunciation (March 25), is represented by vv. 2-11 (1-10), the last seven verses being passed by. Again, psalms that are easily divisible by content are sometimes divided and assigned to different occasions: Ps. 22:2-19 (1-18), the lament, is understandably assigned to Good Friday, while vv. 26-32 (25-31) are assigned to the Fifth Sunday of Easter in the second year (compare the similar division of this psalm and the same assignment in the Roman lectionary).

The range of psalms in this lectionary is impressive: much of the riches of the Psalter becomes available to the alert listener.

Recent Paraphrases of the Psalms

Metrical paraphrases of the psalms continue to be written for hymns, and, indeed, the Psalms continue to be said and sung in a variety of ways in Christian worship; the periodical *The Hymn* recently devoted a whole issue to the matter.[75] I cite here only one author of metrical psalms out of many. The hymnal used at St. Paul (Roman Catholic) Church in Cambridge, Massachusetts, contains metrical paraphrases of fifteen psalms written by the present director of the Boston Arch-diocesan Choir School, John G. Dunn.[76] Of these, three have been adopted in the most recent Presbyterian hymnal.[77] I cite one of them here, a paraphrase of Psalm 91:

> Within Your shelter, loving God,
>   My refuge and my tower,
> I safely walk by day and night
>   Beneath Your guiding power.
> Because I trust in You alone,
>   No evil shall come near.
> The strong defender of my home,
>   With You I have no fear.
> Your holy angels bear me up
>   And keep my feet secure.
> Though fierce and angry foes assail,
>   In You my way is sure.
> As often as I call to You,
>   You kindly hear my prayer.
> In times of trouble and distress
>   I rest in Your own care.
> All those who know Your name on earth
>   Shall life abundant know.
> On all abiding in Your love
>   Your saving grace bestow.[78]

The Taizé Chants

I now turn to an altogether different medium for psalm material, the chants of the Taizé community.

A Protestant monastic community was founded during World War II at Taizé, a village in Burgundy in southeastern France, by Roger Schutz (b. 1915).[79] From the beginning the community has been international and ecumenical, a place of encounter and renewal for both Protestants and Roman Catholics. And one of the most remarkable features of this community is the chants, composed by Jacques Berthier. These are simple, repetitive songs in Latin, suitable for meditation. Latin has been chosen not as a nod to the Roman Catholic Church but simply because Latin is the possession of no present-day nationality. Many of these chants have a specifically Christian content, such as the *Adoramus te, Domine* (We adore you, O Lord), but many of them are verses of the Psalms: *Miserere Mei* (Have mercy on me; Ps. 25:16); *Misericordias Domini* (The steadfast love of the Lord; Ps. 89:2 [1]); *Laudate Dominum* (Praise the Lord, all you nations; Ps. 117:1a); *Miserere Nobis* (Have mercy on us, an adaptation of Ps. 123:3).[80]

Other Musical Works

I now move outside the churches to mention some examples of musical works that draw from the Psalms. Among serious musical works is the *Symphony of Psalms* of Igor Stravinsky (1882–1971), which I mentioned in the Introduction to this work; it was first performed in 1930 and revised in 1948, and it uses Pss. 39:13-14 (12-13); 40:2-4 (1-3); and verses from Psalm 150. And one may mention the *Psalmus hungaricus* of Zoltán Kodály (1882–1967), a work first performed in 1923, which uses the text of Psalm 55 as translated into Hungarian by Michael Vég in the sixteenth century. The *Alleluia* of Randall Thompson (b. 1899) is a remarkable work, first performed in 1940, that uses only the repeated acclamation "Alleluia" until the closing "Amen."

Toward the end of chapter 9, I offered some examples of folk use of the Psalms in Jewish life. In similar fashion, I should like to close this chapter with two examples of Christian folk songs that draw on the Psalms. The first is a spiritual folk song of North America, "Oh He's Taken My Feet," which has recently been revived by the folk singers Jean Redpath and Lisa Neustadt; it is derived from Ps. 40:3 (2). The first stanza is as follows:

> I'll praise Him while He gives me breath
>   I hope to praise Him after death,
> Oh He's taken my feet from the mire and the clay
>   and He's placed them on the rock of ages.[81]

The second is a traditional round in English based on Ps. 137:1: "By the waters, the waters of Babylon; we sat down and wept, and wept for thee, Zion; We remember, we remember, we remember thee, Zion."[82] This round was popularized by the folk singer Tom Paxton in the 1960s. And still another variation on the same psalm verse, a reggae version, was sung by Jimmy Cliff in the reggae film *The Harder They Come.*

In the *Manual on the Liturgy–Lutheran Book of Worship*, published in 1979, there is a section called "The Rediscovery of the Psalter."[83] It does seem as if the present generation, especially the present generation of worshiping communities, has rediscovered the Psalter. But perhaps every generation rediscovers it.

NOTES

1. For a useful survey of scholarship on the Psalms in the first half of the twentieth century, see Aubrey R. Johnson, "The Psalms," in H. H. Rowley (ed.), *The Old Testament and Modern Study* (Oxford: Clarendon, 1951), 162–209; for a more recent assessment of form-critical research, see Erhard S. Gerstenberger, "Psalms," in John H. Hayes (ed.), *Old Testament Form Criticism* (San Antonio: Trinity University Press, 1974), 179–223.

2. Useful for background on lectionaries, particularly for Protestants, are the following articles in *Interpretation* 31 (1977): John Reumann, "A History of Lectionaries: From the Synagogue at Nazareth to Post-Vatican II," 116–30; Gerard S. Sloyan, "The Lectionary as a Context for Interpretation," 131–38; Lloyd R. Bailey, "The Lectionary in Critical Perspective," 139–53.

3. Hermann Gunkel, *Ausgewählte Psalmen* (Göttingen: Vandenhoeck & Ruprecht, 1917).

4. Hermann Gunkel, *Die Psalmen* (Göttingen: Vandenhoeck & Ruprecht, 1926).

5. Hermann Gunkel, *Einleitung in die Psalmen* (Göttingen: Vandenhoeck & Ruprecht, 1933).

6. Sigmund Mowinckel, *Offersang og Sangoffer* (Oslo: H. Aschehoug, 1951); published in English as *The Psalms in Israel's Worship* (New York and Nashville: Abingdon, 1962).

7. See Erhard S. Gerstenberger, review of *The Psalms in Israel's Worship*, by Sigmund Mowinckel, *JBL* 82 (1963):333–36.

8. Artur Weiser, *Die Psalmen* (5th rev. ed.; Göttingen: Vandenhoeck & Ruprecht, 1959); published in English as *The Psalms* (OTL; Philadelphia: Westminster, 1962).

9. See James A. Sanders, review of *The Psalms*, by Artur Weiser, *JBL* 82 (1963):127.

10. Erhard S. Gerstenberger, *Psalms: Part 1, with an Introduction to Cultic Poetry* (Grand Rapids: Eerdmans, 1988).

11. Mitchell Dahood, *Psalms I: 1–50; Psalms II: 51–100; Psalms III: 101–150* (Garden City, N.Y.: Doubleday, 1966; 1968; 1970).

12. Cf. Theodor Gaster, review of *Psalms III*, by Mitchell Dahood, *JBL* 93 (1974): 296–300.

13. James Moffatt (trans.), *The Bible, A New Translation* (New York: Harper, 1934).

14. *The Complete Bible, An American Translation* (Chicago: University of Chicago Press, 1939).

15. Edgar J. Goodspeed, *How to Read the Bible* (Philadelphia: Winston, 1946).

16. For an outline of the history of the RSV, see Luther Weigle, "English Versions since 1611," in S. L. Greenslade (ed.), *The Cambridge History of the Bible*, vol. 3: *The West from the Reformation to the Present Day* (Cambridge: Cambridge University Press, 1963), 377–78.

17. *The Interpreter's Bible* (New York and Nashville: Abingdon, 1951–57).

18. *Gospel Parallels* (New York: Nelson, 1949).

19. *Nelson's Complete Concordance of the Revised Standard Version* (New York: Nelson, 1957).

20. E.g., *Christian Worship: A Hymnal* (St. Louis: Christian Board of Education, 1953); and *Pilgrim Hymnal* (Boston: Pilgrim, 1958).

21. Raymond E. Brown, "Text and Versions," in Raymond E. Brown, Joseph A. Fitzmyer, and Roland E. Murphy (eds.), *The New Jerome Biblical Commentary* (Englewood Cliffs, N.J.: Prentice Hall, 1990), 1111.

22. *The Holy Bible: Revised Standard Version Containing the Old and New Testaments with the Apocrypha/Deuterocanonical Books* (New York: Collins, 1973).

23. *The Jerusalem Bible* (Garden City, N.Y.: Doubleday, 1966).

24. *Biblia de Jerusalén* (Bilbao: Desclee de Brouwer, 1976).

25. *The New Jerusalem Bible* (Garden City, N.Y.: Doubleday, 1985).

26. *The New English Bible with the Apocrypha* (Oxford: Oxford University Press; Cambridge: Cambridge University Press, 1970).

27. *The New American Bible* (Washington, D.C.: Confraternity of Christian Doctrine, 1970). For the background of this translation, see Gerald P. Fogarty, *American Catholic Biblical Scholarship: A History from the Early Republic to Vatican II* (San Francisco: Harper & Row, 1989), 345–48.

28. *The Revised Psalms of the New American Bible* (New York: Catholic Book Publishing, 1991).

29. *Tanakh: A New Translation of the Holy Scriptures according to the Traditional Hebrew Text* (Philadelphia: Jewish Publication Society, 1985).

30. *Good News Bible: Today's English Version, with Deuterocanonicals/Apocrypha* (New York: American Bible Society, 1979).

31. *The Holy Bible: New International Version* (Grand Rapids: Zondervan, 1978).

32. *The Revised English Bible, with the Apocrypha* (Oxford: Oxford University Press; Cambridge: Cambridge University Press, 1989).

33. *The United Methodist Hymnal: Book of United Methodist Worship* (Nashville: United Methodist Publishing House, 1989).

34. John R. Kohlenberger III (ed.), *The NRSV Concordance Unabridged* (Grand Rapids: Zondervan, 1991).

35. *What Bible Can You Trust?* (Nashville: Broadman, 1974).

36. "The New Dutch Translation of the Bible," *Bible Translator* 1 (1950):6–9.

37. Peter Dirksen, personal correspondence.

38. *Traduction oecuménique de la Bible* (Paris: Cerf, 1976); for the background of this translation, see Pierre-Maurice Bogaert, "La Bible en français: Réflexions sur l'histoire et l'actualité," *RTL* 7 (1976):337–53.

39. *Einheitsübersetzung der Heiligen Schrift* (Stuttgart: Katholische Bibelanstalt, 1980); for a review (in French) of this translation, see X. Jacques, review of *Einheitsübersetzung der Heiligen Schrift*, *NRT* 103 (1981):888–89.

40. Egidio Vagnozzi, "Thoughts on the Catholic Intellectual," *American Ecclesiastical Review* 145 (1961):74, 75; see further Fogarty, *American Catholic Biblical Scholarship*, 290–91, and, indeed, all of chap. 13.

41. Fogarty, *American Catholic Biblical Scholarship*, 291–98.

42. Ibid., 322–26.

43. Ibid., 331–33.

44. Ibid., 334–39.

45. Ibid., 339–43; for a summary, see Raymond E. Brown and Thomas Aquinas Collins, "Church Pronouncements," in Brown, Fitzmyer, and Murphy (eds.), *New Jerome Biblical Commentary*, 1169.

46. Raymond E. Brown and others (eds.), *The Jerome Biblical Commentary* (Englewood Cliffs, N.J.: Prentice-Hall, 1968).

47. Frederick R. McManus (ed.), *Thirty Years of Liturgical Renewal: Statements of the Bishops' Committee on the Liturgy* (Washington, D.C.: National Conference of Catholic Bishops, 1987), 3.

48. Clifford Howell, "From Trent to Vatican II," in Cheslyn Jones, Geoffrey Wainwright, and Edward Yarnold (eds.), *The Study of Liturgy* (New York: Oxford University Press, 1978), 246.

49. McManus, *Liturgical Renewal*, 9–16.

50. Ibid., 22.

51. Howell, "Trent to Vatican II," 246.

52. Ibid.; cf. J. D. Crichton, "The Office in the West: The Roman Rite from the Sixteenth Century," in Jones, Wainwright, and Yarnold (eds.), *Study of Liturgy*, 386–88.

53. McManus, *Liturgical Renewal*, 26, 139, 166.

54. See Claude Wiéner, "The Roman Catholic Eucharistic Lectionary," *Studia liturgica* 21 (1991):2–13.

55. I have used *Christian Prayer: The Liturgy of the Hours* (Boston: Daughters of St. Paul, 1976).

56. McManus, *Liturgical Renewal*, 166–67.

57. Pope Paul VI, *Apostolic Constitution, Promulgation* (November 1, 1970): sec. 2, in *Liturgy of the Hours*, 14–15.

58. Psalms 67, 119, 135, 144.

59. Psalms 19, 45, 57, 119.

60. Psalms 16, 86, 88, 130, 143.

61. *Liturgy of the Hours*, 24.

62. C. J. Pfeifer, "Bible and Liturgy," in *NCE* 17:38b.

63. *Nova Vulgata Bibliorum Sacrorum Editio* (Vatican City: Libreria Editrice Vaticana, 1979).

64. For a review in French, see Albert-Louis Descamps, review of *Nova Vulgata Bibliorum Sacrorum Editio, Esprit et Vie* 89 (1979):598–603.

65. Horace T. Allen, Jr., "Consultation on Common Texts," in *NCE* 17:153–54; idem, "*Common Lectionary*: Origins, Assumptions, and Issues," *Studia liturgica* 21 (1991):14–30.

66. *A Liturgical Psalter for the Eucharist* (Minneapolis: Augsburg; Collegeville, Minn.: Liturgical Press, 1976).

67. Standing Liturgical Commission of the Episcopal Church, *Prayer Book Studies 19* (New York: Church Hymnal Corporation, 1970).

68. The Episcopal Church in the United States, *The Book of Common Prayer* (New York: Church Hymnal Corporation and Seabury Press, 1979).

69. Inter-Lutheran Commission on Worship, *The Church Year: Contemporary Worship 6* (Minneapolis: Augsburg, 1973).

70. Inter-Lutheran Commission on Worship, *Lutheran Book of Worship* (Minneapolis: Augsburg; Philadelphia: Board of Publication, Lutheran Church in America, 1978).

71. The Joint Committee on Worship for the Cumberland Presbyterian Church, Presbyterian Church in the United States, and the United Presbyterian Church in the United States of America, *The Worshipbook: Services and Hymns* (Philadelphia: Westminster, 1972).

72. Horace T. Allen, Jr., *A Handbook for the Lectionary, Developed by the Joint Office of Worship of the Presbyterian Church in the United States and the United Presbyterian Church in the United States of America* (Philadelphia: Geneva, 1980).

73. E.g., Perry H. Biddle, Jr., *Preaching the Lectionary: A Workbook for Year A*; idem, *Preaching the Lectionary: A Workbook for Year B*; and idem, *Preaching the Lectionary: A Workbook for Year C* (Louisville: Westminster/John Knox, 1989–91).

74. *Lectionary Homiletics*, P.O. Box 2012, Midlothian, Va., 23112.

75. *The Hymn*, 33, no. 2 (April 1982).

76. Theodore Marier (ed.), *Hymns, Psalms and Spiritual Canticles* (Belmont, Mass.: BACS, 1972), nos. 109, 110, 138, 162, 168, 225, 252, 253, 265, 288, 292, 327, 329, 337, 353.

77. *The Presbyterian Hymnal: Hymns, Psalms, and Spiritual Songs* (Louisville: Westminster/John Knox, 1990), nos. 199, 212, 243.

78. I cite the version in the *Presbyterian Hymnal*; the hymn was revised in 1985.

79. See, e.g., Rex Brico, *Taizé: Brother Roger and His Community* (London: Collins, 1978).

80. Jacques Berthier, *Music from Taizé* (Chicago: G.I.A. Publications, 1978).

81. A recording is Lisa Neustadt and Jean Redpath, "Oh He's Taken My Feet," *Anywhere Is Home* (Library of Congress no. 81-750202). The source is George Pullen Jackson, *Spiritual Folk Songs of Early America* (Gloucester, Mass.: P. Smith, 1975).

82. See, e.g., Peter Blood-Patterson (ed.) *Rise Up Singing* (Bethlehem, Penn.: Sing Out Publication, 1988), 193. This work attributes the tune to William Billings of Boston, *ca.* 1780, but the song does not appear in *The Complete Works of William Billings* (Boston: The American Musicological Society and The Colonial Society of Massachusetts, 1977–90).

83. Philip H. Pfatteicher and Carlos R. Messerli (eds.), *Manual on the Liturgy–Lutheran Book of Worship* (Minneapolis: Augsburg, 1979), 19–21.

PART THREE

CURRENT
THEOLOGICAL ISSUES

15

Toughening Texts: Lament, Recovery, and Praise

Our survey of the history of Jewish and Christian communities through the centuries has revealed a whole array of uses of the Psalms. In the course of this historical survey, we have touched on several issues that need more systematic treatment, questions that revolve around how the Psalms function for worshiping communities, and it is these theological and practical issues that I address in this and the following chapters. I hasten to say, however, that I speak in this part of my work only as a Christian; there is no way I can offer any theological reflection for Jews.

All these issues arise essentially because of the distance between the Psalms and us. In this chapter I want to bring the Psalms directly to bear upon our patterns of worship, to explore not only how the Psalms may be a vehicle for worship but how they may even extend and toughen our experience of worship. Then I reverse the matter in chapter 16, bringing our patterns of worship to bear upon the Psalms, and I there discuss two recurrent issues: how we have excluded from our usage certain psalms or verses of psalms, and whether that exclusion is a good or bad thing. I turn in chapter 17 to the process of translation, dealing with what happens when we move the distance from the Hebrew text of the Psalms to our current languages. Then I move out in chapter 18 from linguistic translation to what might be called "ecclesial translation," that is, the strains that the Psalms undergo in serving as vehicles of worship for communities beyond the original context of the Psalms—as vehicles for Christian worship and as vehicles for women's experience. Finally, I attempt in chapter 19 to make a "theological translation," trying to discern how one might use the entire Psalter today as an expression of God's will for our worship. To be sure, all these issues are closely interrelated, but it is still useful to try to deal with them one by one.

How Not to Use the Psalms

Before we consider how the Psalms may serve as a vehicle for our worship and may even extend our worship, it is useful to ponder how they are *not* to be used. In

The Old Farmer's Almanac, 1991, under an advertisement for hernia trusses, appears an advertisement for a booklet called *Secrets of the Psalms*.[1] The booklet, obtainable from a firm in Chicago that deals in occult supplies, states its author to be Godfrey A. Selig, "Lecturer and Publisher"; its title page sets it forth as "A fragment of the practical Kabbala, with extracts from other Kabbalistic writings, as translated by the Author"; it is published in Arlington, Texas.[2]

Now the Kabbala is an occult esoteric literature, produced by certain groups of Jews in the Middle Ages, that claims to find hidden meaning in the Hebrew Scriptures. But with regard to this particular booklet, I have not been able to find any Kabbalistic work based on the Psalms that might have been an antecedent to it; nor have I been able to learn anything about Selig. Internal evidence from the text of the booklet would indicate that the setting for the original text of this work is the Jewish ghetto life of eastern Europe, perhaps three hundred years ago. Because the booklet, along with its "secrets," contains, oddly, a photo-offset reproduction of the text of the Psalms in the (Protestant) King James Version, and because the firm from which I obtained the booklet advertises among its other goods a "Prayer to St. Michael and Sword," the sword in question being a "14K Gold Plated sword to be worn around the neck," it is clear that we are here in touch with an eclectic approach to religious issues.

The booklet purports to explain how each psalm may be used to further one's success. Thus Psalm 1 is labeled "Psalm for Woman Who Is Pregnant, Psalm for Dangerous Confinement"; Psalm 2, "Psalm for Danger at Sea or Storm"; Psalm 3, "Psalm for Severe Headache or Backache"; Psalm 4, "Psalm for Luck"; Psalm 5 "Psalm for Court Cases"; and so on.

The instructions for Psalm 8, "Psalm to Be Successful in Business," will serve as a sample.

> Psalm 8.—If you wish to secure the love and good will of all men in your business transactions, you should pray this Psalm three days in succession after sundown, and think continually of the Holy name of Rechmial, which signifies great and strong God of love, of grace and mercy. Pronounce at each time the appropriate prayer over a small quantity of olive oil, and anoint the face as well as the hands and feet. The letters, composing the holy name are found in the words: Addir, verse 2; Jereach, verse 4; Adam, verse 5; Melohim, verse 6; Tanischilenu, verse 7. The prayer reads as follows: May it please thee, Oh, Rechmial Eel, to grant that I may obtain love, grace and favour in the eyes of men according to thy holy will. Amen!—Selah!

To this I make several immediate observations. First, there is no obvious connection between the contents of Psalm 8 and the notion of success in business.

Second, the "holy name" for this psalm is given as "Rechmial": for each psalm, it appears, the booklet offers a "holy name," which is a curious matter. In this instance a Hebraist could imagine a divine designation such as "Rachmiel," which in Hebrew would mean "God is my compassion" or the like; this might be the original word, deformed here by mispronunciation or misprinting. The Hebrew spelling of this "holy name," it seems, is made up from consonants that occur successively in the Hebrew words cited in the various verses of the given psalm: thus the first consonant, *r*, is found in the word *'addîr* (the word translated "majestic" in the NRSV: "How *majestic* is your name in all the earth"), and so on for each successive consonant. But again, the Hebrew words in the instructions in the booklet are woefully misspelled: *Tanischilenu*, even in the Germanized spelling of Hebrew words that the compiler employs, should actually be *Tamschilehu*.

Finally and ironically, the verse citations of these Hebrew words, mysterious to the uninformed reader, are given in the Hebrew versification of the Psalms, a different numbering than the versification of the English translation of the Psalms that is appended—namely, the King James Version (on the matter of contrasting versification, see the Introduction). That is, the book does not offer any internal consistency; what we are dealing with here is arbitrary.

Indeed it represents a set of magical procedures. Magic is a practice understood to control and manipulate the forces of nature or the forces governing other persons. In chapter 10 we glimpsed the use of psalm material for magic or talismanic purposes: we recall the use of a psalm verse, written on an apple, to prevent wine from spoiling, and the story of Queen Quendreda, who was said to have cast an evil spell by reciting Psalm 119 backward. Holy things always lie open to manipulation and misuse, and an occult use of the Psalms in our day at least acknowledges in a backhanded way the sense of power understood to reside in the Psalms.

But what are we to say to the adventure driver Tim Cahill? In writing of his adventures attempting to drive the Pan-American highway in record time from south to north, Cahill recalls the advice given him by Michael Morgan, an Episcopal priest who lived next door to him in Montana:

> "Psalm 91," Father Michael said, "is a prayer of protection. It's a good highway prayer." My neighbor gave me a pocket Bible to pack away with my newly purchased knife and borrowed bullet-proof vest. In a pinch, he thought, when quick action is called for, a prayer might consist of simply saying, "Psalm 91, Lord." . . . In Psalm 91, the devout reader is cautioned to make the Most High his or her dwelling: "then no harm will befall you, no disaster come near your tent."[3]

We recall that this very psalm verse was used as an amulet in the Middle Ages (see chapter 10).

So the question arises: Where is the boundary between magic and prayer? Clearly, in the case of the *Secrets of the Psalms* the person who uses a given psalm does not listen to the psalm but simply recites it mechanically, even mindlessly; the assumption is that the very recitation will manipulate God (or fate or the governing force in the world) into bending in the reciter's direction. Further, in this exercise the will of the reciter is central, whereas the will of God is marginal or even absent altogether.

But what of Cahill's simply saying, "Psalm 91, Lord"? Is this magic? Or are these five syllables an encapsulated reminder for him (and for God!) of the whole psalm as it might be recited in a calmer and more leisurely moment? It is a judgment call.

It is obvious that I reject any use of the Psalms for magical purposes: the only "secrets" of the Psalms are the power that is available in the meaning of their phrases to any reader who submits to the biblical faith that gave them birth. And it is to the exploration of the nature of that power that I devote the remainder of this chapter.

Poetry

I begin by setting aside temporarily the specific religious content of the Psalms and concentrating simply on the power of their poetry. In chapter 4 we discussed a bit the poetic skill of the psalmists, and in chapter 17 we ponder the difficulties of transferring that skill into our own languages. And, of course, there is no practical way to separate the poetic power inherent in the Psalms from the power of their religious affirmations—the two are inextricably interwoven. But still it is worth pondering their poetic power for a moment.

The central feature of Old Testament poetry, as we have seen, is parallelism, usually of two adjoining lines. One recent scholar has nicely characterized parallelism as "A, and what's more, B."[4] The reinforcement that the second line gives to the first line creates a sense of spaciousness and richness: it is, in a way, like a pair of stereoscopic photographs, which when viewed together create the effect of three dimensions.

Because this structure is a matter not of rhyme or some other phonetic device but rather of meaning, it can be transferred into English without difficulty. So whether one is worshiping or simply reading aloud, whether one actively believes in God or not, one can respond with emotion, even with awe, in reading the ancient opening lines of Psalm 19:

> The heavens are telling the glory of God;
>   and the firmament proclaims his handiwork.
> Day to day pours forth speech,
>   and night to night declares knowledge.
> There is no speech, nor are there words;
>   their voice is not heard;
> yet their voice goes out through all the earth,
>   and their words to the end of the world.

The scholar Walter Brueggemann, in a recent work on poetry, speaks sadly of our "prose-flattened world." "By prose," he writes,

> I refer to a world that is organized in settled formulae, so that even pastoral prayers and love letters sound like memos. By poetry, I do not mean rhyme, rhythm, or meter, but language that moves like Bob Gibson's fast ball, that jumps at the right moment, that breaks open old worlds with surprise, abrasion, and pace.[5]

The Psalms as Both a Reflection
and a Shaper of Faith

I now turn to the specific religious content of the Psalms. There are all kinds of ways in which one could set forth the variety of religious expression available for Christians in the Psalter, and through the years book after book has been written to help readers appreciate the religious value of the Psalms. Some of these books are scholarly, some devotional; some stress the religious outlook of ancient Israel, whereas others offer stimulus for Christian worship; some deal with the Psalms in general, others with only a selection or even with a single psalm, such as the Twenty-third (see the Epilogue). I refer here to three books that have been important to me.

The first is *Reflections on the Psalms* by C. S. Lewis.[6] Lewis (1898–1963) taught English literature at Oxford and Cambridge Universities; he is perhaps best known for *The Screwtape Letters*, his notion of how the Christian faith looks from the point of view of a subordinate devil in the infernal kingdom. His little book *Reflections on the Psalms* strikes one as very old-fashioned; he uses the King James Version, and clearly his sensibility was shaped by the period before and during the Second World War. But it is a little classic. For example, he offers wise words about how to understand the curses and the self-righteousness in some of the Psalms, and his approach may be discerned in my observations in the course of chapter 4.

The other two books are by Brueggemann; few scholars in our day have done as much to bring an intelligent understanding of the Psalms into Christian sensibility as has Brueggemann. Beyond the book on poetry to which I have already referred, he has written two books that deal specifically with the Psalms: *The Message of the Psalms* (1984)[7] and *Israel's Praise* (1988).[8] Here I would like to draw on some of his ideas.

In *Message of the Psalms*, Brueggemann suggests a connection between ancient Israel and ourselves by deriving from the various genres of psalms (see chapter 6)[9] a threefold scheme of "psalms of orientation," "psalms of disorientation," and "psalms of new orientation." Psalms of orientation are characterized by a lack of movement. These are psalms that do not remind worshipers of any problems in the world; they focus on the equilibrium of things as they are. Among these are psalms of creation, such as Psalm 104; torah psalms, such as Psalms 1 and 119; wisdom psalms, such as Psalm 37; and psalms for occasions of well-being, such as Psalm 133.

Psalms of disorientation are laments either of the individual or of the community. They focus on disequilibrium: life is not as it should be, and in these psalms the psalmists lament, protest, and call God to account.

Psalms of new orientation include songs of thanksgiving. They imply surprise: they mark the occasions of celebration when God has acted to save or liberate.

As for the genre of psalms called "hymns," in Brueggemann's categories they could be classified either as psalms of orientation or of new orientation. If a hymn is descriptive of what God is, if it affirms what is settled and nonnegotiable, then it is a psalm of orientation; whereas if a hymn declares what God has done to liberate or save, it is a psalm of new orientation. But sometimes a given hymn might be classified either way.

This simple scheme is useful for readers or worshipers who in their disorientation could be fed by appropriate psalms but who might reject the notion implied by the word "lament."[10]

Brueggemann's second book, *Israel's Praise*, takes a different tack. He notes that the Psalms are not only responses to the reality of relationship with the biblical God but also expressions that help reshape that relationship with God. That is, the Psalms not only reflect reality but also shift reality (this point of Brueggemann's is one I made briefly in chapter 1).[11]

For example, one may ask, What happens when a community says, "Yahweh is king!" (Ps. 96:10)? The community does not *make* Yahweh king, because Yahweh has always been king. Nevertheless, in declaring that Yahweh is king the community reexperiences that reality and indeed shares the good news of that reality in a way analogous to what happens in the Christian proclamation "Christ is risen!" on Easter: the church's tradition that Christ is risen has been a reality for centuries, but the church still takes the occasion once a year to proclaim the news in all its transforming power. The declaration that "Yahweh is king!" arose in the context of the Pharaoh's oppression of Israel, and Moses' response to that oppression: if Yahweh is king, then Pharaoh is not king. And the declaration that "Yahweh is king!" continued to be made in the new context when Israel was safe in its land, indeed, when the Davidic king in Jerusalem sponsored the declaration that above the Davidic king, Yahweh is king. But then the declaration took on fresh meaning for exiles who were not only deprived of their Davidic king but even of any outward sign that Yahweh is king. Worshipers who continue to make the declaration in times of security and comfort are reminded that for their ancestors, who did not enjoy security and comfort, Yahweh was the liberating God, and that for those who still lack security and comfort Yahweh will be the liberating God. The declaration comes directly as a reassurance to those folk who at the moment lack any outward sign that Yahweh is king.[12]

The Poetry of Lament

One of the most important points Brueggemann makes in his books is the power of the speech of lament psalms. "The lament psalm," he points out, "offers Israel's characteristic way of opening a new world by way of daring protest." He cites Ps. 13:2-3 (1-2), which I give here in the NRSV:

How long, O Lord? Will you forget me forever?
    How long will you hide your face from me?
How long must I bear pain in my soul,
    and have sorrow in my heart all day long?
How long shall my enemy be exalted over me?

Brueggemann continues:

How long indeed. It has been very long, seemingly an eternity. Now the speech explodes with having waited too long. All parties are surprised at the depth of the hostility. That hostility, however, is present both in the text and in the community. The opening speech is about God's failure and neglect in the relationship.

The alienation and the rage have long festered in the silence. Now the speech erupts in indignation and urgency. For a long time things have not been right. Finally there is speech. The speech is on the tongue of the poet. Finally comes the poet to speak the rage and resentment that will tolerate no prosaic utterance. The indignation is not resigned. It is an act of insistence and of hope.

Brueggemann then cites Ps. 39:8-11 (7-10). And he continues:

Indignant hope is sounded because the speaker believes there is still this one to whom speech may be effectively addressed. There still is a serious conversation partner. In the very act of this speech, the world is already reshaped. It is reshaped with a chance of community and communion. It is reshaped with a possibility for dignity and self-respect. There is speaking and a passionate conviction that there is listening.[13]

If poetry may reshape our world, then most emphatically the poetry of the lament psalms has power to reshape our world because of the conviction that God is there, the conversation partner. The psalmist offers a detailed list of complaints, convinced that God will listen and thereby change the psalmist's circumstances for the better.

That awareness of the existence of God the conversation partner is thrown into relief by a "Peanuts" cartoon from Halloween a number of years ago. Linus is out at night in the pumpkin patch. He says, "Oh, Great Pumpkin, why hast thou cast me off? How long, Oh, Great Pumpkin, wilt though hide thyself from me? Mine enemies reproach me all the day! Bring thou me out of my distress!" And then finally, in the last frame, simply, "Rats!" Linus's cult of the Great Pumpkin is idiosyncratic to himself, and his personal conviction, unreinforced by his community of friends, lacks cogency and reinforcement.

These lament psalms, then, are not magic. Of course, the psalmist and his community have a passionate desire to see their circumstances change; but in that passionate desire they have a lively conviction that they are in conversation with God, and that in their circumstances they are struggling with God's will.

The Power of Laments in Worship

I now suggest how the psalms of lament might extend and stretch and toughen our experience of worship. The laments comprise more than one-third of the Psalms, yet they are strikingly underused in our worship. Several scholars have noted this. Thus the Scottish Presbyterian scholar Robert Davidson analyzes in detail the underuse of laments in *The Church Hymnary, Third Edition* (1973), used in the Church of Scotland;[14] and Brueggemann makes the same point from his American perspective.[15]

The matter is worth documenting in detail. I use here the listing of lament psalms of Leopold Sabourin, who builds, as do all scholars of the Psalms, on the work of Hermann Gunkel (see chapter 14).[16] And I analyze the use of laments in both the Roman Catholic lectionary and the "Common Lectionary."

According to Sabourin, there are in the Psalter thirty-eight laments of the individual[17] and eighteen laments of the community,[18] for a total of fifty-six psalms. Of these, twenty psalms (or portions of psalms) are used in the current Roman Catholic lectionary for Sunday Masses,[19] but at least two of them omit the "lament" section;[20] eighteen out of fifty-six is 32 percent. In the Common Lectionary, thirty-four of these psalms appear,[21] but at least ten of these omit the "lament" part or the call for retribution;[22] twenty-four out of fifty-six is 43 percent.

By contrast, Sabourin lists nine psalms of confidence of the individual[23] and three psalms of confidence of the community,[24] for a total of twelve, and of these the Roman Catholic lectionary uses seven[25] and the Common Lectionary, nine.[26] He lists eleven thanksgivings of the individual[27] and six thanksgivings of the community,[28] for a total of seventeen, and of these the Roman Catholic lectionary uses fifteen[29] and the Common Lectionary all seventeen. He lists nineteen hymns,[30] of which the Roman Catholic lectionary uses thirteen[31] and the Common Lectionary, seventeen.[32] Brueggemann remarks:

> It is a curious fact that the church has, by and large, continued to sing songs of orientation in a world increasingly experienced as disoriented. . . . It is my judgment that this action of the church is less an evangelical defiance guided by faith, and much more a frightened, numb denial and deception that does not want to acknowledge or experience the disorientation of life.[33]

Yet if a congregation were thoughtfully guided, the laments could greatly extend its sensibility. In laments the psalmist speaks for those who are innocent, whose rights have been ignored; the laments speak for those who are marginalized in the community. In these psalms, worshipers who are marginalized could find their voice.

Who might these marginalized be among us? There are whole segments of our population that are marginalized: the elderly, often; ethnic minorities, often; women, often. There are the homeless. There are those suffering from AIDS. And, beyond our own communities, there are victims of war, refugees, children. Any folk who are marginalized can be moved to find their voices in these psalms, and any folk who are moved to become sensitized to the marginalized can hear such voices in these psalms.

I begin with laments of the individual, and I explore them through the experience of those in a particularly fearful circumstance—women who are victims of domestic violence.[34] Let us begin with Psalm 41. Verses 2-3 (1-2) affirm that those people are fortunate (or happy) who consider (or are concerned for) the wretched; this verse might lead a woman who has been battered to consider God's concern for those who run a shelter or who offer comfort or therapy. Strikingly, then, the psalm begins by leading the speaker to ponder those who might be helpful to her in a situation of oppression, and the end of v. 3 (2) suggests that God means to protect those who protect the battered.

In v. 5 (4) the original psalmist asks for healing; in the situation I am setting forth, a woman who has been battered may or may not be physically ill, but she will certainly be shattered by her own low self-esteem. Is it too much to see in the words "for I have sinned against you" her present sense of unworthiness—unworthiness that needs to be countered by a knowledge of God's love for her? It is noteworthy that by v. 13 (12) the psalmist no longer confesses to have sinned but instead speaks of "my integrity." In v. 6 (5) the psalmist says, "My enemies wonder in malice when I will die, and my name perish." This may be heard as the voice of a woman who is convinced she loves her partner but who finally in desperation comes to a shelter or seeks help, knowing that her partner wants her dead, psychically and sometimes physically as well. For her to describe aloud the situation of psychic extinguishment, represented by the possibility that her name will perish, is at least to begin to deal with that reality.

Verses 7-9 (6-8) cannot be improved upon as a description by the battered of the batterer and those with whom the batterer consorts:

> And when they come to see me, they utter empty words,
> while their hearts gather mischief;
> when they go out, they tell it abroad.
> All who hate me whisper together about me;
> they imagine the worst for me.
> They think that a deadly thing has fastened on me,
> that I will not rise again from where I lie.

Then, in v. 10 (9), one hears the ultimate horror, the betrayal of domestic concord: "Even my bosom friend in whom I trusted, who ate of my bread, has lifted the heel against me." What, we wonder, does "raised the heel against me" mean, specifically? We recall from chapter 7 that the early Christians remembered Jesus' use of this verse to point to Judas (Mark 14:18; John 13:18). At first hearing it suggests that the ancient psalmist was complaining of being physically kicked. But the Hebrew phrase is probably to be taken metaphorically—the NJB reads, "has taken advantage of me," and the REB reads, "exults over my misfortune." Mitchell Dahood suggests a fresh understanding of the words: "spun slanderous tales about me."[35] We are not sure, but no matter; the most intimate trust, engendered by the sharing of bread, has been utterly shattered.

In v. 11 (10) there comes the first address to God: "But you, O Lord, be gracious to me and raise me up." Indeed! And Jesus' teaching that no sparrow falls without the participation of God in heaven (Matt. 10:29) encourages the battered one to dare to pray to God to raise her up. The last phrase of the verse needs

discussion: "that I may repay them"; the NJB says, "and I will give them their due."
In Israelite culture the phrase implies just retribution. Now, as Christians we tend
to bristle at the notion of "pay him back for what he did to me." But psychologically
the notion is right: what is needed is *parity*; the battered one needs to be in parity
with the batterer. I am not suggesting that the battered one needs to become a
batterer herself, but if there is to be any recovery and healing, then some kind of
parity is absolutely necessary. Given strength from friends (v. 2 [1]) and from God
(the present verse), she may finally be able to look him in the eye. And in vv. 12-13
(11-12) the psalmist is able to affirm this restoration of status: "By this I know that
you [God] are pleased with me; because my enemy has not triumphed over me. But you
have upheld me because of my integrity, and set me in your presence forever." I
suggest, then, that this psalm, a cry for help, is utterly appropriate in the mouth of
a battered woman.

There are other laments that are equally apt for her. We look, for example, at
Ps. 55:13-15 (12-14):

> It is not my enemies who taunt me—
>   I could bear that;
> it is not adversaries who deal insolently with me—
>   I could hide from them.
> But it is you, my equal,
>   my companion, my familiar friend,
> with whom I kept pleasant company;
>   we walked in the house of God with the throng.

Here we are in touch with the grief, the frustration, the fury of someone who
has been betrayed at the deepest level. As an aside, however, I must say that we are
in trouble with Ps. 55:16 (15): "Let death come upon them; let them go down alive
to Sheol; for evil is in their homes and in their hearts." As we learn in chapter 16,
the Roman Catholic Liturgy of the Hours omits this verse in its recitation of the
psalm;[36] I try to suggest a use for this verse by Christians in chapter 19.

Of the laments, none is more awesome than Psalm 22. This psalm has been
incorporated by the theologian Rosemary Ruether into a "Rite of Healing for Wife
Battering." In this rite she sets out a script for two groups of women to recite
antiphonally. The material for the first group is drawn from a "Letter from a
Battered Wife,"[37] while the second group recites Psalm 22, section by section.

In the first speech of the first group, the battered woman introduces herself:
her husband is a college graduate and a professional in his field; they have four
children. "I have everything except life without fear."

Then the second group recites:

> My God, my God, why have you abandoned me? I have cried desperately for
> help, but still it does not come. During the day I call to you, my God, but you
> do not answer. I call at night but get no rest.

The first group continues:

For most of my married life I have been periodically beaten by my husband. What do I mean by beaten? I mean that parts of my body have been hit violently and repeatedly and that painful bruises, swelling, bleeding wounds, and unconsciousness and combinations of these things have resulted. I have been kicked in the abdomen when I was visibly pregnant. I have been punched and kicked in the head, chest, face and abdomen more times than I can count. I have been slapped for saying something about politics, for having a different view about religion, for crying. I have been threatened when I would not do something he told me to do. I have been threatened when he has had a bad day and when he has had a good day. After each beating my husband has left the house and remained away for days.

The second group responds:

But I am no longer a person; I am a worm, despised and scorned by everyone! All who see me make fun of me: they stick out their tongues and shake their heads.

The first group continues:

Few people have ever seen my black-and-blue face or swollen lips, because I stayed indoors afterwards, feeling ashamed. Now the first response to this story, which I myself think of, will be, "Why didn't you seek help?"

And the second group responds:

You relied on the Lord, they say. Why doesn't he save you? If the Lord likes you, why doesn't he help you?

There are more interchanges. The first group recites the words of the battered woman, how she sought help from a clergyman, from a doctor, from the police; and to each of these narratives we hear successive verses of the lament, verses such as "Trouble is near, and there is no one to help."
The final interchange is this one. The first group says:

I have nowhere to go if it happens again. No one wants to take in a woman with four children. Even if there were someone kind enough to care, no one wants to become involved in what is commonly referred to as a "domestic situation."

Then the second group concludes:

O Lord, don't stay away from me! Come quickly to my rescue.

This Rite of Healing is then closed with a reflection prayer by the presider.[38]
Now, Ruether intends this ritual to be celebrated by communities of women, away from men—women who in their solidarity can begin to experience healing.[39] But surely the time must come when those who have been injured directly can begin to share such understandings of the lament psalms with those who have not been injured directly, women and men both; and, ultimately, one must pray with those who have done the injuring. In this way the faith of many Christians can be

toughened. Paul instructs us to rejoice with those who rejoice, weep with those who weep (Rom. 12:15), and these psalms can be a powerful means to lead to lament and to recovery within the whole church.

It is not only for the victims of domestic violence that the lament psalms are appropriate; they can lead us to look out at our world and (alas) find person after person, group after group whose voices need to be heard. Through these laments we may begin to hear them.

There are the politically marginal. The Nicaraguan poet Ernesto Cardenal has taken many of the Psalms and reconceived them in the language of current politics. These reconceptions are too specific to time and place to be a permanent substitute for the lament psalms in question, but their very specificity startles us, even in an English translation. Here is a translation of the beginning of his paraphrase of the same Psalm 22 that we have just considered; it is called, "Why Have You Left Me?"

> Lord O Lord my God
> why have you left me?
> I am a caricature of a man
> People think I am dirt
>   they mock me in all the papers
>
> I am encircled
>   there are tanks all round me
> Machine-gunners have me in their sights
>   there is barbed wire about me
>   electrified wire
> I am on a list
> I am called all day
> They have tattooed me
>   and marked me with a number.

The poem ends:

> Yet
> I shall tell my brothers and sisters
>   about you
> I shall praise you in our nation
> and my hymns will be heard
>   in a great generation
> The poor will go to a banquet
> and our people will give a great feast
>   the new people
>   yet to be born[40]

A reconception such as this one can lead us back to the original Psalms to listen to them with fresh ears, so that they may stretch and toughen our faith.

There are not only laments of the individual but laments of the community, and these, too, may enrich our common worship today, as Brueggemann reminds us.[41] It is true, few who are shaped by worship in our culture are accustomed to public catastrophe, and for that reason our first impulse on hearing a psalm such as Psalm 74, a lament for the destruction of the sanctuary (see chapter 3), might be to dismiss it as something from far away and long ago. But even for us there have been, in the last few decades, sudden emergencies that have at least momentarily jolted our public self-confidence: in the United States there were the assassinations of President John F. Kennedy and his brother Robert Kennedy, and of Martin Luther King, Jr. At such moments the laments of the community can give voice to our dismay:

> We do not see our emblems;
>> there is no longer any prophet,
>> and there is no one among us who knows how long.
> How long, O God, is the foe to scoff?
>> Is the enemy to revile your name forever? (Ps. 74:9-10)

It is reassuring to know that there are psalms not only for times of abundance, but of abasement as well.

Recovery

If the Psalms give voice to lament, then they also give voice to recovery. But it must be admitted that, as with the experience of lament, so the situation is with the experience of recovery and healing: it is spotty in the experience of many of our congregations. It is in the evangelical congregations of Protestantism that the ruling metaphor of healing has been ritualized; corporately, these congregations celebrate their healing from sin, and such communities have often held onto the tradition of "healing services" as well, healing people of their physical ills. By contrast, in many "mainline" Christian communities both the social assumptions and the liturgy have led to a thinning of the craving to be healed from sin and of the conviction that healing from physical ills is a possibility in the context of worship.

As for the matter of sin, I recall with bemusement a fellow member in a congregation to which I once belonged. It was said that if the corporate confession of sin was worded with the plural pronoun "we," he would repeat it with the congregation, but if it was worded with "I," he would remain silent; *his* conscience was certainly clear. Although few Christians might be found who would be so firm and consistent in their convictions as this man was, there are doubtless many who see little in themselves to repent of and therefore little need of healing. But to take one's share of responsibility for the divisions in the church, for the tragedies in our domestic and public life, and for all that renders human existence less than God's will is to share in the new creation brought about by Christ (2 Cor. 5:17). And when a congregation knows itself to be part of that new creation, then it can acknowledge with gladness that it has been healed.

As for physical healing, the onslaught of the epidemic of AIDS has brought a new awareness in many congregations of their corporate need for services of healing, and such events are becoming more common among us. And in all these urgencies of healing the Psalms can find a place.

Psalm 30 is a psalm of thanksgiving of an individual. Look at what God has done for the speaker: "You have drawn me up" (v. 2 [1]); "you have healed me" (v. 3 [2]); "you have brought up my soul [that is, my life] from Sheol [the abode of the dead]" (v. 4 [3])! If Christians are to rejoice with those who rejoice, weep with those who weep, then each member of a congregation who repeats this psalm can be thankful that those who have been ill or grieving or distressed have been brought to healing again by God's grace, and can recall instances in his or her own life when healing has taken place. "Weeping may linger for the night, but joy comes with the morning" (v. 6 [5]); "you have turned my mourning into dancing; you have taken off my sackcloth and clothed me with joy" (v. 12 [11]).

I know of a congregation that has been imaginative in its use of Scripture. One Sunday morning the pastor read the Old Testament lesson, which happened to be Ezek. 37:1-14, the vision of the valley of dry bones. He then asked the members of the congregation to meditate on the passage, and when any member felt his or her bones begin to live, to stand up. And when about two-thirds of the congregation was standing, they sang the doxology together. Perhaps Psalm 30 could be given similar treatment.

Praise

As for the praise of God, the Psalms are filled with it, especially the so-called hymns (see chapter 5). Psalms 146 through 150 are nothing but praise. Some modern Christians are puzzled by the matter of praising God. Why should God need praise? God is infinite; why should our words of praise be necessary, as if God has a poor self-image and constantly needs to be reassured?

Lewis, in his *Reflections on the Psalms*,[42] points out that if God does not need our praise, nevertheless God leads us to be glad to offer praise. We are in a position very much like someone in love: when one is in love, one never tires of saying, "I love you," and one's beloved never tires of hearing the words. The words not only affirm a relationship but deepen that relationship. So it is with praising God: we do it because God is God, because of what God has done for us and continues to do for us.

Now, it is striking that although there is no hesitation on the part of Christian communities to use psalms of praise, nevertheless we do not often enough take our cues from these psalms to praise God on our own. Instead, our praising of God is often limited to those very psalms of praise.

In the Roman Catholic, Episcopalian, and Lutheran liturgies, beyond the use of such psalms, praise is limited to set prayers such as the Gloria Patri, the Gloria in Excelsis, and the doxology. In Calvinist and Free Church traditions, where the order of service usually includes a "pastoral prayer," the prayer usually combines thanksgiving, petition, and intercession. I sometimes challenge theological students to write a pastoral prayer that consists entirely of adoration and praise of God. It is not as easy as it sounds; one is tempted so easily to slide off into offering thanksgiving for what God has done for us, and to set forth further petitions for help.

Now there is certainly no objection to thanksgiving and to petition in pastoral prayers. Indeed, the prayer that Jesus taught his disciples is largely petition—"Thy kingdom come" and the rest—but even that prayer begins with "Hallowed be thy name."

Psalm 139, as we saw in chapter 4, is a hymnic declaration of innocence. Its hymnic material renders it a suitable vehicle of praise. A moment ago we examined the reconception of Psalm 22 in the language of current politics by Ernesto Cardenal; Psalm 139, with its affirmation that God knows the inner life of the one who prays, lends itself to reconception in accordance with all the variety of psychological types that different people represent.

One scheme of analysis of various psychological types that is current today is the "enneagram," a system derived from the Sufi mystical tradition of Islam.[43] This scheme lays out nine personality types, and Kathleen Henry, a spiritual director, has employed the enneagram to adapt Psalm 139 for each of these nine types.

For example, "Ones" are those who avoid expressing anger; they are perfectionists who hate to waste time. For them, the adaptation of Psalm 139 begins,

> Spirit-Source of All Life and All Truth,
> I come from You.
> All that I am is known to You.
>
> Even if I bury, in the soil of resentment,
>   the seeds of my anger, deep,
> Even then,
> You are there—
> Seeing through to my inmost self,
> Claiming me as Your own.

"Fours" are people who perceive themselves to be different, who are isolated, who have often lived through pain and lack a sense of self. The adaptation of Psalm 139 for them begins:

> Indwelling Spirit God
> You are the One I would see
> —if only I could—
> In the mirror backstage.
>
> In the pain—the plummet and pitch—
> You abide in me, vigilant,
> Proclaiming against the empty darkness
> That I am alive.[44]

The psalms of praise remind us of the verbs appropriate to praise: "We praise you, O God; we sing to you, O God; how good you are, O God; you set the stars in their courses; you feed your creatures; you raise up those who are fallen; how great is your name, O God, in all the earth."

These phrases, and phrases in the traditional Christian prayers of praise, can help us find our own voices in praise: "We bless you, we revere you, we worship you, we extol you, we adore you, O God; over and over again we return to you, O God, to lift our voices in praise."

God waits to guide us into ever more authentic worship, and the Psalms have always been a central guide into that worship. They are particularly cogent in stimulating us to modes of worship that are not always diligently cultivated among us, in lament and in recovery and in praise. If we listen carefully to them, we will find them stretching and toughening our prayer and our worship.

NOTES

1. *The Old Farmer's Almanac, 1991* (Dublin, N.H.: Yankee, 1991), 20.

2. Godfrey A. Selig, *Secrets of the Psalms* (Arlington, Tex.: Dorene, 1982).

3. Tim Cahill, *Road Fever: A High-Speed Travelogue* (New York: Random House, 1991), 125–26.

4. This is the formulation of James Kugel, *The Idea of Biblical Poetry: Parallelism and Its History* (New Haven: Yale University Press, 1981), 8.

5. Walter Brueggemann, *Finally Comes the Poet: Daring Speech for Proclamation* (Minneapolis: Fortress, 1989), 3.

6. C. S. Lewis, *Reflections on the Psalms* (London: G. Bles, 1958).

7. Walter Brueggemann, *The Message of the Psalms: A Theological Commentary* (Augsburg Old Testament Studies; Minneapolis: Augsburg, 1984).

8. Walter Brueggemann, *Israel's Praise: Doxology against Idolatry and Ideology* (Philadelphia: Fortress, 1988).

9. This material appeared in an earlier form in Walter Brueggemann, "Psalms and the Life of Faith: A Suggested Typology of Function," *JSOT* 17 (June 1980):3–32.

10. See, e.g., the use made of Brueggemann's scheme in John Craghan, *Love and Thunder: A Spirituality of the Old Testament* (Collegeville, Minn.: Liturgical Press, 1983), chaps. 12–14.

11. It is a point made by many authorities today; see, e.g., Gail Ramshaw, *Christ in Sacred Speech: The Meaning of Liturgical Language* (Philadelphia: Fortress, 1986).

12. Brueggemann, *Israel's Praise*, chaps. 2, 3.

13. Brueggemann, *Finally Comes the Poet*, 52–53; cf. also idem, *Message of the Psalms*, chap. 3; and idem, *Israel's Praise*, 140–45.

14. Robert Davidson, *The Courage to Doubt: Exploring an Old Testament Theme* (London: SCM, 1983), 12–15.

15. Brueggemann, *Message of the Psalms*, 51–52.

16. Leopold Sabourin, *The Psalms: Their Origin and Meaning* (New York: Alba House, 1974).

17. Psalms 5, 6, 7, 13, 17, 22, 25, 26, 28, 31, 35, 36, 38, 39, 42, 43, 51, 54, 55, 56, 57, 59, 61, 63, 64, 69, 70, 71, 86, 88, 102, 109, 120, 130, 140, 141, 142, 143.

18. Psalms 12, 44, 58, 60, 74, 77, 79, 80, 82, 83, 85, 90, 94, 106, 108, 123, 126, 137.

19. Psalms 13, 17, 22, 25, 31, 42, 43, 51, 54, 63, 69, 71, 80, 85, 86, 90, 123, 126, 130, 137.

20. Psalm 69 is represented by vv. 14, 17, 30-31, 33-34 (13, 16, 29-30, 32-33); Psalm 85 is represented by vv. 9-14 (8-13).

21. *Inclusive Language Psalms* (New York: Pilgrim, 1987): Psalms 5, 13, 17, 22, 25, 26, 28, 31, 35, 36, 42, 43, 44, 51, 57, 63, 69, 70, 71, 77, 80, 82, 85, 90, 94, 102, 106, 126, 130, 137, 140, 141, 142, 143.

22. Psalms 25, 36, 44, 63, 69, 77, 85, 94, 106, 143.

23. Psalms 3, 4, 11, 16, 23, 27, 62, 121, 131.

24. Psalms 115, 125, 129.

25. Psalms 4, 16, 23, 27, 62, 121, 131.

26. Psalms 3, 4, 16, 23, 27, 62, 115, 121, 125.

27. Psalms 9–10 (counted as two psalms), 30, 32, 34, 40, 41, 92, 107, 116, 138.

28. Psalms 65, 66, 67, 68, 118, 124.

29. Omitting only Psalms 9–10.

30. Psalms 8, 19, 29, 33, 100, 103, 104, 111, 113, 114, 117, 135, 136, 145, 146, 147, 148, 149, 150.

31. Psalms 8, 19, 29, 33, 100, 103, 104, 113, 117, 136, 145, 146, 147.

32. Omitting only Psalms 136 and 148.

33. Brueggemann, *Message of the Psalms*, 51; and see his whole discussion, 51–53.

34. I am indebted here to a research paper submitted to my colleague Carole R. Fontaine by Dr. Janice P. Leary of Natick, Mass., who has done therapy with battered women.

35. Mitchell Dahood, *Psalms I: 1–50* (Garden City, N.Y.: Doubleday, 1966), 248, 251–52.

36. Daytime Prayer for Wednesday of the Second Week, in *Christian Prayer: The Liturgy of the Hours* (Boston: Daughters of St. Paul, 1976), 728.

37. Del Martin, *Battered Wives* (San Francisco: Volcano, 1981), 1–5.

38. Rosemary Radford Ruether, *Women–Church: Theology and Practice of Feminist Liturgical Communities* (San Francisco: Harper & Row, 1985), 153–59.

39. Ibid., 2–7.

40. Ernesto Cardenal, *Psalms* (New York: Crossroad, 1981), 25, 26.

41. Brueggemann, *Message of the Psalms*, 67–77.

42. Lewis, *Reflections on the Psalms*, chap. 9.

43. Maria Beesing, Robert J. Nogosek, and Patrick H. O'Leary, *The Enneagram: A Journey of Self Discovery* (Denville, N.J.: Dimension, 1984); cf. Kathleen V. Hurley and Theodore E. Dobson, *What's My Type?* (San Francisco: Harper, 1991).

44. Kathleen M. Henry, *The Book of Enneagram Prayers* (privately printed, 1987; obtainable from Alabaster Jar Liturgical Arts, 14 Rockwood St., Jamaica Plain, Mass. 02130), 108, 96.

16

Censored Texts

For centuries, in great sections of the Christian church, every verse of the full Psalter has been recited. This has been the case with the weekly recitation of the Divine Office in the Eastern Orthodox Church (see chapter 10) and was the case in the Roman Catholic Church until 1970 (see chapter 12). The Calvinist churches, too, drew up metrical versions of all 150 Psalms (see chapter 11), though one cannot be sure of the extent to which a given congregation would use each of the 150 systematically.

Yet though the Psalms may nurture and even stretch the sensibility of Christians, as we affirmed in chapter 15, nevertheless Christians have had the tendency to exclude specific psalms, or specific verses of psalms, from their worship, and it is these exclusions that I discuss in this chapter. It is important to discern why these omissions are made and, above all, to ask whether it is appropriate to omit psalms, or portions of psalms, from our worship.

The Omissions in the Liturgy
of the Hours

Central to this question is the current Roman Catholic Liturgy of the Hours. As we learned in chapter 14, the intention of the Liturgy of the Hours, along with the complementary four-week Psalter, is to offer a vehicle by which those who use it may recite the full Psalter in the course of four weeks. Yet three psalms are omitted altogether—Psalms 58, 83, and 109—and there are nineteen other psalms from which one or more verses are omitted. In this regard the *Apostolic Constitution* issued by the pope in 1970 on the Divine Office explains somewhat ingenuously, "in this new arrangement of the psalms some few of the psalms and verses which are somewhat harsh in tone have been omitted, especially because of the difficulties that were foreseen from their use in vernacular celebration."[1] In other words, parts of the Psalms that did not seem offensive to reciters who only half understood them in Latin are now to be omitted when the reciters hear what they really mean in their own language.

I ended chapter 15 by citing the beginning of some modern adaptations of Psalm 139; but it is precisely that same Psalm 139 that offers one of the most notable examples of a censored text: verses 19 through 22 are omitted in the Liturgy of the Hours and, indeed, universally in various liturgical uses made of the psalm.[2] These verses are an expression of hatred of the psalmist's enemies (who are understood to be God's enemies) and the wish that God would kill them. I suggested in chapter 4 that the enemies are not so much "men of blood" as "men of idols," and that the psalmist in vv. 21-22 is affirming his own loyalty to Yahweh. These verses are thus the climax of the psalm, but the loss over the centuries of the listeners' understanding of the innuendo of idol worship (if that interpretation is correct) and, above all, the expression of the wish that God would kill the enemies render these verses unusable without careful reinterpretation (see chapter 19).

I approach the matter of omissions by beginning with the shortest omissions and proceeding to the longest, since it is a consideration of the short omissions that pinpoints the issues precisely. Of the nineteen psalms from which single verses or groups of verses are omitted, six have only one verse omitted: Pss. 5:11 (10); 54:7 (5); 55:16 (15); 110:6; 141:10; 143:12. Four psalms have one and a half or two verses omitted: Pss. 28:4-5; 31:18-19 (17-18); 40:15-16 (14-15); 56:7b-8 (6b-7). There are six that have three to five verses omitted: Pss. 21:9-13 (8-12); 63:10-12 (9-11); 79:6-7, 12; 137:7-9; 139:19-22 (as we have already noted); 140:10-12 (9-11). And there are three psalms that have large-scale omissions: Pss. 35:3a, 4-8, 20-21, 24-26; 59:6-9, 12-16 (5-8, 11-15); 69:23-29 (22-28). Finally, there are the three psalms (58, 83, 109) that are omitted in their entirety.

All the omissions involve imprecations (curses) that occur in laments. But there is no way to reach this conclusion without an examination, somewhat tedious though it may seem, of the omissions.

Psalm 5 is a lament of the individual. As such, it offers many of the expected components of a lament: a plea and invocation (vv. 2-3a [1-2a]); description of worship by the psalmist (vv. 3b-4 [2b-3]); praise of God as the upholder of the righteous (vv. 5-7 [4-6]); a petition (vv. 8-9 [7-8]); and a complaint (v. 10 [9]). The psalm closes with a blessing on the congregation (vv. 12-13 [11-12]). But it is the plea to God against the enemies and the imprecation against them (v. 10 [9]) that have been omitted: "Make them [my enemies] bear their guilt, O God; let them fall by their own counsels; because of their many transgressions cast them out, for they have rebelled against you."

Psalms 54 and 55 are both likewise laments of the individual, and, again, pleas and imprecations are omitted. Ps. 54:7 (5) reads, "He [God] will repay my enemies for their evil. In your faithfulness, put an end to them"; and Ps. 55:16 (15) reads, "Let death come upon them; let them go down alive to Sheol; for evil is in their homes and in their hearts." Inasmuch as I cited the two immediately preceding verses of Psalm 55—namely, vv. 14-15 (13-14)—in chapter 15 as instances of vivid diction that would be helpful for a victim of domestic violence, the breaking of the continuity of the psalm that would result by the omission of v. 16 (15) raises difficult questions; I return to the matter below.

Psalm 110 is a royal psalm, probably for a coronation (see chapter 2). Here v. 6 is omitted, part of an affirmation of God's punishment of enemy nations. The affirmation actually begins in v. 5, but v. 5 is not omitted; it is simply that the diction of v. 6 is too extreme for easy reading: "[v. 5] The Lord is at your right hand; he will shatter kings on the day of his wrath. [v. 6] He will execute judgment among the nations, filling them with corpses; he will shatter heads over the wide earth."

The two remaining single verses that are omitted are Pss. 141:10 and 143:12; both psalms are laments of the individual. Psalm 141:10 is an imprecation—"Let the wicked fall into their own nets, while I alone escape"—and Ps. 143:12 is a plea for God's punishment of enemies—"In your steadfast love cut off my enemies, and destroy all my adversaries, for I am your servant." Both 141:10 and 143:12, as it happens, are the last verses in their respective psalms, and it would be particularly difficult to recite psalms in full that close with seeming self-righteousness and contempt for the enemy.

I move to psalms from which a verse and a half or two verses have been omitted. Psalm 28 is a lament of the individual, and from this psalm vv. 4-5 are omitted. Verse 4 is an imprecation very much like 54:7 (5): "Repay them according to their work, and according to the evil of their deeds; repay them according to the work of their hands; render them their due reward"; and v. 5, the following verse, gives the motive for the imprecation.

In Psalm 31, vv. 18-19 (17-18) are omitted; vv. 16b-18a (15b-17a) are a plea to God on the psalmist's behalf, and vv. 18b-19 (17b-18) are an imprecation. The imprecation is omitted ("Let the wicked be put to shame; let them go dumbfounded to Sheol"), and, for simplicity's sake, the previous half-verse (v. 18a [17a]) as well.

Whether Psalm 40 is a thanksgiving of the individual to which a prayer for deliverance (vv. 14-18 [13-17]) was added, or whether the psalm is a unified lament, in any event vv. 15-16 (14-15), an imprecation, have been omitted. In this instance the imprecation is not particularly offensive, and because Ps. 70:3-4 (2-3) contains essentially the same text, and the full text of Psalm 70 appears in the Liturgy of the Hours, it is likely that 40:15-16 (14-15) was omitted chiefly because of the length of Psalm 40, which, even with the omission of the two verses in question, has been divided into two sections for recitation.

The text of Ps. 56:7b-8 (6b-7), part of a lament, is somewhat difficult to understand, but this omitted sequence contains a plea to punish the enemies ("in wrath cast down the peoples, O God!").

I now turn to psalms with longer omissions, dealing first with the six psalms that omit three to five verses. Psalm 21 is a royal psalm; the context is a battle (see chapter 4). Confusingly, the addressee shifts within the psalm. Thus in vv. 2-7 (1-6) the psalmist addresses Yahweh about the king; but in vv. 9-13 (8-12), which are the verses that are omitted, the addressee is less certain: it would seem to be Yahweh that is addressed in v. 10a (9a) (though v. 10 [9], or part of it, may be a later insertion),[3] whereas in vv. 9, 11-13 (8, 10-12) it is likely to be the king that is addressed. In any event, the omitted verses are a prediction of the king's victory—indeed, a blessing that the king will have victory[4]—and the heightened rhetoric of these verses is distasteful (v. 11 [10]: "You will destroy their offspring from the earth, and their children from among humankind").

From Psalm 63, a lament of the individual, vv. 10-12 (9-11) have been omitted. Verses 10-11 (9-10) are either an imprecation ("may those who seek to destroy my life go down into the depths of the earth," as the new Jewish version [*Tanakh*] translates) or a prediction ("those who seek to destroy my life shall go down to the depths of the earth," as the NRSV renders them); in either case, they speak hopefully of the death of the psalmist's enemies. Verse 12 (11) is, to us, a curious affirmation about the king's adherence to God, but the last line—"for the mouth of liars shall be stopped"—like the closing verses of Psalms 54 and 55, renders the verse a distasteful closing for the psalm.

Psalm 79 is a lament of the community—specifically, a prayer of deliverance from national enemies. From the psalm, vv. 6-7 and 12 have been omitted. Verses 6 and 7 are a plea that God's wrath be poured out on these national enemies, who are portrayed as enemies not only of Israel but of God, and that plea is reinforced in v. 12 ("Return sevenfold into the bosom of our neighbors the taunts with which they taunted you, O Lord!"). As was noted in chapter 4, vv. 6-7 are cited in Jer. 10:25, and his treatment of these verses may be a clue for us in the matter of omissions (see below).

Psalm 137 is another lament of the community, the lament of the exiles in Babylon; vv. 7-9 of this psalm are omitted. Verse 7 is a plea that God punish the Edomites for what they have done to Jerusalem, and vv. 8-9 are a sudden address to personified "daughter Babylon," announcing the speakers' congratulations to those bringing retribution on her ("Happy shall they be who take your little ones and dash them against the rock!"). Like Pss. 54:7 (5); 55:16 (15); and 63:10-12, these words are particularly harsh as an ending for the psalm.

Psalm 139 omits four verses: they are a longer variation on the diction of Ps. 31:7 (6). This is the omission I discussed at the beginning of the chapter.

And in Psalm 140, another lament of the individual, vv. 10-12 (9-11) are omitted, verses that offer imprecations and pleas to Yahweh to destroy the psalmist's enemies ("Let burning coals fall on them! Let them be flung into pits, no more to rise!").

I turn now to Psalms 35, 59, and 69, from which a significant proportion of verses have been removed. Psalm 35 is one of the longest laments of the individual, and the sequence of elements normal to these laments is heard twice: that is, vv. 1-10 offer a tolerably complete lament, and vv. 11-28, another. In this way imprecations are heard in both vv. 4-8 and 24-26 (both sequences omitted in the Liturgy of the Hours); and vv. 20-21, complaints about the behavior of the enemies, are omitted as well. Particularly difficult for present-day liturgical use are the psalmist's quotations of his enemies' jeering: "They say, 'Aha, Aha, our eyes have seen it'" (v.

21); "Do not let them say to themselves, 'Aha, we have our heart's desire'" and "Do not let them say, 'We have swallowed you up'" (v. 25). (Strikingly, the other relevant occurrence of a citation of the enemies "who say 'Aha'" (Ps. 70:4 [3]) has been allowed to stand because the translation paraphrases by rendering "who jeer.")[5] And, finally, v. 3a is also omitted, a plea to God to "draw the spear and javelin against my pursuers."

Psalm 59 is a lament of the individual, and, even more than Psalm 35, it appears to be double, with an identical refrain at the end of each half (vv. 10 [9] and 18 [17]). Though it is the psalm of an individual who testifies to having "blood-thirsty enemies" (v. 3 [2]), the psalm has evidently been broadened to include among the enemies the pagan nations (vv. 6 [5] and 9 [8]). From this psalm, vv. 6-9 (5-8) and 12-16 (11-15) are omitted. Verses 6-9 (5-8) include the two references to the nations: v. 6 (5) is a plea to punish the nations; vv. 7-8 (6-7) are a vivid description of the nations, including a citation of their words ("Each evening they come back, howling like dogs and prowling about the city. There they are, bellowing with the mouths, with sharp words on their lips, for 'Who . . . will hear us?'"); and v. 9 (8) is an affirmation of confidence in God, who holds the nations in derision. A consideration of vv. 12-16 (11-15) is complicated because the text of vv. 11-14 (10-13) seems to be in some disarray: the plea to God not to kill the enemies but just to make them totter (v. 12 [11]) is in direct contradiction with the plea to "consume them" (v. 14 [13]). But both pleas and their related imprecations have been omitted in the Liturgy of the Hours. Further, v. 15 (14) is a repetition of v. 7 (6), and v. 16 (15) is an extension of the simile; these verses too, like the antecedent v. 7 (6), have been omitted.

Psalm 69 is a lament of the individual; from this psalm, vv. 23-29 (22-28) have been omitted. Verses 20-22 (19-21) are a description of the behavior of the enemies, and the omitted seven verses that follow consist of the psalmist's imprecations on the enemies (vv. 23-24, 26, 29 [vv. 22-23, 25, 28]); pleas for punishment of the enemies (vv. 24, 28 [23, 27]); and a motivation for the pleas (v. 27 [26]). The imprecations are distasteful (e.g., v. 24 [23]: "Let their eyes be darkened so that they cannot see, and make their loins tremble continually").

Finally, I turn to the three whole psalms that are omitted. Psalm 58 is a lament of the community. The text of this psalm is somewhat puzzling because of the seeming shifts in the addressee. Though there is a slight text difficulty in v. 2 (1), the psalm seems to begin with a mocking address to pagan gods or, perhaps, to oppressive overlords (see chapter 3). But then v. 7 (6) is addressed to the true God, and v. 10 (9) is addressed to the worshiping community of Israel. Verses 4-6 (3-5) are a description of the wicked, perhaps those sponsored by the pagan gods; they are compared to snakes that cannot be charmed. Verse 7 (6) is a plea to God to disarm the wicked ("O God, break the teeth in their mouths"), and vv. 8-10 (7-9) are an imprecation for their destruction ("let them vanish like water that runs away"). Verse 11 (10) announces the coming victory of the "righteous," that is, the members of the worshiping community, and their retribution is vividly portrayed: they will "bathe their feet in the blood of the wicked." And, finally, v. 12 (11) is a statement of the vindication of the true God of the righteous. The confusing shifts in the identity of the addressee and the preoccupation with enemies, to the exclusion of any expression of trust in God, renders the psalm difficult for Christian worship.

Psalm 83 is likewise a lament of the community: it is a prayer of deliverance from national enemies (see chapter 3). Verse 2 (1) is a petition that God not be passive in the present emergency; vv. 3-9 (2-8) describe the emergency; vv. 10-17 (9-16) are a plea to God for the destruction of the enemies; and vv. 18-19 (17-18) are an imprecation, a wish for punishment of the enemies. Beyond the issue of the imprecations themselves, there is a contributing difficulty in the psalm, namely, the long series of proper names (vv. 7-12 [6-11]).

Psalm 109 is the longest of the three full psalms omitted and, in contrast to Psalms 58 and 83, is a lament of the individual. It contains an imprecation (vv. 6-19) that is uniquely long in the Psalter ("May his children be orphans, and his wife a widow" [v. 9], and so forth). A key question for an understanding of this psalm is whether the psalmist is here cursing his enemy or whether, as many scholars today believe,[6] the psalmist is quoting the curses that the enemies are leveling against him. There are several bits of evidence in favor of the latter suggestion. First of all, vv. 2-4 emphasize the words of enemies (who are referred to in the plural), so that a citation of their words in the following verses would be altogether natural. Then, in v. 5, the psalmist insists that his love for them is answered by their hatred; it would seem inappropriate that this statement be followed by fourteen verses in which he would express his own hatred. Then, in the long imprecation (vv. 6-19), the one who is cursed is referred to in the singular; the singular number would be more appropriate in reference to the psalmist than to the enemies, who were referred to in the plural in vv. 2-4. And in v. 20, after the imprecation, the enemies once more are referred to in the plural; the word "that," which begins v. 20, seems to refer to the long imprecation of vv. 6-19. However, it must be stressed that there is no expression in the Hebrew text corresponding to "they say" at the beginning of v. 6. In any event, the NRSV accepts this understanding of vv. 6-19 as a citation of the psalmist's enemies, in contrast to the RSV, which did not.

Verse 1 is a petition (like Ps. 83:2 [1]) that God not be silent. Verses 2-5 offer a description of the enemies; vv. 6-19, as already set forth, appear to be a long citation of the enemies' words against the psalmist. Verse 20 is a prayer that these words be applied to the enemies; v. 21 is a plea that God act; vv. 22-25 are a description of the psalmist's weakness and humiliation; and v. 26 is a renewal of the plea. Verses 27-29 are an imprecation that the enemies be punished, and vv. 30-31 are a vow to hold a thanksgiving service when God has completed his work with the enemies.

Though the interpretation offered here of vv. 6-19 of this psalm might reassure Christians if they recited it, nevertheless the very length of that section of the psalm militates against its usefulness in worship. (But it should be noted that six verses of the psalm—vv. 21-22, 26-27, 30-31—serve in the Roman Catholic scheme as the responsorial psalm for the weekday Mass for Thursday of the Thirtieth Week of

Ordinary Time, toward the end of October; these six verses make an acceptable lament!)[7]

Now, how may all these omissions be classified? Form-critically, of these twenty-two psalms there are fourteen laments of the individual (Psalms 5, 28, 31, 35, 54, 55, 56, 59, 63, 69, 109, 140, 141, 143) and four laments of the community (Psalms 58, 79, 83, 137). Of the four remaining psalms, Psalm 40 has been classified as a thanksgiving psalm, but it ends with a plea for help, so it, too, may be classified as a lament of the individual. Psalm 21 is a royal psalm, a thanksgiving after battle; Psalm 110, another royal psalm, was perhaps intended as a coronation psalm. And Psalm 139 is a hymnic declaration of innocence.

Strikingly, every one of the omissions refers to the psalmist's enemies, who are assumed to be God's enemies as well (on this, see chapter 4). Most common are the psalmist's third-person imprecations against the enemies, pleas in the second-person to God to act against the enemies, or a mixture of both. The psalmist wishes that God would kill the enemies (Ps. 83:10-11 [9-10]), send them to Sheol (Ps. 31:18 [17]), or otherwise make them vanish (Ps. 35:5); that God would punish them (Ps. 59:6 [5]) or break their power, sometimes in picturesque ways (Ps. 69:23 [22]); that they would be dishonored or shamed (Pss. 35:4; 83:17 [16]; 109:29); or that they would learn that God is God (Ps. 83:19 [18]). Interspersed with these pleas and imprecations are descriptions of the terrible behavior of the enemies: they jeer (Ps. 35:20-21), they are like skulking dogs (Ps. 59:7-8, 15-16 [6-7, 14-15]). Sometimes the psalmist affirms that God will punish the national enemies (Pss. 58:11-12 [10-11]; 59:9 [8]; 110:6); sometimes it is predicted that the king will destroy national enemies (Ps. 58:11-12 [10-11]). But sometimes one cannot be certain whether the psalmist is affirming that the enemies will be destroyed or praying that they may be (Ps. 63:10-12 [9-11]). The psalmist offers congratulations to those who destroy Israel's enemies (Ps. 137:8-9). The psalmist affirms how much he hates God's enemies (Ps. 139:21-22).

Now, we have already noted that Ps. 40:15-16 (14-15) was omitted but that the virtually identical Ps. 70:3-4 was retained. But beyond such an inconsistency in the treatment of essentially the same set of verses, one may ask: Are there pleas and imprecations regarding the enemy that are retained in the Liturgy of the Hours?

In a survey of Psalms 1 through 20, one finds the following such verses (I cite the NRSV): Ps. 10:15, "Break the arm of the wicked and evildoers; seek out their wickedness until you find none"; Ps. 11:6, "On the wicked he will rain coals of fire and sulfur; a scorching wind shall be the portion of their cup"; Ps. 12:4 (3), "May the Lord cut off all flattering lips, the tongue that makes great boasts"; and Ps. 17:13-14:

> Rise up, O Lord, confront them, overthrow them! By your sword deliver my life from the wicked, from mortals—by your hand, O Lord—from mortals whose portion in life is in this world. May their bellies be filled with what you have stored up for them; may their children have more than enough; may they leave something over to their little ones.

These passages offer strong language. Psalm 11:6 may have been retained because "fire and sulphur" there are reminiscent of "sulphur and fire" in the Sodom story in Gen. 19:24 and because of Paul's reference in Rom. 12:20 to heaping burning coals on the heads of one's enemies (though he is in that verse citing Prov. 25:21-22). And to some degree these verses could be retained in the Liturgy of the Hours because the translation was softened. Thus, because "arm" in Ps. 10:15 has a metaphorical reach, the translation "power" is used. And though the meaning of Ps. 17:13-14 appears to be that God should visit on the enemies (and their children) a sample from the riches of his punishments, the Liturgy of the Hours offers a softer rendition of v. 14: "Let your hand, O Lord, rescue me from men, from men whose reward is in this present life. You give them their fill of your treasures; they rejoice in abundance of offspring and leave their wealth to their children."[8]

The Liturgy of the Hours has thus omitted some, if not all, of the harsh language regarding enemies. Such language is felt to be particularly difficult when it closes a psalm (Psalms 63, 137, 141, 143). And citations of the speech of the enemies are sometimes omitted, doubtless because their vividness might appear humorous to a modern reader or listener.

The Stance of Christians toward Enemies

I made an attempt in the course of chapter 4 to set forth the Israelite under-standing of enemies that is offered in the Psalms. But Christians, too, have enemies, both personal and public; I touched on this matter in chapter 15. In any event, the fact does not need to be stressed. It is not only a matter of conflict between Christians and other people of goodwill; there really are people of malice in this world. So the question before us is this: What attitude are Christians to have toward their enemies?

It would not be appropriate here to try to draft a complete answer to that question, but it is necessary at least to offer a provisional answer in the context of these difficult passages in the Psalms. I attempt one in ten propositions.

1. Jesus taught Christians to love their enemies (Matt. 5:44 [Luke 6:27]). Therefore such an expression as Ps. 139:21-22 is excluded from Christian use without a thorough reconception of "hate" and the identity of the enemies (on which, see chapter 19). Such love of enemies can hardly be a matter primarily of the emotions but is more a matter of the will: it would be fair to say that if one does not like one's enemies, one's calling is still to will the best for them. This is certainly implied by the correlative of "love your enemies," namely, "Pray for those who persecute you." Even some of the psalmists sensed what this might mean: "In return for my love they accuse me, even while I make prayer for them. So they reward me evil for good, and hatred for my love" (Ps. 109:4-5; compare 35:12).

2. The call to love one's enemies must be exercised within the context of the claims of justice: if an injustice has been done, then it needs to be made

right. Here the matter becomes complicated, for one must deal with one's own stance, the stance of one's enemies, and the stance of God.

3. The psalmist claims he is "righteous" (or "innocent"); that is, the psalmist claims he is on the side of God, for otherwise he would not be singing a psalm at all. Even a psalm such as Psalm 51 hardly contradicts this statement. By contrast, Christians are warned in many ways against self-righteousness (Matt. 7:11; Rom. 12:3). Christians must never assume that the wrong is all on the side of their enemies. In this regard, passages in the psalms that encourage self-righteousness are misleading to Christians.

4. However, it is a fact that sometimes Christians are abused, oppressed, persecuted, and in such situations they need the help of protectors and, above all, of God; this is what I stressed in chapter 15. The same psalms that might be harmful to Christians who tend to self-righteousness might be empowering for Christians who lack power or self-esteem. How many Christians blame themselves for a bad relationship at home or at work when the fault is really more in their adversaries?

5. Christians who are oppressed by enemies seek not only an end to their oppression but vindication, both among their peers and before their enemies. Here the psalms may be truly helpful (Psalm 54 and *passim*).

6. The crucial question then is: With regard to their enemies, what are Christians to wish for and pray for? Ideally, one would wish for their change of heart (Luke 17:3-4) and for reconciliation with them (Matt. 5:24). Lacking that, one would wish for their recognition that they are in the wrong; that is the burden of the psalmists' prayers that the enemy be shamed (Pss. 6:11 [10]; 31:18 [17]; and *passim*). One would further wish that they might cease their oppression (Ps. 7:10 [9]), or that God would take away their power to oppress (Ps. 59:12 [11]). But any attitude of gloating over one's enemies' fall is excluded; expressions such as that in Ps. 52:8-9 (6-7) can be dangerous: "The righteous will see, and fear and will laugh at the evildoer, saying, 'See the one who would not take refuge in God.'"

7. It is difficult to say whether it is legitimate for Christians to wish for commensurate hurt on their enemies, whether that hurt be exercised by the psalmist empowered by God (Ps. 41:11 [10]) or by God alone (Pss. 28:4; 109:20; 137:8). Jesus' words in Matt. 5:38-39 would seem to exclude the possibility. By contrast, I discussed Ps. 41:11 (10) in chapter 15, and there I suggested how necessary it is that there come to be parity between the one who is oppressed and the oppressor. Commensurate hurt on one's enemy is certainly one kind of parity, but it may not be the best kind; the removal of power from one's enemies may be preferable.

8. It follows from what has been said that it is not legitimate for Christians to wish death on their enemies. Expressions such as are found in Pss. 55:16 (15); 58:11 (10); or 137:9 are excluded for Christians, unless one's notion

of the identification of one's "enemies" is drastically transformed (on which, see chapter 19).

9. Passages in which God is cited as showing contempt toward the national enemies of Israel are likewise questionable. In Ps. 60:10 (8), duplicated in Ps. 108:10 (9), God speaks, "Moab is my washbasin; on Edom I hurl my shoe; over Philistia I shout in triumph." This is a passage, as it happens, that is retained in the Liturgy of the Hours; whether it is retained because the peoples of Moab, Edom, and Philistia are gone from history by those names, so that the expressions are not perceived to be concretely relevant; or whether the listing in the previous verse of peoples of which God is understood to approve (Gilead, Manasseh, Ephraim, Judah) makes it difficult to exclude the disapproved territories; or whether those who prepared the Liturgy of the Hours simply hesitated to censor God's quoted words, would be hard to say. But the mood of contempt put in the mouth of God ("with exultation"; Ps. 60:8 [6]) is difficult to harmonize with the Christian understanding of God.

10. Most difficult is the question of the stance of Christians in a nation at war, when the civil authorities have declared another nation or group of nations to be enemies. One might defend as a legitimate goal for Christians the destruction of enemy military or political institutions, but Christians must always seek to minimize the destruction of human life.

We may tentatively conclude that in Christian worship we are occasionally justified in omitting certain sequences in the Psalms.

A Clue from Jeremiah

Guidance on this matter may come to us from an unexpected quarter, namely, from Jeremiah. Jeremiah 10:25 cites Ps. 79:6-7. Most commentators take that verse in Jeremiah not as a word from the prophet but simply as a secondary addition to the book of Jeremiah from Psalm 79. But, as I have already explained in chapter 4, I propose that Jeremiah himself cites this verse, along with Prov. 16:9 or 20:24, as verses that his fellow citizens should not be reciting, lost as they are in their self-righteousness.[9] Now, if my analysis is sound, it is striking that Jeremiah should have cited these two verses of Psalm 79, since they are two of the three verses of that psalm omitted in the Liturgy of the Hours.

It would be too easy to conclude that we are justified in omitting these two verses, and verses like them, simply because Jeremiah seems to have cited them as showing a wrong attitude. One might argue away the word from Jeremiah by saying that it was a valid judgment in his day but does not necessarily fit our time; or that because the Psalms were not canonized in his day, were not considered Scripture, the prophet is not really criticizing Scripture. But Jeremiah's criticism certainly reinforces a Christian judgment to avoid such expressions of hatred on those outside the worshiping community who are considered enemies.

Omissions in the Common Lectionary

As one might expect, when we turn from the Liturgy of the Hours to other current worship material that uses the Psalter, we find similar patterns of avoidance. As an example we may examine the Common Lectionary (see chapter 14). There are only seven verses that are omitted by the Liturgy of the Hours that are retained in the Common Lectionary: these are Pss. 28:4-5, a relatively mild call for retribution ("Repay them according to their work"), and 35:20-21, 24-26, passages in which the enemy is quoted ("They say, 'Aha, aha'"). But, as one might expect, the Common Lectionary omits the cursing of enemies: it omits Ps. 137:7-9, and it omits not only Ps. 139:19-22 but vv. 23-24 of that psalm as well.

But since the lectionaries are intended to be only a *selection* of the material of the Psalter, other principles of selectivity are at work in them as well, principles that we have noted at several points along the way. Psalms are trimmed when they are too long for lectionary use (in the Roman Catholic lectionary more than in the Common Lectionary). Thus of Psalm 104, the psalm for Pentecost, the Common Lectionary uses vv. 24-34, whereas the Roman Catholic lectionary uses vv. 1, 24, 29-31, 34 (compare the discussion in chapter 14). And laments, as we discovered in chapter 15, are underrepresented in the lectionaries. Neither the Roman Catholic lectionary nor the Common Lectionary hears God say, "Moab is my washbasin" (Pss. 60:10 [8]; 108:10 [9]).

But the ultimate question is how we understand the Psalms to function in worship—whether the Psalms are to stand on their own, as they do in the daily office and in the metrical psalms in the Calvinist tradition, or whether portions of the Psalms are to be used for resonance in a scheme of Christian readings. This is a question that has not received a definitive answer in Christian tradition; it is one to which we return in chapter 19.

Perhaps it is appropriate to close this chapter by considering the constant tendency the church has to bypass material with a negative import. Let me offer an example from hymnody. A hymn that appears in many hymnals today, both Protestant and Roman Catholic, is "The church's one foundation"; it was written by Samuel John Stone in 1866. The hymn celebrates the basis for church unity, "Jesus Christ her Lord"—indeed, as the second stanza says, "one Lord, one faith, one birth."

In most hymnals the hymn is offered in four stanzas, but these are the first, second, fourth, and fifth stanzas of Stone's hymn. The third, crucial stanza is not so often printed:

Though with a scornful wonder,
  Men see her sore oppressed,
By schisms rent asunder,
  By heresies distressed;
Yet saints their watch are keeping,
  Their cry goes up, "How long?"
And soon the night of weeping
  Shall be the morn of song.[10]

In this stanza, the cry of the saints—"How long?"—is a lament, and there is a tendency when singing a hymn not to lament, even when there is a promise that weeping will turn to song. It is tendency it would be good to resist, for the sake of Christian realism.

NOTES

1. Pope Paul VI, *Apostolic Constitution, Promulgation, The Divine Office* (November 1, 1970), sec. 4, in *Christian Prayer: The Liturgy of the Hours* (Boston: Daughters of St. Paul, 1976), 15.

2. E.g., in the *Pilgrim Hymnal* (Boston: Pilgrim, 1958), the responsive reading of Psalm 139 uses vv. 1-12, 17-18, 23-24.

3. Erhard S. Gerstenberger, *Psalms: Part I, with an Introduction to Cultic Poetry* (Grand Rapids: Eerdmans, 1988), 106; Hans-Joachim Kraus, *Psalms 1–59: A Commentary* (Minneapolis: Augsburg, 1988), 287–88.

4. Gerstenberger, *Psalms*, 106.

5. Daytime Prayer, Wednesday of the Third Week, in *Liturgy of the Hours*, 843.

6. So first Hans Schmidt, *Die Psalmen* (HAT I, 15; Tübingen: Mohr, 1934), 200–201; see Artur Weiser, *The Psalms* (OTL; Philadelphia: Westminster, 1962), 690–91; Hans-Joachim Kraus, *Psalms 60–150: A Commentary* (Minneapolis: Augsburg, 1989), 338; against this view is Mitchell Dahood, *Psalms III: 101–150* (Garden City, N.Y.: Doubleday, 1970), 99.

7. I have used *The Vatican II Weekday Missal* (Boston: Daughters of St. Paul, 1975), 1492.

8. This translation is similar in approach to that of the NAB.

9. William L. Holladay, *Jeremiah 1* (Philadelphia: Fortress, 1986), 339, 344.

10. One notes its presence and absence in various hymnals. It is omitted in *The Methodist Hymnal* (Nashville: Methodist Publishing House, 1932); *The Hymnal* (of the Evangelical and Reformed Church) (St. Louis: Eden Publishing House, 1941); *Pilgrim Hymnal* (1958); *Service Book and Hymnal of the Lutheran Church of America* (Minneapolis: Augsburg, 1958); Theodore Marier (ed.), *Hymns, Psalms and Spiritual Canticles* (Belmont, Mass.: BACS Publishing, 1972). It is included in the Episcopal *Hymnal 1940* and *The* (Episcopal) *Hymnal 1982* (New York: The [Episcopal] Church Hymnal Corporation, 1982); Inter-Lutheran Commission on Worship, *Lutheran Book of Worship* (Minneapolis: Augsburg, 1978); *The United Methodist Hymnal: Book of United Methodist Worship* (Nashville: United Methodist Publishing House, 1989); *The Presbyterian Hymnal: Hymns, Psalms, and Spiritual Songs* (Louisville: Westminster/John Knox, 1990).

17

What Makes a Translation?

We pause now in our survey of theological issues raised by our use of the Psalms to make inquiry into a basic matter, that of the process of translation out of Hebrew into current languages—in our case, English. I mentioned briefly in chapter 14 the bewilderment many Christians experience when they are faced with the variety of translations of the Bible in our day. At several points in this work I have dealt with questions of translation of the Psalms, notably in chapters 6, 11, 12, 13, and 14; but there remain some basic issues to be faced.

Specifically, what, really, *is* a translation? This question is not as easy to answer as it seems. One may answer, of course, that a translation is saying the same thing in another language, so that, to use the terms current today, the expression in the receptor language is identical to that in the source language. But the problem is that, for anything more complex than *la plume de ma tante*, what "the same thing" is becomes a fuzzy matter indeed.[1]

First of all, many of the most common expressions of a language cannot be translated literally: I can still remember the astonishment we felt in beginning French class when we learned that to say "How are you?" in French, we had to say *Comment allez-vous?*—literally, "How are you going?" And many years later I would be bemused when I learned that the same question in the vernacular Arabic of Iraq is *šinū lawnak*, contracted to *šlōnak*—literally, "What is your color?" In addition, the corresponding expression in the Hebrew Old Testament was *hăšālôm lĕkā* or *hăšālôm ʾattâ*—literally, "Is it peace to you?" (2 Sam. 20:9; compare Gen. 43:28).

Then, when one becomes acquainted with another current language, one often finds that some simple expression has an important place in the culture of the people speaking that language, and one is hard put to locate the precise equivalent in one's own language. Let me give a couple of examples.

In Dutch one hears the adjective *gezellig* a good deal: the human being is *een gezellige dier*, "a social animal"; *een gezellige avond* is "a pleasant evening"; conversation *bij een gezellig glaasje* is talk "over a cheerful glass"; *een gezellig hoekje* is "a cozy corner." The word then covers notions of sociability, hospitality, comfort, and

316

chumminess, but it is not quite any of these, being tied up with the peculiarly Dutch notion of the safety and warmth of bourgeois family life within the comfort of one's home, in contrast to the (relatively) unknown and threatening world outside.[2]

Again, there is a common Arabic expression that one can hear constantly in Beirut, *in šā' Allāh*, contracted to *inšallāh*—literally, "If God wills." The equivalent Latin phrase was used in the Middle Ages, *Deo volente*, and pious Catholic writers have used the Latin phrase in our day. The Arabic phrase reflects a sensibility that both Muslim and Christian Arabs share: that our days are in the hands of God, and who knows what will intervene to change our plans? Now, the curious thing is that Americans I knew in Beirut, who would never use the English phrase "God willing" in their conversation, would sometimes use the Arabic expression *inšallāh* when talking to a fellow American, as in "I'll meet you for lunch tomorrow, *inshallah*." It would be used even by Americans who had no lively belief in God; it was simply a phrase that fit the circumstances. We Americans doubtless used it with a mocking air sometimes—an indication that we were living in a part of the world where unexpected events often intervened. But it was also used in seriousness: I'll keep the appointment if I can, if the authorities do not impose a curfew or whatever. It was a phrase that was appropriate in Beirut, and no English phrase quite said the same thing, so we used the Arabic expression.

Ultimately, words that fill a need are borrowed in this way from another language—*Blitzkrieg* ("lightning war") from German during the early days of World War II, thereafter shortened to "the Blitz"; *glasnost* ("openness") in our own day from Russian. My point here, however, is that we may find that certain expressions in another language "are hard to translate" or "can't quite be translated" into our own.

If the foreign language is current, one can listen hard and "see how" the Dutch use *gezellig* or the Arabs use *in šā' Allāh*; or one can find an informant who speaks the language as a native, to clear the matter up. But when we are dealing with an ancient text, then, of course, there are no informants: we cannot resurrect King David or one of his wives to ask, "What does this mean?" All we can do is study other contexts in which the expression occurs (if there are any) and look for analogous expressions in related languages; but ultimately we are limited in our ability to be sure we have it right.

Now, when the ancient text is a *sacred* text, as the Bible is, then the matter becomes even more complicated, because there exists a long, steady tradition of the interpretation of the text, whether or not that interpretation is the original intended meaning or even close to it. People who are accustomed to hearing a psalm passage one way may be upset to hear it another way, even if scholars have come to believe that that other way is a more adequate translation.

And finally, when an ancient sacred text is in poetic form, as the Psalms are, then it becomes important to try to bring across from Hebrew to the receptor language not only the intended meaning but also as much as possible of the poetic structure and effects.

So, what makes a translation? It would seem that very often "saying the same thing" is a will-o'-the-wisp. If that is so, then one can say that a translation should communicate in the receptor language the effective content of the text, indeed, the original intention of the writer or speaker, with as little loss or distortion as possible. But loss or distortion there will be; the Italian proverb is profoundly true: *Traduttore traditore*—"A translator is a traitor." There is no perfect congruence between two languages.

Here I should like to discuss three terms: a *literal translation*, a *dynamic equivalent*, and a *paraphrase*. These are not absolute categories but points along a continuum; nevertheless, they are useful distinctions. A literal translation is a word-by-word translation: the literal translation of the Iraqi Arabic phrase for "How are you?" as I have already indicated, is "What is your color?" The dynamic equivalent of that phrase in English is "How are you?"—that is, the equivalent expression in the receptor language. The KJV and, to a lesser degree, the RSV and the NRSV have in many respects approached the category of literal translations; that is, they are as much word-for-word as the differing idioms of Hebrew and English will allow. By contrast, the NEB and the REB have been to a far greater degree translations that seek a dynamic equivalent. Thus in 2 Sam. 20:9a the NRSV offers a translation that is more literal—"Joab said to Amasa, 'Is it well with you, my brother?'"—whereas the REB translates the question as a statement that offers a more dynamic equivalent—"I hope you are well, my brother." One might add that the completely dynamic equivalent in current American English would be "How are you, brother?" The issue that emerges is this: Should expressions in the Bible sound completely current, or should there be a little distance, a little sense of something other than current English idiom? This is particularly pertinent in the case of the Psalms, where there is a sense of awesome poetry. It is a judgment call.

If a translation communicates the content of the text and the intention of the writer or speaker in expressions as close to the original as possible, then a paraphrase is a looser equivalent that is shaped to a greater degree by the expected forms of the receptor language. Some years ago J. B. Phillips published a paraphrase of the Epistles of the New Testament in a work called *Letters to Young Churches*.[3] Phillips pointed out that the form of modern letter-writing style is looser and more discursive than Paul's tight rhetoric; he therefore expanded and extended the phrases of the Epistles—and in so doing, he greatly heightened an understanding of them by modern readers. For example, the NRSV for Rom. 2:3-4 reads, "Do you imagine, whoever you are, that when you judge those who do such things and yet do them yourself, you will escape the judgment of God? Or do you despise the riches of his kindness and forbearance and patience?" For this passage Phillips offers: "What makes you think that you, who so readily judge the sins of others, can consider yourself beyond the judgment of God? Are you, perhaps, misinterpreting God's generosity and patient mercy towards you as weakness on His part?"

Sometimes a rendering is on the edge between a dynamic equivalent and a paraphrase. For example, because of the restrictions on vocabulary of the TEV, it is often too much of a paraphrase for careful study.

I described in chapter 11 one important class of paraphrases of the Psalms, namely, the metrical psalms that were written in the period of the Reformation and thereafter. Here the paraphrase was necessary in order to achieve regularity of meter and rhyme, so that the psalms could be sung by congregations.[4]

Now I discuss several specific kinds of problems that emerge in translating the Psalms. I mostly deal with problems of putting the Psalms into English, but on occasion I refer to other languages as well.

The Problem When the Receptor Language Has No Equivalent

Frequently, an item to be translated simply does not exist in the receptor language. Sometimes it may be as simple as a concrete noun. For example, Eskimos have no sheep. The only solution is to borrow the word into Eskimo from English or some other modern language and perhaps append a note such as this: "Sheep are gentle domesticated animals raised for wool and meat."[5] Thus, in a language such as Eskimo, "The Lord is my shepherd" will be a problem, and one must find a paraphrase. Another solution was possible in the Maya language, which likewise did not know "sheep"; there the descriptive phrase "cotton deer" was used.[6]

It may be that an Old Testament custom is unknown. The familiar phrase in Ps. 23:5, "You anoint my head with oil," literally means, "You put olive oil on my head"; it suggests the hospitality of the divine host and, conceivably, God's consecration of the king as well (see chapter 1). But given the fact that this custom may be considered outlandish in the receptor language, a more effective translation may need to be a dynamic equivalent, such as "You welcome me as an honored guest" (TEV).

Or a theological, cultural, or psychological term may not find a *precise* equivalent in the receptor language. A famous problem has been the best translation of the word "God" in Chinese; it was a problem for Roman Catholic missionaries in China in the seventeenth century and a problem for Protestant missionaries in the nineteenth century.[7] The Jesuits, beginning with Matteo Ricci, used two terms that were traditional in the Chinese classics, *Tian* and *Shangdi*. *Tian*, often translated into English as "heaven," also suggests "nature," "time," "providence," and "virtue." It is the benevolent source of sustenance for all. The term certainly suggests what is real and vast in the governance of the universe, but the entity to which it refers is not personal. The second term Ricci adopted was likewise indigenous, *Shangdi*: *shang* means "over" or "above" and *di* means "ruler," "sovereign," so that the phrase means "Supreme Ruler." In imperial China the emperor worshiped *Shangdi*. But the question was raised whether Christians should use terms that already had indigenous (and thus pagan) connotations, and with the term *Shangdi* the matter was complicated by the fact that the term could refer not only to a deity but to deceased emperors as well.

The Dominicans favored the phrase *Tian-Zhu*, a phrase that Ricci had also employed. Though this combination was not an indigenous Chinese expression, it is perfectly comprehensible. *Tian* is the word meaning "heaven" and the like, and

Zhu is a term for "lord" or "master," marking a human status of authority; the phrase *Tian-Zhu* would then mean "Divine Master."

The discussion over these two approaches—indigenous terms or a fresh phrase—continued for nearly a century and was eventually referred to Rome; a papal bull in 1715 decreed that the Dominican phrase, *Tian-Zhu*, was to be the Chinese term for God. The decision had long-term consequences: the Chinese emperor himself was irritated by the fact that foreigners took it upon themselves to settle a question of Chinese idiom, and that irritation prompted an edict a few years later that prohibited the Christian faith within the empire and enjoined the confiscation of church property.

The first Protestant missionary in China in the nineteenth century, Robert Morrison, used the term *Shen*, a general term meaning "Good Spiritual Being." The difficulty with the term is that it is generic: in Chinese belief there are many good spiritual beings (and many *guei*—"bad spiritual beings"). Later Protestant translators took up the expression *Shangdi*, one of Ricci's expressions that had been rejected by Rome. Protestant missionaries were greatly exercised over the choice between these two terms, and the Bible societies actually published separate Chinese editions of the Bible in each term, leaving the choice to the reader. Thus we have the situation in which Chinese Roman Catholics use one expression for "God" and Chinese Protestants use either of two others. (But it should also be noted that Chinese Christians use other expressions as well: thus *Tien Fu* [Heavenly Father], an expression made habitual by its occurrence in the Lord's Prayer, is current in the language of prayer.)

I turn now to a Hebrew noun that appears frequently in the Psalms, the word *nepeš*: this noun refers to the total human being in both physical and psychological manifestations. Thus in Prov. 23:2 the phrase "lord of *nepeš*" refers to someone with a large appetite; similarly, "those who are seeking after my *nepeš*" (Ps. 35:4 and *passim*) are "seeking after my life." Sometimes the word means one's "will" (thus it is used in the NRSV in Ps. 27:12—"Do not give me up to the will of my enemies"). The word may be used not only of the will of an individual but of the will of the whole community: in Ps. 33:20 we read, "Our *nepeš* waits for Yahweh; he is our help and shield." Very often the term means something like "one's total being" or "the total being of the community," but again, "my *nepeš*" may mean little more than "I myself." Now, the KJV and the translations that follow in its train (the RSV and the NRSV) have often translated the word by "soul," but "soul" in English carries with it Hellenistic overtones that suggest something ethereal, in *contrast* to the body (as when we say, "She doesn't have enough to keep body and soul together"). So when Ps. 23:3 says, "He brings back my *nepeš*," is it a good translation or a misleading one to say, "He restores my soul"? In Ps. 42:2 (1) we read, "As a deer longs for flowing streams, so my *nepeš* longs for you, O God"; and this is reinforced by the next verse—"My *nepeš* thirsts for God, for the living God." Now, shall we do as the NRSV does and translate in these verses "my soul," when the metaphor of thirst is used with a word that implies "my total being"? Or shall we translate with "I," as the REB and the TEV do? Furthermore, "our soul" (Ps. 33:20, NRSV), seems very odd without the kind of complicated explanation offered here; the REB and TEV have simply "we" in that verse. It is clear that translating even a simple psychological term may be far from easy.

I turn now to another Hebrew word. In Ps. 94:1, God is twice described (NRSV) as "God of vengeance." But the Hebrew word *nĕqāmôt* is not quite "vengeance." It has become clear that the word is used to describe the exercise of sovereign power on behalf of the disadvantaged.[8] "Vengeance" in English suggests the actions taken by feuding enemies against each other, whereas the matter would seem to be covered better by a word such as "vindication": the "judge of the earth" (v. 2) is asked to "give to the proud what they deserve"; the "proud" are identified as the "wicked" (v. 3). The rights of humble, innocent people have been trampled on; it is time for the sovereign God to intervene. It may be noted that the new Jewish version (*Tanakh*) translates "God of retribution," and TEV translates "a God who punishes." I suggest that this is an important point, because the idea that the Old Testament portrays God as a "God of vengeance" often leads Christians to reject it.

The mention of the "wicked" in Ps. 94:3 reminds us of the discussion in chapter 4 regarding Psalm 1; there I suggested that the Hebrew terms translated "righteous" and "wicked" might better in some contexts be translated as "innocent" and "guilty," respectively. If the word were translated "guilty" in Ps. 94:3, it would help make the situation clear.

Hebrew "Tenses"

A different sort of problem is presented by the fact that Hebrew verbs do not really have the clear distinctions of tense that verbs in European languages do. It is not the place here to offer a lesson in Hebrew grammar; I will simply state that finite verbs in Hebrew (more exactly, verbs other than imperatives, infinitives, and participles) are classified either as "perfect," a form that in prose (among its other uses) expresses completed action, usually in the past, or "imperfect," a form that in prose (among its other uses) expresses habitual or potential action; but there may also be other nuances in these forms that are lost on us. (This question is among the most controverted in Hebrew grammar.)[9] But in poetry, particularly in early poetry, these two forms often appear side by side, in parallelism with each other as stylistic differences, sometimes even with the identical verb; and the meanings perhaps offer very little more contrast than the English "he sits" and "he is sitting" do.

For example, in Ps. 29:5 the verb (meaning "break") in the first half of the verse is a participle, whereas the verb in the second half is a finite form of a different stem of the same verb (meaning, perhaps, "shatter"). Because the two half-verses both have "Yahweh" (the Lord) and "cedars," it is regrettable that the NRSV does not take account of the shift of verb form, instead offering the word "breaks" for both verbs: some shift would be useful; perhaps "The voice of the Lord breaks the cedars; the Lord has broken [or, shattered] the cedars of Lebanon." Again, in v. 10 one might translate, "The Lord has sat [or, the Lord sat] enthroned over the flood; the Lord sits enthroned as king forever" (the NAB and the new Jewish version have "sat" and "sits," respectively).

Appropriate Level of Diction

One needs to make decisions about the "tone" or "level" of language into which to translate the Psalms. In general, if the Gospels in the New Testament are written in the ordinary marketplace Greek of the first century of our era, then the Psalms are at the other extreme: they are stately, formal poems. Here I deal with one example of the problem, and that is the choice of pronoun to be used in the Psalms in addressing God.

It is true, in neither Hebrew nor Greek are there any special pronouns by which to address God; in Hebrew there are four forms of "you," for masculine singular, feminine singular, masculine plural, and feminine plural, and the "you" used in addressing God is the normal (masculine) singular form used also in addressing an individual (male) human being. (I do not here deal with the use of specifically masculine forms in reference to God; I take up this matter in chapter 18.) Now, in the English of the seventeenth century "thou" was the ordinary singular pronoun of address (with its related forms "thee," "thy," and "thine") and was used in addressing both God and individual human beings; and, at the same time, "ye" was the plural pronoun of address (with its related forms "you," "your," and "yours"), though the usage varied in this period and, indeed, beginning in the fourteenth century, "ye" could be used as a form of respect to address an individual, especially someone of higher rank.[10] But by the twentieth century, outside of poetic diction, "thou" was used only in prayer in addressing God. Accordingly, as I indicated in chapter 14, in the RSV "thou" (and its appropriate verb forms) was confined to addressing God, while "you" was used for individual human beings; and now the NRSV has abandoned "thou" altogether and used "you" in addressing God as well. I think this is a sound decision, but there is no doubt that in this matter what these new translations gain in immediacy of language in the Psalms they lose in awesomeness.

There is a similar issue in Dutch: the pronoun *Gij* has for centuries been used only for God (curiously, this pronoun is etymologically related to the English plural form "ye"), and the usage was retained in the "New Translation" of 1951. But the diction of prayer in the Protestant churches of Holland has been shifting, and more and more the pronoun *U* (the pronoun used in formal situations to address either one or more persons, a form etymologically related to the English "you") is used to address God, and any future revision of the Dutch Bible must deal with the matter.[11] (It may be noted in passing that in the French and German languages there is no analogous issue: the French *tu* and the German *du*, second-person pronouns for familiar address to an individual, have always served as the pronouns for addressing God.)

The situation becomes far more complicated in languages such as Burmese, where there is a whole range of grammatical options from which to draw in addressing the deity. (Compare my remarks in chapter 13 on the perceived defects in the translation made by Adoniram Judson of the Bible into Burmese.)

The Historical Baseline from Which to Translate

The question may emerge, out of what time-point in the source language shall we translate a psalm? That is, if one assumes that a given psalm comes from the pre-exilic period, shall it be translated out of the set of meanings current at the time when the psalm was originally composed and sung? Or should it be translated out of the set of meanings current in the post-exilic period, when that psalm became part of a canonical collection? Or, indeed, shall it be translated out of the set of meanings current for New Testament Christians?

This is by no means a purely theoretical problem. What shall we do about the traces of polytheism to be found in the Psalms? Those who are addressed in Ps. 29:1 are in Hebrew the *bĕnê 'ēlîm* ("sons of gods," according to the NRSV footnote). Because this psalm is evidently a Yahwistic adaptation of a Canaanite hymn to Baal (see chapter 2), an address to the assembled gods is not surprising. But, then, is the translation of the NRSV, "heavenly beings," justified—a translation that for us carries the implication of angels?

Again, I have become convinced that Psalm 1 was written in the pre-exilic period (see chapter 4). At that time the Hebrew word *tôrâ* (v. 2) meant "teaching" (see the NRSV for the same word in Isa. 1:10); it was "instruction" on the norms of covenant behavior. Then, in the post-exilic period, the word became much more "law," implying even "written law," and so v. 2 came to be understood as referring to meditation on the written law of the Pentateuch. So how shall we translate the two occurrences of the word in v. 2—as "teaching" or "law"?

We may ask the same question about the "valley of the shadow of death" in Psalm 23, so dear to Christians but now abandoned in the NRSV.

The Problem When Familiarity Misleads

How, indeed, shall we translate a psalm when the traditional translation is so familiar (Psalm 23 being the prime example), but when translators are convinced that the traditional rendering is less than accurate?

The Hebrew expression *'ašrê* has traditionally been translated "blessed"; it is the first word of Psalm 1 (and Psalm 32 and others; see the RSV). But the translation "blessed" is best saved for the Hebrew word *bārûk* and related words (see Ps. 18:47 [46]). The word in Ps. 1:1 really means "to be congratulated" or "fortunate"; hence the translation "happy" in the NRSV and other recent translations. How many of such shifts in translation are appropriate when a worshiping community is familiar with a traditional rendering?

I now shift to more technical questions.

The Poetic Devices of Hebrew

To what extent should one try to reproduce in the receptor language what may loosely be called "poetic effects" in the Hebrew? Again, I illustrate from Psalm 1. Commentators are fond of pointing out the sequence of verbs in the Hebrew of v. 1—literally, "walk," "stand," and "sit"—and the KJV and the RSV reproduced this sequence: the RSV rendered, "Blessed is the man who *walks* not in the counsel of the wicked, nor *stands* in the way of sinners, nor *sits* in the seat of scoffers." But each of these verbs is used metaphorically: "walk" in Hebrew frequently implies a life-style—that is, to "live" in a particular way—and "way" likewise suggests one's life-style; further, "sit in the seat of" suggests "participate in the deliberations of." All these implications of the Hebrew words are out of focus if in current English one translates literally "walk," "stand," and "sit," so the NRSV has abandoned the effect of the sequence and offers instead, "Happy are those who do not follow the advice of the wicked, or take the path that sinners tread, or sit in the seat of scoffers"; and the new Jewish version abandons all three verbs—"Happy is the man who has not followed the counsel of the wicked, or taken the path of sinners, or joined the company of the insolent" (the translation is similar in other recent versions). It is difficult to be firm about what to do in a situation like this: whether to retain the poetic effect of the sequence of literal verbs and thereby increase the obscurity of meaning for the current reader, or to increase comprehension by abandoning the sequence.

There is another matter in v. 1., a small matter but one worthy of consideration nevertheless. In the three parallel clauses, the verb in the first clause *precedes* its prepositional phrase while the verbs in the last two clauses *follow* their respective prepositional phrases: the word order in Hebrew is "Happy is the man who does not walk in the counsel of the wicked, and in the way of sinners does not stand, and in the seat of scoffers does not sit." This word order gives the last two clauses a kind of closure. Word order is not altogether fixed in English, particularly for poetry. Why could a translation not replicate this word order?

Again, in the same verse the verb "sit" in Hebrew (*yāšāb*) is echoed by the related words "seat of" (*môšab*), and here the NRSV has preserved the wordplay by the related words "sit" and "seat" in English—indeed, increasing the alliteration with "scoffers," the Hebrew antecedent for which does not offer any particular wordplay. But there are other wordplays in the Hebrew psalm that cannot be replicated in English. One in particular is the play between *ba'ăṣat* (in the counsel of [the wicked]) in v. 1 and *ba'ădat* (in the congregation of [the righteous]) in v. 5; there is no way I know of to reproduce this effect in English.

Again, the word *derek* (way, or path) is found in v. 1 ("way of sinners") and twice in v. 6 ("way of the righteous" and "way of the wicked"). The NRSV has varied the words, however, using "path" in v. 1 and "way" in v. 6; but because the two English words "way" and "path" are virtually identical in meaning, and because the Hebrew word both opens and closes the psalm, it might be important to consider staying with the same word in an English version.

Double Meanings in Hebrew

I now turn from what is sometimes possible to what is usually impossible, and that is the matter of the rendering in the receptor language of double meanings in the Hebrew. I give three examples. In Ps. 103:12, the NRSV correctly translates, "As far as the east is from the west, so far he removes our transgressions from us"; but the expression "from us" (Hebrew, *mimmennû*) also means "from him(self)," and the context of vv. 11 and 13 suggest that both meanings are present. But there is obviously no way to render the double meaning in English.

A lovely double meaning occurs in Ps. 137:2. In v. 1 the Hebrew says, literally, "By the watercourses of Babylon, there we sat and even wept, in our remembering Zion." Then v. 2 continues, "On willows in her midst we hung our lyres." But the word translated "in her midst" (*bĕtôkāh*) also means "in her oppression." In the meaning "in her midst" the word is parallel with the word "there" in v. 1; in the meaning "in her oppression" it points ahead to v. 3, which reads, literally, "For there our captors asked us words of song." This kind of double meaning has been called "Janus parallelism" by scholars, since the single word looks both backward to one parallelism and forward to another, like the Roman god Janus whose two faces faced in opposite directions. But there is no way this double meaning can be put into English; at most, the second meaning can be given in a footnote.

Again, in Ps. 148:6b the Hebrew plays on the extended meaning of *ḥōq*, both "limit," and "law," and on two rather different meanings of *'ābar* (pass): God established the heavenly bodies forever; "he fixed their limit, which cannot be passed" *and* "he fixed their law, which cannot pass away." The implication is both of a limit that cannot be crossed and of a law that will never cease. Here the NRSV has given the second meaning in a footnote, but the footnote unfortunately implies that it offers an alternative meaning, rather than the second possibility in a double meaning.

Inability of the Receptor Language to Accept Hebrew Poetic Structure

I now consider the extent to which one should look for poetic structures in the receptor language into which to render the Hebrew poetic structures of the Psalms. Essentially, this was what was done in the metrical paraphrases of the Psalms in the Calvinist churches (see chapter 11): the Psalms were rendered into French or English meter and rhyme for singing. Every receptor language will have traditional poetic diction and structures; in the case of translations into languages for which the biblical faith is new, speakers sometimes resist the use of such chant forms or other poetic patterns because of their pagan connotations.[12]

The matter is more complicated when the receptor language cannot accept the basic poetic structure of Hebrew poetry, that is, the structure of parallelism (see chapter 4). This circumstance may arise for different reasons; I offer here two types of situations. The first arises when there are restrictions on the range of vocabulary in the translation. This is the case with the TEV, which was intended for readers for whom English is a second language or who have difficulty in reading (see chapter 14). Occasionally the restricted vocabulary or style of this translation will not allow for as many synonymous expressions as are found in the Hebrew original, and the translation has thus simply compressed the original diction. For example, where in Ps. 19:11 (10) the NRSV has "More to be desired are they than gold, even much fine gold; sweeter also than honey, and drippings of the honeycomb," the TEV has simply "They are more desirable than the finest gold; they are sweeter than the purest honey."[13] Again, in Ps. 90:1-2 the NRSV has "Lord, you have been our dwelling place in all generations. Before the mountains were brought forth, or ever you had formed the earth and the world, from everlasting to everlasting you are God." Here the poet has gloried in repetition: "the earth and the world," "from everlasting to everlasting." But here the TEV renders v. 1 as "O Lord, you have always been our home" and compresses "the earth and the world" into "the world" (evidently "earth" is not part of the vocabulary of the TEV). Again, the last verse of this psalm repeats the words "the work of our hands, establish it" (see the NRSV), but the TEV omits the line.

One more example: in Ps. 27:12 the NRSV translates, "Do not give me up to the will of my adversaries, for false witnesses have risen against me, and they are breathing out violence"; here the TEV has compressed the verse to "Don't abandon me to my enemies, who attack me with lies and threats."

The other type of situation is the problem posed by some receptor languages in which any repetition by synonyms may sound childish or absurd.[14] "In most parts of the world no such poetic parallelism exists, and receptors are often irked by what they regard as obnoxious repetition and tautology in Semitic poetic forms."[15] In such instances there is no recourse but in some way to combine the parallel expressions into a single one; at the same time, the translator must be alert to appropriate patterns of poetry in the receptor language and give attention to the possibility of shaping the material into these patterns, as I have already suggested.

Instances in Which the Hebrew Text
Has Evidently Been Misunderstood
or Damaged

All of the points I have so far discussed have assumed that one understands a given passage of Hebrew. But there are many passages in the Hebrew Bible whose meanings are uncertain or disputed; there are passages that appear to have been damaged by copyists' errors in ancient times. We remind ourselves that in the earliest centuries the manuscripts of the Psalms were written with consonants only, and that the signs for the Hebrew vowels were only fixed in the Middle Ages (see chapter 9); in such texts there were many opportunities for mistakes and misunderstandings. In this respect the book of Psalms is no different from the rest of the Hebrew Bible; in translations like the NRSV, such passages often carry a footnote such as "The meaning of the Hebrew is uncertain."

But a translation of the Psalms has to translate *something* in every case. Detailing the understanding of the Hebrew text of the Psalms is the task of commentaries, but I offer here two examples of passages that, in my opinion, have not been understood correctly.

The first example is from Psalm 2, a royal psalm discussed in chapter 2. The difficulty is in v. 12; the first expression in that verse is a famous problem. The previous verse is startling but yields sense: "Serve Yahweh with fear, and shriek with trembling"—that is, the kings and rulers of the earth who are addressed (v. 10) are told to submit in craven fear to the rule of Yahweh. But the first two words of v. 12 yield no sense: as they stand, *naššĕqû-bar* consists of an imperative plural verb, *naššĕqû* (kiss), followed evidently by a noun, *bar* (traditionally understood as "son"). The command to "kiss the son" might seem to make sense, given the statement in v. 7 that the new king has been declared the son of God; but *bar* is actually the Aramaic word for "son," rather than the Hebrew *bēn*, which occurs in v. 7. The translation of the end of v. 11 and the beginning of v. 12 that appears in the NRSV, "with trembling kiss his feet," is only a guess, based on a complete reconstruction of the Hebrew text.

I suggest that the consonants of the expression at the beginning of v. 12 have been correctly transmitted but that the words have been wrongly divided and that the wrong vowels have been given to the consonants. I read the sequence not as *naššĕqû-bar* but as *nōšê-qeber* ([you] who forget the grave). By this reading, vv. 11-12a would be "Serve Yahweh with fear, and shriek with trembling, O you who forget the grave, lest he be angry and you perish on the way, for his wrath is quickly kindled." The plausibility of this reading is reinforced by Ps. 50:22, where a similar warning is found with a more common Hebrew synonym for "forget": "Mark this, then, you who forget God, lest I tear (you), and there be no savior." But this solution, which I published in a biblical journal a number of years ago,[16] has not to my knowledge been taken up by any commentary on the Psalms, to say nothing of being accepted in a translation of the Psalms. If the suggestion has merit, the process could take many years.

In the other example, both the consonant and vowel traditions of the Hebrew text are correct, I believe; it is simply that our understanding of the grammar of the passage needs to be shifted. The example is one I offered in chapter 8, namely, Ps. 45:7a (6a); vv. 7-8 (6-7), we recall, are cited in the Septuagint translation in Heb. 1:8, where the author of Hebrews understands the passage to be addressed to Jesus Christ as the Son of God. But in the original context of Psalm 45, the proposal of Mitchell Dahood in his commentary (for this commentary, see chapter 13) is surely correct: that the half-verse, addressed to the king, means, "God has enthroned you forever and ever." In this way the half-verse is parallel to v. 8b (7b)—"Therefore God, your God, has anointed you with the oil of gladness beyond your companions."[17] This proposal by Dahood has now been taken up by the REB; it has, of course, the difficulty for the Christian reader of being in tension with the understanding of Heb. 1:8 (though this is not the only pair of Old Testament and New Testament passages in such tension; one thinks of Isa. 7:14 and Matt. 1:23).

So, what makes a translation, when the translation is to be made from an ancient Hebrew poetic text that carries with it a continuous history of interpreta-tion? It is not simply a matter of looking up a series of words in a dictionary; rather it is a whole combination of judgment calls. And the questions with which I deal in the next chapter raise still further questions about what a translation of the Psalms should be.

NOTES

1. There is an enormous literature on biblical translation. A useful presentation of the issues involved in translating the Bible is Barry Hoberman, "Translating the Bible: An Endless Task," *Atlantic* 255, no. 2 (February 1985):43–58; and see the articles in *Interpretation* 32 (1978):115–57. The works of Eugene Nida are particularly to be recommended for further reading: see Eugene A. Nida, *God's Word in Man's Language* (New York: Harper, 1954); and, on a more technical level, idem, *Toward a Science of Translating, with Special Reference to Principles and Procedures Involved in Bible Translating* (Leiden: Brill, 1964); Eugene A. Nida and Charles R. Taber, *The Theory and Practice of Translation* (Leiden: Brill, 1974); and the bibliographies in the last two works. The suggestions above in chap. 13 n. 66 are likewise useful. And see the publication *The Bible Translator*, and the publications of the United Bible Societies and the American Bible Society.

2. Simon Schama, *The Embarrassment of Riches: An Interpretation of Dutch Culture in the Golden Age* (Berkeley: University of California Press, 1988), esp. 399–400, 570, 611–12.

3. J. B. Phillips, *Letters to Young Churches: A Translation of the New Testament Epistles* (New York: Macmillan, 1947).

4. For this whole question, see Nida, *Toward a Science of Translating*, 18–26.

5. Eugene A. Nida, *Bible Translating: An Analysis of Principles and Procedures, with Special Reference to Aboriginal Languages* (New York: American Bible Society, 1947), 136.

6. Nida, *Toward a Science of Translating*, 216.

7. See Kenneth Scott Latourette, *A History of the Expansion of Christianity* (7 vols.; New York: Harper, 1937–45), 3:340–52; G. W. Sheppard, "The Problem of Translating 'God' into Chinese," *Bible Translator* 6 (1955):23–30 (reprinted from *Hibbert Journal* 43, no. 1). I have shifted the older Wade–Giles transliteration of Chinese into the current *pingyin*.

8. George E. Mendenhall, *The Tenth Generation: The Origins of the Biblical Tradition* (Baltimore: Johns Hopkins University Press, 1973), 69–104.

9. See, recently, Bruce K. Waltke and Michael Patrick O'Connor, *Biblical Hebrew Syntax* (Winona Lake, Ind.: Eisenbrauns, 1990), 479–563.

10. See the examples in the *Oxford English Dictionary*, s.v. "ye."

11. Peter Dirksen, personal correspondence.

12. H. van der Veen, "The Use of Literary or Poetic Language in Poetic Parts of the Bible," *Bible Translator* 3 (1952):212–18.

13. For a discussion of the issues involved in the TEV translation of this verse, see William D. Reyburn, "Poetic Parallelism: Its Structure, Meaning and Implication for Translators," in Philip C. Stine (ed.), *Issues in Bible Translation* (United Bible Societies Monograph Series 3; London: United Bible Societies, 1988), 109–10.

14. Heber F. Peacock, *A Translator's Guide to Selected Psalms* (Helps for Translators; London: United Bible Societies, 1981), 1.

15. Nida, *Toward a Science of Translating*, 211.

16. William L. Holladay, "A New Proposal for the Crux in Psalm ii 12," *VT* 28 (1978):110–12.

17. Mitchell Dahood, *Psalms I: 1–50* (Garden City, N.Y.: Doubleday, 1966), 273.

18

Psalms for Whom?

Having explored the issue of translation of the Psalms—that is, the issue of their transfer from one language to another—I raise the question of what might be called ecclesial transfer, that is, the transfer of the Psalms from one historical community to other subsequent communities.

One can raise the question most basically: For whom have the Psalms been written? The first and easiest answer is "For their first users and hearers." As we learned in chapters 2 through 5, those first users and hearers were the people of Israel who lived in the period extending from perhaps the eleventh to the fifth centuries B.C.E. And, as we have seen, though not all the psalms presuppose a locale at either the temple of Solomon in Jerusalem or the post-exilic temple, most of them do. But as we know, the Psalms have had a life that has extended far beyond the context of the first users and hearers, and it is the problems raised by that extended life that I address in this chapter.

For Jews, as we have seen (chapter 9), the Psalms have had an extended life beyond the existence of any temple in Jerusalem—that is, beyond 70 C.E. For Jews in the centuries thereafter, the Psalms have been vehicles for personal and communal prayer in home and synagogue. That extension of usage by Jews beyond the period of worship in the temple could be sustained without any serious distortion or strain in the texts; the references to the king and to the temple could be understood to point toward the messianic age.

But two other extensions in the use of the Psalms have indeed brought strain. The first of these is their use by Christians: from the very beginning of the existence of Christian communities, Christians have retained the Psalms as a primary vehicle for their worship, to express their own distinctive experience, with all the questions of appropriateness and adequacy that that retention has raised. The second of these, which has become acute in our own day, is the question of the degree to which the Psalms are appropriate and adequate to express the experience of women, and how that experience might be heard. It is these two extensions of usage that I explore in this chapter.

How Do the Psalms Function
for Christians?

Christians have been using the Psalms as an expression of worship for the entire period of Christian history, as chapters 8 and 10 through 14 have amply demonstrated, so it might seem as if there were nothing more to talk about. But still, there are strains; for instance, we examined in chapter 16 the psalm material that Christians tend to bypass. So we need to ask the question systematically: How is Christian experience reflected in the Psalms?

To simplify our search for an answer, I confine myself to laying two sources side by side: the first, a traditional Protestant one, and the second, a current Roman Catholic one. The Protestant one is the commentary on the Psalms of John Calvin (see chapter 11); the Roman Catholic one is the context provided for the Psalms in the current Liturgy of the Hours (see chapter 14). The use of Calvin's commentary needs no further explanation, but the context of the Liturgy of the Hours does. The commission that was appointed by Pope Paul VI to prepare the current Liturgy of the Hours provided various aids to meditation on a given psalm, such as a title; an appropriate short quotation from the New Testament or from one of the church fathers; and, to close the psalm, a "psalm-prayer," that is, a brief prayer that offers a Christian reading of the psalm.[1] These aids offer easy access to current Roman Catholic interpretation of the psalm in question.

Now, it must be said in the first instance that a whole range of psalms provide splendid vehicles for Christian worship, without any adaptations or shifts. If one accepts the New Testament convictions that the God who created the world and who covenanted with Israel is the same God who sent Jesus to redeem the world, and that there is a continuity as well as a discontinuity between Israel in the Old Testament and the church in the New Testament (as Gal. 6:15-16 indicates), then psalm after psalm speaks without strain to the condition of Christians. Indeed Calvin takes that identity of Israel and the church so much for granted that he regularly uses the word "Church" for the nation Israel, side by side with "David," a usage that seems anachronistic to us; for example, in speaking of Psalm 14, Calvin writes:

> We have much need to be fortified from the example which David here sets
> before us: so that, in the midst of the greatest desolations which we behold in
> the Church, we may comfort ourselves with this assurance, that God will
> finally deliver her from them.[2]

By the same token, the psalm-prayer after this psalm in the Liturgy of the Hours reads, "God of wisdom and truth, without you neither truth nor holiness can survive. Safeguard the Church you have gathered into one and make us glad in proclaiming you."[3]

This identification prevails in the many instances where there are specific references to "Zion" or "Jerusalem." Thus for Psalm 125, Calvin writes, "When the Church is emblematically described by the situation of the city of Jerusalem, the design of the Prophet is to encourage each of the faithful to believe, that the safety promised in common to all the chosen people belongs to him."[4] By the same token the psalm-prayer for this psalm in the Liturgy of the Hours reads:

> Surround your people, Lord, within the safety of your Church, which you preserve on its rock foundation. Do not let us stretch out our hands to evil deeds, nor be destroyed by the insidious snares of the enemy, but bring us to share the lot of the saints in light.

It thus ends with a paraphrase of Col. 1:12.[5]

Because the advent of Jesus Christ has signaled for Christians the decisive victory of God in the world, expressions that occur in certain psalms of God's victory over Israel's enemies are reappropriated in the light of the advent of Jesus Christ, so that the person of God the Father and the person of Jesus Christ overlap. For example, Calvin is at pains in his comment on Ps. 143:10—"Teach me to do your will, for you are my God; let your good spirit lead me on a level path"—to insist that the grace of God does not simply allow us to hear the word, does not simply make us capable of doing good, but "he effectually influences the consent of our hearts, and as it were leads us by the hand."[6] And the Liturgy of the Hours offers before this psalm a citation of Gal. 2:16—"A man is not justified by obser-vance of the law but only through faith in Jesus Christ"—and subjoins to it the following psalm-prayer:

> Lord Jesus, early in the morning of your resurrection, you made your love known and brought the first light of dawn to those who dwell in darkness. Your death has opened a path for us. Do not enter into judgment with your servants; let your Holy Spirit guide us together into the land of justice.[7]

Similarly, Psalm 51, a prayer for renewal after sin, is reconceived in the light of the Christian affirmation that Christ, without sin, has rescued us from our sins. Thus Calvin writes of this psalm, "The truth is, that we cannot properly pray for the pardon of sin until we have come to a persuasion that God will be reconciled to us." And again:

> The mention which is here made of *purging with hyssop*, and of *washing* or *sprinkling*, teaches us, in all our prayers for the pardon of sin, to have our thoughts directed to the great sacrifice by which Christ has reconciled us to God. . . . This, which was intimated by God to the ancient Church under figures, has been fully made known by the coming of Christ.[8]

The Liturgy of the Hours heads this psalm with a citation from Eph. 4:23-24— "Your inmost being must be renewed, and you must put on the new man"—and the psalm-prayer thereafter reads:

> Father, he who knew no sin was made sin for us, to save us and restore us to your friendship. Look upon our contrite heart and afflicted spirit and heal our troubled conscience, so that in the joy and strength of the Holy Spirit we may proclaim your praise and glory before all the nations.[9]

I now turn to psalms whose original context has been more radically recon-ceived by Christians. In the original Old Testament context of the Psalms, it is normally clear who is speaking: it is the psalmist, speaking as an individual or on behalf of the worshiping congregation. And it is normally clear that it is God who is addressed or spoken about; there is no confusion or blending of identities. But in the advent of Jesus Christ, Christians in using various psalms have developed a variety of fresh identifications in hermeneutical shifts, shifts that begin with the New Testament itself.

1. Christians sometimes understand the psalmist to be Jesus Christ himself, crying out to God to relieve him of his distress. This is notably the case with Psalm 22, given Jesus' own cry on the cross (Mark 15:34; see chapter 8). In his comment on this psalm, Calvin distinguishes between the psalmist and Jesus Christ this way:

> David complains in this psalm, that he is reduced to such circumstances of distress that he is like a man in despair. . . . At the same time, he sets before us, in his own person, a type of Christ, who he knew by the Spirit of prophecy behoved to be abased in marvellous and unusual ways previous to his exaltation by the Father.[10]

Similarly, the Liturgy of the Hours titles Psalm 22 "God hears the suffering of his Holy One" and cites the cry from the cross in Matt. 27:46. The psalm-prayer that follows the psalm reads:

> Father, when your Son was handed over to torture and seemed abandoned by you, he cried out to you from the cross and death was destroyed, life was restored. By his death and resurrection, may we see the day when the poor man is saved, the downtrodden is lifted up and the chains that bind people are broken. United to the thanks that Christ gives you, your Church will sing your praises.[11]

There are other psalms in commenting on which Calvin writes in similar fashion of the way David speaks both of himself and by prophecy of Jesus Christ, and whose speaker the Liturgy of the Hours identifies with Jesus Christ; they include Psalms 2, 16, 27, 41, 57, and 140. And the Liturgy of the Hours takes still others in this way: Psalms 3, 6, 28, 30, 31, 35, 55, 56, 59, 86, and 88.

When the psalmist is king and speaks of preparation for war, as in the case of Psalm 144, the Liturgy of the Hours understands the speaker to be Jesus Christ and the warfare to be spiritual; it quotes Hilary, who himself cited Jesus' word in John 16:33: "Take courage; I have conquered the world!"

A special instance is the poem to the king and queen on the occasion of their wedding (Psalm 45); though Calvin understands the king in the first part of the psalm to be Solomon, he also understands the king to refer to Christ, and he understands the queen in the second part of the psalm to refer to the church.[12] The Liturgy of the Hours understands the king to be Christ and the address to the queen to be to the Virgin Mary as exemplar of the church.[13]

Another special instance is Psalm 8. Hebrews 2:7 cites v. 6 (5)—"You have made him little lower than God [or, the angels]"—to apply to Jesus Christ, and

Eph. 1:22—"He has put all things under his feet"—is a paraphrase of v. 7 (6) of the psalm, again applying the words to Jesus Christ. Given these citations, both Calvin and the Liturgy of the Hours take over the identification.

2. Contrariwise, the identification of Jesus Christ as the Second Person of the Trinity has made it possible to understand affirmations about God or addresses to God specifically as affirmations about or addresses to Jesus Christ, almost to the exclusion of God the Father. This identification is aided by the fact that in the Psalms the expression "the Lord" refers to God, either as a translation of the Hebrew "Adonay" or as a substitute for "Yahweh," whereas "the Lord" in the New Testament usually refers to Jesus Christ. The identification is preeminently the case with Psalm 23. Calvin says, "God, in the person of his only begotten Son, has exhibited himself to us as our shepherd, much more clearly than he did in old time to the fathers who lived under the Law."[14] The Liturgy of the Hours titles the psalm "The Good Shepherd," appends Rev. 7:17 ("The Lamb himself will be their shepherd and will lead them to the springs of living waters"), and the psalm-prayer that follows reads:

> Lord Jesus Christ, shepherd of your Church, you give us new birth in the waters of baptism, anoint us with saving oil, and call us to salvation at your table. Dispel the terrors of death and the darkness of error. Lead your people along safe paths, that they may rest securely in you and live for ever in your Father's house.[15]

And the Liturgy of the Hours takes other psalms in this way: Psalms 60, 98, 101, 124, and 131.

But even given all this adaptation of the Psalms by the Christian community, nevertheless, as we saw in chapter 16, Christians have tended to omit psalm sequences that call down God's wrath on personal enemies, sequences that encourage attitudes of hatred and self-righteousness in the worshiper. The Christian ethic of forgiveness of enemies is not furthered by such psalms.

The question can be posed in many ways. Is the Psalter adequate for Christian prayer? Does the Psalter, however reinterpreted, strike the emphases of the Christian gospel? In what ways does the phraseology of the Psalter mislead Christians? I try here to offer a personal assessment of the situation, saving until chapter 19 my suggestions as to how Christians might best use the Psalter.

1.   The Psalter has been drawn on universally by Christians. This use has been either in whole (or almost in whole), as in the Roman Catholic and Orthodox rounds of corporate prayer (the Divine Office) and in the metrical psalms of the Calvinists, or in part, as in the selection of verses or short sequences of verses from the Psalms in various portions of the Roman Catholic Mass, Orthodox liturgy, or Protestant worship services and in the selection of various psalms or parts of psalms for Protestant responsive readings.

2. Stimulated by the usage of the New Testament and the affirmations of Christian theology, Christian communities have shaped a new understanding of many psalms.

3. The Gospel of Luke offers three fresh canticles, or psalmlike poems: the Magnificat, attributed to Mary (Luke 1:46-55); the Benedictus, attributed to Zechariah, the father of John the Baptist (Luke 1:68-79); and the Nunc Dimittis, attributed to Simeon (Luke 2:29-32). These canticles have always been used alongside the Old Testament Psalms in Christian worship; in the Anglican *Book of Common Prayer* they are part of daily worship, and in the present-day Roman Catholic Liturgy of the Hours the Benedictus is a part of morning prayer, the Magnificat is a part of evening prayer, and the Nunc Dimittis is a part of night prayer, each prayer thus being offered once a day. In this way the specific tone of Christian worship in these canticles reinforces the Old Testament Psalms. And in a similar way Christians through history have produced hymns that reflect specific Christian emphases, particularly in Protestant worship but now more and more in Roman Catholic worship as well. The very production and singing of these hymns suggests that, at many points in Christian history, Christians have perceived the Psalter by itself to be insufficient to sustain Christian worship (compare in this regard the eventual adoption of hymns alongside the Psalter by the various Calvinist churches, described in chapter 13).

4. Psalms in which one's enemies are cursed and psalms in which one prays for military victory over national enemies have been avoided, both in various lectionaries and in Protestant responsive readings. This circumstance, explored in chapter 16, points to the perception of Christians that using these psalms without a total shift of metaphor is not appropriate. I return to this question in chapter 19.

One may represent the emphases of the Old Testament Psalms and the emphases of Christian worship as two circles that overlap to a great degree but are not entirely congruent: whether Christians can shift to a complete congruence of the two circles is a question we ask in chapter 19. But in the meantime, we can ponder the consequences if the answer to the question at the beginning of this chapter, "For whom have the Psalms been written?" is to be, "For Christians as well as for Jews."

How Do the Psalms Function for Women?

I now turn to a far more difficult and controversial topic, that is, the degree to which the Psalter is an appropriate and adequate vehicle to express the experience of women. The topic is difficult and controversial because it has been raised urgently only in our own time, and women and men are just beginning to think the matter through.

I begin with what is incontrovertible: that the Israelite faith emerged in a patriarchal culture, that is, a culture in which power was overwhelmingly in the hands of men—both domestic authority within the household and clan and political authority in Israel as a whole—and that the faith of Israel, which challenged so many assumptions in the ancient Near East about the way one apprehends the divine and about the nature of history, evidently did not challenge the assumptions of male supremacy.[16] The institutions of Israel, those of monarch, priest, and prophet, were either entirely or overwhelmingly male. There is no need here to document this statement; and the rare emergence of powerful women such as Deborah the judge, Athaliah the queen, and Huldah the prophet and the inclusion in the canon of the books of Ruth and the Song of Solomon, which reflect women's perspectives, do nothing to contradict it. There were cultural and historical reasons for this circumstance, but this is not the place to explore them.[17]

As to Christian history, there is evidence, particularly in the Gospel of Luke, that Jesus himself challenged the assumptions of patriarchy at many points, and there is evidence that in the earliest church, women filled roles of leadership.[18] But patriarchy reasserted itself, and aside from the practice of some "heretical" sects, such as the Montanists in the late second century, and some Protestant communities such as the Society of Friends, the Shakers, and the Salvation Army, there was no parity between the sexes in church leadership until the middle of the nineteenth century.

As to the Psalms specifically, one may point to the probability that Psalm 131 was written by a woman (see chapter 4), but such a circumstance does not change the fact that the overwhelming majority of the Psalms must have been written by and were used primarily by men. As we saw in chapter 4, there are many Psalms in which the psalmist is the king. In other psalms the psalmist refers to himself by masculine pronouns, adjectives, or verbs. For example, in Ps. 16:10 the adjective translated "faithful one" is masculine singular, and in Ps. 41:6 (5) the verbs in Hebrew are masculine singular (see the "he" in the RSV of that verse). Furthermore, this masculine cast to the Psalms is reinforced by the Hebrew linguistic habit of using masculine nouns and adjectives as generics (see, e.g., the RSV for Ps. 1:1: "Blessed is the man").

Now, let it be said, and said clearly, that there have surely been countless women through the ages (and Jews as well as Christians) who have been able to use the Psalms for their worship without any conscious sense of deprivation. The words of the Psalms have been perceived to "speak to their condition," as Quakers say (compare similar perceptions in chapter 15). We recall the Countess of Pembroke, who wrote exquisite metrical paraphrases of the Psalms (chapter 11), and the testimony of Thérèse of Lisieux and of Dorothy Day (chapter 12). And there are countless such women today: anyone who has given talks to church groups about gender-specific and nongender-specific language in biblical translation or in religious discourse will have heard the firm testimony of many women as to their glad use of the traditional language of worship, without any sense of unease (e.g., "To me 'man' refers to either sex" and "I have no trouble referring to God as 'he'").

Whether such women are simply reflecting the assumptions of the dominant patriarchy that they have internalized, or whether they have found genuine access to God through masculine-dominated language, or both, such testimony may be heard on every hand.

Nevertheless, a growing number of women and men have become uncomfortable with the traditional situation. I hasten to say that I cannot claim to speak for Jews on this matter; there have been some significant recent works by Jewish women that deal with the reconception of Jewish traditions,[19] but I do not attempt to contribute to that discussion. What I do here is deal with the question from a Christian perspective, especially as it bears on the Psalms.

I begin by making a linguistic point, which I frame by speaking of "Dialect A" and "Dialect B" in current English. In Dialect A the word "man" refers to either sex, whereas in Dialect B the word "man" refers to the adult male human only. The first dialect is the traditional usage of English; but my point here is that what is at issue is not whether Dialect A is "correct" or "incorrect," but simply that Dialect B is a different dialect. And as far as usage is concerned, it is clear that more and more people, both male and female, have shifted from speaking Dialect A to Dialect B. The reason for this shift is the fresh concern in our day for women's perceptions.

Now, if the Psalms are to speak to the existence of both women and men within the worshiping community, and if more and more people speak Dialect B, then a translation that refers to the worshiping community by the word "men" cannot meet current usage. This became one of the major concerns in the committee that produced the NRSV, as I explained in chapter 14.

I have already made mention of Ps. 1:1, which in the RSV begins "Blessed is the man"; this reflects the Hebrew *'îš* (man, or adult male human). The psalm is clearly contrasting the life-styles of the "righteous" (plural) and the "wicked" (plural)—compare vv. 5 and 6, where the Hebrew words are plural and where English translations imply a plural. The Hebrew "man" in v. 1 is simply a stylistic variation, so the NRSV is quite justified in a translation that pluralizes in vv. 1-3: "Happy are those who do not follow the advice of the wicked."

Sometimes this kind of Hebrew diction offers more difficulty. In Ps. 8:5 (4) the RSV reflected the Hebrew idiom: "What is man that thou art mindful of him, and the son of man that thou dost care for him?" Here "son of man," an idiom that implies "a single (male) human being," is in parallelism with "man." The NRSV translates, "What are human beings that you are mindful of them, mortals that you care for them?"

In Ps. 71:10-11 the RSV has a whole series of masculine pronouns referring to the psalmist: "For my enemies speak concerning me, those who watch for my life consult together, and say, 'God has forsaken him; pursue and seize him, for there is none to deliver him.'" In the NRSV the committee managed to rephrase with minimum awkwardness; v. 11 now reads, "They say, 'Pursue and seize that person whom God has forsaken, for there is no one to deliver.'"

But in Ps. 41:6 (5), which is a similar verse, the solution was not so simple. The RSV translated, "My enemies say of me in malice: 'When will he die, and his name perish?'" I recall the morning the NRSV committee was working on that verse; the substitution of "that person" resulted in a monstrosity, "When will that person die, and that person's name perish?" I pointed out that this is not how enemies talk. But I also pointed out that indirect questions, although not common in Hebrew poetry, are possible in English poetry, and that possibility became our solution: "My enemies wonder in malice when I will die, and my name perish." In these ways both women and men may find themselves equally in the worshiping community of the Psalms.

But there are related issues to pursue. A major one is the gender-tagged references to God. Biblical descriptions portray God as personal, but they are offered as similes or metaphors rather than literal descriptions; indeed, sometimes the non-literal nature of these descriptions is made explicit. Thus in Ezekiel's great vision of the throne-chariot of God the prophet states that what he saw was "something that seemed like a human form" (Ezek. 1:26, NRSV), and even so, his description is four steps removed from reality ("This was the appearance of the likeness of the glory of Yahweh"; Ezek. 1:28). And one occasionally reads the recognition that God can be compared to a woman as well as to a man: in one verse of the Psalms, God is compared to a mistress as well as to a master (Ps. 123:2). And Jesus, according to Luke 15:3-10, told a parable about a shepherd who goes after a lost sheep, with the implication that the shepherd represents God, and then matched it with a parable about a housewife who goes after a lost coin. (I suspect Christians have heard more sermons about God the Good Shepherd than about God the Good Housewife.)

Nevertheless, the patriarchal culture of the Bible offers metaphors for God that are overwhelmingly male: God is portrayed as Master, Lord, Judge, King, Shepherd, and Father.

Now, because neither Hebrew nor Greek has a third-person singular personal pronoun that is not gender-specific, the pronoun used to refer to God, in both the Old Testament and the New Testament, is "he." And because English, like Hebrew and Greek, lacks a third-person singular personal pronoun that is not gender-specific, the translation in English Bibles for the "he" that refers to God is likewise "he." Given what we have said about the metaphorical nature of the descriptions for God, this "he" may imply "he, as it were," but the rendering is still "he." (It is worth pondering how different our situation would be if the biblical languages were Armenian, for example, or Hungarian or Turkish, and if English were similar— these languages, like many across the world, have a third-person singular pronoun that serves for both "he" and "she.") The result, then, is that English-speaking Christians have inherited the whole mind-set of male references to God, and although, when they think about it, they usually understand that God is not a sexual being, they are usually bewildered at first when the specific male metaphors and pronouns for God are challenged.

But why, one may ask, should these metaphors and pronouns be challenged? The answer is that our habits of language shape our thoughts and attitudes in ways far beyond our reckoning; this has become clear in recent years. If women have been denied effective power in the household or in the community or in the world, and then if they sit alongside men and worship a God who is known by male attributes and male references, then women easily become marginalized in their own awareness (and in the awareness of men). The theologian Mary Daly wrote some years ago, "If God in 'his' heaven is a father ruling 'his' people, then it is in the nature of things and according to divine plan and the order of the universe that society be male dominated."[20] Judith Plaskow, a professor of religious studies, notes that a student of hers (in an "Introduction to Religion" class at Wichita State University) reported that when she asked her boss why there were no female executives in the company she worked for, he replied, "Because God is a man."[21] That such an affirmation is alive and well is demonstrated by the front-page headline in the *New York Post* for June 17, 1991: "God is a Man." The headline was an oversimplified summary of a homily on the subject of feminism preached the previous day (Father's Day) by Cardinal John O'Connor of New York.

Christian theologians have always recognized that God cannot be visualized as exclusively male. To take only a single example, the Lutheran theologian Johann Arndt, in his work *True Christianity* (1606), describes God this way: "In his word God addresses us in more friendly a fashion than the fashion by which any father, any mother can address her crying children. . . . As a mother surrounds her child with love, so the goodness of the Lord surrounds us."[22]

But in our own day, women and men who are concerned for a change of awareness on these issues have become less and less comfortable with praying to a God who is steadily referred to as "he." I know devout Roman Catholics who tell me that they can no longer pray the Psalms as given in the Liturgy of the Hours, and I know Protestants who similarly have vowed no longer to use such language in worship. What solutions might be forthcoming for this crisis in people's hearts?

There has been an edition of the "Common Lectionary" (see chapter 14), prepared in 1983–1985 by the Division of Education and Ministry of the National Council of the Churches of Christ in the U.S.A., that adapts the readings according to the RSV into inclusive language.[23] The result for the Psalms, where there are so many third-person pronouns for God, is awkward: "God restores my soul; God leads me in paths of righteousness for God's name's sake."

A more graceful solution is that of a member of the Carmelite order, who has taken the Liturgy of the Hours and has adapted it, using "all-inclusive language."[24] How has this adaptation been done? The expression "the Lord," which, as we know, is usually a substitute for the name "Yahweh," has often been restored to "Yahweh." Frequently, third-person description of God has been replaced by second-person address. It is noteworthy that in the Hebrew original of the Psalms there is often a shift from third-person reference to second-person reference or vice versa: for example, in Psalm 23—"The Lord is my shepherd" (third person); "I shall fear no evil, for you are with me" (second person); "I shall dwell in the house of the Lord my whole life long" (third person once more). So the Carmelite member's adaptation of Psalm 23 simply stays with the second person through the whole psalm:

Yahweh, you are my shepherd;
there is nothing I shall want.
Fresh and green are the pastures
where you give me repose.
Near restful waters you lead me,
to revive my drooping spirit.
You guide me along the right path;
you are true to your name.
If I should walk in the valley of darkness
no evil would I fear.
You are there with your crook and your staff,
with these you give me comfort.
You have prepared a banquet for me
in the sight of my foes.
My head you have anointed with oil;
my cup is overflowing.
Surely goodness and kindness shall follow me
all the days of my life.
In your own house shall I dwell for ever and ever.[25]

But it may be asked: Even though it may be justifiable to shift singular to plural, as in the NRSV of Ps. 1:1-3, is it justifiable to shift the personal reference from third to second person like this? I would answer as follows. If one wants a translation that translates third person as third person and second person as second person for a study Bible—for example, for an analysis of the poetry that is patterned by such shifts—then no. But if one wants the translation of a psalm through which one is praying, an act in which one's stance is address to God anyway, and if an adaptation such as we have been examining allows a sister or brother to pray without stumbling (compare Rom. 14:21), then such an adaptation is altogether justifiable.

Psalm 76 is adapted similarly by the Carmelite member. In the Hebrew of vv. 2-4 (1-3) the references to God are in the third person; they shift in vv. 5-11 (4-10) to second person and revert to third person in vv. 12-13 (11-12). In the adaptation, vv. 2-4 (1-3) are shifted to the second person, while the references in vv. 12-13 (11-12) are retained in the third person because of the address to fellow worshipers there. The psalm thus begins: "You are made known in Judah, O God; in Israel your name is great."[26]

By the same token, the first four verses of Psalm 24 are shifted to the second person: vv. 1-2 read, "Yours is the earth and its fullness, the world and all its peoples. It is you who set it on the seas; on the waters you made it firm." In v. 6, "the God of Jacob" has become "the God of their ancestors"; in vv. 7-10, the phrase "the King of glory" has become "the God of glory."[27]

I provide here one more example. We saw earlier what the NRSV has done with Psalm 8 to avoid the use of "man" and "son of man." The inclusive language adaptation by the Carmelite member shifts these terms to the first person:

When I see the heavens, the work of your hands,
the moon and the stars which you arranged,
who are we that you should keep us in mind,
mortal flesh that you care for us?
Yet you have made us little less than a god;
with glory and honor you crowned us,
giving us power over the works of your hand,
putting all things under our feet.[28]

In this kind of graceful way the material of the Psalms is reshaped for those who are becoming sensitized to the nature and power of language to refer to God.

But beyond finding nongender-specific language for the people of God and nongender-specific language for God in the existing Psalms, there are still further concerns to ponder as one becomes aware of the distinctive experience of women. Recent studies indicate that women develop psychological maturity in a way different from men,[29] and that the pattern of women's conversation differs in striking ways from the pattern of men's conversation.[30] These differences, it would appear, are not specific to a given culture (though a given culture may shift them in significant ways) but are transcultural. Thus where men compete with each other and move toward individuation, women involve themselves in networks with each other and move toward community. These differences raise profound questions about the theological perspectives that we have derived from the Bible and from Christian tradition. How might these matters be addressed in connection with the Psalms? Just as we asked whether the Psalms are an adequate expression of Christian experience, we can ask whether the Psalms are an adequate expression of women's experience.

One can assume that there would have been a specific experience of women in Israelite times that would have resonance with women's experience today. Unfortunately, that experience of Israelite women has left little written trace in the biblical record. We have already noted the probability that Psalm 131 was written by a woman, but we have no assurance that the experience of women has left any direct trace in other psalms. There is one psalmlike poem in the Old Testament attributed to a woman, the "Song of Hannah" (1 Sam. 2:1-10). Whether or not one can trust the attribution to the extent of taking the poem as the words of a woman, it is noteworthy that the song mentions barrenness and giving birth (v. 5) as Psalm 131 mentions a weaned child with its mother (v. 2), surely preoccupations of women. But one could carry the hermeneutic of suspicion to the extent of raising the question whether a psalm or psalmlike poem of a woman that is included in a collection made and used by men does not embody the concerns of men as those concerns have been internalized by the female poets.

I have already mentioned the Magnificat in the New Testament (Luke 1:46-55), but one may raise similar questions about it: Did it really come from a woman, and if so, does it embody women's concerns? Or is it the work of a woman who has internalized men's concerns? That the Magnificat has been integrated into evening prayer for Roman Catholics and Anglicans, a vehicle for men as well as women, says nothing directly about the question either way. (The song in Jth. 16:1-17, in the Deuterocanonical books, raises similar questions.)

The perception that the Psalter is skewed in the direction of men's experience has produced at least one attempt by a woman to frame new psalms, such as would be appropriate for various women in the Old Testament;[31] but the production of these psalms, useful as they may be for devotional purposes, leaves untouched the questions we address to the canonical Psalter on its adequacy to reflect women's experience.

My own suspicion is that the most useful way to proceed is simply to raise a series of questions about women's experience and the Psalms. Obviously, I cannot speak firsthand on the matter, and in any event the questions as they are raised today are too new to have settled answers. Here, then, are a set of questions to ponder.

1. Central to the culture of biblical Israel is what has been called "corporate personality,"[32] that is, the idea that a family, clan, or nation manifests a group identity (compare the Hebrew word *nepeš*, discussed in chapter 17). Are there aspects of the notion of corporate personality that resonate with the experience of women, who work toward community? The Psalms emerged in experiences of corporate worship and have been preserved in corporate worship. Do they then reinforce the craving of women to build community?

2. There is plenty in the Psalms about war and victory in battle, typical male concerns. Are there other motifs in the Psalms that specifically reinforce women's experience? One thinks, for example, of the sensitivity to creation in Psalm 104; there is also the expression of pride in children in Ps. 128:3, and the joy in the harmony of the family (Psalm 133), though these are worded from a male point of view. What others might there be?

3. I suggested in chapter 15 that the lament psalms could be useful in setting forth the experience of abused women and in pointing the way toward healing. In what ways could these psalms express the experience of women in general who suffer under sexism? The experience of discrimination is not something confined to women, but the usefulness of such psalms in combating sexism is a matter to be pursued.

4. Is a valid experience of God's presence and guidance something that, to some degree at least, transcends the contrasting psychological development of men and women? That is to say, does the "vertical" experience of God cover both women's and men's experience? The experiences of men and women in the use of spiritual reading or spiritual direction from the other sex suggest that the answer might be in the affirmative. But this begs the question whether the Psalter offers an adequate or balanced reflection of the experience of God. If men have trusted, as vehicles for their worship, psalmlike poems that (at least purport to) express women's experience (the Song of Hannah, the Magnificat), can women trust men's psalms?

5.   Does Jesus offer direction that is as adequate to women's experience as to men's? One is tempted to give a theological answer that is a quick "yes," but there may be historical evidence in the Gospels to flesh out such an answer. I have already indicated that Jesus seems occasionally to have used female images as well as male images for God, and there are many notices in the Gospels of his conversing with women and healing women. But one can press the matter more deeply. I revert to Deborah Tannen's study on the patterns of female and male conversation and raise the question: Was Jesus' conversation less "male" and more "female" than men ordinarily manifest? It is impossible to frame an answer, given the limitations of the Gospel accounts and their distance from the historical Jesus, but I would suggest nevertheless that Jesus in his noncompetitive mode, his willingness to honor children, and his concern for other individuals pointed the way toward a stance that may resonate with women's experience. And the noncompetitive "fruit of the Spirit" set forth in Galatians ("love, joy, peace, patience, kindness, generosity, faithfulness, gentleness, self-control"; Gal. 5:22-23) reinforces our suspicion. If, then, we read the Psalms "through Jesus Christ our Lord," as I suggest in chapter 19, can the Psalms in this fashion be heard to resonate with women's experience?

It is in these and similar directions that the discussion must go if we are to fulfill the vision of Paul that "there is no longer male and female; for all of you are one in Christ Jesus" (Gal. 3:28).

NOTES

1. Pope Paul VI, "Promulgation: The Divine Office," *Apostolic Constitution* (November 1, 1970), sec. 3; see *Christian Prayer: The Liturgy of the Hours* (Boston: Daughters of St. Paul, 1976), 15.

2. John Calvin, in *Calvin's Commentaries: Psalms*, tr. James Anderson (Edinburgh: Calvin Translation Society, 1843–55; reprint, Grand Rapids: Eerdmans, 1948–49), 1.189.

3. Daytime Prayer, Tuesday of the First Week, in *Liturgy of the Hours*, 596.

4. Calvin, *Psalms*, 5.89.

5. Evening Prayer, Tuesday of the Third Week, in *Liturgy of the Hours*, 831.

6. Calvin, *Psalms*, 5.257.

7. Morning Prayer, Thursday of the Fourth Week, in *Liturgy of the Hours*, 966, 967–68.

8. Calvin, *Psalms*, 2.297–98.

9. Morning Prayer, Friday of the Second Week, in *Liturgy of the Hours*, 754, 756.

10. Calvin, *Psalms* 1.356.

11. Daytime Prayer, Friday of the Third Week, in *Liturgy of the Hours*, 877.

12. Calvin, *Psalms*, 2.173–94; see esp. 189.

13. Evening Prayer, Monday of the Second Week, in *Liturgy of the Hours*, 699.

14. Calvin, *Psalms*, 1.396.

15. Daytime Prayer, Sunday of the Second Week, in *Liturgy of the Hours*, 676.

16. On this, see Norman K. Gottwald, *The Tribes of Yahweh* (Maryknoll, N.Y.: Orbis, 1979), 685.

17. See Carol L. Meyers, *Discovering Eve: Ancient Israelite Women in Context* (Oxford: Oxford University Press, 1988). Also useful are John H. Otwell, *And Sarah Laughed: The Status of Women in the Old Testament* (Philadelphia: Westminster, 1977); Athalya Brenner, *The Israelite Woman: Social Role and Literary Type in Biblical Narrative* (Sheffield: JSOT, 1985); Peggy L. Day (ed.), *Gender and Difference in Ancient Israel* (Minneapolis: Fortress, 1989).

18. Elisabeth Schüssler Fiorenza, *In Memory of Her: A Feminist Theological Reconstruction of Christian Origins* (New York: Crossroads, 1983).

19. See esp. Judith Plaskow, *Standing Again at Sinai: Judaism from a Feminist Perspective* (San Francisco: Harper & Row, 1990), and bibliography in that work; but she does not deal specifically with the Psalms.

20. Mary Daly, *Beyond God the Father: Toward a Philosophy of Women's Liberation* (Boston: Beacon, 1973), 13.

21. Plaskow, *Standing Again at Sinai*, 156 n. 10.

22. Johann Arndt, *True Christianity*, 2.42; I have consulted *Vier Bücher von wahren Christenthume* (Nurnberg: Heinrich Haubenstricker, 1826), 468.

23. *Inclusive Language Psalms* (New York: Pilgrim, 1987).

24. *Companion to the Breviary: A Four-Week Psalter Featuring All-Inclusive Language* (1985), and *Seasonal Supplement with Special Feasts and Commemorations for Use with Companion to the Breviary: A Four-Week Psalter Featuring All-Inclusive Language* (1986), both prepared by Teresa M. Boersig, O.C.D.; available from Carmelite Monastery, 2500 Cold Spring Road, Indianapolis, Ind. 46222.

25. *Companion to the Breviary*, 29–30.

26. Ibid., 30.

27. Ibid., 9–10.

28. Ibid., 51–52.

29. Judith V. Jordan and others, *Women's Growth in Connection: Writings from the Stone Center* (New York and London: Guilford, 1991).

30. Deborah Tannen, *You Just Don't Understand: Women and Men in Conversation* (New York: Ballantine, 1990).

31. Miriam Therese Winter, *WomenWisdom, A Feminist Lectionary and Psalter*, parts 1 and 2, *Women of the Hebrew Scriptures* (New York: Crossroad, 1991).

32. For the classic expression of the idea, see H. Wheeler Robinson, "The Hebrew Conception of Corporate Personality," in Paul Volz (ed.), *Werden und Wesen des Alten Testaments: Vorträge gehalten auf der Internationalen Tagung Alttestamentlicher Forscher zu Göttingen vom 4.–10. September 1935* (BZAW 66; Berlin: Töpelmann, 1936), 49–62; republished as *Corporate Personality in Ancient Israel* (Facet Books, Biblical Series 11; Philadelphia: Fortress, 1964).

19

Through
Jesus Christ Our Lord

We have surveyed the history of the use of the Psalms, and in chapters 15 through 18 we explored from a Christian perspective a variety of issues that the use of the Psalms implies. Now it is time to raise the ultimate normative theological question: How *should* we use the Psalms? What does God intend us to do with the Psalms?

There can be as many answers to this question as there are belief systems. For those who are convinced that God does not exist, the question is nonsense; for those who are not sure that God exists, or are fairly certain we cannot know whether God exists, the question again will be beside the mark. For those numberless folk across the world who adhere to faiths other than the Jewish or Christian ones, the question will be irrelevant; these folk might read the Psalms as Christians might read the Hindu Bhagavad-gita, as significant religious poetry of an alien faith but irrelevant for their understanding of God. Superstitious folk of whatever declared faith may put passages of the Psalms to occult or manipulative use (see the beginning of chapter 15).

For secularized Jews, the Psalms may be read as a precious portion of the Jewish tradition (compare the remarks in chapter 9 on the use of the Psalms in secular contexts by Israeli Jews). For those whose religious outlook has emerged out of the Christian tradition but who now do not derive their revelation of God from the Bible, such as Quakers and Unitarians, particular psalms may be moving testimonies of a specific tradition about God, but the Psalms are not authoritative.

Again, there are a variety of faith communities that in different ways find authority in the Hebrew Scriptures or in the Christian Bible. For some Orthodox Jews the answer to the question "What does God intend us to do with the Psalms?" would be "Recite them in Hebrew." But this is not practical for most Christians. And for the great majority of Christian communities that find their authority in the Bible, there will be a variety of answers to the question.

Let us remind ourselves of the total situation. What we have is a series of Hebrew poems that were vehicles for the worship of God for the Old Testament people, composed for the most part between the eleventh and the fifth centuries

B.C.E. These poems were collected and became part of a standard repertoire for worship (the "Psalter"); this collection, in turn, by the third and second centuries B.C.E., became authoritative and eventually part of the canon of Jewish Scripture—that is, part of a unique literature understood to have been revealed by God and therefore something other than a purely human construct. This Psalter was taken over without question by Christians in various translations and has been for all of Christian history a uniquely important vehicle for both the Christian understanding of God and the Christian worship of God. And because of its double identity—namely, poetry that had its origin at a particular time in the past and Scripture that is understood to be of permanent (and even timeless) meaning and importance—the Psalms are constantly in tension between what they *meant* and what they *mean*, to use the useful distinction of the theologian Krister Stendahl.[1] And that tension has been explored in various ways in chapters 15 through 18.

One of the genres to which we keep returning as we ponder our use of the Psalms is that of the laments. Christian communities have tended to avoid using the laments, even though, as I have suggested, using them could deepen our faith (chapter 15). However, those same laments often use language in regard to one's enemies that, when taken literally, is excluded for Christians, so that the churches have avoided specific verses and even whole psalms (chapter 16). Indeed the distance of the language and culture of biblical Hebrew from our own is great enough (chapter 17), and the perceived spiritual needs of Christian communities from Old Testament ones are different enough (chapter 18), to raise a profound uneasiness about how the Psalms are to function for us.

We seem to be caught in a dilemma. Either we read and recite the full Psalter as it comes to us in translation in our Bibles and risk more than one shudder at the savage wishes expressed there toward personal and national enemies—and risk, too, an occasional chuckle at the descriptions of the behavior of one's enemies that remind us of nothing so much as the behavior of children with each other on school playgrounds—or else we read and recite a bowdlerized Psalter as it comes to us sanitized by some lectionary or hymnal committee and risk missing the grittiness of the biblical faith. In the first instance, one tries to hold onto the canonical principle reflected in 2 Tim. 3:16, that "all scripture is inspired by God and is useful for teaching, for reproof, for correction, and for training in righteousness," while wondering what is useful about celebrating the bashing of Babylonian babies' brains (Ps. 137:9). In the second instance, one seems to be setting one's own notions above the canon. Is there any way out of this dilemma?

I propose one here; it is essentially a reading of the Psalms that is christological. I propose to do in our day what the church fathers and the Reformers did less systematically in their day. I believe the proposal has theological integrity, and I offer it as a possibility for the consideration of Christians.

The Reality of Evil

The psalmist is aware of the reality of evil—thoroughly aware. The reality of evil is clear in the whole Bible; it is particularly apparent in the New Testament, where God's solution to the reality of evil is set forth in the victory of Jesus Christ over sin and death (1 Cor. 15:57). The psalmist, for his part, catalogues in great detail the evil work of his enemies, who talk against him, plot against him, betray him, shame him. For the psalmist the ultimate scandal is that these enemies are not only against him but against God (Ps. 139:21). And Christians agree that there are often people who do plot and betray; indeed, there are whole structures of society that conspire to neglect the needs of human beings and even conspire to oppress them (see chapter 15).

If the psalmist's descriptions of evil can be pointed toward the centers of evil in our present world, then those passages would certainly be "useful for teaching."

The Location of Evil

As we saw in chapter 4, the psalmist had a clear conscience. The Israelites tended to look upon a human being as onefold: one was either for or against God. The idea of mixed motives or hypocrisy, the notion of saying one thing and doing another, is not common in the Old Testament in the way it is in the New Testament. The psalmist's conscience was clear: he was on the side of God, or he would not be singing a psalm. And because evil was real, he located it elsewhere than in himself: among his fellows, among his enemies, among the enemies of the nation.

For Christians, shaped by the New Testament, evil is real, but it is not necessarily only "out there," outside of ourselves. First we take the log out of our own eyes, and then we will see clearly to take the speck out of our neighbor's eye (Matt. 7:5). As Pogo, the protagonist of an American cartoon strip a number of years ago, once said, "We have met the enemy, and it is us." Paul gave classic shape to the matter in Rom. 7:14-25: in his understanding, the evil that he did was done not by himself but by the "sin" that dwells within him (vv. 17, 20). There are both a "law of God" within him and a "law of sin" within him (vv. 22-23), each struggling with the other, and his only rescue from the paralysis of the struggle between these two "laws" is afforded by God "through Jesus Christ our Lord" (v. 25).

Whereas for the psalmist the struggle is between the good within him and the evil in others, for the Christian the struggle is between the good and the evil within oneself, as well as outside oneself. If we as Christians are to make use of the recognition of the reality of evil in the Psalms, then we must find ways to locate that evil within ourselves, as well as outside ourselves.

Jesus Christ as the One Who Prays
the Psalms

The historical Jesus knew the Psalms: he is remembered as arguing about the meaning of Psalm 110. He prayed through the Psalms; we know this because devout Jews have always done so, and because of the specific Christian memory of the words he uttered on the cross, Ps. 22:2 (1) (Matt. 27:46 [= Mark 15:34]) and Ps. 31:6 (5) (Luke 23:46; see chapter 8).

Christian testimony has been that Jesus Christ was obedient to God (Phil. 2:8), that he was tested as we are yet without sin (Heb. 4:15). We may conclude that only for him was evil completely external: he is remembered as having struggled with evil, personified as the devil, in the temptations in the wilderness (Matt. 4:1-11; Luke 4:1-13), after which the devil left him.

From the Christian point of view, then, Jesus Christ is the only person who may safely pray the Psalms that speak of the evil that dwells in the enemies. Christians frequently end their prayers with the ascription "through Jesus Christ our Lord," by which I assume we mean that Jesus Christ is both the mediator and the censor of our prayers: he sponsors our prayers, but what is unworthy of him we are asking him to block.

Could we, then, more consistently than we now do, pray the Psalms through Jesus Christ our Lord? As we ourselves pray the Psalms, can we hear him not only pray Psalm 22, as the church has always done (see chapter 18), but other psalms as well, psalms of praise and psalms of lament? He whom the church has known as son of David can be heard to pray the royal psalms. The church that is the body of Christ (1 Cor. 12:27) can hear him praying the thanksgivings of the community and the laments of the community.

His praying of the Psalms can stretch our praying of them. He can adore and praise God fully, while by comparison we can adore and praise God only faintly and fitfully. He can lament the sin in the world, which he took upon himself (John 1:29; Rom. 5:21), in ways we cannot begin to imagine.

"The Enemies" for Jesus Christ

Who were the enemies of the historical Jesus? We can think of many who figure in the Gospel accounts—Judas, the high priest Caiaphas, Pontius Pilate, others. But the testimony in the Gospels centers on the devil (the evil one, Satan, Beelzebul) and on demons (unclean spirits; compare Mark 1:23), who are understood to be ruled by the devil (Mark 3:22)—indeed, who are called "children of the evil one" (Matt. 13:38); it is they who loom as Jesus' steady enemies. (Compare Jerome's commentary on Psalm 2; see chapter 10.) Jesus taught his disciples to pray that God rescue them from "the evil one" (such, evidently, is the meaning of that clause in the Lord's Prayer—Matt. 6:13, NRSV; compare John 17:15).

In the Gospels people are said to be possessed by demons, and a crucial element in Jesus' calling is to cast these demons out (Matt. 10:8); usually it is understood that a person may be possessed by a single demon (Mark 1:23), but it is said that Mary Magdalene had seven demons (Luke 8:2), and the Gerasene demoniac was possessed by "many" (Mark 5:9), who are said to have exchanged words with Jesus (Matt. 8:29-32). Indeed Jesus told a wry parable about a demon that was expelled from a person and later came back with seven worse ones to take up residence within the person (Matt. 12:43-45 [= Luke 11:24-26]).

The scribes at one point accused Jesus, since he dealt effectively with demons, of being in league with Beelzebul himself, and Jesus had to refute the notion, implying that he must tie up Satan (Mark 3:22-27; compare John 8:44-49).

At climactic moments it is said that Satan himself entered into particular people: when Peter protested at Jesus' prediction of his death, Jesus said, "Get behind me, Satan!" (Mark 8:33 and par.); and when Judas determined to betray Jesus, it is said that Satan entered into him (Luke 22:3; John 13:27). Jesus' disciples could report with joy that the demons submitted to them, and Jesus reported to them a vision that Satan had already fallen: "I watched Satan fall from heaven like a flash of lightning" (Luke 10:17-18). It is clear, then, that Jesus, his disciples, and the Galilean crowds that followed them saw their world shaped not only by God and God's angels (Matt. 4:11 and *passim*) but by Satan and Satan's demons as well. For Jesus and his followers, the world is a battleground between God and the angels on the one hand and Satan and the demons on the other.[2]

Satan and the Demons:
A Distinctive Belief System

I defer for the moment a discussion of the reality or unreality of Satan and demons; I deal first with the specific belief system that posits their existence. It is certainly a belief system that continued past New Testament times; one thinks of Antony of Egypt (251?–356), beset in the wilderness by demons in the guise of wild beasts.[3] It is a belief system that continued through the Reformation: one of the stanzas of Martin Luther's hymn "A Mighty Fortress Is Our God" proclaims it:

And though this world, with devils filled,
   Should threaten to undo us;
We will not fear, for God hath willed
   His truth to triumph through us:
The prince of darkness grim,
   We tremble not for him;
His rage we can endure,
   For lo! his doom is sure,
   One little word shall fell him.[4]

And it is a belief system that continues in various circles today (see below), though it is not one, it is safe to say, that will be shared by many readers of this work. Just as important, it is not a belief system to be found in the Old Testament; the Psalms are by and large innocent of it. It is true, one finds Ps. 106:37—"They sacrificed their sons and their daughters to demons"; but these "demons" are identified with Canaanite idols (vv. 36, 38), which are powerless (Ps. 115:4-8).

It is clearly a belief system, however, of the New Testament and of the Deuterocanonical works that were written in a time near that of the New Testament (see Tob. 6:14-18), and, indeed, it was a widespread belief system in the Hellenistic civilization of the time. Although the question of its ramifications is an important one, it is one into which we cannot enter here.[5] The central matter here is to identify what it is to which the belief system referred: it appears, in large measure at least, to be an explanation for mental illness.[6]

It was not only those around the afflicted person who were convinced the person was possessed by a demon: the afflicted one often affirmed it too. And for a nonscientific culture it was a plausible belief: if there is a shift in personality, if a person is no longer "himself" or "herself," if the person behaves in a destructive or violent way, then that person is understood to be possessed by an alien, destructive spirit, that is, a demon. An incident is related in Mark 9:17-27 (= Matt. 17:14-20; Luke 9:38-43a) of a boy possessed by a spirit that made him unable to speak; it is clear that the boy suffered from epilepsy. In the case of the Gerasene demoniac (Mark 5:1-20), it has been suggested that he suffered from a manic-depressive psychosis.[7] When the demons that possessed the demoniac are perceived to speak out, therefore, it is the speech of the victim of a mental illness that is reported.

Now, whether there was a higher incidence of mental illness in Palestine in Jesus' day than at other times and in other places across the world would be impossible to say, but the frustration suffered by those who in the face of Roman imperial power dreamed of God's restoration of the glory of Israel would certainly have reinforced any such illness. The speech of those who were demon-possessed was often heavy with religious expectation (compare Mark 1:24).

To sum up so far: the New Testament presents us with a worldview in which God is struggling against the kingdom of Satan, in which Jesus is proclaiming the victory of God over the kingdom of Satan. One manifestation of the kingdom of Satan was the perceived phenomenon of demon-possession, and Jesus is reported to have represented the victory of God over Satan by casting out the demons of those who were possessed, that is to say, by healing them.

The Psalms as Expressions of God's
Victory over the Enemies of God

Given a belief system no longer shared by most Christians in our day and not shared by the Psalms, my attempt to offer it as a theological solution to the dilemma presented to us by the treatment of enemies in the Psalms would seem quixotic indeed. Nevertheless, let us persevere and see how it might work.

The psalmist looks upon his enemies, we remind ourselves, as the enemies of God. The demons described in the New Testament are the enemies of God. The words of the psalmist regarding his enemies therefore fit Jesus' attitude toward the demons. Jesus does all he can to defeat them; he wishes to see them dead. He wishes to see God rule supreme: he teaches his disciples to pray, "Thy kingdom come."

The demons defy Jesus (Mark 1:24; 5:7) just as the psalmist's enemies did who "open wide their mouths against me; they say, 'Aha, Aha, our eyes have seen it'" (Ps. 35:21). All the harshest words against the psalmist's enemies are appropriate against the demons: "But you, O God, will cast them down into the lowest pit; the bloodthirsty and treacherous shall not live out half their days. But I will trust in you" (Ps. 55:24 [23]).

Our Attitude toward the Reality
of Demons

But it will not be easy for most of us to persuade ourselves that what I have been proposing is a useful way to proceed. For most of us, demons are the stuff of cartoons in *The New Yorker* or of sensational films such as *Rosemary's Baby*. The narratives of Jesus' exorcisms, as we listen to them or read them, hardly register in our minds and hearts; we ignore them, or else we turn away from them in puzzlement, assuming them to be part of the furniture of the Bible, from far away and long ago. Some years ago a Christian missionary in Africa is supposed to have reduced Christian theology to a single affirmation: "Jesus is stronger than the demons." This proclamation functioned well for those who heard him and responded, but it does not do for most of us. It is true, a recent survey indicated that one in ten Americans claims to have talked with the devil in the flesh.[8] It is true, Roman Catholics who testify to visionary experiences of the Virgin Mary often testify to the work of Satan and the demons as well. But if someone comes to our attention who believes in demons, we normally take the belief as evidence of a delusional system.

And, clearly, I do not want to reinforce delusional systems. But perhaps we should not be too dismissive about the matter of demons. In a book called *People of the Lie*, the physician M. Scott Peck takes seriously the existence of demons and the exorcism of demons.[9] I am reminded of the remark in a rather different direction by the comedian Lily Tomlin: "Why is it," she once asked, "that when we talk to God it is called prayer, and when God talks to us it is called schizophrenia?" In particular, I think it is important for us not to confine our associations with demons to the psychiatrist's office or the mental hospital.

But instead of insisting either that demons do or do not exist, what I would suggest for us is a kind of *what if* attitude. In chapter 18 the suggestion was made that the pronouns for God in the Bible are metaphorical, that we are saying, "God, he, as it were." Now I am suggesting that we beg the question of the reality of demons, and use the concept at least as a powerful metaphor: we can say, "We pray the downfall of the demons, as it were."

The note struck in *The Screwtape Letters* of C. S. Lewis[10] is exactly what I have in mind. That work, which I mentioned in passing in chapter 15, purports to be a series of letters to a junior demon named Wormwood from his superior (Screwtape) on the best ways to tempt a new Christian.

I suggest, then, that we develop a respect for the power that demons—as it were—hold over human life; but in the knowledge of the power of God we can laugh at them and hold them—as it were—in contempt, as the psalmist did his enemies.

I propose, then, a reading of the Psalms that takes seriously the centrality of Jesus Christ in the life of the church as the struggle against evil is pursued. In the rite of baptism according to the *Book of Common Prayer*, the following questions, among others, are asked of the person to be baptized or on behalf of the infant to be baptized: "Do you renounce Satan and all the spiritual forces of wickedness that rebel against God?"; "Do you renounce the evil powers of this world which corrupt and destroy the creatures of God?"; "Do you renounce all sinful desires that draw you from the love of God?" And the questions are similar in Roman Catholic baptism: "Do you reject Satan, and all his works, and all his empty promises?" Indeed for Roman Catholics the questions are renewed each Easter Vigil in the reaffirmation of baptismal promises, as if Christians are really only capable of making such a renunciation a year at a time. I propose that we enlist the Psalms in the struggle to make permanent that renunciation of evil.

Roman Catholic and Protestant
Modes of Prayer

But I must digress for a moment to indicate some contrasts in theological style that bear on the spiritual life, that is, on the active daily intercourse between the Christian and God, because Roman Catholics and various communities of Protestants have differed in their understanding of how the struggle against evil is pursued, and in their practices of prayer. An outline at least of these differences is necessary here.

The roots of these differences are to be found in the New Testament itself. Paul stressed the justification of the believer by faith in the action of God in the crucifixion and resurrection of Jesus Christ (Rom. 5:1). The emphasis here is on what God has *already* done for the believer and for the world: in God's act of justification, the crucial battle has already been fought and won. "He has rescued us from the power of darkness and transferred us into the kingdom of his beloved Son" (Col. 1:13). The Fourth Gospel, in different vocabulary, has the same stress: the believer has eternal life, having passed from death to life (John 5:24). And if God has done the crucial action for the believer, the believer does not have a crucial need to "work" at the relation with God.

By contrast, there is a strand in the New Testament, especially in the later epistles, that stresses the necessity of believers to prepare themselves for the eventual return of Christ, when God will make all things right. Here the emphasis is on the *not yet*, and it is incumbent on believers to be zealous in preparation—in short, to be disciplined in the process of sanctification.

> Our struggle is not against enemies of blood and flesh, but against the rulers, against the authorities, against the cosmic powers of this present darkness, against the spiritual forces of evil in the heavenly places. Therefore take up the whole armor of God, so that you may be able to withstand on that evil day, and having done everything, to stand firm. (Eph. 6:12-13)

> Therefore prepare your minds for action; discipline yourselves; set all your hope in the grace that Jesus Christ will bring you when he is revealed. . . . Be holy yourselves in all your conduct. (1 Pet. 1:13, 15)

As the Christian faith became the official faith of the population of Europe, and as the church became worldly in many ways in its style of life, it was sanctification that was stressed, and this became the traditional stance of the Roman Catholic Church. The daily office became the discipline of prayer for the clergy and monastic communities and for those of the upper classes with the leisure and taste for it. For various monastic orders and for the nobility that wished it there were teachers who developed various traditions of spiritual discipline. And in the meantime, the devotional life of the laity was nurtured by such exercises as the saying of the rosary. For Roman Catholics, both clergy and laity, the power of God is mediated preeminently in the sacraments, especially in the Eucharist, which strengthen the faithful.

The Protestant Reformation reaffirmed both the centrality of the Bible and the doctrine of God's justification of believers. Indeed the Calvinist wing of the Reformation pressed this stress on the power and the initiative of God to the point of the doctrine of predestination—the belief that God had willed the salvation of believers from the foundation of the world. Evangelical Protestants have emphasized the importance of a conversion experience in the life of the believer, often in the years of adolescence; the conversion signals the acceptance of God's grace in their lives. And the Protestant stress on the priesthood of all believers led the discipline of private prayer in a different direction: it was not something for the clergy and for the leisured class but something for all believers, and it has been centered in the reading of the Bible. Typically, Protestants would read each day a chapter of the Bible, either alone or in the family circle. This reading of the Bible has been devotional; it has been reading for the purpose of hearing God's immediate word to the readers. By and large, Protestants have not used prayer books, the Anglican *Book of Common Prayer* being an exception. And, by and large, Protestants have not had a tradition of "practicing the presence of God" or of self-examination in the Roman Catholic sense: God is already present, and the task of believers is to be open to God's work in their lives. Vocal prayer then has tended to center on thanksgiving and on intercessions that reflect personal concerns.

It is instructive to look for a moment at that classic of Protestant spirituality, *Pilgrim's Progress* by John Bunyan (1628–1688); it is an allegory of the journey of the pilgrim, Christian, from the "City of Destruction" to the "Heavenly City." It does not set forth a system for attaining one's spiritual goal but is rather a symbolic depiction of the progress made by a typical soul toward the heavenly goal; along the way Christian meets such tempters as "Mr. Worldly-Wiseman," "Mr. Facing-Both-Ways," and the like.

By contrast, Roman Catholics have developed, as I have indicated, systems of spiritual discipline such as the spiritual exercises of Ignatius Loyola (1491?–1556), the founder of the Jesuits, and spiritual writings such as those of Teresa of Ávila (1515–1582), which encourage self-examination and the systematic development of progress in prayer. And in our present century, just as Roman Catholics have rediscovered the Bible, so some Protestants have discovered the kind of spiritual direction associated with Roman Catholics. This Protestant search for spiritual direction is in part the result of a weakening grip on the doctrine of justification and the discipline of Bible reading.

The Battles of Present-Day Christians

Now, whether we emphasize the prior power and grace of God manifest in our lives in conversion or whether we emphasize our obligation to work at responding to God day by day, it is clear that we are called to grow in grace and knowledge of our Lord and Savior Jesus Christ (2 Pet. 3:18). Even if the crucial battle has already been fought and won, there are still mopping-up operations to pursue.[11] And it is in this process of growth in grace that I propose enlisting the Psalms in a fresh way.

Before we examine the Psalms as a help in these battles, however, it is useful to name some of the enemies that present-day Christians confront. A previous generation would have been satisfied with a single designation: we are battling against *sin*. But it is characteristic of the steadily increasing secularism of our present age that "sin" is a word spoken mostly in church, and the battles, if fought, are given other names.[12] And though a complete answer is out of the question, I can at least indicate the terrain.

I turn first to interior battles. I have already pointed out that Paul understood the war within (Rom. 7:23). I could reproduce the list of the "works of the flesh" offered in Gal. 5:19-21—"fornication, impurity, licentiousness, idolatry," and the rest. Or I could examine the traditional seven deadly sins—pride, covetousness, lust, envy, gluttony, anger, sloth—though some people in our day have thought those sins to be ones to which men are particularly prone, to the neglect of those besetting women.[13] What I do is offer some present-day examples of interior enemies, in no particular order.

1. Crippling memories from childhood. For many of us, memories of neglect or abuse in childhood continue to cripple our effectiveness as adults— with ourselves, with family members, with colleagues.

2. Unresolved anger. Many of us lash out at or abuse family members or employees in ways that suggest a deep-seated anger that has never been dealt with. There is a lot of free-floating anger around.

3. Depression. Many of us are depressed some or all of the time, finding no energy or zest for living. It is true, some depression appears to be caused by abnormal brain chemistry, but some of it may be relieved by a shift in spiritual stance.

4. Low self-esteem. Some of us have so low a view of ourselves as to be paralyzed when it comes to attempting new tasks and developing new skills. How many people introduce themselves with a sentence that begins, "I'm just a (housewife, salesman, student)"?

5. Boredom. Many of us feel "stuck," wondering what to do for large stretches of time. We lack any resources to initiate activity either by ourselves or with others.

6. Addictions. Many of us feel trapped by addictive habits: wrong patterns of eating; damaging consumption of tobacco, alcohol, or drugs; obsessive sexual indulgences; and the like. Those with a drug addiction have been heard to say they "have a monkey on their backs."
7. Inappropriate struggles for power. It is usually men, but sometimes it is women, who cannot rest until they have exerted power over other people. Sometimes it is exercised sexually. Sometimes it is the struggle for economic or political power.

Then there are the exterior enemies against which to do battle. These are easier to recognize; the newspapers and nightly television news are full of them, and I suggested a few of them in chapter 15. There is sexism—the attitude of devaluing women, and the institutional structures that prevent women from achieving the life to which they have been called. There is ethnocentricity and racism—the attitude that devalues those outside one's own ethnic group or culture or race, and the institutional structures that prevent those outside the dominant ethnic group or culture or race from achieving the life to which they have been called. Indeed, these "-isms" are simply different manifestations of a more basic attitude of devaluation or contempt for anyone or any group that is different, that is "other," and of the actions that result from these attitudes, such as scapegoating.

And there are institutionalized patterns in political and economic structures that bring about injustices of many sorts. With all these external enemies the Christian is called to do battle.

The Enemies of Present-Day Christians as "Demons"

It is noteworthy that not only do the original *Spiritual Exercises* of Ignatius Loyola speak of "the enemy," "the evil one," and "the evil spirit,"[14] but the same terminology is used in a contemporary reading of the exercises.[15] So if the term "demons" is a convenient one for the forces that work on us against God, whether demons are a reality or not, the question becomes: Is it appropriate to look upon those enemies that we perceive today, those that I have mentioned and those that I have not, as demonic? My answer is yes, at least to the degree that it is a useful assumption as we consider our use of the Psalms.

For example, addictions in our day are often described as demons. I have already mentioned the expression "monkey on my back"; that monkey is not benign but malign, and "monkey" and "demon" could be seen as equivalent metaphors. In one recent interview with a recovered alcoholic who is an Episcopal priest, he stated, "Addiction is a hole in the soul. Addicts are the walking dead. My alcoholism was sick, depraved, like being possessed by the devil. I know what demon possession means." Again, "recovering from alcohol addiction . . . is a spiritual journey, learning to worship the right God and not the one in a bottle."[16]

One resource that many addicts of various sorts have found useful in our day is groups that make use of the "twelve steps," exemplified by Alcoholics Anonymous. One of those twelve steps is the seeking of help from a "higher power." The implication therefore is that we are dealing with something more than a purely psychological problem.

Again, boredom might not sound particularly demonic, but I suggest that it is simply a modern name for the deadly sin called "sloth" or "accidie" in the Middle Ages. One of the affirmations in the Statement of Faith of the United Church of Christ is "You seek to save your people from aimlessness and sin"; it would seem to be a besetting spiritual issue in our time. Similar observations might be made about the other enemies I have mentioned. Could we in prayer confront the demons that beset us, face them down, hurl imprecations at them roundly and wholeheartedly in the words the psalmists used against their enemies of old? I suggest it is an enterprise worth pursuing.

The Psalms as Spiritual Exercises

I now return to the question posed in this chapter: How might the Psalms be used by Christians?

I suggest that Roman Catholics might want to try reading the Psalms sequentially, from Psalm 1 to Psalm 150, without leaving out any sequences that are "somewhat harsh in tone" (see chapter 16). The advantage of the present canonical order is precisely that it is *not* a very "logical" order—the sequence catches us unawares, forcing us to ponder the sudden actions of God in our lives. I suggest that Protestants return to a sequential reading of the Psalms and take seriously the spiritual struggle with the forces of darkness that the Psalms reflect. I suggest that Christians who embark upon a reading of the Psalms listen to them christocentrically, watching Christ do battle with the enemies of God.

As I have said, this is analogous to the way the church fathers and the Reformers read the Psalms (compare the observations in chapters 10, 11, and 18), though I propose that we do it quite systematically. I propose that we naively, uncritically listen to them being recited by Jesus Christ. How might this reading be done? Let us take the first three psalms as examples.

Psalm 1

As I explained in chapter 18, the Hebrew text of the first verse of Psalm 1 uses "the man"—as the RSV had it, "Blessed is the man"—but because for the psalmist "the man" is representative of all those who love God's law, the NRSV is justified in pluralizing—"Happy are those." If we hear Jesus Christ reciting the psalm, he can use "the man"; if we read the psalm as part of the body of Christ (Rom. 12:5), we can use the plural. In either case, how are we to listen as Jesus Christ uses the psalm? He is the righteous one (1 John 2:1) who does not take the path that sinners tread. And not only does he meditate on the law day and night; he teaches us the true meaning of the law (Matthew 5 and *passim*) and exemplifies what God has intended in the law (Rom. 8:3). Can we pray to stay faithful to Jesus Christ, so that we are not like the chaff that the wind drives away? Can the triune God watch over our ways, that they remain righteous?

Psalm 2

In this royal psalm the new king speaks; he cites the words of the pagan rulers (v. 3) and the words of God (vv. 6, 7-9). Christian tradition has it that the words of v. 7b were spoken at Jesus' baptism by John the Baptist, so that it is altogether appropriate for us to listen to Jesus Christ recite the psalm. Who are the nations and the rulers that conspire against him? They are not only Pilate and others who conspired to kill him; we, too, are the Gentiles, adopted as children of God (Gal. 4:5). So we must no longer live as the Gentiles live but must clothe ourselves with the new self (Eph. 4:17-24). The reference is also to the rulers who are cosmic powers of this present darkness (Eph. 6:12), the demons, in fact, who beset us day by day. Jesus Christ recites the psalm as a sublime affirmation of God's designation of him as King of the nations (Rev. 15:3), indeed, King of kings (Rev. 17:14; 19:16). We, too, by God's grace will share in his kingdom (Matt. 25:34). "Happy are all who take refuge in him"; we ask, "O God, are we truly in that company? And if so, do we acknowledge how lucky we are?"

Psalm 3

One can hear Jesus Christ reciting this psalm in the Garden of Gethsemane. Listen to his foes mock him, saying, "There is no help for you in God." It would be demons who could put into his mind the passing prayer that night, "Father, if you are willing, remove this cup from me" (Luke 22:42); the next day the demons entered into the leaders in the crowd who mocked at him on the cross: "He saved others; let him save himself" (Luke 23:35). We, too, may pray the psalm, aghast at the number of demons who mock our affirmations of trust in God and who lead us to wonder whether there is any help from God at all.

Nevertheless, Jesus at Gethsemane could put his trust once more in God; the psalmist says, "But you, O Lord, are a shield around me," and Jesus said in Gethsemane, "Not my will but yours be done" (Luke 22:42). Could Jesus shout within him a prayer to God, "Rise up, O Lord! Deliver me, O my God!" (v. 8 [7])? Can we? Did he pray in that wonderful imprecation that God might break the teeth of the demons who haunted him (again, v. 8 [7])? Can we? Psalm 3 ends in trust, and so the next day, as he was dying, he is said to have used the trustful words of another psalm: "Father, into your hands I commend my spirit" (Luke 23:46). The wording of the end of our psalm—"Deliverance belongs to the Lord; may your blessing be on your people!"—reminds us that we may not only reaffirm our trust in God but have our thoughts finally directed away from ourselves to our fellow Christians.

In such a way we might work our way through the whole Psalter, alert to the ways of God within the covenant community. We can listen for Jesus' voice psalm by psalm; we can ponder our own stance before God; we can be aroused to the ways of the demons in our own lives and in our world, and even more aroused by the strength God manifests in destroying the power of those demons, in our own lives and in the world.

NOTES

1. Krister Stendahl, "Biblical Theology, Contemporary," in *IDB* 1:419–20.

2. See Werner Foerster, *"daimōn,* etc.," in *TDNT* 2:16–20; Walter Wink, *Unmasking the Powers: The Invisible Forces That Determine Human Existence* (Philadelphia: Fortress, 1968), 41–68, and references there.

3. Athanasius, *The Life of St. Antony* (Westminster, Md.: Newman, 1950), secs. 3–10, 51–53.

4. Translation of Frederick Henry Hedge, 1852.

5. Useful is James Kallas, *The Significance of the Synoptic Miracles* (London: SPCK, 1961), 38–76.

6. S. Vernon McCasland, *By the Finger of God: Demon Possession and Exorcism in Early Christianity in the Light of Modern Views of Mental Illness* (New York: Macmillan, 1951).

7. Ibid., 38–39.

8. A Gallup "Mirror of America" poll, reported in the *Los Angeles Times,* 12 August 1991, sec. B, p.3.

9. M. Scott Peck, *People of the Lie: The Hope for Healing Human Evil* (New York: Simon and Schuster, 1983).

10. C. S. Lewis, *The Screwtape Letters* (New York: Macmillan, 1943).

11. Oscar Cullmann, *Christ and Time* (Philadelphia: Westminster, 1950), 84.

12. Karl Menninger, *Whatever Became of Sin?* (New York: Hawthorn, 1973).

13. Valerie Saiving Goldstein, "The Human Situation: A Feminine View," *JR* 40 (1960):100–112; reprinted (with name of author Valerie Saiving) in Carol P. Christ and Judith Plaskow (eds.), *Womanspirit Rising: A Feminist Reader in Religion* (San Francisco: Harper & Row, 1979), 25–42.

14. Secs. 315, 325–27, and often; see, conveniently, Elisabeth Meier Tetlow (trans.), *The Spiritual Exercises of St. Ignatius Loyola: A New Translation* (College Theology Society, Resources in Religion 3; Lanham, Md.: University Press of America, 1987).

15. David L. Fleming, *Modern Spiritual Exercises: A Contemporary Reading of the Spiritual Exercises of St. Ignatius* (Image Books; Garden City, N.Y.: Doubleday, 1983).

16. Interview with the Rev. Monte Pearse, *The Boston Globe,* 3 September 1991, 28, 31. See further Gerald G. May, *Addiction and Grace* (San Francisco: Harper & Row, 1988); Patrick McCormick, *Sin as Addiction* (New York: Paulist, 1989).

How the
Twenty-third Psalm
Became an American Secular Icon

Chapter 1 of this work is a short consideration of Psalm 23, and there I mentioned Garrison Keillor's sketch in which Psalm 23 was linked with Lincoln's *Gettysburg Address* and John McCrae's poem "In Flanders Fields" as the three alternative recitations appropriate for the Memorial Day observances at Lake Wobegon. It is clear that the Twenty-third Psalm holds a unique position in American popular culture, and it is a matter of curiosity how it gained that position.

The first thing to say is that it is always the King James Version that is used in the recitation of the psalm. It is therefore through Protestant Americans, and through the Protestant imprint on American secular culture, that the psalm has become unique; there has been no corresponding preoccupation with this psalm among Roman Catholics. A Catholic friend tells me that in the 1950s and 1960s, when he was a pupil in the public schools in Lynnfield, Massachusetts, school prayer consisted simply of a recitation by all the pupils, in every classroom, every day, of the Twenty-third Psalm, led in each school by the loudspeaker. He said the Catholic kids found it hard to understand what was going on.

I begin with a point I made in Chapter 1: that Psalm 23 was reinforced in the New Testament by the words in John 10, in which Jesus identifies himself as the Good Shepherd. This identification led, in turn, to the popularity of depictions of Jesus the Good Shepherd in Christian art, beginning with the catacombs in Rome. The image of Jesus as the Good Shepherd is therefore a possession of the whole church, leading, for example, to the German evening hymn *Hirte deiner Schafe* (Shepherd of your sheep) of Johann Crüger (1653).

The importance of the psalm was both reflected and reinforced in the English-speaking world by two publications in the seventeenth century. One is the Scottish metrical paraphrase "The Lord's my shepherd, I'll not want" (1650), which has been enormously popular (see chapter 11). The other is the occurrence of the phrase "Valley of the Shadow of Death," the location of an episode in Part 1 of John Bunyan's *Pilgrim's Progress* (1678): as Christian walks through the Valley, he recites, "Though I walk through the valley of the shadow of death, I shall fear no evil."[1] But one should note that there the Valley was the symbol not of death but of the dark night of the soul, where hell seems so near.[2]

In the course of the nineteenth century, however, the psalm became intertwined with changing American views of death. Death was certainly a preoccupation of Americans through the whole of the century, as one can see in a perusal of Sunday-school literature from the first half of the century. Children were constantly being reminded in the literature of the time of the importance of Christian discipleship, in order to be afforded a happy death.

> If sex is the common preoccupation of Americans in the mid-twentieth century, then death was the obsession of evangelical Protestants in the first half of the nineteenth. Their stories teemed with dying people; Sunday school books moved toward the predictable, climactic death of a pious hero.[3]

But in this literature the Twenty-third Psalm played no part.

Nor was it the inevitable psalm to use at a funeral. In its service for the burial of the dead, the form of the *Book of Common Prayer* in use in the United States in the nineteenth century used Ps. 39:5-14 (4-13) or Psalm 90 or both, but not Psalm 23; the Twenty-third Psalm entered the service for burial of the dead only in the revision of 1979. Similarly, the funeral ceremony of the Methodists in 1836 offered a delicate balance between fear and hope; Psalm 23 was only added in 1916, as the ceremony shifted radically toward hope.[4]

Furthermore Psalm 23 was not a staple of the earliest revival preaching. Thus Charles G. Finney (1792–1875), in the course of his *Memoirs*, mentions preaching from John 3:16 but not from Psalm 23.[5]

And the psalm was not a convention of popular culture before the Civil War. McGuffey's *Readers*, drafted in the 1830s, included passages from the Bible: the *Second Reader* included the Lord's Prayer and the Ten Commandments, and the *Third Reader*, the Sermon on the Mount and Psalms 19 and 104; but the Twenty-third Psalm does not appear.[6]

As we shall see, by the end of the nineteenth century there were many popular books about the Bible penned by writers who had visited Palestine, books describing Palestinian shepherd life and thereby making reference to the Twenty-third Psalm; but that was not the case in the first part of the century. Horatio B. Hackett, who was a professor of Bible at the (Baptist) Newton Theological Institution in Massachusetts, wrote in 1855 a little book that offered illustrations of biblical matters from current Palestinian life after having visited the region.[7] Though in that work he mentions the pilgrim psalms (Psalms 121–134)[8] and the "pastures of the wilderness" (Ps. 65:13 [12]),[9] he does not mention the Twenty-third Psalm.

The psalm was not a convention of deathbed scenes before the Civil War. For example, at the death of Little Eva in Harriet Beecher Stowe's *Uncle Tom's Cabin* (1852), Tom quotes Matt. 25:6: "At midnight there was a great cry made, Behold, the bridegroom cometh."[10] But Psalm 23 does not appear in that scene.

Nor, as far as I can determine, was the psalm a convention of pious soldiers during the Civil War. Hackett published in 1864 a little book of anecdotes about

Christian piety and bravery among the soldiers.[11] The anecdotes he relates in that book of dying soldiers mention Psalm 91 ("A thousand shall fall at thy side"),[12] the hymn "Nearer, My God, to Thee,"[13] even the prayer "Now I lay me down to sleep,"[14] but not the Twenty-third Psalm. By the same token, the report of a Granville, Ohio, minister who had been among the Northern prisoners in the Confederate prison at Andersonville, Georgia, mentions many prayer meetings, texts on which sermons were preached, and the like, but he does not mention the Twenty-third Psalm.[15]

It was not cited in the prayers or addresses at the funeral and burial of Abraham Lincoln;[16] and it does not appear to figure in Memorial Day services in the period 1868–1870.[17]

It is true that I have located two accounts of deathbed scenes from before the Civil War in which the Twenty-third Psalm is crucial. One is the death of John Steele, a physician who was a missionary of the American Board of Commissioners for Foreign Missions in the Madura (now called Madurai) Mission in south India, on October 6, 1842. During the day preceding his death he made several brief affirmations of faith that were either verses of Scripture or reflections of biblical faith. Then, on the evening preceding his death, he repeated the first four verses of the Twenty-third Psalm. But the interesting thing about the account of the scene, written by a fellow missionary, is that the latter did not so describe it ("he repeated the first four verses of the Twenty-third Psalm"), as he might well have done if such a recitation were a convention of the deathbed; instead he writes, "Towards morning he repeated, 'The Lord is my shepherd, I shall not want,'" and goes on to record the wording of the four verses in full.[18] That is, the manner of the telling suggests that the Twenty-third Psalm was part of Steele's own deep piety rather than the automatic and conventional resort of a dying Christian.

The other deathbed scene is just as notable; it is the recollection of Gilbert J. Greene, in his old age, of an incident involving Abraham Lincoln when the latter was a young lawyer in Springfield, Illinois, in the years 1837 to 1847.[19] Greene was a friend of Lincoln, a printer at that time, and Lincoln asked him one day to ride out into the country to witness the oral will of a dying woman. After she had dictated her will, she made a pious comment about how relieved she would be to join her family members in heaven, and she asked Lincoln to read to her from the Bible.

> They offered him the Book but he did not take it, but began reciting from memory the Twenty-third Psalm, laying special emphasis upon "Though I walk through the valley of the shadow of death, I will fear no evil, for Thou art with me, thy rod and thy staff they comfort me." Without using the book, he took up the first of the fourteenth chapter of John—"In my Father's house are many mansions." After he had given these and other quotations from the Scriptures, he recited several hymns, closing with "Rock of Ages, Cleft for Me." . . . The woman was more sick than we realized, and died while we were there. Riding home, I expressed surprise that he should have acted as pastor as well as attorney so perfectly, and Mr. Lincoln replied, "God and eternity and heaven are very near to me today."[20]

Now this narrative may reflect Lincoln's own piety—he had read Bunyan's *Pilgrim's Progress* as a boy[21]—but it could simply be a reflection of Greene's post-Civil War piety put back onto Lincoln decades before.

By 1880 the psalm had triumphed. In the revision of the initiation ceremony for the lodge of (the Independent Order of) Odd Fellows, made in that year, the reading of the Twenty-third Psalm was included.[22]

And, in 1885, Mary Baker Eddy published her *Science and Health with Key to the Scriptures*;[23] in her "Key to the Scriptures" she offers her interpretation of verses from Genesis 1–4 and from Revelation 10, 12, and 21; and to her remarks on the book of Revelation she appends an interpretation of Psalm 23. It is almost as if, having explained from her perspective chapters from both the beginning and the end of the Bible, she was impelled to offer finally a comment on what was for her the central chapter from the middle of the Bible. "In the following Psalm one word shows, though faintly, the light which Christian Science throws on the Scriptures by substituting for the corporeal sense, the incorporeal or spiritual sense of Deity:— [Divine Love] is my shepherd; I shall not want."[24]

The psalm was a cliché for dying soldiers in the Spanish–American War (1898). In a fulsome tribute to American Red Cross nurses in that war, Franklin B. Hussey of Chicago wrote:

> [The nurse] carried balm and healing not only to broken and bleeding bodies, but to broken and bleeding hearts as well, and stood through long pestilential nights, like a ministering angel of heaven, beside the weary pillow of pain, and when all that human hands could do had been done, and the dying soldier murmured last words to mother, wife or sweetheart, hers the ear that caught the last faint whisper, hers the fingers that penned the last letter home, hers the voice that read from the thumb-worn page, "The Lord is my Shepherd, I shall not want. . . . Yea, though I walk through the valley of the shadow of death"—while with his hand clasped in hers, his soul passed on through the "valley" and the "shadow" up to "the sandals of God." . . . that woman's form, with melting heart and nerves of steel, against the soft blue of the summer sky, with her lint and bandages in one hand and her Bible in the other, the sign of the cross upon her sleeve, and the glory of the countenance of the "Son of Man" reflected on her face.[25]

It is therefore in the two decades after the Civil War that we must look for the appropriation of the Twenty-third Psalm by American secular culture. The initial trigger, I would suggest, was a tribute to the psalm voiced by Henry Ward Beecher (1813–1887) in the period 1856 to 1858. Beecher was an enormously popular preacher, arguably the greatest influence on the piety of the time; in the period in question he was pastor of the Plymouth Congregational Church in Brooklyn, New York. His tribute to Psalm 23 is part of a longer sequence, delivered as a sermon or lecture at the church, on the way in which Scripture reflects the "sacred joy of souls in trial." He mentions Job and Isaiah and then turns to David, and his words were influential enough that they must be quoted in full.

David has left no sweeter psalm than the short twenty-third. It is but a moment's opening of his soul; but—as when one, walking the winter street, sees the door opened for some one to enter, and the red light streams a moment forth, and the forms of gay children are running to greet the comer, and genial music sounds, though the door shuts and leaves the night black, yet it cannot shut back again all that the eye, the ear, the heart, and the imagination have seen—so in this psalm, though it is but a moment's opening of the soul, are emitted truths of peace and consolation that will never be absent from the world.

Beecher then turns to the psalm itself, and the ensuing two paragraphs became an enormous encouragement for the affection that Americans ultimately manifested for the psalm.

The twenty-third psalm is the nightingale of the psalms. It is small, of a homely feather, singing shyly out of obscurity; but, O, it has filled the air of the whole world with melodious joy, greater than the heart can conceive. Blessed be the day on which that psalm was born.

What would you say of a pilgrim commissioned of God to travel up and down the earth singing a strange melody, which, when one heard, caused him to forget whatever sorrow he had? And so the singing angel goes on his way through all lands, singing in the language of every nation, driving away trouble by the pulses of the air which his tongue moves with divine power. Behold just such an one! This pilgrim God has sent to speak in every language of the globe. It has charmed more griefs to rest than all the philosophy of the world. It has remanded to their dungeon more felon thoughts, more black doubts, more thieving sorrows, than there are sands on the sea shore. It has comforted the noble host of the poor. It has sung courage to the army of the disappointed. It has poured balm and consolation into the heart of the sick, of captives in dungeons, of widows in their pinching griefs, of orphans in their loneliness. Dying soldiers have died easier as it was read to them; ghastly hospitals have been illumined; it has visited the prisoner and broken his chains, and, like Peter's angel, led him forth in imagination, and sung him back to his home again. It has made the dying Christian slave freer than his master, and consoled those whom, dying, he left behind mourning, not so much that he was gone as because they were left behind, and could not go too. Nor is its work done. It will go singing to your children and my children, and to their children, through all the generations of time; nor will it fold its wings till the last pilgrim is safe, and time ended; and then it shall fly back to the bosom of God, whence it issued, and sound on, mingled with all those sounds of celestial joy which make heaven musical forever.[26]

This characterization of the psalm was cited, without attribution, in *The Shepherd Psalm* of Frederick B. Meyer (1889). Meyer (1847–1929) was an English Baptist preacher and author of popular studies on the Bible who accompanied Dwight L. Moody in preaching tours of the United States on many occasions (for Moody, see below). In the *Shepherd Psalm* he writes, "Before me lies a page that describes it [the Twenty-third Psalm] in some such terms as these: that it is a pilgrim minstrel commissioned of God to travel up and down through the world," and he paraphrases the first five sentences of Beecher's last paragraph. Then he directly cites, with quotation marks, from "It has remanded" through to the end.[27] In passing it may be noted that Meyer's biographer reports that Meyer's last Sunday morning sermon (February 10, 1929) was devoted to the "Shepherd Psalm," and the biographer remarks, "The tens of thousands, throughout the world, he has helped by that message!"[28]

Those two paragraphs by Beecher, called "The Singing Pilgrim, A Characterization of the Twenty-third Psalm, Henry Ward Beecher," were then reprinted in William A. Knight's *The Song of Our Syrian Guest* (1904),[29] a book that sold two million copies; and the same two paragraphs, called "A Pilgrim of God, A Characterization of the Twenty-third Psalm," appeared in Leslie D. Weatherhead's *A Shepherd Remembers* (1938).[30] And, curiously, Meshack P. Krikorian, in his book *The Spirit of the Shepherd* (1938), cites the last two sentences of Beecher's words but misattributes the words to Meyer![31] (For a discussion of the books of Knight, Weatherhead, and Krikorian, see below.) In short, Beecher's tribute to the Twenty-third Psalm was enormously influential, striking a chord in the sensibilities of American readers and being cited again and again.

A further reinforcement of the psalm may have been Louisa May Alcott's *Little Women* (1868), a work that went through two editions in six weeks. *Little Women* was a feminized and domesticated retelling of *Pilgrim's Progress*, told through the eyes of the protagonist Jo. In the first chapter Jo's mother proposes to Jo and her sisters that the girls take *Pilgrim's Progress* seriously, and there are many parallels to Bunyan's work throughout the book. Now, I have already noted the "Valley of the Shadow of Death" in *Pilgrim's Progress* itself, so it is notable for our purposes that chapter 40 of *Little Women*, wherein Jo witnesses the death of her younger sister Beth, is titled "The Valley of the Shadow." Indeed that very phrase became a cliché for the nearness of death: Franklin Lane, the Secretary of the Interior under President Woodrow Wilson, when recovering from a serious illness, stated, "Never before have I been called to deliberately walk into the valley of the shadow."[32]

Before we delineate the shifts in American life and thought in the period from 1865 to 1900 that brought the Twenty-third Psalm to prominence, let us remind ourselves of the nature of the psalm. It is short and therefore easily memorized. It is undemanding. It does not mention sin or suggest the appropriateness of participating in any ecclesial community. It simply seems to affirm that God (or, alternatively, Jesus) accompanies the speaker and takes care of him or her. The psalm could be appropriated for a rite of passage, since it appears to move from references to life ("He leadeth me beside the still waters") to death ("Yea, though I walk through the valley of the shadow of death, I will fear no evil, for thou art with me") to eternal life ("and I shall dwell in the house of the Lord for ever"). It is a psalm that could be used in public contexts, acceptable to both Jews and Christians and giving no offense to anyone.

Now, the emergence of the Twenty-third Psalm as a staple of American popular culture would appear to be the effect of the combination of three interwoven
developments: the shift from the old Calvinist theology into both liberal theology
and individualistic evangelicalism; the feminization and sentimentalization of both
church and culture; and the continued evolution of "civil religion." Though these
are, as I say, interwoven, I discuss them one by one.

There is no way even to summarize the theological developments among Protestants in the United States in the nineteenth century, but there was a strong trend
away from the traditional Calvinism, with its emphasis on the sovereignty of God
in human lives and on a high Christology, a theology that engendered in Christians
a fear of damnation, toward a new emphasis on the goodness of God's creation, on
the human life of Jesus as an influence for good, and on a hope for the progressive
amelioration of the affairs of humankind. Two events in the first half of the nineteenth century may symbolize the trend. One is the Unitarian split from Congregationalists across New England: the American Unitarian Association was formed in
1825.[33] Unitarians rejected the doctrine of the Trinity and espoused a more liberal
outlook than Congregationalists did. The other is the publication in 1847 of *Christian Nurture* by Horace Bushnell (1802–1876), a Congregational pastor in Hart-
ford, Connecticut; in this work the author argued for the quiet unfolding of the
Christian nature of the child under appropriate influences instead of conversion as
the normal entrance to the kingdom of God.[34]

In the 1850s, Beecher became the prime spokesperson for the liberal gospel to
the American public. "I would not, for the world, bring up a child to have that
horror of death which hung over my own childhood," claimed Beecher.[35] In 1877,
Beecher renounced the doctrine of hell,[36] and nine years later the American Board
of Commissioners for Foreign Missions at its annual meeting devoted a full day to a
debate over whether it was necessary for missionaries sent out by the board to
believe in hell, a debate then published in full by Houghton Mifflin.[37] Six years
later the board quietly ceased to enforce the requirement.[38]

But if the Twenty-third Psalm was a favorite of Beecher's, it was equally attrac-
tive to those evangelical Christians who emphasized an individualistic piety. One
reflex of the psalm was the gospel hymn "He leadeth me." This hymn, the leading
phrase of which is, of course, taken from a line in v. 2 of the psalm, was written in
1862 by Joseph Henry Gilmore (1834–1918), a Baptist minister and writer; it was
written in connection with a sermon he was preaching on Psalm 23 at the First
Baptist Church of Philadelphia. Without his knowledge his wife submitted it for
publication, and three years later Gilmore was surprised to hear it sung in the
Second Baptist Church of Rochester, New York.[39] There are only the lightest of
other references to the psalm in the hymn ("by waters calm"), and it carries other
biblical images ("Eden's bowers," "Jordan") and reminiscences of other hymns
("death's cold wave" may reflect "death's cold sullen stream" in the hymn "My faith
looks up to thee," written by Ray Palmer in 1830), but its uncomplicated individualistic message struck a popular chord, as the antecedent Twenty-third Psalm was
likewise doing.

The second development was what Ann Douglas has called the "feminization" of American culture[40] and its concomitant sentimentalization, particularly in the period after the Civil War. It is important to insist that the term "feminization" is not intended as pejorative but simply as a description of what was happening as the reigning Calvinism receded in American Protestant churches. In 1888, Warren C. Hubbard, rector of St. Paul's Protestant Episcopal Church in Brooklyn, New York, complained that whereas men cursed, pursued money relentlessly, and neglected religion, the "average woman," though overburdened with domestic chores, found time to go to church: "Men seem to think that religion is meant for women and children."[41] Men flocked instead to lodges such as the Masons and Odd Fellows, where they could hold secret rituals away from women and contemplate the fact of death and the benevolence of a deistic God.[42]

Especially after the Civil War, American popular culture was shaped to a greater and greater degree by the literary efforts of ministers and of women, whose writings were overwhelmingly of the sentimental sort. Beecher's description of the psalm (1858) and Hussey's tribute to Red Cross nurses (1898) nicely bracket that process.

There was an extraordinary preoccupation in this period with the nature of heaven; a prime example of this preoccupation is a now forgotten novel by Elizabeth Stuart Phelps, *The Gates Ajar* (1868),[43] which Douglas analyzes in detail. This work is a semibiographical novel that draws on many biblical passages (though not, as it happens, on Psalm 23) to offer descriptions of heaven; its scenes delighted hundreds of thousands of Americans[44] and was later mocked by Mark Twain in his book *Extract from Captain Stormfield's Visit to Heaven* (1909).[45] Phelps's novel illustrates a trend: heaven is no longer the place to meet God (or Jesus) but the place for reunion with family members who have died. Contributing to this development was undoubtedly the enormous burden of grief left by the Civil War: hardly a household was left untouched by death. "The liberals' conception of death as a casual stroll into a domesticated heaven further suggested that if woman did not inherit the earth, she would at least hold sway in heaven."[46]

It was a period in which women became dominant in teaching in both Sunday schools[47] and public schools[48] and were moving into nursing. It was a period when mothers were idealized. Thus in the preaching of the revivalist preacher Dwight L. Moody (1837–1899), the godly mother often assumed Christ-like qualities: in a sermon in 1876 he describes a mother seeking and finding her daughter who has "fallen"—"See how that mother sought for her and forgave her."[49] The rhetoric recalls "The Son of Man came to seek out and to save the lost" (Luke 19:10) and the shepherd that seeks the lost sheep (Matt. 18:10-14 [= Luke 15:3-7]). The Twenty-third Psalm, it scarcely need be said, was an ideal expression of the faith in this context.

The third development is the continued evolution of "civil religion," that is, the shared national beliefs, symbols, and rituals that are borrowed (in the American experience) from Protestantism but which are free of association with any single religious community and which function as a source of meaning and social solidarity.[50] The extent to which Americans in the nineteenth century used biblical images to describe the American experiment and, in general, blended (Protestant) faith and politics is a surprise to our generation, sensitive as we are to any sponsorship of Christian symbols by the state. Prayer in the public schools was universal. As late as 1892 the United States Supreme Court upheld the laws prohibiting commerce on Sundays (the so-called Blue Laws) on the grounds that "this is a Christian nation."[51]

It was a period in which Protestants and American secular culture felt the need to defend themselves against Roman Catholicism, given the large Catholic immigration between 1870 and 1885; the reigning American culture of the time looked upon Catholicism as "regressive" and "uncivilized," given the declaration of the doctrine of papal infallibility (1870). And perhaps it is well to recall the economic uncertainty of those years as well: one thinks of the "panics" (depressions) of 1873 and 1893. People craved security against economic disaster, as well as from other threats. In this context the Twenty-third Psalm thrived.

Washington Gladden (1836–1918) was for many years pastor of the First Congregational Church of Columbus, Ohio, and became moderator of the National Council of Congregational Churches in 1904. He was a leader in the social gospel movement, and he was typical of those who would identify church and civic contexts. "A faith that is at war with patriotism needs . . . to be scrutinized. Such was not the faith of the early prophets; and in all the later centuries, love of God and love of country have finely blended in the characters of the noblest of earth."[52]

Gladden was also a pastor for whom the Twenty-third Psalm loomed large. In his description of the psalms which he offered in a book he wrote in 1891, *Who Wrote the Bible?*, he clearly had the Twenty-third Psalm in mind, among others.

> Jewish saints and patriots chanted [the psalms] in the synagogue and on the battle-field; apostles and evangelists sung them among perils of the wilderness, as they traversed the rugged paths of Syria and Galatia and Macedonia; martyrs in Rome softly hummed them when the lions near at hand were crouching for their prey: in German forests, in Highland glens, Lutherans and Covenanters breathed their lives out through their cadences; in every land penitent souls have found in them words to tell the story of their sorrow, and victorious souls the voices of their triumph; mothers watching their babes by night have cheered the vigil by singing them; mourners walking in lonely ways have been lighted by the great hopes that shine through them, and pilgrims going down into the valley of the shadow of death have found in their firm assurances a strong staff to lean upon.[53]

In any event, the women and ministers won out, if the insertion of the Twenty-third Psalm into the revised initiation ritual of the Odd Fellows in 1880 is any indication.

And suddenly little books about the psalm were everywhere: books for use in Sunday schools and books for the development of personal piety. I have already cited Frederick B. Meyer's *Shepherd Psalm* (1889). Ten years later we have Josephine L. Baldwin's work, *The Shepherd Psalm for Children*;[54] this work offers a reproduction of "David the Shepherd Boy Overcomes the Lion" as a frontispiece and closes with a song, the first stanza of which is:

Like obedient lambs, who follow
  Where their shepherd leads each day,
We will follow God, our Leader,
  Gladly His commands obey.[55]

I also cite here the work of a Congregational minister, Oliver Huckel (1864–1940), *The Melody of God's Love: A New Unfolding of the Twenty-third Psalm*.[56]

But no work had more influence than one that I have already mentioned as citing the Beecher paragraphs, Knight's *Song of Our Syrian Guest*. As I have stated, the book sold more than two million copies; after almost ninety years it is still in print.[57] Knight was a Congregational minister who wrote other books with a Near East locale, such as *On the Way to Bethlehem*,[58] but *Song of Our Syrian Guest* was overwhelming in its impact. It sets itself forth as an explanation of the psalm by a Syrian friend: "'The Lord is my shepherd; I shall not want.' There is the opening strain of its music; in that chord is sounded the keynote which is never lost till the plaintive melody dies away at the song's end. All that follows is that thought put in varying light."

More recently there have been attempts to rescue the psalm from sentimental treatment, even while recognizing its unique appeal. Thus there appeared a little book in Great Britain, for the National Sunday School Union, evidently in the 1930s, called *The Eastern Colour of the Bible*, which helps to give the reader the texture of Near Eastern life and along the way offers a description of Palestinian shepherds.[59] Then Leslie D. Weatherhead (1893–1976), an outstanding British Methodist preacher who would also write the book *Psychology, Religion and Healing*,[60] wrote the book in 1938 that quotes the Beecher paragraphs, *A Shepherd Remembers: Studies in the Twenty-third Psalm*, with ten photographs of Palestinian shepherds and sheep.

There have even been books written about the psalm by actual shepherds, who can describe the reality and hardship of what it is like to herd sheep: one from an Armenian pastor (Krikorian) who had been a shepherd in his youth,[61] and one from a European who grew up in east Africa among herdsmen and later was himself a sheep owner and sheep rancher for eight years.[62]

And even before the appearance of books that communicated this reality principle, there was a recognition that an overindividualized interpretation of the psalm is off the mark: in a Congregational journal in 1918 a young pastor from Detroit writes of a conversation he had with a carpenter friend who was "by birth a Russian Jew, by adoption an American and by conviction a Christian." His friend says, "Your children and your old men and women all know the Twenty-third Psalm. They call it 'The Shepherd's Psalm.' We call it 'The People's Song.'" The friend then goes on to explain the psalm from the point of view of the corporate experience of the Jewish people: "Perhaps it would be better to use the plural throughout." He then does so, beginning with "Jehovah is our Shepherd; we shall not want."[63]

Yet the process of sentimentalization that the psalm has undergone has not been confined to the United States: it has spread to England, as the writing and preaching of Meyer indicate (and compare Weatherhead's book, which attempts to counter the sentimentalization), and to Germany as well—I have already cited the remarks of the German scholar Hans-Joachim Kraus on the matter.[64]

And evidently, by extension, the sentimentalization process has affected some American Jews as well. Across from the Reform Jewish Temple in Chelsea, Massachusetts, is a Jewish funeral home. When guests enter to attend a funeral, they receive a card printed with the name of the deceased together with the Twenty-third Psalm in English; and on the wall in the chapel, facing visitors, the psalm is inscribed in Hebrew. The Jewish novelist John Hollander, whom I cited at the end of chapter 9, recalls:

> For a long time there was only one psalm. I can still hear the tones of my father's voice identifying a puzzling string of utterances: "That's the *twenty-third* psalm," stressed just like that. It seemed the name of only one thing, and since I didn't know what the set "psalm" comprised, the poem remained *sui generis*.[65]

And so it has become.

NOTES

1. There is no numeration of the sections of *Pilgrim's Progress*: the event takes place about 40 percent along the way in Part 1.

2. Henri Talon, *John Bunyan, The Man and His Works* (London: Rockcliff, 1951), 150.

3. Robert W. Lynn and Elliott Wright, *The Big Little School* (New York: Harper & Row, 1971), 41.

4. James J. Farrell, *Inventing the American Way of Death, 1830–1920* (Philadelphia: Temple University Press, 1980), 94–95.

5. Garth M. Rosell and Richard A. G. Dupuis (eds.), *The Memoirs of Charles G. Finney: The Complete Restored Text* (Grand Rapids: Zondervan, 1989); see 99.

6. William H. McGuffey, *The Eclectic Second Reader* (Cincinnati: Truman & Smith, 1836); and idem, *The Eclectic Third Reader* (Cincinnati: Truman & Smith, 1837); see, conveniently, John H. Westerhoff III, *McGuffey and His Readers: Piety, Morality, and Education in Nineteenth-Century America* (Nashville: Abingdon, 1978), 112–13, 125–26, 136–37.

7. Horatio B. Hackett, *Illustrations of Scripture, Suggested by a Tour through the Holy Land* (Boston: Heath & Graves, 1855).

8. Ibid., 21–23.

9. Ibid., 26–27.

10. Harriet Beecher Stowe, *Uncle Tom's Cabin*, chap. 26.

11. Horatio B. Hackett, *Christian Memorials of the War: or, Scenes and Incidents Illustrative of Religious Faith and Principle, Patriotism and Bravery in Our Army* (Boston: Gould & Lincoln, 1864).

12. Ibid., 71.

13. Ibid., 85.

14. Ibid., 156–57.

15. T. J. Sheppard, "Religious Life and Work in Andersonville," in John McElroy, *Andersonville: A Story of Rebel Military Prisons* (Toledo: D. R. Locke, 1879), chap. 81.

16. *Our Martyr President: Voices from the Pulpit of New York and Brooklyn* (New York: Tibbals & Whiting, 1865), 393–420.

17. *Memorial Ceremonies at the National Cemetery, Arlington, Virginia, May 30, 1868* (Washington, D.C.: McGill & Witherow, 1868); *The National Memorial Day* (Washington, D.C.: Headquarters of the Grand Army of the Republic, 1870).

18. *The Missionary Herald* 39 (1843):170.

19. The recollection may be found in Carl Sandburg, *Abraham Lincoln: The Prairie Years* (New York: Harcourt Brace, 1926), 416; and in James Francis Goodman, *Lincoln at Heart, or, His Moral and Religious Life* (Stockbridge, Mich.: James Francis Goodman, 1931), 41–42.

20. Goodman, *Lincoln at Heart*, 42.

21. William H. Herndon, *Herndon's Lincoln: The True Story of a Great Life* (New York: Belford Clarke, 1889; reprint, Cleveland: Fine Editions, 1949), 36.

22. Mark C. Carnes, *Secret Ritual and Manhood in Victorian America* (New Haven: Yale University Press, 1989), 122.

23. Mary Baker Eddy, *Science and Health with Key to the Scriptures* (Boston: Christian Science Publishing Society, 1885).

24. Ibid., the close of chap. 16.

25. Franklin B. Hussey, "A Tribute to the Red Cross Nurses," in Clara Barton, *The Red Cross: A History of This Remarkable International Movement in the Interest of Humanity* (Washington, D.C.: American National Red Cross, 1898), 678–79.

26. Henry Ward Beecher, *Life Thoughts* (Boston: Phillips Sampson, 1858), 8–10.

27. Frederick B. Meyer, *The Shepherd Psalm* (New York: Revell, 1889), 14–15.

28. A. Chester Mann (pseudonym for Philip I. Roberts), *F. B. Meyer: Preacher, Teacher, Man of God* (New York: Revell, 1929), 213.

29. William A. Knight, *The Song of Our Syrian Guest* (Boston: Pilgrim, 1904).

30. Leslie D. Weatherhead, *A Shepherd Remembers: Studies in the Twenty-third Psalm* (New York: Abingdon, 1938).

31. Meshack P. Krikorian, *The Spirit of the Shepherd: An Interpretation of the Psalm Immortal* (Grand Rapids: Zondervan, 1938), 21.

32. Ibid., 71.

33. See Gaius Glenn Atkins and Frederick L. Fagley, *History of American Congregationalism* (Boston: Pilgrim, 1942), 122–44.

34. Ibid., 174–77.

35. Cited in Farrell, *American Way of Death*, 80.

36. Ibid., 82.

37. *The Great Debate: A Verbatim Report of the Discussion at the Meeting of the American Board of Commissioners for Foreign Missions Held at Des Moines, Iowa, Thursday, October 7, 1886* (Boston and New York: Houghton Mifflin, 1886).

38. For the whole episode, see Lyman Abbott, *Reminiscences* (Boston: Houghton Mifflin, 1915), 469–77.

39. *The Hymnal 1940 Companion* (New York: The [Episcopal] Church Pension Fund, 1949), 267.

40. Ann Douglas, *The Feminization of American Culture* (New York: Knopf, 1977).

41. This was in a sermon to Masons in Brooklyn, New York, by Warren C. Hubbard ("Sermon to Members of Aurora Grata Lodges" [New York: Nathan Lane's Sons, 1888], 6–8, 18–21); cited in Carnes, *Secret Ritual*, 77.

42. Carnes, *Secret Ritual*, chap. 3.

43. Elizabeth Stuart Phelps (Ward), *The Gates Ajar* (Boston: Fields Osgood, 1870).

44. Douglas, *Feminization*, chap. 6.

45. Mark Twain, *Extract from Captain Stormfield's Visit to Heaven* (New York: Harper, 1909).

46. Carnes, *Secret Ritual*, 78.

47. Douglas, *Feminization*, 112; and, in more detail, Anne M. Boylan, *Sunday School: The Formation of an American Institution, 1790–1880* (New Haven: Yale University Press, 1988), 114–23.

48. Carnes, *Secret Ritual*, 112, with references.

49. Dwight L. Moody, *Great Joy* (New York: E. B. Treat; Chicago: Palmer Augir, 1877), 475; cited in Darrel M. Robertson, *The Chicago Revival, 1876: Society and Revivalism in a Nineteenth-Century City* (Metuchen, N.J.: Scarecrow, 1989), 130.

50. See Russell E. Richey and Donald D. Jones (eds.), *American Civil Religion* (New York: Harper & Row, 1974); esp. in that collection Will Herberg, "America's Civil Religion: What It Is and Whence It Comes," 76–88, and, more recently, Ralph C. Wood and John E. Collins, *Civil Religion and Transcendent Experience: Studies in Theology and History, Psychology and Mysticism* (Religion and the Social Crisis 3; Macon, Ga.: Mercer University Press, 1988).

51. So Associate Justice David J. Brewer; see Robert T. Handy, *Undermined Establishment: Church–State Relations in America* (Princeton: Princeton University Press, 1991), 12–13.

52. Washington Gladden, *Ruling Ideas* (Boston and New York: Houghton Mifflin, 1895), 223.

53. Washington Gladden, *Who Wrote the Bible?* (Boston and New York: Houghton Mifflin, 1891), 205–6.

54. Josephine L. Baldwin, *The Shepherd Psalm for Children* (New York: Revell, 1899).

55. Ibid., 64.

56. Oliver Huckel, *The Melody of God's Love: A New Unfolding of the Twenty-third Psalm* (New York: Crowell, 1905).

57. William A. Knight, *The Song of Our Syrian Guest* (1904; reprint, New York: United Church Press, 1972).

58. William Allen Knight, *On the Way to Bethlehem* (Boston: Pilgrim, 1912).

59. George H. Scherer, *The Eastern Colour of the Bible* (London: The National Sunday School Union, n.d.), 26–27.

60. Leslie D. Weatherhead, *Psychology, Religion and Healing* (New York: Abingdon, 1951).

61. Krikorian, *Spirit of the Shepherd*.

62. W. Phillip Keller, *A Shepherd Looks at Psalm 23* (Grand Rapids: Zondervan, 1970).

63. I. Paul Taylor, "A People's Song: Beautiful Interpretation of the 23d Psalm," *Congregationalist and Advance* 103, no. 49 (December 5, 1918):619–20.

64. Hans-Joachim Kraus, *Psalms 1–59: A Commentary* (Minneapolis: Augsburg, 1988), 309.

65. John Hollander, "Psalms," in David Rosenberg (ed.), *Congregation: Contemporary Writers Read the Jewish Bible* (New York: Harcourt Brace Jovanovich, 1987), 293.

Appendix 1

Psalms in the
Divine Office in the
Roman Catholic Church
Just before the Reformation

There were eight times of prayer: (1) Vigils at midnight, often called "Matins" or "Nocturns"; (2) Lauds at daybreak; (3) Prime at roughly seven o'clock; (4) Terce at roughly nine o'clock; (5) Sext at roughly noon; (6) None at roughly three o'clock; (7) Vespers in the evening; and (8) Compline on retiring. Sunday Vigils consisted of three "nocturns" (divisions of recitation), the first (here marked "I") containing twelve psalms, the second and third (here marked "II" and "III") consisting of three psalms each. Vigils on the weekdays consisted of the first nocturn only.

Beyond the Psalms, Lauds contained seven canticles from the Old Testament, one each day. All of these are part of the Hebrew and Protestant canon except the Song of the Three Young Men in the furnace (Dan. 3:35-66; versification sometimes given as 57-88), which was an addition in the Septuagint and is therefore Deuterocanonical. In addition, the three canticles from Luke are included: the Benedictus to close Lauds, the Magnificat to close Vespers, and the Nunc Dimittis to close Compline. All other biblical references in the table are from the Psalms, and all numeration of the Psalms is regularized to the Hebrew (and Protestant) numeration (see the Introduction).

It should also be noted that for Lauds on the Sundays from the third Sunday before Lent (Septuagesima Sunday) through Palm Sunday, Psalm 51 was substituted for Psalm 93 and Psalm 118 was substituted for Psalm 100; for Prime on those same Sundays, Psalm 93 was substituted for Psalm 118.[1]

	Sunday	Monday	Tuesday	Wednesday	Thursday	Friday	Saturday
Vigils	95 as an introductory psalm every day ———————————————————————						
I	1–3,	27–38	39–42	53–62,	69–80	81–89,	98–109
	6–14		44–50	64, 66, 68		94, 96, 97	
			52				

	Sunday	Monday	Tuesday	Wednesday	Thursday	Friday	Saturday
II	16–18						
III	19–21						

Lauds
93 (51), 51 every weekday ———————————————————————

100	5	43	65	90	143	92
(118)						

63 every day ———————————————————————
67 every day ———————————————————————

Dan. 3:	Isa. 12:	Isa. 38:	1 Sam. 2:	Exod. 15:	Hab. 3:	Deut. 32:
35–66	1-6	1-20	1-10	1-19	2-19	1-43

148–150 every day ———————————————————————
Luke 1:68-79 every day ———————————————————————

Prime
22–26
54 every day ———————————————————————
118
(93)
119:1-32 every day ———————————————————————

Terce
119:33-80 every day ———————————————————————

Sext
119:81-128 every day ———————————————————————

None
119:129-176 every day ———————————————————————

Vespers

110–15	116–117,	127–131		132, 133,	138–142	144–147
	120, 121			135–137		

122–126 (Tuesday)

Luke 1:46-55 every day ———————————————————————

Compline
4 every day ———————————————————————
31:2-6 every day ———————————————————————
91 every day ———————————————————————
134 every day ———————————————————————
Luke 2:29-32 every day ———————————————————————

NOTE

1. Adapted from Pierre Riché and Guy Lobrichon (eds.), *Le Moyen Age et la Bible* (Bible de Tous les Temps 4; Paris: Beauchesne, 1984), 546–47.

Appendix 2

Psalms in the
Divine Office in the
Eastern Orthodox Church

The recitation of the Psalms in the Orthodox Divine Office is organized by "cathisms" (literally, "sessions"); the Psalter consists of twenty cathisms. Each cathism consists of three "stanzas," a grouping of one to four psalms. Each stanza of psalms is closed by appropriate Christian prayer phrases. In the listing of cathisms that follows, the numeration of Psalms follows the Hebrew (and Protestant) numeration (see the Introduction).[1]

A. Composition of the Cathisms of the Psalter

Cathism	Stanza	Psalms
I	1	1, 2, 3
	2	4, 5, 6
	3	7, 8
II	1	9, 10, 11
	2	12, 13, 14
	3	15, 16, 17
III	1	18
	2	19, 20, 21
	3	22, 23, 24
IV	1	25, 26, 27
	2	28, 29, 30
	3	31, 32
V	1	33, 34
	2	35, 36
	3	37

Cathism	Stanza	Psalms
VI	1	38, 39, 40
	2	41, 42, 43
	3	44, 45, 46
VII	1	47, 48, 49
	2	50, 51
	3	52, 53, 54, 55
VIII	1	56, 57, 58
	2	59, 60, 61
	3	62, 63, 64
IX	1	65, 66, 67
	2	6
	3	69, 70
X	1	71, 72
	2	73, 74
	3	75, 76, 77
XI	1	78
	2	79, 80, 81
	3	82, 83, 84, 85
XII	1	86, 87, 88
	2	89
	3	90, 91
XIII	1	92, 93, 94
	2	95, 96, 97
	3	98, 99, 100, 101
XIV	1	102, 103
	2	104
	3	105
XV	1	106
	2	107
	3	108, 109

Cathism	Stanza	Psalms
XVI	1	110, 111, 112
	2	113, 114–115, 116:1-9
	3	116:10-19, 117, 118
XVII		119
XVIII	1	120, 121, 122, 123, 124
	2	125, 126, 127, 128, 129
	3	130, 131, 132, 133, 134
XIX	1	135, 136, 137
	2	138, 139, 140
	3	141, 142, 143
XX	1	144, 145, 146
	2	147:1-11, 147:12-20
	3	148, 149, 150

B. Recitation of the Cathisms of the Psalter

In general, the recitation of the cathisms of the Psalter begins with the first cathism in Vespers on Saturday night and continues through the week. But there are six patterns for a week of recitation: (1) from the Sunday of St. Thomas (the First Sunday after Easter) until the close of the Exaltation of the Holy Cross (21 September); from the forefeast of the Nativity (20 December) until the close of Theophany (Epiphany, the afterfeast of which is completed 14 January); and during the two weeks before Lent, the so-called week of carnival and the so-called week of cheese-eating (closing on Quinquagesima Sunday, that is, the Sunday before Lent and the seventh Sunday before Easter, called "Sunday of Forgiveness"); (2) from the close of the Exaltation of the Holy Cross (21 September) until the forefeast of the Nativity (20 December); and from the close of Theophany (14 January) until the Sunday of the Prodigal (ninth Sunday before Easter); (3) during the first, second, third, fourth, and sixth weeks of Lent (which begins on Monday after the seventh Sunday before Easter, not on [Ash] Wednesday, as in the West); (4) during the fifth week of Lent, when the recitation of the Great Canon, a penitential hymn of Andrew of Crete (eighth century), takes place on Thursday (the normal pattern); (5) during the fifth week of Lent, when the Great Canon is recited on Tuesday; and (6) during Holy Week. Among these patterns there are three by which the whole Psalter is completed once in the week (patterns 1, 2, and 6) and three by which the Psalter is completed twice within the week (patterns 3, 4, and 5). It is sufficient to set forth patterns 1 and 3 here; the cathisms are here given in Arabic numerals, not Roman.

Pattern 1:

	Matins	*Vespers*
Sun.	2, 3	
Mon.	4, 5	6
Tues.	7, 8	9
Wed.	10, 11	12
Thurs.	13, 14	15
Fri.	19, 20	18
Sat.	16, 17	1

Pattern 3:

	Matins	*Prime*	*Terce*	*Sext*	*None*	*Vespers*
Sun.	2, 3, 17					
Mon.	4, 5, 6		7	8	9	18
Tues.	10, 11, 12	13	14	15	16	18
Wed.	19, 20, 1	2	3	4	5	18
Thurs.	6, 7, 8	9	10	11	12	18
Fri.	13, 14, 15		19	20		18
Sat.	16, 17					1

NOTE

1. Adapted from Feuillen Mercenier and François Paris, *La Prière dans les églises de rite byzantin, I: L'Office divin, la liturgie, les sacrements* (Prieuré d'Amay-sur-Meuse, Belgium, 1937), 195–97.

INDEXES

There are two indexes, an Index of Scripture and Other Early Writings and an Index of Authors and Historical Persons. But in a work that treats the origin of the Psalms and all the use that is made of the Psalms in subsequent years, it is difficult to draw anything but an arbitrary line between these two. Therefore I have divided the material in the following way.

The Index of Scripture and Other Early Writings consists first of references to passages of the Old Testament (in the English order of books), of the New Testament, and of the Deuterocanonical books; these references disregard subdivisions of verses (v. 1b is treated as if v. 1). It is to be noted that references to full books of Scripture are not indexed; this exclusion extends to Deuterocanonical books and books in the Pseudepigrapha. References to the supernumerary psalms retained in some traditions (Psalms 151–155) are indexed in the Deuterocanonical books. It is to be noted that this index does not include references to Psalms and other Scriptures that occur in the Appendixes. The index then includes references to the Ugaritic texts; Qumran sectarian writings; Josephus; the writings of the early church fathers (1 Clement, Barnabas, Didache, Ignatius of Antioch, Polycarp, Justin Martyr, Irenaeus); the Mishnah and the Babylonian Talmud; and the Qur'ān. It does not include references to the works of the later fathers (such as those of Origen and Augustine) or to the Jewish commentaries of the Middle Ages (such as Rashi).

The Index to Authors and Historical Persons does not include any biblical persons (David, Jeremiah, Paul), or any persons contemporaneous with the Bible (Alexander the Great, Hillel, Philo of Alexandria). It does include later church fathers (Origen, Augustine) and historical figures from that time forward (Charlemagne, various popes), and it is to be noted that the entries of early figures employ the conventional spelling (Jerome, Rashi). This index also includes composers of musical works. It does not include references to editors of standard editions (Migne is not listed), but it does include the editors of remote or difficult material, such as those of Qimḥi's commentary. No hymnals are listed, and there are no references to modern translations (KJV, NRSV).

Index of Scripture and Other Early Writings

Index of Authors
and Historical Persons